The Mexico Reader

THE LATIN AMERICA READERS

A Series Edited by Robin Kirk and Orin Starn

Also in this series:

THE
MEXICO
READER

History, Culture, Politics

Edited by Gilbert M. Joseph and Timothy J. Henderson

DUKE UNIVERSITY PRESS   DURHAM AND LONDON 2002

© 2002 Duke University Press   All rights reserved
Printed in the United States of America on acid-free paper ∞
Designed by Rebecca M. Giménez   Typeset in Monotype Dante
by Tseng Information Systems   Library of Congress Cataloging-
in-Publication Data appear on the last printed page of this book.
*Publication of this book has been made possible with the assistance
of the Frederick W. Hilles Publication Fund of Yale University.*
Acknowledgment of copyright begins on page 763.

Dedicated to the memory of Pat Bradley,

colleague and friend

Contents

IV   *Trials of the Young Republic*

Special Section

V   *Revolution*

VI   *The Perils of Modernity*

VII   *From the Ruins*

VIII   *The Border and Beyond*

Acknowledgments

Producing a book this big on a country as diverse as Mexico necessarily incurs many debts. We are grateful to the many friends and colleagues—*mexicólogos todos*—who over the past four years shared their ideas, enthusiasm, and favorite selections with us—and taught us a great deal about Mexico in the bargain. We are particularly indebted to those who helped to translate and edit selections, wrote new pieces or customized essays for the volume, or contributed photographs and other graphics: Chris Boyer, Wayne Cornelius, Ray Craib, Amy Ferlazzo, Alejandra García Quintanilla, Gabriela Gómez-Cárcamo, Salvador Lemus, John Mraz, Karren Pell, Marián Peres Tsu, Jeffrey Pilcher, Matt Roller, Anne Rubenstein, Jeff Rubin, Jan Rus, Andrew Sackett, Michael Simmons, and Heather Williams.

Others provided invaluable research and administrative support. In New Haven, Alison Bruey and Andrew Sackett hunted for appropriate graphics in published collections and on line; Masha Salazkina patiently tracked down permissions; and Beatriz Riefkohl and Sarah Morrill helped to prepare a behemoth of a manuscript. In Montgomery, the Technology Resource Center at Auburn University Montgomery scanned scores of photographs. Thanks to all of the student workers who did the scanning, and to Carolyn Rawl, the center's director. Thanks also to the AUM Library's interlibrary borrowing department, and to Janice Willis for help with typing.

We also received timely financial support at the beginning and end of our work. The Joint Center for Latin American Studies at the University of Illinois–Champaign and the University of Chicago generously provided Timothy Henderson with a Summer Visiting Scholar Grant in the summer of 1997 to research and photocopy rare Mexican materials in the University's Regenstein Library. Auburn University Montgomery provided financial support in the form of a Faculty Grant-in-Aid. Yale's Center for International and Area Studies supported a variety of editorial costs as the volume took form.

Finally, we are extremely grateful to two colleagues at Duke University Press: Kay Robin Alexander, who did much to streamline the onerous process of researching copyrights and seeking out permissions, and Valerie Millholland, our extraordinary editor, who provided warm encouragement and her characteristic brand of therapy throughout the process.

A Note on Style

In doing the translations for this volume we have attempted as much as possible to remain true to both the flavor and meaning of the original text. We have tried to choose English words that are as close as possible to the Spanish counterparts, though translation is an inexact science. In instances where it seemed essential to provide some further explanation, we have used brief and unobtrusive brackets whenever possible. At times, however, a brief footnote was in order. Many of the selections were substantially abridged, and for this we offer apologies to the authors. With respect to proper names, we have made a practice of rendering these as they appeared in the original text. Some names—for example, Moctezuma—have many different spellings, and several of those spellings appear in the pages to follow. We hope readers will bear with us.

Tijuana · · Mexicali

Juárez

Chihuahua

Gulf of California

Monterrey

PACIFIC OCEAN

GULF OF MEXICO

Tampico

León

Guadalajara · · Querétaro

Gulf of Campeche

Mérida

FEDERAL DISTRICT Veracruz

Puebla

Mexico

Oaxaca

· San Cristóbal de Las Casas

Acapulco

Gulf of Tehuantepec

0   100   200   300
Miles

Introduction

Mexico has always exercised a tremendous hold on the imagination of out-siders. Over the centuries, visitors have marveled at its tremendous economic possibilities and been lured by its "exotic," expressive cultures. Standing atop one of the great pyramids of the Aztec capital of Tenochtitlán (now Mexico City) in 1519, one of Hernán Cortés's Spanish lieutenants was barely able to contain his awe at the tableau that spread out before him:

> We were astounded at the great number of people and the quantities of merchandise, and at the orderliness . . . that prevailed, for we had never seen such a thing before. . . . Every kind of merchandise . . . had its fixed place . . . with dealers in gold, silver, and precious stones, feathers, cloaks, and embroidered goods, and male and female slaves to be sold in the mar-ket. . . . We saw pyramids and shrines in these cities that looked like gleam-ing white towers and castles: a marvelous sight to behold.[1]

Three centuries later, a "scientific conquistador," the German Alexander von Humboldt (hailed in his time as "the monarch of the sciences"), spent a year of intense investigation in Mexico, then published a book in 1810 that celebrated the virtually boundless economic potential of Mexico's agricultural and mineral resources. Observing that there was not a single plant in the rest of the world that could not grow in its soil, Baron von Humboldt predicted a bright future for Mexico.[2] Almost two hundred years later, in the early 1990s, U.S. political and business leaders regaled the American public with latter-day images of a cornucopia of trade and investment that would be realized as soon as the United States ratified NAFTA (the North America Free Trade Agreement).

Mexico's cultural complex — that is, both its aesthetic realm and its political culture — has riveted foreigners at least as much as its enticing landscapes and natural resources. Enlightenment philosophes and nineteenth-century liberal intellectuals were obsessed by the intriguing mixture of artistic achievement and bloodcurdling brutality — of "civilization and barbarism" — that they saw as the hallmark of Mexico's pre-Columbian societies, most notably the Aztec empire. In the aftermath of Mexico's epic Revolution (1910–1917), *norteameri-*

canos, titillated (and unsettled) by the violent careers of telluric revolutionary chiefs like Pancho Villa and Emiliano Zapata and captivated by revolutionary artists like Diego Rivera, reencountered Mexico, celebrating the cultural and political triumphs of *La Revolución.* The "enormous vogue of things Mexican" among U.S. artists, intellectuals, and activists in the 1920s and 1930s, for example, played itself out on one level in a "discovery" of Mexico's "timeless" and exotic popular culture. Rustic songs and dances, folk cuisine and handicrafts, the exuberant murals painted on the walls of public ministries and cantinas alike, "primitive" *retablos,* and the evocative woodcuts of Mexican revolutionary artist José Guadalupe Posada—all generated a powerful romantic appeal among waves of "revolutionary tourists" disaffected with the excesses of U.S. capitalist society and modernity itself.[3] Significantly, the new Mexican revolutionary state did what it could to promote these desires, eager to perpetuate notions of *mexicanidad* (Mexican-ness) rooted in an "authentic" *mestizo* rural culture of which it was the legitimate custodian and beneficiary.

In the decades that followed, as postrevolutionary governments "institutionalized" the revolution and "modernized" the country under the aegis of an immovable party, the message that the nation's leaders wished to convey to the world was that Mexico was now, all at once, cosmopolitan, folkloric, and *safe.* Thus, the "Amigo Country" was both on the cutting edge of modernization and laid back; capable of staging high-profile events like the Olympics and the World Cup but also impromptu dawn serenades by mariachis; a mecca simultaneously for high-powered investors and countercultural tourists seeking a road less traveled.[4] As this essay was being written, following the turn of the new millennium, one multinational tourist promotion trumpeted the attractions of the "new, exclusive Explorian Resort in tropical Mexico." Here, tourists in the post–Indiana Jones mold could rise early to bask in nature's secluded, early-morning splendors; ride motor bikes deep into the recesses of a Mayan jungle, spotting parrots and monkeys and unearthing ancient artifacts and treasures along the way; and then return in the afternoon to sample all the comforts and excitements of a luxurious hotel and sports complex.[5]

In the world beyond the rhetoric of state builders and tourist promoters, however, modernity has been fraught with perils for Mexico. *The Mexico Reader* has assembled a wealth of materials that afford the reader an opportunity to reflect on the broader, uneven process whereby Mexico became "modern." Read together, these selections call into question linear notions of modernization as an inexorable and overwhelming historical current. They show how Mexicans at all points on the social spectrum have shaped the content, pace, and direction of modernization. In the process, the anthology unpacks the enduring images of Mexican political economy and culture that many foreigners nurture of Mexico—images that are themselves an important dimension of Mexican history and in whose shaping both Mexicans and outsiders have often colluded. Longtime *New York Times* correspondent Alan Riding has remarked in his book *Distant Neighbors* that no two countries that share a common border understand each other less than the United States and Mexico.[6] This collection aims to provide a deeper understanding in the north of our neighbor south of the Rio Grande.

Any deeper understanding of Mexico must begin with acknowledgment that, for all of its historic economic potential and its much-publicized entry into an "integrated" North American economy in 1994, Mexico remains closer to its Third World past than to its supposedly inexorable First World destiny. Despite its continuing recovery from the economy's disastrous "meltdown" in 1995—a recovery that has witnessed a rise in exports and wages—per capita income is barely $5,000 a year, and 40 million of Mexico's 90 million citizens are poor by any standard. Mexico has become the United States' second largest business partner (Canada is no. 1, Japan no. 3). It has produced fabulous fortunes in business, politics, oil, and the drug trade, with more billionaires in recent decades than any other country save the oil emirates. Still, as many as 150,000 Mexicans are driven to migrate illegally to the United States each year, owing to a lack of real economic opportunities in the countryside or the cities. Quite simply, most Mexicans have remained outside the periodic booms of recent decades while participating fully in the busts that have preceded and followed them. Moreover, despite the pronouncements by Baron von Humboldt and others regarding the country's agricultural and mineral abundance and the rich cultural endowments of its people, it has always been thus.

These perpetual frustrations are partly explained by the country's history, geography, and politics. Mexico has always presented formidable challenges to economic development and governance, in part owing to the tremendous diversity of its peoples, languages (even today there are still almost sixty indigenous languages spoken), and regions. No doubt the country's notoriously difficult topography—particularly the existence of two rugged cordilleras that run from north to south, effectively cutting off the western and eastern portions of the country from the central corridor, while isolating many of the center's fertile valleys from one another—has played an important role in the regionalization of the country. Even today in an age of globalization, the small farmer of Tamaulipas, who cultivates flat, irrigated fields of sorghum and speaks the mixed Spanish–English border patois, can hardly recognize a fellow countryman in the highland *campesino* of Chiapas, who speaks a Maya-inflected version of *castellano,* if he speaks Spanish at all, and who tends a miserable plot of corn. In Mexico City, the teeming urban heart of Mexican civilization, high-rise buildings loom above colonial churches, which in turn overshadow the blackened ruins of the destroyed indigenous civilization. The city is home to the rich and powerful, but also to shantytown dwellers and street beggars. All of this makes Mexico difficult to grasp as an abstraction; it must be appreciated in its specificity. As made clear in the title of Lesley Byrd Simpson's classic history, there are indeed "many Mexicos"—and ruling them effectively has never been easy.[7]

The task of governing Mexico and unleashing its economic potential was made more formidable still by the lingering trauma of the Spanish conquest, and by a colonial legacy of exploitation, racism, and paternalistic authoritarian rule. It was further complicated by the extraordinary economic, political, and ideological power of the Roman Catholic Church, which has played dramatic, ambiguous, and often contradictory roles in the nation's history. And it was embittered by the fact that, since independence at least, Mexico's leadership has shown itself determined to doggedly pursue the chimera of "modernity." Generations of would-be reformers and social engineers—liberals, revolutionaries, and technocrats—have found themselves repeatedly frustrated by stubborn Mexican realities. It has seemed to them that each time they have had their nation poised to make its debut in the company of "developed," "First World" countries, they have been blindsided by some manifestation of what anthropologist Guillermo Bonfil Batalla has called "*México profundo*" (the old, "deep Mexico").[8] The recent indigenous rebellion of the Zapatista National Liberation Army in Chiapas, which followed hot on the heels of the signing of NAFTA, is only the most recent case in point. And if the modernizers' hopes have not been undone by recalcitrant internal forces, they have often been dealt the *golpe de gracia* by the perverse logic of the modern world economy itself, and Mexico's highly vulnerable, dependent status in it. Thus, in the 1980s, the oil-export boom evaporated, leaving only a mountain of debt; more recently, the nation's overvalued peso collapsed immediately after NAFTA was signed, with countless millions of dollars of portfolio ("hot money") investment fleeing the country at the stroke of a keyboard. Indeed, there have been few periods in Mexico's national history that have *not* been characterized as times of "crisis." Of course, for those Mexicans who do not share the "developmentalist" vision of their leaders, or whose families' livelihoods and mores have been disrupted by it, terms such as *crisis* (and *modernity* itself) take on a very different meaning.

While Mexico is certainly a unique and extraordinary country, it is also true that the multistranded examination of Mexican history, culture, and politics presented in this volume can shed a good deal of light on central problems facing the so-called "developing world" as a whole. Specifically, Mexico provides a compelling case study for examining such nations' historical struggles to achieve effective modes of governance and sustainable economic growth. Although Americans often take these things for granted (especially in times of economic prosperity!), throughout most of the so-called "Third" or "developing" world, and certainly in Latin America, almost two hundred years after the achievement of formal independence there is still no tried-and-true formula for political stability and broad-based economic development. Why is this the case? Why, on virtually every economic and social indicator, are the Latin American nations (not to mention their African and Asian counterparts) so far behind the United States, which won its independence at roughly the same time? Why — despite the dazzling fortunes of a favored few — is the gap between North and South apparently widening, notwithstanding all the optimistic forecasts that were made at the onset of NAFTA and the "New World Order"? And finally, what roles have the United States (and other foreign powers) played in the quest of countries such as Mexico to attain effective, representative governance and balanced economic development?

We believe that the themes explored by our contributors will provide grist for discussion and debate of these and many other questions. At the core of the volume lies an attempt to convey something of the multiple histories of Mexico's development as a nation — histories "from above," "from below," and in between; histories shaped by forces and agents inside and outside the country. Unlike much of the prevailing pedagogical literature on Mexico, *The Mexico Reader* seeks to show how these histories intersect, illuminating the tension between long-running processes of global economic expansion, national state-formation, and the responses these larger trends have produced at the grass roots. In this sense, the volume will likely pose a challenge to many introductory texts on Mexico, since the linkages between the state's political-economic and cultural projects of transformation, on the one hand, and local equations of resistance, accommodation, negotiation, and popular empowerment, on the other, are at once central to the Mexican past yet still not adequately understood.

Thus, like *The Peru Reader,* which initiated this series, this volume seeks to integrate political-economy and cultural approaches in an effort to understand the past and present of a complex society and to tease out the manner in which the former has shaped the latter. And like our Andean predecessor, while we strive to present a broad range of perspectives and eschew "totalizing" renditions of history, such as overwrought theories of "imperialism" or "dependency," we also seek to avoid a "postmodern carnival of polyphony."[9] This anthology examines a country whose history is bound up with what Mexico's late Nobel Laureate Octavio Paz described as "cycles of conquest."[10]

Not for nothing, then, do we take pains to examine the structures of power and privilege—caste and class, ethnoracial, and gendered—that have undergirded Mexican society. Some of the readings focus on enduring forms of class exploitation; others suggest how gender ideologies interlock with hierarchies of class and ethnicity, giving the lie to the kind of unitary notions of Mexicanness that postrevolutionary state builders advanced throughout the twentieth century. The collection underscores that class oppression does not eliminate ethnic, gendered, or generational identities, though it may speak through them with important consequences for collective political action. The volume also demonstrates that although it is fashionable these days to bash Marxist theories of imperialism and dependency—and, to be sure, their simple correlation of Third World ills with First World domination often caricatures more than it explains—foreign intervention runs throughout the course of Mexican history and has been an unmistakable factor in the nation's poverty and internal conflicts.

Guided by these larger questions, goals, and assumptions, our criteria for selecting pieces for this anthology have been relatively straightforward. First, we have sought to evoke a variety of actors and environments, so that the patterned complexity of *muchos Méxicos* will emerge vividly over the centuries, in a manner that inflects the country's class, ethnic, gender, generational, regional, and ideological axes of difference. Second, we have put a premium on Mexican voices that are of critical importance but presently inaccessible to English-speaking readers. Many of the selections, therefore, appear for the first time in translation. Finally, we have made every effort to avoid readings that are arcane, overly technical, or require extensive previous knowledge of a given topic. Most of the pieces we have chosen were originally written for a general audience; each, we hope, will be successful in clarifying issues, piquing interest, and stimulating thought. Most of the readings presented herein are relatively short, but we have included a final section offering suggestions for further reading for those who wish to delve more deeply.

The timing of this anthology is quite propitious. In the elections of July 2, 2000, the virtual political monopoly of Mexico's ruling party, the Institutional Revolutionary Party (PRI)—long besieged by the growing assertiveness of nongovernmental organizations, indigenous rebels, opposition forces on the right and left, and a public weary of crisis and corruption—was definitively broken. Writers in Mexico and throughout the world lauded the transparency of the elections and welcomed a new era of openness and democracy under the iconoclastic leader of the center-right National Action Party (PAN), Vicente Fox. Along with a flurry of well-deserved congratulations and premature predictions of cataclysmic change, we have seen the beginnings of serious efforts within the government and civil society to sort out long-standing problems, to comprehend the mistakes of the past in order to take full advantage of the apparent new opportunities. We hope that this anthology can play a role in this process by introducing a new generation of Americans to Mexico in a way that will make them at once more sympathetic toward Mexico's historical problems and more appreciative of its cultural richness and transformative potential.

THE BOOK CONTAINS eight parts. Part I examines the theme of *mexicanidad*. It inquires into the reasons behind the national obsession with "Mexican-ness" and chronicles the attempts by generations of thinkers and politicians to celebrate or deconstruct the national essence, to find some sort of Mexican archetype. While consensus on the issue is obviously impossible, more certain is the construction or politicization of "national character" by the postrevolutionary state to legitimize its rule. Parts II through V examine Mexico's history from pre-Columbian times through the consolidation of the Mexican revolution at the conclusion of the administration of President Lázaro Cárdenas in 1940. The country's historical evolution has profoundly influenced present-day Mexico and will powerfully shape the nation's prospects in the twenty-first century. These sections are designed to be of interest in themselves, but they also foreground the themes we take up in parts VI through VIII, which are almost entirely dedicated to Mexico since 1940. These final sections, which focus on the contradictions and costs of postrevolutionary modernization, the rise of civil society (particularly since 1968), and the dynamic transcultural zone that is articulated by the two-thousand-mile U.S.–Mexican border, are designed to resonate with one another. They are also intended to provoke discussion about a new Mexico — and a new United States — whose citizens, as anthropologist Arjun Appadurai puts it, are no longer as "tightly territorialized [and] spatially bounded," and where such fundamental categories as "foreign" and "domestic" become increasingly blurred.[11]

Notes

1. Bernal Díaz del Castillo, *The Conquest of New Spain,* translated by J. M. Cohen (Baltimore: Penguin Books, 1963), 232–35. More of Díaz del Castillo's classic eyewitness account appears in Part III of this volume.

2. José Miranda, *Humboldt y México* (Mexico City: Universidad Nacional Autónoma de México, 1962).

3. Helen Delpar, *The Enormous Vogue of Things Mexican: Cultural Relations between the United States and Mexico, 1920–1935* (Tuscaloosa: University of Alabama Press, 1992).

4. Gilbert M. Joseph, Anne Rubenstein, and Eric Zolov, eds., *Fragments of a Golden Age: The Politics of Culture in Mexico since 1940* (Durham, N.C.: Duke University Press, 2001); see, especially, the editors' introduction and the essay by Zolov, "Discovering a Land 'Mysterious and Obvious': The Renarrativizing of Postrevolutionary Mexico."

5. This promotion was aired frequently on New York radio stations in 2000.

6. Alan Riding, *Distant Neighbors: A Portrait of the Mexicans* (New York: Vintage Books, 1986), ix–xi.

7. Lesley Byrd Simpson, *Many Mexicos,* 4th ed. (Berkeley: University of California Press, 1974).

8. Guillermo Bonfils Batalla, *México Profundo: Reclaiming a Civilization,* translated by Philip Dennis (Austin: University of Texas Press, 1996). A selection from *México Profundo* appears in Part I of this volume.

9. Orin Starn, Carlos Iván Degregori, and Robin Kirk, eds., *The Peru Reader: History, Culture, Politics* (Durham, N.C.: Duke University Press, 1995), 9.

10. Octavio Paz, *The Labyrinth of Solitude and Other Writings,* translated by Lysander Kemp, Yara Milos, and Rachael Phillips Belash (New York: Grove Press, 1985). A selection from *The Labyrinth of Solitude* appears in part I of this volume.

11. Arjun Appadurai, "Global Ethnoscapes: Notes and Queries for a Transnational Anthropology," in *Recapturing Anthropology: Working in the Present* (Santa Fe, N.M.: School of American Research, 1991), 191; see also Gilbert M. Joseph, "Close Encounters: Towards a New Cultural History of U.S.-Latin American Relations," in *Close Encounters of Empire: Writing the Cultural History of U.S.-Latin American Relations,* edited by Gilbert M. Joseph, Catherine C. LeGrand, and Ricardo D. Salvadore (Durham, N.C.: Duke University Press, 1998), 3–4.

I

The Search for "Lo Mexicano"

Since the concepts of "nationality" and "nationalism" came into existence some two centuries ago, it has been a common presumption that different peoples exhibit characteristics peculiarly their own. The term *nation* itself, which is derived from the Latin *natio,* meaning "birth," suggests something innate and inevitable, traits which are shaped by genetics and environment—traits which can be analyzed, but changed only with great difficulty.

Mexicans, perhaps more than most peoples, have long been preoccupied with defining what it means to be Mexican, such that the terms *lo mexicano* and *mexicanidad* have become standard intellectual fare. Yet musings on the topic have seldom been celebrations of Mexico's vibrant national spirit; they have more typically been tortured reflections on the country's apparent inability to emerge from a prolonged and troubled adolescence. Some have sought explanations in the social structures inherited from centuries of colonial rule; others have located the problem in the unique attributes of the Mexican "race." Among the first to adopt this latter perspective were foreigners like U.S. Ambassador Joel Poinsett, who held that the Mexican "race" was weak and degenerate. The advent of modern psychology led to more nuanced and sympathetic analyses, such as those of Octavio Paz and his mentor, the psychologist Samuel Ramos. These have been criticized for exaggerating supposed personality traits and reifying culture. Recent "postmodern" thinkers tend likewise to be skeptical of analyses which find unalterable attributes of different nationalities, since often "nationality" comes to seem a polite code word for "race." Race, these thinkers claim, is more a "social construction" than a matter of biology. Moreover, the postrevolutionary Mexican state seized upon some of the supposed elements of *"mexicanidad"* to legitimize and sustain its rule, adding an unfortunate political dimension to the question.

While consensus on so slippery an issue is clearly impossible, we present in this section several classic statements on the topic of the Mexican character. Fundamentally, all seek to account for the apparent fact that Mexico has not quite become "modern," positing characteristics that are profoundly at odds with those commonly attributed to North Americans or Northern Europeans. The final reading by Alma Guillermoprieto poses a crucial question: In this age of globalization of capital and media, could the image of *"lo mexicano"* — whether we view it as a good or bad thing — be threatened finally with extinction?

The Mexican Character

Joel Poinsett

Today, Joel Roberts Poinsett's chief claim to fame in the United States is as the man who brought home the Mexican "Christmas flower," which came to be called the poinsettia. Despite this innocent association, however, few figures in Mexican history have excited quite such passionate controversy. Born in Charleston, South Carolina, Poinsett (1779–1851) first became involved in Latin American affairs in 1811 as special envoy from President James Monroe to Chile. Returning to the United States in 1813, he pursued a political career in the South Carolina legislature and in the U.S. House of Representatives, to which he was elected in 1821. In 1822 he traveled to the Mexico of Agustín Iturbide and authored a short book on the subject, Notes on Mexico. *In 1825 he was appointed U.S. Ambassador to Mexico. He later would serve as Secretary of War in the cabinet of President Martin Van Buren.*

From the outset of his tenure as ambassador to Mexico, Poinsett was an outspoken proponent of U.S.-style liberalism: decentralized, constitutional, republican government; anticlericalism; and free trade. A substantial number of influential Mexicans found such activity decidedly pernicious, and their antipathy toward him was exacerbated by the fact that the ambassador advocated extending the southern boundary of the United States to the Rio Grande. Poinsett found like-minded cohorts in the York Rite Masonic Lodge, which he helped to organize in Mexico. The York Rite Masons (or Yorkinos) were rivals of the Scottish Rite Masons (or Escoceses), and the two lodges increasingly emerged as bitter, secretive political clubs. The sub rosa nature of these political organizations was conducive to conspiratorial thinking, and Conservative Escoceses became increasingly convinced that Poinsett was a subversive foreign agent seeking deliberately to weaken and undermine Mexico.

As will be seen from the following excerpt from an 1829 letter to Secretary of State Martin Van Buren, Poinsett had a pessimistic view of the Mexican character and of the nation's potential for progress. Poinsett's generalizations might serve as a compendium of North American stereotypes of Mexicans to this day.

The character of this people cannot be understood, nor the causes of their present condition be fully developed without recurring to the oppression under which they formerly laboured. It would lead you into error to compare them with the free and civilized nations of America and Europe in the Nineteenth Century. They started from a period nearer to the age of Charles the fifth, and it is even a matter of some doubt whether this Nation had advanced one step in knowledge and civilization, from the time of the conquest to the moment of declaring themselves Independent. No portion of the Spanish dominions in America was watched over by the Mother Country with such jealous care as Mexico. Its comparatively dense population, its extensive and fertile territory, its rich and varied productions, and especially its mineral wealth, rendered it a source of great profit to Spain; while the history of the ancient splendour of Mexico, and the glory of its conquest could not fail to enhance the value of its possession in the eyes of that chivalrous people. In order to preserve that possession every precaution was taken that human prudence could devise to prevent the access of strangers to Mexico and to keep the people in profound ignorance of their own strength and resources as well as of their relative position with regard to other Nations. . . .

The nobility and gentry then as now, inhabited spacious hotels, built after the fashion of those of the mother Country, solid and substantial; but still more destitute of all comfort or convenience. Their style of living was not generous or hospitable, although they sometimes gave costly and ostentatious entertainments. From their absurd pretensions to rank and from their unmeaning jealousy of each other, there never did exist that social intercourse among the higher orders, which in every other Country forms the chief charm of life. Here every man of distinction considered it beneath his dignity to visit his friends or neighbours, and remained in his own house, where in a large gloomy apartment dimly lighted and miserably furnished he received a few visitors of inferior rank who formed his tertulia [social gathering] of every night. It is not to be wondered at therefore that the sons of these men, equally uneducated with themselves, fled from the gloomy mansions of their fathers to the Theatre, the coffee houses or the gambling table; and this circumstance united to the absence of all excitement to industry, from the preference given by the Council of the Indies to Europeans for all appointments, rendered the Aristocracy of Mexico an ignorant and immoral race. The same state of society existed among the higher orders of the clergy and marked their character in the same unfavorable manner. The regular clergy formed from the very dregs of the people, was then and is now disgustingly debauched and ignorant. They have lost the influence they formerly possessed over the common people, and so sensible are they of the universal contempt which they have brought upon themselves by their unworthy conduct, that they would

The Cosmic Race

José Vasconcelos

José Vasconcelos (1882–1959) was among the most important and influential Mexican intellectuals of the twentieth century. His childhood was spent partly on the U.S.–Mexican border, where he attended schools in Eagle Pass, Texas. During his formative years, Vasconcelos developed a profound suspicion of Americans, whom he viewed as crassly pragmatic, arrogant, shallow, aggressive, and lacking in spirituality. Undoubtedly, he was also offended by the fact that many Americans continued to endorse ideas like those espoused earlier in the century by their compatriot Joel Poinsett. Like certain other Latin Americans of the turn of the century—such as the Uruguayan philosopher José Enrique Rodó, the Nicaraguan poet Rubén Darío, and the Cuban patriot José Martí—Vasconcelos's thought developed in part as a reaction against North America and its materialistic values. He felt that Latin Americans must avoid imitating American culture, and that in order to do that successfully they would need a guiding philosophy, one that celebrated their strengths and virtues. In this spirit, he argued that the Latin American mestizo constituted a new race, a "cosmic race," which combined the virtues of Indians and Europeans. This, Vasconcelos believed, would be the race of the future.

While Vasconcelos's theory turned the white supremacist racism of the day on its head, it remains at heart a racist theory. By imputing inevitable characteristics to the various races of the earth, Vasconcelos engages in rather reckless stereotyping. His romantic notion of the spiritual essence of his people and of the soullessness of Anglo-Saxon culture, together with his increasing bitterness at the course of events in Mexico, would lead him to embrace fascism and anti-Semitism during World War II.

For all his failings, Vasconcelos remains a uniquely engaging figure. Active in the Mexican revolution from its earliest days, he would serve as Mexico's secretary of education, and in this capacity he acted with boundless energy and idealism. An advocate of Indian literacy, he greatly increased the presence of education in the countryside; his Ministry of Public Education produced massive quantities of inexpensive workbooks and textbooks; and the ministry's department of fine arts sponsored the work of some of Mexico's greatest modern artists, including the muralists Diego Rivera, José Clemente Orozco, and David Alfaro Siqueiros, as well as musicians Manuel M.

Cortés and La Malinche, a mural by José Clemente Orozco.
(National Preparatory School, Mexico City)

Ponce and Julián Carrillo. At odds with the Mexican government after 1924, he ran
unsuccessfully for president in 1929 in an energetic campaign plagued by violence and
fraud on the part of the newly formed official government party.

Greece laid the foundations of Western or European civilization; the white
civilization that, upon expanding, reached the forgotten shores of the American continent in order to consummate the task of re-civilization and re-popu-
lation. Thus we have the four stages and the four racial trunks: the Black,
the Indian, the Mongol, and the White. The latter, after organizing itself in
Europe, has become the invader of the world, and has considered itself destined to rule, as did each of the previous races during their time of power. It
is clear that domination by the whites will also be temporary, but their mission is to serve as a bridge. The white race has brought the world to a state in
which all human types and cultures will be able to fuse with each other. The
civilization developed and organized in our times by the whites has set the
moral and material basis for the union of all men into a fifth universal race,
the fruit of all the previous ones and amelioration of everything past. . . .

Let us recognize that it was a disgrace not to have proceeded with the cohesion demonstrated by those to the north, that prodigious race which we are accustomed to lavish with insults only because they have won each hand at the secular fight. They triumph because they join to their practical talents the clear vision of a great destiny. They keep present the intuition of a definite historical mission, while we get lost in the labyrinth of verbal chimeras. It seems as if God Himself guided the steps of the Anglo-Saxon cause, while we kill each other on account of dogma or declare ourselves atheists. How those mighty empire builders must laugh at our groundless arrogance and Latin vanity! They do not clutter their mind with the Ciceronian weight of phraseology, nor have they in their blood the contradictory instincts of a mixture of dissimilar races, but they committed the sin of destroying those races, while we assimilated them, and this gives us new rights and hopes for a mission without precedent in History.

For this reason, adverse obstacles do not move us to surrender, for we vaguely feel that they will help us to discover our way. Precisely in our differences, we find the way. If we simply imitate, we lose. If we discover and create, we shall overcome. The advantage of our tradition is that it has greater facility of sympathy toward strangers. This implies that our civilization, with all defects, may be the chosen one to assimilate and to transform mankind into a new type; that within our civilization, the warp, the multiple and rich plasma of future humanity is thus being prepared. This mandate from History is first noticed in that abundance of love that allowed the Spaniard to create a new race with the Indian and the Black, profusely spreading white ancestry through the soldier who begat a native family, and Occidental culture through the doctrine and example of the missionaries who placed the Indians in condition to enter into the new stage. . . . Spanish colonization created mixed races, this signals its character, fixes its responsibility, and defines its future. The English kept on mixing only with the whites and annihilated the natives. Even today, they continue to annihilate them in a sordid and economic fight, more efficient yet than armed conquest. This proves their limitation and is indication of their decadence. The situation is equivalent, in a larger scale, to the incestuous marriages of the pharaohs which undermined the virtues of the race; and it contradicts the ulterior goals of History to attain the fusion of peoples and cultures. To build an English world and to exterminate the red man, so that Northern Europe could be renovated all over an America made up with pure whites, is no more than a repetition of the triumphant process of a conquering race. This was already attempted by the red man and by all strong and homogeneous races, but it does not solve the human problem. America was not kept in reserve for five thousand years for such a petty goal.

The purpose of the new and ancient continent is much more important. Its predestination obeys the design of constituting the cradle of a fifth race into which all nations will fuse with each other to replace the four races that have been forging History apart from each other. The dispersion will come to an end on American soil; unity will be consummated there by the triumph of fecund love and the improvement of all the human races. In this fashion, the synthetic race that shall gather all the treasures of History in order to give expression to universal desire shall be created. . . .

The so-called Latin peoples . . . are the ones called upon to consummate this mission. . . . [They] insist on not taking the ethnic factor too much into account for their sexual relations, perhaps because from the beginning they are not, properly speaking, Latins but a conglomeration of different types and races. Whatever opinions one may express in this respect, and whatever repugnance caused by prejudice one may harbor, the truth is that the mixture of races has taken place and continues to be consummated. It is in this fusion of ethnic stocks that we should look for the fundamental characteristic of Ibero-American idiosyncrasy. . . . In Latin America . . . a thousand bridges are available for the sincere and cordial fusion of all races. The ethnic barricading of those to the north in contrast to the much more open sympathy of those to the south is the most important factor, and at the same time, the most favorable to us, if one reflects even superficially upon the future, because it will be seen immediately that we belong to tomorrow, while the Anglo-Saxons are gradually becoming more a part of yesterday. The Yankees will end up building the last great empire of a single race, the final empire of White supremacy. Meanwhile, we will continue to suffer the vast chaos of an ethnic stock in formation, contaminated by the fermentation of all types, but secure of the avatar into a better race. In Spanish America, Nature will no longer repeat one of her partial attempts. This time, the race that will come out of the forgotten Atlantis will no longer be a race of a single color or of particular features. The future race will not be a fifth, or a sixth race, destined to prevail over its ancestors. What is going to emerge out there is the definitive race, the synthetical race, the integral race, made up of the genius and the blood of all peoples and, for that reason, more capable of true brotherhood and of a truly universal vision. . . .

How different the sounds of the Ibero-American development [from that of the Anglo-Saxons]! They resemble the profound scherzo of a deep and infinite symphony: Voices that bring accents from Atlantis; depths contained in the pupil of the red man, who knew so much, so many thousand years ago, and now seems to have forgotten everything. His soul resembles the old Mayan *cenote* [natural well] of green waters, laying deep and still, in the middle of the forest, for so many centuries since, that not even its legend remains any more. This infinite quietude is stirred with the drop put in our blood by the Black, eager for sensual joy, intoxicated with dances and unbridled lust. There also appears the Mongol, with the mystery of his slanted eyes that see everything according to a strange angle, and discover I know not what folds and newer dimensions. The clear mind of the White, that resembles his skin and his dreams, also intervenes. Judaic striae hidden within the Castilian blood since the days of the cruel expulsion now reveal themselves, along with Arabian melancholy, as a remainder of the sickly Muslim sensuality. Who has not a little of all this, or does not wish to have all? There is the Hindu, who also will come, who has already arrived by way of the spirit, and although he is the last one to arrive, he seems the closest relative. . . . So many races that have come and others that will come. In this manner, a sensitive and ample heart will be taking shape within us; a heart that embraces and contains everything and is moved with sympathy, but, full of vigor, imposes new laws upon the world. . . .

We in America shall arrive, before any other part of the world, at the creation of a new race fashioned out of the treasures of all the previous ones: The final race, the cosmic race.

The Sons of La Malinche

Octavio Paz

Without a doubt, the most famous essay ever written about "mexicanidad" is Octavio Paz's The Labyrinth of Solitude, *which first appeared in the influential journal* Cuadernos Americanos *in 1950. Paz (1914–1998) was by then already a major figure in Mexican poetry, and the book marked his brilliant debut as an essayist. The essay is a dizzying intellectual exercise, seeking to explain the Mexican's "hermetic" personality through an allusive, though at times opaque, combination of Jungian psychology, poetic imagery, and historical analysis. Paz held that Mexico was intent on denying its true heritage, that its evolution was retarded by repeated cycles of conquest, violation, and revolution, and that centuries of history were embedded in the Mexican character.*

Paz's literary career began in the early 1930s. He fought on the Republican side in the Spanish Civil War and later undertook a diplomatic career, which included posts in France, India, Japan, and Switzerland. He quit this career in 1968 in protest against the government killings of student protestors at the Plaza de Tlatelolco (see part VII of this volume). While he remained very critical of the Mexican political system, he became increasingly conservative in his later years, which often placed him at odds with other Latin American intellectuals. In 1990 he was awarded the Nobel Prize for Literature.

All of our anxious tensions express themselves in a phrase we use when anger, joy, or enthusiasm cause us to exalt our condition as Mexicans: *"¡Viva México, hijos de la chingada!"* This phrase is a true battle cry, charged with a peculiar electricity; it is a challenge and an affirmation, a shot fired against an imaginary enemy, and an explosion in the air. Once again, with a certain pathetic and plastic fatality, we are presented with the image of a skyrocket that climbs into the sky, bursts in a shower of sparks and then falls in darkness. Or with the image of that howl that ends all our songs and possesses the same ambiguous resonance: an angry joy, a destructive affirmation ripping open the breast and consuming itself.

When we shout this cry on the fifteenth of September, the anniversary of our independence, we affirm ourselves in front of, against and in spite of the "others." Who are the "others"? They are the *hijos de la chingada:* strangers, bad Mexicans, our enemies, our rivals. In any case, the "others," that is, all those who are not as we are. And these "others" are not defined except as the sons of a mother as vague and indeterminate as themselves.

Who is the *Chingada?* Above all, she is the Mother. Not a Mother of flesh and blood but a mythical figure. The *Chingada* is one of the Mexican representations of Maternity, like *La Llorona* or the "long-suffering Mexican mother"[1] we celebrate on the tenth of May. The *Chingada* is the mother who has suffered—metaphorically or actually—the corrosive and defaming action implicit in the verb that gives her her name. . . .

In Mexico the word [*chingar*] has innumerable meanings. It is a magical word: a change of tone, a change of inflection, is enough to change its meaning. It has as many shadings as it has intonations, as many meanings as it has emotions. One may be a *chingón,* a *gran chingón* (in business, in politics, in crime or with women), or a *chingaquedito* (silent, deceptive, fashioning plots in the shadows, advancing cautiously and then striking with a club), or a *chingoncito.* But in this plurality of meanings the ultimate meaning always contains the idea of aggression, whether it is the simple act of molesting, pricking or censuring, or the violent act of wounding or killing. The verb denotes violence, an emergence from oneself to penetrate another by force. It also means to injure, to lacerate, to violate—bodies, souls, objects—and to destroy. When something breaks, we say: *"Se chingó."* When someone behaves rashly, in defiance of the rules, we say: *"Hizo una chingadera."*

The idea of breaking, of ripping open, appears in a great many of these expressions. The word has sexual connotations but it is not a synonym for the sexual act: one may *chingar* a woman without actually possessing her. And when it does allude to the sexual act, violation or deception gives it a particular shading. The man who commits it never does so with the consent of the *chingada. Chingar,* then, is to do violence to another. The verb is masculine, active, cruel: it stings, wounds, gashes, stains. And it provokes a bitter, resentful satisfaction.

The person who suffers this action is passive, inert and open, in contrast to the active, aggressive and closed person who inflicts it. The *chingón* is the *macho,* the male; he rips open the *chingada,* the female, who is pure passivity, defenseless against the exterior world. The relationship between them is violent, and it is determined by the cynical power of the first and the impotence of the second. The idea of violence rules darkly over all the meanings of the word, and the dialectic of the "closed" and the "open" thus fulfills itself with an almost ferocious precision.

The magic power of the word is intensified by the fact that it is prohibited. No one uses it casually in public. Only an excess of anger or a delirious enthusiasm justifies its use. It is a word that can only be heard among men or during the big fiestas. When we shout it out, we break a veil of silence, modesty or hypocrisy. We reveal ourselves as we really are. The forbidden words boil up in us, just as our emotions boil up. When they finally burst out, they do so harshly, brutally, in the form of a shout, a challenge, an offense. They are projectiles or knives. They cause wounds. . . .

If we take into account all of its various meanings, the word defines a great part of our life and qualifies our relationships with our friends and compatriots. To the Mexican there are only two possibilities in life: either he inflicts the actions implied by *chingar* on others, or else he suffers them himself at the hands of others. This conception of social life as combat fatally divides society into the strong and the weak. The strong—the hard, unscrupulous *chingones*—surround themselves with eager followers. This servility toward the strong, especially among the *políticos* (that is, the professionals of public business), is one of the more deplorable consequences of the situation. Another, no less degrading, is the devotion to personalities rather than to principles. Our politicians frequently mix public business with private. It does not matter. Their wealth or their influence in government allows them to maintain a flock of supporters whom the people call, most appositely, *lambiscones* (from the word *lamer:* "to lick").

The verb *chingar*—malign and agile and playful, like a caged animal—creates many expressions that turn our world into a jungle: there are tigers in business, eagles in the schools and the army, lions among our friends. A bribe is called a "bite." The bureaucrats gnaw their "bones" (public employment). And in a world of *chingones,* of difficult relationships, ruled by violence and suspicion—a world in which no one opens out or surrenders himself—ideas and accomplishments count for little. The only thing of value is manliness, personal strength, a capacity for imposing oneself on others.

The word also has another, more restricted meaning. When we say, *"Vete a la chingada,"*[2] we send a person to a distant place. Distant, vague and indeterminate. To the country of broken and worn-out things. A gray country, immense and empty, that is not located anywhere. . . . The *chingada,* because of constant usage, contradictory meanings and the friction of angry or enthusiastic lips, wastes away, loses its contents and disappears. It is a hollow word. It says nothing. It is Nothingness itself.

After this digression, it is possible to answer the question, "What is the *Chingada*?" The *Chingada* is the Mother forcibly opened, violated or deceived. The *hijo de la Chingada* is the offspring of violation, abduction or deceit. If we compare this expression with the Spanish *hijo de puta* (son of a whore), the difference is immediately obvious. To the Spaniard, dishonor consists in being the son of a woman who voluntarily surrenders herself: a prostitute. To the Mexican it consists in being the fruit of a violation.

Manuel Cabrera points out that the Spanish attitude reflects a moral and historical conception of original sin, while that of the Mexican, deeper and more genuine, transcends both ethics and anecdotes. In effect, every woman —even when she gives herself willingly—is torn open by the man, is the *Chingada*. In a certain sense all of us, by the simple fact of being born of woman, are *hijos de la Chingada,* sons of Eve. But the singularity of the Mexican resides, I believe, in his violent, sarcastic humiliation of the Mother and his no less violent affirmation of the Father. A woman friend of mine (women are more aware of the strangeness of this situation) has made me see that this admiration for the Father—who is the symbol of the closed, the aggressive— expresses itself very clearly in a saying we use when we want to demonstrate our superiority: "I am your father." . . .

The *macho* represents the masculine pole of life. The phrase "I am your father" has no paternal flavor and it is not said in order to protect or to guide another, but rather to impose one's superiority, that is, to humiliate. Its real meaning is no different from that of the verb *chingar* and its derivatives. The *macho* is the *gran chingón.* One word sums up the aggressiveness, insensitivity, invulnerability and other attributes of the *macho:* power. It is force without the discipline of any notion of order: arbitrary power, the will without reins and without a set course. . . .

The essential attribute of the *macho*—power—almost always reveals itself as a capacity for wounding, humiliating, annihilating. Nothing is more natural, therefore, than his indifference toward the offspring he engenders. He is not the founder of a people; he is not a patriarch who exercises *patria potestas;* he is not a king or a judge or the chieftain of a clan. He is power isolated in its own potency, without relationship or compromise with the outside world. He is pure in communication, a solitude that devours itself and everything it touches. He does not pertain to our world; he is not from our city; he does not live in our neighborhood. He comes from far away: he is always far away. He is the Stranger. It is impossible not to notice the resemblance between the figure of the *macho* and that of the Spanish conquistador. This is the model— more mythical than real—that determines the images the Mexican people form of men in power: caciques, feudal lords, hacienda owners, politicians, generals, captains of industry. They are all *machos, chingones.*

The macho has no heroic or divine counterpart. Hidalgo, the "father of the fatherland" as it is customary to call him in the ritual gibberish of the Republic, is a defenseless old man, more an incarnation of the people's helplessness against force than an image of the wrath and power of an awe-inspiring father. Among the numerous patron saints of the Mexicans there is none who resembles the great masculine divinities. Finally, there is no especial veneration for God the Father in the Trinity. He is a dim figure at best. On the other hand, there is profound devotion to Christ as the Son of God, as the youthful God, above all as the victimized Redeemer. The village churches have a great many images of Jesus—on the cross, or covered with thorns and wounds— in which the insolent realism of the Spaniards is mingled with the tragic symbolism of the Indians. On the one hand, the wounds are flowers, pledges of resurrection; on the other, they are a reiteration that life is the sorrowful mask of death. . . .

The Mexican venerates a bleeding and humiliated Christ, a Christ who has been beaten by the soldiers and condemned by the judges, because he sees in him a transfigured image of his own identity. . . . And this brings to mind Cuauhtémoc, the young Aztec emperor who was dethroned, tortured, and murdered by Cortés.

Cuauhtémoc means "Falling Eagle." The Mexican chieftain rose to power at the beginning of the siege of México-Tenochtitlán, when the Aztecs had been abandoned by their gods, their vassals and their allies. Even his relationship with a woman fits the archetype of the young hero, at one and the same time the lover and the son of [a] goddess. . . . He is a warrior but he is also a child. The exception is that the heroic cycle does not end with his death: the fallen hero awaits resurrection. It is not surprising that for the majority of Mexicans Cuauhtémoc should be the "young grandfather," the origin of Mexico: the hero's tomb is the cradle of the people. This is the dialectic of myth, and Cuauhtémoc is more a myth than a historical figure. Another element enters here, an analogy that makes this history a true poem in search of fulfillment: the location of Cuauhtémoc's tomb is not known. To discover it would mean nothing less than to return to our origins, to reunite ourselves with our ancestry, to break out of our solitude. It would be a resurrection.

If we ask about the third figure of the triad, the Mother, we hear a double answer. It is no secret to anyone that Mexican Catholicism is centered about the cult of the Virgin of Guadalupe. In the first place, she is an Indian Virgin; in the second place, the scene of her appearance to the Indian Juan Diego was a hill that formerly contained a sanctuary dedicated to Tonantzin, "Our Mother," the Aztec goddess of fertility. We know that the Conquest coincided with the apogee of the cult of two masculine divinities: Quetzalcóatl, the self-sacrificing god, and Huitzilopochtli, the young warrior-god. The defeat of these gods—which is what the Conquest meant to the Indian world, because it was the end of a cosmic cycle and the inauguration of a new divine kingdom—caused the faithful to return to the ancient feminine deities. This phenomenon of a return to the maternal womb, so well known to the psychologist, is without doubt one of the determining causes of the swift popularity of the cult of the Virgin. The Indian goddesses were goddesses of fecundity, linked to the cosmic rhythms, the vegetative processes and agrarian rites. The Catholic Virgin is also the Mother (some Indian pilgrims still call her Guadalupe-Tonantzin), but her principal attribute is not to watch over the fertility of the earth but to provide refuge for the unfortunate. The situation has changed: the worshipers do not try to make sure of their harvests but to find a mother's lap. The Virgin is the consolation of the poor, the shield of the weak, the help of the oppressed. In sum, she is the Mother of orphans. All men are born disinherited and their true condition is orphanhood, but this is particularly true among the Indians and the poor in Mexico. The cult of the Virgin reflects not only the general condition of man but also a concrete historical situation, in both the spiritual and material realms. In addition, the Virgin—the universal Mother—is also the intermediary, the messenger, between disinherited man and the unknown, inscrutable power: the Strange.

In contrast to Guadalupe, who is the Virgin Mother, the *Chingada* is the violated Mother. . . . Both of them are passive figures. Guadalupe is pure receptivity, and the benefits she bestows are of the same order: she consoles, quiets, dries tears, calms passions. The *Chingada* is even more passive. Her passivity is abject: she does not resist violence, but is an inert heap of bones, blood and dust. Her taint is constitutional and resides . . . in her sex. This passivity, open to the outside world, causes her to lose her identity: she is the *Chingada*. She loses her name; she *is* no one; she disappears into nothingness; she is Nothingness. And yet she is the cruel incarnation of the feminine condition.

If the *Chingada* is a representation of the violated Mother, it is appropriate to associate her with the Conquest, which was also a violation, not only in the historical sense but also in the very flesh of Indian women. The symbol of this violation is doña Malinche, the mistress of Cortés. It is true that she gave herself voluntarily to the conquistador, but he forgot her as soon as her usefulness was over. Doña Marina[3] becomes a figure representing the Indian women who were fascinated, violated, or seduced by the Spaniards. And as a small boy will not forgive his mother if she abandons him to search for his father, the Mexican people have not forgiven La Malinche for her betrayal. She embodies the open, the *chingado,* to our closed, stoic, impassive Indians. Cuauhtémoc and Doña Marina are thus two antagonistic and complementary figures. There is nothing surprising about our cult of the young emperor—

"the only hero at the summit of art," an image of the sacrificed son—and there is also nothing surprising about the curse that weighs against La Malinche. This explains the success of the contemptuous adjective *malinchista* recently put into circulation by the newspapers to denounce all those who have been corrupted by foreign influences. The *malinchistas* are those who want Mexico to open itself to the outside world: the true sons of La Malinche, who is the *Chingada* in person. Once again we see the opposition of the closed and the open.

When we shout "*¡Viva México, hijos de la chingada!*" we express our desire to live closed off from the outside world and, above all, from the past. In this shout we condemn our origins and deny our hybridism. The strange permanence of Cortés and La Malinche in the Mexican's imagination and sensibilities reveals that they are something more than historical figures: they are symbols of a secret conflict that we have still not resolved. When he repudiates La Malinche—the Mexican Eve, as she was represented by José Clemente Orozco in his mural in the National Preparatory School—the Mexican breaks his ties with the past, renounces his origins, and lives in isolation and solitude.

The Mexican condemns all his traditions at once, the whole set of gestures, attitudes and tendencies in which it is now difficult to distinguish the Spanish from the Indian. For that reason the Hispanic thesis, which would have us descend from Cortés to the exclusion of La Malinche, is the patrimony of a few extremists who are not even pure whites. The same can be said of indigenist propaganda, which is also supported by fanatical criollos and mestizos, while the Indians have never paid it the slightest attention. The Mexican does not want to be either an Indian or a Spaniard. Nor does he want to be descended from them. He denies them. And he does not affirm himself as a mixture, but rather as an abstraction: he is a man. He becomes the son of Nothingness. His beginnings are in his own self.

This attitude is revealed not only in our daily life but also in the course of our history, which at certain moments has been the embodiment of a will to eradicate all that has gone before. It is astonishing that a country with such a vivid past—a country so profoundly traditional, so close to its roots, so rich in ancient legends even if poor in modern history—should conceive of itself only as a negation of its origins.

Our shout strips us naked and discloses the wound that we alternately flaunt and conceal, but it does not show us the causes of this separation from, and negation of, the Mother, not even when we recognize that such a rupture has occurred. In lieu of a closer examination of the problem, we will suggest that the liberal Reform movement of the middle of the last century seems to be the moment when the Mexican decided to break with his traditions, which is a form of breaking with oneself. If our Independence movement cut the ties that bound us to Spain, the Reform movement denied that the Mexican nation as a historical project should perpetuate the colonial tradition. Juárez and his generation founded a state whose ideals are distinct from those that animated New Spain or the pre-Cortesian cultures. The Mexican state proclaimed an abstract and universal conception of man: the Republic is not composed of criollos, Indians, and mestizos (as the Laws of the Indies, with a great love for distinctions and a great respect for the heterogeneous nature of the colonial world, had specified) but simply of men alone. All alone.

The Reform movement is the great rupture with the Mother. This separation was a necessary and inevitable act, because every life that is truly autonomous begins as a break with its family and its past. But the separation still hurts. We still suffer from that wound. That is why the feeling of orphanhood is the constant background of our political endeavors and our personal conflicts. Mexico is all alone, like each one of her sons.

Notes

1. *La Llorona* is the "Weeping Woman," who wanders through the streets late at night, weeping and crying out. *Trans.*
2. Somewhat stronger than "Go to Hell." *Trans.*
3. The name given to La Malinche by the Spaniards. *Trans.*

The Problem of National Culture

Guillermo Bonfil Batalla

Like Octavio Paz, anthropologist Guillermo Bonfil Batalla (1935–1991) believed that Mexico suffers from a crisis of identity. However, for Bonfil the nature of that crisis is quite different. For the earlier thinkers, the Indian remained a shadowy presence who constituted a "problem," the only apparent solution to which was assimilation into the Westernized culture of the dominant, usually urban groups. By contrast, Bonfil Batalla argued that the true Mexico, which he labels "México profundo," is represented by Indians, rural mestizos, and a portion of the urban poor, whose culture is Mesoamerican. The values of this culture are incompatible with those of the elite, who have consistently sought to imitate the culture of Western Europe and to deny the social realities of their own country. Far from an inert mass, Mexico's Indians remain the bearers of a true, alternative civilization which needs to be reclaimed rather than denied or suppressed.

Bonfil Batalla was among Mexico's most distinguished anthropologists. He served as director of the National Institute of Anthropology and History (INAH), founded and directed the National Museum of Popular Culture, and directed the Center for Research and Advanced Study in Social Anthropology (CIESAS). In 1975 he helped to organize Mexico's first National Congress of Indian Peoples, which reflected his conviction that Indian peoples would profit more from autonomy and self-determination than from efforts, however well intentioned, at assimilation or social welfare.

What explains the absence of a common Mexican culture is the presence of two civilizations that have never fused to produce a new civilizational program. Neither have they coexisted in harmony, to each other's reciprocal benefit.

To the contrary, the groups of Mesoamerican origin and the successive hegemonic groups dominant in Mexican society, with their versions of Western civilization, continue to be opposed. There has never been a process of convergence, but, rather, one of opposition. There is one simple and straightforward reason: certain social groups have illegitimately held political, economic, and ideological power from the European invasion to the present. All have been affiliated through inheritance or through circumstance with Western civilization, and within their programs for governing there has been no place for Mesoamerican civilization. The dominant position of these groups originated in the stratified order of colonial society. It has expressed itself in an ideology that conceives of the future only in terms of development, progress, advancement, and the Revolution itself, all concepts within the mainstream of Western civilization. Cultural diversity and, specifically, the omnipresence of Mesoamerican civilization have always been interpreted within that scheme in the only way possible. They are seen as an obstacle to progress along the one true path and toward the only valid objective. The mentality inherited from the colonizers does not allow perception of or invention of any other path. Mesoamerican civilization is either dead or must die as soon as possible, because it is of undeniable inferiority and has no future of its own.

The presence of two distinct civilizations implies the existence of different historical plans for the future. We are not dealing simply with alternatives within the framework of a common civilization, proposals that might alter current reality in many ways but that do not question the ultimate objectives or the underlying values that all share as participants in the same civilizational project. We are, rather, dealing with different projects, which are built on different ways of conceiving of the world, nature, society, and humankind. They postulate different hierarchies of values. They do not have the same aspirations nor do they understand in the same way how the full realization of each human being is to be achieved. They are projects that express two unique concepts of transcendence. Throughout, attempts at cultural unification have never suggested unity through creation of a new civilization that would be the synthesis of the existing ones. Rather, unity has been attempted through the elimination of one (Mesoamerican civilization, of course) and the spread of the other.

The colonial enterprise engaged in destroying Mesoamerican civilization and stopped only where self-interest intervened. When necessary, whole peoples were destroyed. On the other hand, where the labor force of the Indians was required, they were kept socially and culturally segregated. Indirectly and in a contradictory fashion, the minimum conditions for the continuity of Mesoamerican civilization were created, in spite of the brutal decline in population during the first decades after the invasion. This decline was one of the most violent and terrible demographic catastrophes in the history of humanity. Its intrinsic nature prevented the colonial regime from posing a project of cultural fusion that might have amalgamated the Mesoamerican and the Western civilizational planes. The ideology that justified colonization was that of a redemptive crusade, thus revealing the conviction that the only path to salvation was that of Western civilization.

The Westernization of the Indian, nevertheless, turned out to be contradictory, given the stubborn necessity of maintaining a clear distinction between the colonizers and the colonized. If the Indians had stopped being Indians in order to be fully incorporated into Western civilization, the ideological justification for colonial domination would have ended. Segregation and difference are essential for any colonial society. Unification, on the other hand, whether by assimilation of the colonized to the dominant culture or through the perhaps improbable fusion of two civilizations, denies the root of the colonial order.

The birth and consolidation of Mexico as an independent state in the turbulent course of the nineteenth century did not produce any different plan, nothing that deviated from the basic intention of taking the country along the paths of Western civilization. The struggles between the liberals and the conservatives reflect different conceptions of how to achieve that goal, but those struggles never question it. The new nation was conceived as culturally homogeneous, following the dominant European conviction that a state is the expression of a people with a common culture and the same language and is produced by having a common history. Thus, consolidating the nation was the goal of all groups contending for power. They understood consolidation as the slow incorporation of the great majority to the cultural model that had been adopted as the national plan.

The ruling groups of the country, who make or impose the most important decisions affecting all of Mexican society, have never admitted that to advance might imply liberating and encouraging the cultural capacities that really exist in the majority of the population. . . . In this way of thinking about things, the majority of Mexicans have a future only on the condition that they stop being themselves. That change is conceived as a definite break, a transformation into someone else. It is never conceived as bringing up to date through internal transformation, as liberating cultures that have been subject to multiple pressures during five centuries of colonial domination.

The constitutional history of Mexico is an example that illustrates this schizophrenic posture in a striking way. In all cases it has led to the juridical construction of a fictitious state from whose norms and practices the majority of the population is excluded. . . . We must admit [that it is] a great dominating fiction. Otherwise, how do we explain a system of democratic elections based on the recognition of political parties as the only legitimate vehicles for electoral participation in a country in which an absolute majority of the population does not belong to any party or exercise its right to vote? One would look in vain for a single example demonstrating an intention to understand and recognize the real systems that various groups use to obtain and legitimize authority. One would look in vain for an attempt to structure a national system in which local political forms would have a place and in which, at the same time, they might encounter the stimulus and the possibilities for progressive development. There are no such examples. The country must be modern right now, made so by virtue of law, and if reality follows other paths, it is an incorrect and illegal reality.

This schizophrenic fiction, manifest in all aspects of the country's life and culture, has grave consequences, which do not seem to worry the proponents of the imaginary Mexico. In the first place, the fiction produces the marginalization of the majority, a marginalization that is real and not imaginary. . . . This is not . . . a marginalization that is expressed only in reduced access to goods and services, but, rather, a total marginalization, an exclusion from one's own way of living. Many Mexicans thus have a choice: they can live on the margin of national life, related to it only by the minimal, inevitable relations between their real world and the other, which appears as different and external; or they can live a double life, also schizophrenic, changing between worlds and cultures according to circumstances and necessities; or, finally, they can renounce their identity from birth and try to be fully accepted in the imaginary Mexico of the minority.

The notion of democracy was established two centuries ago as one of the central aspirations of Western civilization. However, upon being mechanically transplanted into a postulate of the imaginary Mexico, it converted itself into a series of mechanisms of exclusion, whose effect was to deny the existence of the population. It is a curious democracy that does not recognize the existence of the people themselves, but, rather, sets itself the task of creating them. Afterward, it would, of course, put itself at their service. It is a surprising democracy of the minority, a national program that begins by leaving out the majority groups of the country. It is a project that ends by making illegitimate the thoughts and actions of the majority of Mexicans; the people themselves wind up being the obstacle to democracy.

A second consequence is also inevitable. By making reality a blank page, one chooses not to make use of the greater part of the cultural capital of Mexican society. It becomes an absolute impossibility to recognize, appreciate, and stimulate the development of the extensive and varied cultural patrimony that history has placed in Mexican hands. The old colonial blindness remains, the notion that here there is nothing with which a future can be built. If the people have to be created to substitute for the nonpeople who exist, it follows that a culture also has to be created to substitute for the existing nonculture. The elements that ought to constitute the core of the new culture are not here, and they are important: ideas, knowledge, aspirations, technology, what to do and how to do it. Once more we find the dishonest task of substituting for reality instead of transforming it.

Does It Mean Anything to Be Mexican?

Roger Bartra

The classic writings on "lo mexicano" have been heavily criticized in recent years for their tendency to generalize about what is unarguably a vast number of people. Relatively few of those people, we might surmise, conform to the image of the eternal adolescent or the wounded, angry macho described by the likes of Octavio Paz. Nor may it be helpful, beyond a certain point, to generalize, in rather dichotomous fashion, as Bonfil Batalla does, about the existence of two Mexicos inhabited by circumscribed dominant and subordinate groups. Some have suggested that these pensadores *(grand thinkers), whatever their motives, have only created and perpetuated stereotypes of the Mexican that have been manipulated for political ends. Anthropologist-sociologist Roger Bartra takes the argument a step further, suggesting that the stereotype of the* pelado, *as featured in Mexican popular culture, serves the interests of the Mexican state. Bartra finds this popular stereotype exemplified by Mario Moreno, better known as Cantinflas (1911–1993), the beloved comedic everyman of the Mexican cinema.*

Roger Bartra received his doctorate in Sociology from the University of Paris and is currently an investigator with the Institute of Social Studies of the National Autonomous University of Mexico (UNAM). For many years he was the editor of La Jornada Semanal, *one of the nation's most prominent literary magazines. Bartra has been a pioneer in the field of Mexican cultural studies and is the author of many influential writings on the intersection of culture and power in both rural and urban Mexico.*

My mind is bent to tell of bodies changed into new forms. —Ovid, *Metamorphoses*

The deplorable conditions in which the working classes are born and raised have for a long time inspired a feeling of horror and revulsion in the bourgeoisie, who are afraid to recognize the proletariat as creatures they themselves have created. Although no one can deny that they are a necessary and inevitable result of industrialization, they continue to be seen by the dominant class as "a malignant chancre on the flanks of modern society," according to Albert Dandoy in a noteworthy book on the French working class published just after the Second World War. The book is dreadful, but it does pick up the old bourgeois tradition of horror at a proletariat whose mentality is tinged with resentment, distrust, immorality, mimicry, and complexes of inferiority and dispossession. These, we notice, are the same features attributed to the Mexican by Samuel Ramos and his school. The new urban landscape fills these observers of the Mexican spirit with terror. For them the Mexican is a figure without meaning, who denies everything for no reason, who lacks principles, distrusts everyone, and disdains ideas. Ramos asks anxiously: "But then, why does the Mexican live?" He can live because he leads a nonreflective existence, without a future, so that Mexican society is no more than "a chaos in which individuals gravitate at random like scattered atoms." This metaphor applies perfectly to the typical functioning of modern capitalist society.

From 1844, Friedrich Engels tried to understand and describe the terrible "culture of poverty," as it is called today. In his classic study of the situation of the working class, he showed that the typically proletarian tendencies to impulsiveness, improvidence and, of course, to the abuse of alcohol and sex are a necessary counterweight to ease the privations, instability, and degradation characteristic of their everyday lives. Today, the strange proletarian subculture of the nineteenth century has almost ceased to exist in the most-developed capitalist countries; but it has surfaced on the backward periphery, where the pains of a deferred industrial revolution are made more acute by the consequences of colonial and imperial oppression. It is not surprising that cultural stereotypes arise which are to a certain degree similar to those used by the European bourgeoisie to illustrate their idea of the proletariat.

What is odd about the Mexican situation is that there is a curious departure from the proletarian prototype, with the object of fomenting the development of a national identity. After the Revolution, the Mexican nationalists, orphans of native bourgeois traditions, had only the peasants and the proletariat as sources of inspiration. An ideological dissection had to be performed in order to extract some features of popular culture for elevation to the category of national ideology; other aspects, considered irrelevant, were to be disposed of. It was not simply a Manichaean operation to get rid of those elements considered harmful, as was undertaken by the positivists of the *porfiriato*.[1] Rather, it meant the emergence of a complex, contradictory image of the Mexican, in great measure forged as a reflection of the condition of the urban proletariat. I have already mentioned the prototype of the Mexican as sentimental and violent, passionate and aggressive, a resentful and rancorous figure. Another essential element must now be recognized: the Mexican also appears as a man in flight, seeking refuge from the sad reality around him. This evasion has been described and assessed from many different perspectives—from the idleness and lack of willpower that lead him to shun work to the creation of complex mechanisms of elusion and dissimulation. For many it is a senseless flight, contributing to the chaos of industrial society. One result of this evasion is the creation of an image having a long history in picaresque literature. The Mexican *pelado,* however, is not just a variant of the social type created by the Spanish picaresque tradition. Thus Augustín Yáñez has claimed that the *pelado* lacks the roguish acuity of the *pícaro,* a cleverness that is essentially language-based and "acquired through adventure, example, and practical observation." The *pelado,* jettisoned by modern urban industrialization, is . . . one for whom language is not a means of communication but, rather, a barrier of elusion designed for self-defense and concealment. Thus, one of the best descendants of the old *pícaro* is a hero of the silent movies rather than of the novel: Charlie Chaplin, who with his helpless simplicity and gentle guile manages to awaken waves of sympathy for those living in the misery of the twentieth century. The elusive language of gestures, with every kind of movement of the eyebrows and moustache, is the best barrier against the aggressiveness of reality.

The Mexican equivalent of Chaplin is Cantinflas, one of whose most important characteristics is precisely the elusive language that allows him to slip out of any predicament. One observer of the Mexican character, César Garizurieta, claims that Cantinflas is the most representative example of the Mexican psychological type. Unlike Chaplin, whose formal dress reveals a Utopian desire for change, Cantinflas has no aspirations to better himself and "does not want a better world even as a dream; he is happy with life as it is." The Mexican of the modern age has remained at the level of a caricature of man. The energy, aggressiveness, and life force, so fervently exalted by various illustrators of the Mexican Revolution as characteristic of the new man, fade away before the prototype of Cantinflas. This frustrated Mexican Prometheus fails to bring with him not only the secret of fire, but also the gift of the word. According to Garizurieta,

> Cantinflas expresses himself in self-defense through an artificial, subtle language, resulting from aspects of his incompetence. Faced with his exaggerated feeling of inferiority, he knows that he is equally compromised whether he affirms or denies. Therefore, he neither affirms nor denies: he oscillates between affirmation and denial. Without intending it, he elicits laughter or tears when he speaks, since there are no frontiers delimiting the tragic from the comic.

Without a doubt the great popularity of Cantinflas stems from the fact that, in his mockery, he is also criticizing social injustice. For example, when

Cantinflas *(left)* became a major movie star during the 1940s,
often playing the role of a *pelado*. La Cineteca Nacional

he is asked if work is a good thing, he answers: "If it were any good, the
rich would have cornered the market in it." But he is a conformist critic who
proposes escape rather than struggle, slipping away rather than fighting. The
Mexican becomes a teacher of feints and puns. He becomes a twisted, subtle,
evasive, and indirect character, dominated by "the goal of circumlocution"
thanks to a language having such a prodigious store of evasions, elusions,
wastefulness, and deviousness that it appears made to order for the art of
punning, "pointing to one extreme only to turn up at the other, and later re-
versing the direction."[2] It is highly unlikely that the Cantinflas stereotype can
be applied to many Mexicans; however, it is obvious that it could be useful
in defining the political style of Mexico's government bureaucrats. It is also
an excellent metaphor for describing that peculiar mediating structure which
legitimizes one-party dictatorship and government despotism. That structure
is a labyrinth of contradictions, puns, and feints which allow the most radical
popular demands to be accepted—before, inevitably, they are lost in the maze
of corridors, anterooms, and offices, and their original meaning vanishes. In

this aspect, above all others, it can be easily appreciated that the definition of the national character obeys political motives more than anything and can be understood better if we seek its roots not in the people, but in the hegemonic classes. Consider the following definition:

> It is imminence that is the determining characteristic of the Mexican, the provisional man, and everyday events that are not suspended on the edge of it leave him unconcerned: to lose his job or his love; to have money or not to have it; to fulfill a promise or not, for him everything *importa madre* [doesn't really matter].[3]

This is an outline of *importamadrismo*, whose antecedents as a metaphor one must seek as far back as in the book *El no importa de España* (1668), by the Spanish writer of novels of customs and manners, Francisco Santos. There Santos referred to the Spanish indolence that justified everything which turned out wrong with a dry *no importa* (it doesn't matter). Menéndez Pidal tells of the German count who, around 1599, was exasperated by Phillip II's unperturbable ministers (nicknamed the "ministers of eternity") and who greatly suffered with the "come back tomorrow" attitude so well described by Mariano José de Larra in 1833.

We are confronted with a complicated phenomenon: in some moments in history, the ruling classes appropriate what they think is popular culture and develop a curious mimicry of it. In this way the national culture drinks at the wells of popular culture. But it is not a linear process; the popular components of the national culture are mere fragments (frequently very distorted ones) of what is in reality the everyday life of the social class whence they are taken. We can recognize the proletarian (even lumpenproletarian) origin of the feints, elusions, puns, and laziness that are said to contribute to the formation of the Mexican character; we can even observe behavior worthy of Cantinflas in many politicians. But it must be emphasized that there is a wide gap between the real life of a *pelado* in the inner-city community of Tepito and the model that cinema, television, literature, or philosophy proposes to society as a point of reference. The situation grows in complexity owing to the fact that the mass media recycle the popular stereotypes fabricated by the hegemonic culture so that, in their turn, they exercise an influence on the lower classes' way of life. If this last stage did not occur, then the national culture would have no part in the legitimation of the dominant system. This legitimizing function endows power with a species of dynamism, so that we are constantly encountering the birth of new forms of culture. The same stereotype that can, at first, have a markedly antihegemonic character is transformed until it acquires almost unrecognizable facets: thus, the workers in the revolutionary murals become existentialist hieroglyphs representing anguish, and the comedy of the humbler classes' outdoor theaters is continued in the stammerings of Cantinflas. At last, for the hegemonic classes, the potentially dangerous and revolutionary *pelados* and proletarians end up as a bunch of grotesque characters who know only to jabber and who, in most cases, express their emotions in song.

The dialects that arise in the working-class barrios are originally forms of defense. Not only are they language that allow the members of a social group to identify with their own way of life, but they also act as barriers that impede others from understanding their conversations. Understandably, the popular dialects are highly influenced by the speech of the underworld and the prisons, where cryptic forms of communication are developed to hinder understanding. These are languages *with no meaning* for those who do not belong to the social group which creates them, and that is precisely why they are developed: they make sense only *here* (in the streets), rather than *out there* (in refined, bourgeois society). From this need to identify and differentiate oneself came the so-called *arte-acá* (art-here) of Tepito, a poor Mexico City barrio in which popular forms for the defense of the local culture have arisen. But the moment the popular slang is removed from its natural environment it loses its sense, and the phenomenon I have noted occurs: what is *meaningless* becomes the *new meaning* of popular speech. The slang's new function is to confuse meanings and reveal only the defensive, evasive aspects of the popular language. So the speech of Cantinflas drains the language of meaning and converts it into a method for avoiding predicaments; in contrast, the popular slang that Cantinflas takes as his point of departure is a deeply committed form (i.e., it is coherent to him and the world around him). In this way the Mexican stereotype adopts elements that have a popular origin, but when the scene shifts — as when barrio slang emerges from the mouth of Cantinflas — they acquire another meaning.

The myth of the *pelado* in its Cantinflas version is particularly interesting because it clearly reveals the relationship that the political culture establishes between government and people. Cantinflas is not only the stereotype of the poor Mexican from the city; he is also a harmful simulacrum of the strong structural link that necessarily exists between state despotism and popular corruption. Cantinflas's message is transparent: misery is a permanent state of mindless primitivism that must be vindicated through laughter. This is expressed principally in his corruption of speech, through a veritable implosion of meanings; it is the delirium of a metamorphosis in which everything changes without any apparent meaning. It is understood that there is a correspondence between the corruption of the people and the corruption of the government: the people get the government they deserve. Or, put the other way round, the authoritarian, corrupt government has the people that suit it: namely, those whom the nationalism of Cantinflas offers as objects of domination.

A frequent theme in the Cantinflas movies is the confusion of roles: the bullfighter is a petty thief (*Ni sangre ni arena*); the policeman is a *pelado* (*El gendarme desconocido*); and the judge and lawyers end up talking like Cantinflas (*Ahí está en detalle*). The intrinsic corruption of the *pelado* is found throughout the political system; given that the regime of the Revolution is of the people, it must behave in accord with the Mexican character (with "national idiosyncrasy," as politicians like to refer to this corruption of character). The cheap morals and vulgarity with which the exploits of Cantinflas are usually presented cannot obscure the fundamental fact that they are a simulacrum of the *pelado* converted into a policeman, the people transformed into government, and nonsense enthroned as political discourse.

The verbal confusion of Cantinflas, rather than serving to criticize the demagogy of the politicians, actually legitimizes it. With gestures and mime (running parallel to the nonsense of the verbal effluence) it is insinuated that there is another interpretation, something hidden; that other reality, invoked by the nodding of the head and the movement of the eyebrows and hips, is a world of illegal profits, sexuality without eroticism, power without representation, wealth without work. There is in the punning and the feints a subtle invitation to bribery: the rules of the game are founded in a common venality that allows the Mexican to evade the police, swindle the feebleminded, escape from homosexuality, obtain intercourse easily with other women while avoiding being made a cuckold by one's own. The *pelado* lives in a world that, in order to function, needs to be oiled regularly: thus, a shifting society is built in which, at any moment, everything can lose meaning, and civility becomes slick and lubricious. When things freeze up, it is necessary to smear them with what in Europe is called the "Mexican ointment": a bribe. When a problem or obstacle arises, it is necessary to rub into the appropriate hands the ointment that will keep the permanent delirious metamorphosis of the senses under way.

The stereotype of the *pelado* living immersed in the corrupt world must, nevertheless, move us and touch our heartstrings. We cannot avoid glimpsing in the *pelado* the presence of a spirit pierced by emotions, impulses, afflictions, and excitements. So, when the spirit is questioned about the meaning of being Mexican, the answer is obvious: the Mexican has no sense . . . but he does have sentiments.

Notes

1. *Porfiriato:* the dictatorship of General Porfirio Díaz (1876–1911).

2. Salvador Reyes Nevares, *El amor y la amistad en el mexicano* (Mexico City: Porrúa y Obregón, 1952), 2–3, 28.

3. Jorge Carrión, *Mito y magia del mexicano* (Mexico City: Editorial Nuestro Tiempo, 1970), 55.

Mexico City 1992

Alma Guillermoprieto

Journalist Alma Guillermoprieto, one of the most insightful chroniclers of contempo-
rary Latin America, contributed the following "letter" to The New Yorker *at a time*
when the government of President Carlos Salinas de Gortari—a Harvard-educated
technocrat who packed his government with individuals of similar backgrounds and
outlooks to his own—was feverishly promoting the North American Free Trade Agree-
ment. The relentless pursuit of North American–style modernity, however, was a
double-edged sword: many Mexicans not only doubted that NAFTA *would bring the*
many blessings it promised, but they also feared it would impoverish Mexico's rich and
unique culture. In the following excerpt from Guillermoprieto's letter, the centerpiece
is one of the touchstones of Mexico's popular culture, the ranchera *song.*

Mexicans know that a party has been outstandingly successful if at the end
of it there are at least a couple of clusters of longtime or first-time acquaintances leaning on each other against a wall, sobbing helplessly. The activities
one normally associates with a party—flirting and conversation, and even the
kind of dancing that leads to an amnesiac dawn in a strange bed—are considered here mere preludes to or distractions from the ultimate goal, which
is weeping and the free, luxurious expression of pain. A true celebrant of the
Mexican fiesta will typically progress along a path that leads from compul-
sive joke-telling to stubborn argumentativeness to thick-tongued foolery, all
in pursuit of a final, unchecked, absolving wash of tears, and a casual observer
of this voluptuous ritual might conclude that the essential Mexican *fin de fiesta*
cannot happen without alcohol. Not so. It cannot happen without *ranchera*
music. People may cry admirably with little help from booze, but a drunk
who begins to whimper without the benefit of song produces only mediocre
tears. He cries out of self-pity. The man or woman who, with a few tequilas
packed away, bursts into tears to the strains of a *ranchera* hymn—"Let My
Bed Be Made of Stone," for example—weeps for the tragedy of the world,
for a mother, for a father, for our doomed quests for happiness and love, for

life. Sorrow on such a magnificent scale is in itself redeeming, and—an added benefit—its glory leaves little room for embarrassment the morning after.

Now that Mexico is carpeted with Kentucky Fried Chicken, Denny's, and McDonald's outlets, and Coca-Cola is the national drink; now that even low-paid office workers are indentured to their credit cards and auto loans; now that the government of President Carlos Salinas de Gortari has approved a North American Free Trade Agreement, which promises to make Mexico commercially one with its neighbors to the north, there is little scope for magnificent sorrow in the average citizen's life. In the smog-darkened center of Mexico City, or in its monstrous, ticky-tacky suburban spokes, the average citizen on an average day is more concerned with beating the traffic, making the mortgage payment, punching the clock. Progress has hit Mexico in the form of devastation, some of it ecological, much of it aesthetic. Life is rushed, the water may be poisoned, and the new industrial tortillas taste terrible. Favorite ornaments for the home include porcelain dogs and plastic roses, and for the two-thirds of the population which is confined to the cities recreation usually takes the form of a couple of hours with the latest imported sitcom or the local *telenovelas*. Hardly anyone knows anymore what it is to live on a ranch or to die of passion, and yet, when it comes to the defining moments of *mexicanidad*, *ranchera* music, with its odes to love, idyllic landscapes, and death for the sake of honor, continues to reign supreme.

It is a hybrid music. Sung most often to the accompaniment of a mariachi ensemble, *rancheras* generate tension by setting the classic formality of the trumpets and violins against the howling quality of the vocals. The lyrics of many of the best-known songs—"Cielito Lindo," say—include verses that were inherited in colonial days from Spain. Many of the rhetorical flourishes—"lips like rose petals," "eyes like stars"—are Spanish also. But when *rancheras* turn, as they do obsessively, to the topics of death and destruction, alcohol and defeat, and the singer holds up his dying heart for all to see, or calls for the stones in the field to shout at him, he is bleeding from a wound that is uniquely Mexican.

The spiritual home of *ranchera* music is in the heart of Mexico City—in a raucous plaza surrounded by ratty night clubs and forbidding ancient churches. The plaza, which is not far from where I grew up, is named after Giuseppe Garibaldi, the nineteenth-century Italian revolutionary, but the central statue is of José Alfredo Jiménez (1926–1973), who wrote more songs about weeping, alcohol, and women than any other *ranchera* composer. José Alfredo's statue is wearing mariachi costume, because that is what he wore when he sang, and because the plaza is home to dozens, if not hundreds, of men who are themselves mariachis, and who stroll the plaza at all hours of the day

Man with a Violin. (Photo by Henri Cartier-Bresson. Reprinted by permission of Magnum Photos, Inc.)

and night, singing José Alfredo's songs and those of other *ranchera* composers to anyone who pays to listen.

On three of the plaza's irregular sides are vast cantinas and a food market, where vats of highly seasoned soup are sold throughout the night to ward off or cure hangovers. At the plaza's dissonant center is a constantly moving swarm of blurry-eyed revellers and costumed mariachis. The people in mufti stroll, wail at the moon, stagger into each other's arms, or gather around a group of musicians and sing along with them, striking defiant poses as they belt out the words. The mariachis tag after potential customers and negotiate prices, play checkers with bottle tops, shiver in the midnight cold, and, thirty or forty times an evening, play their hearts out for the revellers. Here and there, an electric-shock vender wanders through the crowd, offering a brightly painted box of programmable current to those who, for the equivalent of a couple of dollars, want to take hold of a pair of wires and test their endurance of electricity. A gaggle of tall, goofy-looking foreigners applauds and smiles at the mariachis who have just finished playing for them, and the mariachis smile, too, because tourists pay well. The people from Stand P-84, a wholesale outlet for guavas and mangoes in the city's gigantic central produce market, think the tourists are pretty funny.

Chuy Soto and his guava-selling colleagues arrived here around eight-o'clock on this particular drizzly evening, and now, five hours later, they have reached the euphoric, sputtering stage at which the spirit invariably moves a Mexican to reach for extravagant metaphors and sing the glories of his country. There is a little pile of plastic glasses and empty bottles to mark the site where Chuy's group has been standing all this time, and the singer for the mariachi ensemble that has been accompanying them has just about lost his voice, but Chuy and his friends are full of vigor. "We come here to sing, and after a while emotions come out of us, and Mexicanness," Chuy says, blinking and pursing his lips as he struggles to focus. An adolescent tugs at my elbow, teary-eyed and anxious to share his own thoughts, but he can't get out a single coherent phrase, and he vanishes. One of Chuy's warehouse partners is trying to dance with a plump young woman whose acquaintance he has just made, but he's holding on too tight, and she pushes him away. The woman's friend is singing along with the mariachi (the name refers both to the group and to its individual members), for perhaps the fifth time, a song called "Dos Almas" (Two souls), but by now she can't get anyone to listen to her and she weaves off in a huff. The amiable Chuy is still explaining Mexicanness to my companion, who is Peruvian. "A Mexican's heart is always open and full of music," he stammers, but a buddy of his, who spouts profanity and has in general a sharper-edged vision of things, butts in. "A Mexican knows that life is worthless," he declares.

The mariachi singer Ismael Gutiérrez and his group charge twenty-five thousand pesos, or about eight dollars, per song, but they offered Chuy and his friends the wholesale rate after serenading them with thirty *rancheras.* This meant that for a lucky evening of solid work each of the members of the Mariachi Real del Potosí, as the group Gutiérrez belongs to is called, got about thirty dollars. The group is small, and not first-rate. There's only one of each of the essential components of a mariachi: a violin; a guitar; a trumpet; a *guitarrón,* or fat bass guitar; a *vihuela,* or small plinking guitar; and the singer — Gutiérrez. Like many of his fellow-musicians who have land or a family trade in the provinces, Gutiérrez comes to Mexico City every fortnight or so from his home state — San Luis Potosí, in his case — and puts up at one of the scarred buildings around the plaza, where, he says, the old-fashioned, high-ceilinged rooms are crowded with bunk beds stacked as many as five high. There, he makes sure he gets at least eight hours' sleep a day, to keep his voice going. That is also where he stores his costume, which is as essential to his occupation as any instrument.

In the old days, before the movies, mariachis used to dress like what they were: peasant musicians. But when the Mexican movie industry began producing musicals, back in the thirties, mariachis in Indian dress — big white shirts and trousers, and straw hats — came to seem too ordinary, and someone decided to outfit them in the elegant *mestizo* dress of the *charro,* or horseman. It basic elements are a broad-brimmed felt hat, a short, fitted black jacket, and tight black trousers with double seams running down the outside of the leg. For show, *charros* decorated the seams with brass or silver fittings and with fancy embroidery. Mexico's Hollywood kept the ornaments and the embroidery and added color. The majority of Garibaldi's mariachis wear silver-trimmed black, but now they do this to signify that they are free-lancers, which means that if a customer approaches a *guitarrón* player, say, requesting a song, the musician has to pull an ensemble together from the other black-clad free-lancers standing around. Ismael Gutiérrez is a significant step up in the hierarchy: he belongs to a formally constituted group, and all the members of his Mariachi Real wear sober Prussian blue. Gutiérrez—stout, cheerful, courtly, and equipped with a remarkable handlebar mustache—looks reassuring in his outfit, like a character out of an old-time movie.

Because Gutiérrez belongs to an established mariachi, he has been able to weather a disaster that has affected Garibaldi since the beginning of the year: construction of a new subway line began then, shutting off the main access road to the plaza and cutting down the number of potential customers so drastically that on any given Friday night the ratio of mariachis to revellers appears to be almost one to one. Gutiérrez and his mates have discovered the advantages of business cards, and by handing them out (printed with a more prosperous relative's phone number) around local office buildings and to friendly customers, they have been able to make up for the loss of walk-by trade. Not so the free-lancer Jesús Rosas. Although he plays what his colleagues describe as "a very pretty trumpet," all he can do now is dream of joining a group or landing a permanent job with the mariachis who play inside one of the huge cantinas, such as the famous Tenampa, that face on the plaza. Rosas is only twenty-five, but he has been playing Garibaldi since he left home, more than a decade ago. He used to be in demand, because he plays well, knows a lot of songs, and has a particular affability, at once alert and courteous, friendly and firmly reserved, that is much prized by Mexicans. Now times are bad, but he is stubborn. While dozens of lesser mariachis are coping with the subway crisis by heading for the Reforma, a few blocks away, to flag down cars and hustle for customers, Rosas, who finds such a procedure completely undignified, remains in Garibaldi. "The plaza is here," he says, but that means that by noon on most days he is already cruising it, his trumpet protectively cradled in a beat-up vinyl carrying case, trying to make up in long hours for the clients he has lost.

Mexico's subway is a tremendous achievement: it is now one of the longest urban railroads in the world; it allows millions of people to crisscross the sprawling city to get to work on time every day; it did not collapse, or even buckle, during the earthquake that shattered much of the city seven years ago; it is clean; it runs smoothly. Its expansion has forced dozens of shop owners along the path of its construction into bankruptcy and brought the Garibaldi mariachis to the brink of despair, but if everything goes according to the official plan, once the station opens in 1993 Garibaldi will be overrun by *ranchera* devotees, and mariachi income will soar. Gutiérrez doesn't think this will happen, because people who can afford mariachis travel by car. Nevertheless, this is the kind of promise that Mexico's rulers are constantly making to their subjects these days: severe sacrifices are being asked, and times are hard, but the country is being modernized, and when modernity arrives it will bring great rewards.

"MODERNITY" IS THE buzzword, and, although hardly anyone knows how to define it, even the people in Garibaldi can recognize its presence in their lives. Modernity is what makes the mariachi Guadalupe González—a man who boasts that he beats his woman regularly, out of a traditional sense of duty ("She misses it if I don't," he explains)—welcome the subway that Jesús Rosas dislikes. *"Hay que modernizarse,"* he admonishes Rosas, citing the contemporary imperative. Modernity is what makes Rosas look uncomfortable at the mention of wife-beating by his elders, and it is also what makes his young fellow-mariachis finish their *ranchera* practice and immediately tune in a rock station on the radio, to Rosas's distress. Modernity is the guiding impulse behind the latest gambit by the travel agencies, which consists of bringing tourists to Garibaldi by the busload to be serenaded by musicians permanently under agency contract, instead of letting the tourists wander about in time-honored fashion until they find a mariachi who strikes them as *simpático*. It used to be, Guadalupe González says, that first-rate mariachis like him could deliver the traditional *ranchera* serenade outside the window of a house where a party was going on, and then prove their versatility by playing boleros, polkas, and even cha-cha-chas for the partygoers to dance to. Now, thanks to modernity, mariachis deliver their serenade and are waved away, and the party continues to the sound of a rock band, a *cumbia* group, or, worst of all, one of those tootling electronic organs with programmable rhythms and sound effects. Modernity, as it is understood here, means speed and high productivity and the kind of cost analysis that leads to one electronic organ rather than half a dozen friendly but expensively thirsty mariachis. Now that a finished text of the proposed North American Free Trade Agreement has been initialled by the trade ministers of Canada, the United States, and Mexico, the arrival of full-scale modernity is assumed to be imminent. The terms of the treaty state that fifteen years after its final approval all tariffs and barriers to trade between the three countries will disappear. In effect, this means that the continent will become a single, gigantic market, and the government officials are already trumpeting the estimated benefits: great tonic shots of foreign investment that will make the economy roar. Less powerful people worry that they, like the mariachis, will lose their jobs to electronic substitutes. But a more common undercurrent of worry and doubt, in the endless private jokes, offhand conversational references, editorial cartoons, and television chat-show allusions to the free-trade treaty, is more abstract, and strikes deeper. What people want to know about the coming onslaught of modernity is: How Mexican is it to be modern? Or, rather, since everything modern comes from a large, powerful country to the north, how Mexican is it to be like the United States?

There is nothing new about such fears of cultural takeover, of course: Mexico has been under invasion from the United States in one form or another since the war in 1847 that cost the country half its territory, and since then the arrival of each new fad or technological improvement has been used by pessimists to herald the death of Mexican tradition. Rosas's worry that the *ranchera* is a dying form is hardly original, but it is not paranoid. Rock-music stations *are* increasingly numerous. Mariachi serenades *are* far less frequent. This doesn't mean that Rosas's rock-humming contemporaries are less Mexican than he is; it simply means that their culture is more fragmented. The remarkable psychic sturdiness shared by the inhabitants of a city that often looks like the morning after the apocalypse may or may not owe something to cultural coherence, but, as every Latino teen-ager in Los Angeles knows, the combination of cultural fragmentation and social disadvantage can be poisonous. To the whiz kids from Harvard and the Sorbonne who are currently running the Mexican government, though, the diversification of Mexican culture is also rich with promise. Nationalism and tradition are *retardatarios,* cosmopolitanism is creative, and what used to be called cultural imperialism is now known as "the inevitable future." . . .

Whether economic *apertura* will lead to a final drowning of Mexican culture in United States sauce is not an entirely idle question—at least, not when one is sitting in a Kentucky Fried Chicken outlet and eating some of the first fast-food tacos that Taco Bell is hoping to find a mass market for in Mexico City. . . .

I WENT TO SEE the postmodern *ranchera* singer Astrid Hadad's show . . . , and as she worked her way to a tiny stage through the crowded bar where she was performing she peddled tacos from a basket. "What kind would you like?" she asked her customers. "Now that we have the free-trade treaty, I can offer you hamburger tacos, hot-dog tacos, chili-con-carne tacos. . . ." For her presentations, Hadad likes to wear red lipstick with carnival glitter in it—on her eyelids—and a Jean Paul Gaultier–like cone-shaped bra, which she later rips off and replaces with a big, anatomically accurate foam-rubber heart. Her show, which has been attracting ever more loyal audiences over the last few years, relies heavily on the nostalgia value of *ranchera* music and on its inherent campiness, but it would not be so energetically appealing if her powerful voice were not a perfect vehicle for *rancheras* or if her understanding of a *ranchera* prototype—the brassy, hard-drinking, love-wounded dame—were not intuitive. Hadad belted out, "As if I were a sock, you step on me all day," and her audience howled with laughter and the acid pleasure of recognition. When, in a frenzy of Mexican passion, she asked what would become of her heart— "this bleeding, burning, conquered, crunched, roasted, ground, blended, anguished heart"—a couple of people in the audience rose to give her a standing ovation. Hadad had come onstage with peasant-style braids and wearing a typical *china poblana* embroidered skirt. Now she loosened the braids, tore off the skirt to reveal a slinky black dress underneath, removed the heart from the dress's strapless bodice, added long gloves, checked her image in an empty mirror frame, and retold the well-known myth of Quetzalcoatl, the god-king of Tula, and his rival Tezcatlipoca, or Smoking Mirror. "Tezcatlipoca is jealous because Quetzalcoatl is blond, so he gives him some pulque. Quetzalcoatl gets drunk, screws his own sister, wakes up with a terrible hangover, and sees his image in Tezcatlipoca's mirror. He heads for the beach and sets sail, and as he leaves he promises to return. So he does, the blond, blue-eyed god, and that's how we discovered the joys of"—here Hadad licked her lips lasciviously—"cultural penetration."

Offstage, Hadad turned out to be a tiny woman with a sharp Lebanese profile (it is a curious fact of cultural life here that many of the most devoted *mexicanistas* are themselves—like Hadad and like Frida Kahlo—first- or second-generation Mexicans) and an intellectual manner. Not surprisingly, she declared that what first attracted her to *rancheras* was that they are so essentially Mexican. "I think it has to do with the attitude toward suffering that we inherited from the Aztecs," she said. "It's not that we have an extraordinary capacity for suffering—everyone does. It's the way we *relish* it. I think only Russians compare with us in that. And then there's the element of machismo. Again, it's not that men here beat their wives more, because I'm sure that Germans do it just as much; it's that here they boast about it. Obviously, I'm very critical of that, but what keeps me coming back to the music is the passion. Now that we're all becoming so rational and sensible, it's getting harder and harder to find passion in our lives; I think that's what we all seek in the *ranchera*."

I asked Hadad why she cracked so many jokes about the Free Trade Agreement in her show, and why she thought her audience was so responsive to them, and she said it was because of the enormous apprehension that people are feeling about it. She pointed out that even the great Mexican movie goddess María Félix had taken the unusual step of speaking out publicly against the treaty, warning that it might cause Mexican values—not to mention factories—to collapse. Like nearly everyone else who is fearful of the treaty, Hadad confessed that she had no idea what was in it. "But it seems obvious to me that the little guys—us—are not going to be the ones calling the shots," she said. "The government gets all excited describing the wonderful things that will result from the treaty, but I say '*What* wonders?' As far as I can make out, all it means is that in the future we're going to be more like South Korea and less like us."

THIS IS, IN FACT, precisely what one of Salinas de Gortari's bright young intellectuals described to me some time ago as his best hope: that if Mexico's debt situation remains stable, if its workers can be persuaded to let wage increases remain just below the rate of inflation, if monetary policy and inflation itself continue under tight government control, enough foreign investment will land here "to turn this country into South Korea or maybe Taiwan." . . .

I FLEW FROM Mexico City to Tijuana, a scorching-hot border town that can be seen either as the hideous, seedy product of more than a century of cultural penetration or as the defiant, lively result of a hundred years of cultural resistance. Just a few miles south of San Diego, Tijuana reigns as the world capital of Spanglish, shantytowns, and revolting souvenirs, yet, despite it all, remains completely Mexican. The United States may be just an imaginary line away, but on this side of the line driving becomes more creative, street life improves, bribes are taken, and hairdos are more astonishing. I thought Tijuana would be a good place to catch a show by Juan Gabriel, a singer and prolific composer who is the most unlikely heir to the mantle of *ranchera* greatness that could ever be imagined.

Juan Gabriel likes to perform at *palenques*, or cockfight arenas, which are a traditional element of state fairs. When I arrived at the Tijuana *palenque*, around midnight, several hundred people were watching the last fight, perched on chairs in a coliseumlike arrangement of concrete tiers surrounding a small circular arena. Those in the know say that hundreds of thousands of dollars' worth of bets are placed in the course of a fight, but all I saw was half a dozen men with little notebooks standing in the arena, catching mysterious silent signals from the audience and scribbling down figures, while the two fighting cocks were displayed by their handlers. After a few minutes, the men with notebooks left, and the cocks, outfitted with razorlike spurs, were set on the ground. The cocks flew at each other, spurs first, while the audience watched in tense, breathless silence. In a matter of minutes, one of the animals lay trembling on the ground, its guts spilling out, and the other was proclaimed the victor, to a brief, dull cheer. Instantly, Juan Gabriel's roadies moved in.

The instruments they set up—electric organ and piano, two sets of drums —are not the ones normally associated with *ranchera* music, but then Juan Gabriel is not what one would think of as a typical mariachi singer. For starters, he is from the border himself—from Ciudad Juárez, where he was born, and where he was raised in an orphanage. When he burst on the pop-music scene, in the early seventies, radio audiences often mistook his high-pitched voice for a woman's. His fey mannerisms became the subject of crude jokes. He has been press-shy ever since a scurrilous book by a purported confidant fed hungry speculations about his sexual preferences. Yet, in this nation of self-proclaimed machos, Juan Gabriel has been able to perform before a standing-room-only crowd in the Palacio de Bellas Artes, Mexico's Carnegie Hall. He lives in Los Angeles, uses electronic backups and percussion, and writes songs that never mention drunkenness or two- or three-timing women, but when men in Garibaldi drink and fall into the confessional mode these days their musical inspiration invariably includes songs composed by Juan Gabriel.

As the first, wailing *ranchera* chords tore through the din and Juan Gabriel emerged from the bullpen, there was a roar from the *palenque,* and in the roar there was a call for blood. The composition of the audience had changed: a majority of women, mostly middle-aged and in girls'-night-out groups, had filled the stands, along with a large minority of romantic couples and a dense sprinkling of men in groups. A lot of the men were wearing big *norteño* hats, and in the front row a group of couples and male buddies in big hats and heavy gold chains had set up beer cans and bottles of tequila along the concrete ledge that defined the arena space. The women in the audience were shouting their love for Juan Gabriel hysterically, but a couple of men behind me were shouting something quite different, and so were a lot of the men in big hats. *"Marica!"* and *"Jotón!"* they yelled, meaning "Fag!" or "Queer!" They yelled this over and over, and, because the cherub-faced Juan Gabriel in his graying middle age has put on something of a paunch, someone improvised an insult that was quickly copied: "You're pregnant, you faggot! Go home!" The men had paid between forty and sixty dollars a head to indulge in this pleasure, and Juan Gabriel, circling the arena slowly to acknowledge the majority's applause, also acknowledged this generosity with a small, graceful curtsy before he began to sing.

His music is proof of the fact that the *ranchera* has changed as much as Mexico has, and that in doing so it has survived. His backup singers at the *palenque* were two skinny, curvy black women in tight dresses: they chimed in on the chorus as required, but with distinctly gringo accents. Standing between them and his electronic band, Juan Gabriel sang and twirled to music from his pop repertoire, punctuating some of the jazzier songs with belly rolls and shimmies that drove the women and the machos wild in opposite ways. There was rather a lot of this cheerful music, and then he slowed down and began to sing a real *ranchera,* a song of bad love, loss, and pain, in which the composer makes abject offers to his departed love. In case the fugitive should ever decide to return, Juan Gabriel sang, "You'll find me here, in my usual spot, in the same city, with the same crowd, so you can find everything just as you left it." By the second verse, there was no need for him to sing at all, because the members of the audience were chanting the words for themselves with the rapt reverence accorded an anthem. "I just forgot again," the audience sang, "that you never loved me." I glanced at a couple of the big guys sitting in the front row, armed with their bottles of tequila, who had earlier folded their arms protectively across their chests and smirked whenever Juan Gabriel wiggled in their direction. Now they were singing.

A dozen fawn-colored *charro* hats wobbled at the entrance to the bullpen, and the audience, seeing the mariachis arrive, roared itself hoarse with welcome. Gold decorations along the musicians' trousers caught the light. The men lined up facing Juan Gabriel's band, adjusted their hats, took up their instruments, and filled the *palenque* with the ripe, aching, heart-torn sound of the mariachi. Juan Gabriel, singing this time about how hard it is to forget, was now not queening at all. The big guys sitting across from me leaned into each other, swaying companionably to the music, like everyone else in the audience. Behind me, the last heckler had finally shut up. Juan Gabriel sang a lilting *huapango* and a couple of *sones,* without pausing once for chatter. He segued from one song to the next or went through long medleys, the doo-wop girls bursting in occasionally with a trill or two. Then the girls left the stage, and so did the band. Juan Gabriel, alone with the mariachis, slowed down for the introductory chords of a song that begins, "Podría volver," and, recognizing these, the audience squealed in ecstatic pain. "I could return, but out of sheer pridefulness I won't," the lyrics say, in what is perhaps the most perfect of a hundred *ranchera* hymns to the unbending pride of the loser. "If you want me to come back you should have thought of that before you left me." Here and there, his listeners yelped as if some very tasty salt had just been rubbed into their national wound. Life hurts. I hurt. The hell with you: I'll survive, Juan Gabriel sang. In the front row, the two big guys looked immensely happy, and just about ready to weep.

Two *Ranchera* Songs

José Alfredo Jiménez and Cuco Sánchez

As Alma Guillermoprieto so eloquently points out, the lyrics of ranchera *songs are most often concerned with heartbreak, loss, betrayal, revenge, and self-pity—and all this to the accompaniment of soaring horns and violins. While cautioning readers to bear in mind that there is tremendous variety within the genre, we here include a small sample of the* ranchera: *very popular songs by two of the most renowned* ranchera *composers, José Alfredo Jiménez (1926–1973) and Cuco Sánchez (1921–2000).*

THE HORSEMAN, *by José Alfredo Jiménez*

In the far-off mountains rides a horseman,
Wandering alone in the world and wishing for death.
In his breast he carries a wound, his soul is destroyed.
He wants to lose his life and be reunited with his beloved.
He loved her more than his own life,
And he lost her forever.
That's why he is wounded, that's why he seeks death.
He spends whole nights singing with his guitar,
Man and guitar weeping by the light of the stars.
Then he loses himself in the night, and although the night is very beautiful,
He asks God to bear him away to her,
The woman he loved more than his own life,
And lost forever.
That's why he is wounded, that's why he seeks death.

THE BED OF STONE, *by Cuco Sánchez*

Let my bed and headboard be made of stone.
The woman who loves me must love me truly.
Ay yay yay, my love, why don't you love me?

I went to the courtroom and asked the judge if it's a crime to love you.
He sentenced me to death.
Ay yay yay, my love, why don't you love me?

The day they kill me, may it be with five bullets,
And I will be very close to you, so as to die in your arms.
Ay yay yay, my love, why don't you love me?

For a casket, I want a *sarape,*
For a crucifix, my crossed ammunition belts.
And upon my tombstone, write my final farewell with a thousand bullets.
Ay yay yay, my love, why don't you love me?

II

Ancient Civilizations

If the analysts of *"lo mexicano"* agree on anything, it is that Mexico was home to magnificent civilizations and cultures prior to the coming of the Europeans, and that much of the country's subsequent history has witnessed attempts to deny, suppress, and, more recently, politically incorporate the vestiges of those civilizations and cultures. During the independence period, some thinkers invoked the glories of ancient Mexico, but their sincerity is difficult to judge: they seem to have regarded those glories largely as a convenient rhetorical device to deny the legitimacy of the Spanish conquest and colonial rule, not to suggest that Mexico's indigenous cultures be revived or even respected. The twentieth century, however, saw tremendous advances in understanding and appreciation of ancient Mexico, particularly after the Mexican revolution, through the National Institute of Anthropology and History (INAH, in its Spanish acronym). Today, a visit to the National Museum of Anthropology in Mexico City cannot help but overwhelm the visitor, and the ruins of the indigenous civilizations annually attract and impress countless thousands of tourists.

The earliest civilizations of Mesoamerica began to take shape around 2000 B.C.; by 1200 B.C. impressive cities had been built and a distinctive Mesoamerican religion had evolved. Around A.D. 300, the region entered its so-called "classical period," a time when huge cities such as Teotihuacán in central Mexico, and the Zapotec city of Monte Albán, in the southern state of Oaxaca, dominated large territories. In the jungles and mountains to the southeast, the Maya erected splendid city-states, created elaborate ceramics, studied the stars and planets, and developed a system of writing. By around A.D. 800–900, the classical civilizations entered into a decline that has still not been adequately explained. Subsequent cultures tended to be more fragmented and bellicose than their predecessors, but they nevertheless achieved a high degree of sophistication. In central Mexico, the region of the largest populations and highest development, successive waves of *chichimecas,* or nomadic peoples, moved in from the north to enjoy the good life on the fertile central plateau.

The Aztecs—easily the best known of Mexico's indigenous cultures—were one such group. After migrating into the lake region of central Mexico in the mid-1200s, they endured years of tribulation before establishing what would become their awe-inspiring capital city of Tenochtitlán. By the mid-1400s, in alliance with other city-states of the region, the Aztecs launched a campaign of imperial domination that would win them a precarious control of much of central and southern Mexico.

Mesoamerican cultures were complex and sophisticated, but they also earned a reputation for brutality. The following readings aim to provide readers with a brief introduction to the mythology, religious beliefs and practices, values, and enduring legacy of these cultures, which, while certainly subordinated, continue to resonate in modern Mexico.

The Origins of the Aztecs

Anonymous

Mesoamerican peoples believed that time moved cyclically. In contrast to the Western notion that time began at a certain moment and has developed in linear fashion ever since, for the Mesoamericans time was created and extinguished at regular intervals. The Aztecs believed themselves to be living in the epoch of the Fifth Sun, since four suns had existed and been extinguished prior to their appearance on earth. The belief that time could end gives insight into the seriousness with which Mesoamericans viewed their religious life: if either humans or gods failed to perform their functions faithfully and precisely, the light of day would be devoured and the world would cease to exist.

The following excerpt is a brief account of the legend of the five suns. It was translated by anthropologist Thelma D. Sullivan from the Anales de Cuauhtitlán, *part of the* Codex Chimalpopoca. *This account was written by Aztec authors some forty to fifty years after the Spanish conquest, but was based on certain older texts and traditions. It gives a clear sense of the fatalism and pervasive pessimism that tended to characterize the Mesoamerican worldview.*

. . . They had been wandering about shooting their arrows;
they had no houses, they had no land,
they had no woven capes as clothing;
only hides, only Spanish moss did they use to cover themselves.
And their children grew up in mesh bags,
in cagelike crates used for carrying things.

They ate the prickly pear, the barrel cactus,
the *tetzihoactli,* and the bitter prickly pear.
They suffered great hardships for 364 years
until they arrived in the city, Quauhtitlan.
In that year it began, it originated
the rule of the Chichimeca,
the people of Quauhtitlan.

It must told, it must be understood. . .
that while on their way they gave themselves a king.

During these years, of the Chichimeca's wandering.
It is said, it is recounted
that it was still the time of darkness.
They say that it was still the time of darkness
because as yet no fame, no glory was theirs;
there was no joyousness.
They wandered from place to place. . . .

In the first age,
according to accounts, according to the recollections
of the ancients for they knew it . . .
the earth, the world,
came into existence, was established. . . .

It is recounted, it is said
that four kinds of life were created. . . .

The old men knew that in 1-Rabbit,
in that year the earth and heaven were established,
and they also knew that
when the earth and heaven were established
there were four kinds of beings,
four kinds of life were created.
They knew that each one was a Sun.
And they said that he created,
he fashioned their gods from ashes;
they attributed this to Quetzalcoatl. . . .

In the beginning was the first Sun,
4-Water was its sign;
it was called the Sun of Water.
In this Sun all was carried off by water,
the people were transformed
into dragonfly larvae and into fish.

The second Sun was established.
4-Jaguar was its sign;
it was called the Jaguar Sun.
In this Sun it happened that the heavens collapsed,
that the Sun did not move on its course from its zenith.

It began to darken, when all was dark,
then the people were devoured.

And Giants lived in this Sun.
The elders say that their greeting to each other was
"May you not fall,"
because everyone who fell,
fell forevermore.

The third Sun was established.
4-Rain was its sign;
it was called the Sun of Rain.
In this Sun it occurred that it rained fire
and the people were consumed by fire. . . .
It rained stones.
They now say that this was when the stones we now see fell,
and the lava rock boiled up.
And also, it was when the great rocks formed into masses,
and became red.

The fourth Sun:
4-Wind was its sign;
it was called the Sun of Wind.
In this Sun all was carried off by the wind,
the people turned into monkeys.
And afterward the monkey men
that lived there dispersed about the forests.

The fifth Sun:
its symbol is 4-Motion.
It was called the Sun of Motion
because it moves, it follows a course.
And say the ancients:
that in this Sun it shall come to pass
that the earth shall move,
that there shall be famine,
and that we all shall perish. . . .

In the year 13-Reed,
they say that the Sun that now exists was created.
At that time the Sun of Movement
arose at dawn, gave its light. . . .

In this fifth Sun the earth shall move,
there shall be famine,
then we shall perish.

The Cost of Courage in Aztec Society

Inga Clendinnen

Without a doubt, the most famous aspect of Aztec culture is its propensity for violent ritual, most notably human sacrifice on a grand scale. This fact has presented historians with a dilemma, for it seems that too much emphasis on such gory practices promotes sensationalism and only serves to distract readers from more noble and seemly aspects of Aztec society, as well as from the everyday life and culture of the people. Although the point is well-taken, it must also be recognized that to gloss over or ignore Aztec ritual is to overlook the very thing that the Aztecs themselves viewed as their most important function on earth. For the Aztecs, particularly the ruling elites, warfare and ritual were functions of their religion — a religion which, like any other, was at heart a complex expression of humanity's place in nature and the cosmos.

The best historians, of course, seek not to sensationalize but to explain. Few in recent years can rival cultural historian Inga Clendinnen, professor at La Trobe University in Australia. In the following article, she examines the remarkably complex rituals of warfare and sacrifice in order to achieve some understanding of what these rituals actually meant to the Aztecs.

> Proud of itself
> is the city of Mexico-Tenochtitlán.
> Here no one fears to die in war.
> This is our glory. . . .
>
> Who could conquer Tenochtitlán?
> Who could shake the foundation of heaven?

Today we are tempted to read this fragment of an Aztec song-poem as a familiar piece of bombast: the aggressive military empire which insists on its invincibility, its warriors strangers to fear. In what follows I want to indicate how the business of war was understood in the great city of Tenochtitlán, and then . . . to enquire into how warrior action was sustained and explained, in the hope of drawing closer to an Aztec reading of this small text.

THAT TENOCHTITLÁN WAS the creation of war and the courage and stamina of its young fighting men was indisputable. The splendid city which Cortés and his men saw shimmering above its lake waters in the autumn of 1519 had been founded as a miserable collection of mud huts less than two hundred years before. . . .

[By the mid-1400s, under Emperor] Moctezuma the Elder, the armies of the Triple Alliance of Tenochtitlán, Texcoco and Tlacopan spilled beyond the valley to carve out the broad shape of their magnificent if unstable tribute empire. That expansion was paralleled by the increasing magnificence of Tenochtitlán. In 1519, the last year of its grandeur, it contained perhaps 200,000 to 250,000 people, with many more densely settled around the lake margin. (Seville, the port of departure for most of the conquistadores, numbered in the same year not more than 60,000 persons.) The city lived more by trade than tribute, but that trade had been stimulated and focused by war, just as its war-fed splendor attracted the most skilled artisans and most gifted singers to embellish its glory further. The one-class society of the early days of hardship had given way to an elaborately differentiated hierarchy. But that hierarchy had been created through the distribution of the spoils of war, and success in combat remained its dynamic. Performance on the field of battle was as central for the confirmation of an elevated position as for escape from a lowly one, and concern regarding that performance gripped young males of all social ranks.

It also concerned those who directed the city. From the age of ten or eleven all commoner youths save those few dedicated to the priesthood came under the control of the "House of Youth," the warrior house in their own *calpulli* [lineage group]. These were not exclusively military schools: each lad was expected to master a range of masculine skills, most particularly the trade of his father. The great mass of Aztec warriors were essentially part-time, returning from campaigns to the mundane pursuits of farming, hunting or fishing, pulque brewing and selling, or the dozen other trades the city supported. Few commoners were so successful in battle as to emancipate themselves entirely from such labor. Nonetheless it was war and the prospect of war which fired imagination and ambition. At fifteen the lads began intensive training in weapon-handling, gathering every evening in the warrior house with the mature warriors — local heroes — to learn the chants and dances which celebrated warriors past and the eternal excitements of war. Assigned labors became a chance to test strength, as boys wrestled logs from the distant forest to feed the never-dying fires in their local temple or to meet their ward's obligations at the central temple precinct. But war provided the crucial and indeed the sole consequential test. Performance in that test was measured in a quite straightforward, arithmetical kind of way. Movement through the ranks of the warrior grades depended on taking alive on the field of battle a specified number of captives of specified quality. Each promotion was marked by the award of designated insignia and by a distinctive cutting and arranging of the hair, although the "warrior lock," at the center and slightly to the back of the head, was always kept intact. (Some of the most elevated warriors, the "shaven-headed Otomí," kept only that lock, bound with bright cord close to the scalp so that it floated banner-like above the shaven pate.) It was possible for the commoner who distinguished himself over several campaigns to graduate into the lower ranks of the royal administration, or even to enjoy the perquisites of lordship, at least for his lifetime. . . .

The conditions of warrior training for the sons of the lords are less clear. . . . It was probably significantly more rigorous. For a noble in the later years of empire the cost of cowardice was high. Access to office and the perquisites of office—its tribute fields, its dependent laborers—depended on adequate performance in battle, and the higher the office the more spectacular the required performance. . . .

A dramatic toughening in the required warrior performance for the nobility had come in the middle years of the rule of Moctezuma the Elder, just before the Aztec expansion beyond the valley. Tlacaelel, a young general under Itzcoatl, adviser of Moctezuma and to three rulers after him, and chief architect and strategist of empire, made the new rules clear. The most coveted jewels, the richest cloaks and shields could no longer be bought in the marketplace. They could be purchased only with valorous deeds. Any male who failed to go to war, even if he were the king's son, would be deprived of all signs of rank and would live as a despised commoner, while great warriors would eat from the king's dish. This was a sufficiently crucial matter to breach the hardening divisions of class: should a legitimate son prove cowardly, and the son of a slave or servant excel him in battle, the bastard would replace the coward as legitimate heir. Furthermore Tlacaelel proclaimed the initiation of a particular kind of warfare against five precariously independent provinces across the mountains—provinces noted, as were the Aztecs, for the toughness of their fighting men. In these so-called "Flowery Wars" the sole end would be the mutual taking of warrior captives for ritual killing. At the same time Tlacaelel was preparing the great campaigns of subjugation which would bring hundreds, even thousands, of prisoners to Tenochtitlán. The building of the Great Temple was already in train. In the next years the Aztecs were to become notorious among their neighbors for the mass ceremonial killings, and for the extravagant theatricalism in which those killings were framed. . . . They were intended as the most efficacious of political acts; the most direct demonstration of the high legitimacy of Aztec supremacy. . . .

The declarations made in that theater of dominance were understood by the Aztecs' neighbors, although few found them permanently compelling, as Cortés was to discover to his advantage. But in the Aztec politics of spectacle the great ceremonies which consumed so great a part of the fruits of war constituted the final, necessary and consummatory act of war; they transformed human victory into sacred destiny.

AZTECS WERE NOT soldiers, at least not in the modern European sense. . . . They had no organized "army," nor officers either. But the Aztec warrior, like the European soldier, was a social product: it should be possible to discover how he was made. He faced, again and again, the threat of injury or death deliberately inflicted: it should be possible to discover something of how that threat appeared to him. And, a man trained to violence, he moved constantly in and out of civilian society: it should be possible to discover how he made that passage. The benefits of warrior action and warrior status were manifest, and not all material. What concerns me now is to count the costs of Aztec courage.

There was, of course, the obvious and familiar cost of war: the grief attending the death of a loved father, son, husband, brother, friend. . . . The kin had been well disciplined for the relinquishment. Childbed was conventionally designated a battlefield, where a woman could "take a captive" by capturing a baby. The midwife greeted the birth of a male child with war cries and a formal exhortation, addressed to the child, but directed, of course, to the panting, newly delivered mother, who was emphatically not given the baby to hold:

> My precious son, my youngest one . . . heed, hearken: thy home is not here, for thou art an eagle, a jaguar . . . here is only the place of thy nest . . . out there thou has been consecrated . . . War is thy desert, thy task. Thou shalt give drink, nourishment, food to the sun, lord of the earth . . . perhaps thou wilt receive the gift, perhaps thou wilt merit death by the obsidian knife . . . The flowered death by the obsidian knife [that is, death on the killing stone].

A sufficiently explicit intervention by society in a zone we might consider private. It was the parents who then formally dedicated the infant to war, presenting him to the "Rulers of Youth" at the local warrior house, where he would live from puberty to marriage. . . .

If success had its negative aspects . . . failure could be a lifetime of bitterness. One strength of the Aztec system was that it was not necessary to succeed to survive: it was possible to live by one's own labor, saved from want by periodic handouts from the tribute warehouse or from a successful neighbor or kinsman. But failure was public, publicly marked, at an age when such marks burn deep. From about ten each lad grew a long lock of hair at the nape of the neck, which remained uncut until he had participated in the taking of a captive on the field of war. If after two or three campaigns he still had not forced himself to enter the fray—and it was always possible to hang back— he was thrown out of the warrior house, his head shaven in a tonsure to dramatize the loss of the warrior lock and to prepare him for the carrying pad of humble labor: forever a peripheral man. . . .

Aztec combat was highly individualistic, and depended utterly on the courage of the individual. For his first venture into war the fledgling warrior went only as an observer, to "carry the shield" of an experienced warrior whose technique he was to study. On his second time out he was expected to participate in a group capture: up to six novices could combine to drag a warrior down. The body of the victim of the joint assault was later exquisitely portioned out: torso and right thigh to the major captor, left thigh to the second; right upper arm to the third; left upper arm to the fourth; right forearm to the fifth; and left forearm to the sixth. With that initial capture, cooperation was at an end: from that time on the youth was in direct competition with his peers, as he searched through the dust-haze and the mind-stunning shrieking and whistling to identify and engage with an enemy warrior of equal, or preferably just higher, status. The nice portioning out of the first captive suggests that even there in-group ranking was more important than any notion of team spirit.

The lads of each warrior house had lived and trained together, and we could expect some camaraderie to have developed. Discipline within the houses was maintained by a kind of extreme prefect system, with peers set to watch peers and to punish delinquents with savage beatings, or with the searing from the head of the treasured warrior lock. Would male bonding have survived all that—or, perhaps, thrived on it? Certainly sentiment toward one's companions on the field of battle was firmly and officially discouraged. To go to the aid of a threatened comrade would probably provoke a charge of having tried to steal his captive, and not only the false claiming of a captive, but the giving of one's captive to another, was punishable by death. . . .

It was on that field of battle that the Aztec aesthetic of war could be most perfectly displayed and most profoundly experienced; and here "aesthetic" must be understood to comprehend moral and emotional sensibilities. Glimpses in both the painted and written sources suggest that combat was initiated by a formal rhetoric of gesture, with a "presentation stance" of the club arm dropped and the body in a half-crouch. Since each warrior had an interest in not damaging his opponent too severely, there being no honor to be won by killing in the field, and a maimed man being useless for the most engrossing rituals, it is likely there was an initial preference for using the flat side of the club to stun, resorting to the cutting edges only when faced with a singularly difficult antagonist.

The action, when it came, was very fast: the clubs, although heavy, were handy. Even against the quite unfamiliar bulk and speed of a Spanish horseman native warriors could calculate their blows for maximum effectiveness through a remarkable combination of speed, strength, balance, and timing. The aim was to stun or sufficiently disable one's opponent so that he could be grappled to the ground and subdued. . . .

The dramatic shape of the combat, its "style," was poised stillness exploding into violent action. Aztecs described the two creatures most closely associated with warriors in the following terms: "the eagle is fearless . . . it can gaze into, it can face the sun . . . it is brave, daring, a wingbeater, a screamer . . ." The lordly jaguar, "cautious, wise, proud . . . reserved," if troubled by a hunter first seats itself, casually deflecting the flying arrows, and then "stretches, stirs . . . and then it springs." And so dies the hunter. . . .

Explosions of anger, paralyzing eruptions of rage, transformations from the stillness of perfect control to furious violence—great Aztec warriors would seem to be uncomfortable people to be with. And lesser warriors had less control. Young men kept at a pitch for war and trained to a style of touchy arrogance were hard to maintain peaceably in a city. To an outsider there was a startling incidence of violence tolerated within Aztec society, much of it generated from the young men in the warrior houses. So-called "ritual combats" . . . raged through the streets. . . . On those occasions, ordinary people had to do their best to keep out of the way. On other occasions—playful occasions, but Aztecs had very rough notions of play—the townsfolk were themselves the victims, likely to be despoiled of their cloaks, or intimidated into offering "tribute" to a squad of young men. . . .

So, it would seem, society strove to contain and limit the undesired costs of courage by a determined effort to impose order on the unruly men of war. Penal codes were savage, with swift and violent retribution laid down for all socially disruptive acts, from drinking and adultery to theft and extortion, and the higher the rank the more strenuous the punishment. Public rhetoric insisted on the virtues of humility, modesty, frugality, and self-control. . . . These recommendations were made in a society which rewarded its warriors with the opportunity to bask in public adulation. . . . On the one hand we have high and gaudy rewards for aggression: on the other, formal denunciations of aggressive behaviour and of personal vanity. Is this simply a "contradiction," the manifestation of the strain imposed on a society avid for the material rewards of empire but unprepared for its social costs, and so developing a rhetoric of control to net a violent reality of its own making?

So to see it is to miss the opportunity to explore Aztec understandings of violence, and the deeper bonds between warrior and society. The most extreme forms of violence were, after all, officially imported into the city, in the great killing rituals which marked the most collective occasions. Nor were these remote top-of-the-pyramid affairs. The victims, living and dead, were endlessly moved about the neighbourhoods; in one festival the lieutenant of Huitzilopochtli [the patron deity of the Aztecs, associated with war and conquest] ran through the streets slaughtering slaves staked out like goats along his way; in the Feast of the Flaying of Men . . . men in newly flayed human skins skirmished through the streets—and then went on to penetrate individual houses. . . .

A simple notion of the unforeseen and undesired consequences of military expansion will not penetrate far into [the nature of violence in Aztec society]. Only through the glass of ritual, smoky and obscure as that glass is, do we have much chance of discerning how violence, on the field of battle and off it, was understood, and how warrior and civilian society cohered.

. . . WITH THE FIRST gathering of the agricultural harvest and the onset of the frosts the Aztec season of war began. Eighty days after that harvest, the first crop of warrior captives was killed, and eighty days after that, as the first signs of spring indicated the beginning of the planting season, came the Feast of the Flaying of Men. It was an important festival in that its first two days and all the evenings of the twenty days to follow required the attendance of those in authority in Tenochtitlán. It starred the warriors, especially the great warriors, and it honored Xipe Totec, the Flayer or the Flayed One, who was associated with the east, a zone of plenty, and with the early spring, and who was represented by a priest wearing a flayed human skin, and a mask of a flayed human face.

The first day of the festival saw the killing of the less important war captives. The victims, decked in elaborate regalia, were brought from the local warrior houses in which they had been kept, tended and displayed since their capture, and delivered by their captors to the priests waiting at the foot of Xipe's pyramid in the main temple precinct. Ideally they were meant to go leaping up the steps of the pyramid, shouting the chants of their city as they went, and some did: others had to be dragged up by the priests. At the top, before the shrine, they were flipped on their backs over a small upright stone, a priest securing each limb, while a fifth priest struck open the chest with a flint knife, took out the heart, and raised it toward the sun. The body was sent hurtling and tumbling down the stairs to be collected at the bottom by old men from the appropriate ward temple, where they carried it to be flayed and dismembered, probably by the captor. One thigh was reserved to Moctezuma, the other and most of the rest of the body going to the captor, who summoned his kin to a feast at his house. There, amid weeping and lamentations, the kinsmen of the captor each ate a small piece of flesh served with a dish of "dried" (unsoftened?) maize kernels. The captor himself, whose splendid captor's regalia had been replaced by the white chalk and feathers which marked the victim destined for the killing stone, did not participate in the feast.

The killings at the pyramid went on for much of the day. It is difficult to establish the numbers usually killed—presumably that varied according to the fortunes of war—but perhaps sixty or so died. . . . But it is what happened later on that second day which seems to have been the most compelling sequence in the whole complex affair. It also involved a mode of killing specially identified with the Aztecs, revived in Tenochtitlán to mark the victory of Moctezuma the Elder over the Huastecs.

For this ritual only the greatest captives were selected, their captors being accordingly the more honored. The victims were chosen to die on what the Spaniards later dubbed the gladiatorial stone, at the base of Xipe's pyramid. They had been rehearsed for the occasion. Their captors had presented them to the people in a sequence of different regalias over the preceding four days, at the place where they were to die. There they were forced to engage in mock combats, and then to submit to a mock heart excision, the "hearts" being made of unsoftened maize kernels. The night before their deaths they spent in vigil with the captors, their warrior lock being cut and taken at midnight. Then early in the afternoon of that second day of Xipe's festival they were marshalled close to the stone, their captors still beside them, before assembled dignitaries and as many other people as could fit into the temple precinct, as four of the greatest Aztec warriors, two from the order of Jaguar warriors, two from the order of Eagles, presented their weapons in dedication to the sun. Then down from Xipe's pyramid came in procession the high priest of Xipe Totec in the regalia of his lord, followed by the other high priests as representatives of their deities, to take their seats around the gladiatorial stone. This was a performance worthy of the contemplation of the gods.

The stone was about waist high, and a meter and a half wide, but set on an elevated platform about the height of a man. The first victim, now stripped of his regalia and clad only in a loincloth, was given a draught of "obsidian wine"—*pulque,* the Aztec alcoholic drink, probably spiked with a drug from

Gladiatorial sacrifice. (Codex Magliabechiano, Biblioteca Nazionale, Florence)

their ample pharmacopoeia — and tethered by the waist to a rope fastened at the center of the stone. He was presented with weapons; four pine cudgels for throwing, and a war club. The club was studded not with flint or obsidian blades, but with feathers. Then the first Jaguar warrior, equipped with a real club, advanced and engaged him in combat.

There must have been a system of timing of rounds or of counting passes or exchanges, although it is not recorded, because exceptionally fine fighters were sometimes able to survive the assaults of all four warriors. In those cases a fifth warrior, a left-hander, was brought into play to bring him down. When he was down, the lord Xipe advanced, struck open the breast and cut out the heart, which was raised "as a gift" to the sun, and then placed in the eagle vessel in which it would be later burned. The priest then submerged a hollow cane in the blood welling in the chest cavity, and raised the cane, so, as it was said, "giving the sun to drink." The captor was given the cane and a bowl of the blood which he carried throughout the city, daubing the blood on the mouths of the stone idols in all the temples. The circuit completed, he went to Moctezuma's palace to return the magnificent regalia of he who offers a victim at the gladiatorial stone, and from there went back to his local temple to flay and dismember his captive's body. And then, later in the day, he watched his lamenting kin eat the maize stew and the flesh of his captive, while they wept for their own young warrior. He did not participate, saying "Shall I perchance eat my very self?" Meanwhile at the foot of Xipe's pyramid other victims had been tethered to the stone, and had fought and died. At the end of the day, when the last of the victims had been dispatched, the priests performed a dance with the severed heads, which were then skewered on the skull rack beside the stone.

It is obvious even from this sketchy account that a great many things were going on, but I want to focus on what was understood to be happening on the actual stone. There are a thousand ways of killing a man, but why tether him to a stone, restricting his movements but giving him the advantage of height? Why arm him with a club, a formidable weapon in its weight and reach, but with its effectiveness reduced by the replacement of its cutting blades with feathers? And why, given this finely calculated inequality, did the victim co-operate? It was clearly imperative that he fight, and fight as well as he was able: for this ritual only warriors from tribes fully participant in Aztec understandings of war were chosen. He could not fight for his life, for that was forfeit. Why then?

He, like his Aztec counterparts, had been long prepared. From his earliest days those who spoke for society had made his mission plain: to give the sun the hearts of enemies, and to feed the insatiable earth with their bodies. Every lad training in the warrior houses knew that access to the warrior paradise in the House of the Sun was restricted to those who died in either of two ways: on the field of battle, where death was rare, given that the end of combat was the taking of captives, or on the killing stone. That death he had to strive to desire, or at least to embrace. Just as only ritual action made "victory" from the outcome of battle, so for the individual warrior action on the field of battle was consummated only later, and ritually. Behind the desperate excitements of battle lay the shadow of the killing stone, and a lonely death among strangers. This is why the captor, in the midst of the adulation accorded him for having taken a victim for the sun, wore at the cannibal feast of his kin the chalk and down of the victim; why the kin lamented; why he could not eat of what was indeed his "own flesh," for he too, ideally, would die on the stone, and his flesh be eaten in another city. In the rhetoric of Aztec ideology the battlefield was as much a sacred space as the temple precinct—or as much as human confusions and the terrible contingency of war permitted. But it was only on the stone that the meaning of the death could be made manifest.

To be overcome in battle was not fortuitous: it was the sign that the warrior was a warrior no longer, and had begun the transition to victim. From the moment of the seizing of the warrior lock his separation from the ordinary world began. The "rehearsals," as we might cynically call them—the garments changed again and again, the mock combats at the stone, the mock heart excisions—all marked his passage to increased sacredness. Then, with the taking of his warrior lock of hair, "the eagle man was taken upwards"—that is, the warrior made his flight to the sun: before his physical death the individual was extinguished, the transition completed. It was as victim that he watched other men from his city, men he had known when they were alive, fight and die on the stone, until it was his turn for a last display of maximum valor, the exemplary passionate acceptance of his fate. And if he died well his praises would be sung in the warrior houses of his home place.

The deeper fascination [of] that combat was the most comprehensive metaphor for Aztec understanding of how human society, the world and the cosmos worked. The endless repetitious struggles between the natural elements were endlessly replicated in the ritual ball game, in the mock combats which studded the ritual cycle, and in this most solemn contest on the gladiatorial stone.

The victims were called "the striped ones," and the action on the stone "the striping." What the assailants strove to do was not to club or to stun, but to wound delicately; to slit the skin with an obsidian blade so that blood would spring forth. Xipe, who himself wore a human skin, represented the early spring, when the husk of the seed must be pierced if the sprouting life within is to break through, and when the winter-hardened skin of the earth is pierced by the new growth. Certainly the offerings bestowed on the skin-wearers—the garlands of flowers and the necklaces of maize ears—make the agricultural connection plain. But the most important aspect and the dominant meaning of "the striping" for those who performed and for those who watched was the effusion of warrior blood. . . .

Spaniards and the Europeans who came after them have presented an urban-imperial image of Tenochtitlán, with its splendid hierarchies of priests and warriors and its whole sections of artisans and merchants. But it was a city green with growing things, banked with the *chinampas,* the ingenious system of shallow-water agriculture which had brought the Aztecs their first prosperity. The bulk of the population were not agriculturalists, but those specialist artisans and priests and warriors lived in a vegetable-growers' world, and the centrality of agriculture to their lives could not have been in doubt.

The *chinampas* required men's exquisite manipulations of earth, seeds, sun and water in an alchemy of vegetable abundance. It was highly precise cultivation, its small stages laid out from when each seed in its individual block of earth, covered against frost, watered by hand, was raised until it was brought to sprout, and then transferred to the only slightly less intensive cultivation of the *chinampa.* The *chinampa* itself was formed by the piling of thick mats of water weed, which provided a fibrous, permeable, and slowly composting base for the rich silt dredged up from the lake bottom. More water could be scooped up at need. . . .

I would argue . . . that the *chinampas* not only made Tenochtitlán experientially an agricultural city, and that the plants so raised provided essential ritual equipment — models of what was to come — for ceremonies designed to influence growth in the open fields, but that those highly visible *chinampa* manipulations provided the model for men's part in the natural order, and for their role in aiding the growth of essential foods. In the Feast of the Flaying of Men, when the *chinampa* city turned from the business of war to the growing of things, those manipulations of earth, water, sun, and seed through which men found their sustenance were explored through the symbolic medium of the human body, and the interdependence between agriculturalist and warrior set out.

Aztecs called human blood, most particularly human blood deliberately shed, "most precious water." They understood it to be a non-renewable resource, so its value was enhanced. It was thought to have extraordinary fertilizing power. The creation myths, confused and contradictory as they might be on the role of particular "deities," pivot on the creative efficacy of shed blood, as when the great darkness which preceded this Fifth Sun was dispersed only when a little pustular god threw himself into the fire, to be transformed into the Sun. But the Sun only came to move — that is to be alive — when the other gods had spilled their blood, some voluntarily, others unwillingly. A singularly terrifying creation story, and the one most often assumed in Nahuatl texts, tells of the gods Quetzalcoatl and Tezcatlipoca gazing down on the great earth monster swimming in the primeval waters. They went down and seized her by her giant limbs, and wrenched her body in half, one part forming the sky, the other the earth. Then the other gods descended, and from her hair they created trees, flowers, and herbs; from her skin, grass and flowers; from her eyes, wells, springs, and small caverns; from her mouth, rivers and large caves; from her nose mountain valleys; from her shoulders, mountains. This terrible creature cried out in the night and refused to bring forth fruit until she was soaked in human blood and fed with human hearts. When satisfied, she brought forth the plants which provide man's sustenance. It is she who is obsessively represented on the underside of the ritual vessels designed to receive human blood and hearts. Whatever icons they bear on their upper surfaces, whatever great forces they invoke, underneath she is there, her insatiable maw wide open, great claws at elbows and knees, in the squatting position Aztec women adopted to give birth.

So much, for the moment, for blood. Consider now the experience which participation in the gladiatorial ritual brought the captor. The conventional rewards for the warrior were public adulation, the presentation of insignia by the ruler, gifts of capes, flowers, tobacco pipes, which could then be proudly displayed. For many evenings after Xipe's festival young warriors gathered to adorn themselves and to dance before Moctezuma's palace. Sometimes Moctezuma himself, flanked by the other two rulers of the Triple Alliance, came dancing slowly out though the gates to join them: the might of the Aztec empire on display. Later came more exuberant dancing with the women of the city.

From all that festivity the captor was excluded. For all those days he and his kin were in a state of penance, eating meagerly, prohibited from washing, living secluded from the ordinary pleasures. For those days he was engaged in a different zone. The young man he had captured had been close to him in age, aspirations, prowess. He had tended him through the days before the ceremony, through his unmaking as the warrior, his making as the victim. And he had watched his captive's performance in an agony of identification: it was his own prowess being tested there on the stone. Then came a different intimacy, as he flayed the young body he had known in life and saw youths who sought to participate in his glory clamber into the dank skin. In a society which passionately valued cleanliness and treasured sweet scents, he and his kin had to live in a stench of corruption for the full twenty days. Then, at the end of the period of penance, he struggled for the last time into the crumbling, stinking shroud, to experience its transformation, its slow turning into matter, until, like the pierced casing of the maize seed, it was cast off and sealed away in a cave at the base of Xipe's pyramid, and so returned to the earth.

The explosion of relief which followed the casting off of the skins—the great cleansing and washing, initially with cornmeal to get off the grease, and then a sequence of progressively more playful and rowdy re-enactments of the festival—suggests the strain for those warriors "privileged" to be taken through the ritual glass to confront what lies on the other side of the adulation, the tobacco pipes, the plumes, the grand display. Just as the captive was rehearsed at the stone, so his captor rehearsed through those days his own death and decay; for the transformation of his own flesh into vegetable matter. The Nahuatl word *tonacayotl* means "things of the sun's warmth," that is, the fruits of the earth. It is also used metaphorically to mean "our flesh." When the kin took into their mouths the morsels of human flesh and the stew of dried maize kernels—maize in its least modified form—the lesson they were being taught was that the two substances, perceptually so different, were of the same stuff, although at different points in the cycle. While we transmute bread and wine into flesh and blood, reflecting the centrality of man in our cosmology, they saw human flesh and human blood as transmuted into sacred maize and sacred water. Our "man is dust and will be dust again" focuses on the pathos of the brief reign of the flesh: for them man's flesh has been, is and will be again part of the vegetable cycle. (Maize was the only deity always represented in the terms of a natural human biography.) The Flayed Lord Xipe Totec sang of the identity of the tender maize and the warrior flesh it would become:

> I am the tender corn
> Of jade my heart is made
> The gold of rain I'll see
> My heart will be refreshed
> The fledgling man grow firm
> The man of war be born.

The "man of war" was Cinteotl, Young Lord Maize Cob, who would at his harvesting at the end of the agricultural season lead his warriors out to war.

The body of the warrior captive was disassembled with extraordinary care, and allocated very deliberately: the warrior lock to the captor; the heart, the "precious Eagle Cactus fruit," offered to the Sun; the blood to give drink to the Sun and all the stone images; the skin to be worn through all the days of the festival, and then laid away; the flesh to the captor's kin and to Moctezuma; the head skewered on the skull rack. Further, the thighbone, scraped or boiled clean of flesh, was draped with the captive's warrior jacket and victim's heron plume and set up as a sacred object in the courtyard of the captor. Only small parts of that so careful disassembling had to do with the human and social world. . . .

[The Florentine Codex describes blood as] "Our blood, our redness, our liquid, our freshness, our growth, our life blood . . . it wets the surface . . . it strengthens one . . . one is greatly strengthened. . . ." Blood vessels are likened to reeds. The analogies between the movement of blood through the flesh and that of water through the earth are vivid. The description of the heart relates it closely to the sun: it is "round, hot, that by which there is existence. It makes one live. . . ." [There is also some evidence in myth that bone was identified with seed.] . . .

What we have in that careful analysis of the human body, an analysis at once physical and conceptual, is the setting out in terms of its components of those elements the Aztecs saw as being manipulated in *chinampa* agriculture, and which they identified as those which made up the world: human flesh being equated with maize, vegetable foods and the earth itself; human blood with rain and flowing water; the human heart with the sun's heat; and (this less confidently) human bone with seed. Note that this analysis was performed upon the body of a great warrior. While the same essential understanding must have informed all accounts of the relationship between the human and the natural order, the Aztecs, specialists in warfare, chose to render it most explicitly when dramatizing the unobvious but crucial connection between the feats of warriors and the food of men.

Notions of an afterlife have their place here. Aztecs understood that men who died by water-related accident or disease returned to a springtime world with Tlaloc, He who Makes Things Sprout, and who manifests himself in rain and the mountains. . . . Babies who died so young that they had not been committed to this world were buried by the grain bins, and thought to have returned, still unblemished, from whence they came. Those who died in battle (including women dead in childbirth) and those who died on the killing stone went to a warrior paradise. And all others, regardless of rank, travelled for four bitter and bleak years through the increasingly chill nine layers of the underworld until they arrived at the lowest level, presented their gifts to the Death Lord, and dissolved into Nothingness — or, rather, into Everything, for "there is our common home, there is our common place of perishing; there, there is an enlarging of the earth where forever it [the individual life] hath ended. . . ." After that four year journey, the "person" had quite gone. For all of the four years kin made offerings of garments and equipment to ease the pains of the journey: the journey completed and the four years passed, the ceremonies ceased. . . .

There was nothing "personal" in the relationship between men and those powers which, for want of a better term, we call by the altogether misleading word "gods". . . . There is a growing consensus that what Aztecs meant by all these names and images was the invocation of different aspects of relatively few great natural forces or principles, and a commentary on the relationships between them — as when Earth was addressed as Our Grandmother, Mother of the Sacred Ones, She who Eats our Filth, Heart of the Earth, Mother of our Sustenance, and so on. Aztec sculpture (like the Aztec language and like the construction of ritual objects) exhibits the same compiling mode whereby icons, most of the sturdily naturalistic representations of hearts, flowers, skulls, serpents, are compiled into remarkably abstract commentaries on the nature of things: a kind of metaphysical poetry in stone.

The great forces thus invoked and reflected upon had no engagement with man, with one exception. The exception was Tezcatlipoca, invoked as the Night Wind, the Enemy on Both Sides, the Youth, the Lord of the Close Vicinity. He was arbitrary, the personification of capricious power, coming

among men from time to time to wreak casual havoc and dispense casual rewards. He was associated with sorcerers, who injure men wantonly and by
stealth, and with the jaguar, with its superb annihilating power. He was also
the deity associated with human rulership. Neither with him, nor with the
more abstract natural elements, was there any hint of a contract. There was
instead a key word in Nahuatl, *tequitl*, which can be roughly translated as
"debt," "levy" or "tribute," but carrying with it a strong implication of what
we might call "vocation," being applied to the whole-hearted performance of
one's obligatory occupation in the world. It was used most insistently, however, to describe the offerings made of one's own blood, in the routine daily
offerings, or on the battlefield or the killing stone. Only in those places did the
individual wholly and completely pay his or her "debt." But all forms of the
payment were penitential, and some grievously so. In a great warrior festival
midway through the season of war, a representation of Huitzilopochtli was
moulded out of a rich dough of maize and seeds. . . . It was killed by a blow
to its vegetable heart in the presence of all the military chiefs, and the heart
presented to the ruler. Each year the body was divided in rotation between
the paired warrior houses in Tenochtitlán and the sister but subordinate city
of Tlatelolco. All the members of the two warrior houses ate a fragment of
the dough. The ingestion initiated a year of such strenuous penance and obligation that men were driven to pawn their land or their labor, or even to seek
a once-for-all settlement of their "debt" through death in battle rather than
endure it to the end.

To eat the flesh of Huitzilopochtli was a heavy thing. Thus the young warriors began to learn the lesson—a lesson only to be learnt in the ritual zone,
not on the field of battle—of what it was to be a warrior. The lesson took
time to learn, and had been learnt best by those who had risen to eminence
and so, for example, had had the dark experience of offering a captive at the
gladiatorial stone. The rough exuberance of the warrior youth gave way to
sedate melancholy for those who knew how fleeting were the pleasures of
this life, its riches, its public acclaim, and how heavy the burden of humanity.

The tempo and dramatic structuring of the ritual at the gladiatorial stone,
as of many other Aztec rituals, reiterated the same understanding. . . . The
Aztecs characterized their universe as composed of heavens above and underworlds below this seen world, those heavens and underworlds being stable
and enduring. This layer, Tlalticpactli, "on earth," the layer manifest to the
senses, they characterized as chronically unstable, and called it "that which
changes." That understanding of the fragility of the perceived world, and of
human arrangements within it, could be dramatized by making human sta-
tuses uncertain: the triumphant warrior does not display his status as his cap-

tive fights there on the stone; he strives to achieve it afresh. That constant challenge and testing structured all the hierarchies.

The deliberate insertion into ritual of the problematical and the unpredictable, like the capriciousness attributed to the sole interventionist god Tezcatlipoca, spoke of the uncertainty of the things of this world. Ephemerality made those things the more treasured. Aztec "lyric poetry" strikes an easy and mistaken response from the European reader, with its pretty imagery of falling flowers and misty patios (in Aztec reality, images of death on the stone). But the elegiac "where have all the flowers gone?" note is correctly recognized. Only briefly were men warmed by the sun in this world, between the dark and the dark. The particular beauties which most profoundly moved them — the shimmer of feathers, the shaped sounds of a chanted poem, the scent of a flower, the translucence of fragile jade — were moving precisely because they were as ephemeral as the lives of men.

"Courage," in such a context, becomes a complex notion. There seem to have been two kinds of bravery recognized in the Aztec fighting man which, although touched by the connotations of class, were far from exhausted by them. One was the attribute of those warriors like the "shorn ones" or the "shaven-headed Otomí" who hurled themselves heedlessly into the fray. Such men were richly rewarded and highly valued. But they were not accorded positions of authority, nor unqualified social approval. In one of the great homilies in which a father instructs his son in correct and controlled social demeanor, the "so-called furious in war" who goes "foolishly" encountering his death is classified along with the clown and buffoon as one who understands nothing and lives for vanities and acclaim. He knows no fear because he has no knowledge. Admiration is reserved for the warrior who is morally informed; who understands his obligation. He will go humbly and quietly in this world, watchful, prudent; but when the Earth Lord Tlatecuhtli stirs, "openeth his mouth, parteth his lips," when the flame of war is kindled, he will be ready. The same great prayer to Tezcatlipoca which acknowledges the anguish of the bereaved kinsfolk also acknowledges that anguish of the true warriors, "those who suffer pain, who suffer torment in their hearts" and ask that they be given their only release, their only ease — the final encounter with Tezcatlipoca:

> Show him the marvel. May his heart not falter in fear. May he desire, may he long for the flowery death by the obsidian knife. May he savor the scent, savor the freshness, savor the sweetness of the darkness . . .
> Take his part. Be his friend.

And this to the "Enemy on Both Sides."

When we hear an official rhetoric of acute self-control, and watch scenes

of extraordinary public violence, we are not confronting some unresolved social dilemma of how to enjoy the profits of military expansion without having
to bear with socially disruptive warriors. Aztec rhetoric and Aztec ritual were
unified in the endeavor to sustain a social order sufficiently in harmony with
the natural order to survive within it. To describe as "violence" the deliberate
sequence of bloody acts which we see brought into the frame and focus of
ritual action is to assume that their point lay in their destructiveness. But the
crucial understandings which grounded those killings and slow dismember-
ings were that human flesh and maize—"maize" as metonym for all vegetable sustenance—were the same matter in different transformations; that
the transformations were cyclic, and the cycles constantly in jeopardy; and
that men's actions played a part recognized as small but, given the delicacy of
the balance, always potentially decisive in maintaining the sequence of those
transformations, and so men's slight purchase on existence.

They were bleak understandings, reducing men to objects, and declaring
human society to be peripheral, important only to itself. It took courage
enough, and long years of training, to accept them.

Popol Vuh

Anonymous

Maya civilization reached its apogee prior to the year 900 in the rainforests of southern Mexico and northern Central America. Overpopulation, environmental degradation, and chronic warfare led to a decline in Maya civilization and the abandonment of many of the major Maya cities. Surviving cultures clustered in two separate regions: the lowlands of northern Yucatán and the highlands of Guatemala. The founders of the kingdom of Quiché carried the classical legacy with them. Although they worked in difficult circumstances—during the mid-sixteenth century, when European conquerors and missionaries were challenging the old ways with a vengeance—they aimed to preserve the wisdom of their ancestors—or, as translator Dennis Tedlock puts it, to "preserve the story that lay behind the ruins." The stories of the Popol Vuh, although associated primarily with the Maya of highland Guatemala, contain many of the fundamental elements of Maya culture.

What follows is a Maya story of the origin of human beings. It follows the creation of the earth, when a handful of gods were dissatisfied with their handiwork and hoped to fashion beings who would walk, work, talk, and, especially, honor their creators. As we shall see, it took them several tries to get it right.

Now they planned the animals of the mountains, all the guardians of the forests, creatures of the mountains: the deer, birds, pumas, jaguars, serpents, rattlesnakes, yellowbites, guardians of the bushes.

A Bearer, Begetter [god] speaks:

"Why this pointless humming? Why should there merely be rustling beneath the trees and bushes?"

"Indeed—they had better have guardians," the others replied. As soon as they thought it and said it, deer and birds came forth.

And then they gave out homes to the deer and birds:

"You, the deer: sleep along the rivers, in the canyons. Be here in the meadows, in the thickets, in the forests, multiply yourselves. You will stand and walk on all fours," they were told.

So they established the nests of the birds, small and great:

"You, precious birds: your nests, your houses are in the trees, in the bushes. Multiply there, scatter there, in the branches of trees, the branches of bushes," the deer and birds were told.

When this deed had been done, all of them had received a place to sleep and a place to stay. So it is that the nests of the animals are on the earth, given by the Bearer, Begetter. Now the arrangement of the deer and birds was complete. . . .

And then the deer and birds were told by the Maker, Modeler, Bearer, Begetter:

"Talk, speak out. Don't moan, don't cry out. Please talk, each to each, within each kind, within each group," they were told—the deer, birds, puma, jaguar, serpent.

"Name now our names, praise us. We are your mother, we are your father. Speak now . . . speak, pray to us, keep our days," they were told. But it didn't turn out that they spoke like people: they just squawked, they just chattered, they just howled. It wasn't apparent what language they spoke; each one gave a different cry. When the Maker, Modeler heard this:

"It hasn't turned out well, they haven't spoken," they said among themselves. "It hasn't turned out that our names have been named. Since we are their mason and sculptor, this will not do," the Bearers and Begetters said among themselves. So they told them:

"You will simply have to be transformed. Since it hasn't turned out well and you haven't spoken, we have changed our word:

"What you feed on, what you eat, the places where you sleep, the places where you stay, whatever is yours will remain in the canyons, the forests. Although it turned out that our days were not kept, nor did you pray to us, there may yet be strength in the keeper of days, the giver of praise whom we have yet to make. Just accept your service, just let your flesh be eaten. . . ."

And so their flesh was brought low: they served, they were eaten, they were killed—the animals on the face of the earth.

AGAIN THERE COMES an experiment with the human work, the human design, by the Maker, Modeler, Bearer, Begetter:

"It must simply be tried again. The time for the planting and dawning is nearing. For this we must make a provider and nurturer." . . .

So then comes the building and working with earth and mud. They made a body, but it didn't look good to them. It was just separating, just crumbling, just loosening, just softening, just disintegrating, and just dissolving. Its head wouldn't turn, either. Its face was just lopsided, its face was just twisted. It couldn't look around. It talked at first, but senselessly. It was quickly dissolving in the water.

"It won't last," the mason and sculptor said then. "It seems to be dwindling away, so let it just dwindle. It can't walk and it can't multiply, so let it be merely a thought," they said.

So then they dismantled, again they brought down their work and design. Again they talked:

"What is there for us to make that would turn out well, that would succeed in keeping our days and praying to us?" they said. Then they planned again:

"We'll just tell Xpiyacoc, Xmucane, Hunahpu Possum, Hunahpu Coyote, to try a counting of days, a counting of lots," the mason and sculptor said to themselves. Then they invoked Xpiyacoc, Xmucane.

THEN COMES THE naming of those who are the midmost seers: the "Grandmother of Day, Grandmother of Light," as the Maker, Modeler called them. These are names of Xpiyacoc and Xmucane.

When Hurricane had spoken with the Sovereign Plumed Serpent, they invoked the daykeepers, diviners, the midmost seers:

"There is yet to find, yet to discover how we are to model a person, construct a person again, a provider, nurturer, so that we are called upon and we are recognized: our recompense is in words.

Midwife, matchmaker,
our grandmother, our grandfather,
Xpiyacoc, Xmucane,
let there be planting, let there be dawning
of our invocation, our sustenance, our recognition
by the human work, the human design,
the human figure, the human mass. . . .

You have been called upon because of our work, our design. Run your hands over the kernels of corn, over the seeds of the coral tree, just get it done, just let it come out whether we should carve and gouge a mouth, a face in wood," they told the daykeepers.

And then comes the borrowing, the counting of days; the hand is moved over the corn kernels, over the coral seeds, the days, the lots.

Then they spoke to them, one of them a grandmother, the other a grandfather.

This is the grandfather, this is the master of the coral seeds: Xpiyacoc is his name.

And this is the grandmother, the daykeeper, diviner who stands behind others: Xmucane is her name.

And they said, as they set out the days:

"Just let it be found, just let it be discovered,
say it, our ear is listening,
may you talk, may you speak,
just find the wood for the carving and sculpting
by the builder, sculptor.
Is this to be the provider, the nurturer
when it comes to the planting, the dawning?
You corn kernels, you coral seeds,
you days, you lots:
may you succeed, may you be accurate,"

they said to the corn kernels, coral seeds, days, lots. "Have shame, you up there, Heart of Sky: attempt no deception before the mouth and face of Sovereign Plumed Serpent," they said. Then they spoke straight to the point:

"It is well that there be your manikins, woodcarvings, talking, speaking, there on the face of the earth."

"So be it," they replied. The moment they spoke it was done: the manikins, woodcarvings, human in looks and human in speech.

This was the peopling of the face of the earth:

They came into being, they multiplied, they had daughters, they had sons, these manikins, woodcarvings. But there was nothing in their hearts and nothing in their minds, no memory of their mason and builder. They just went and walked wherever they wanted. Now they did not remember the Heart of the Sky.

And so they fell, just an experiment and just a cutout for humankind. They were talking at first but their faces were dry. They were not yet developed in the legs and arms. They had no blood, no lymph. They had no sweat, no fat. Their complexions were dry, their faces were crusty. They flailed their legs and arms, their bodies were deformed.

And so they accomplished nothing before the Maker, Modeler who gave them birth, gave them heart. They became the first numerous people here on the face of the earth.

Again there comes a humiliation, destruction, and demolition. The manikins, woodcarvings were killed when the Heart of the Sky devised a flood for them. A great flood was made; it came down on the heads of the manikins, woodcarvings.

The man's body was carved from the wood of the coral tree by the Maker,

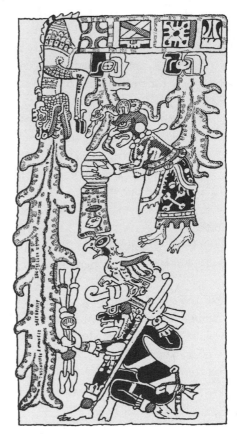

The destruction of the world by water.
(Dresden Codex)

Modeler. And as for the woman, the Maker, Modeler needed the pith of reeds for the woman's body. They were not competent, nor did they speak before the builder and sculptor who made them and brought them forth, and so they were killed, done in by a flood:

> There came a rain of resin from the sky.
> There came the one named Gouger of Faces: he gouged out their eyeballs.
> There came Sudden Bloodletter: he snapped off their heads.
> There came Crunching Jaguar: he ate their flesh.
> There came Tearing Jaguar: he tore them open.

They were pounded down to the bones and tendons, smashed and pulverized even to the bones. Their faces were smashed because they were incompetent before their mother and their father, the Heart of Sky, named Hurricane. The earth was blackened because of this; the black rainstorm began, rain all day and rain all night. Into their houses came the animals, small and great.

Their faces were crushed by things of wood and stone. Everything spoke: their water jars, their tortilla griddles, their plates, their cooking pots, their dogs, their grinding stones, each and every thing crushed their faces. . . .

The stones, their hearthstones, were shooting out, coming right out of the fire, going for their heads, causing them pain. Now they run for it, helter-skelter.

They want to climb up on the houses, but they fall as the houses collapse.

They want to climb the trees; they're thrown off by the trees.

They want to get inside caves, but the caves slam shut in their faces.

Such was the scattering of the human work, the human design. . . . And it used to be said that the monkeys in the forests today are a sign of this. They were left as a sign because wood alone was used for their flesh by the builder and sculptor.

So this is why monkeys look like people: they are a sign of a previous human work, human design—mere manikins, mere woodcarvings. . . .

AND HERE IS the beginning of the conception of humans, and the search for the ingredients of the human body. So they spoke, the Bearer, Begetter, the Makers, Modelers named Sovereign Plumed Serpent.

"The dawn has approached, preparations have been made, and morning has come for the provider, nurturer, born in the light, begotten in the light. Morning has come for humankind, for the people of the face of the earth," they said. It all came together as they went on thinking in the darkness, in the night, as they searched and they sifted, they thought and they wondered.

And here their thoughts came out in clear light. They sought and discovered what was needed for human flesh. It was only a short while before the sun, moon, and stars were to appear above the Makers and Modelers. Broken Place, Bitter Water Place is the name: the yellow corn, white corn came from there.

And these are the names of the animals who brought the food: fox, coyote, parrot, crow. There were four animals who brought the news of the ears of yellow corn and white corn. They were coming from over there at Broken Place, they showed the way to the break.

And this was when they found the staple foods.

And these were the ingredients for the flesh of the human work, the human design, and the water was for the blood. It became human blood, and corn was also used by the Bearer, Begetter.

And so they were happy over the provisions of the good mountain, filled with sweet things, thick with yellow corn, white corn, and thick with pataxte and cacao, countless zapotes, anonas, jocotes, nances, matasanos, sweets—

the rich foods filling up the citadel named Broken Place, Bitter Water Place. All the edible fruits were there: small staples, great staples, small plants, great plants. The way was shown by the animals.

And then the yellow corn and white corn were ground, and Xmucane did the grinding nine times. Corn was used, along with the water she rinsed her hands with, for the creation of grease; it became human fat when it was worked by the Bearer, Begetter, Sovereign Plumed Serpent, as they are called.

After that, they put it into words:

the making, the modeling of our first mother-father,
with yellow corn, white corn alone for the flesh,
food alone for the human legs and arms,
for our first fathers, the four human works.

It was staples alone that made up their flesh.

The Meaning of Maize for the Maya

J. Eric Thompson

The Popol Vuh makes clear the importance of maize for the Maya culture: it was of maize that the gods fashioned human beings, and maize has been the staff of life for the Maya ever since. Even knowing this, however, we may have some difficulty understanding precisely what maize meant—and means—in a vulnerable agricultural society such as that of the Maya. In the following reading, a distinguished British anthropologist reflects movingly on the Maya worldview, and how it differs from our own.

Maize was a great deal more than the economic basis of Maya civilization; it was the focal point of worship, and to it every Maya who worked the soil built a shrine in his own heart. Without maize the Maya would have lacked the leisure and the prosperity to erect their pyramids and temples; without their mystical love for it, it is improbable that the peasants would have submitted to the unceasing and stupendous program of building directed by the hierarchy. The Maya laborer knew that he was building to conciliate the gods of sky and soil, on whose care and protection his maize field was dependent.

Love of the soil is found among peasants the world over, but I doubt that there is a more strongly mystical attitude toward its produce than in Middle America. To the Maya, corn is peculiarly sacred. Even today, after four centuries of Christian influence, it is still spoken of with reverence and addressed ritualistically as "Your Grace." It is the gods' supreme gift to man, to be treated with full respect and not a little humility. Before clearing the land or sowing, the Maya fasted, practiced continence, and made his offerings to the gods of the soil. Each stage in the farming round was religious celebration.

More than two hundred years ago a friar summed up the highland Maya's attitude toward maize in these words: "Everything they did and said so concerned maize that they almost regarded it as a god. The enchantment and rapture with which they look upon their milpas is such that on their account they forget children, wife, and any other pleasure, as though the milpas were their final purpose in life and source of their felicity." This is very much to the point, but the writer made one mistake. The Indians did regard the maize as a god, although they took good care not to let the friars know it.

A somewhat similar attitude is revealed by the comment of a Mam Maya from western Guatemala on the white custom of burying in niches. The Indians, he said, consider it better to feed the earth with their dead bodies in payment for the products it gives them when they are alive — "The earth gives us food; we should feed it."

In our urban civilization the productivity of the land is something rather remote which is taken for granted. It is associated more with chain stores and can openers than with the soil, and, if our thoughts go a step back of that, we envision a man on a tractor or behind a team of horses, something picturesque, but unrelated to our efforts to earn our daily bread.

The Maya, who has to struggle against climate, tropical pests, and a too exuberant vegetation, sees things in a very different light. His livelihood depends literally on the sweat of his brow, not on the steaming flanks of a pair of horses. Even now, with the benefit of crops introduced from the Old World to vary his diet, 80 percent of his food is maize. He eats it with every meal year in and year out, and so the failure of that one crop is a disaster to him. The maize seems to be fighting beside him in an unending defense against every kind of enemy, trying to survive in order that the man and his family may also live.

The conception of a crop as a live being, an ally striving at our side, is utterly alien to our way of thinking, but it was and is fundamental in the Maya pattern of thought. No wonder that the Maya personified the maize and regarded it with a reverential love which we could never feel for anything inanimate. Maize is the gift which the gods could bestow on man only after considerable effort. The story is given in Maya legend:

Maize was once stored beneath a great mountain of rock. It was first discovered there by the marching-army ants, which made a tunnel to its hiding place beneath the rock and began carrying the grains away on their backs. The fox, who is always curious about his neighbors' doings, saw the ants carrying this strange grain and tried some. Soon the other animals and then man learned of this new food, but only the ants could penetrate to the place where it was hidden.

Man asked the rain gods to help them get at the store. In turn, three of the rain gods tried, but failed, to blast the rock apart with their thunderbolts. Then the chief rain god, the oldest of them all, after many refusals, was prevailed upon to try his skill. He sent the woodpecker to tap the surface of the rock to find the weakest spot. When it had been discovered, he told the woodpecker to take cover under an overhanging ledge while he tried to split the rock. With all his strength he hurled his mightiest thunderbolt against the weak point, and the rock was riven asunder. Just as the thunderbolt struck, the woodpecker, disobeying orders, stuck out his head. A flying fragment of rock hit him on the [top of his head], causing it to bleed freely, and ever since the woodpecker has had a red head. The fiery heat was so intense that part of the maize, which had been entirely white, was charred. Some ears were slightly burned, many were discolored with smoke, but some escaped all damage. There resulted four kinds of maize — black, red, yellow, and white. . . .

BEFORE EACH TASK the Maya makes his offering to the gods who guard his field. Ceremonies at sowing time among the Mopan Maya of southern [Belize] will illustrate the religious setting.

The night before sowing, the helpers gather at the hut of the owner of the field. At one end of the hut the sacks of seed are laid on a table before a cross, and lighted candles are placed in front and to each side of a gourd containing cacao and ground maize. The seed is then censed with copal, and afterwards the hut, inside and out, is completely censed. The men, who have brought their own hammocks, lounge in them, passing the night in conversation and music and the enjoyment of a meal served at midnight. Sometimes the group prays in the church for a good crop. The purpose of this vigil is to ensure that the crop will not be endangered by the incontinence of any member of the group (the Mam, the Chorti, the Kekchi, and other Maya groups observe periods of continence of up to thirteen days at sowing time).

Looking back thirty years, I can see the group, most of them deep in shadow, for the guttering candles throw only a small circle of light. One or two are sitting in their hammocks; a third is lying back in his hammock with one foot dangling over the edge. Everyone is wrapped in a thin blanket, for the April night is cold and the chill air has no trouble in finding the spaces between the poles that form the walls of the hut. Conversation in soft, sing-song Maya starts and dies like puffs of wind. Outside, the constellations of the tropics dawdle across the sky; they seem so close, one feels like raising his hand to push them on their course. Curiosity can hardly be delaying them; they have seen such vigils for many centuries. At daybreak the owner of the land goes to his field ahead of the rest of the party. There, in the center of the field, he burns copal and sows seven handfuls of maize in the form of a cross oriented to the four world directions, and recites this prayer:

O god, my grandfather, my grandmother, god of the hills, god of the valleys, holy god. I make to you my offering with all my soul. Be patient with me in what I am doing, my true God and [blessed] Virgin. It is needful that

Religious ritual celebrated in Yaxuná, Yucatán, in 1986. The ritual is descended directly from pre-Columbian practice. (Photo by Debra S. Walker)

you give me fine, beautiful, all I am going to sow here where I have my work, my cornfield. Watch it for me, guard it for me, let nothing happen to it from the time I sow until I harvest it.

Rites of the same general type precede clearing the land and burning off the scrub when it is dry. Typical of the religious context of the agricultural year are the ceremonies to the Chacs still held in villages of Yucatán when rain is needed. Not a man in the village fails to attend. The first task is to fetch the water needed in the preparation of the food offerings. This has to be virgin water from a sacred cenote where women never go. Once this has been brought, no one must return home, for if anyone had intercourse with a woman during the ceremony, the rains would not come. Accordingly, the men sling their hammocks within the cleared area, usually on the outskirts of the village.

Following two days of preliminary ceremonies, the shaman offers at dawn of the third day thirteen tall gourds and two shallow gourds of *balche* [Mayan wine] to the Chacs and the guardians of the milpas. Following a chant by four assistants, the *balche* is distributed among the assembly, and everyone must take a little, for the *balche* purifies one of evil. Birds are then brought forward. Four assistants called chacs hold each bird in turn by its wings and legs while the shaman pours *balche* nine times down its throat and dedicates it to the rain gods. After that the birds are killed.

Thirteen times *balche* is sprinkled on the altar, and after each sprinkling is offered to the members of the congregation. By noon the food is ready, and the main ceremony can commence.

A boy is tied by his right leg to each post of the altar. These four boys represent frogs, the attendants and musicians of the rain gods. As the ceremony proceeds, they croak in imitation of frogs announcing the approach of a storm. An older man, selected to impersonate the chief Chac, is reverently carried to a cleared space a few yards east of the altar. He is provided with a calabash and a wooden knife, for . . . calabashes are carried by the Chacs and water sprinkled from them causes rain. The wooden knife represents the implement with which they produce the lightning.

From time to time this impersonator makes sounds like thunder and brandishes his wooden knife. Sometimes in place of a single impersonator of the chief Chac, four men, one at each corner of the altar, represent the four Chacs of the world directions. Each time the shaman recites a prayer or offers *balche,* they dance nine times around the altar.

The altar is piled with food and drink. Thirteen tall gourds and two dishes of *balche,* nine pails of broth from the sacrificial birds, four lots each of nine piles of tortillas made of maize and squash seeds, and nine piles of various other kinds of tortillas are placed on it.

After this provender has been offered to the gods (a time-consuming ceremony), all retire so that the gods can feast on the offering without interruption. When it is judged that the gods have concluded their repast, the shaman returns and pours *balche* on the head of the impersonator of the chief Chac. The food, minus the spiritual essence already extracted from it, is divided among the men, and except for one or two minor ceremonies the rain petition is finished.

Great stress is laid on imitative magic. The croakings of the frogs, the noises like thunder, the impersonation of the rain god with the symbols of rain and lightning are basically magic. Important, too, is the use of the sacred numbers seven, nine, and thirteen. The purification pattern runs through the ceremony: virgin water must be used, theoretically the sacrificed birds are virgin, continence is essential, and *balche* is a purifier. In ancient times this ceremony would probably have been not a village, but a district, rite, and children might have been offered instead of turkeys.

Yet, these rites must not be regarded as so many ethnological data; they are the expressions of Maya preoccupation with the living maize and the gods who nourish him and give him drink. Much of the ancient pomp and ceremony is no more, but we can be sure that the Maya peasants, gathered in the courts of Tikal or Palenque for some ceremony, recognized with satisfaction the representations of the maize god, the Chacs, and the earth gods carved on the façades and roof combs of the temples, and were content to continue building to their glory and serving the priests who served them. They had given their hearts to the land and could have anticipated Kipling's lines: "And Memory, Use, and Love make live us and our fields alike."

Omens Foretelling the Conquest

Anonymous

The cultures of Mesoamerica shared a strong sense of fatalism: astrology and divination were much prized skills, a means of piercing the veil and discovering what caprices nature held in store. It is hardly surprising, then, that after the Conquest people recalled the impressive omens that had foretold the event. We will, of course, never know if the following occurrences were genuine. In any case, it was clear that so momentous an episode as the European invasion could not have taken place unannounced. The omens described in the following passages are from the Florentine Codex, collected from native informants in central Mexico during the 1550s by the Franciscan friar Bernardino de Sahagún.

The first bad omen: Ten years before the Spaniards first came here, a bad omen appeared in the sky. It was like a flaming ear of corn, or a fiery signal, or the blaze of daybreak; it seemed to bleed fire, drop by drop, like a wound in the sky. It was wide at the base and narrow at the peak, and it shone in the very heart of the heavens.

This is how it appeared: it shone in the eastern sky in the middle of the night. It appeared at midnight and burned till the break of day, but it vanished at the rising of the sun. The time during which it appeared to us was a full year, beginning in the year 12-House.

When it first appeared, there was great outcry and confusion. The people clapped their hands against their mouths; they were amazed and frightened, and asked themselves what it could mean.

The second bad omen: The temple of Huitzilopochtli burst into flames. It is thought that no one set it afire, that it burned down of its own accord. The name of its divine site was Tlacateccan [House of Authority].

And now it is burning, the wooden columns are burning! The flames, the tongues of fire shoot out, the bursts of fire shoot up into the sky!

The flames swiftly destroyed all the woodwork of the temple. When the fire was first seen, the people shouted: "Mexicanos, come running! We can put it out! Bring your water jars . . . !" But when they threw water on the

Among the omens foretelling the conquest were a bird with a mirror for a head and the temple of Huitzilopochtli in flames. (Florentine Codex)

blaze it only flamed higher. They could not put it out, and the temple burned to the ground.

The third bad omen: A temple was damaged by a lightning-bolt. This was the temple of Xiuhtecuhtli [fire god], which was built of straw, in the place known as Tzonmolco [part of the main temple of Tenochtitlán]. It was raining that day, but it was only a light rain or a drizzle, and no thunder was heard. Therefore the lightning-bolt was taken as an omen. The people said: "The temple was struck by a blow from the sun."

The fourth bad omen: Fire streamed through the sky while the sun was still shining. It was divided into three parts. It flashed out from where the sun sets and raced straight to where the sun rises, giving off a shower of sparks like a red-hot coal. When the people saw its long train streaming through the heavens, there was a great outcry and confusion, as if they were shaking a thousand little bells.

The fifth bad omen: The wind lashed the water until it boiled. It was as if it were boiling with rage, as if it were shattering itself in its frenzy. It began from far off, rose high in the air and dashed against the walls of the houses. The flooded houses collapsed into the water. This was in the lake that is next to us.

The sixth bad omen: The people heard a weeping woman night after night. She passed by in the middle of the night, wailing and crying out in a loud voice: "My children, we must flee far away from this city!" At other times she cried: "My children, where shall I take you!"[1]

The seventh bad omen: A strange creature was captured in the nets. The men who fish the lakes caught a bird the color of ashes, a bird resembling a crane. They brought it to Motecuhzoma in the Black House.[2]

This bird wore a strange mirror in the crown of its head. The mirror was pierced in the center like a spindle whorl, and the night sky could be seen in its face. The hour was noon, but the stars and the *mamalhuaztli*[3] could be seen in the face of that mirror. Motecuhzoma took it as a great and bad omen when he saw the stars and the *mamalhuaztli*.

But when he looked at the mirror a second time, he saw a distant plain. People were moving across it, spread out in ranks and coming forward in great haste. They made war against each other and rode on the backs of animals resembling deer.

Motecuhzoma called for his magicians and wise men and asked them: "Can you explain what I have seen? Creatures like human beings, running and fighting . . . !" But when they looked into the mirror to answer him, all had vanished away, and they saw nothing.

The eighth bad omen: Monstrous beings appeared in the streets of the city: deformed men with two heads but only one body. They were taken to the Black House and shown to Motecuhzoma; but the moment he saw them, they all vanished away.

Notes

1. Apparently a reference to Cihuacoatl, an ancient earth goddess, who wept and cried out in the night. She is one of the antecedents of the llorona (weeping woman), who is still heard in rural Mexico.
2. The house of magical studies. Motecuhzoma, the king, was a devoted amateur wizard.
3. Three stars in the constellation Taurus. They were extremely important in the Nahuatl religion: the Nahuas performed various ceremonies in their honor and offered them copal incense three times each night.

III

Conquest and Colony

The Spaniards who arrived on the shores of Mexico in 1519 bent on glorious conquest were in fact undertaking a dangerous enterprise of dubious legality. Their leader, Hernán Cortés, had defied the orders of his sponsor, Cuban governor Diego Velázquez, and appealed directly to King Charles I of Spain (who was also Emperor Charles V of the Holy Roman Empire) for recognition as the rightful conqueror of the mainland. His surprising success in this endeavor is one of history's greatest adventure stories. Firsthand Spanish chronicles of the conquest of Mexico continue to inspire awe, not only for their accounts of Spanish derring-do, but also for their descriptions of the magnificent civilizations that were destroyed. Once the city-states of the valley of Mexico were conquered, the Spaniards set their sights on subduing the other indigenous civilizations of the Americas. While Spanish accounts of these events celebrate the heroism of the conquerors, native chronicles of the same events describe the initiation of a long period of forced labor, disease, hunger, and cultural weakening.

The colonial period of New Spain, while presenting an outward façade of stability most of the time, was in fact rife with hardship, rivalries, and conflict. Indigenous groups that had allied with the Spaniards, making the Conquest possible, ultimately received treatment from the conquerors that was no more humane than that which the Spanish accorded the vanquished: all became part of the reward given to the conquerors, which consisted of Indian labor and tribute, and the related possibility of encroaching on indigenous lands. While the methods for extracting Indian labor varied over time and place, the Indians often found themselves reduced to the status of dependent laborers in this new society. What's more, they succumbed in massive numbers to disease and abuse, such that the decades following the Conquest must be reckoned as one of history's greatest demographic holocausts. The friars who came as missionaries to convert the natives, expecting thereby to bring about the millennium of the New Testament, were the greatest defenders of indigenous peoples; and yet, in easing the harshness of the Conquest, they helped to consolidate and perpetuate it. They were also instrumental in instituting special protections for the Indians, but those protections were by no means an unqualified blessing: they had the ironic effect of consolidating the Indians' status as perpetual minors in the eyes of the colony's rulers, which would have significant political and social consequences in the post-Independence era. To make matters worse, the clerics who followed that first generation of missionaries were seldom equal to the example of the pioneers: the hierarchy lived parasitically, luxuriating in Baroque excess, while parish priests lived miserably from fees collected for performing the sacraments. While these same parish priests became extremely influential figures at the local level, reports were widespread of their casual disregard for the niceties of their calling.

The ironies multiplied. Despite the royal government's best efforts to maintain the "purity" of the races, race mixing was under way from the earliest days of the colony, and mestizos—persons of mixed race—gradually emerged as the dominant racial group. Spain's zealous efforts in other spheres had similar unintended consequences: although the mother country tried mightily to control every aspect of colonial society and economy, it ended by losing its grip upon those colonies and permitting the emergence of a powerful landowning class of creoles, or American-born whites. Those creoles would later lead the movement for independence, but only with great reluctance and trepidation, since the exploitative system that they inherited left them vulnerable to the wrath of Indians, mestizos, and blacks. As we shall see, the legacy of that system of power and privilege and the backlash it wrought would powerfully shape the course of independent Mexico. In a host of ways, then, the selections that follow underscore the thrust of much recent research on the colonial period. They suggest the numerous ways that diverse groups and actors consigned to colonial domination ended up evading or putting to their own use the institutions and norms of the imperial regime.

The Spaniards' Entry into Tenochtitlán

Bernal Díaz del Castillo and Hernán Cortés

The small force of Spaniards led by Hernán Cortés arrived on the Mexican main-land in the spring of 1519. After four months on the coast, during which time Cortés and his men collected information about the Aztec capital, México-Tenochtitlán, and fomented alliances with the Aztecs' enemies, the band of about 450 adventurers jour-neyed inland. This act violated the orders given Cortés by his sponsor, Cuban governor Diego Velázquez, that Cortés should restrict his mission to fact-finding and that under no circumstances was he to venture inland. The march to the Aztec capital took nearly three months, for it involved crossing some formidable terrain and fighting several skirmishes with hostile Indians, most notably those of the Tlaxcala region. Eventu-ally, the Spaniards were able to convert the Tlaxcalans into staunch allies and to continue their march to Tenochtitlán. The Aztec emperor Moctezuma (whose name is rendered in a variety of spellings) tried his best to persuade the invaders to turn back, but they were determined, and toward the end of 1519 they arrived finally at the magnificent capital city of the Aztecs. Their initial impressions are recorded in the following excerpts by two of the most famous chroniclers of the conquest, Cortés himself, and his lieutenant, Bernal Díaz del Castillo.

THE FIRST SIGHT OF TENOCHTITLÁN,
as described by Díaz del Castillo

We came to a broad causeway and continued our march towards Iztapalapa. And when we saw all those cities and villages built in the water, and other great towns on dry land, and that straight and level causeway leading to Mexico, we were astounded. These great towns and *cues* [pyramids] and buildings rising from the water, all made of stone, seemed like an enchanted vision from the tale of Amadis.[1] Indeed, some of our soldiers asked whether it was not all a dream. It is not surprising therefore that I should write in this vein. It was all so wonderful that I do not know how to describe this first glimpse of things never heard of, seen or dreamed of before.

When we arrived near Iztapalapa we beheld the splendor of the other *Ca-*

ciques [chiefs or nobles] who came out to meet us, the lord of that city whose name was Cuitlahuac, and the lord of Culuacan, both of them close relations of Montezuma. And when we entered the city of Iztapalapa, the sight of the palaces in which they lodged us! They were very spacious and well built, of magnificent stone, cedar wood, and the wood of other sweet-smelling trees, with great rooms and courts, which were a wonderful sight, and all covered with awnings of woven cotton.

When we had taken a good look at all this, we went to the orchard and garden, which was a marvelous place both to see and walk in. I was never tired of noticing the diversity of trees and the various scents given off by each, and the paths choked with roses and other flowers, and the many local fruit-trees and rose-bushes, and the pond of fresh water. Another remarkable thing was that large canoes could come into the garden from the lake, through a channel they had cut, and their crews did not have to disembark. Everything was shining with lime and decorated with different kinds of stonework and paintings which were a marvel to gaze on. Then there were birds of many breeds and varieties which came to the pond. I say again that I stood looking at it, and thought that no land like it would ever be discovered in the whole world, because at that time Peru was neither known nor thought of. But today all that I then saw is overthrown and destroyed; nothing is left standing.

The *Caciques* of that town and of Coyoacan brought us a present of gold worth more than two thousand pesos; and Cortés thanked them heartily for it, and he showed them great kindness, telling them through our interpreters something about our holy faith, and declaring to them the great power of our lord the Emperor. . . .

Early next day we left Iztapalapa with a large escort of these great *Caciques*, and followed the causeway, which is eight yards wide and goes so straight to the city of Mexico that I do not think it curves at all. Wide though it was, it was so crowded with people that there was hardly room for them all. Some were going to Mexico and others coming away, besides those who had come out to see us, and we could hardly get through the crowds that were there. For the towers and *cues* were full, and they came in canoes from all parts of the lake. No wonder, since they had never seen horses or men like us before!

With such wonderful sights to gaze on we did not know what to say, or if this was real that we saw before our eyes. On the land side there were great cities, and on the lake many more. The lake was crowded with canoes. At intervals along the causeway there were many bridges, and before us was the great city of Mexico. As for us, we were scarcely four hundred strong, and we well remembered the words and warnings of the people of Huexotzinco and Tlascala and Tlamanalco, and the many other warnings we had received to beware of entering the city of Mexico, since they would kill us as soon as they had us inside. Let the interested reader consider whether there is not much to ponder in this narrative of mine. What men in all the world have shown such daring? But let us go on.

We marched along the causeway to a point where another small causeway branches off to another city called Coyoacan, and there, beside some tower-like buildings, which were their shrines, we were met by many more *Caciques* and dignitaries in very rich cloaks. The different chieftains wore different brilliant liveries, and the causeways were full of them. Montezuma had sent these great *Caciques* in advance to receive us, and as soon as they came before Cortés they told him in their language that we were welcome, and as a sign of peace they touched the ground with their hands and kissed it.

There we halted for some time while Cacamatzin, the lord of Texcoco, and the lords of Iztapalapa, Tacuba, and Coyoacan went ahead to meet the great Montezuma, who approached in a rich litter, accompanied by other great lords and feudal *Caciques* who owned vassals. When we came near to Mexico, at a place where there were some other small towers, the great Montezuma descended from his litter, and these other great *Caciques* supported him beneath a marvelously rich canopy of green feathers, decorated with gold work, silver, pearls, and *chalchihuites,* which hung from a sort of border. It was a marvelous sight. The great Montezuma was magnificently clad, in their fashion, and wore sandals of a kind for which their name is *cotaras,* the soles of which are gold and the upper parts ornamented with precious stones. And the four lords who supported him were richly clad also in garments that seem to have been kept ready for them on the road so that they could accompany their master. For they had not worn clothes like this when they came out to receive us. There were four other great *Caciques* who carried the canopy above their heads, and many more lords who walked before the great Montezuma, sweeping the ground on which he was to tread, and laying down cloaks so that his feet should not touch the earth. Not one of these chieftains dared to look him in the face. All kept their eyes lowered most reverently except those four lords, his nephews, who were supporting him.

When Cortés saw, heard, and was told that the great Montezuma was approaching, he dismounted from his horse, and when he came near to Montezuma each bowed deeply to the other. Montezuma welcomed our Captain, and Cortés, speaking through Doña Marina,[2] answered by wishing him very good health. Cortés, I think, offered Montezuma his right hand, but Montezuma refused it and extended his own. Then Cortés brought out a necklace which he had been holding. It was made of those elaborately worked and colored glass beads called *margaritas* . . . and was strung on a gold cord and dipped in musk to give it a good odor. This he hung round the great Montezuma's neck, and as he did so attempted to embrace him. But the great princes who stood round Montezuma grasped Cortés' arm to prevent him, for they considered this an indignity. . . .

THE MEETING WITH MONTEZUMA (MUTEZUMA),
as described by Cortés

When at last I came to speak to Mutezuma himself I took off a necklace of pearls and cut glass that I was wearing and placed it round his neck; after we had walked a little way up the street a servant of his came with two necklaces, wrapped in a cloth, made from red snails' shells, which they hold in great esteem; and from each necklace hung eight shrimps of refined gold almost a span in length. When they had been brought he turned to me and placed them about my neck, and then continued up the street in the manner already described until we reached a very large and beautiful house which had been very well prepared to accommodate us. There he took me by the hand and led me to a great room facing the courtyard through which we entered. And he bade me sit on a very rich throne, which he had had built for him and then left saying that I should wait for him. After a short while, when all those of my company had been quartered, he returned with many and various treasures of gold and silver and featherwork, and as many as five or six thousand cotton garments, all very rich and woven and embroidered in various ways. And after he had given me these things he sat on another throne which they placed there next to the one on which I was sitting, and addressed me in the following way:

"For a long time we have known from the writings of our ancestors that neither I, nor any of those who dwell in this land, are natives of it, but foreigners who came from very distant parts; and likewise we know that a chieftain, of whom they were all vassals, brought our people to this region. And he returned to his native land and after many years came again, by which time all those who had remained were married to native women and had built villages and raised children. And when he wished to lead them away again they would not go nor even admit him as their chief; and so he departed. And we have always held that those who descended from him would come and conquer this land and take us as their vassals. So because of the place from which you claim to come, namely, from where the sun rises, and the things you tell us of the great lord or king who sent you here, we believe and are certain that he is our natural lord, especially as you say that he had known of us for some time. So be assured that we shall obey you and hold you as our lord in place of that great sovereign of whom you speak; and in this there shall be no offense or betrayal whatsoever. And in all the land that lies in my domain, you may command as you will, for you shall be obeyed; and all that we own is for you to dispose of as you choose. Thus, as you are in your own country and your own house, rest now from the hardships of your journey and the battle which you have fought, for I know full well of all that has happened to you from Pununchan to here, and I also know how those of Cempoala and Tlascalteca have told you much evil of me; believe only what you see with your eyes, for those are my enemies, and some were my vassals, and have rebelled against me at your coming and said those things to gain favor with you. I also know that they have told you the walls of my houses are made of gold, and that the floor mats in my rooms and other things in my household are likewise of gold, and that I was, and claimed to be, a god; and many other things besides. The houses as you see are of stone and lime and clay."

Then he raised his clothes and showed me his body, saying, as he grasped his arms and trunk with his hands, "See that I am of flesh and blood like you and all other men, and I am mortal and substantial. See how they have lied to you? It is true that I have some pieces of gold left to me by my ancestors; anything I might have shall be given to you whenever you ask. Now I shall go to other houses where I live, but here you shall be provided with all that you and your people require, and you shall receive no hurt, for you are in your own land and your own house."

I replied to all he said as I thought most fitting, especially in making him believe that Your Majesty was he whom they were expecting; and with this he took his leave. When he had gone we were very well provided with chickens, bread, fruit and other requisites, especially for the servicing of our quarters. In this manner I spent six days, very well provisioned with all that was needed and visited by many of those chiefs."

THE MARKETPLACE OF TENOCHTITLÁN,
as described by Díaz del Castillo

On reaching the market-place, escorted by the many *Caciques* whom Montezuma had assigned to us, we were astounded at the great number of people and the quantities of merchandise. . . . Let us begin with the dealers in gold, silver, and precious stones, feathers, cloaks, and embroidered goods, and male and female slaves who are also sold there. They bring as many slaves to be sold in that market as the Portuguese bring Negroes from Guinea. Some are brought there attached to long poles by means of collars round their necks to prevent them from escaping, but others are left loose. Next there were those who sold coarser cloth, and cotton goods and fabrics made of twisted thread, and there were chocolate merchants with their chocolate. In this way you could see every kind of merchandise to be found anywhere in New Spain, laid out in the same way as goods are laid out in my own district of Medina del Campo, a center for fairs, where each line of stalls has its own particular sort. So it was in this great market. There were those who sold sisal cloth and ropes and sandals they wear on their feet, which are made from the same plant. All these were kept in one part of the market, in the place assigned to them, and in another part were skins of tigers and lions, otters, jackals, and deer, badgers, mountain cats, and other wild animals, some tanned and some untanned, and other classes of merchandise.

There were sellers of kidney-beans and sage and other vegetables and herbs in another place, and in yet another they were selling fowls, and birds with great dewlaps [turkeys], also rabbits, hares, deer, young ducks, little dogs, and other such creatures. Then there were the fruiterers; and the women who sold cooked food, flour and honey cake, and tripe, had their part of the market. Then came pottery of all kinds, from big water-jars to little jugs, displayed in its own place, also honey, honey-paste, and other sweets like nougat. Elsewhere they sold timber too, boards, cradles, beams, blocks, and benches, all in a quarter of their own.

Then there were the sellers of pitch-pine for torches, and other things of that kind, and I must also mention, with all apologies, that they sold many canoe-loads of human excrement, which they kept in the creeks near the market. This was for the manufacture of salt and the curing of skins, which they say cannot be done without it. I know that many gentlemen will laugh at this, but I assure them it is true. I may add that on all the roads they have shelters made of reeds or straw or grass so that they can retire when they wish to do so, and purge their bowels unseen by passers-by, and also in order that their excrement shall not be lost.

But why waste so many words on the goods in their great market? If I describe everything in detail I shall never be done. Paper, which in Mexico they call *amal,* and some reeds that smell of liquid amber, and are full of tobacco, and yellow ointments and other such things, are sold in a separate part. Much cochineal[3] is for sale too, under the arcades of that market, and there are many sellers of herbs and other such things. They have a building there also in which three judges sit, and there are officials like constables who examine the merchandise. I am forgetting the sellers of salt and the makers of flint knives, and how they split them off the stone itself, and the fisherwomen and the men who sell small cakes made from a sort of weed which they get out of the great lake, which curdles and forms a kind of bread which tastes rather like cheese. They sell axes too, made of bronze and copper and tin, and gourds and brightly painted wooden jars.

We went on to the great *cue,* and as we approached its wide courts, before leaving the market-place itself, we saw many more merchants who, so I was told, brought gold to sell in grains, just as they extract it from the mines. This gold is placed in the thin quills of the large geese of that country, which are so white as to be transparent. They used to reckon their accounts with one another by the length and thickness of these little quills, how much so many cloaks or so many gourds of chocolate or so many slaves were worth, or anything else they were bartering.

Now let us leave the market, having given it a final glance, and come to the courts and enclosures in which their great *cue* stood. Before reaching it you passed through a series of large courts, bigger I think than the Plaza at Salamanca. These courts were surrounded by a double masonry wall and paved, like the whole place, with very large smooth white flagstones. Where these stones were absent everything was whitened and polished, indeed the whole place was so clean that there was not a straw or a grain of dust to be found there.

When we arrived near the great temple and before we had climbed a single step, the great Montezuma sent six *papas* [priests] and two chieftains down from the top, where he was making his sacrifices, to escort our Captain; and as he climbed the steps, of which there were one hundred and fourteen, they tried to take him by the arms to help him up in the same way as they helped Montezuma, thinking he might be tired, but he would not let them near him.

The top of the *cue* formed an open square on which stood something like a platform, and it was here that the great stones stood on which they placed the poor Indians for sacrifice. Here also was a massive image like a dragon, and other hideous figures, and a great deal of blood that had been spilled that day. Emerging in the company of two *papas* from the shrine which houses his accursed images, Montezuma made a deep bow to us all and said: "My lord Malinche,[4] you must be tired after climbing this great *cue* of ours." And Cortés replied that none of us was ever exhausted by anything. Then Montezuma took him by the hand, and told him to look at his great city and all the other cities standing in the water, and the many others on the land round the lake; and he said that if Cortés had not had a good view of the great market-place he could see it better from where he now was. So we stood there looking, because that huge accursed *cue* stood so high that it dominated everything. We saw the three causeways that led into Mexico: the causeway of Iztapalapa by which we had entered four days before, and that of Tacuba along which we were afterwards to flee on the night of our great defeat, when the new prince Cuitlahuac drove us out of the city . . . , and that of Tepeaquilla. We saw the fresh water which came from Chapultepec to supply the city, and the bridges that were constructed at intervals on the causeways so that the water could flow in and out from one part of the lake to another. We saw a great number of canoes, some coming with provisions and others returning with cargo and merchandise; and we saw too that one could not pass from one house to another of that great city and the other cities that were built on the water except over wooden drawbridges or by canoe. We saw *cues* and shrines in these cities that looked like gleaming white towers and castles: a marvelous sight. All the houses had flat roofs, and on the causeways were other small towers and shrines built like fortresses.

Having examined and considered all that we had seen, we turned back to the great market and the swarm of people buying and selling. The mere murmur of their voices talking was loud enough to be heard more than three miles away. Some of our soldiers who had been in many parts of the world, in Constantinople, in Rome, and all over Italy, said that they had never seen a market so well laid out, so large, so orderly, and so full of people.

Notes

1. A medieval romantic adventure story very popular among the generation of *conquistadores*. *Ed.*
2. Doña Marina was an Indian woman who served the conquerors as translator. She later became Cortés's mistress and mother of his son, Martín. *Ed.*
3. A red dye made from the dried bodies of insects that nest in nopal cacti. *Ed.*
4. Although the name "Malinche" has come to be associated with Doña Marina, Cortés's translator and mistress, it was originally the Indians' name for Cortés himself. Since Doña Marina was always with Cortés and since it was she who actually spoke to the Indians, the Indians referred to Cortés as "Marina's captain," which was shortened to "Malinche." *Ed.*

Cortés and Montezuma

J. H. Eliott

Like any document, the chronicles written by the conquistadores *must be read with caution, since their authors were hardly objective observers. In the following excerpt, British historian John H. Eliott, an eminent authority on the relations between Spain and its New World colonies, seeks to find the truth of Cortés's own narrative by placing the conqueror in the context of his times.*

There was no lack of resourcefulness in Cortés's approach to the conquest of Mexico, which was as much a political as a military operation, and one conducted simultaneously against the Aztec emperor and the governor of Cuba. The contemporary chronicler Fernández de Oviedo refers at one point to Cortés's capacity to "construct romances (*novelar*) and devise schemes appropriate to a resourceful, astute, and cunning captain." Recent work on Cortés . . . has helped to confirm his extraordinary skill in the constructing of romances and the devising of schemes. The first letter of relation . . . is a brilliant fictional reconstruction which draws heavily on the political and juridical ideas embedded in the *Siete Partidas.*[1] The governor, Velázquez, is painted in the darkest colors as a man consumed by greed and personal interest, whereas Cortés himself emerges as the faithful servant of the Spanish Crown and a staunch upholder of the common weal.

But it is in his account of the confrontation with Montezuma that Cortés's powers of imagination and invention are revealed at their best. Although the whole episode remains deeply mysterious, it at least seems clear that Cortés's account of what passed between the two men should not be taken, as it has long been taken, at face value. In all probability, two distinctive layers of legend now surround the relationship between Cortés and Montezuma. The outer layer, which forms the basis of modern interpretations of the conquest of Mexico, holds that Cortés was the unwitting beneficiary of an Aztec tradition that the priest-king Quetzalcóatl would one day return from out of the east and reclaim his own. No evidence has apparently been found, however, to prove the existence of any pre-conquest tradition of Quetzalcóatl leading his followers to the land of Anáhuac. It is possible that the stories of a return from the east, like those of the omens which paralyzed Montezuma's powers of decision sprang up *after* the conquest; and the identification of Cortés with Quetzalcóatl (who is never mentioned in the writings of Cortés), may first have been made in the 1540's by the Franciscans Motolonía and Sahagún.

But wrapped within this legend lies another, for which Cortés himself may have been largely responsible—a legend similar in theme but less specific in its details. Cortés retails two speeches by Montezuma, both of them so improbable in content and tenor as to suggest that they were founded more on fantasy than facts. The two speeches are couched in tones quite alien to an Aztec but familiar enough to a Christian Spaniard; for they subtly combine the themes of the coming of a Messiah and the return of a natural lord to his vassals, in order to lead up to the grand climax of Montezuma's renunciation of his imperial heritage into the hands of Charles V. "We give thanks to our gods," says Montezuma, "that in our time that which was long expected has come to pass." [Eulalia] Guzmán has shrewdly pointed out how this whole passage echoes the strains of the *Nunc Dimittis.*[2] But the New Testament analogies do not end here. Montezuma ends his first speech of welcome with the dramatic gesture of lifting his clothes to show Cortés his body, saying: "you see that I am of flesh and bones like yourself and everyone else, mortal and tangible." Does not this contain overtones of Jesus's words to the disciples ("a spirit hath not flesh and bones as ye see me have") and of Paul and Barnabas at Lystra ("we also are men of like passions with you")?

It is hard to avoid the impression that Cortés was drawing on all his very considerable reserves of imagination in order to paint for Charles V a solemn and spectacular picture of a scene that may never have occurred. If the scene had a faintly Biblical setting, it would be all the more impressive, especially as Montezuma's forefathers were now in the process of being endowed with distant Christian origins; and, with a nice irony, Cortés introduces his account of Tenochtitlán with words that themselves have a Biblical ring: "I know that [these things] will seem so remarkable that they cannot be believed, for what we behold with our own eyes, we cannot with our understanding comprehend." But if Cortés drew on the Bible for his general setting, and on Castilian legal codes for the ideas of suzerainty and vassalage which he put into Montezuma's mouth, there still remains a third crucial element in the story—the myth of the ruler returning from the east. It has been suggested that Cortés heard some such story from the Indians in the Antilles, but it seems equally possible that he heard it on his march to Mexico, and stored it up for future use. According to Bernal Díaz, two *caciques* at Tlaxcala told Cortés of a prophecy that men would come from the region where the sun rises and would subjugate the land. If so, the prophecy may have related not to Quetzalcóatl but to Huitzilopochtli, the god of war, who appears in the writings both of Cortés and Bernal Díaz, under the guise of "Orchilobos." In a letter written by Don Antonio de Mendoza, the first viceroy of New Spain, to his brother, it is specifically stated that the Aztecs welcomed Cortés thinking that he was "Orchilobos"—not Quetzalcóatl. Fernández de Oviedo, commenting on the letter, disbelieves the stories both of Orchilobos coming from the north-east, and of Cortés being mistaken for him; but this does not affect the possibility that Cortés picked up some local legend, which he then proceeded to embellish and turn to account with his customary skill.

Whatever the exact origins of the myth of the returning ruler, the whole Montezuma episode, as related to Charles V, bears witness to Cortés's remarkable fertility of invention. This creative ability, the capacity to build on a grand scale, often starting from the most slender foundations, is perhaps the most striking of all the characteristics of Cortés. It carried him through the delicate problems involved in the defiance of Velázquez; it carried him through the conquest of Mexico itself; and it inspired his approach to the work of reconstruction when the Aztec empire had fallen.

His plans for the New Spain to be established on the ruins of the old Mexico were deeply influenced by his experiences in the Antilles where he had seen the Indian population destroyed. A repetition of the Antilles experience must at all costs be avoided, and he wrote, like the great Renaissance builder he was, of the conservation of the Indian as being "the foundation on which all this work has to be built." But behind his schemes for the creation of an ordered society of Spaniards and Indians lay a vision which he had borrowed from the friars. It was in August 1523 that the first three Franciscan missionaries (all Flemings) arrived in Mexico, to be followed in May 1524 by the famous "twelve apostles" headed by Fray Martín de Valencia. In the fourth and fifth letters of relation, dated October 1524 and September 1526, there are clear signs of Franciscan influence on Cortés's thought. The Franciscans, the majority of whom seem to have been less influenced by Erasmus than by Italian apocalyptic traditions and the doctrines of Savonarola,[3] arrived with a burning desire to establish, in a Mexico still uncorrupted by European vices, a replica of the church of the apostles. Cortés, in the first of his letters, had emphasized the importance of informing the pope of his discoveries, so that measures could be taken for the conversion of the natives. But now, in his fourth letter, he couples his pleas for assistance in the work of conversion, with an attack on the worldliness of the church and the pomp and avarice of ecclesiastical dignitaries. His diatribe, so typical of contemporary European protests against the wealth and corruption of the church, is clearly inspired by the friars, for whom he requests exclusive rights in the conversion of Mexico. It is the Franciscans, too, who inspire the prophecy in the fifth letter that there would arise in Mexico a "new church, where God will be served and honored more than in any other region of the earth."

The Franciscans provided Cortés with an enlarged vision, not only of the new church and the new society to be built in Mexico, but also of his own special role in the providential order. He had already, in his first letter, been careful to insist that God had arranged the discovery of Mexico in order that Queen Juana and Charles V should obtain special merit by the conversion of its pagan inhabitants. It followed from this that he himself, as the conqueror of Mexico, enjoyed a special place in the divine plan. The attitude of the Franciscans was bound to encourage him in this belief, for to them he inevitably appeared as God's chosen agent at a vital moment in the ordering of world history—the moment at which the sudden possibility of converting untold millions to the Faith brought the long-awaited millennium almost within sight. It was, therefore, with the concurrence of the Franciscans that Cortés could now designate himself as the "agency" (*medio*) by which God had been pleased to bring the Indians to an understanding of Him.

Notes

1. Law code devised by King Alfonso X, king of Castile and León from 1252 to 1284. The *Siete Partidas* was a compilation of Spanish legal knowledge of the day, and it is often looked to as the supreme statement of the notion of "natural law," which sees God as the only infallible source of justice. *Ed.*

2. *Nunc Dimittis:* Luke 2:29–32: "This day, Master, thou givest thy servant his discharge in peace; now thy promise is fulfilled. For I have seen with my own eyes the deliverance which thou has made ready in full view of all the nations: a light that will be a revelation to the heathen, and glory to thy people Israel" (New English Bible). *Ed.*

3. Girolamo Savonarola (1452–1498), Italian religious reformer. A Dominican friar, he preached heatedly against laxity in religious matters, defied Pope Alexander VI, and was hanged for heresy. *Ed.*

The Battles of Tenochtitlán and Tlatelolco

Anonymous

The events of the conquest are familiar: The Spaniards, after entering the city of Tenochtitlán, hoped to force the surrender of the city by taking the emperor Montezuma hostage. When they had kept him in captivity for several months to little profit, the tension was broken by the news that a group of Spaniards sent by Diego Velázquez, governor of Cuba, had arrived at the coast, intent on punishing Cortés for his insubordination. Cortés and part of his army left Tenochtitlán to deal with this matter; meanwhile, back in the city, forces under the command of Cortés's lieutenant, Pedro de Alvarado, fearing a conspiracy against them, attacked their hosts during a celebration of the lords of Tenochtitlán, committing a frightful massacre. Cortés returned to find the city in an uproar, and soon the Spaniards were driven out. They sought refuge among their allies to the east of the volcanoes, and there, together with those allies, they carefully prepared for the siege of Tenochtitlán.

The following excerpt, written in Nahuatl in 1528 by anonymous authors from Tenochtitlán's neighboring, allied city-state of Tlatelolco, describes the valiant, doomed, resistance of the Aztecs and their allies during the final siege and subjugation of the city.

Now the Spaniards began to wage war against us. They attacked us by land for ten days, and then their ships appeared. Twenty days later, they gathered all their ships together near Nonohualco, off the place called Mazatzintamalco. The allies from Tlaxcala and Huexotzinco set up camp on either side of the road.

Our warriors from Tlatelolco immediately leaped into their canoes and set out for Mazatzintamalco and the Nonohualco road. But no one set out from Tenochtitlan to assist us: only the Tlatelolcas were ready when the Spaniards arrived in their ships.[1] On the following day, the ships sailed to Xoloco.

The fighting at Xoloco and Huitzillan lasted for two days. While the battle was under way, the warriors from Tenochtitlan began to mutiny. They said: "Where are our chiefs? They have fired scarcely a single arrow! Do they think they have fought like men?" Then they seized four of their own leaders and put them to death. The victims were two captains, Cuauhnochtli and Cua-pan, and the priests of Amantlan and Tlalocan. This was the second time that the people of Tenochtitlan killed their own leaders.

THE SPANIARDS SET UP two cannons in the middle of the road and aimed them at the city. When they fired them, one of the shots struck the Eagle Gate. The people of the city were so terrified that they began to flee to Tlatelolco. They brought their idol Huitzilopochtli with them, setting it up in the House of the Young Men. Their king Cuauhtemoc also abandoned Tenochtitlan. Their chiefs said: "Mexicanos! Tlatelolcas! All is not lost! We can still defend our houses. We can prevent them from capturing our storehouses and the pro-duce of our lands. We can save the sustenance of life, our stores of corn. We can also save our weapons and insignia, our clusters of rich feathers, our gold earrings and precious stones. Do not be discouraged; do not lose heart. We are Mexicanos! We are Tlatelolcas!" . . .

The captains from Tenochtitlan cut their hair short, and so did those of lesser rank. The Otomies and the other ranks that usually wore headdresses did not wear them during all the time we were fighting. The Tlatelolcas sur-rounded the most important captains and their women taunted them: "Why are you hanging back? Have you no shame? No woman will ever paint her face for you again!" The wives of the men from Tenochtitlan wept and begged for pity.

When the warriors of Tlatelolco heard what was happening, they began to shout, but still the brave captains of Tenochtitlan hung back. As for the Tlatelolcas, their humblest warriors died fighting as bravely as their captains.

A SPANIARD NAMED Castañeda approached us in Yauhtenco. He was accompa-nied by a group of Tlaxcaltecas, who shouted at the guards on the watchtower near the breakwater. These guards were Itzpalanqui, the captain of Chapul-tepec; two captains from Tlapala; and Cuexacaltzin. Castañeda shouted to them: "Come here!"

"What do you want?" they asked him. "We will come closer." They got into a boat and approached to within speaking distance. "Now, what have you to say to us?"

The Tlaxcaltecas asked: "Where are you from?" And when they learned that the guards were from Tlatelolco, they said: "Good, you are the men we are looking for. Come with us. The 'god' has sent for you."

The guards went with Castañeda to Nonohualco. The Captain [Cortés] was in the House of the Mist there, along with La Malinche [Doña Marina], The Sun [Alvarado] and Sandoval. A number of the native lords were also present and they told the Captain: "The Tlatelolcas have arrived. We sent for them to come here."

La Malinche said to the guards: "Come forward! The Captain wants to know: what can the chiefs of Tenochtitlan be thinking of? Is Cuauhtemoc a stupid, willful little boy? Has he no mercy on the women and children of his city? Must even the old men perish? See, the kings of Tlaxcala, Huexotzinco, Cholula, Chalco, Acolhuacan, Cuauhnahuac, Xochimilco, Mizquic, Cuitlahuac and Culhuacan are all here with me."

One of the kings said: "Do the people of Tenochtitlan think they are playing a game? Already their hearts are grieving for the city in which they were born. If they will not surrender, we should abandon them and let them perish by themselves. Why should the Tlatelolcas feel sorry when the people of Tenochtitlan bring a senseless destruction on themselves?"

The guards from Tlatelolco said: "Our lords, it may be as you say."

The "god" said: "Tell Cuauhtemoc that the other kings have all abandoned him. I will go to Teocalhueyacan, where his forces are gathered, and I will send the ships to Coyoacan."

The guards returned to speak with the followers of Cuauhtemoc. They shouted the message to them from their boats. But the Tlatelolcas would not abandon the people of Tenochtitlan.

THE SPANIARDS MADE ready to attack us, and the war broke out again. They assembled their forces in Cuepopan and Cozcacuahco. A vast number of our warriors were killed by their metal darts. Their ships sailed to Texopan, and the battle there lasted three days. When they had forced us to retreat, they entered the Sacred Patio, where there was a four-day battle. Then they reached Yacacolco.

The Tlatelolcas set up three racks of heads in three different places. The first rack was in the Sacred Patio of Tlilancalco [Black House], where we strung up the heads of our lords the Spaniards. The second was in Acacolco, where we strung up Spanish heads and the heads of two of their horses. The third was in Zacatla, in front of the temple of the earth-goddess Cihuacoatl, where we strung up the heads of Tlaxcaltecas.

The women of Tlatelolco joined in the fighting. They struck at the enemy and shot arrows at them; they tucked up their skirts and dressed in the regalia of war.

The Spaniards forced us to retreat. Then they occupied the market place. The Tlatelolcas—the Jaguar Knights, the Eagle Knights, the great warriors— were defeated, and this was the end of the battle. It had lasted five days, and two thousand Tlatelolcas were killed in action. During the battle, the Span-

The Battle of Tenochtitlán as envisioned by an anonymous seventeenth-century Spanish artist. (From the collection of the Yale Art History Department)

iards set up a canopy for the Captain in the market place. They also mounted a catapult on the temple platform.

AND ALL THESE misfortunes befell us. We saw them and wondered at them; we suffered this unhappy fate.

> Broken spears lie in the roads;
> we have torn our hair in our grief.
> The houses are roofless now, and their walls
> are red with blood.

> Worms are swarming in the streets and plazas,
> and the walls are splattered with gore.
> The water has turned red, as if it were dyed,
> and when we drink it,
> it has the taste of brine.

> We have pounded our hands in despair
> against the adobe walls,
> for our inheritance, our city, is lost and dead.
> The shields of our warriors were its defense,
> but they could not save it.

We have chewed dry twigs and salt grasses;
we have filled our mouths with dust and bits of adobe;
we have eaten lizards, rats and worms. . . .

When we had meat, we ate it almost raw. It was scarcely on the fire before we snatched it and gobbled it down.

They set a price on all of us: on the young men, the priests, the boys and girls. The price of a poor man was only two handfuls of corn, or ten cakes made from mosses or twenty cakes of salty couch-grass. Gold, jade, rich cloths, quetzal feathers—everything that once was precious was now considered worthless.

Note

1. During the sojourn in Tlaxcala, Cortés ordered that thirteen small ships be built to maneuver on Lake Texcoco and aid in the siege of Tenochtitlán. *Ed.*

The Spiritual Conquest

Fray Jerónimo de Mendieta

*No account of the conquest would be complete without some consideration of the key
role played by the first Christian missionaries. Cortés, as J. H. Eliott points out, was a
pious man who fancied himself "God's chosen agent" in the evangelization of the New
World. He was also a practical man who had witnessed the destruction of the Indian
populations of the Caribbean islands. Both from religious conviction and a determination that the experience of the islands not be repeated on the mainland, he specifically
requested that a group of Franciscan monks be sent from Spain to protect and evange-
lize the Indians. The Franciscans, who were heavily influenced by Erasmus's writings
and other currents in Renaissance humanism, emphasized poverty and humility in
all their works, and this attitude seems to have aided them in winning over a substantial portion of the Indian population. They went about their task of evangelization
with remarkable zeal and determination—although, as later selections in this section will attest (see particularly the readings by Florescano and Leonard), the Church
and its clergy were by no means always humble and righteous in their dealings with
Indians.*

*The following selection seeks to claim for the friars their fair share of the credit
for securing Spanish domination of New Spain. It was written by Jerónimo de Mendieta, a Franciscan monk who arrived in New Spain in 1554. Although he was not
an eyewitness to the events he describes, he is regarded as one of the most reliable
historians of this early period of evangelization, for he was well acquainted with the
leader of the original "Twelve," Fray Toribio de Benavente (more commonly known
as Motolinea or Motolinía), as well as with many other participants and witnesses.
He was also able to utilize the writings of the earliest missionaries, as well as the
archives of the convent of San Francisco in Mexico City. Mendieta wrote his classic
account,* Historia eclesiástica indiana, *between 1571 and 1596.*

> *On the devotion and reverence with which the governor,*
> *Fernando Cortés, received the twelve friars*

When the governor, Fernando Cortés,[1] heard of the arrival of the friars he
had sent for, he was greatly pleased; and rejoicing in his soul, he gave thanks

to Our Lord for this blessing. He then ordered some of his servants to go out and greet them in his name, and to look after them, so that they should lack nothing and so that no misfortune should befall them, for things in that land were not yet quite stable and settled, it having been won by only a few Spaniards who were at that time all gathered in Mexico City and fearing some mishap. . . .

While these friars, eschewing all comfort, walked barefoot to Mexico, which is sixty leagues from the port where they disembarked, the governor ordered that all of the principal Indian caciques from the largest villages around Mexico be called before him, so that they would all be together to receive the ministers of God who came to teach them His law and show them His will, and to guide them along the path to their salvation. When these servants of God passed through Tlaxcala, they stopped for a day to rest from their journey and to see that renowned and populous city, and they awaited the market day when most of the people of that province would come together to buy provisions for their families. The friars marveled at seeing such a multitude of souls, more than they had ever in their lives seen gathered together. They praised God with the greatest joy at seeing the bounteous harvest He had placed before them. And since they could not speak to the Indians, for they lacked knowledge of their language, they spoke like mutes, using signs to indicate heaven, hoping to make them understand that they had come to show them the treasures and glories that were up there. The Indians walked behind them, just as children will follow someone who brings them some novelty, and they marveled to see the friars wearing such ragged clothing, so different from the elegance and ostentation they had seen in the Spanish soldiers. They said to one another: "Who are these men who are so poor? What sort of clothing are they wearing? They are not like the other Christians of Castile." And they kept repeating a word of theirs, saying, *"motolinea, motolinea."* One of the fathers, whose name was Toribio de Benavente, asked a Spaniard what this word meant that the Indians kept repeating. The Spaniard answered: "Padre, *motolinea* means 'poor,' or 'poverty.'" And from that time forward, Fray Toribio always called himself "Fray Toribio Motolinea."

When they got to Mexico, the governor, accompanied by the Spanish gentlemen and Indian nobles who had been gathered for the occasion, went forth to receive them. And kneeling on the ground, one by one the governor kissed each of their hands. Pedro de Alvarado did likewise, as did all of the Spanish captains and gentlemen. Upon seeing this, the Indians followed suit, and in imitation of the Spaniards they too kissed the friars' hands. Such is the power of the example of one's superiors.

This most memorable act is now commemorated in many paintings throughout New Spain, for it was the best thing that Cortés ever did. He acted not as a mere man, but as an angelic and heavenly being, and through him the Holy Spirit built a firm foundation for the preaching of the divine word. So it was that, through men who appeared poor and lowly in the eyes of the world, as well as through others just as poor, broken and despised, the word was introduced into this new world, and broadcast among those infidels who were present, and thence to the innumerable villages and peoples at their command. And certainly this deed of Cortés is the best thing he ever did, for in the rest of his deeds he conquered others, but in this he conquered his own self. Such a conquest, according to the words of all the saints and wise men, is stronger, more powerful, and more difficult to achieve than any other in the world. For what other man who, finding himself at such a high summit, lord of a New World, feared and respected by that world's greatest lords, regarded by them as another god Jupiter, would lower and humble himself to the point of kneeling before some poor and ragged men, who to the world seemed worthy of scorn, and kissing their hands? Truly this was the act of a man who was very catholic at heart, who understood well the honor due to priests, unworthy though they may have appeared, for they are the ministers of God on earth, his vicars and delegates. Such respect was not observed in other parts of the world, and there the faith has been allowed to collapse and fall into countless errors. And if this honor is due to all of the priests of Christ everywhere, it is especially due in those places which are new to the faith, where tender shoots attentively note how the old Christians deal with the priests, and if the old Christians give the priests the honor that their dignity warrants, then those new to the faith will be guided by their example.

Then the governor, having greeted his new guests with such great humility, turned to the caciques and Indian nobles, who were stunned and astonished at seeing the extraordinary act just described, and said to them: "Do not marvel at what you have seen, that the captain-general, governor and delegate of the Emperor of the world should show obedience and subjugation to these men who arrived from Spain poor and in rags. For we have dominion and may govern all those under our command—although it be true that everything comes from the supreme God—because the Emperor, who is the greatest Lord in this world, grants us such power. But this power is limited, it extends no farther than the bodies and goods of men, and to that which is visible and tangible, and which in this world is perishable and subject to corruption. But these men, though they be poor, have power over immortal souls, each and every one of which is of greater value and esteem than anything of the world, including gold and silver and precious stones, and even the sky over our heads. Because God grants them the power to guide to heaven the souls of all who seek their aid, and there they shall enjoy everlasting glory. Those who do not seek their aid will be lost and will go to hell to suffer eternal torment, like that which is now suffered by your ancestors who did not have ministers like these to instruct them in the knowledge of the God who created us, and whose knowledge we must keep so that we will come to reign with him in heaven. And in order that a like fate should not befall you, and that you should not, out of ignorance, go to the same place where your fathers and grandfathers have gone, these priests of God, whom you call *teopixques,* have come to show you the way to salvation. Hold them, therefore, in the highest esteem and reverence, for they are guides for your souls, the messengers of the most high Lord, and your spiritual fathers. Hear their doctrine and obey their counsels and commands, and see that all others attend and obey them, for this is my will and that of our lord and Emperor, as well as the will of God Himself, Who we live for and serve, and Who sent us to this land."

On how the Religious, with the help of their disciples,
destroyed the temples of the idols

Although on the one hand these servants of God were heartily content at seeing how the people attended their sermons and listened to their doctrine, on the other hand they suspected that the Indians might be attending church merely to comply superficially with the orders given them by their nobles in order to deceive the friars, and that this might not be a sincere movement by the people to seek the remedy for their souls by renouncing the worship of the idols. And the friars persuaded themselves that this was indeed the case, for they were told that, while in public the Indians no longer made their old sacrifices, which usually involved the killing of men, in the secret spaces of the hills and in fearful, remote places, and at night in the temples of the demons which were still standing, they continued to make their sacrifices, and in the temples they performed their old ceremonies, chants, and drunken celebrations. Seeing this, the friars wrote to the governor Don Fernando Cortés, who at that time had left for Las Higueras,[2] asking him to give rigorous orders that the sacrifices and services of the demons be stopped, because as long as they went on, the preaching of the ministers of the church would be in vain. The governor very swiftly did as they asked. But the secular Spaniards, who had to execute the punishments and search out the delinquents, and who were occupied in building their houses and in taking their tribute from the Indians, were satisfied as long as no one committed a public homicide before their eyes; as to the rest, they cared nothing about it. So business went on as usual, and the idolatry continued; and yet the friars saw that time was being lost and work being done in vain so long as the temples of the idols were standing. Because it was clear that the ministers of the demons had to go there to exercise their offices, and to convoke and preach to the people, and to make their accustomed ceremonies. And attentive to this, the friars agreed to begin destroying the temples, and not to stop until they were all burned to the ground, and the idols likewise destroyed and eradicated, even though in doing this they would place themselves in mortal danger. They carried out their plan, beginning in Texcuco, where there were very beautiful temples with fine towers, and this was in the year 1525, the first day of the year. And then they destroyed the temples of Mexico, Tlaxcala, and Guexozingo. The friars took with them the children and young men they had raised and instructed, the sons of the Indian lords and nobles . . . and they also received help from the common people who were already converted and wanted to prove that they were confirmed in the faith. And this they ordered done at a time when those who might have opposed them were distracted by other things. And since in most cases they used fire, which burned rapidly, there could be no resistance. And so fell the walls of Jericho, with voices of praise and shouts of joy from the faithful children, while those who remained outside of the faith were frightened and stupefied, and the wings of their hearts (as they say) were broken at seeing their temples and gods brought down. Regarding this heroic exploit, some wished to argue with the friars by saying, first, that it was a rash deed, for it might anger and incite the Indians who might kill them; and second, that they could not in good conscience do such damage to the buildings they destroyed, and to the clothing and finery and things that decorated the idols and the temples that now burned and were lost. To which the friars responded with many good reasons that we will make clear in the following section.

On the great benefit that followed upon the destruction of the principal
temples and idols, in both the spiritual and temporal realms
The account I heard regarding the blame that some placed upon the friars in this case seems to suggest that those who muttered and opposed them were moved by envy, for the friars had taken charge of the destruction of idolatry, they had undertaken this dangerous task without asking for help. . . . Since the secular Spaniards had arrived with Captain Don Fernando Cortés, . . . they judged themselves to be conquerors in the spiritual as well as in the temporal realm, and they did not want others to take from them the honor and glory of which they boasted. . . . I believe, however, that the secular Spaniards were moved to censure the work of the friars mostly out of fear that the Indians would rise up against them. For since they were few and the governor was absent, they feared they might all be killed. This fear endured for many years among the secular Spaniards. The friars, however, were not afraid, first be-

cause they were not afraid of dying for the love of God, and second because they knew the quality and condition of the Indians, who, if they sensed fear or cowardice in those with whom they had dealings, would take heart and grow bold. If, on the other hand, they saw valor and fortitude in their adversaries, then they would lose their spirit and turn cowardly, as the friars learned from experience. At this very time, the Indians were conspiring to rise up against the Spaniards; they wished to offer new sacrifices to the idols, demanding that their gods favor them against the Christians, whom they held in low regard since they were few and poorly adjusted, and they issued proclamations about who would lead the Indians in their efforts to get the better of the Spaniards. Cortés (whom they feared and respected) was not present in the land. But seeing how the friars, with such daring and determination, set fire to the Indians' principal temples, and destroyed the idols they contained, and seeing that this was immediately preceded by the governor's rigorous command that no further sacrifices be made to the demons, it seemed to the Indians that this order was not unfounded, that the governor would return shortly, or perhaps more people were on their way from Castile. And the Indians ceased their plotting, for they saw that the Spaniards did not fear them. If before they were of a mind to rebel, it was because they felt the Spaniards were frightened; for some twenty or thirty days the city of Mexico was guarded closely, its inhabitants in such fear they dared not travel even amid the thunder of horses' hooves, but they watched and waited, not even daring to leave Mexico City. . . . But then the infidels, seeing their principal temples laid waste, lost heart in the performance of their idolatry, and from that time forward the way was opened to demolish what remained of idolatry. Now the many, the conquered, did not even try to resist when the friars went themselves, or sent their disciples, to search for and confiscate idols, and to destroy the few temples that remained. Indeed, these acts inspired in them such timidity and fear that a friar could simply send some children with rosary beads or some other sign, and those children, upon finding idolatry or witchcraft or drunkenness, would say that the fathers sent them to make them stop doing such things. And this incredible subjection and respect accorded to the religious was essential to the fulfillment of their Christian mission.

On the two things for which the conquistadores *and other Spaniards are greatly indebted to the religious of the Order of San Francisco*
In view of the material offered in the last section, and because it is right to acknowledge and express gratitude for men's good works, I would like here to mention two things for which the Spaniards of New Spain are particularly obliged to the friars of San Francisco, and therefore have reason to show their

thanks. The first is a matter we have just touched upon, although we did not declare it so boldly as we do now: the conservation of this land, and the fact that is was not lost once won, is due to the friars of San Francisco, just as much as the initial conquest was the work of Don Fernando Cortés and his companions. I will not address the issue of whether this was just or unjust, licit or illicit. Rather, I will discuss the similarity of one conquest to the other insofar as thanks are due. I dare affirm this truth by citing the authority of Father Toribio Motolinea, one of the twelve, who was a participant and eyewitness. He was my guardian and I knew him always to be a holy man, a man who would never say anything other than the plain truth. In those early days, he said, there were very few Spaniards in Mexico, barely 200 . . . and the Spaniards had ill feelings toward one another, owing to dark ambition and greed, and they would not consider the manifest danger they were in, being surrounded by millions of Indians who resented the Spaniards for having forcibly enslaved them. When they were advised by the friars of this apparent fact, they in fact became quite afraid. Yet despite all of this, they were so impassioned and blind that they took up arms; and they were so headstrong that none among them sought peace, or intervened in their disputes, or placed themselves in front of their swords, lances, and artillery, except for the friars. Our Lord granted these men the grace to bring peace. Had it not been for them, the Spaniards would have continued in their blindness and begun to kill each other, and then the Indians would have come along to finish them all off, for they were waiting for just that opportunity. This venerable father [Motolinea] affirms that, although the lords and nobles of these kingdoms had, in their infidelity, always been enemies of one another and making war among themselves, at this time they were very much united and allied, and fully prepared to make war. But the Indians whom the friars had nurtured warned them of what was happening, and using whatever means they thought best they managed to detain and obstruct the intentions of the nobles and to warn the Spaniards. . . .

As for my second proposition, it is not necessary to find witnesses, for it is the best-known thing in all the world: had there been no friars (who ceaselessly implored our Catholic kings, the Emperor and his son), there would have been no people in the world poorer and more miserable than the Spaniards who lived in New Spain, once the Indians had been finished off. And they would have had no Indians were it not for the tenacity of the friars in defending those Indians: otherwise, how many years would it have been before all of the Indians died, just like the Indians of the islands had done? Who can doubt this? Yet instead of thanking the friars for this, the Spaniards have always borne ill will toward them, complaining and muttering among themselves that the friars were taking away their slaves and would not allow them to use the Indians as they saw fit. What they wanted was to help themselves to the Indians in such a way that would have promptly annihilated them, for they took account of nothing but the present moment. One can clearly see, then, that the friars have been the cause of the conservation of the Indians wherever they have been. Because it is only in those places where they have had charge of indoctrination that there are Indians in large numbers; elsewhere, they have all been consumed by forced servitude. We have examples of this in Nicaragua and Honduras, and on the southern and northern coasts, where for many years there have been practically no people, since they did not have the religious to protect them.

Notes

1. Cortés's first name is variously rendered as "Hernán," "Hernando," or "Fernando." *Ed.*
2. In 1522, shortly after the conquest of Tenochtitlán, Cortés dispatched an expedition under the leadership of Cristóbal de Olid with orders to establish a Spanish settlement at Las Higueras, in the north of Honduras. Olid followed Cortés's own example and disavowed the authority of his patron, whereupon Cortés fitted up an elaborate expedition to punish the renegade. He was away from Mexico City for a full two years on this disastrous adventure. *Ed.*

Why the Indians Are Dying

Alonso de Zorita

For all the purported good intentions of Cortés and the early friars to avoid a demographic catastrophe like that which had plagued the Caribbean islands, the early decades of Spanish colonization in the Americas proved to be one of history's greatest holocausts. In central Mexico, according to one estimate, the indigenous population declined by about 85 percent in the century after the military conquest. While it is generally agreed that the main cause of this decline was epidemics of Old World diseases to which the Indians had little immunity, it must also be recognized that the harsh system of tribute and labor extraction devised by the conquistadores *and early settlers also played a significant, interactive role. Apart from the more egregious cases of exploitation, overworked and undernourished bodies were even more susceptible to the vectors of European disease.*

Early on, the Spanish crown had ruled decisively that Indians could not be enslaved. Nevertheless, persistent demands by conquerors and settlers that they be rewarded for their efforts led to the system of encomienda, *royal grants under which groups of Indians were obliged to provide tribute and labor to a Spanish trustee, or* encomendero, *who was supposed to be responsible for their spiritual conversion and welfare. As abuses of the system mounted, the Crown, both to stem the assault on the Indian community and to avert the threat of an autonomous American nobility, issued a series of laws and decrees that aimed to do away with the* encomienda. *Despite some success in this endeavor, exploitation of Indian labor became an enduring feature of colonial society.*

Alonso de Zorita (ca. 1511–1585) was trained as a lawyer. He first came to the Americas in 1548 to take up a position on the Audiencia (the High Court and governing board) of Española, the Caribbean island where Columbus had established the first American settlement but which had since seen the near extinction of its native population. From his first days in the colonies, he angered the Spanish settlers with his denunciations of their cruelty to the Indians. In 1556 he was made an oidor [judge] of the Audiencia of New Spain, the most important in the colonies. Zorita would spend the next ten years in Mexico, a decade during which the Spanish crown accelerated its efforts to wrest power from the encomenderos. *After returning to Spain in 1566, he commenced work on his* Brief and Summary Relation of the Lords of New Spain, *which he completed in 1585. Clearly, Zorita exaggerates the joys of the Indians' pre-Conquest life, and he badly overstates their supposed submissiveness and docility. Like his predecessor, the great defender of the Indians Bartolomé de las Casas, Zorita likely reckoned that the threat to the Indian population was sufficiently grave and immediate to demand a strategy of exaggerated and overwrought rhetoric.*

In the old days [the Indians] performed their communal labor in their own towns. Their labor was lighter, and they were well treated. They did not have to leave their homes and families, and they ate food they were accustomed to eat and at the usual hours. They did their work together and with much merriment, for they are people who do little work alone, but together they accomplish something. . . .

The building of the temples and houses of the lords [*principales*] and public works was always a common undertaking, and many people worked together with much merriment. They left their houses after the morning chill had passed, and after they had eaten what sufficed them, according to their habits and means. Each worked a little and did what he could, and no one hurried or mistreated him for it. They stopped work early, before the chill of the afternoon, both winter and summer, for they all went about naked or with so few clothes it was like wearing none. At the slightest rainfall they took cover, because they tremble with cold when the first drops fall. Thus they went about their work, cheerfully and harmoniously.

They returned to their houses, which, being very small, were cozy and took the place of clothing. Their wives had a fire ready and laid out food; and they took pleasure in the company of their wives and children. There was never any question of payment for this communal labor. In this same way, with much rejoicing and merriment and without undue exertion, they built the churches and monasteries of their towns. These are not as sumptuous as some have said, but accord with what is necessary and proper, with moderation in everything. . . .

Neither drunkenness nor their well-organized communal labor is killing [the Indians] off. The cause is their labor on Spanish public works and their personal service to the Spaniards, which they fulfill in a manner contrary to their own ways and tempo of work. To make this clear, I shall relate some things that have been and are being done to the Indians. . . .

What has destroyed and continues to destroy the Indians is their forced labor in the construction of large stone masonry buildings in the Spaniards' towns. For this they are forced to leave their native climates, to come from tierra fría to tierra caliente, and vice versa, 20, 30, 40, and more leagues away.

Their whole tempo of life, the time and mode of work, of eating and sleeping, are disrupted. They are forced to work many days and weeks, from dawn until after dusk, without any rest.

Once I saw, after the hour of vespers, a great number of Indians hauling a long heavy beam to a construction site owned by a very prominent man. When they stopped to rest, a Negro overseer went down the line with a leather strap in hand, whipping them all from first to last to hurry them on and keep them from resting; he did this not to gain time for some other work, for the day was over, but simply to keep up the universal evil habit of mistreating the Indians. Since the Negro struck with force and they were naked, with only their genitals covered, the lashes must have caused them cruel pain; but no one spoke or turned his head, for they are ever long-suffering and submissive. It is a routine thing to drive them, to work them without letting them pause for breath, and to harass them in every possible way. . . .

They have been destroyed by the great and excessive tribute they have had to pay, for in their great fear of the Spaniards they have given all they had. Since the tribute was excessive and continually demanded, to make payment they sold their land at a low price, and their children as slaves. When they had nothing left with which to pay, many died for this in prison; if they managed to get out, they emerged in such sorry state that they died in a few days. Others died from being tortured to tell where there was gold or where they had hidden it. They have been treated bestially and unreasonably in all respects.

Their numbers have also been diminished by their enslavement for work in the mines and in the personal service of the Spaniards. In the first years there was such haste to make slaves that they poured into Mexico City from all directions, and throughout the Indies they were taken in flocks like sheep to be branded. The Spaniards pressed the Indian lords to bring in all the slaves, and such was the Indians' fear that to satisfy the Spaniards they brought their own vassals and even their own children when they had no others to offer. Much the same thing happens today in the provision of Indians on the pretext that they had risen in rebellion, contrary to Your Majesty's orders.

They have been reduced by the thousands by their toil in the gold and silver mines; and on the journey to the mines 80 or 100 leagues away they were loaded with heavy burdens to which they were not accustomed. They died in the mines or along the road, of hunger and cold or extreme heat, and from carrying enormous loads of implements for the mines or other extremely heavy things; for the Spaniards, not satisfied with taking them so far away to work, must load them down on the way. Although the Indians brought some food from home, the amount was scanty, for they had no more; and it ran out on their arrival at the mines or on the return journey home. Countless numbers died, and many fled to the woods, abandoning their homes, wives, and children, and thus the towns on the way to the mines or around them became depopulated. The Spaniards still compel the Indians to go to the mines on the pretext that they are being sent to construct buildings there and are going voluntarily; these Spaniards claim that Your Majesty does not prohibit such labor, but only forbids work in the mines. In actual fact the Indians never go voluntarily, for they are forced to go under the repartimiento system[1] by order of the Audiencia, contrary to Your Majesty's orders. . . .

The Indians have also been laid low by the labor of making sheep, cattle, and pig farms, of fencing these farms, of putting up farm buildings, and by their labor on roads, bridges, watercourses, stone walls, and sugar mills. For this labor, in which they were occupied for many days and weeks, they were taken away from their homes, their accustomed tempo of work and mode of life were disrupted; and on top of everything else they had to supply the materials for these projects at their own cost and bring them on their own backs without receiving any pay or even food. Now they are paid, but so little that they cannot buy enough to eat, for they are still used for such labor with permission from the Audiencias. . . .

They have [also] been destroyed by the household service they have had to give to the Spaniards. They still give this service in some places, or are hired out to the mines. Those whose turn it was to serve a week and provide the Spaniards with food and fuel sometimes had to start out two weeks beforehand; thus in order to serve one week they must spend four weeks in coming and going. The roads were filled with Indian men and women, exhausted, dying of hunger, weary and afflicted; and the roads were strewn with the bodies of men, women, and even their little ones, for they used them to carry food—something these people had never before done.

Yet another multitude has been killed off and continues to be killed off by being taken as carriers on conquests and expeditions, and still others to serve the soldiers. They were taken from their homes by force and separated from their women and children and kin, and few if any returned, for they perished in the conquests or along the roads, or died on their return home. . . .

Needless to say, they were taken in collar chains, and mistreated along the way; and when an Indian, man or woman, was worn out from the burden he was carrying, the Spaniards cut off his head so as not have to stop to unchain him, and his load was distributed among the rest.

Yet another multitude perished in the seaports building ships for the Marqués [Cortés] to send to California and the Spice Islands. By the thousands they were made to carry provisions, materials, and rigging on very long journeys of 40, 50, and more leagues. They trudged through forests and mountains and over wretched roads, crossing rivers and marshes far from their native lands, without food, clothing, or shelter. Wherever they went the alcaldes mayores and corregidores, and their lieutenants and alguaciles, worked them unmercifully, and fined them, and took their food and whatever else they pleased. These officials also took part of the supplies the Indians had gathered for the ships, so the Indians' work was never done. For when they had brought what was required of them, a Spanish judge would take what he pleased for his own trafficking, and order them to gather more for the ships.

Then there was the dike that was built in Mexico City,[2] and the fencing of a large part of the Valley of Toluca to protect the Spaniards' cattle, from which the Indians suffered incalculable damage. The dike, several Spaniards told me, was of no use whatever. All the people of the land were summoned, and they came from 30 and 40 leagues away. It was built at the Indians' expense, although it meant nothing to them even if it had been of use. It is always thus, for it is not enough that they give their labor and provide their own food; they must also bring and pay for all the materials for these public works. It was an incalculable waste of people as well as of their pitifully small means. They provided the earth, the stone, the stakes; thus they contributed both the labor and the materials though they received no benefit from this dike, whose cost has been estimated at 300,000 ducats.

It is said the numbers of laborers and masons occupied in this work was well over two million. Since the causeway is very long, the work took about four months, and each day a very great number of people were engaged in it. They worked hard all day in the water, mud, and cold, having no shelter by day or night. As a result, at the end of the week they returned home exhausted and fell ill from their ordeal. Countless numbers died. . . .

These are the things that have worn down the people of this land. They have resulted in disrupting their way of life, their routine of work, diet, and shelter, and in taking them from their towns and homes, their wives and children, their repose and harmony. I believe that their excessive labor, their exposure to hunger, cold, heat, and wind, their sleeping on the ground in the open, in the cold and the night dew, are the cause of their plague of *cámaras* [a disease characterized by diarrhea]. There is no cure or relief for the disease, and they die on the fourth or fifth day. Death brings an end to their suffering, from which they are never free as long as they are alive.

I could mention other things that are causing the extinction of these wretched people, but the great increase in the number of farms owned by Spaniards is in itself a sufficient cause. Then, fifteen, and twenty years ago there were fewer farms, and there were many more Indians. The Indians were forced to work on them and suffered hardships therefrom, but since they were many and the farms few, it was not so noticeable. Now the Spanish farms are many and large and the Indians very few, and they must clear, cultivate, and weed as well as harvest and store the crops, so that all this labor now falls on the few that remain. There are ten times more Spaniards and Spanish farms and estates and ranches than there were, while there is barely one third as many Indians. And these few are continually being attacked by plagues, of which many die, whereas the work is continually increasing. Seeking escape from their oppression, many flee to the woods and mountains, leaving their fields, towns, and homes, and wander from place to place in search of a spot where they may find rest. But wherever they go they find hard work, want, and misfortune.

The Audiencias continually instruct the provincial capitals to send repartimientos of Indians for labor in the Spanish towns of their districts. On construction sites, farms, and cattle ranches, the Spaniards pay each Indian 2 1/2 or 3 reales a week. Some Indians come a distance of 20, 25, and more leagues, depending upon the provincial capital to which they are subject and the distance from that capital to the place where they must go to be assigned to employers. Consequently, to arrive on Monday they must leave their homes on Wednesday or Thursday of the week before. The Spaniards dismiss most of their Indians on Sunday, after Mass; those who worked very well, in the employers' opinion, they let go Saturday evening. As a result, the Indians do not reach their homes until the following Wednesday or Thursday. But many never see their homes again; they die on the road from the hardships and excessive labor they have had to endure almost without food, for the food they bring from home does not last them for so many days. Moreover, they have had to work without their poor mantles, for when they enter the employer's house or other place of work, he takes their mantles from them on the grounds that he must keep them as security that his Indians will not run away. In fine, in order to serve a week for 2 1/2 or 3 reales, the Indians must spend two weeks or longer away from home.

Since the Spanish construction projects, farms, ranches, and herds are so numerous and large, the Audiencias outdo themselves dispatching orders to the corregidores and alcaldes mayores to provide Indian laborers for the Spaniards. These officials fully understand the injury this is causing and know that the Indians are dying out, but their only concern is to aid the Spaniards. It avails the principales naught to complain and cry out that they cannot provide all the people that are demanded of them; indeed, they are arrested, fined, and mistreated for their pains.

The religious warn of the consequences of what is taking place, but no one believes them. The invariable reply is: Let the order be carried out, let the Indians go and help the Spaniards. On account of this intolerable abuse the Indians are dying like flies; they die without confession and without religious instruction, for there is no time for such things. The fewer the Indians, the more burdens the Spaniards load on those who remain. Because of this and the ill treatment they receive, the Indians return home with their health shattered. Thus disease preys on them all year long, nay, all their lives, for its causes never cease.

When they go to the construction projects or other places of labor, they bring from home certain maize cakes or tortillas that are supposed to last them for the time they are gone. On the third or fourth day the tortillas begin to get moldy or sour; they grow bitter or rotten and get as dry as boards. This is the food the Indians must eat or die. And even of this food they do not have enough, some because of their poverty and others because they have no one to prepare their tortillas for them. They go to the farms and other places of work, where they are made to toil from dawn to dusk, in the raw cold of morning and afternoon, in wind and storm, without other food than those rotten or dried-out tortillas, and even of this they have not enough. They sleep on the ground in the open air, naked, without shelter. Even if they wished to buy food with their pitiful wages they could not, for they are not paid until they are laid off. At the season when the grain is stored, the employers make them carry the wheat or corn on their backs, each man carrying a fanega, after they have worked all day. After this, they must fetch water, sweep the house, take out the trash, and clean the stables. And when their work is done, they find the employer has docked their pay on some pretext or other. Let the Indian argue with the employer about this, and he will keep the Indian's mantle as well. Sometimes an enemy will break the jar in which an Indian carries water to his master's house, in order to make him spill the water on the way, and the employer docks the Indian's wages for this.

So the Indian returns home worn out from his toil, minus his pay and his mantle, not to speak of the food that he had brought with him. He returns home famished, unhappy, distraught, and shattered in health. For these reasons pestilence always rages among the Indians. Arriving home, he gorges himself because of his great hunger, and this excess together with the poor physical condition in which he returns help to bring on the cámaras or some other disease that quickly takes him off. The Indians will all die out very quickly if they do not obtain relief from these intolerable conditions.

There is another injury — and it is not a small one — that results from their journeys. Because the Indians are now so few and the demands for their labor so numerous, each Indian is assigned many turns at compulsory labor. Moreover, contrary to what Your Majesty has ordered, the officials make the Indians go at the season when they should be sowing or weeding their fields, which are their sole wealth and means of support. The Indian must plant and weed his field within eight days or risk the loss of all his crops. If he returns from work when the time for seeding or cultivation is past, it does him little good to seed or cultivate, for he does not reap half the crop he would have, had each task been done at the proper time. Moreover, most of the Indians return sick or fall sick upon their arrival, and since they cannot cultivate or clear their fields, they harvest nothing or very little. As a result they suffer hunger all year long, and they and their families fall ill and die. On top of this, the officials fine them for not working their fields, though this is not their fault, and they are jailed and have to pay the costs. . . .

The ancient kings and lords never ruled in this way, never took the Indians from their towns, never disrupted their way of life and labor. I cannot believe that Your Majesty or the members of Your Majesty's Council know or have been informed about what is taking place. If they knew of it, they would surely take steps to preserve Your Majesty's miserable vassals and would not allow the Indians to be entirely destroyed in order to gratify the wishes of the Spaniards. If the Indians should die out (and they are dying with terrible rapidity), those realms will very quickly become depopulated, as has already happened in the Antilles, the great province of Venezuela, and the whole coast of northern South America and other very extensive lands that have become depopulated in our time. The wishes of Your Majesty and his Royal Council are well known and are made very plain in the laws that are issued every day in favor of the poor Indians and for their increase and preservation. But these laws are not obeyed and not enforced, wherefore there is no end to the destruction of the Indians, nor does anyone care what Your Majesty decrees. How many decrees, cedulas, and letters were sent by our lord, the Emperor, who is in glory, and how many necessary orders are sent by Your Majesty! How little good have all these orders done! Indeed, the more laws and decrees are sent, the worse is the condition of the Indians by reason of the false and sophistical interpretation that the Spanish officials give these laws, twisting their meaning to suit their own purposes. It seems to me that the saying of a certain philosopher well applies to this case: Where there is plenty of doctors and medicines, there is plenty of ill health. Just so, where there are many laws and judges, there is much injustice.

We have a multitude of laws, judges, viceroys, governors, presidentes, oidores, corregidores, alcaldes mayores, a million lieutenants, and yet another million alguaciles. But this multitude is not what the Indians need, nor will it relieve their misery. Indeed, the more such men there are, the more enemies do the Indians have. For the more zeal these men display against the Indians, the more influence do they wield; the Spaniards call such men Fathers of the Country, saviors of the state, and proclaim them to be very just and upright. The more ill will such men show against the Indians and friars, the more titles and lying encomiums are heaped upon them. But let an official favor the Indians and the religious (who are bound together, one depending upon the other), and this alone suffices to make him odious and abhorrent to all. For the Spaniards care for one thing alone, and that is their advantage; and they give not a rap whether these poor and miserable Indians live or die, though the whole being and welfare of the country depend upon them.

God has closed the eyes and darkened the minds of these Spaniards, so that they see with their eyes what is happening, yet do not see it, so that they perceive their own destruction, yet do not perceive it, and all because of their callousness and hardheartedness. I have known an oidor to say publicly from his dais, speaking in a loud voice, that if water were lacking to irrigate the Spaniards' farms, they would have to be watered with the blood of Indians. I have heard others say that the Indians, and not the Spaniards, must labor. Let the dogs work and die, said these men, the Indians are numerous and rich. These officials say such things because they have not seen the Indians' sufferings and miseries, because they are content to sit in the cool shade and collect their pay. They also say these things to win the good will and gratitude of the Spaniards, and also because they all have sons-in law, brothers-in-law, relatives, or close friends among them. These friends and relatives are rich in farms, ranches, and herds; and the officials control a major part of this wealth. That is what blinds them and makes them say what they say and do what they do.

Notes

1. *Repartimiento* system: a system of compulsory, paid labor drafts. This officially sanctioned, rotating labor draft was supposed to provide a more humane and controllable means of extracting Indian labor than the *encomienda*. *Ed.*

2. The greatest and most labor-intensive public-works project of the colonial period in New Spain was the so-called *desagüe*, a series of ambitious operations aimed at ending the periodic flooding with which the lake region of central Mexico was plagued. The *desagüe* was an off-and-on project involving, at various times, the building of dikes, drainage canals, and subterranean tunnels. Here, Zorita appears to refer to building of the Albarradón de San Lázaro, a new dike built in 1555–1556 (see Charles Gibson, *The Aztecs Under Spanish Rule: A History of the Indians of the Valley of Mexico, 1519–1810* [Stanford, Calif.: Stanford University Press, 1964], 236–52; and also the reading by Joel Simon in part VI of this volume). *Ed.*

The Colonial Latifundio

Enrique Florescano

*One of the most representative (and notorious) aspects of the colonial Mexican land-
scape (and of that of the first century after Independence) is the great landholding, or
latifundio. The concentration of land in relatively few hands, and the inefficient and
exploitative fashion in which it was used, often had dire consequences, as the following selection, by one of Mexico's most prominent rural historians, makes abundantly
clear. The large landholding, and its tendency to expand and profit at the expense of
indigenous communities, would be a fundamental issue in Mexican life and politics
until its virtual destruction during the 1920s and 1930s. It is well worth emphasizing,
however, that Indians (and the poor population in general) were not merely passive
victims of exploitation: as Florescano points out, they resisted in many ways, often
with great tenacity and creativity.*

The Indian and the Latifundio

In the indigenous mentality, there was no concept of individual property. The
land belonged to the community; the individual only had the right of usufruct, and only so long as he complied with the duties and obligations that
the community imposed. Even then, the concept of usufruct was restricted
to the use of an amount of land necessary for subsistence and the payment of
individual and communal tributes. So the appearance and development of lati-
fundism—the concentration in one person or family of enormous extensions
of land, of which they cultivated only a small portion—was something inexplicable and essentially unjust for the Indians. For the Indians, as Wistano Luis
Orozco aptly put it, "under the colonial regime, *proprietor* was a synonym for
conqueror, and *property,* a synonym for *violence.*" That violence is impossible to
quantify, because the Spaniards exercised it over all aspects of the indigenous
world: over all their lands, villages, labor, children, women, and the system
of values that made up their universe: religion, customs, fiestas, rituals. . . .
Nothing was spared, everything was attacked, altered, submitted to a process
of constant devaluation. But perhaps the violence that most affected the Indi-

ans was that exercised over the lands of their communities, because it was land that gave cohesion and order to all of indigenous life. Without community lands, one cannot imagine the basic unit of indigenous society, the Indian village. . . . The Indian village *was* the land: the land was the foundation that maintained the community, and on it rested the family and the individual. So as long as the villages retained their lands, they maintained their integrity as villages, their social cohesion, and even their traditions and customs. By contrast, the villages that lost their lands disintegrated rapidly, and their inhabitants were absorbed by the haciendas or European-style cities. They ceased being Indians. Thus, the tenacious and incorruptible struggle that the Indians waged every day of the three centuries of the colonial regime was more than a struggle for land: it must be considered a battle for survival. Paradoxically, that unequal and quotidian struggle for the land came to be, among the hundreds of factors that weakened and threatened the integrity of the communities, a positive factor in maintaining the social cohesion of the indigenous villages.

We here reproduce part of a document that narrates the foundation of the village of Santo Tomás Ajusco (D.F.), in 1531. In it we see the general violence that the Spaniards unleashed on the indigenous world immediately after the conquest, the vulnerability and impotence of the conquered, the anguish at losing their lands, and the will to survive, reflected in the foundation of the new village:

> My beloved children: today is the fourth day of the second month: February, in the year of the one and true God, 1531 . . . Beloved children, it is well that you should know that in all parts, all of those governors who protect the villages are growing sad because of what the white people from Castile have been doing and continue to do. We know about the punishment of the superior governors, patrons of the villages. . . . [The Spaniards] ask them for their riches and if they do not give up all of the yellow metal and the shiny glass, they are punished. You know that [the Spaniards] take away their beautiful women and also their young maidens. They are never content . . . How much blood was spilt! Blood of our fathers! And for what? . . . Know this: because they want that only they should rule. Because they are starved for the metal and wealth of others. And because they want us under their heel. And because they want to insult our women and our young maidens; and because they want to make themselves the owners of our lands and all our wealth. . . . There, Junto al Agua, Mexico, it is known that the man Cortés of Castile . . . was authorized to come to divide up our lands . . . Thus it is said, it is spoken that this Marquis will come to take away the lands; and also he will point out to us lands that will form

new villages. Now, as for us, where will they throw us? Where will they put us? Too much sorrow has come upon us. What shall we do, my children? But despite everything, my heart revives, and I agree to form here a village, at the foot of this hill of Axochco Xaltipac [today the village of Ajusco, D.F.]. . . . And I agree to build a temple of worship where we shall place the new God that the Castilians have brought us. They want us to worship him. What shall we do, my children? It is best that we be baptized, that we surrender ourselves to the men of Castile, to see if then they will not kill us . . . And in order that they not kill us, it is best that we no longer have all of our lands. It is best that we reduce our boundaries . . . So now, I cut back and reduce our lands, which is as it must be, and my will is that our boundaries begin where the sun comes up . . . I calculate that for this small amount of land, perhaps they will not kill us. What difference does it make that we used to have more land! But this is not because of my will; only because I do not want that my children be killed, there is no more than this little bit of land and on this land we shall reside, ourselves and our children after us. And we shall work no more than this land, to see if now they will not kill us. . . .

The same fears and hopes that moved the founders of the village of Ajusco to reduce the boundaries of their lands are present in the majority of the indigenous villages that refused to abandon their ancient sites, or that were "congregated" into new villages. The nearness of the Spaniards' towns and haciendas continually threatened them and kept them in a permanent state of anxiety. The villages that had the misfortune of being situated on lands that were well irrigated and close to the large population centers suffered constant deterioration, and gradually they were expelled from the lands that they had occupied for generations. Others were literally hemmed in by the growth of the haciendas and they could not acquire more lands when their populations increased. The majority suffered from the inexorable whittling away of the community lands and the gradual loss of their rivers and woods. Nevertheless, the diminutive *"fundos legales"* which constituted their refuge were sufficient to resist the Spanish assault. Thanks to those lands, they could overcome the bloodletting caused by the *encomienda* and the *repartimiento,* survive the epidemics and famines, resist the disintegration that threatened them upon the reestablishment of free contract labor, and make a united front against the unstoppable expansion of the latifundios. But not all of the Indians agreed to live under the tension of permanent anxiety and threat. The most resolute took refuge in hostile and remote regions far from all contact with the Spaniards. . . .

The majority of the Indian villages exposed to the aggression of the conquerors decided to defend their right to the land through recourse to Spanish legislation. It is well known that royal authority, by itself or through the
colonial authorities, always tried to defend the Indian, the weakest member
of society. But all of those who have confronted the reality of that protective
legislation know also that . . . interminable disputes over the land were the
rule, not the exception.

A recurring problem throughout the sixteenth century was the penetration of the Spaniards' livestock into the Indians' open and cultivated lands,
which launched the wide-scale, often sterile and legalistic, debate over the
rights of the Indians to the land. The list of grievances regarding these invasions that the Indians presented between 1530 and the start of the seventeenth
century is almost as bulky as the list of royal decrees and orders prohibiting
the granting to Spaniards of livestock ranches which would damage the Indians' interests. And if in the first decades of the seventeenth century the flood
of grievances about livestock on Indian lands diminished, it is due above all to
the fact that in those years the livestock found a more favorable environment
for their development in the desolate plains of the north.

At the same time, the largest and most important dispute involving the land
problem was growing: disputes over property. During the sixteenth and seventeenth centuries the Indians accumulated lawsuits against the Spaniards about
all of the problems involving land, but especially about the losses that they suffered of their communal and individual properties; against the Indian *caciques*
who used their posts to usurp lands from the *macehuales* [commoners]; against
other villages and communities that tried to take over their lands, and finally
against the convents and religious persons who frequently tried to increase
their territorial patrimony at the expense of the Indians.

During the eighteenth century, in addition to fighting on all of these fronts,
the Indians witnessed an increase in aggression against their properties at the
precise moment when their population was recovering from the demographic
disasters of the preceding centuries. As the numerous lawsuits of this epoch
demonstrate, the Indians had to fight not only for the land itself, but for all of
the elements linked to it which permitted its productive use. To the common
complaints about property were added those which sought to reclaim water,
woodlands, pasturelands, and other community resources threatened by the
growth of the cities, the founding of new towns, and the unchecked expansion of the haciendas and Church properties. A superficial examination of the
copious documentation found in the archives is enough to convince the re-
searcher that the diverse ways in which colonial legislation sought to protect

Indian property were, in reality, useless. But despite the constant failures, the Indians continued accumulating their complaints in the different offices of the colonial administration, bequeathing lawsuits from fathers to sons. Nevertheless, there were many who, in view of the inefficacy of the law, had recourse to mutinies and rebellions in order to secure justice for themselves. But those revolts were always spontaneous, and above all, too local to provoke a campesino movement of a more generalized nature.

At the end of the eighteenth century other factors, in addition to the oppression of the latifundios, made things still more difficult for the Indian villages. In the first place, their population grew, and that brought an increase in the demand for land, which at that time the communities could not satisfy since they were hemmed in by the great haciendas and latifundios. And above all, the population of mestizos and *castas* [mixed-race persons] grew enormously, and they also set their sights on the Indians' lands. In these years, in central Mexico and in the regions of greatest economic activity, indigenous properties were constantly reduced by the thousands of fraudulent proceedings that Europeans, creoles, mestizos, and *castas* undertook to appropriate them. . . .

With the encroachments of Spaniards, creoles, mestizos, and *castas* on indigenous property, the circle was completed, enclosing the Indians within the limits of subsistence and putting a brake on their possibilities for development. From 1560 onward, agriculture managed by Spaniards began to displace indigenous production in the markets. In the eighteenth century the production of the haciendas and latifundios completely dominated the restricted urban markets, and through tenancy and sharecropping contracts their proprietors managed to control a large part of the indigenous production that went onto the market. The rest of the Indians' harvest went to feeding their families and paying the intermediaries (mestizos, *castas,* and Spaniards) who in a thousand ways took the Indians' products and sold them on the market. On the other hand, the haciendas and latifundios installed themselves in the valleys and irrigated lands, displacing the Indians from these places. Thus, at the end of the colonial period the haciendas were located on the outskirts of the urban centers of greatest population and near the mining camps, at the sides of roads, or near the key distribution points. That strategic situation favored their dominion over the commercialization of products and permitted many hacendados and merchants to monopolize or take better advantage of the systems of transportation (mule trains, carts, or canoes in the Valley of Mexico). In sum, while indigenous farmers found the markets increasingly closed to them, farms managed by Spaniards and creoles had within their reach all of the means to control those markets. They had a monopoly on credit, which the Church only granted to those who had the security of landed property. All of this, in addition to the employment of superior agricultural techniques and instruments, opened an immense breach between indigenous agriculture and that managed by creoles and Spaniards. From that time on, the Indian villages remained condemned to being simple suppliers of the field labor required by the haciendas and cities.

At the end of the eighteenth century, the situation of the Indians was so desperate and anguished that the most prudent men of the colony saw in this class a sector potentially disposed to heed the calls to do away with that situation. Here is a prophetic report from Viceroy Revillagigedo about the situation of the Indians, dated 1790:

> The miserable Indians, by nature, for want of education and due to the extreme poverty and decadence in which they find themselves, breathe nothing more than humiliations and discouragement, and they deem themselves happy when they have enough to barely satisfy the most basic needs of food. . . . In such a situation . . . an extraordinary lack of maize, or more impositions that they absolutely cannot pay, would be capable of putting them in a state of desperation that would oblige them to undertake some sort of excess.

The Effects of Agricultural Crises

Agricultural crises were undoubtedly the most spectacular and terrible result of the [climatic conditions of Mexico]. Naturally, in the colonial era agricultural crises meant the loss of the maize crop, the most important and widely cultivated grain. Maize was the essential and at times only food for the immense majority of the indigenous population, as well as for a large number of mestizos, *castas,* and poor Spaniards, and of nearly all beasts of burden, poultry, and pigs. The reduction or total loss of the maize harvest would bring about, therefore, in addition to an intense agricultural crisis, a general economic crisis. . . .

The economic effects of agricultural crises were many, since they affected the urban as well as the rural population; they affected the many different activities that depended directly on maize, as well as those who suffered indirectly from the general increase in prices and diminished buying power.

In the most populous cities, in addition to the fact that prices would rise immediately upon the loss of the maize crop, and that this would lead to a rise in the price of all other foodstuffs, there were other factors that made the situation more dramatic for the urban consumer. First was the structure of the city populations, which were composed for the most part of individuals who depended on maize as their principal food. Second was the extreme poverty of these groups, for their incomes were minimal, sporadic, or nonexistent in the case of those who lived by begging and who formed the legions of 20 to 30 thousand unemployed . . . in the capital, sleeping wherever nighttime found them and wandering about the plazas and sidewalks during the days. For these many poor people, the increase of 5, 10, 15 or more reales per fanega of maize meant immediate hunger. On the other hand, from the first days of the crisis people would be seized by panic, which would bring a state of tension and anxiety to the entire city. In the crisis of 1785–1786, this compelled many desperate people to sack and burn "the granaries of many hacendados accused by the public of not wanting to distribute their grains." The first victims of the famine, the poorest population of the cities, were also . . . the first to fall victim to the epidemics that accompanied the crises.

Another portion of the city population—those employed in day labor on the nearby haciendas or in different jobs in the city—felt the crisis years with a similar intensity, and often swelled the ranks of the unemployed. This was, first, because the price of maize would increase by 100, 200, and even 300 percent relative to its lowest price in the good years, while wages remained the same. Second, many of these laborers were fired by their bosses or were left without work when the factories or workshops closed down.

On the other hand, the fate of artisans and workers in more specialized activities (cloth makers, tobacco workers, carpenters, cobblers, etc.), although difficult, was less onerous. With wages of three, five and even eight or ten reales per day, they could defend themselves against the threat of hunger. But the crises . . . took away all or most of their wages, since these had to be used to buy subsistence articles. And the same occurred with middle-income consumers. . . .

Finally, the speculators, the *"regatones"* [resalers], the pork-raisers who needed large quantities of maize to fatten their swine, and the great landowners who did not cultivate maize but who needed it to feed their workers, greatly increased the shortages in the cities by buying huge quantities of maize in anticipation of the most difficult times ahead.

If crises meant shortages, want, hunger, unemployment, and social tension in the cities, in the countryside they were simply catastrophic. Principally, this was because there were no institutions such as public granaries or warehouses which, in the cities, would distribute maize at low prices; nor were there charitable institutions to care for the unfortunate, nor authorities who would check the rise in prices. And above all, the distribution of land, which was as unequal as the distribution of wealth in the cities, increased the debility of rural structures. The immense peasant population lacked lands in proportion to their needs, and those lands they did have (communal lands, tiny garden plots, or small properties) were non-irrigated lands, or in any case lands whose output could barely satisfy the needs of a family.

Precarious in normal times, the equilibrium of the rural structure collapsed during times of crisis. The food policies of the colony were the first to weaken it, for news of an unfavorable harvest would scarcely reach the city before the granary administrators and the viceroy himself would order that large purchases be made in the principal centers of production, and that that grain be brought to the big cities and mining camps. And even when care was taken to avoid hoarding and panic, the great hacendados would hasten to guard their grains in anticipation of high prices, and they spread the news that their harvest was lost. Who would people go to then, if not to the small farmers and Indians, who always needed money and were willing to sell? And the worst of all was that behind the granary officials came the speculators and carters, who carried off the stocks of even the poorest peasants.

Thus, when the crisis had not yet reached its maximum intensity, already the small and medium farmers found their reserves exhausted and the prices risen to unaccustomed heights in the countryside. At that point they had no recourse other than to sell their assets: perhaps two or four burros, a team of oxen, their plows, their hens, until they had been reduced to misery. Afterward they would be obliged to migrate to the cities or wander in the woods in search of food. In the most serious crises (1749–50, 1785–86, 1809–10), to this terrible situation was added the fact that the hacendados fired their least indispensable workers so as to save the ration of maize that they would have been obligated to give them. . . . In the mines and other labor centers the shortage of essential foodstuffs forced a halt to activities, causing massive migration of the laboring population. During the crisis of 1749–50, the shortage was so great in the mining zone, in the west and center of the country, that the population abandoned the mines and villages en masse, flooding in great waves into the less affected zones. The Indians of the most remote villages and those of the non-cereal producing zones, compelled by hunger, joined the unemployed of the mines and together ravaged the countryside, eating fruits and wild herbs, spreading epidemic diseases, invading the principal cities of the West and even the capital. . . .

The fact that [the great latifundio] had good and extensive lands, large warehouses to accumulate grain, and the capital necessary to await the times of the highest prices, gave it powerful tools to help it get the greatest benefit from the years of crisis. In general, their function during these years was as follows:

Once the news was out of the loss of the harvest, the first reaction of the great hacendados was to hide their grain and declare that they had no grain to sell. The consequences of these measures were felt immediately in the principal cities and mining camps, since the granaries of those places were supplied by those same large haciendas. Thus, to the natural shortage due to the loss of the harvests was added the artificial shortage that the hacendados created in order to raise the prices and obtain better profits. These maneuvers, generally practiced by the great hacendados in the crisis years, are explained by the monopoly on supply that the latifundio enjoyed. In those years, inasmuch as the scarce reserves of the Indian or of the small and medium farmer would be soon used up or very close to being so, only the colossal granaries of the great haciendas had grain enough to meet consumer demand, since although a bad year was bad for all farmers, the storage capacity of the great hacienda permitted it to hold onto the surpluses of previous years. In other words, in times of crisis the latifundio was not only the principal seller, but practically the only one, and therefore the hacendados resisted selling in the first months of the shortage and waited for the most critical months, when consumers were practically at their mercy and would pay whatever price they set for their grain.

In some cases the authorities of the cities and the viceroy tried to counter these maneuvers. . . . It is hardly surprising that, during the gravest crises, the antagonism that pitted the great hacendados, on one side, and the authorities and consumers on the other, took on the intensity of a serious social conflict. The case that best illustrates this situation is the crisis of 1785–86. During that crisis all of society—the authorities, the urban poor, merchants, miners, and all of the members of the Church—declared war on the great hacendados and speculators. The viceroy initiated the hostilities by issuing a declaration on October 11, 1785, that if the hacendados did not keep "the granaries open for provisioning of the poor," or if they tried to unjustly raise the price, he would be obliged to take "the serious measures that the case demands, in order to help out those unfortunate people who, although poor, are the ones who allow the rich to grow fat . . . and are the ones who enrich the Kingdoms with their labor, with their persons in time of war, and with the taxes on consumption." One month later, the Bishop of Puebla circulated a letter to all dioceses: "Monopolies of any kind are illicit and reprehensible, as are any negotiations aiming to horde grain and seeds." . . .

Thus, twenty-four years before the insurrection of 1810, the agricultural crisis of 1785–86 revealed to all of the inhabitants of New Spain the tremendous inequality of the social structure, the immense harm derived from the great hacienda, and it contributed to forming a generation that was aware of those imbalances. From that time forward . . . the attacks on the latifundio were more constant and more violent.

A Baroque Archbishop-Viceroy

Irving Leonard

Less than a century passed between the time when twelve humble, raggedly dressed Franciscan monks had walked barefoot from Veracruz to the capital (1524), and the time when a new Archbishop, Fray García Guerra, made the same voyage, albeit in less-ascetic fashion (1608). In that intervening time, much had changed. The Spanish Church had gone from the gentle optimism of the Catholic humanists to the rigid doctrines of the Counter-Reformation and the ornate spectacle of the Baroque Age. The Spanish colonies had changed from a dangerous frontier into a colony governed by one of the world's most elaborate bureaucracies. Spain itself had gone from the world's most vast and powerful empire to one that was overdrawn and clearly in decline.

In the following vignette, Irving Leonard, who was a distinguished professor of Spanish-American literature and history at the University of Michigan, vividly brings to life many of the cultural trends, sights, and sounds that characterized New Spain in the Baroque Age. In Leonard's account, Archbishop García Guerra embodies the spirit of his age: haughty and ostentatious, skilled in the "verbalistic intellectualism" so typical of the time, yet with a taste for profane pleasures and an unquenchable thirst for power. García illustrates the blurring of civil and ecclesiastical jurisdictions and the eclipse of the energetic missionary spirit of the early colonial clergy. Yet some things did not change: nature, in central Mexico, remained capricious, and people were still quick to give a mystical interpretation to out-of-the-ordinary phenomena.

Surrounded by a numerous retinue and mountainous luggage, an imposing figure, in the panoply of high ecclesiastical office, stood on the foredeck of [a ship] slowly picking its way toward [shore]. Among the swarm of expectant inhabitants lining the shore word had quickly passed that the conspicuous personage was no less than a great Prince of the Church, the Archbishop newly appointed to the See of Mexico, Fray García Guerra by name and renowned for his vast learning and stirring eloquence. Increasingly visible to these eager onlookers, as the vessel hove to, was the commotion on deck caused by the obsequious crew and personal servants who scurried about to initiate the for-

midable task of lightering ashore the distinguished dignitary and his multi-
tudinous effects. . . .

The [port city of] Vera Cruz, at which the travelers were disembarking,
had an aspect of raw newness for, indeed, it was not yet a decade old. An
earlier site of the port farther south was abandoned at the close of the sixteenth century because the fortified rock of San Juan de Ulloa offered better
protection from the heavy gales which descended from the north and from
the fierce pirates who might descend from anywhere. Otherwise, there was
little to commend the location for human habitation and, important as the
settlement was as a trading center and entrance to an opulent viceroyalty, its
population barely exceeded two thousand. Situated in a dreary stretch of sand
broken by tiny, sluggish streams, swampy bogs, and shallow pools of stagnant
water, the moist heat, swarms of mosquitoes, gnats, and other noxious insects
made the vicinity singularly unhealthy. The frequent, heavy downpours during the long rainy season, now approaching its end when the fleet put in, left
a humid, dank atmosphere that was almost suffocating, and in it every sort
of pest and repulsive creature seemed to proliferate. . . .

Fray García Guerra hardly wished to linger in these unhealthy surroundings and, as everything was in readiness for his journey to Mexico City, he
began the slow advance inland accompanied by a long caravan of horses, pack
mules, coaches, litters, creaking carts, and pedestrians. It was a triumphal
march and the progress of his carriage was deliberately slow to permit all his
flock along the way to behold the majesty of a Prince of the Church and to
pay homage to this intermediary of God. Well over a month elapsed before
he made his ceremonious entry into the viceregal capital.

Meanwhile, the bright-hued caravan halted at each Indian village and ham-
let where the natives, doubtless prompted by the local *cura,* or parish priest,
proffered their most colorful entertainments, often a curious mixture of aboriginal folkloric elements and those acquired from the Spaniards. These festivities were unfailingly accompanied by a noisy salute of fireworks. Between
these stops the Archbishop's carriage passed under an endless series of floral
arches, erected scarcely a musket-shot distance apart. As the episcopal con-
veyance approached these Indian communities a small band of villagers came
forth to meet it, each individual bedecked in the peculiar attire of the locality
and blowing odd strains on trumpets and other wind instruments. Escorted in
this manner the Archbishop's coach rolled into the tiny village square invariably adorned with floral chains and varicolored bunting, and there its occu-
pant witnessed the colorful *mitotes,* the most solemn of the ceremonial dances
and songs of the natives. Fray García Guerra vastly enjoyed these strange inter-
ludes in which these primitive members of his flock, arrayed in picturesque

costumes and adornments, performed the most ritualistic of their pagan rites, for he had a special fondness for music in all its forms, and the novelty of these curious strains left him undisturbed by their non-Christian origins. In his train were clergymen from Castile who were gifted instrumentalists, and the Cathedral council, doubtless informed of the new prelate's predilection, had thoughtfully sent down skilled musicians from Mexico City to lighten the tedium of his journey. Thus the Archbishop found delight in the variety of harmonies that charmed his ears along the way.

In this pleasant fashion Fray García Guerra neared his destination. Scarcely a dozen leagues from Mexico City he paused briefly in the small Indian town of Apa where a personal representative of the viceroy, in behalf of that magistrate, welcomed the new head of the Mexican church. Only the fact that his feet hurt, so ran the message, prevented Don Luis de Velasco, viceroy for the second time of this great realm of the Spanish empire, from coming in person to kiss the ring of the chief primate and place himself unreservedly at the Archbishop's disposal. Despite his gouty extremities Don Luis de Velasco assured the prelate that he would not fail to meet him in person before the triumphal entry into the capital.

Mexico City, situated amidst lakes in the lofty valley of Anahuac, suffered periodic inundations that had long called for drastic remedy. Only the year before so destructive a flood had descended upon this administrative center that a transfer of the municipality to another site was seriously contemplated. Commercial and other interests, however, strongly resisted this solution and the viceroy, on the advice of a German cosmographer, Enrico Martínez, and of others, had authored a gigantic engineering project designed to carry off the excess waters in a series of cuts and channels. The most ambitious part of this undertaking was a huge notch in the hills near the village of Huehuetoca. It occurred to Don Luis de Velasco that a joint inspection of this work would be an admirable occasion for the first meeting of the respective heads of Church and State, and necessary arrangements were, accordingly, made. In due course Fray García Guerra alighted from his carriage at the viceroy's temporary quarters whereupon the king's surrogate in New Spain hobbled out to the front staircase and demonstratively welcomed the new prelate. After dining together the two most powerful dignitaries in the land drove away to inspect the progress made on the large cut. It was on this excursion that the first of an ominous series of mishaps befell the proud Fray García Guerra.

The rise of this Dominican clergyman to the eminence he now claimed in one of the richest archbishoprics in Spain's enormous empire had been foreordained and rapid. Singularly propitious were the auguries of the stars at his birth in 1560 in a village of Old Castile. Of noble ancestry, it was soon apparent that his studious temperament admirably equipped him for the verbalistic intellectualism of the age and culture in which he lived. His native talents splendidly adapted him for a luminous career in the Church, then so powerful in the affairs of man, and at the age of fifteen he sought to don the Dominican habit. In May, 1578, he was duly admitted to the order of his choice at the Convent of St. Paul in Valladolid, and almost immediately he gained distinction in philosophy, metaphysics, and theology. His extraordinary gifts as a dialectician and his consummate skill as an orator quickly brought wide acclaim. His brilliance as an expounder of the doctrines then hardening under the pressures of the Counter Reformation brought recognition from the secular rulers of the land as well as from his Dominican superiors. After filling chairs of theology in monasteries at Avila, Burgos, Segovia and Valladolid, he became prior of the convent where he had taken his first vows. When the weak monarch, Philip III, was induced to transfer his Court from Madrid to Valladolid in 1600, Fray García Guerra attracted the approving eye of the king's influential favorite, the Duke of Lerma, who soon elevated the talented clergyman to the lofty eminence of the *Patronato* of Castile. After the birth of a royal prince destined, as Philip IV, to preside over the dissolution of the political glory that was Spain, Fray García Guerra officiated at the baptism.

With Madrid once again the capital a few years later, Philip III did not forget the churchman whose eloquence and administrative ability he had admired in Valladolid. When death created a vacancy in the archbishopric of Mexico, it was the royal will that Fray García should accept it. If the clergyman's hesitation was sincere, his Dominican superiors soon convinced him that it was a duty to fulfill his destiny. After papal confirmation Fray García was consecrated on April 5, 1608, and, two months later, he embarked for his New World post. Fate had smiled steadily upon this son of Old Castile and now had placed him in one of the most important offices to which a clergyman might aspire.

The shift of activities from the Old to the New World seemed to mark, however, the turning point in the unbroken good fortune which had attended his career from birth. Almost imperceptibly portents of the future began to gather like clouds on the horizon, and the brightness of the day slowly dimmed until the darkness of death blotted all. The first of these omens, which hardly seemed to have any import, occurred when the new Archbishop and the Viceroy of New Spain rode together to inspect the drainage project at Huehuetoca. The road through the pass, over which they were driving, had been traveled again and again without mishap of any sort, and it appeared free of any hazards to the safety of these heads of the absolute government of the land. Suddenly and without warning their carriage turned completely over, spilling the august occupants by the wayside in a most undignified manner. Attendants hurried to their aid. Though both victims of the accident were badly shaken and slightly injured, they were able to resume the journey the next day. This incident seemed insignificant enough, but Fray García was to remember it as the beginning of his misfortunes.

Again his caravan took up the slow pilgrimage toward Mexico City, stopping in each of the intervening villages for the customary ceremonies of fealty, homage, and entertainment so obsequiously provided by the inhabitants. Meanwhile, the viceroy sped ahead to oversee the final arrangements for the sumptuous reception of the Archbishop in the capital. Even slower than before was Fray García's progress, for he was repeatedly administering the sacrament of confirmation, and the festive journey from Vera Cruz had stretched into a full month. But at last he reached Santa Ana, a suburb of the city, where he alighted from his ornate carriage and mounted a mule to make his entry with the simulated humility of the Founder of Christianity. A group of municipal officials, in brightest livery and astride gaily caparisoned horses, had come out to accompany the Archbishop on this final stage of his travels. As the small procession entered the outskirts of the capital it stopped at the Dominican monastery. Near a platform, erected by the members of this religious body to do honor to a distinguished brother of their Order, Fray García dismounted from his mule and climbed upon the shaky staging where the Dean, councilors of the Cathedral, and other dignitaries were seated. Scarcely had the Archbishop begun to acknowledge the rejoicing of the assembly when the improvised rostrum trembled ominously and, with a loud crash, the entire structure collapsed, flinging its respected occupants to the ground and crushing a luckless Indian beneath it. Once again, as when he was thrown from the carriage at Huehuetoca, Fray García was badly shaken but received no severe injury, and presently the interrupted ceremonies were resumed. There were those, however, who, having heard of the earlier mishap, shook their heads gravely. These signs did not augur well for the new prelate.

The arrangements for the crowning event went forward—the magnificent spectacle of the entry into the Cathedral under the episcopal pallium. The liveried magistrates, who had met Fray García on the outskirts of the city, now took positions as a guard of honor. Each held an ornate staff supporting the purple and gold pallium with brocade trimmings which sheltered the Archbishop robed in glittering vestments. So massive was this canopy that it required twenty-two of the uniformed *regidores* to hold it aloft in this fashion. This dazzling tableau moved slowly through the streets lined with the awed populace. From the walls, windows, and balconies of the buildings on either side hung rich tapestries and bright-hued bunting. At length the procession

Our Lady of Ocotlán Sanctuary, Tlaxcala, a fine example of the ultra-Baroque style. (Photographer Ichiro Ono. Reprinted by permission of Ichiro Ono.)

halted in front of the Cathedral, still far from completion. Before the ponderous portal stood a gigantic arch with a Baroque profusion of sculptural details, of complex symbols, of ornamental figures, and of erudite quotations.

Leaving the pallium on the Cathedral steps the Archbishop, with attendant priests and acolytes, moved majestically into the gloomy splendor of the interior and advanced toward the gleaming effulgence of the candlelit altar while the great nave resounded with the swelling paeans of the *Te Deum Laudamus,* sung by an augmented choir. To the edification of all assembled this mighty Prince of the Church prostrated himself before the Cross with ostentatious humility. After an appropriate pause in this position Fray García Guerra slowly arose to his feet and the profound solemnity of the moment yielded to an almost gay burst of melodious song, secular and festive in character. This sudden transition heightened the emotional effect and drama of the scene, filling the audience with a kind of rapture. The Archbishop, a dazzling figure in the magnificence of his episcopal robes, then seated himself near the high altar to witness a brief, allegorical play ingeniously staged in the chancel. Elaborately costumed performers, in witty dialogues of prettily worded phrases, explained and interpreted the fanciful designs and symbols embellishing the enormous arch at the Cathedral door. At the conclusion of this sprightly interlude the Dean, prebendaries, and other ecclesiastical dignitaries approached the prelate in single file to offer their obeisance with impressive humility. The object of this adulation was now more than ever the cynosure of admiring and reverent eyes.

For Fray García it was a supreme moment. His fortunate career had brought him to a pinnacle of glory in the neomedieval world that Spain was expending its blood and treasure to maintain and that it passionately believed was the fulfillment of God's will on earth. But like the civilization that he personified, he was already an anachronism and his own fate epitomized the destiny of that age. Unforeseen by all that throng was the certainty that, in a few brief years, his dissected and decomposing body would lie interred in the very place where he now sat amid so much pomp and circumstance. Long after in the same century a distinguished citizen of Mexico City, moved by other portents, would exclaim: "O sacred and most just God, how removed from human reason are Thy incomprehensible and venerable judgments! And how true are the Scriptures when they state that laughter is mingled with tears and that sorrow follows upon the greatest joys!"

The newly inaugurated Archbishop did not fail to display the piety, benevolence, and oratorical gifts that so clearly justified his designation to the richest See of the New World. To his flock he seemed the perfect embodiment of an exemplary minister of the Gospel and a saintly administrator of the Church of God. In those first months of his office he appeared to strive for justice for all with an impartiality, a lack of precipitation, and a compassionate rectitude. His varied duties he performed with punctuality, and so zealous was he in distributing alms personally from his vast income that his meals were often delayed. Faithfully he visited all parts of his broad diocese, and in the churches he preached with that moving eloquence and great learning that unmistakably marked him as one set apart to do God's work.

All who came into the presence of this ecclesiastical Prince acquired a conviction that Fray García was, indeed, an inspired person happy in fulfilling a great destiny. Yet a close observer might have perceived that, with all the homage daily bestowed upon him, with all the Croesus-like wealth at his disposal, and with all the assurance of an eternal reward at the end of his earthly existence, a disquieting urge vaguely stirred deep within his consciousness. Omnipotent as he was in the social and economic as well as the spiritual lives of his flock, an unspoken longing, which was growing in intensity, possessed him to dominate the political affairs of the realm as well. Don Luis de Velasco, the reigning viceroy, was a great proconsul of his Majesty who had served with great distinction in both Mexico and Peru. His long experience, proven skill, and sound judgment were indispensable to the weak and vacillating Philip III, sorely needing in Spain such able administrators to manage an empire already betraying symptoms of decay and disintegration. It was but a matter of time before royal summons would compel the return of Don Luis to the homeland. In such an eventuality the viceregal office commonly devolved upon the Archbishop as an interim appointment at least, and Fray García found himself dwelling on this possibility with increasing insistency.

Like most at the summit of human institutions, the prelate's existence was essentially a lonely one. As the accepted instrument of God he was the recipient of obsequious demonstrations of awe, veneration, and fear wherever he went. Nowhere did his basically gregarious nature find the intimate companionship and confidence that it craved. With all his appearance of piety and of a dedicated servant of the Lord, and with all his ascetic ostentation, he longed for the milder sensual delights of his flock. He loved the sweet melody of instrumental music, the singing of ballads and folk songs, the gustatory pleasures of the table, and the strong tonic of spectacles of the bull ring. To satisfy the first of these tastes Fray García had fallen into the habit of dropping into the Royal Convent of Jesus and Mary in the afternoon to visit Sister Mariana de la Encarnación and Sister Inés de la Cruz, whose company he found especially congenial. Both nuns were skilled instrumentalists and singers who infallibly charmed the Archbishop by lively renditions of popular airs. With perfect mastery they played liturgical music on the convent organ, and with effortless ease they shifted to the guitarlike *laúdes* and *rabeles*, strumming accompaniments to worldly songs that told of sentimental longings, of blighted loves, and of forsaken hopes. This musical potpourri they interlarded with sprightly chatter most relaxing to a prelate surfeited by the ceremonious formality of his daily life. The culinary arts of these talented ladies, manifested in sweetmeats and dainty dishes, added delight to these restful occasions, and rarely did Fray García miss these agreeable afternoon visits. . . .

Even this gentle and harmless association did not exempt Fray García entirely from the solicitation and importunity that often beset the powerful and influential, for the hospitable nuns were not wholly without guile. They, too, had dreams and ambitions. Long cherished was their hope of founding a new convent under the rule of the reformed Carmelites, and already a wealthy patron had willed a sufficient sum for a building and given part of the endowment. The benefactor had named the Archbishop an executor, and only the approval and a supplementary grant of funds by Fray García were needed to convert a dream into reality. Hence the devout ladies exerted themselves to charm their opulent guest who remained curiously immune to their overtures. This intimate communion with the nuns, however, had brought forth a confession of his own aspirations of becoming the viceroy of Mexico, and whenever pressed for action on the beloved project of his hostesses he invariably put them off by exclaiming: "Ah, my dear sisters, if God is pleased to bestow upon me the office of viceroy, I shall surely help you to start the convent that you so rightly desire! And what a splendid one I shall make it!"

"Must we wait until then, Sire?" the anxious nuns pleaded.

"Yes, my dears," was his constant answer. "It can only be when I become the viceroy."

Fray García's afternoon visits continued regularly and with equal regularity, as they plied him with appetizing tidbits, melody, and conversation, the nuns repeated their pleas. Invariably the obdurate Archbishop vouchsafed the same reply: "When I am the viceroy . . ." Even when Sister Inés de la Cruz professed to have had a vision in which the viceregal office was bestowed upon the ambitious prelate, Fray García remained unmoved. Until the prophecy was fulfilled he would make no commitment, and the impatient nuns could only pray more fervently for divine intercession.

Another favorite diversion of the Archbishop were the drives in his ornate, mule-drawn carriage to outlying churches and congregations. The upset near Huehuetoca, when he had accompanied the viceroy on a tour of inspection, had in no way diminished his enjoyment of such excursions, which were of frequent occurrence. One day, however, in returning from the Santa Mónica monastery it happened that the well-trained mules suddenly took fright and dashed pell-mell through the streets of the city. Frantically the coachman tried to bring the careening carriage under control, and a few bystanders bravely attempted to check the flight of the maddened beasts. Fray García clung desperately to his seat in an effort to ride out the fury of the mules but, as his equipage plunged wildly about the thoroughfare, panic seized him. In a convulsive attempt to save himself he started to leap. Unfortunately, his foot caught in the carriage step, hurling him to the ground where he lay senseless. Though in time he seemed to recover from this mishap, so much more severe than the preceding ones, it had fatal consequences.

Fateful for Fray García was the year 1611 which witnessed his greatest triumph and greatest disaster. It was as if the Fates, having bestowed their bounties so generously on the Spanish clergyman, were growing weary of his claims on their prodigality. His gnawing desire for secular power, after rising so high in the ecclesiastical sphere, appeared to turn his wheel of fortune downward. The series of accidents befalling him were unheeded warnings and now Nature itself was offering disturbing admonitions.

The spring of that year brought the long-expected summons to Don Luis de Velasco to vacate his viceregal office and return to Spain to serve as president of the Royal Council of the Indies. The same decree formally designated Fray García Guerra as his successor in Mexico. The prayerful and seemingly modest acquiescence of the Archbishop did not wholly conceal his inner delight, and his ostentatious humility hardly veiled his keen pleasure in supervising the elaborate plans for a second triumphal entry into the capital, this time with the full panoply of the viceregal office. He gave his closest personal attention to the details of erecting an ornate arch, of selecting the sonorous verses and Latin inscriptions to adorn it, of preparing the magnificent display of fireworks and the illuminations of the facades of public buildings by night, of rehearsing the *Te Deum Laudamus* and the lighter music that so delighted him, and of the construction of the grandstands along the line of march. Absorbed in these pleasurable activities all thought of his promises to the hospitable nuns at the Convent of Jesus and Mary fled from his mind. Indeed, the financial assistance pledged for the new Carmelite establishment was diverted to a pastime close to Fray García's heart—bullfights. To celebrate his elevation to the supreme rank of Archbishop-Viceroy he decreed that these taurine spectacles should take place every Friday for an entire year. And presently he prevailed upon a reluctant city council to construct a private bull ring within the Palace since it hardly seemed fitting for one of his ecclesiastical eminence to attend such functions in public places.

The first of these *corridas* occurred on Good Friday. The choice of the date, curiously symptomatic of the juxtaposition of the sensate and the spiritual in the Baroque age, apparently inspired no adverse comment except from one source. Sister Inés de la Cruz, whose protest possibly arose as much from disappointed hopes as from scandalized disapproval, begged the Archbishop-Viceroy in a note not to encourage such diversions on the day commemorating the Passion of Jesus Christ. But Fray García was too elated to heed this plea and the spectacle took place as scheduled. But a similar event the following Friday brought possible signs of divine displeasure. Just before the appointed hour of the bullfight earth tremors shook the city so severely that the *corrida* was postponed. Undaunted by this warning Fray García comfortably seated himself the following week to witness his favorite sport. Hardly was the first bull charging into the ring when the city experienced another earth spasm so violent that the grandstand and the neighboring houses collapsed. The stone coping of the balcony where the Archbishop was sitting suddenly cracked and a portion of it fell, narrowly missing him and killing several onlookers below. But even so pointed a hint did not deter Fray García, who refused to revoke his decree calling for a weekly exhibition of the popular pastime.

Before assuming his new office Fray García had retired to an outlying village to await formal notification of the departure of his predecessor from Vera Cruz and to make a ceremonial entry into Mexico City as viceroy. When the welcome word arrived that Don Luis de Velasco had sailed the Archbishop's first act was to abase himself publicly before the shrine of the Virgin of Guadalupe. This rite performed, he permitted his attendants to address him by the coveted secular title "Your Excellency."

The inaugural march into the capital on June 19, 1611, duplicated the pomp and splendor of his earlier entry as Archbishop with, however, features of a more secular character. This time he rode a beautiful mare of the most pure blooded stock of the realm, the gift of the city council. Beneath the episcopal pallium supported by the *regidores* on foot, who were dressed in velvet uniforms of brilliant crimson, the Archbishop-Viceroy presented a gallant figure. Next in order came the judges of the Royal Audiencia, the magistrates of other tribunals, and the flower of the viceregal aristocracy, each group vying with the other in theatrical splendor. Slowly the pageantlike procession filed through the streets hung with garlands and past the bordering houses almost concealed by the tapestries and hangings draped from their balconies. But again, as Fray García tasted anew the wine of earthly fame and glory, a tragic note jarred the festive moment.

On the little Santiago square, the Indian community had erected a tall pole called a *volador* from which, as a feature of the celebration, acrobatic members swung high in the air as if from a lofty merry-go-round. This circus-like performance was a death-defying act which thrilled the spectators and added a note of expectancy to the general excitement. Just as the Archbishop-Viceroy drew abreast of this plaza a performer, whirling through the air, lost his grip on the rope and fell, his body horribly shattered, almost at the feet of Fray García. Once again in the midst of rejoicing and at a moment of proud fulfillment tragedy struck, a sinister warning, perhaps, that the Fates were losing patience with the excessive ambition of a favored mortal.

But this macabre incident scarcely interrupted the colorful inauguration. The glittering procession resumed its course toward the triumphal arch which simulated a huge fortress gate decorated by an intricate pattern of symbolic figures painted on its facade. Here the Corregidor administered a ceremonious oath to the new viceroy and handed him a large golden key. The ponderous doors of the imitation stronghold then swung open and the bright column, with Fray García in the lead, wended its way to the Cathedral where the thunderous *Te Deum Laudamus* reverberated through the nave. Presently the Archbishop-Viceroy, accompanied by the city's principal magistrates, departed by another door and entered the Viceregal Palace on the east side of the central square. There his accompaniment of judges of the Royal Audiencia and other officials obsequiously took their leave and Fray García retired into the chambers of his secular predecessors to relish the first moments of his ascent to the supreme authority of the State as well as of the Church in the fairest of the Spanish realms. Outside, in the plaza, deafening explosions of bombs and artillery-pieces saluted the new viceroy. That night the whole city seemed ablaze with lanterns in doorways and windows and roaring bonfires in the streets and squares.

These noisy demonstrations and the general rejoicing found the Archbishop-Viceroy vaguely troubled. His satisfaction was tinged with disillusionment, a sort of *desengaño*. Realization, somehow, fell short of anticipation. The series of mishaps had engendered haunting forebodings, and already a recurrence of physical pain depressed his spirits. Ever since that dreadful day when he had leaped from the carriage drawn by runaway mules, the pain in his side had become increasingly severe. Also a series of strange phenomena of nature in recent months had filled him and his subjects with uneasiness. Were they harbingers of impending disaster? Oppressed by bodily discomfort and superstitious fears, he confronted with deepening anxiety the heavier obligations which his pride and ambition had thrust upon him.

The disturbing aberrations of nature did not cease as Fray García took up his duties. The very month of his inauguration witnessed a total eclipse of the sun which terrified the masses. An unnatural darkness engulfed the city at noon, and it seemed to deepen as the afternoon advanced. "This phenomenon," wrote a chronicler, "which the astronomers had predicted, produced an effect upon Spaniards and Indians such that both raced frantically to the shelter of the churches to implore God's mercy, and they did not venture out until nightfall." The seismic disturbances coinciding with Fray García's bullfights were followed in August by the severest earthquake in the memory of the oldest inhabitant. With seeming pointedness it wreaked heavy damage on religious establishments where many inmates were crushed beneath the rubble. To everyone this disaster appeared especially terrifying because an inordinate number of tremors had preceded it. More than forty were experienced within thirty hours and all were exceedingly violent.

Weeks and months passed without dissipating the dread and anxiety that pervaded the city. Christmas day brought even more menacing indications of divine displeasure. About half past two in the afternoon the whole sky over the Valley of Mexico turned a dark, reddish black and a shower of ashes fell, sifting a thin layer over the houses and the fields. This strange manifestation lasted until the great, crimson bowl of the sun dipped over the western rim. Just as it disappeared, a frightful downpour of rain deluged the city, transforming its streets into rushing torrents of water. Clearly, these were unmistakable signs of heavenly wrath and inexorable summonses to repentance, most of all, perhaps, for the ailing Archbishop-Viceroy.

Fray García Guerra's symptoms, meanwhile, had worsened, and it was clear that he was gravely ill. Attacks of pain alternated with high fever and confined him to his bed. The best physicians in the land, whose medical knowledge derived almost wholly from the ancients, Galen and Hippocrates, could prescribe no other remedies than repeated purges and bloodletting which further weakened the afflicted prelate. Early in January, 1612, a stormy dispute arose among the doctors in consultation regarding the necessity of an operation. Three of them were promptly dismissed while the others performed some crude surgery which doubtless hastened the patient's demise. In sick despair Fray García had even turned to his good friend, Sister Inés de la Cruz, whose hopes for a new convent he had so long defrauded, and he begged for her prayers. He assured her of his deep repentance and pledged himself to keep his promise to her if he could but be restored to health. The response of the disappointed nun was hardly consoling to the doomed Archbishop-Viceroy, for she merely urged him to prepare for death and to voice thanks to God that his sorrow was only in the temporal realm. Fray García now knew that he must resign himself to the inevitable. Calling his confessor, he received the last Sacrament and thereafter, with the feeble strength left to him, he performed such acts of humility and contrition as he could. Further bloodletting doubtless shortened his period of suffering. With Christian fortitude he endured his afflictions until "he surrendered his spirit to the Lord on February 22, 1612."

The chronicler gives a gruesome account of the autopsy performed upon the noble cadaver hardly had life departed. With morbid satisfaction he describes the advanced decomposition of various organs and the removal of the skull top and the emptying of the brains into a container for separate burial. This writer seemed to share the view of a contemporary Baroque poet Jerónimo de Cáncer that "también en lo horrible hay hermosura" (there is also beauty in the horrible). These repellent details, following almost immediately the recital of the colorful pageantry of the Archbishop-Viceroy's years in Mexico, provide an abrupt transition. Sharpening the contrast still further is the rapid shift from the vital, dynamic scenes of Fray García's existence to the minute description of the veritable orgy of mourning at the public funeral. With morose zest the eulogist tells of streets and public buildings draped in black, of the mournful monotony of endlessly tolling bells, of the almost exuberant frenzy of the chapel decorations, and of the corpse lying in state, of the interminable processions of dignitaries, nobles, officials, monks, and soldiers marching to the rhythm of muffled drums and hoarse fifes, of downcast throngs of the kaleidoscopic society of Mexico, and of the all-pervading solemnity of Death and the futility of things mortal. All of this tremendously heightened the tragic sense of drama infusing the spirit of that age.

The death of the chief of Church and State and the ensuing funeral obsequies increased the mounting tension and anxiety of the inhabitants of the capital. Scarcely were the remains of Fray García deposited beneath the altar by which, a few short years before, he had sat at his episcopal installation flushed with the joy of adulation, when dread rumors and alarms gripped the nervous citizenry. With no successor to wield the absolute power of government to which all were accustomed, the more privileged elements of society especially fell prey to a panic [of] fear. Like a noisome vapor, dark threats against law and order seemed to rise from every quarter. The judges of the Royal Audiencia assumed the executive functions, but their collective rule failed to offer the security that the single figure of the Archbishop-Viceroy, endowed with the legal sanction of the distant Spanish monarchy and, seemingly, of God Himself, embodied in the minds of all. The apprehension of the upper classes spawned vague intimations of plots against the regime, of uprisings in the provinces, particularly of Negroes who had escaped from slavery and had taken refuge in the hills. These *cimarrones* were ever suspected of conspiring with the exploited Indian masses to throw off white supremacy. So great was the terror of Europeans and Creoles that they did not dare to venture out upon the streets and they barricaded themselves within their homes.

This community neurosis became acute one night when a herd of hogs was heard rooting and squealing about the city thoroughfares. These sounds were interpreted as an assault launched by runaway Negroes and they created near panic among the judges of the Royal Audiencia as well as the citizenry. Even the coming of daylight failed to dissipate the general hysteria, and fear-ridden officials rounded up twenty-nine Negro men and four women as alleged conspirators. In a desperate effort to deter subversive elements, the authorities barbarously executed the wretched suspects in the public square before a huge gathering. The severed heads were conspicuously displayed on pikes until the stench of decomposition caused their removal. Similar spasms of uncontrollable fear had shaken Europeans before between the terms of viceroys, but the simultaneous disappearance of both the head of the State and of the Church in one person had let loose a more violent wave of unreasoning fright and terror. Thus, in death as in life, this Spanish Archbishop-Viceroy singularly epitomized an aspect of that strange spirit of the Baroque which subtly dominated the entire seventeenth century and long after.

On Men's Hypocrisy

Sor Juana

Women, by all accounts, occupied a decidedly subordinate position in colonial Mexico. It is ironic, then, that one of the most distinguished poets and intellectuals of the period was a Jeronymite nun, Sor [Sister] Juana Inés de la Cruz (not to be confused with Fray García's solicitous friend in the previous selection). Born in 1648 in a small village in Puebla, to unmarried parents in very modest economic circumstances, she early evidenced precocious talents that brought her to the attention of the viceroy and his wife, who took the prodigy into their court as a maid-in-waiting. Her natural brilliance and insatiable thirst for knowledge led her to shun the accepted course for women in her day — marriage — opting instead to enter a convent (in 1669) where she would be relatively free to pursue her intellectual and artistic inclinations. The cloistered life in colonial Mexico was not necessarily ascetic, and Sor Juana was able to build a substantial library, read and write prodigiously, and socialize with many of the most illustrious personages of the day. In 1690 the Bishop of Puebla censured her for neglecting religious in favor of profane subjects, and for behaving in ways inappropriate to her sex and vocation. In response, she wrote an intellectual autobiography, the "Reply to Sor Philothea," perhaps her most famous single piece of writing. In this remarkable letter, Sor Juana ostensibly repents her aberrant ways, even while clearly celebrating the life of the mind. The Bishop's chastisement, however, compelled her to cease her writing, give away her books and musical and scientific instruments, and devote herself to charitable work and extreme acts of penance and mortification. She died in 1695, the victim of a plague that swept Puebla in that year.

While much of Sor Juana's poetry contains the flowery language and intricate symbolism characteristic of the Baroque style, the poem we include here — a comment on the famous sexual double-standard — is written in a playful vein, even while it is quite serious in its intent.

Silly, you men — so very adept
at wrongly faulting womankind,
not seeing you're alone to blame
for faults you plant in woman's mind.

After you've won by urgent plea
the right to tarnish her good name,
you still expect her to behave —
you, that coaxed her into shame.

You batter her resistance down
and then, all righteousness, proclaim
that feminine frivolity,
not your persistence, is to blame.

When it comes to bravely posturing,
your witlessness must take the prize:
you're the child that makes a bogeyman,
and then recoils in fear and cries.

Presumptuous beyond belief,
you'd have the woman you pursue
be Thais[1] when you're courting her,
Lucretia[2] once she falls to you.

For plain default of common sense,
could any action be so queer
as oneself to cloud the mirror,
then complain that it's not clear?

Whether you're favored or disdained,
nothing can leave you satisfied.
You whimper if you're turned away,
you sneer if you've been gratified.

With you, no woman can hope to score;
whichever way, she's bound to lose;
spurning you, she's ungrateful;
succumbing, you call her lewd.

Your folly is always the same:
you apply a single rule
to the one you accuse of looseness
and the one you brand as cruel.

What happy mean could there be
for the woman who catches your eye,
if, unresponsive, she offends,
yet whose complaisance you decry?

Still, whether it's torment or anger —
and both ways you've yourselves to blame —
God bless the woman who won't have you,
no matter how loud you complain.

Sor Juana Inés de la Cruz. Miranda, 1651. (University of Mexico City)

It's your persistent entreaties
that change her from timid to bold.
Having made her thereby naughty,
you would have her good as gold.

So where does the greater guilt lie
for a passion that should not be:
with the man who pleads out of baseness
or the woman debased by his plea?

Or which is more to be blamed—
though both will have cause for chagrin:
the woman who sins for money
or the man who pays money to sin?

So why are you men all so stunned
at the thought you're all guilty alike?
Either like them for what you've made them
or make of them what you can like.

If you'd give up pursuing them,
you'd discover, without a doubt,

you've a stronger case to make
against those who seek you out.
    I well know what powerful arms
you wield in pressing for evil:
your arrogance is allied
with the world, the flesh, and the devil!

Notes

1. Thais: Semi-historic Athenian courtesan who is said to have been mistress of Alexander on his Asiatic conquests, and later mistress of the king of Egypt. *Ed.*
2. Lucretia: In Roman legend, a matron renowned for her virtue, who stabbed herself to death after being raped. *Ed.*

The Itching Parrot, the Priest,
and the Subdelegate

José Joaquín Fernández de Lizardi

One of the most unforgettable characters of late colonial Mexico is the fictional Pedro Sarmiento, whose name was corrupted by his schoolmates to "Périco Sarniento," or "Itching Parrot." The protagonist of The Itching Parrot *embodies many of the characteristics of the Mexican* pelado, *described earlier in this volume by Roger Bartra, although he also has many traits of the* pícaro, *the wandering rogue of the Spanish picaresque tradition. Although born to a fairly reputable family, he proves too lazy to train for the "respectable" professions such as law and theology. He likewise disdains honorable trades, hoping instead to live by his wits, which consistently prove inadequate. He inhabits a colorful and corrupt world of gamblers, rascals, confidence men, charlatans, beggars, and thieves. His adventures pointedly satirize the society of late colonial Mexico, where pompous claims and highfalutin phrases substitute for both competence and compassion (among the colorful figures that populate the book, for instance, we find one Doctor Purgante, who spouts random terms in Latin but whose only remedy consists of prescribing laxatives).*

Fernández de Lizardi (1776–1827) was born into a creole family of modest means. By the time the movement for Mexico's independence broke out in 1810, he had begun to write for and to publish political newspapers. While he was late to fully embrace the cause of independence, his writings—which came to comprise fiction, poetry, and numerous essays—were consistently critical of the Spanish colonial system. Fernández de Lizardi took special aim at the suffocating fiscal and administrative bureaucracy that marked the enlightened despotism of the Spanish Bourbon kings who had succeeded Hapsburg rule in the early eighteenth century. He espoused many of the reforms that would come to be identified with the Liberal cause: he decried corruption and incompetence in government, the Church, and the professions; he denounced slavery and racial oppression; and he favored the impartial and impersonal rule of law. His 1816 book, from which the following chapter is taken, is widely regarded as the first genuine Spanish-American novel. In the following excerpt, we get a glimpse of corruption in both petty officialdom and the priesthood in late colonial Mexico.

If when the boys in school named me the Itching Parrot, they had called me Jumping Jack, I could say now they foresaw my adventures, so quickly did I hop from one occupation to another, out of bad luck into good: first sacristan, then beggar; and now scrivener to the Subdelegate at Tixtla, with whom I got along so well from the first day that he began to show real fondness for me; and, to crown my felicity, after a little while he quarreled with his clerk, who left the village.

My master was of the mercenary kind of subdelegate and he was trying, he told me, not only to reimburse himself for the expense he had incurred in obtaining his appointment, but to make a small fortune out of the district during his five years there. With such honest, straightforward intentions, he did not omit even the most wicked and illegal means of fattening his pockets. He was a merchant and owned parcels of land; he sold his goods on credit at a good price to the farmers, and made them pay in grain at less than the harvest-time value; he collected his own bills punctually and exactly, but he gave no quarter where other creditors were concerned, and these poor men, when they were forced to ask his aid, always gave up a good share of their collections to him. Although it was no longer the custom for subdelegates to collect a silver mark by way of fine from persons denounced for incontinence, my master paid no attention and kept spies, who informed him fully as to the private life and miracles of all his neighbors; and not only did he collect the silver mark from the accused but he also imposed exorbitant fines in proportion to their means; always warning them to be careful about repetition of the offence, because they would pay double for it. In a few days he would fall upon them suddenly and get more money out of them. There was one poor farmer among them whose abundant harvest for a year all went in fines; another lost his little farm for the same reason; a shopkeeper went bankrupt; the very poor were without a shirt.

In the villages there are always some shameless toadies who comb the beard of the Subdelegate for all they are worth, and who stoop to any filth in their efforts to gain his good will. The Subdelegate gave money, through me, to one of these men to set up a monte game. This scoundrel took the money, gathered in as many players as he could, and sent us word as to where he could be found. We made up the round, fell upon them, shut them all up in jail, and emptied their pockets by means of fines. Counter to all the royal orders protecting the Indians, we abused these unhappy people at our pleasure, making them work for us as much as we liked without paying them a centavo. We issued proclamations on any pretext and pitilessly exacted the penalties imposed for infractions. What proclamations they were! We proclaimed that donkeys, pigs, and chickens should not be permitted to run loose outside the corrals, that shopkeepers must keep cats, that no one might go to Mass barefoot, and other things as strange.

The priest rivalled us in exploiting the wretched villagers. I should like to pass over the deeds of this churchman, but I must say something about them because of the part he played in my leaving that village. He was well instructed, a doctor of canons, not scandalous in his private life, and almost too courtly in his manners. He was energetic in the pulpit, punctual in his ministry, sweet and affable in his conversation, considerate to his household, modest in the street, and would have been an excellent pastor, if such a thing as money were not known in this world; but he was ruled by avarice and covetousness. He had plenty of charm to make himself loved, but where money was concerned, he could not dissemble and was inexorable; the miseries of the unfortunate did not move him, the tears of the widow and orphan did not soften his heart.

But so you may see there is something of everything in this world, I must relate an episode which I witnessed. Our priest invited the priest from Chilapa, don Benigno, a virtuous man without hypocrisy, to visit Tixtla during the festival. One afternoon while they were amusing themselves playing manille until dinner time, a poor woman entered, clothed in rags, crying bitterly, with one little creature at her breast, and another about three years old holding her hand.

"What do you want, daughter?" the priest of Tixtla asked her.

The poor woman, drinking her own tears, responded, "Father, my husband died night before last. He has left me nothing except these children. I have nothing to sell and I can buy neither shroud nor candles for him. I have gathered by begging alms these twelve reals I bring your grace; and neither I nor this little girl have eaten today. I beg you, Father, by the life of your mother, in God's name, do me the kindness of burying my husband, for I will work my spinning wheel and pay you two reals on account every week."

"Daughter," said the priest, "what was your husband?"

"A Spaniard, sir."

"Then," said the priest, "according to the regulations you lack six pesos to complete paying the fees. Here, read this," and he put the list of fees in her hands.

The unhappy widow, weeping, said, "Oh, Father! I don't know how to read. What I beg of you is that in God's name you bury my husband."

"Daughter," said the priest with great elegance, "I cannot do such favors. I have to maintain myself and pay the vicar. Go see don Blas, don Agustín, or any of the rich gentlemen, and beg them to let you have the money, which you may pay back later in work; and then I will order the body buried."

"Father," said the poor woman, "I have seen all those gentlemen already and they will not help."

"Then go into service," said the priest.

"Who would take me, sir, with these babies?"

"Well, go along, see what you can do, and don't annoy me," said the priest, angrily. "This curacy was not given me to run on trust. The merchant and the butcher do not trust me."

"Sir," the unhappy woman insisted, "the corpse is beginning to spoil and it cannot remain much longer in the neighborhood."

"Then eat it, for if you don't bring me exactly seven pesos and a half, don't think I'll bury it for the plague itself! You shameless swindlers are all alike! You have money for fandangos and dinner parties, you can wear shoes and petticoats every day, while your husbands live; but you can never afford to pay the poor priest his fees. Get out, curse you; and don't bother me any more."

The unhappy woman went, confused, tormented, and shamed by the harsh treatment of her priest, whose lack of charity scandalized everyone present. But in a little while the widow entered again hurriedly and putting seven and half pesos on the table said to the priest, "Here is your money, sir. Do me the favor of sending the vicar to bury my husband."

"What do you think of this, brother?" said the priest to don Benigno. "You see how this little cheat brought her money with her all prepared in case I should not yield, and pretended to be in misery so I would bury her husband for nothing? Another priest with less experience than I have might have let her deceive him with those whines and tears."

Don Benigno lowered his eyes, was mute, and changed color from time to time, as if the prelate were rebuking him; then he looked at the widow earnestly, as if he wished to speak to her. We were all hanging on this scene, mystified at don Benigno's disturbed countenance, but the Tixtla priest dropped the money into his pocket and faced the woman severely, "You shameless creature. Your husband will be buried, but not until tomorrow, to punish you for your deceit."

"I did not deceive you, Father," said the widow humbly. "I am really in distress. The money was given me just now as alms."

"Just now? That's another lie," said the priest. "Who gave it to you?"

The woman, letting loose of the little girl's hand and holding on one arm the child at her breast, threw herself at the feet of don Benigno, embraced his knees, leaned her head upon them, and melted in weeping, unable to speak. The child who could walk cried also on seeing her mother cry. Our priest was astonished. The priest from Chilapa bent over, tears rolling from his eyes, and raised the woman up. We were all silent at such a spectacle. Finally, the woman calmed herself a little and turning to us, she said, "Gentlemen, this Father, who is not only a priest but an angel from Heaven, called to me as I was alone in the hallway, gave me twelve pesos, and said, 'Go now, little daughter. Pay for the burial and do not tell who has helped you.' But I would be the most ungrateful woman in the world if I did not cry out the name of him who has done me such great charity!"

Both priests were scarlet and confused, not daring to look at each other. The vicar, with great prudence, took the woman away with him, saying he would attend to the burial at once; and the Subdelegate, hoping to divert the minds of the guests from this episode, invited them to resume the card game.

The Subdelegate and the priest being so well matched in greed, there was little peace between the two. They were always at it tooth and claw, for two cats cannot be kept peaceably in one sack. Both of them worked with all possible speed to squeeze the village for his own benefit; competition developed, and quarrels resulted. The priest, without its pertaining to his duties, persecuted such incontinent persons as were unmarried, trying to force them to marry and pay him the fees; the Subdelegate did the same thing to get fines. When the priest caught victims, the secular arm claimed them; the churchman refused to give them up, and a conflict of jurisdictions arose. The poor were always the losers, and they paid either with imprisonment or silver; the miserable Indians were the main objects of both traffickers. With the exception of the few spoiled rich men who could afford to buy immunity, everyone hated the priest and the Subdelegate. Some had already complained against them in Mexico [City], but their accusations were easily refuted, as witnesses could always be found to discredit the accusers and make them appear as slanderers.

But crime cannot go forever without punishment. The principal Indians and the Governor went to the capital, in bitter rebellion against the rule of the judges, the priest and the Subdelegate. Without troubling to name the priest this time, they formally accused the Subdelegate, presenting in the Royal Audiencia a terrible declaration, containing many damning clauses: The Subdelegate engaged in commerce and owned lands. He obliged the natives of the village to buy on credit and exacted payment from them in grain at a lower price than that current on the market. He forced them to work at his labors for whatever wage he wished and whoever refused to work for him was lashed and jailed. He permitted those who could afford to bribe him to lead unchaste lives, but he fined and imprisoned the poor for the same offence. For five hundred pesos he had protected and freed a murderer. Through a third party, he set up games and then fined the men caught playing. He forced the Indians to work as house servants, without pay. He used the Indian women as he pleased, taking three of them to his house each week, and did not exempt from this service even the daughters of the [Indian] Governor. He exacted from the Indians the same fees he collected from the Spaniards. On market days he was the first haggler to seize the scarcest goods, hoarding them to sell to the poor at raised prices. Lastly, he speculated with the royal tribute monies. The Indians concluded their charges by asking that the Subdelegate be recalled to answer in the capital; that a commissioner be sent to Tixtla to investigate these charges; and that, if the accusations were proved, the Subdelegate be removed from his office, and obliged to make retribution for the private damages he had inflicted on the villagers. The Royal Audiencia appointed and despatched a commissioner at once.

All this tempest was brewing in Mexico [City] without our knowledge. The Indians' absence did not arouse any suspicion in us, for they told us they were going to order an image made. A notification from the Commissioner took my master by surprise one afternoon when he was airing himself on the balcony of the royal house. It was a simple statement to the effect that his functions were to cease from that moment, he was to name a lieutenant in his place, leave the village within three days, and within eight present himself in the capital to answer charges against him. My master was struck cold at this order, but since there was no help for it, he obeyed, leaving his affairs in my hands.

When I found myself alone, with all the authority of the Subdelegate at my back I ran wild at my own pleasure. I first banished from the village a pretty girl because she lived in incontinence. So I said, but it was really because she refused my ad-interim protection. Afterwards, thanks to a gift of three hundred pesos from the lover in the case, I incriminated a poor man whose only offence was to have a pretty but dishonorable wife; and I cleverly arranged to despatch him to prison, leaving his wife free to live with her paramour. Next, I summoned and threatened all those whom I suspected of incontinence; and they, afraid I would banish their mistresses also if I took the notion, paid me the fines I demanded and sent gifts so I would not put them through the mill too often. I annulled the most formal legal documents, revised testaments, and destroyed public records. In the month that I lasted as vice-subdelegate, I was a more devilish nuisance than the Subdelegate had been, and I ended by making myself hated thoroughly.

To crown my labors, I began to gamble publicly in the royal house, and on the evening that luck turned against me, I went out with the patrol and persecuted the private gamblers by way of revenge; so that on some nights my fellow gamblers left my house at twelve and at one numbers of poor fellows caught playing in other houses went to jail; and I replaced the greater part of my losses by the fines I extracted from them. One night my guests gave me such a plucking that, not having a real of my own, I unlocked the public moneyboxes and lost all there was in them. I did this with so little discretion that the other players noticed and tattled to the priest and the Governor of the Indians, who, being responsible for the money and knowing I could not replace it, immediately sent a report of my doings to the capital, backed by individual declarations that they collected not only from the honorable residents of the village, but from the Commissioner himself. All this was done with such secrecy that no smell of it came to my nostrils.

The priest was the principal agent of my ruin, and this not because of his love for the village nor his jealousy for its well-being, but because he had hoped to get the great part of that money for himself, under pretext of repairing the church. He had already proposed this to the Indians, and they, it seems, had almost agreed. When he learned how I had forestalled him, he exploded and determined to get rid of me. To add to my griefs, the Subdelegate, being unable to answer the charges against him, resorted to the excuse of fools and declared it was news to him that those things were crimes: He was a layman, had never been a subdelegate before and knew nothing at all about the duties of that office; I had suggested all these expedients to him, he told them, and so I should be held responsible, for he had trusted me completely. These excuses, prepared by the pen of a clever lawyer, influenced the final judgment of the Audiencia, not enough to convince them of the Subdelegate's innocence, but enough to lessen the blame placed upon him, especially since at this very time they received the priest's report, which proved to them that I had committed more atrocities than the Subdelegate himself. Then they bore down upon me with all the rigor of the law that formerly had threatened my master; they excused his misdeeds; decided he was a fool and unfit to be a judge; deposed him from his employ, and exacted from his guarantors replacement of the royal monies, leaving private citizens' rights open for them to repeat charges against the Subdelegate when his fortunes bettered, because in this case he proved himself insolvent; and they sent seven soldiers to Tixtla to conduct me to Mexico [City].

So far was I from dreaming of disaster that I was playing country manille with the priest and the Commissioner at a real a point the afternoon the soldiers came for me. I was thinking only how to make up for four tricks they had won in succession; just when I had played a solo and was inflated with pride, the soldiers entered the room. Such people know nothing about the proprieties; they asked for the lieutenant; when I was pointed out, they informed me I was under arrest, and, without allowing me even to play out my hand, got me up from the table and handed the priest a letter. The letter, I suppose, must have contained the instructions of the Royal Audiencia as to who should govern the village. I was conducted to jail and the prisoners there made a great deal of fun at my expense and revenged themselves on me in short order for all the troubles I had caused them in a short month.

The next day, before breakfast, they clothed me heavily in irons, mounted me on a mule, and conducted me to Mexico [City], where they lodged me in the Court jail. When I entered this gloomy place, I remembered the cursed shower of urine with which other prisoners had bathed me the first time I had the honor of entering there; the ferocious treatment of the trusty; my friend don Antonio, the Eaglet, and all the sorry events of my life in that place. I consoled myself that this time it might not go so badly with me, for I had six pesos in my pocket. . . . But the six pesos were soon spent and I passed through all the kinds of discomfort poverty can inflict, especially in such places. Meanwhile, my case ran the usual course; I had no defense; I confessed, was convicted, and sentenced to join the King's troops for eight years in Manila, which arm of the service was at that time flying a recruiting flag in Mexico.

IV

Trials of the Young Republic

The dawn of the nineteenth century found Bourbon New Spain in a state of agitation. Age-old problems—the elite's monopoly of the land, the vast gulf between rich and poor and between the races, corruption in administration, tensions between church and state—persisted. Adding to these tensions was the fact that the mother country had come to be ruled by the modernizing Bourbon dynasty, which sought to reform the colonial system so as to minimize the participation of creoles (as American-born whites were called), to expand the imperial supervision of colonial affairs, and especially to increase revenues accruing to the crown of Spain, which were largely used to finance Spain's expensive participation in European wars. Creole discontent might well have reached a breaking point sooner had it not been for the fact that the Mexican elite presided over a highly exploitative system. The vast majority of the population—Indians and *castas*—tended to make little distinction between creoles and *peninsulares:* all seemed to be oppressors. Bloody rebellions of Indians in Peru and black slaves in Haiti served as object lessons regarding the high cost of dissension among the ruling classes.

In late 1807 Napoleon Bonaparte's troops occupied Spain. Bonaparte forced the abdication of King Charles IV and the renunciation of the throne by Charles's successor, Ferdinand VII. The removal of the one factor that, more than any other, had given legitimacy and cohesion to the Spanish colonial system—namely, the Spanish monarchy—plunged the colony into confusion and violence that would last for more than a decade. And even when independence was achieved, peace and order were not. The first two-thirds of the nineteenth century in Mexico would be characterized by government penury, political instability and corruption, peasant unrest, civil wars, and foreign invasions. Ideological differences arose between those who wished to preserve and ennoble such Spanish traditions as monarchy, hierarchy, Roman Catholicism, and centralism; and those who favored a sweeping move in the direction of republicanism, egalitarianism, federalism, and secularism. Eventually, the factions would be denominated "Conservative" and "Liberal," respectively.

Not until the last quarter of the century was peace and a modicum of conciliation achieved. Even then, problems lurked beneath the placid veneer of an
entrenched "order and progress" regime, and many of these problems would
eventually erupt in the epic Mexican revolution of 1910.

The readings included in this section seek to give readers something of the
flavor of those times and to explain why peace, order, and progress remained
so elusive.

The Siege of Guanajuato

Lucas Alamán

Spanish conservatives seized control of Mexico City shortly after receiving news of the Napoleonic usurpation in 1808. From that time, Mexico was alive with creole conspiracies. The most famous of the creole conspirators was Miguel Hidalgo, the restless, reform-minded parish priest of the small town of Dolores in the intendancy of Guanajuato. When his plotting was discovered, he was forced to launch his revolution months ahead of schedule, and without benefit of proper planning. On September 16, 1810 — today celebrated as Mexican Independence Day — he gathered the people of Dolores and environs together and proclaimed the "Grito de Dolores," which called for revolution in the name of Ferdinand VII and the Roman Catholic Church, but which also invited Indians and castas to avenge nearly three centuries of wrongs perpetrated against them by the Spaniards. The masses of Indians and mixed castes responded enthusiastically — so enthusiastically, in fact, that the rebellion quickly fell out of Hidalgo's control, and there followed episodes like that narrated in the following excerpt. At these first clear signs of popular rage, creoles became horrified that what they had long feared had finally come to pass. Most quickly withdrew their support.

Clearly, Father Hidalgo was neither a gifted military man nor a meticulous planner; his armies were rather quickly dispersed, and he was captured and executed in 1811. He did, however, live on as a powerful symbol. For some, he became an icon of liberation; for others, his was a cautionary tale that proved the dangers of rousing the restive masses. Lucas Alamán (1793–1853), who would become a distinguished historian and the most important voice for Conservatism in early republican Mexico, was 17 years old in 1810, scion of a wealthy and influential family of Guanajuato. He witnessed the siege of the wealthy mining city firsthand, and the violent spectacle influenced his later conviction that irresponsible demagoguery would provoke anarchy, which would in turn spell doom for property and civilization (something he tended to equate with religion and the Spanish heritage). While his elitism can surely be questioned, his vivid, often gruesome descriptions make it clear why these nightmarish events haunted him throughout his life.

Don Miguel Hidalgo y Costilla was born in the year 1747 in the town of Pénjamo, in the province of Guanajuato. His father, Don Cristóbal Hidalgo, was
a native of Tejupilco in the intendancy of Mexico. After establishing himself
in Pénjamo, he married Doña Ana María Gallagamandarte, with whom he
had four children, the second of whom was Miguel. . . .

Miguel distinguished himself in his studies at the . . . College of San Nico-
lás [in Valladolid, Michoacán, today known as Morelia], where he later gave
highly renowned courses in philosophy and theology, and also served as rector. His fellow students called him "the fox" [*el zorro*], a name that perfectly
suited his crafty character. He spent the years 1778 to 1779 in Mexico City,
where he received the holy orders and the degree of bachelor of theology.
It is said that the ecclesiastical council of Valladolid had earlier granted him
four thousand pesos to meet the expenses and gratuities of the doctoral degree, and that he went to Mexico to solicit the degree but en route he lost
the money in a card game at Maravatio. He served in several parishes, and
when his elder brother Joaquín died he was given the parish of Dolores, in
the province of Guanajuato where Joaquín had served, and which produced
an income of perhaps eight or nine thousand pesos per year.

Miguel was hardly straitlaced in his daily life and was quite unorthodox in
his opinions, and he did not concern himself with spiritual ministrations to
his parishioners. These duties fell, together with half the parish income, to
a cleric named Francisco Iglesias. Miguel spent his time translating French,
which was very rare in those days, especially among the clergy. He also took
great pains to foment several agricultural and industrial pursuits in the parish.
He greatly extended the cultivation of grapes, which today are harvested in
considerable abundance in that territory, and he began planting mulberry
trees for the raising of silkworms. . . . He also had a factory built for making
china and another for bricks; he built vats for tanning hides, and he set up
workshops for diverse crafts. He was not merely generous, but a spendthrift
in matters of money, which made him highly esteemed by his parishioners,
especially the Indians, whose languages he spoke. He was also much appreciated by all those who—like the bishop-elect of Michoacán, Abad y Queipo,
and [Juan Antonio de] Riaño, the intendant[1] of Guanajuato—were interested
in the true progress of the country. Even so, it would seem that in some of
these fields his knowledge was deficient, as was the orderliness which would
have been indispensable to make them achieve real progress. Once Bishop
Abad y Queipo asked him what method he had adopted for chopping and distributing the leaves to the silkworms in accordance with their ages, separating
out the dry leaves, and keeping the furrows cleaned—matters about which
the books on the topic give so many and such scrupulous instructions. Miguel

answered that he followed no order at all, that he threw the leaves out just as they came off the tree and the worms would eat whatever they wanted. The bishop, who told me this anecdote, later told me that Hidalgo's revolution was like his silkworm raising, and it had similar results!

Nevertheless, Hidalgo brought about many improvements, even using the silk of his harvests to make a few pieces of clothing for his use and that of his father's last wife. He also augmented the keeping of bees, moving many swarms to the hacienda of Jaripeo after he bought that property. He was very fond of music, and even made the Indians of his parish learn it. He formed an orchestra, and had it perform all over, from the battalion of Guanajuato to the frequent parties he held in his home. The proximity of his place of residence to the capital city allowed him to go there often and to stay for long periods, which afforded me the chance to see him up close. He was of middling stature, stoop shouldered, dark complected and with lively green eyes, his head a bit slumped over his chest, his hair very white and balding, as if he had already passed the age of sixty, but vigorous, although neither active nor quick in his movements: a man of few words in ordinary dealings, but animated when arguing in the collegial style, as when he entered heatedly into some dispute. Rather disheveled in his dress, he did not wear anything but what the small town priests normally wore at that time. (This was a cloak of black wool with a round hat and a large walking stick, and a suit of knee breeches, waistcoat and jacket made from a kind of wool that came from China and was called Rompecoche).

IN HIS PLAN of revolution, Hidalgo followed the same ideas as the backers of independence in [Viceroy] Iturrigaray's councils.[2] He proclaimed allegiance to King Ferdinand VII: he sought to sustain the king's rights and to defend them against the designs of those Spaniards who had negotiated their country's surrender to the French and who were then in control of Spain, men who would have destroyed religion, profaned the churches and extinguished the Catholic cult. Religion, then, played the principal role, and inasmuch as the image of Guadalupe is the cherished object of the cult of the Mexicans, the inscription put on the revolution's banners read: "Long live religion. Long live our most holy mother Guadalupe. Long live Ferdinand VII. Long live America and death to bad government." But the people who rushed to follow this banner simplified the inscription and it became the simple cry, "Long live the Virgin of Guadalupe and death to the *gachupines!*" What a monstrous pairing of religion with murder and robbery! It is a cry of death and desolation, one I heard thousands and thousands of times in the early days of my youth, and after so many years it still resounds in my ears with a frightful echo!

Among a people to whom religion is disgracefully reduced to mere super-ficial practices; where many ministers, especially in the smaller towns, devote themselves to the most licentious lifestyle; where the dominant vice of most people is an inclination toward theft; it is not surprising that one should find, among such people, partisans for a revolution whose first steps were to free the criminals, to open the properties of the richest citizens to unlimited plun-der, to incite the common people against everything that until then they had feared and respected, and to give free rein to all vice; a revolution which, moreover, later gave out military ranks freely, opening an immense field for the workers' ambitions. So it was that in all of the villages, the priest Hidalgo found so favorable a predisposition that he needed only to show himself in order to drag the masses of people along behind him. But the methods he employed to gain such popularity destroyed the foundations of the social edi-fice and suffocated all principles of morality and justice, and all the evils that the nation now laments flow from that poisoned fountain.

As Hidalgo, on this and later marches, passed through the fields and vil-lages, he was joined by people who formed diverse groups or mobs. They carried sticks to which they had tied banners or multi-colored handkerchiefs displaying the image of Guadalupe, which was the standard of the enterprise and which those who adhered to the party also wore as an emblem on their hats. The cowboys and other mounted men from the haciendas, nearly all of whom were of mixed blood, formed the cavalry. They were armed with the lances that Hidalgo had had made beforehand, and with swords and ma-chetes which they customarily carried in their daily work; very few had pistols or carbines. The infantry was made up of Indians, divided by villages or bands, armed with sticks, arrows, slings and lances. Since many of them took their women and children along, they looked more like the barbarous tribes, who emigrate from place to place, than like an army on the march. The *caporales* and *mayordomos* [overseers] from the haciendas who took part became chiefs of the cavalry. The Indians took their orders from their village governors or from the captains of the hacienda work gangs. Many carried no weapons at all, and were prepared for nothing but plunder. Mounted men each earned a peso per day, while those on foot got four reales; but since no reviews were held and there was no formal enlistment, this led to great theft and mayhem, even though a treasury was established in the charge of Don Mariano Hidalgo, the priest's brother. Mariano Hidalgo did not trouble himself to provide supplies or means of subsistence for the disorderly mob. In the middle of September, when the revolution began, the corn was ripening in the fields, and in that era of wealth and prosperity for agriculture, especially in the opulent province of Guanajuato, the haciendas abounded in livestock and all sorts of foodstuffs.

How unfortunate was the farm of a European which Hidalgo and his army chanced to pass by: with a tremendous cry of "Long live the Virgin of Guadalupe and death to the *gachupines!*" the Indians would scatter amid the cornfields and quickly gather in the harvest; they would open the granaries, and the grains stored there would be gone in moments; the stores, which nearly all of the haciendas had, were looted down to the bare bones. The insurgents would kill all of the oxen they needed, and if there were some Indian village nearby, they would destroy even the buildings in order to cart away the roof beams and doors. The haciendas of the Americans suffered less at the start of the war, but as it progressed all came to be treated in the same way.

THE CITY OF Guanajuato is situated at the base of a deep, narrow valley which is dominated on all sides by high rugged mountains. . . . The town had perhaps seventy thousand inhabitants including those of the mining camps. Of these, the Valenciana mines, which had been for many years enjoying uninterrupted prosperity, had something like twenty thousand people. The region enjoyed great abundance: the huge sums that were distributed each week among the people as wages for their work in the mines and related haciendas sparked commercial activity; the great consumption of foodstuffs by the people, and the pasturing of the many horses and mules used in the mining operations, had caused agriculture to flourish for many leagues around. In the city there were many rich homes, and many more which enjoyed a comfortable middle-class existence: commerce was almost exclusively in the hands of the Europeans, but many creole families supported themselves easily from mining-related activities, and they were all respectable in the orderliness of their dress and in the decorum they observed. The people, occupied in the hard and risky labor of the mines, were lively, happy, prodigal, and brave.

So populous a city, situated amid the craggy hills which have been aptly compared to a sheet of crumpled paper, could not defend itself unless the mass of its inhabitants were united; so it was essential that its defense have the support of the common people. This was made fully clear when the intendant sounded the general alarm on September 18: a large number of people came armed with rocks, and they occupied the hills, streets, plazas, and rooftops in the early morning of the 20th, when the advance guard at Marfil believed Hidalgo was drawing near, which is why the alarm was sounded, and the intendant with his troops and armed peasants rode down the glen to meet him. The intendant, however, believed from that moment that the people were changing their minds, and he feared that the lower classes of the city would join Hidalgo when he arrived; thus, he changed his plan, deciding instead to take cover at a strong, defensible point while awaiting aid from the Viceroy or from the troops which [General Félix] Calleja [commander-in-chief of the royalist forces] was supposed to recruit from San Luis Potosí.

In order to ensure the provision of corn, a food of primary necessity for the people and for many of the beasts employed in the mines, the intendant had built a spacious public granary, or *alhóndiga,* in which a quantity sufficient for a year's consumption could be stored, thus avoiding the inconvenience of frequent fluctuations in the price of this grain, which was caused especially by the difficulty of traveling the roads during the rainy season. He came up with this plan in 1783, which came to be known as "the year of hunger" due to the terrible shortages. He chose to construct this building on a site at the entrance to the city, on the slope where El Cuarto Hill ends to the west, which is the point where the river that passes through the town meets the one that flows down from the mines. . . . In building this structure, intendant Riaño hoped to show not only that he cared greatly about supplying the needs of the capital and of the province that it governed, but also that he had good taste in architecture. . . .

The Alhóndiga de Granaditas, which acquired so much and such lamentable celebrity on this occasion, was very sturdily built and it dominated the principal entrance to the city, but it was itself dominated by El Cuarto Hill . . . and by San Miguel Hill, which was a greater distance off to the south. This was the point where the intendant resolved to make a stand, and on the night of the 24th, without anyone realizing it, he moved his troops and armed peasants, as well as the entire royal treasury, the treasuries of the municipalities, and all of the archives of the government and city council [to the Alhóndiga]. . . .

At dawn on the 25th, the town was surprised to see the moats closed off and the trenches demolished, and [immediately] they knew everything that had happened the preceding night. There was general consternation at seeing the city abandoned, for nearly all of the Europeans with their treasures, as well as many creoles, had gone to the Alhóndiga and shut themselves in. As near as can be determined, the sum gathered there in silver ingots, cash, mercury from the royal treasury, and valuable objects was worth no less than three million pesos. So great was the wealth of the country back then that such a large sum was gathered in a few moments in one provincial city!

The city council of Guanajuato, in the explanation they sent to the Viceroy to vindicate their own conduct and that of the city's inhabitants, attributed the loss of the city and all the misfortunes that followed to the intendant's decision. They claimed that the lower classes would have remained faithful and resolute and that their spirit would not have strayed had they not noticed that they were being mistrusted, whereupon they began to say that the *gachupines* and high-toned gentlemen wanted to defend only themselves, abandoning the common people to the enemy, and therefore they began to disperse among the neighborhoods and hills in groups. . . .

The defenders took all measures necessary to make the Alhóndiga ready to withstand a siege. The siege would not be a long one, since [General] Calleja, in reply to the note of alarm that Riaño had sent him on the 23rd, said he would send assistance by Monday the 24th, and he and his troops would be in Guanajuato all the following week; he also said that he would advise [Riaño] as his troops drew near. In addition to 5,000 fanegas of corn that were stored in the Alhóndiga, the intendant had a large quantity of flour and provisions of all sorts brought, as well as twenty-four women to make tortillas. That was more than enough to sustain five to six hundred men gathered there for several months. Nor did they lack water, for the building had a capacious cistern on its patio, which was full at the time since the rainy season had just passed. More than thirty very large rooms . . . were full of food, gold, silver ingots and coins, mercury, and other things of value. They built three trenches to close off the principal avenues leading to the Alhóndiga. . . . All of these dispositions were directed by Don Gilberto de Riaño, the elder son of the intendant, who held the rank of lieutenant and served in the regular line regiment of Mexico City and who was on leave in his father's house. His father greatly respected his son's knowledge in such matters, for this gallant young man had diligently studied the works of the marquis of Santa Cruz and other military authors. Understanding the resolution to abandon the city and concentrate the defense exclusively in the Alhóndiga, Gilberto came up with the idea of making flasks of mercury into hand grenades. These are iron cylinders, about a foot tall and six inches in diameter, with narrow mouths closed with a screw: they are filled with powder and grapeshot, and a small hole is made for a wick, which is ignited at the proper time. Having assembled all of the arms and munitions in the city at the Alhóndiga, the east door was sealed off with an adobe wall; thus there was no way of getting in except by the principal door, which opened onto the small plaza to the north.

In order to win the people's hearts, the intendant, with great solemnity, published a proclamation on the morning of the 26th, abolishing the payment of tribute. This favor, which had been conceded by the regency back on the 26th of May, had not been put into effect on the pretext that a study had to be made first. Now, given the circumstances under which it was published, it was not only viewed coldly, but the lower classes of Guanajuato took it as a concession made from fear: it was met with mockery and jokes, and it ended up swaying the minds of the crowd against the government. In the moments of a revolution, the most beneficent actions done out of convenience, produce a result entirely contrary to the one desired. . . .

Hidalgo . . . returned from Celaya toward Guanajuato, at every step augmenting the crowd that followed him. Riaño knew well the difficulty of his position. "The people," he told Calleja on the 26th, "voluntarily surrender themselves to the insurgents. They already did so in Dolores, San Miguel, Celaya, Salamanca, Irapuato; the same shall soon happen at Silao. The seduction spreads here, there was no security or confidence. I have fortified myself in the most suitable place in the city, and I will fight to the death, if the five hundred men I have at my side do not forsake me. I have very little gunpowder, because there absolutely is none, and the cavalry is poorly mounted and armed, with no weapons but their glass swords,[3] and the infantry their mended rifles, and it is not impossible that these troops might be seduced [by the rebels]. The insurgents are bearing down on me, supplies are impeded, mail is intercepted. Sr. Abarca is working actively, and Your Excellency and he together must come to my assistance, because I fear being attacked at any moment. I must not continue, because since the 17th I have not been able to rest or get undressed, and it is three days since I slept for a whole hour." Such was the anguish of spirit and bodily fatigue that [Riaño] suffered in these grievous circumstances. The Europeans had grown dispirited, many of them abandoning the city and heading for Guadalajara, and the ones at the frontier of the sierra, at Santa Rosa and Villalpando, did the same, as they were unprotected.

[Translator's summary: At this point, Hidalgo sends two agents to demand that the city be surrendered and that all Spaniards be turned over to the insurgents. Intendant Riaño puts the proposal to a vote, and the defenders of the Alhóndiga declare that they will resist to the death. They make ready for a siege.]

The people of Guanajuato watched from the surrounding heights, some now deciding to join Hidalgo, others, no fewer in number, only watching so they would be ready when it came time to pillage. The people from the mines occupied the hill next to El Cuarto; these were mostly workers from the Valenciana mine who were roused by their administrator, Dasimiro Chovell, who was believed to have reached a prior agreement with Hidalgo.

A little before twelve o'clock, in the avenue of Our Lady of Guanajuato, which is the entrance to the city from the plains of Marfil, there appeared a huge crowd of Indians with few rifles; most were carrying lances, sticks, slings, and arrows. The first of this group passed the bridge . . . and arrived in front of the adjoining trench, at the foot of Mendizábal Hill. Gilberto de

Riaño—to whom his father had entrusted the command of that point, which he deemed the most hazardous—ordered them to stop in the name of the king, and since the crowd continued to advance, he gave the order to open fire, whereupon some Indians fell dead and the rest retreated hurriedly. In the avenue, a man from Guanajuato said they should go to El Cuarto Hill, and he showed them the way. The remaining groups of Hidalgo's footsoldiers, perhaps 20,000 Indians, joined by the people from the mines and the lower classes of Guanajuato, were occupying the heights and all of the houses around [the Alhóndiga de] Granaditas, in which they placed soldiers from Celaya armed with rifles; meanwhile a corps of around two thousand cavalrymen, composed of country people with lances, mixed in among the ranks of the dragoons of the Queen's regiment led by Hidalgo, climbed along the road called Yerbabuena and arrived at [the top of San Miguel Hill], and from there went down to the city. Hidalgo went to the headquarters of the Prince's cavalry regiment, where he remained throughout the action. The column continued crossing through the town in order to station itself at Belén Street, and as they passed by they sacked a store that sold sweets, and they freed all the prisoners of both sexes who were locked up in the jail—no fewer than three or four hundred persons, among them serious criminals. They made the male prisoners march on the Alhóndiga.

The intendant, noting that the largest number of the enemy rushed to the side of the trench at the mouth of Los Pozitos Street . . . thought it necessary to reinforce that point. He took twenty infantrymen from the company of the peasants to join the battalion, and with more boldness than prudence he went with them to station them where he wanted them to be, accompanied by his assistant, José María Bustamante. Upon returning, as he was climbing the stairs to the door of the Alhóndiga, he was wounded above the left eye by a rifle bullet and he immediately fell dead. The shot came from the window of one of the houses of the little plaza to the east of the Alhóndiga, and is said to have been fired by a corporal of the infantry regiment from Celaya. Thus, a glorious death ended the spotless life of the retired frigate captain Don Juan Antonio de Riaño, knight of the Order of Caltrava, intendant, *correjidor,* and commandant of the armies of Guanajuato. . . .

The intendant's death introduced division and discord among the defenders of the Alhóndiga at the moment when it was most necessary that they act in unison and with firm resolution. The counselor of the intendancy, Manuel Pérez Valdés, citing the fact that in the ordinance of the intendancy leadership falls to the counselor when the [intendant] is accidentally removed, claimed that since he was now the superior authority of the provinces, nothing should be done except by his command. He was inclined to surrender. Major Ber-

The Alhóndiga de Granaditas, Guanajuato. (Photo by Tim Henderson. Reprinted by permission of Tim Henderson.)

zabal argued that, since this was a purely military situation, according to the ordinance he should take charge, since he was the veteran officer of the highest rank. He was resolved to keep up the defense. While this dispute could not be resolved, the confusion of the attack meant that everyone was giving commands and no one was obeying them, except for the soldiers who always recognized their old leaders. The crowd on El Cuarto Hill began a barrage of stones, hurling them by hand and shooting them with slings, a barrage that was so continuous it exceeded the thickest hail storm. In order to keep the combatants supplied with stones, swarms of Indians and the people of Guanajuato unceasingly picked up the round stones that covered the bottom of the Cata River. So great was the number of stones launched in the short time that the attack lasted, that the floor of the Alhóndiga's balcony was raised about a quarter above its ordinary level. It was impossible to defend the trenches, and the troops that garrisoned them were ordered to withdraw; Captain Escalera of the guard ordered that the door of the Alhóndiga be closed. With that, the Europeans who occupied the Hacienda of Dolores were left isolated and with no recourse but to sell their lives dearly, and the cavalry on the slope of the Cata River was in the same situation or worse. Nor could the people on the roof defend themselves for long, since it was dominated by the hills El Cuarto and San Miguel, although since the latter was farther away, less damage was done from there. And despite the havoc caused by the continuous fire of the troops of the garrison, the number of assailants was so great that those who fell were very promptly replaced by others, and they were not missed.

Once the trenches were abandoned and the troops who defended the roof withdrawn, that wild mob rushed to the base of the building: those in front were pushed by those who followed, unable to turn around, as in an ocean storm when some waves are impelled by others till they dash against the rocks. The brave man could not show his mettle, nor could the coward find a way to flee. The cavalry was completely routed, unable to use its weapons and horses. Captain Castilla died, some soldiers perished; the rest joined the conquerors. The valiant José Francisco Valenzuela, turning his horse about, rode up the hill three times, opening a path with his sword; he was dragged from his saddle and suspended on the points of the lances of those who surrounded him in large numbers; even so, he killed some of those closest to him before receiving his death blow, shouting "Long live Spain!" until he gave up his final breath. He was a native of Irapuato and a lieutenant of the company of that village.

There was a store at the corner of Los Pozitos Street and Mount Los Mandamientos where they sold *ocote* [pine] chips, which the men who worked the mines by night used to illuminate the road. The crowd broke down the doors [of the store] and, loading up that fuel, they brought it to the door of the Alhóndiga and set it ablaze. Others, who were experienced at subterranean labors, approached the back of the building, which was surrounded by earthen walls, . . . [and they] began to drill holes to undermine the foundation. Those inside the building hurled iron flasks, of which we have spoken, through the windows down into the crowd. These would explode and bring down many people, but immediately the mob would close in tight and snuff out the flasks that had fallen under their feet, which is why there were so few wounded among the assailants, even though a large number were killed. The discord among those under siege was such that, at the very moment when Gilberto Riaño (who was thirsty for vengeance in his father's death), Miguel Bustamante, and others were hurling flasks at the assailants, the counselor held up a white handkerchief as a sign of peace. The people, attributing to perfidy what was nothing more than the effect of the confusion that prevailed inside the Alhóndiga, redoubled their furor and began to fight with greater cruelty. The counselor then ordered a soldier to climb down from a window to parley; the unfortunate man fell to the ground, broken to bits. Then Martín Septiem tried to leave, confident in his priestly vocation and in the Holy Christ he carried in his hands; the image of the Savior flew into splinters as stones struck it, and the priest, using the crucifix in his hand as an offensive weapon, managed to escape through the crowd, though badly wounded. The Spaniards, meanwhile, hearing only the voice of terror, tossed money from the windows in hopes of sparking the people's greed and thus placating the mob; others shouted their capitulation, and many, persuaded that their final hour had arrived, threw themselves at the feet of priests to receive absolution.

Berzabal, seeing the door ablaze, gathered what soldiers he could of the battalion and stationed them at the entrance: as the door was consumed by flames, he ordered his soldiers to fire at close range, and many of the assailants perished. Still, those in back of the crowd pushed forward, and the ones in front trampled over the dead, sweeping everything before them with an irresistible force. The patio, stairs, and corridors of the Alhóndiga were very soon filled with Indians and common people. Berzabal, retreating with a handful of men who remained with him to a corner of the patio, defended his battalion's banners along with the standard-bearers Marmolejo and González. When these men fell dead at his side, he gathered up the banners and held them tightly with his left arm, and he held out with a sword—even though it had been destroyed by a pistol shot—against the multitude that surrounded him, until he fell pierced by many lances, still without abandoning the banners he had sworn to defend. What a worthy example for Mexican soldiers, and a well-earned title of glory for the descendants of that valiant warrior!

[With Berzabal's death] all resistance ceased, and no more than a few isolated shots were heard from some who still held out, such as the Spaniard Raymayor, who did not let the Indians come near till all of his cartridges were spent. The Europeans at the Hacienda of Dolores tried to save themselves through a back door that opened upon the log bridge over the Cata River, but they found that the assailants had already taken that bridge. They then retired to the well, where—since it was a high, strong spot—they defended themselves until the last of their ammunition ran out, causing much carnage among the insurgents. . . . The few Europeans who remained alive at the end fell or were thrown into the well, and they drowned.

The taking of the Alhóndiga de Granaditas was entirely the work of the common people of Guanajuato, together with numerous bands of Indians led by Hidalgo. As for Hidalgo and his fellow leaders, there was not, nor could there have been, any disposition other than to lead the people to the hills and begin the attack. But once it had begun, it was impossible to maintain any order at all: there was no one to receive or follow orders, for there was no organization at all in that riotous crowd, nor were there lesser chiefs to lead the people. They rushed with extraordinary valor to take part in the first action of the war, and, once committed to combat, the Indians and people of the villages could not turn back, for the crowd surged forward upon those who went first, obliging them to win land and to instantaneously occupy any space left by those who died. The resistance of the besieged defenders, though intrepid, was without order or plan, since the intendant died before anyone else, and it is to this we may attribute the quick termination of the action, for by five in the afternoon it was all over.

The insurgents, after taking over the Alhóndiga, gave free reign to their vengefulness. Those who had surrendered begged their conquerors in vain for clemency; on their knees, they prayed that their lives be spared. Many of the soldiers of the battalion were dead; others escaped by taking off their uniforms and mixing with the crowd. Of the officers, many young men of the city's most distinguished families perished, and others were gravely wounded, among them Gilberto Riaño who died a few days later, and José María and Benigno Bustamante. Of the Spaniards, many of the richest and most important citizens died. . . . Some managed to hide in granary number 21, where the corpses of the intendant and several others lay, but they were discovered and killed without mercy. All were despoiled of their clothes. When the rebels stripped the corpse of José Miguel Carrica, they found he was covered with haircloth, which gave rise to the rumor that a *gachupín* saint had been found. Those who remained alive — naked, covered with wounds, tied up with rope — were taken to the public jail, which had been empty since the prisoners were freed. To get there, they had to cross the long expanse from the Alhóndiga while the unruly crowd threatened them with death at each step. It is said that, in order to avoid this menace, Captain José Joaquín Peláez managed to persuade his captors that Hidalgo had offered a cash reward if he were brought in alive, and thus he was guarded with greater care in that treacherous transit.

There are various calculations of the number of dead on both sides. The insurgents took pains to hide their dead, burying them that night in ditches they dug in the Cata River bottom. The city council, in its statement, estimated the dead at three thousand; Abásolo, at his trial, said that there were very few. The latter claim does not strike me as plausible, and the former I think is rather exaggerated. Some two hundred soldiers died, as well as one hundred and fifty Spaniards. Their naked corpses were seized by the feet and hands and carried or dragged to the nearby cemetery of Belén, where they were buried. The intendant's body spent two days exposed to the mockery of the mob: the people wished to investigate for themselves an absurd fable that had been circulating, which said that the intendant had a tail because he was a Jew. (This same ridiculous fable ran through the mob with respect to all of the Spaniards, even among those who had seen their naked corpses. Such is the ignorance of the common people!) . . . The [intendant's] body was then buried in a mean shroud that had been placed there by the monks of that convent, receiving none of the honor that should have been due the mortal remains of a noble conqueror. No sign of compassion was permitted: one woman in the crowd, who expressed sympathy when the corpse of a European was carried by, was wounded in the face by the men who carried it.

The people devoted themselves to pillaging everything that had been gathered at the Alhóndiga, and it all disappeared within a few moments. Hidalgo wanted to reserve the ingots of silver and money for himself, but he could not prevent the people from taking them. Later some of the ingots were found and taken back, for they belonged to the army's treasury and so could not be included in the general looting. The Alhóndiga presented the most dreadful spectacle: the food that had been stored there was scattered all around; naked corpses were found half-buried in corn and money, all of it stained with blood. The looters killed one another fighting among themselves for booty. A rumor spread that the granaries holding the stores of gunpowder had been burned, and that the castle — which is what the people called the Alhóndiga — was about to blow up; the Indians fled, and the people on horseback sped through the streets to escape. With that, the common people of Guanajuato, who may have been the ones who spread this rumor, remained sole owner of the prize — at least until the rest, their fear having evaporated, came back to take their share.

The people who had stayed on the hilltops awaiting the results now came down to take part in the despoliation, even though they had not been involved in the combat. Together with the rest of the townspeople and the Indians who had come with Hidalgo, they began the general looting of the stores and homes of the Europeans of the city, which began that same afternoon and continued all through the night and all the next day. They ransacked more pitilessly than any foreign army could have done. The sad scene on that mournful night was lit by many torches of candlewood and *ocote,* and nothing was heard but the blows of doors being battered down, and the ferocious howls of the rabble who applauded upon seeing them fall and then charged as if in triumph to steal the merchandise, furniture, clothing, and all kinds of things. Women fled in terror to their neighbors' homes, crawling across the roofs, and, still not knowing if they had lost a father or a husband in the Alhóndiga that afternoon; they watched as the treasures their men had collected during many years of work, industry, and economy were snatched away in an instant. Whole families who had awakened that day under the protection of a father or husband, some enjoying opulence, others taking pleasure in an honorable yet moderate lifestyle, lay down that night in a deplorable orphanhood and misery. It was not as if many people ceased being rich while just as many emerged from poverty: no, all those treasures that in active and industrious hands fomented commerce and mining, now went up in smoke without leaving any trace but a memory of ancient prosperity. It has taken many years to recover that prosperity, plus the great boost that Guanajuato later received from foreign mining companies and the fortuitous bonanzas some of these have enjoyed.

The looters grabbed the most valuable things from one another. The astute and clever people of Guanajuato took advantage of the ignorance of the Indians to take their loot away from them, or to buy it at a low price. They persuaded the Indians that ounces of gold were not coins, but copper medallions, and they bought them for two or three reales; they did the same with the jewelry, the value of which they themselves did not know. On the 29th, Hidalgo's birthday, Guanajuato presented the most lamentable aspect of disorder, ruin, and desolation. The plaza and the streets were full of fragments of furniture, the remains of the goods looted from the stores, and liquor that had been spilled once the people had drunk their fill. The people abandoned themselves to all manner of excess. Hidalgo's Indians made the strangest figures of all, for on top of their own clothing they wore the clothes they had taken from the homes of the Europeans, including the uniforms of magistrates, so that the Indians adorned themselves with embroidered dresscoats and gilded hats while barefoot and in the most complete state of inebriation.

The pillage was not limited to the homes and stores of the Europeans of the city; the same thing was done in the mines, and the looting became extensive at the metal-refining haciendas. The commoners of Guanajuato, having already killed in the Alhóndiga the industrious men of these establishments—the men who had enabled them to earn their keep by paying them considerable wages—now ruined the establishments themselves, dealing the death blow to that branch of mining that had been the source of the wealth not just of the city of Guanajuato, but of the whole province. Mexicans, too, were affected by all this devastation by virtue of the business relations they had with the Spaniards, especially in the field of metal refining. Some banking houses owned by Mexicans would advance the Spaniards funds at a discount on the value of the silver that they received in payment, according to the rules established in the mining ordinance for advances on the price of silver.

Hidalgo wanted to put a stop to this disorder, so he published a proclamation on Sunday, September 30. Not only was this proclamation not obeyed, but inasmuch as there was nothing left to loot in the houses and stores, the commoners began to drag the iron trellises down from the balconies, and they broke into the homes of Mexicans whom they suspected of hiding goods belonging to Spaniards. Among the homes so threatened was that of my own family, which was located atop a store that had belonged to a Spaniard who had died in the well at Dolores, a man named José Posadas. Although the home had already been sacked, one of Posadas's trusted porters let it be known that in an interior patio there was a storeroom that he himself had stocked with money and goods. It was very difficult to hold the people back: they entered through the mezzanine and made their way to the foot of the stairway. I was in no little danger myself, having been raised European. Amid this conflict, my mother resolved to go and see the priest Hidalgo, with whom she had longtime friendly relations, and I went with her. It was quite risky for a decently dressed person to walk the streets among that mob, drunk with rage and liquor. We nonetheless arrived without incident at the headquarters of the Prince's regiment, where Hidalgo was staying. We found Hidalgo in a room filled with people of all classes. In one corner there was a considerable stack of silver ingots that had been recovered from the Alhóndiga, and which were still stained with blood; in another corner was a stack of lances, and haphazardly suspended from one of the walls was the painting of the image of Guadalupe, which served as the symbol of this enterprise. The priest was seated on his field cot with a small table in front of him, wearing his ordinary costume, but with a purple shoulder-belt on top of the jacket, which appeared to be some portion of a priest's stole. He received us gladly, assuring my mother of their longtime friendship. Once made aware of our fears for the house, he gave us an escort commanded by a muleteer from the Cacalote Ranch near Salvatierra, Ignacio Centeno, whom Hidalgo had made a captain and whom he ordered to defend my house and to guard the belongings of Posadas. Hidalgo told the escort to bring those things to his lodgings as soon as possible, for he needed them to meet the expenses of his army. Centeno thought it would be impossible to hold back the growing tumult, for at each instant more and more people gathered determined to join in the looting. He sent one of his soldiers to Hidalgo, thinking the priest's presence would contain the disorder which the public proclamation had not been sufficient to do.

Hidalgo came on horseback to the plaza where my house was located, accompanied by his generals. At the head of the group was the painting of the image of Guadalupe, and an Indian on foot banging a drum. Some country people followed on horseback, along with some of the Queen's dragoons in two ranks. The priest and his generals presided over this procession-of-sorts, dressed in jackets like those worn by small town militia officers; in place of the insignia of the Queen's regiment, they had hung silver cords and tassels from their epaulets, which no doubt they had seen in some picture of the French generals' aides-de-camp; they all wore the image of the Virgin of Guadalupe on their hats. When Hidalgo's retinue arrived in front of the Posadas store where the largest mob was gathered, they ordered the mob to withdraw. When the people did not obey, [one of the officers] tried to keep them away from the doors of the store by forcing his way into the midst of the crowd. Nearby, the flagstones formed a sharp slope, and at the moment they were covered with all sorts of filth and were very slippery. [The officer] fell off his horse, and while trying to get up, he angrily drew his sword and began to wield it at the crowd; people fled in terror, leaving one man gravely wounded. Hidalgo continued circling the plaza, ordering that the men who were dragging the balconies off the houses be fired upon. With that the crowd began to disperse, though for some time large groups remained selling the objects they had ransacked for outrageous prices.

Hidalgo did his best to keep some things hidden from the people. Captain Centeno and the guards stayed for several days in my house at my family's expense, and they spent those days removing the money and other belongings from Posadas's interior storeroom and bringing them to the cavalry headquarters. It was determined that they were worth around 40,000 pesos. As Centeno became a familiar presence in my house, he was once asked for his views of the revolution in which he had taken part. He replied, with the sincerity of a humble man of the country, that his wishes could easily be summed up as follows: to go to Mexico City and place the priest on the throne, and then, with the rewards that Hidalgo would pay him for his services, he would return to working in the fields. What happened in my house with the belongings of Posadas was repeated in many other houses, since although there were faithful servants who helped to salvage what remained of their masters' treasures, others betrayed their masters and denounced the places where they had hidden their money and jewelry. . . .

When the tumult of the siege and sacking of the city had calmed somewhat, Hidalgo lodged his cavalrymen in the ransacked haciendas. The Indians remained scattered throughout the streets, and many of them, content with the loot they had taken, returned to their villages and *rancherías*. Desertion did not bother the priest at all, however, because he was sure he would find plenty of new recruits in all of the villages he passed through. . . .

Notes

1. Intendant: One of the reforms carried out by the Spanish Bourbons was the implementation of the intendancy system, wherein government-appointed, professional, salaried administrators oversaw the affairs of their districts. *Ed.*

2. Viceroy José de Iturrigaray (r. 1803–1808), after receiving news of the Napoleonic usurpation, allowed Mexican creoles to form a pro-creole junta, or caretaker government, in the name of Ferdinand VII. This junta, along with the viceroy himself, was overthrown by conservative *peninsulares* on September 15, 1808. *Ed.*

3. The armaments of the regiment were bad, and the swords broke easily, which is what the intendant referred to.

Sentiments of the Nation, or Points Outlined by Morelos for the Constitution

José María Morelos

After Hidalgo's death, another parish priest, José María Morelos, emerged as the most prominent military leader of the revolutionary forces. Morelos was a mestizo (some have described him as a mulatto) from Michoacán, who had studied briefly with Hidalgo and who joined the rebellion in its early stages. He was a far more competent disciplinarian and military strategist than Hidalgo had been, but his forces, too, were eventually scattered, and he was captured and executed in 1815. In 1813 he declared independence and convoked a Constitutional Congress at Chilpancingo, Guerrero, where he presented a summary of his political and social ideas. They make for curious reading today, since they feature many concepts that would soon be clearly identified with "liberalism"—for example, the equality of individuals before the law, popular sovereignty, fair taxation, and an end to slavery and servitude—while at the same time upholding strict religious intolerance and established hierarchies.

1. That America is free and independent of Spain and of all other Nations, Governments, or Monarchies, and it should be so sanctioned, and the reasons explained to the world.

2. That the Catholic Religion is the only one, without tolerance of any other.

3. That all ministers of the Church shall support themselves exclusively and entirely from tithes and first-fruits (*primicias*), and the people need make no offering other than their own devotions and oblations.

4. That Catholic dogma shall be sustained by the Church hierarchy, which consists of the Pope, the Bishops and the Priests, for we must destroy every plant not planted by God: *minis plantatis quam nom plantabir Pater meus Celestis Cradicabitur.* Mat. Chapt. XV.

5. That sovereignty springs directly from the People, who wish only to deposit it in their representatives, whose powers shall be divided into Legislative, Executive, and Judiciary branches, with each Province electing its representa-

tive. These representatives will elect all others, who must be wise and virtuous people. . . .

6. [Article 6 is missing from all reproductions of this document. *Ed.*]

7. That representatives shall serve for four years, at which point the oldest ones will leave so that those newly elected may take their places.

8. The salaries of the representatives will be sufficient for sustenance and no more, and for now they shall not exceed 8,000 pesos.

9. Only Americans shall hold public office.

10. Foreigners shall not be admitted, unless they are artisans capable of teaching [their crafts], and are free of all suspicion.

11. That the fatherland shall never belong to us nor be completely free so long as the government is not reformed. [We must] overthrow all tyranny, substituting liberalism, and remove from our soil the Spanish enemy that has so forcefully declared itself against this Nation.

12. That since good law is superior to all men, those laws dictated by our Congress must oblige constancy and patriotism, moderate opulence and indigence, and be of such nature that they raise the income of the poor, better their customs, and banish ignorance, rapine, and robbery.

13. That the general laws apply to everyone, without excepting privileged bodies, and that such bodies shall exist in accordance with the usefulness of their ministry.

14. That in order to dictate a law, Congress must debate it, and it must be decided by a plurality of votes.

15. That slavery is proscribed forever, as well as the distinctions of caste, so that all shall be equal; and that the only distinction between one American and another shall be that between vice and virtue.

16. That our ports shall be open to all friendly foreign nations, but no matter how friendly they may be, foreign ships shall not be based in the kingdom. There will be some ports specified for this purpose; in all others, disembarking shall be prohibited, and 10% or some other tax shall be levied upon their merchandise.

17. That each person's home shall be as a sacred asylum wherein to keep property and observances, and infractions shall be punished.

18. That the new legislation shall forbid torture.

19. That the Constitution shall establish that the 12th of December be celebrated in all villages in honor of the patroness of our liberty, the Most Holy Mary of Guadalupe. All villages shall be required to pay her monthly devotion.

20. That foreign troops or those of another kingdom shall not tread upon our soil unless it be to aid us, and if this is the case, they shall not be part of the Supreme Junta.

21. That there shall be no expeditions outside the limits of the kingdom, especially seagoing ones. Expeditions shall only be undertaken to propagate the faith to our brothers in the remote parts of the country.

22. That the great abundance of highly oppressive tributes, taxes and impositions should be ended, and each individual shall pay five percent of his earnings, or another equally light charge, which will be less oppressive than the *alcabala* [sales tax], the *estanco* [crown monopoly], the tribute, and others. This small contribution, and the wise administration of the goods confiscated from the enemy, shall be sufficient to pay the costs of the war and the salaries of public employees.

23. That the 16th of September shall be celebrated each year as the anniversary of the cry of independence and the day our sacred liberty began, for on that day the lips of the Nation parted and the people proclaimed their rights, and they grasped the sword so that they would be heard, remembering always the merits of the great hero, señor don Miguel Hidalgo y Costilla, and his *compañero,* don Ignacio Allende.

Chilpancingo, 14 September 1813.

José María Morelos

Plan of Iguala

Agustín de Iturbide

After more than ten years of sporadic violence, when the fighters for independence had been reduced to little more than guerrilla bands, Mexican independence was quickly and unexpectedly consummated when a royalist general, Agustín de Iturbide, reached an understanding with rebel leaders and issued a vague declaration of independence in the town of Iguala (in what is now the southern state of Guerrero). Former royalists and rebels joined forces and rallied around this plan of the "Three Guarantees," which celebrated the broadest points of agreement among the contending factions: independence, the union and equality of creoles (American-born whites) and Spaniards, and Roman Catholicism. Iturbide, whose reputation as a military leader was for brutality rather than prescience, failed to anticipate the many challenges and difficulties that came with Mexico's new political autonomy. His relations with the Constituent Congress created by the plan were troubled from the outset. They reached a breaking point when Iturbide, trumpeting the fact that neither Ferdinand VII nor any other European prince showed any interest in becoming Emperor of Mexico, had himself crowned Emperor Agustín I. Resistance to this presumptuous move culminated in a rebellion headed by another former royalist officer, Antonio López de Santa Anna, the young commander of the Veracruz garrison—a rebellion that ousted Iturbide in March 1823. Thus began a long period of penury and chronic political turbulence that quickly shattered the exuberant optimism apparent in the Plan of Iguala.

24 February 1821

Americans:

When I speak of Americans, I speak not only of those persons born in America, but of the Europeans, Africans, and Asians who reside here. May they all have the good grace to hear me!

The largest Nations of the Earth have been dominated by other Nations, and so long as they were not permitted to form their own opinions, they were not free. The European countries, although they achieved great heights in education and politics, were once slaves to the Roman Empire. That Empire, the most renowned in history, was like a father who, in his dotage, watched as his children and grandchildren left home, for they were of an age to start homes of their own and to fend for themselves, though they maintained all the respect, veneration and love due their father.

For three hundred years, North America was under the tutelage of Spain, the Most Catholic and pious, heroic and magnanimous of Nations. Spain educated and aggrandized it, forming its opulent cities, its beautiful villages, its remote provinces and kingdoms, increasing its population and splendors, knowing every aspect of the natural opulence of its soil, its rich minerals, the advantages of its geographical situation. We have seen the damage caused by our great distance from the center of the Empire, and we know that the branch is now the equal of the trunk: public and general opinion declare that we should be absolutely independent from Spain and from all other Nations. Europeans and Americans from all regions likewise believe this to be so.

That same voice which sounded in the village of Dolores in 1810, and which caused the people so much hardship due to the disorder, abandonment, and a multitude of vices, also convinced the people that a general union between Europeans, Americans, and Indians, is the only solid basis upon which our common happiness can rest. After the horrible experience of so many disasters, is there anyone who is now unwilling to support that union through which so much good can be achieved? European Spaniards: your fatherland is America, because you live here; here you shall have commerce and possessions! Americans: Who among you can say that you are not descended from Spaniards? We are held together by a dulcet chain formed by links of friendship, common interests, education and language, and a unity of sentiments. You shall see that these are close and powerful links, and that the happiness of the Kingdom depends on everyone uniting in a single opinion and speaking with a single voice.

The time has come to manifest the uniformity of your sentiments, so that our union can be the powerful hand that emancipates America without the need of foreign help. At the head of a valiant and resolved army, I have proclaimed the Independence of North America! It is now free, it is now its own Master, it no longer recognizes or depends upon Spain or any other Nation. All shall greet it as an Independent Nation, and, with gallant hearts, we shall raise our voices, together with those of the troops that have resolved to die before abandoning this heroic enterprise. The Army is not animated by any desire other than to keep pure the Holy Religion we profess, and to preserve the general happiness. Listen, here is the firm basis upon which we found our resolution:

ART. 1. The Roman, Catholic, Apostolic Religion, without tolerance of any other.

ART. 2. The absolute Independence of this Kingdom.

ART. 3. Monarchical Government, limited by a Constitution suitable for the country.

ART. 4. Ferdinand VII or someone of his dynasty, or some other prince, shall become Emperor. We shall have an established monarchy so as to prevent acts of ambition.

ART. 5. There shall be an interim committee [*junta*] which shall convoke a Congress [Cortes] to enact this Plan.

ART. 6. This committee shall name a Governing body, and it will be composed of the representatives already proposed to the Viceroy.

ART. 7. It shall govern in accordance with the oath already made to the King, until the King shall come to Mexico, whereupon all previous orders shall be suspended.

ART. 8. If Ferdinand VII decides not to come to Mexico, the Committee of the Regency shall govern in the name of the Nation until the matter of who shall be crowned king is resolved.

ART. 9. This Government shall be sustained by the Army of the Three Guarantees.

ART. 10. The Congress shall decide if the Committee should continue or be replaced by a Regency until the arrival of the Emperor.

ART. 11. As soon as it is completed, the Constitution of the Mexican Empire shall enter into effect.

ART. 12. All of the inhabitants of that Empire, with no considerations except those of merit and virtue, are citizens qualified to accept any employment.

ART. 13. All persons and properties shall be respected and protected.

ART. 14. The Regular and Secular Clergy shall retain all of their properties and privileges.

ART. 15. All Government officers and public employees shall remain in office, and shall be removed only if they oppose this plan. Those opposed to the plan shall be replaced by those who distinguish themselves by their adhesion to the plan, as well as by their virtue and merit.

ART. 16. A protecting Army shall be formed, which shall be called the Army of the Three Guarantees. Any of its members, from the highest to the lowest ranks, shall be executed if they violate any one of the Three Guarantees.

ART. 17. This Army shall observe their Orders to the letter, and its Chiefs and Officers shall continue on the same footing as before.

ART. 18. The troops that compose the Army shall be considered as troops of the line, as shall all who come to embrace this Plan: all other citizens shall be considered a National Militia, and the rules for this and the form it shall take shall be decided by Congress.

ART. 19. Military ranks shall be determined by reports from the respective Chiefs, and shall be granted provisionally in the name of the Nation.

ART. 20. The interim Congress shall meet and proceed against crimes in complete accordance with the Spanish Constitution.

ART. 21. Those who conspire against Independence shall be consigned to prison; no further measures shall be taken against them until Congress dictates the punishment corresponding to the most serious crimes, including treason against His Divine Majesty.

ART. 22. Those who try to spread division and who are reputed to be conspirators against Independence shall be subject to close vigilance.

ART. 23. Inasmuch as the Congress which has been formed is a constituent Congress, Deputies must be elected with this understanding. The Committee will decide on the rules and the time necessary for the task [of writing a Constitution].

Americans:

Herewith, the establishment and the creation of a new Empire. Herewith, the oath of the army of the Three Guarantees, whose voice is that of he who has the honor of leading it. Herewith, the object for which I ask your cooperation. I ask of you no more than what you yourselves have wished and longed for: union, fraternity, order, interior calm, vigilance, and horror toward any turbulent movement. These warriors want nothing more than the common happiness. Join us to bravely advance an enterprise that in all aspects (excepting, perhaps, the small role I have played in it) must be called heroic. Having no enemies to combat, we trust in the God of the Armies, who is also the God of Peace, that those who make up this armed force, which brings together Europeans and Americans, dissidents and royalists, will be mere protectors, simple spectators to the great task that I have outlined today, which the fathers of the Nation shall retouch and perfect.

May the great Nations of Europe marvel at seeing how North America frees itself without shedding a single drop of blood. In your joyful celebrations, say: Long live the Holy Religion we profess! Long live Independent North America, among all the Nations of the Earth! Long live the union that brings our happiness!

Agustín de Iturbide

Women and War in Mexico

Frances Calderón de la Barca

The most famous of all foreigners' accounts of life in nineteenth-century Mexico is that of Fanny Calderón de la Barca, the Scottish-born wife of the first Spanish Minister to Mexico. Her lively letters to friends and family on both social and political matters, written between 1839 and 1842, form the basis of her enduring volume, Life in Mexico (1843).

Calderón's remarks on elite Mexican women consist, as she herself admitted, of sweeping generalizations, and they betray her for what she was—an upper-class foreigner who believed strongly in certain social conventions, albeit one with a droll sense of humor and a witty writing style. Nor did Mrs. Calderón shrink from reporting on the political affairs of her day. To lightly paraphrase her remarks below: "When a woman's head is about to be blown off, it's quite natural for her to ask why." Her account here of a failed rebellion by the Liberal forces of Valentín Gómez Farías in 1840 affords considerable insight into the nature of Mexican politics in the early days of the republic. While Calderón joins the participants in the event in speaking of "revolution," the matter hardly deserves such lofty terminology. Only a small portion of the population is involved in the fray. Most of the common folk scurry to get out of the way of the contenders, apparently caring little for the stirring pronouncements issued by both sides. The reader gets the sense of witnessing a bit of political theater rather than a meaningful attempt to set the nation upon a worthy course.

July 5, 1840

You ask me how Mexican women are educated. In answering you, I must put aside a few brilliant exceptions, and speak en masse, the most difficult thing in the world, for these exceptions are always rising up before me like accusing angels, and I begin to think of individuals, when I should keep to generalities. Generally speaking, then, the Mexican Señoras and Señoritas write, read and play a little, sew, and take care of their houses and children. When I say they read, I mean that they know how to read; when I say they write, I do not mean that they can always spell; and when I say they play, I do not assert that they have generally a knowledge of music. If we compare their education with that of girls in England, or in the United States, it is not a comparison, but a contrast. Compare it with that of Spanish women, and we shall be less severe upon their *far niente* descendants. . . . [As] to schools, there are none that can deserve the name, and no governesses. Young girls can have no emulation, for they never meet. They have no public diversion, and no private amusement. There are a few good foreign masters, most of whom have come to Mexico for the purpose of making their fortune, by teaching, or marriage, or both, and whose object, naturally, is to make the most money in the shortest possible time, that they might return home and enjoy it. The children generally appear to have an extraordinary disposition for music and drawing, yet there are few girls who are proficient in either.

When very young, they occasionally attend the schools where boys and girls learn to read in common, or any other accomplishment that the old women can teach them; but at twelve they are already considered too old to attend these promiscuous assemblages, and masters are got for drawing and music to finish their education. I asked a lady the other day if her daughter went to school. "Good heavens!" said she, quite shocked, "she is past eleven years old!" It frequently happens that the least well-informed girls are the children of the cleverest men, who, keeping to the customs of their forefathers, are content if they confess regularly, attend church constantly, and can embroider and sing a little. Where there are more extended ideas, it is chiefly amongst families who have traveled in Europe, and have seen the different education of women in foreign countries. Of these the fathers occasionally devote a short portion of their time to the instruction of their daughters, perhaps during their leisure evening moments, but it may easily be supposed that this desultory system has little real influence on the minds of the children. I do not think there are above half-a-dozen married women, or as many girls above fourteen who, with the exception of the mass-book, read any one book through in the whole course of the year. They thus greatly simplify the system of education in the United States, where parties are frequently divided between the advocates for solid learning and those for superficial accomplishments; and according to whom it is difficult to amalgamate the solid beef of science with the sweet sauce of *les beaux arts.*

But if a Mexican girl is ignorant, she rarely shows it. They have generally the greatest possible tact; never by any chance wandering out of their depth, or betraying by word or sign that they are not well informed of the subject under discussion. Though seldom graceful, they are never awkward, and always self-possessed. They have plenty of natural talent, and where it has been thoroughly cultivated, no women can surpass them. Of what is called literary society, there is of course none. . . .

There is a little annual lying beside me called *"Calendario de las Señoritas Mejicanas,"* of which the preface, by Galván, the editor, is very amusing.

"To none," he says, "better than to Mexican ladies, can I dedicate this mark of attention — (*obsequio*). Their graceful attractions well deserve any trouble that may have been taken to please them. Their bodies are graceful as the palms of the desert; their hair black as ebony, or golden as the rays of the sun, gracefully waves over their delicate shoulders; their glances are like the peaceful light of the moon. The Mexican ladies are not so white as the Europeans, but their whiteness is more agreeable to our eyes. Their words are soft, leading our hearts by gentleness, in the same manner as in their moments of just indignation they appall and confound us. Who can resist the magic of their song, always sweet, always gentle and always natural? Let us leave to foreign ladies (*las ultramarinas*) these affected and scientific manners of singing; here, nature surpasses art, as happens in everything, notwithstanding the cavillings of the learned.

"And what shall I say of their souls? I shall say that in Europe the minds are more cultivated, but in Mexico the hearts are more amiable. Here they are not only sentimental, but tender; not only soft, but virtuous; the body of a child is not more sensitive, (*no es mas sensible el cuerpo de un niño*), nor a rose-bud softer. I have seen souls as beautiful as the borders of the rainbow, and purer than the drops of dew. Their passions are seldom tempestuous, and even then they are kindled and extinguished easily; but generally they emit a peaceful light, like the morning star, Venus. Modesty is painted in their eyes, and modesty is the greatest and most irresistible fascination of their souls. In short, the Mexican ladies, by their manifold virtues, are destined to serve as our support whilst we travel through the sad desert of life. . . ."

There are in Mexico a few families of the old school, people of high rank, but who mingle very little in society; who are little known to the generality of foreigners, and who keep their daughters entirely at home, that they may not be contaminated by bad example. These select few, rich without ostentation, are certainly doing everything that is in their power to remedy the evils occasioned by the want of proper schools, or of competent instructresses for their daughters. Being nearly all allied by birth, or connected by marriage, they form a sort of *clan;* and it is sufficient to belong to one or other of these families, to be hospitably received by all. They meet together frequently, without ceremony, and whatever elements of good exist in Mexico, are to be found amongst them. The fathers are generally men of talent and learning, and the mothers, women of the highest respectability, to whose name no suspicion can be attached.

But, indeed, it is long before a stranger even suspects the state of morals in the country, for whatever be the private conduct of individuals, the most perfect decorum prevails in outward behaviour. . . .

They are besides extremely *leal* [loyal] to each other, and with proper *esprit de corps,* rarely gossip to strangers concerning the errors of their neighbours' ways; indeed, if such a thing is hinted at, [they] deny all knowledge of the fact. So long as outward decency is preserved, habit has rendered them entirely indifferent as to the *liaisons* subsisting amongst their particular friends; and as long as a woman attends church regularly, is a patroness of charitable institutions, and gives no scandal by her outward behaviour, she may do pretty much as she pleases. As for flirtations in public, they are unknown.

I must, however, confess that this indulgence on the part of women of unimpeachable reputation is sometimes carried too far. We went lately to a breakfast, at which was a young and beautiful countess, lately married, and of very low birth. She looked very splendid, with all the . . . diamonds, and a dress of rose-coloured satin. After breakfast we adjourned to another room, where I admired the beauty of a little child who was playing about on the floor, when this lady said, "Yes, she is very pretty—very like my little girl, who is just the same age." I was rather surprised, but concluded she had been a widow, and made the inquiry of an old French lady who was sitting near me. "Oh, no!" said she—"she was never married before; she alludes to the children she had before the count became acquainted with her!" And yet the Señora de——, the strictest woman in Mexico, was loading her with attentions and caresses. I must say, however, that this was a singular instance. . . .

There are no women more affectionate in their manners than those of Mexico. In fact, a foreigner, especially if he be an Englishman, and a shy man, and accustomed to the coolness of his fair countrywomen, need only live a few years here, and understand the language, and become accustomed to the peculiar style of beauty, to find the Mexican Señoritas perfectly irresistible.

And that this is so, may be judged of by the many instances of Englishmen married to the women of this country, who *invariably* make them excellent wives. But when an Englishman marries here, he ought to settle here, for it is very rare that a *Mexicaine* can live out of her own country. They miss the climate—they miss the warmth of manner, that universal cordiality by which they are surrounded here. They miss the *laissez-aller* and absence of all etiquette in habits, toilet, etc. They find themselves surrounded by women so differently educated, as to be doubly strangers to them, strangers in feeling as well as in country. A very few instances there are of girls, married very young, taken to Europe, and introduced into good society, who have acquired European ways of thinking, and even prefer other countries to their own; but this is so rare, as scarcely to form an exception. They are true patriots, and the visible horizon bounds their wishes. In England especially, they are completely out of their element. A language nearly impossible for them to acquire, a religion which they consider heretical, outward coldness covering inward warmth, a perpetual war between sun and fog, etiquette carried to excess, and insupportable stiffness and order in the article of the toilet; rebosos unknown, *cigaritos* considered barbarous. . . . They feel like exiles from paradise, and live but in hopes of a speedy return. . . .

July 15, 1840

Revolution in Mexico! or *Pronunciamiento,* as they call it. The storm which has for some time been brewing, has burst forth at last. Don Valentín Gómez Farías and the banished General Urrea have pronounced for federalism. At two this morning, joined by the fifth battalion and the regiment of *comercio,* they took up arms, set off for the palace, surprised the president in his bed, and took him prisoner. . . . Some say that it will end in a few hours—others, that it will be a long and bloody contest. Some are assured that it will merely terminate in a change of ministry—others that Santa Anna will come on directly and usurp the presidency. At all events, General Valencia, at the head of the government troops, is about to attack the pronunciados, who are in possession of the palace. . . .

The firing has begun! People come running up the street. The Indians are hurrying back to their villages in double-quick trot. As we are not in the centre of the city, our position for the present is very safe, all the cannon being directed towards the palace. All the streets near the square are planted with cannon, and it is pretended that the revolutionary party are giving arms to the *léperos* [the urban poor]. The cannon are roaring now. All along the street people are standing on the balconies, looking anxiously in the direction of the palace, or collected in groups before the doors, and the azoteas, which are out of the line of fire, are covered with men. They are ringing the tocsin—things seem to be getting serious.

Nine o'clock, P.M.—Continuation of firing without interruption. I have spent the day standing on the balcony, looking at the smoke, and listening to the different rumours. Gómez Farías has been proclaimed president by his party. The streets near the square are said to be strewed with dead and wounded. There was a terrible thunderstorm this afternoon. Mingled with the roaring of the cannon, it sounded like a strife between heavenly and earthly artillery. We shall not pass a very easy night, especially without our soldiers. Unfortunately there is a bright moon, so night brings no interruption to the firing and slaughter. . . .

17th. — The state of things is very bad. Cannon planted all along the streets, and soldiers firing indiscriminately on all who pass. Count C——— [is] slightly wounded, and carried to his country-house at Tacubaya. Two Spaniards have escaped from their house, into which the balls were pouring, and have taken refuge here. The E——— family have kept their house, which is in the very centre of the affray, cannons planted before their door, and all their windows already smashed. Indeed, nearly all the houses in that quarter are abandoned. We are living here like prisoners in a fortress. The Countess del V———e, whose father was shot in a former revolution, had just risen this morning, when a shell entered the wall close by the side of her bed, and burst in the mattress. . . .

18th. — There is a great scarcity of provisions in the centre of the city, as the Indians, who bring in everything from the country, are stopped. We have laid in a good stock of *comestibles,* though it is very unlikely that any difficulties will occur in our direction. While I am writing, the cannon are roaring almost without interruption, and the sound is anything but agreeable, though proving the respect entertained by Farías for "the lives, properties, and interests of all." We see the smoke, but are entirely out of the reach of the fire.

I had just written these words, when the Señora ——— who lives opposite, called out to me that a shell had just fallen in her garden, and that her husband had but time to save himself. The cannon directed against the palace kill people in their beds, in streets entirely out of that direction, while this ball, intended for the citadel, takes its flight to San Cosme! Both parties seem to be *fighting the city* instead of each other; and this manner of firing from behind parapets, and from the tops of houses and steeples, is decidedly safer for the soldiers than for the inhabitants. It seems also a novel plan to keep up a continual cannonading by night, and to rest during a great part of the day. One would think that were the guns brought nearer the palace, the affair would be sooner over. . . .

19th. — . . . My writing must be very desultory. Impossible to fix one's attention on anything. We pass our time on the balconies, listening to the thunder of the cannon, looking at the different parties of troops riding by, receiving visitors, who, in the intervals of the firing, venture out to bring us the last reports — wondering, speculating, fearing, hoping, and excessively tired of the whole affair.

Gómez Farías, the prime mover of this revolution, is a distinguished character, one of the *notabilities* of the country, and has always maintained the same principles, standing up for "rapid and radical reform." He is a native of Guadalajara, and his literary career is said to have been brilliant. He is also said to be a man of an ardent imagination and great energy. His name has appeared in every public event. He first aided in the cause of Independence, then, when deputy for Zacatecas, showed much zeal in favour of Yturbide — was afterwards a warm partisan of the federal cause — contributed to the election of General Victoria, afterwards to that of Pedraza — took an active part in the political changes of '33 and '34; detests the Spaniards, and during his presidency endeavoured to abolish the privileges of the clergy and troops — suppressed monastic institutions — granted absolute liberty of opinion — abolished the laws against the liberty of the press — created many literary institutions, and whatever were his political errors, and the ruthlessness with which in the name of liberty and reform he marched to the attainment of his object, without respect for the most sacred things, he is generally allowed to be a man of integrity, and even by his enemies, an enthusiast, who deceives himself as much as others. Now in the hopes of obtaining some uncertain and visionary good, and even while declaring his horror of civil war and bloodshed, he has risen in rebellion against the actual government, and is the cause of the cruel war now raging, not in the open fields or even in the scattered suburbs, but in the very heart of a populous city.

This morning all manner of opinions are afloat. Some believe that Santa Anna has started from his retreat at Manga de Clavo, and will arrive to-day — will himself swallow the disputed oyster (the presidential chair), and give each of the combatants a shell apiece; some that a fresh supply of troops for the government will arrive to-day, and others that the rebels must eventually triumph. Among the reports which I trust may be classed as doubtful, is, that General Urrea has issued a proclamation, promising *three hours' pillage* to all who join him. Then will be the time for testing the virtues of all the diplomatic *drapeaux*. . . .

20th. — We were astonished this morning at the general tranquillity, and concluded that, instead of having attacked the rebels, the government was holding a parley with them, but a note from the English minister informs us that a skirmish has taken place between the two parties at one of the gates of the city, in which the government party has triumphed. So far the news is good.

Our street has a most picturesque and lively appearance this morning. It is crowded with Indians from the country, bringing in their fruit and vegetables for sale, and establishing a temporary market in front of the church of San Fernando. Innumerable carriages, drawn by mules, are passing along,

packed inside and out, full of families hurrying to the country with their children and movables. Those who are poorer are making their way on foot—
men and women carrying mattresses, and little children following with baskets and bird-cages—carts are passing, loaded with chairs and tables and beds,
and all manner of old furniture, uprooted for the first time no doubt since
many years—all are taking advantage of this temporary cessation of firing to
make their escape. Our stables are full of mules and horses sent us by our
friends in the centre of the city, where all supplies of water are cut off. . . .

21st.—After passing a sleepless night, listening to the roaring of cannon,
and figuring to ourselves the devastation that must have taken place, we find
to our amusement that nothing decisive has occurred. The noise last night
was mere skirmishing, and half the cannons were fired in the air. In the darkness there was no mark. But though the loss on either side is so much less
than might have been expected, the rebels in the palace cannot be very comfortable, for they say that the air is infected by the number of unburied dead
bodies lying there; indeed there are many lying unburied on the streets, which
is enough to raise a fever, to add to the calamitous state of things. . . .

It is now evening, and again they announce an attack upon the palace, but
I do not believe them, and listen to the cannon with tolerable tranquillity. All
day families continue to pass by, leaving Mexico. The poor shopkeepers are to
be pitied. Besides the total cessation of trade, one at least has been shot, and
others plundered. A truce of two hours was granted this afternoon, to bury
the dead, who were carried out of the palace. . . .

26th.—. . . Firing continues, but without any decided result. It is a sound
that one does not learn to hear with indifference. There seems little doubt that
ultimately the government will gain the day, but the country will no doubt
remain for some time in a melancholy state of disorder. Bills are fastened today on the corners of the streets, forbidding all ingress or egress through the
military lines, from six in the evening till eight in the morning. Gentlemen
who live near us now venture in towards evening, to talk politics or play at
whist; but generally, in the middle of a game, some report is brought in, which
drives them back to their houses and families with all possible haste. . . .

Last night the archbishop paid a visit to the president, in the convent of San
Agustín, to intercede in favour of the *pronunciados*. The mortars have not yet
played against the palace, owing, it is said, to the desire of the general-in-chief
to avoid the further effusion of blood.

The tranquillity of the sovereign people during all this period, is astonishing. In what other city in the world would they not have taken part with one
or other side? Shops shut workmen out of employment, thousands of idle
people, subsisting, Heaven only knows how, yet no riot, no confusion, appar-

Death Attacks Even the Young Woman. (From Joaquín
Bolaños, *La portentosa vida de la muerte, emperatriz de los
sepulcros . . .* [1792])

ently no impatience. Groups of people collect on the streets, or stand talking
before their doors, and speculate upon probabilities, but await the decision of
their military chiefs as if it were a judgment from Heaven, from which it were
both useless and impious to appeal.

27th. — "Long live the Mexican Republic! Long live the Supreme Government!" Thus begins the government bulletin of to-day, to which I say Amen!
with all my heart, since it ushers in the news of the termination of the revolution. And what particularly attracts my attention is, that instead of the usual
stamp, the eagle, serpent, and nopal, we have to-day, a shaggy pony, flying
as never did mortal horse before, his tail and mane in a most violent state of
excitement, his four short legs all in the air at once, and on his back a man
in a jockey cap, furiously blowing a trumpet, from which issues a white flag,

on which is printed "News!" *in English!* and apparently in the act of springing over a milestone, on which is inscribed, also in English—"100 *to New York!*"

"We have," says the government, "the grateful satisfaction of announcing that the revolution of this capital has terminated happily. The rebellious troops having offered, in the night, to lay down arms upon certain conditions, his Excellency, the Commander-in-Chief, has accepted their proposals with convenient modifications, which will be verified to-day; the empire of laws, order, tranquillity, and all other social guarantees being thus re-established," etc. Cuevas, Minister of the Interior, publishes a circular addressed to the governors of the departments to the same effect, adding, that "in consideration of the inhabitants and properties which required the prompt termination of this disastrous revolution, the guarantees of personal safety solicited by the rebels have been granted, but none of their pretensions have been acceded to; the conspiracy of the fifteenth having thus had no other effect but to make manifest the general wish and opinion in favour of the government, laws, and legitimate authorities." A similar circular is published by General Almonte.

Having arrived at this satisfactory conclusion, which must be as agreeable to you as it is to us, I shall close this long letter, merely observing, in apology, that as Madame de Stael said, in answer to the remark, that "Women have nothing to do with politics,"—"That may be, but when a woman's head is about to be cut off, it is natural she should ask *why?*" so it appears to me, that when bullets are whizzing about our ears, and shells falling within a few yards of us, it ought to be considered extremely natural, and quite feminine, to inquire into the cause of such *phenomena.*

The Glorious Revolution of 1844

Guillermo Prieto

Anastasio Bustamante, the president against whom the 1840 rebellion was fought, succumbed to a successful rebellion the following year. This one resulted in the provisional presidency of Antonio López de Santa Anna, Mexico's most durable caudillo. Santa Anna ruled in very intemperate and imperious fashion, disbanding Congress when it tried to pass a constitution guaranteeing human rights and an end to special privileges and monopolies, and granting himself, as president, powers that were practically absolute. The rebellion against Santa Anna, declared in 1844, went quickly and smoothly, ending in his arrest and, supposedly, permanent exile (though in fact, he would continue to be a force in Mexican politics for another ten years).

The following excerpt, by one of Santa Anna's many detractors, describes the decadence of Santa Anna's "Court," and celebrates the 1844 rebellion (in the hyperbolic fashion of the time) as one of the purest and noblest in Mexico's history. Guillermo Prieto (1818–1897) was a poet, educator, historian, and political supporter of liberal causes. He would later act as finance minister in the Liberal government of Benito Juárez.

The peculiar conditions that our society inherited from colonial tradition meant that all power and life were centered in Mexico City. The city was the source of jobs and favors, the wellspring of business, the center of entertainment and fashion, the meeting place for wealthy people from all over, and the ledger where civilization recorded its achievements and treasures.

The court of Santa Anna had much luster, and although discontent and misery reigned in the provinces, around the dictator there were daily dances and banquets, and the meetings in the home of Señora Vallejos in San Angel were among the best and most exclusive ever seen in Mexico. Of course, everything was designed to suit the tastes of the arbiter of the country's destiny.

Were it possible to present a scene which would reveal Mexico at a single glance, it would have to be the Easter week festivities in San Agustín de las Cuevas. There were grand church celebrations, with bells chiming, fireworks, and chamber music. There were taverns, ice-houses, inns, and shops everywhere; dice games and roulette wheels, card games and little colored balls . . . games with all their many complications and tricks. There were banners hung between the rooftops of the *pulquerías* and cantinas bearing announcements of all kinds.

At the outskirts of town, under the trees or among the workers' huts, there were mules, horses, coaches, small canopied carriages and carts, all bearing wanton, angry people. On the sidewalks and in the streets, there were nothing but dense crowds; one would be inundated, as if swimming in a sea of people dressed in all colors, wearing button-down trousers, long overcoats, large hats — the ridged hats of the priests, the round hats of the friars, and the straw hats of the lower-class people.

There were games of monte like the one at the Hospicio, where they displayed a large slab of gold weighing many ounces and had a pot of a hundred thousand pesos. The gaming salon opened onto a delightful flower garden, full of leafy fruit trees and exquisite flowers, surrounded by crystalline fountains and enchanting waterspouts. Under the trees were tables with liquors and refreshments, and in the tavern lunches and magnificent meals were always served, along with chocolates, coffee, sweets, and whatever whetted the appetites of the opulent gamblers.

The trick was to bet enormous sums, and to greet loss with studied indifference. Thus, stories were told of Manuelito Rodríguez, who one Easter, with his profit from selling a pair of scissors, won two hundred thousand pesos playing *la dobla;* and of Matías Royuela, who once, while chatting away, placed a twenty thousand peso bet; when it was announced that he had lost, he did not for one moment interrupt the interesting tale with which he was regaling his friends.

The most illustrious members of society, eminent figures in the court and the Church, in public affairs and commerce, gave themselves over to the gambler's cult. The shepherds of souls, along with everyone else, gathered 'round the green felt. So did the fathers of families and merchants jealous of their credit. There was one hacendado who condemned himself to privations for an entire year just so he could award himself the pleasure of losing 40 or 50 thousand pesos at the Easter festivities de San Agustín.

The center of this frantic revel was the plaza, with its large building containing an ice-house, an inn, public and private games, and on the ground floor, the great plaza of fighting cocks where huge sums were ventured.

Santa Anna was the heart and soul of this emporium of disorder and excess. It was something to see him at the fights, surrounded by the money-lending potentates, throwing down his bets, taking other people's money, mingling with minor employees and even with inferior officers; he borrowed money

Drunkenness, murder, and mayhem as depicted by an anonymous nineteenth-century
Mexican artist. (Detail of a painting, Instituto Nacional de Bellas Artes, collection Museo
Nacional de Arte Moderno, Mexico City)

and did not repay it, and the people applauded him as though they were unworthy of such favors. And when the pace flagged, the fairer sex would bestow
their smiles and join Santa Anna in his pranks. The cockfights presented the
most repugnant of spectacles, full of those lawless *léperos,* provocateurs and
cheats, shouting, fighting, and always passing around pitchers and bowls of
pulque.

It was there that Santa Anna would preside. He knew the gamecock from
Tlacotalpán and the one from San Antonio el Pelón or Tequixquiápam; he
would set the rules for the fight, and check the birds to see that the spurs were
fitted right.

There were moments when the emcee's cries, the music, the applause and
jeers were overwhelming, when drunkards with roosters under their arms

rubbed elbows with the great Supreme Chief. In such surroundings, Santa Anna would laugh and was truly in his glory. . . .

ALTHOUGH THESE DAYS were full of political events, neither those events nor the commentaries upon them were matters for serious study or even close attention. Foreigners saw to their businesses and interests, priests and the faithful clung to their beliefs or so-called traditions, exploiting the fear of purgatory; and the carriage rolled on, among political movements of lawyers without clients, idle and diffident people, reckless and vicious mobs, all vying, with greater or lesser success, for the spoils of government jobs, usurious lending operations, and other contemptible industries, all seeming to say "I will take from you and give to me. . . . You've already eaten, so get out of here, we're hungry."

Thus, whenever someone spoke of politics to J. Velente Baz, he would say: "Bah! Politics! Politics is like a lousy beanery that's been invaded by some audacious customers who threaten the hostess with importunings and insults. At the door to this miserable beanery stands a hungry crowd, who at first watch the diners in silent envy, then grow irritable and agitated, then finally drive the diners out and install themselves in their place, sitting down to satisfy their appetites. But they don't count on the fact that the ones who ate before will return after a while, and the same scene is repeated, for all the same reasons."

Of course, as the scene changes, so does the decor: On one side are crucifixes and candlesticks, three-cocked hats, counts and marqueses with their retinues of monks, ascetics, confraternities, brotherhoods, etc., etc.; and on the other are the national guardsmen, impromptu heretics, every patriotic booster with his "plan," and every *sans cullotte* planning to disembowel monks, kill nuns, clear away the cobwebs of superstition, and declare heaven itself to be national property, exiling the saints, angels and seraphim and converting it into a place of fandangos, drunken sprees, and disorders.

So most people shielded themselves from politics as against a virus carried by the inhabitants of the moon. Ladies and gentlemen of business deemed it to their credit to say that they understood nothing of politics, while government employees and military men, with the utmost cynicism, boasted that they would support whoever paid them, putting aside their conscience and their pride.

There were newspapers, like the *Lima de Vulcano de los Escoseses,* edited by Luis Espino, and *El Mexicano,* by Pablo Sánchez, a military man employed in the Ministry of War . . . ; and yet these were very few, and if one of them had two hundred subscribers they thought it a marvel, which should give an idea of the trends in opinion and of the attention merited by political events. . . .

In the dark depths of society, fanaticism ruled in close alliance with soldiers and the old *encomenderos*-turned-soldiers. Notions of the sciences and social sciences appeared only intermittently in isolated groups, or rather among separate and undistinguished individuals. They were like buried treasures, or fertile seeds locked up in sterile boxes. Knowledge was like wealth held in gold and silver ingots which were owned by a few powerful people, when what was needed was liquid currency — not a handful of wealthy people, but many people with money to provide for their urgent needs. . . . It was necessary to divulge knowledge, to turn vast wealth into small change.

WHILE THE PEOPLE sought solace, and while the hero [Santa Anna] surrounded himself with noisy merriment, in very hushed voices people would call their Caesar "the fifteen claws," a reference to his love of money. In Congress, unnoticed, a determined and conscientious opposition movement took shape, aiming to vindicate rights and honor, among good patriots who would eventually make the glorious revolution of December 6, [1844]. . . .

The revolution of December 6, which can be called popular *par excellence,* which began in the most obscure neighborhoods and spread to the highest levels of society, was, so to speak, prepared, nurtured, and determined by Santa Anna, by a bloody and ridiculous Caesarism, and by that stupid militarism that gave brute force preponderance over the sacred rights of man.

And the most remarkable thing was the way those who believed themselves to be men of principle would change their colors at a whim. Although this was due in large part to their great ignorance, it was also due to Santa Anna, who was a Proteus, assuming all shapes and enlisting under all banners, now casually joining the men of aristocracy and privilege, now joining the liberals who proclaimed equality, religious toleration, and the ideas of Farías, without ever properly understanding those ideas. The revelry in the palace, the despotism of satraps, the robbery of the money-lender, the whore, the gambler . . . all helped to determine that celebrated revolution.

Discontent burned in every corner of the country, and the very reticence of the stifled press was like oil that silently ignites a bonfire. [General Valentín] Canalizo, who was Santa Anna's toy soldier [vice-president], authorized all the arbitrary measures, even taking command of the Army in outrageous defiance of the law, ordering that the keys to Congress be confiscated, and demanding that everyone swear obedience to the dictatorial order of November 29, which immediately preceded the coup d'état.

Congress adopted a resolute and praiseworthy attitude. The deputies Alas and Llaca made accusations against Canalizo and Santa Anna.

Agitation spread violently, the Government employees and soldiers leading the revolt . . . the powerful went through impotent convulsions, and Santa Anna, drunk with power and opulence, persisted in his scorn of the people and in his absurd faith in the use of force.

The most notable and visible personages in that revolution . . . had already prepared the operation admirably. The newspaper *Siglo XIX* could be considered the protagonist of this glorious moment. . . .

Canalizo had gagged the press and ordered Congress closed; Santa Anna, at the head of the army, issued tyrannical orders, and the most casual happenstance had strong resonance as dawn broke on December 6, the day of the great popular revolution.

As soon as he heard of the rebellion, Canalizo, who was bold and reckless, ordered an attack on the [Congressional] Palace, an order that was not carried out thanks to the efficacious mediation of an army officer called Falcón, who, at great risk to his own life, lent a very valuable service.

The response inside the [Congressional] Palace was tumultuous. In the immense atrium of San Francisco, men gathered, armed with rifles, fire-locks, pistols, and sabers, assuming a warlike attitude. . . . Currents of people swelled by the moment till they covered the ground, swinging to and fro on the street-light poles. Impudent, wild eyes, bloodthirsty howls and rowdy laughs, straw hats and sparks flying through the air, disheveled hair, indescribable noises, all surging violently amid a moving forest of clubs, rifles, swords, hammers, and who knows what else.

Deputies and senators followed, beaming. The rabid crowd went to the theater and quickly demolished the plaster statue erected to Santa Anna. They ran furiously to the Pantheon of Santa Paula and with savage ferocity exhumed Santa Anna's leg, playing games with it and making it an object of ridicule; then they turned toward the Alameda, and when the gatekeeper stubbornly refused to open the gate, they tore the iron gates up from their foundations and bent them like tree branches felled by a mighty storm. Somehow they toppled the statue of Santa Anna in the Plaza del Volador off of its high column, smashing it on the ground.

Around four in the afternoon, in the midst of that inexpressable deluge, deputies and senators began a parade from San Francisco to the [Congressional] Palace. People stood on rooftops and balconies, others ran through the streets, among horses and carriages, steering a course through that turbulent river and drawing near to the fathers of the nation, shouting their names, waving their hats in the air, throwing down flowers.

"Look, that pale skinny guy, it's Llaca." . . . "Long live Llaca!" . . . "That guy who's walking half stooped over, who is he?" . . . "He's the great Pedraza." . . . "And him?" . . . "Don Luis de la Rosa." . . . "Long live Alas!"

The retinue arrived at the Palace. The crowd scattered in all directions, and an enormous group entered the Chamber, where the deputies and senators took their seats. The people wanted to tear up a large painting depicting Barradas's surrender in Tampico,[1] a work by the painter París, which featured General Santa Anna in the foreground. Llaca opposed this because the painting was a national glory, and the people, with enchanting docility, obeyed and followed him, meek and genial as a fiery horse when it feels its owner's hand caress its neck.

At night there were cockfights and parties, unmarred by robberies, fights, and disorder. From Querétaro, Santa Anna cursed the rebels, even while the new Government in Mexico received a hail of letters pledging support.

Note

1. A reference to Santa Anna's defeat of the Spanish, who invaded Tampico under General Isidro Barradas in July 1829. *Ed.*

Décimas Dedicated to Santa Anna's Leg

Anonymous

The ornate funeral ceremonies that General Santa Anna ordered performed in 1842 for his leg, which was lost fighting the French at the Battle of Veracruz in 1838, are often seen as the culmination of that caudillo's vainglory and megalomania. After being amputated, the leg spent four years buried at Santa Anna's hacienda, Manga de Clavo, in the state of Veracruz. When Santa Anna resumed the presidency in late 1841, he had the limb dug up, placed in a crystal vase, and taken amid a full military dress parade to Mexico City, where it was buried beneath an elaborate monument in the cemetery of Santa Paula. The funeral involved cannon salvos, speeches, and poems in the general's honor. As recounted by Guillermo Prieto in the previous selection, irreverent crowds in 1844 demolished the monument, dug up the leg, and played games with it.

Such events provided grist for broadsides known as décimas, predecessors of the popular topical ballads known as corridos. Décimas were often satirical in tone, and they represented a variety of viewpoints. The following décimas present divergent viewpoints on the matter of Santa Anna's leg.

I.

Why should anyone criticize
If a funeral is performed
for the foot, arm, or hair
of an illustrious General?

Passions always tarnish
merit with malevolence
and really do not wish
true merit celebrated;
So answer quickly
and with confidence:
Why should we not honor
merit in the lifeless limb

of a great and heroic caudillo?
Why should anyone criticize?

To make this fitting obsequy
to a sacrificed limb —
not to the man, but to what he has given
fearlessly for the Fatherland —
it would be unjust,
ungrateful, foolish and disloyal
to claim it is not lawful and right
that a lone foot have
a tomb or mausoleum,
that a funeral is performed.

Did Artemisia not hide
the ashes of Mausolus[1]
in her breast and believe this
the only remedy?
She did her duty.
So today Mexico erects
a tomb reaching to the sky,
covering with ardent hope
a jewel of History,
and giving glory
to the foot, arm or hair.

There is a maxim which states
a cherished principle:
If one kisses the hem of a robe
it is because of the Saint who wears it;
thus, it is not for the foot itself, on the contrary,
though traitors may complain,
that we say, for good or ill,
"Viva!" and be assured
that the people are grateful
to an illustrious General.

II.
Nothing in life is permanent,
God alone remains,
so the things of this world
are here today and gone tomorrow.

If we search through all of history
we will not find a single soul
whose triumphs and glory
last for all eternity.
Even so, our memory
of great heroes is eternal;
though no one can be constant
in their conduct or their lives
for until death arrives,
nothing in life is permanent.

Such may be said of Santa Anna's foot
which was placed in Santa Paula
with such solemn
pomp and majesty;
and today the Mexican populace,
after rising in rebellion,
full of enthusiasm and zeal,
took the foot from the sepulchre;
so it is clear that on the earth
God alone remains.

At that hour and moment
the foot's owner was far away;
but around here his FOOT was
walking around with the rebels.
It is certain that no one
felt any pain from this;
but I believe
that such an unthinkable act
could only have been done by
the things of this world.

At other times this foot
was earnestly respected;
but that was when its owner
still held us in subjugation;
today the people have treated it
like a dirty old bone,
because the nation
no longer wishes to stand for it;

because, in the end, good and evil
are here today and gone tomorrow.

Note

1. Mausolus: Persian satrap who ruled over Caria from c. 376–353 B.C. Known for his personal aggrandizement, he designed a splendid tomb for himself which his wife, Artemisia, built after his death. He thus gave his name to the mausoleum. *Ed.*

War and Finance, Mexican Style

Juan Bautista Morales

While Liberals and Conservatives battled one another in scenes such as that described by Frances Calderón, other observers wryly ridiculed the pretensions of both parties. Civil strife was expensive, as was the country's more constructive business. Mexico's colonial treasure trove — the silver mines — had collapsed with Independence. A series of weak governments found it impossible to institute a functional tax-collection system, and when Mexico defaulted on the interest payments on British loans in 1826, Mexico's credit in European capital markets suffered irreparable damage. The country's only reliable source of revenue was taxes on overseas trade, but as the volume of Mexico's trade declined, this source became increasingly precarious. In desperation, Mexico's governments took to contracting loan after loan from Mexican moneylenders known as agiotistas, *who charged exorbitant rates of interest for the use of their capital. The country's chronic indebtedness became a key feature of its nineteenth-century history.*

Juan Bautista Morales (1788–1856) published his book El Gallo Pitagórico *(The Pythagorean Rooster) between 1845 and 1849 in the newspaper* El Siglo XIX. *In the following excerpt, he concocts a satirical dialogue in which a foreign visitor — presumably a European — comes to understand something of Mexican war and finance.*

"In what manner do you make war among yourselves?" I asked a Mexican.

My Mexican interlocutor answered me thus. "Although among us there are many parties, the belligerents close ranks into only two: the government and the rebels [*pronunciados*]. Each of these parties manages to fill its ranks, beginning with those who are most sympathetic to it, and each tries to neutralize its opponents. If conditions favor the government, then the government wins; but if they are favorable to the rebels, the government loses completely, though Achilles himself may come to its aid. Our strategy works better in the preliminary stages than in open campaign. Let me explain.

"It all begins with each side discrediting the other in the official and opposition newspapers. Once one side loses prestige, the intrigues begin. Troops are seduced with promises of rank and position, and whatever money is available is distributed among subaltern agents and emissaries. For this purpose, the *agiotistas* open their coffers at the very moderate rate of five or six percent monthly. Once the thing is "fried and cooked," as the saying goes; that is, once it is known for certain which leaders and which troops are in and at what hour the officers will announce their rebellion, then the commanding officer, if he does not wish to follow his party, must be tied up. Then it's to arms, to war, war on them all . . . ! A skirmish ensues, a contra dance in which some of the dancers go from one party to the other. . . . The next day comes the first granting of prizes, which consist of military ranks. The sergeants become second lieutenants, the second lieutenants become first lieutenants, the first lieutenants become captains, and so forth; bellies that yesterday were colorless now wear red sashes, the red sashes give way to green, and the green give way to blue. Following that, a motion is made in the Chamber that the ranks be approved, the debt contracted with the *agiotistas* is acknowledged, and a crucifix or coat-of-arms is granted those who have distinguished themselves in the campaign. Everything requested is conceded, and a second round of prizes is planned. . . . Each person receives a prize in accordance with his deeds. That is our strategy. . . .

"Now, this requires a bit of explanation. . . . A poor man may manage to feed himself and his family for a day, but in order to do so he is forced to sell a jewel or a bond worth a hundred pesos, for only five or six pesos. Doubtless you have known in Europe another class of *agiotistas* who are very different from the ones in this republic. There they are formed into companies that speculate in commerce, such that when some member or creditor of the business wants to sell off a share or a bond, the transaction takes place, the price of the shares rising or falling depending on whether the funds are soluble or the hopes for the success of the transaction are reasonably sound. Among us there is nothing of the sort. The *agiotista* usually confines himself to lending money to the government when it finds itself hard up. So among us every *agiotista* is a usurer, although not every usurer is an *agiotista*. The reason is clear: those who lend money to the government make their profits by loaning cash in exchange for paper, in order to be repaid in cash; so the cheaper they buy the paper, the larger the profit they make. . . .

"You have been to England and France, where they have national commerce: here that does not exist, it is all foreign. The foreigners are more interested in their own countries than in ours: what matters to them is to take out silver, and it matters nothing to them whether the nation's industry progresses or does not. Indeed, if one examines this impartially, he will find that they are interested in seeing that this country does *not* progress. The less able the Mexicans are to meet their needs from the products of their own soil, the more they need the foreigners, for foreigners have more articles of consumption. Our national merchants are hucksters for the foreigners, and thus they are allied in their interests to the foreigners. So greed and egoism are the common vices of merchants, and Mexicans and foreigners both possess these traits in heroic proportion. When any one of them opens his cash box or his warehouse, he swears by the wand of Mercury, his tutelary deity, to make as much profit as he can; and don't imagine that he is in any way troubled by his conscience, for he has no private morality in this area. You will see these merchants attending mass, doing the rosary, and even acting as brothers of the holy school, but even so they have no scruples about bribing guards, falsifying bills and invoices, and other ingenious little pranks. . . . Small wonder that in ancient times merchants were given Mercury as their protector deity. Mercury was not the god of thieves, he was the god of immense looting. And yet all of these merchants, just like the *agiotistas,* exude honor, probity, good faith, and even patriotism from every pore in their bodies. Nevertheless, despite these virtues, if the impoverished government, in its dire need, should establish a tax, no matter how small, then it's *flectere si nequeo superos, Acheronta movebo* — If they cannot bend Heaven, they shall move Hell. They send petitions to congress and to the government containing the signatures of two or three hundred of the leading merchants protesting the tax: they try to bribe the ministers, the deputies, the senators, and anyone who can wield influence in their favor. If this is not enough, they goad some rebel to jump into the fray . . ."

A Conservative Profession of Faith

The Editors of El Tiempo, February 12, 1846

Even before it was fought, the war between the United States and Mexico would become the crucible for Mexican nationhood. As Mexico moved ever closer to war, Liberals and Conservatives, both painfully aware of Mexico's centrifugal tendencies, its chronic debility, its poverty, and its political paralysis, groped for explanations. For Conservatives, the problem was quite simply republicanism, an insidious virus that had infected the national organism and weakened the noble Hispanic legacy of monarchism and Roman Catholicism.

El Tiempo was the most important newspaper of conservatism, and its editorial board included the most illustrious Conservatives of the mid–nineteenth century. In the following excerpt, written two months before the outbreak of the war—a time of high tensions—the newspaper's editors eloquently and succinctly stake out their position.

We promised to publish a complete and explicit manifesto of our political principles. We shall now fulfill our promise. . . .

We believe that our independence was a grand and glorious feat, and also a necessary and inevitable one. When kingdoms and provinces which are far from the metropolis reach a certain level of development and growth, when the culture has created interests and the capacity to govern, then the time has come to loosen the ties that bind the young nations to the more ancient and advanced ones, which, like mothers, gave them their education and strength, initiating them into the life of civilization. So independence had to come sooner or later, and though ten years of cruel wars could not secure it, a military movement of seven months in 1821 was enough to make the words of Iguala the country's banner. Why? Because the guarantees contained in that plan united all spirits, all sympathies; because the clergy, the army, and the people were assured of a future full of glory and prosperity for the fatherland. That is why many Spanish priests, military men and merchants remained in Mexico, performing their tasks and services; that is why this important revolution was not consumed by blood and ruin, and why independence united so many sentiments. It was because the general welfare was considered, and because the ties that bound past and present and future were loosened but not broken.

The plan of Iguala was not carried out. Iturbide wished to create a dynasty for his own benefit; and this empire, lacking foundation, lacking legitimacy, lacking respect for time and tradition, fell into ruins at the first revolutionary stirrings. The lamentable tragedy that took Iturbide's life, took from the fatherland a faithful servant who was misled by inexperience and dazzled by flattery. The United States then began to build an empire of a different sort in Mexico: its books and ideas, the promises made by its representatives, the fraudulent spectacle of its prosperity, dragged our noble trustful nature down new and dangerous roads. Republican ideas took control of the nation's destiny, and were formulated into government.

We then started down this fatal path upon which we still walk. Overlooking our differences of origin, of religion, and of history; without considering that our social, political, and religious unity made us best suited for the monarchical form of government—just as the Americans are suited for republicanism and federalism by their diversity of cults, peoples, and languages—we believed that the quickest way to assure political liberty was to throw ourselves into the arms of the United States, servilely imitating its institutions and slavishly following its perfidious advice. Thus, the absurd constitution of 1824 was written, and the American representative[1] founded, in the name of liberty, secret societies which tyrannized and destroyed the country. The treasury was disorganized, administration was ruined. We should have had enough resources to satisfy all of our ambitions, but the people's wealth was squandered, and we began to contract increasingly ruinous loans. The nation was weakened by the expulsion of the peaceful and hardworking Spaniards, along with their Mexican families and the immense wealth that they possessed. Civil liberty was drowned amid continuous revolts, which turned a disciplined and long-suffering army into a tool of ambition and anarchy. Presidents and Congresses fell before bloody revolutions. From that time, civil war in the countryside and disorder in the cities practically became our normal state. Meanwhile, barbarous Indians dared to pillage our territory with impunity, and the United State grabbed Texas and prepared to usurp California.

This description is not exaggerated: official documents, speeches by the country's representatives, articles in the newspapers—all present a much grimmer picture of our situation.

So, what do we now contemplate? What is the situation within and outside of the country?

An administration disorganized, a treasury lost, enormous debts that consume us, revenues pledged to our creditors, the soldier begging the usurer for his scant subsistence, justice neglected, barbarians threatening the borders of our civilization, Yucatán emancipated, the United States occupying our territory; and all this without a navy with which to defend our coasts, and without the power to allocate the resources that our valiant army would need to expel the zealous invaders from the nation's soil.

And what about overseas?

Our reputation in Europe is lost; one is accustomed to hearing about the perpetual scandal of our revolutions, and we are seen as a nation condemned to the fate of the turbulent and semi-barbarous republics of the south, or one destined to be the prisoner and slave of the federation of the North. This country, so rich in natural resources, no longer has credit in any market; and the instability of our governments discredits our institutions, obstructing any political alliance that we might establish in Europe to help us resist invasions from the United States. No nation will sign treaties with the unfortunate republics of Spanish America, which are condemned by fate to wallow in anarchy and convulsion; where diplomacy is impossible, secrets impracticable; where neither treasons nor guarantees exist or can exist within its precarious governments.

Very well, then. We know this sad situation and, unlike many others, we do not try to deceive our country. Since the Mexican nation has the greatest elements of grandeur and prosperity of any nation in the world, and since men here, like men everywhere, are made by education, institutions and habits, we do not believe and do not repeat the vulgar notion that we are incapable of political existence, or that we cannot govern ourselves. We believe that republican institutions have brought us to a state close to despair and prostration, just as they would have done to Spain, England, and France. We believe that at the present time we are not merely heading for ruin, demoralization, and anarchy; we are approaching the complete dissolution of the nation, and the loss of our territory, our name, and our independence.

Holland, France, England have, in bygone epochs, experimented with republicanism, and, in order to survive, they shook off that political form with disgust and fear, for it undermined their existence just as it does ours. In those countries, republican revolutions left glorious, if not prosperous, memories. Holland freed itself from the Spanish yoke and built up a navy. England, under the iron-fisted administration of Cromwell, conquered Dunkirk and Jamaica. France made Europe tremble, and in its revolutionary delirium brought its tricolored banner triumphantly to Germany, Italy and Switzerland. The three nations, nonetheless, were consumed by internal divisions, and they sought the remedy for their ills in monarchy. Today these brilliant and fertile civilizations enjoy all the benefits of liberty and order, and they see their vain utopias as a foolish delirium: the republican parties no longer exist; they are dead. Where are the educated men who still proclaim republican doctrines in those free countries?

But if the republic could not take root in those countries, then what will become of Mexico, where we have experienced nothing but humiliation and disaster? Instead of conquering foreign territories, the eternal dissensions of our republic have caused us to lose Texas and Yucatán,[2] both of which pertained to Mexico when we began our independence. Every day, instead of triumphing over our enemies, we are threatened with the loss of more territory: the French flag has waved over Ulúa and Veracruz, the American stars float above the Rio Bravo [or Rio Grande, as it is known in the United States]. The republic has created nothing, it has destroyed everything; and our proud national character chafes at the impotence to which our great country has been reduced.

We repeat that it is for this reason that we believe the republic has been a costly experiment, a harsh warning; but it might still be remedied. Now, if you ask what we want and desire, we will say it frankly. We want Representative Monarchy; we want National Unity; we want order along with political and civil liberty; we want the integrity of Mexican territory; we want, in the end, all of the promises and guarantees of the Plan of Iguala, in order to ensure that our glorious independence has stable foundations. If the most advanced and civilized countries of the world have, after lengthy convulsions, adopted a certain form of government, then that form of government is suitable for us. It is what the army at Iguala and its heroic caudillo promised would lead to our happiness and prevent our destruction; it is toward this that we wish to move; it is what we long for, what we defend.

We want a regimen of government in which justice is administered with impartiality, because it is independent of all parties; in which the government has the stability and strength to protect society, and where the laws, respected by everyone, guarantee the rights of all citizens. We want a regimen in which chambers are elective and royal power is hereditary, in order to ensure both political liberty and to maintain the existing order. We want an order of things that regularizes commerce, protects industry, develops the intellectual activity of the nation, and in whose ordered hierarchy all eminent men shall have a place.

We want what exists in all of the respected monarchies of Europe, where there is no aristocracy other than one of merit, skill, education, wealth, and military and civil service; where a man is not asked who his parents are, but what he has done to make himself worthy of positions and honors.

We want a strong and vigorous army that can cover itself with laurels by nobly defending its country, in which military hierarchies are respected and those who shed their blood for the fatherland receive the consideration they are due; we want that army to win victories overseas; and we want the soldier to be assured of a comfortable and stable retirement after his difficult life, not the abandonment and misery with which revolutions reward his services.

We want decorous and dignified support for the Catholic cult of our fathers, not the anarchy that continually threatens Church property. We were born into the bosom of the Church, and we do not wish to see the cathedrals of our religion become temples of those sects that scandalize the world with their religious complaints; nor do we wish to see the hateful starry banner flying from their towers.

We want a representative monarchy that can protect the distant regions as well as those nearby, defend them against the assaults of savages, and extend the borders of civilization that are besieged by barbarism. We want a stable government that inspires confidence in Europe, making possible overseas alliances that might help us to resist the United States, if it persists in trying to destroy our nationality.

All of the legal parties can find a place around this banner, so long as they wish to see the independence and liberty of the country affirmed; so long as they want our sad and unfortunate fatherland to become the premier nation of America. We have faith in our country's future, in its aggrandizement; and we do not believe that so vast, so rich, and so privileged a territory must always be prisoner to dissolution and anarchy.

But we do not want reaction of any sort. Conservatives of conviction and character, we ask protection for all interests regardless of their origin. It is madness to believe that a prince of royal blood should come to Mexico to establish a dynasty with the support of foreign governments. Such a thing could have happened three centuries ago, but it cannot happen today, especially in a country with representative government. We do not want a single job or a single military rank that is not in Mexican hands: whoever hopes to bring stability to our country must be supported only by the army and by the Mexican people.

We have completed our profession of Faith. It is at last clear and complete. Convinced that our ideas are the only ones that can save the nation, we sustain them with decorum and civility, but also with determination and energy. We are not at all disturbed by the calumnies which always follow those who fight against disorder, prejudice and abuse: we scorn the calumniators and we carry on our work without fear. What is certain is that we will never be accomplices of foreign ambition, and, in our newspaper, the stars of the United States will never eclipse the colors of our national flag.

Notes

1. A reference to Joel Poinsett, the first American ambassador to Mexico, who helped to found the liberal York Rite Masonic Lodge, and whose views on Mexicans appear in this volume's first section. *Ed.*

2. Following the example of Texas and repelled by Santa Anna's highly centralist Constitution of 1836, the remote state of Yucatán, which had always had tenuous relations with Mexico, declared its independence in 1840. It rejoined Mexico in 1843, then separated again in 1845, but reunited with Mexico permanently in 1848, while in the throes of a bloody race war. *Ed.*

Considerations Relating to the Political and Social Situation of the Mexican Republic in the Year 1847

Mariano Otero

Liberals had their own explanations for Mexico's woes. Whereas the Conservatives felt that Mexico had grown weak to the extent that it had deviated from the examples of its mother country, Liberals insisted that many of the unfortunate remnants of the colonial system were to blame. Mexico, if it were to prosper, would have to make itself more, not less, like the "modern" nations of the world.

Undoubtedly one of the most eloquent and unflinching spokesmen for the Liberal view was Mariano Otero (1817–1850). Otero was widely read in political philosophy. He served in the national Congress and, for a brief time, in the cabinet of President José Joaquín Herrera as secretary of the interior and of foreign relations. Like the editors of El Tiempo, *Otero was staunchly nationalistic and eager to find a solution to Mexico's continuing vulnerability. Yet unlike those Conservatives, he found his country's weakness had less to do with the particular system in place (that is, a monarchy vs. a republic) than with the realities of the social and psychological makeup of Mexico and Mexicans.*

The fact that a foreign army of ten or twelve thousand men should have penetrated from Veracruz to the very capital of the republic; the fact that, with the exception of the bombarding of that port, the action at Cerrogordo, and the minor encounters that it had with Mexican troops in the immediate environs of the capital, this army has not found enemies with whom to fight— while it has swept across three of the most important and populous states of the Mexican federation, states with more than two million inhabitants— these facts assume such proportions that they cannot but give rise to the most serious reflections.

Petty-minded men, those who judge events solely on the occurrences themselves, usually fall into serious error. For this reason it is not strange that, as we have already seen in some foreign journals, the Mexican people have been characterized *as an effeminate people, a degenerate race that does not know how to govern or to defend itself.*

But the man of thought . . . cannot consider the Mexican republic in its present sad situation to be composed of a people who suffer from defective origins through the effeminacy or degradation of their race but rather of a people who have been the victims of a defective education and a worse organization. From this point of view, we believe that Mexico, far from deserving the deprecation and mockery of the other nations, merits, if not the assistance which as a nation it might hope for from the other nations of the world in the name of universal justice, at least the sympathy which any good heart should feel toward a nation that sustains a just cause. . . .

We will not exhaust ourselves in useless protestations. . . . Instead, let a simple account of the component parts that make up the nation suffice to explain its present situation. . . . [W]e might calculate the population as reaching seven million, of whom, according to the least exaggerated reports, four million are Indians and three million Europeans, mixed, for the most part, with the indigenous strain.

The Indians are spread throughout the entire territory of the republic, grouped in small communities and forming really a family apart from the white and mixed races. The miserable way of life of the Indians today differs little or not at all from what it was when they were subjects of the great emperor Montezuma. . . . Neither in the time of the viceroys nor later, after independence, has there been adopted an adequate system of education for this race, an education which would on the one hand improve the condition of the individual, raising him from the brutalized state in which he exists, and on the other hand make him useful to society. Neither early nor late have these people been taught anything more than to fear God, the priest, and the mayor, and the ignorance in which they live is such that perhaps three quarters of the Indians have not yet received the news of the attainment of national independence. That they remain in this error is all the more credible in view of the fact that in many places they are still charged tribute for the king of Spain in the same spirit in which they are asked for donations for the ransoming of captives and for the holy places of Jerusalem.

The work that they are generally put to is cultivating the earth for a small daily stipend, and since this pay is not always sufficient to cover the costs of their sad existence, they often ask the owner of the hacienda on which they work for wages in advance to be paid back by their labor, thus obliging them to stay put until they have paid their debt. . . .

In addition, there is a system which *so happily* prevails among the Mexican clergy by which, while the so-called higher clergy and bishops live opulently in the capital, the parish priests find that their very survival depends upon the income from their parish *rights*. For this reason, these representatives of the God of goodness and mercy make it a point not to allow any Indian to be born, to marry, or to die with impunity, that is, without paying the *established rights*. In this way, the parish priests take their cut from the scant resources that the Indians count on for their livelihood.

Those Indians who live close to the great population centers go to them to sell vegetables, poultry, firewood, coal, and other such goods which fetch them a small price, but even this paltry sum is further reduced by the cut taken at the city gate by collectors who, in the name of the nation, commit against these people the most infamous and repugnant extortions.

To put the finishing touch on this canvas, which faithfully portrays the sadness of Indian life, we need but add that the only active part that the Indians take in the public life of the country is to serve as soldiers in the army, a role which is forced upon them. And in this capacity, rather than serving their country, they act as instruments for the aggrandizement of their officers, who in times of peace give them little bread but a big stick *(poco pan y mucho palo)* and in war often abandon them at the moment of danger. For all these reasons, it is easy to understand why this important sector of the population has no interest in preserving an order of things of which it is the victim. Certainly the Indians have watched the entrance of the North American army with the same indifference with which they watched in the past the Spanish armies taking dominion of the country, and with the same calm with which, after independence, they have watched the comings and goings of our troops engaged in continual revolutions. Without any further necessities than those demanded by their semi-savage level of existence, without relationships or pleasures of any kind which might arise out of a contact with society, with neither interests nor affections that tie them to it, and with the confidence that their abject condition could not be worsened, they look upon all that might happen with the most apathetic indifference.

We shall now proceed to examine the 3 million inhabitants of European or mixed descent who comprise the populations of the capitals and other cities and towns of importance in the republic. . . . With the exception of about three hundred thousand men, the top figure for those employed in agriculture, industry, mining, business, and certain trades and offices, the nine hundred thousand remaining account for the unproductive classes, such as the clergy with all of its subordinates and dependents, the military, the bureaucracy, lawyers, doctors, and finally that multitude of loafers and vagabonds that abounds in the main cities of the republic.

From this unexaggerated estimate, we might judge the sad situation that afflicts that quarter of the population which works and produces and therefore must necessarily support the other three quarters. What an enormous disproportion! Here is the origin of the backwardness and discouragement encumbering all sources of the national wealth. Here is sufficient cause for the destruction of the nascent Mexican republic; indeed, it would suffice to destroy the most flourishing nation on earth! . . .

There is little good to be said about the standing of those Mexicans who dedicate themselves to the skills and trades. Unfortunately, there still persists among us the error inherited from the Spaniards who, with their lofty notions of chivalry and nobility, taught us to look down upon any man who follows a trade. To be a man of respectability it was necessary to be a military man, a government official, a clergyman, a lawyer, or at least a doctor. All others in society were considered to be the inferior classes, and even businessmen were looked upon with contempt, being referred to as rag dealers. As a result of such ridiculous, not to say pernicious ideas, no father of any means, however moderate, wanted, nor still does want, his sons to learn a trade. He would even be ashamed to apprentice them to a commercial house or to any other business, because the idea of *serving a master,* as the saying goes, whether in a workshop or in a store, would seem to him to be a very denigrating thing.

This concern about status reaches such a proportion that many artisans who have lived decent and honorable lives in their trades, far from teaching them to their sons, put them in a college to learn law or medicine; or, as soon as they get out of school knowing something of reading, writing, and arithmetic, they try to get some influential person to prevail upon the government to bestow upon [their] sons a civil or military post. . . . There are many fathers also who, before apprenticing their sons to any trade, would prefer that they had no profession at all and would abandon them to the fate of searching out their livelihood in any way that *God might give them to understand,* but without, of course, giving up their status as gentlemen — *hombres decentes* — that is to say, without working at any job that might dishonor them, because for this class of men working itself is dishonorable, and they do not think that this is true of spending their entire lives as vagabonds and swindlers.

And so it has come about that, while the republic is plagued by hundreds of generals, thousands of superintendents and officials, bureaucrats, clergymen, and doctors, one cannot find a single distinguished Mexican in any art, skill, or trade: and it is certain that, in any of the important population centers, the best architect, the most able painter, the best sculptor, the best carriage maker, the most intelligent upholsterer, the most painstaking cabinet maker, and even the best cobbler will turn out not to be a Mexican but a foreigner.

This is a truth all the more sad when one considers that there is no lack of ability among the Mexicans and that they are even famous for their skills in making fine reproductions. . . .

In view of this simple and true account of the state in which the productive classes — the smallest part of the Mexican republic — find themselves, it is easy to understand the sense of permanent malaise in which they live. And this, in turn, sufficiently explains the detachment and indifference with which these classes, on the whole, have looked upon the present war through which the republic is suffering. Say what one might, patriotism, that noble and chivalrous sentiment which in other countries moves the people and raises them to such a pitch of fervor that they would a thousand times prefer death to permitting the slightest offense against their country — that sentiment cannot exist in a country without education and in one which has been lacerated by thirty-seven years of travail and misery. . . .

The men who have figured in the directing of our public affairs have shown neither the proper science nor the consciousness of the great duties imposed upon them by the high posts that their ambitions have elevated them to. None of them have shown the least concern for the removal of those strong obstacles to the welfare and happiness of the nation. All of this is very natural in a country where men never ascend to power through the free vote of the citizenry but are always placed there either through intrigues on the part of one or another faction or, as is often the case, by revolutionary action on the part of the armed forces.

This system, certainly original in a republic, of presenting the people with their rulers without first consulting them and obtaining their consent, has necessarily resulted in the emergence of picked officials whose least concern is with the welfare of the people. It could not be otherwise in view of the fact that the parties, which represent this or that special interest, do not seek in their candidates independent men devoted to the general interest of the country but rather men who will adhere strictly to the special interests of [their] party. Accordingly, these same men in taking power feel obligated to honor their commitment to serve faithfully the party that elevated them to office.

For these reasons we have seen that some governments have decidedly protected the army, others the clergy, others the bureaucrats, and some others all three classes at once. However, there has never been a government which has put a brake on the pretensions of the privileged classes while reforming or destroying their abuses. None has dedicated itself to the protection of the industrious classes which most merit the attention of any government that would be enlightened or patriotic. For these classes there has been nothing but pompous promises which have never been fulfilled. In order to discredit the government which they have wanted to overthrow, factions in revolt have hurled charges to the effect that this government has not protected industry or commerce. . . .

One would have to concede that such a system, practiced for twenty-six years, could only bring about the most profound disgust between the industrious classes and their governments. What bonds or sympathies could possibly exist between these classes and the various governments, considering that the latter, instead of lending them some support, have burdened them daily with more taxes of all kinds in order to satisfy the ambitions of thousands of men of the privileged classes who, with no decent title to it, have proposed to live at the expense of the nation? None, certainly. . . .

As the inevitable result of so many cruel and repeated deceptions, [the productive classes] are now in a state of mortal discouragement. This being the case, could anyone maintain that they should now go on to sacrifice what remains of their fortunes as well as their very lives for their country? And in defense of what? . . .

To these definite considerations, which should certainly suffice to explain, at least to enlightened men, the apathy which has characterized most members of the industrious classes during the present war, should be added the observation that the United States army has not [spread] terror and death everywhere, robbing or destroying property, violating women, and, in short, perpetrating all kinds of crimes against the conquered populace. On the contrary . . . the American army, sustaining itself on its own resources and paying good prices for whatever it needed for its subsistence, has respected private property. No peaceful Mexican has been persecuted. Everyone has been allowed to continue working freely in his trade or occupation. And finally, far from oppressing the people with heavy taxes, the American army has considerably reduced import duties in the occupied ports, and in the cities and towns of the interior; [moreover], it has abolished the customs houses and tax-collecting stations which had formerly vexed and harassed all who sought their livelihoods in the mercantile trades. . . .

Can it be demanded of the property-owning and industrious Mexicans that they bring about their own ruin or even death in defense of those same abuses of which they are the victims? . . . And yet, despite all these reasons cited, the industrious classes of Mexico have, in fact, given no little proof of the extent to which they esteem the honor and good name of their country. . . .

It now remains for us to consider the three classes which are the true masters of the country: the army, the clergy, and the government bureaucracy. Since these are the only groups that have enjoyed its privileges and have decreed, according to their whims, its fate, it would seem that they should have taken on the present battle as a personal cause, being well persuaded that in any new and enlightened order of things all those abuses by which they have lived up until now would, undoubtedly, be swept away. However, in examining the particular modus of these classes among themselves, we shall see that—although they have been very potent in imposing upon the country a static condition, heading it in the direction of total ruin—they have been utterly without force when it has come to uniting against a foreign invasion, convinced though they must be that that thrust will be more fatal to them than to the rest of the country. . . .

We will start with the army because this class is the most immediately responsible for the loss of national honor, for whose defense this same army has been continually maintained at a cost to the country of millions of pesos in the twenty-six years that have elapsed from independence to the present.

We have said elsewhere that the soldiers, in general, are Indians, forcibly made to serve, and we have also observed that these Indians have little or no conception of nationality, and no interest whatever in maintaining an order of things in which they figure only as beasts of burden. Nevertheless, it must be truthfully said that as soldiers they are really quite good, because—aside from not being cowards—they have great endurance in the campaign. They have shown that they can cross hundreds of leagues over bad roads, barefoot, badly clothed and worse fed, and this without complaining or committing any notable act of insubordination. Without doubt, if these same Indians were led by officers with good training and some sensibility, they would be as good as the soldiers of any other country. The trouble, therefore, with the Mexican army is not with the soldiers but with the officers, who, with a few and honorable exceptions, are assuredly the most ignorant and demoralized on earth. Nor could it be otherwise, when the attainment of military rank among us has nothing to do with competence or valor but rather with appointments based on the most contemptible favoritism.

From the time in which we gained our independence, a multitude of obscure and ignorant men have been presenting themselves to the new government, alleging the important services and immense sacrifices that they are supposed to have made in defense of the national cause, and asking to be given, in recompense for these services, high military posts. . . . In this way men were brought into the army who had had no previous experience of military service and were absolutely ignorant of the art of war and therefore worthless in terms of the careers they were presumed to be following. Later, the abuse of handing out military posts reached such a point of scandal that any Mexican who would consent to remain a peasant would seem to be positively admirable, so easy had it become for anyone who wanted a military post to get one.

Above all, during twenty years of this kind of thing, the favorite occupation of the army has been, with but a few intervals, the making of revolution. Consequently, the disorder within the military has reached its culmination. Every new government, elevated to power through a military revolt—as they all have been—has felt obliged to immediately reward that part of the army which installed it, and thus preferments are awarded to all the leaders and officers of that faction. On the other hand, the government that was about to fall had given new posts to the other part of the army that had remained faithful to it before its fall. These last-minute promotions have always been recognized by the new government in order to keep everybody happy. In this way, each revolution has resulted in a swelling of the officer corps and at the same time in a new wave of promotions for those officers already in grade. In the light of this, it should not appear at all strange that those farces known as *pronunciamientos* should recur so frequently, because it is clear that by this route a former second lieutenant, for example, who has taken part in six consecutive revolutions, will undoubtedly have made it to the rank of general. . . .

As a consequence of so much disorder and also of the facile appointments and promotion of officers, it is not surprising that one can hardly find, although there are hundreds of generals, thousands of colonels, lieutenant colonels, commanders, and so forth, a single general in whom one would confide the command of a small division, because many of them do not even know the rudiments of the art of war, and they would be in a dilemma should they be put in charge of a company on patrol. Also, one could count on the fingers of the hand the number of colonels in whom one could trust the command of a single regiment in combat; and finally, as for junior officers, there are very few good ones because, along with their other defects, they are given to insubordination, which makes them useless for any sort of service.

One is forced to conclude that such an army, when faced with its first national war against a foreign army that is at least tolerably well organized, is bound to play the same ridiculous role that was played by the Pope's soldiers before the armies of Napoleon.

It is not in the least difficult to count the number of defeats which our army has suffered in the present war. One has only to know beforehand how many engagements it has had with the enemy, because each battle has been a defeat, with some of the skirmishes lasting only a few minutes. But, however disgraced our military has been at arms, it has not been sparing in giving out proclamations, manifestos, and explanations to the public, because, on the "literary" side, our army surely has no equal in the world. There are generals who have felt called upon to issue a proclamation upon taking charge of their troops. This has been followed by another proclamation each time they have passed through a city or town en route. They even make proclamations, upon getting out of bed in the morning, to their valiant comrades in arms. . . .

This total lack of truth and justice naturally discourages all good officers, or perhaps converts them into bad ones because in the present scheme of things even the basic motives for human action are missing: the hope of reward and the fear of punishment.

Furthermore, in all well-organized societies an officer knows that should he die in battle his family, at least, will be taken care of by the government, and if he should be incapacitated he can count on a soldier's home where he can pass the rest of his life comfortably and decently. In Mexico these things do not obtain. Though a veterans' institution and a pension fund for military widows exist in name, any incapacitated veteran can be sure that he will perish, at the end, in utter poverty, after having begged for his subsistence from public charity. If, on the other hand, he is killed in action, his family will without doubt be the victims of misery or of the prostitution which is its consequence, and his cadaver will serve as meat for the birds and animals because frequently, if not always, it is allowed to remain stretched out on the field of battle without anyone taking the trouble to bury it. . . .

Let us go on now to examine the situation of the clergy, in whose hands resides the largest portion of the property of the republic — a fact which accounts for the great and baneful influence the clergy has exercised upon society. In view of this vast ownership, it would seem only natural that the clergy would ardently defend the nation or, more precisely, these same properties, being persuaded that any other even half-enlightened government that establishes itself in the country must necessarily despoil it of all these immense holdings and reduce it to the simple exercise of its purely spiritual mission upon earth. The clergy should be the more determined to resist with all its capacities the advance of the enemy forces because this army represents a people for which the absolute toleration of various religions forms the very basis of its social system. This being so, it is evident that should Mexico succumb in the fight the clergy here would not only have to fear the loss of its material interests but also of that sole and absolute power which it has exercised without opposition in a country in which no other religion but theirs is tolerated.

In view of all this, the blind self-centeredness which the clergy has shown in a cause that one would have thought to have been its very own would seem inexplicable were it not for two considerations. The first of these is the very ignorance of the individuals involved, by which they have shown themselves to be incapable of comprehending the difficult times in which they are living, being unable to foresee the dire consequences which lie in store for them as a result of the stupidity and egotism of their present conduct. Secondly, and more importantly, one must consider the inequality that exists within this privileged class itself, by which a small minority lives surrounded by the greatest abundance while the rest are left with hardly enough to sustain themselves in a decent manner. One has only to survey the disproportion that exists among the various groups making up the clergy in order to substantiate the exactness of these observations.

The Mexican clergy consists of bishops and canons, curates and vicars, private clerics or chaplains, and members of religious orders—of both sexes. The bishops and canons, who make up what is known as the high clergy, are supported by tithes. Although the income from this source has been reduced a good deal since the workers have been relieved of the obligation to pay them, it is still a considerable sum. . . . In the great cities such as Mexico City, Puebla, Guadalajara, Querétaro, Orizaba, and others, there is a multitude of clergy who are quite useless, and in these same cities the bishops and canons lead comfortable and even sumptuous lives, remote from all inconveniences and enjoying all the pleasures that riches can provide. In contrast, those who really give a service to religion, the curates and vicars, with rare exceptions, must endure lives overburdened with work and destitute, sometimes to the point of sheer misery. . . .

The parish priests suffer all kinds of privations, being constantly on call and having to travel long distances to say mass and dispense the sacraments in remote places. Sunday, the day of rest for all others, is their heaviest day. Yet for all this travail they receive only the donations that might be forthcoming from the faithful for baptisms, weddings, funerals, and so forth. As observance of these sacraments is on the decline, so too is the livelihood of the poor parish priests. . . .

As for the bureaucrats, their history is very similar to that of the military. Amidst the perpetual disorder and dissolution of our governments, nevertheless, public jobs continue to be handed out in great profusion—perhaps to truckle to this or that personage who has made a recommendation or maybe to reward the slightest service given to one of the people in government. Seldom, or very rarely, is there an effort to establish the honesty or capacity of the person being considered for a job, but what is certainly taken into account is whether the recommender has some degree of influence. Once this is established, the applicant is, of course, given a position—without further inquiry. There are also many cases of important jobs being obtained through the donation of money to those who have access to the government and enjoy its favor.

The result of this facile manner of handing out jobs is that there are many people in public employment who cannot handle the grammar of their own language or do simple arithmetic, nor can they write at even a medium level of proficiency. As for morality, the examples are as many as they are scandalous of employees who have made tremendous fortunes, abusing the confidence which the government has so ineptly reposed in them. Corruption of this kind has become so well-established and generally accepted—even in society—that nobody is scandalized to see a public employee who earns an annual salary of between two or three thousand pesos buy himself haciendas, furnish his townhouse with the most exquisite and costly appointments, and generally maintain his family at an extravagant level of luxury. None of this attracts any attention because such cases are innumerable, and the public has become accustomed to seeing that all employees—with very few exceptions—who have any access to public funds spend three or four times more than they earn.

Despite this scandalous corruption and ineptitude on the part of most bureaucrats, the government, even if it wants to, is powerless to remedy the situation. According to the laws of the Republic, the employee who is given a government office acquires in the act of being hired a *property,* which nobody, not even the government itself, can deprive him of without establishing just cause. The posing of this condition, given the way justice is administered in the country, is tantamount to declaring that the bureaucrats can do anything they want, secure in the knowledge that nothing will dislodge them from their jobs. . . .

Moreover, a dismissed employee, no matter how justified the government might have been in discharging him, is always well received by the opposite party, whose newspapers immediately begin a clamor against the *horrible attempt* on the part of the government to attack the employee's property without respect for due process of law. The government accused of taking such an action is branded as arbitrary, despotic, and tyrannical. . . .

From the above it would seem that the best office one could aspire to in Mexico would be that of government employee, and in effect these employees would have veritable sinecures if it were not for the fact that their very excess in number jeopardizes their situation as a group. In those countries that boast some kind of order, the number of employees hired corresponds to the number needed for specific offices; but in Mexico, where everything tends to go in reverse, the offices are created to accommodate the employees. . . .

For all these reasons, it can be seen that in this class of government employees, as with the military and the clergy, there does not exist, nor can there exist, an *esprit de corps*. Consequently, although this group is potentially strong enough to put a great deal of pressure upon society, it does not have the incentive to promote its individual interests by resort to concerted action, not even in defense of the very abuses upon which it thrives.

We have now brought to a conclusion this sad description of the state in which all classes of society in the republic now find themselves. . . . To discover that we have been guilty of error would indeed be cause for celebration, because we are, after all, Mexicans and would like nothing better than to see our fatherland happy and respected throughout the world; but we cannot indulge in illusions, and we do not believe that, in the picture we have traced of our society, we have told anything but those truths which nobody can deny, because they are visible to all who, free of emotional bias or delusion, are willing to see the reality of things.

Therefore, it seems utterly useless for foreign writers to seek feverishly such explanations as the *feminization or degradation of the Mexican race* in order to account for the indifference which this nation has shown toward the present war. It is equally ridiculous for Mexicans to engage in mutual recrimination over what has happened. For our part, we believe that everything is to be explained in these few words: IN MEXICO THERE IS NOT, NOR IS THERE A POSSIBILITY OF DEVELOPING A NATIONAL SPIRIT, BECAUSE THERE IS NO NATION. In effect, if a nation cannot call itself such without having all the elements that make for its happiness and well being internally while being at the same time respected abroad, then Mexico cannot properly call itself a nation.

It is useless to point out that the Mexican Republic possesses an immense territory of more than [840,000 square miles], bathed by two great oceans, with a multitude of navigable rivers, with the most varied climates in which all the fruits of the globe can be produced, with virgin territories whose astonishing fertility gives the farmer practically a 100 percent yield; where, as a culmination to the special bounty bestowed upon this land, there are great hills and mountains loaded with the most precious metals. All of this only serves to prove that this country has all the natural elements to make up a great and happy nation and that in the passage of time, on this very ground that we now tread upon, there will be a people who will without doubt occupy one of the prime positions among the most rich and powerful nations of the earth. But as long as fanaticism, ignorance, and laziness continue being the basis of our education and as long as we do not have a government which is truly enlightened and energetic, taking all the measures necessary to ensure the advancement of this society, the Mexican people, although treading on gold and silver, will be a weak and unfortunate people and will continue to present to the world the humiliating spectacle of a beggar emaciated by misery and hunger, living in a beautiful palace full of gold and all types of riches which he does not know how to make use of, not even for his own well being and happiness.

Liberals and the Land

Luis González y González (1925–2003)

Following the war with the United States and several more years of turmoil, a new, younger generation of Liberals, including Ignacio Comonfort, Miguel Lerdo de Tejada, and Benito Juárez, came to power determined to enact sweeping reforms that they hoped would propel their country headlong into the modern world. After seizing power in the Revolution of Ayutla (1854) — which overthrew Santa Anna for the last time — they immediately issued a series of decrees that came to be known collectively as "La Reforma" (the period of Reform) and would have long-range, and some dire, consequences. Among other things, they sought to transform Mexico's agriculture. Their failure to realize their dream of creating an enterprising, modern, scientific countryside, as we shall see, would be a major factor in the genesis of the Mexican revolution of 1910.

In the following selection, one of Mexico's most eminent social historians explains the problems the Liberals sought to overcome, what they hoped to accomplish, and why, in the end, they failed.

The creed of the Reform was defined on the same day the insurgents of Ayutla began calling themselves "Liberals," and the paladins of the Santa Anna dictatorship Conservatives and "crabs." That creed borrowed, in true Mexican style, from the fetishes and phobias of European and North American liberalism: the will to riches, freedom, order, democracy and science, and an end to tradition. It also featured a pair of purely national dogmas. One, formulated by Miguel Lerdo in 1856, held that: "Mexico's soil is some of the most fertile in the world." The other, in the words of don José María Vigil, maintained that "we Mexicans are unable to effectively exploit the physical and material gifts with which we have been blessed." Behind our natural greatness we glimpse the work of Providence; in our human failings, the work of History. . . .

The Liberal vision was comprised of a half-dozen freedoms — economic, political, intellectual, religious, pedagogical, and the freedom to work. This version of laissez-faire advocated the suppression of Tyrants, substituting the noble tyranny of the Law; this, in turn, in order to keep itself equidistant between despotism and chaos, required democracy, understood as government of the people, by the people, and for the people—but only once the people were capable of making good use of reason. Our reformers feared that Mexicans would not fulfill this requirement. "How can we establish and affirm liberal institutions?" asked Castillo Velasco in the Constituent Congress of 1856, "if for the majority of citizens liberty is a chimera and perhaps an absurdity?" . . .

The fact that the Reform was born in the tiny town of Ayutla and was initially led by an hacendado[1] should not lead us to conclude that its authors were farmers. Most had been educated in the city, where they were bureaucrats, doctors, lawyers, journalists, or poets. They were urban, middle-class people of modest means who were not entirely ignorant of country life. Some came by their knowledge of agriculture through childhood experiences; others had associated briefly with peasants during the civil strife [of the early nineteenth century]. Their knowledge of the countryside made them aware of the bad situation of the peasants, but it did not help them to appreciate the true magnitude of Mexico's agricultural resources. Thus, the Liberals could cling to their idea of a Mexican paradise "where not only is there eternal spring, but eternal too are the elements of life, prosperity, and progress."

These peculiarities do not exhaust the theme of the attitudes and worldview of the men of the Reform. But they are enough to provide an introduction to the three features of that party: their determination to find the route to wealth through agriculture, their image of the agrarian problem, and (given the timidities of their ideology) the audacity of their agrarianism. While similar governments of Europe heroically resisted the temptation to meddle in rural matters, ours undertook to convert virgin lands into fertile fields, miserable landless peasants into prosperous landowners, victims of peonage into free people, and slaves of myth into men of positive science.

The reformers divided the agrarian problem into several parts. In the technical sphere, they lamented the shortage of labor to cultivate the land, the rudimentary use of fertilizer and irrigation, the backwardness of cultivation, the felling of woods, the lack of capital, and the rickety means of communication and transportation. In the institutional sphere, they decried the abundance of unused land, the Indian communities, the depredations of "barbarians" [nomadic Indians], tithes, the "dead hand" [of the Catholic Church], the latifundio, peonage, civil discord, and the military draft. In the intellectual sphere, they bemoaned the magical and animistic notions of the peasants, their religiosity combined with an indifference toward science, ignorance of the Spanish language in some, and the lack of literacy in all. . . .

In a pamphlet of 1848, attributed to Mariano Otero, there appear words that would later be repeated endlessly: "Until now, all of the discoveries and improvements made in other countries to make agricultural operations faster and more economical have had no effect on the farmers of Mexico." The tools and the systems of cultivation remained as antiquated as they were ineffective. Very few farmers irrigated and fertilized their lands, and no one knew of the modern methods for procuring water and using chemical fertilizers in their fields. They were men of the past, and even the administrators of the haciendas were afraid of the technical improvements in production methods introduced by the North Americans.

To the farmers' backwardness was added their lack of capital: agricultural credit banks were unknown, and agricultural income did not permit capitalization. Not even the few wealthy farmers obtained appreciable profits, except when a fertile year was followed by two or three sterile ones, assuming their fields were close to some city or port that consumed or shipped these products. Generally each community, ranch, or hacienda produced no more or less than necessary to satisfy strictly local consumption. To violate this norm was to expose oneself to the risks of overproduction, while failing to cultivate enough to live on might bode famine. . . .

Several factors contributed to this misfortune. One was "the hateful servitude of the system of *alcabalas*" [duties on internal commerce]. Another was the dispersal, shortage, and indolence of the national population. And above all, there was the inefficacy of the means of communication and transportation. The muletrains and oxcarts did not permit agricultural surpluses, for they were expensive, slow and insufficient, making it unaffordable to transport merchandise from the centers of production to the markets of the country, let alone to overseas markets. The lack of railroads, navigable rivers, and shipping was lamentable, and the wretched state of the few existing roads added the final, grim touches to this picture.

To this list of adverse factors we might add rural institutions, which were obstacles to the economy as well as to freedom, democracy, and order. In this category were the "vacant lands" [*terrenos baldíos*] administered by Spain during the colonial era, and by the Mexican government from 1821. It was known that these occupied a large part of the country, but their exact location, size, and quality were not known. Most were virgin lands; a few were cultivated by indigenous occupants without title to the property, and a larger portion were frequented by the Apaches, nomadic peoples who made life, agriculture, and livestock raising very difficult in the [northern] states of Sonora, Chihuahua and Coahuila.

The Apaches, who were quite skilled with horses, lances, arrows, and firearms, knew the art of war and were incomparable as hunters. In the middle

The Hacienda Blancaflor, Yucatán. (*Mexico: A Higher Vision* [La Jolla, Calif.: Alti Publishing, 1990], 41.)

of the nineteenth century, when Yankee pioneers began to occupy their lands, they grew enraged to the point that they became the worst threat to lives and fortunes on both sides of the border. . . . In groups of ten, fifteen, or twenty individuals, they would fall upon caravans, haciendas and villages. They would customarily kill the men and take the animals, women and scalps of their victims. Due to their devastating efficiency, the populating of the North was delayed and the few inhabited, cultivated zones were quickly de-populated. . . . [Meanwhile,] Yaqui and Mayo Indians [of Sonora] were on a war footing against possible invaders of their lands. . . .

At the other end of the country, the belief that "Indians only hear with their backsides," put into practice by the landowners of Yucatán, caused the out-break in 1847 of an extremely cruel race war. For three years there was killing, robbery, and burning without truce and without pity. At the end of that time, it was tacitly agreed that the rebels would occupy the south of the peninsula, and the old masters, with their faithful Indians, the north. The southerners organized free states, invented a new religion, and established amicable rela-tions with the British of Belize. With the weapons given them by the British in exchange for hardwoods, they periodically invaded and devastated the hacien-das of their old masters who, for their part, also made frequent incursions into the strongholds of their ex-servants; any Indians they captured, they sold to the slaveowners of Cuba. These comings and goings of one and the other led to countless evils and to a new agricultural activity: the henequen industry.

The majority of the Republic's sedentary Indians (Nahuas, Otomís, Tarascans, Zapotecs, Mixtecs, Totonacs, Huaxtecs, etc.) were distributed among five thousand small villages which, instead of considering themselves part of a national whole, seemed like closed worlds. Each one owned a little land of poor quality, which was divided into "fundos" (the place where the village homes were located), "propios" (lands which were supposed to sustain the town leaders), "ejidos" (for the common uses of the population), and "lands of common distribution," used individually by the inhabitants and owned in common. When special protection of the Indians was ended by [the Liberal] regime of juridical equality, the haciendas seized part of the villages' lands, leaving them insufficient land to support the residents and obliging them to sell their labor as day workers. . . .

The stagnant wealth of the clergy, the so-called "dead hand," included property that was movable and immovable, productive and unproductive, rural and urban, all destined to benefit the religious orders, secular priests, seminaries, religious brotherhoods, and educational institutions. According to the calculations of Miguel Lerdo de Tejada . . . the value of those goods at mid-century amounted to around three billion pesos. The fact that they were not for sale was considered harmful to the public treasury and to private enterprise. The public treasury got no revenues from property transactions, and private entrepreneurs could not invest their money in buying properties from among the eight or nine hundred farms the Church rented to private parties, who, in addition to not being able to own those farms outright, did not work them properly.

The individually owned lands were called, according to their size, ranchos or haciendas. The ranchos (small properties) were viewed sympathetically by the leading lights of liberalism; the haciendas, which were over a thousand hectares in size and with populations of more than a hundred, were less well regarded. In 1854 there were 6,092 haciendas and a significantly smaller number of *hacendados*. The haciendas of the North and of the coasts were so vast that it would have taken several days to walk from one end to the other. Ponciano Arriaga, an orator of slow locution and hard phrases, railed against them in the Constituent Congress: "The accumulation by one or a few persons of great landed possessions, unworked, uncultivated, and unproductive, prejudices the common welfare and is contrary to the spirit of republican and democratic government." . . .

"The evidence has convinced me," wrote Luis de la Rosa, "that the system of cultivating the great landed properties by means of day laborers, who are called *peones,* is very harmful to public morality, and every day it becomes more prejudicial to the interests of the great landowners." The farm laborers worked poorly. They were furnished only with bad food, little clothing, and a hut made of sticks and straw. The worst thing was that they were paid partly in cash and another part in certificates exchangeable in the hacienda stores. Debt servitude was a truly anti-liberal system. In order to cover extraordinary expenses (marriages, baptisms, festivals and funerals) the peon indebted himself to the point of being sold to the patron, whom he could leave only through flight or because another master would pay the sum of his debt. In the first case, he would be pursued by the authorities and sometimes returned; in the second, he would gain nothing.

Administrators and majordomos [overseers] were nearly all the same. . . . They paid little, and punished much. With whippings and beatings they hoped to overcome the perpetual laziness of the peons and to punish their small crimes, above all that of getting drunk on Mondays. However much the Liberals defended the workers—saying that the blame lay with the miserable wage, debt servitude, the grinding workdays from sunup to sundown, and physical punishments—the overseers insisted on their tactics. . . .

The laborer, victim of peonage, was avenged by the bandit, who "never robs the poor/but only gives them money." "Highway robbers," their detractors called them; "heroes of the royal highway," said some Liberals, who recognized the justice of their cause. No one dared to defend them openly, since there was no moral defense for their armed assaults against the lives, properties and honor of landowners and travelers. They gathered for the purpose of murder and robbery. The gangs, which numbered in the dozens in the central states, had no political banner although at times they sought the protection of some political movement so as to avoid risks. At the head of every gang was a "robust captain, browned by the sun and the weather," skilled with horses, ropes, and weapons. . . .

We must not confuse bandits . . . with seditious chieftains or *"pronunciados,"* the tireless redeemers of the army in the first fifty years of independence. . . . The sum of all the *pronunciamientos* since the consummation of independence until the Liberal victory is generally given the mild name "civil struggle." . . . Among other evils, this "civil struggle" lubricated the forced military draft which, apart from violating human freedom, robbed agriculture of its best workers. In order to recruit troops—there was already an abundance of officers and chiefs—both the seditious parties and the tyrants would have their "draft commissions" fall upon the pueblos and haciendas. There they would round up the small farmers, selecting the most robust and leaving weeping mothers, widows and orphans behind. They would then take their new recruits to a barracks, from whence, after some instruction in the use of weapons, they would sally forth toward "all the slaughterhouses of the country," to die without glory, without ever knowing the "cause" they fought for, and leaving their families to fend for themselves.

There is yet a third point of rural life that the Reform condemned energetically: the survival of myth. Indian groups, especially those farthest from the center of the country, were still devoted to . . . a magical, animistic tradition. The rest of the peasantry, if less superstitious, clung to religious beliefs and attitudes that, at least in part, were incompatible with scientific progress. . . .

Superstition was compounded by ignorance of Spanish. Instead of the idiom of the majority, the Indians used poor minority languages. . . . Each ethnic group spoke in its own way, and there were more than a hundred aboriginal ethnic groups. Nearly a million and a half Indians spoke Nahuatl; around 500,000, Otomí; a quarter of a million spoke Maya; an equal number spoke Zapotec idioms; a few less, Mixtec; some 100,000, Tarascan, and smaller groups in some of the remaining tongues: Totonac, Tzotzil, Tzeltal, Huaxtec, Popoloc, Rarámuri, Zoque, Yaqui, Chontal, and so forth. None of these old languages was written. . . .

The remaining cultivators, although Spanish speakers, also failed to fulfill the requirements of modernity. Their religious ideas were not founded in gospel, were contaminated by superstition, and sanctioned intolerant and backward attitudes. Their secular knowledge was very slight; their lack of letters, total. And they did not even have opportunities to become educated. The children of the countryside did not attend the urban schools, while a school in the countryside was an extraordinary thing. The education efforts of Alamán, Mora, Alcocer, the Lancasterian Society, and other people and institutions during the first half of the nineteenth century, stand out both for the nobility of their objectives and for their failure. . . .

Liberal agrarianism proposed to remake the life of the countryside. With respect to economics, it tried to attract foreign capital, introduce new crops, modernize farming methods, suppress the *alcabalas,* and especially to increase the population, sowing virgin zones with foreign colonists, and building railroads, canals, highways and telegraphs. In social matters, the Liberals called for the survey and sale of "vacant" lands, the distribution of Indian communal lands among their co-owners, the amortization of ecclesiastical property, the division of the latifundios, freedom of labor, and war against Apaches, rebellious Indians, bandits, and troublemakers. The problem in the intellectual sphere it hoped to resolve by secularizing, spreading, and making compulsory primary education, and by creating an institute of agricultural studies. . . .

Writings by Luis Robles, José María Iglesias, Sebastián Lerdo de Tejada, Francisco Zarco, and Francisco Zamacona show a blind faith in the redemptive and profitable capabilities of modern means of communication, especially railroads. Robles said: "Peace, the increase of the population, equilibrium between public revenues and expenditures, and the export of the various fruits of our soil, are Mexico's necessities: all of them will be satisfied when we have a network of railroads that unites our producing districts with the coasts." Zamacona asserted: "The iron roads will solve all of the political, social and economic questions that the want and bloodshed of two generations have not been able to solve." . . .

By 1856, most European countries and the United States had a vast network of iron rails. Mexico, by contrast, had not even united its capital with its major port. Railroad building began to be taken seriously when the Liberal Party took power. While Ignacio Comonfort was president, concessions were granted to several construction companies. Political discord and the inexperience of some concessionaires retarded the task. The storm passed; new concessions were granted; and the older ones began to bear fruit. On December 20, 1872, at the Peak of Maltrata, the rails that went from Veracruz to Mexico City were united. On January 1, 1873, President [Sebastián] Lerdo de Tejada inaugurated the route. . . .

"Immigration has been the abiding dream of our governments," wrote Juvenal in 1871. Since Mexico had gained its independence it called for agricultural immigrants from the most advanced countries. In the age of Santa Anna very few came for fear of disorder and Mexico's religious intolerance, or so they said. The Constituent Convention of 1856, after heated debates, decided in favor of religious freedom. . . .

Immigration [the Liberals believed,] would bring incalculable benefits to the country: it would improve, for example, the moral situation of the Mexicans, and, above all, it would make our nation "one of the richest agricultural countries in the world." It would also colonize the virgin lands in a matter of years. . . .

Once Maximilian's Empire was defeated, the Liberals crowed: "Everything has changed, the masses of the country want colonization and colonization shall come, because foreigners know perfectly well that the Mexico of today is very different from what it was before." The years passed and the colonists did not come; people grew worried; and Congress passed the law of May 31, 1875, which gave the task of colonization to private enterprise and not exclusively to the State. [Under the terms of the law, the government] offered the immigrants lands at moderate prices with long-term financing, help in acquiring Mexican citizenship, and various economic incentives and privileges. In order to provide for the first expenditures of colonization, Congress approved an appropriation of 250,000 pesos.

To assist with colonization, the Liberals proposed to divide and sell the *terrenos baldíos* . . . On July 20, 1863, when the republican government found itself in San Luis Potosí, it expedited a general law of alienation of "vacant" lands which hoped to foment colonization and the small property. . . . Among the "illegitimate" owners of vacant lands were indigenous peoples whose lands were "denounced" and adjudicated to the denouncer. . . . The policy of *baldíos* did not favor the Indians, nor did it produce small property owners. It certainly did benefit the great latifundistas, as did the "Lerdo Law." The Lerdo Law had been passed on June 25, 1856 by [Treasury Secretary] Miguel Lerdo de Tejada. It ordered that properties belonging to civil and ecclesiastical corporations be adjudicated to their tenants or, in their absence, to those who denounced them or bought them at public auction. Article 8 of that order exempted the village *fundos* and *ejidos,* but it abandoned to fate the *propios* and the land of *común repartimiento,* and despoilments were in fact perpetrated. . . .

The Indians opposed all of these measures, both because they lacked the spirit of individualism and because they feared abuses. *El Constitucional* wrote: "A multitude of lands that are called 'communal' and which are cultivated by the Indians on their own account, have passed into the hands of denouncers, leaving the Indians, overnight, without a patch of ground on which to walk, and exposing them to the whims of the new owners." Ignacio Ramírez asked in 1868 that the parcelization of Indian property be suspended, since "communal lands had been usurped through a variety of means . . . , including buying judges and obtaining the complicity of superior authorities."

In the ten years of the Restored Republic [1867–1876], only a few villages had their lands divided; others, through hard efforts, managed to impede the division. These usually lost their lands later. The Indian, owner of his parcel of land, might find himself confronted one day by a cacique who would threaten to take the parcel from him for failing to pay his taxes. The Indian might consult a bad lawyer who was in connivance with the cacique. The bad lawyer would counsel the Indian to sell his land before losing it. The Indian would accept and cede the land to the cacique in exchange for . . . whatever. And this was only one of the multiple forms in which the despoilment was consummated.

The first law of divestment (that of June 25, 1856) sought, in addition to dividing the Indian communities, to take land from the "dead hand" of the Church and divide it up, thereby putting into circulation large amounts of stagnant wealth through a wise strategy which not only would not harm the clergy, but would actually help them. The clergy would be assured of the proceeds of their capital, and their property would be [improved] simply by changing its form. In addition, this would increase the funds of the public treasury, and bring other lesser benefits. But all of the bishops—if not the parish priests—protested against the law, and were not without influence in its application and results.

The majority of the tenants on the clergy's farms, and small farmers in general, refused to buy church property, some for lack of money, others due to the scruples of conscience. Not a single poor person escaped from poverty thanks to the Lerdo Law; but many rich landowners and merchants increased their fortunes without caring a bit about the excommunications thrown their way by the bishops, who, determined to do themselves in, fomented the wars of the Reform. In reply to that bellicose attitude, and in order to obtain a loan from the United States, Juárez ordered the nationalization of clerical property. The clergy, doubly wounded, remained on a war footing, but when they were defeated, they began to sell pardons at a low price to those who had added to their wealth with that of the church.

No energetic measures were taken against the secular latifundio. The majority of the Constituent Congress of 1856 was deaf to the propositions of men like Isidro Olvera, José María Castillo Velasco, and Ponciano Arriaga. Olvera proposed that the landowners with more than ten square leagues of cultivable land, or twenty of pastureland, be prohibited from acquiring more land. Castillo Velasco asked for the government's help in increasing the number of landowners. Arriaga went the farthest in his celebrated vote . . . in favor of the distribution of "our fertile and currently idle lands among the hardworking men of our country." He proposed that the owners of farms of more than fifteen square leagues be forced to enclose and cultivate them, under threat of losing them; to give *ejidos* to the villages that lacked them; and to distribute lots according to the census, buying the lands of surrounding haciendas for this purpose.

[More than] eighty *hacendados,* all of them "indifferent to political movements" . . . denounced the opprobrious words of Olvera, Castillo, and Arriaga against the sacred right of property; they held that for economic reasons, not merely those of justice, such words must be ignored. Congress, in the end, left the big landowners alone. . . . Apart from confiscating the farms of some of Maximilian's supporters and distributing one of them among 700 day laborers, [Congress] did nothing to demolish the secular latifundio, and nothing to slow its growth.

The Liberals' aversion to the system of peonage was translated into some measures of a juridical nature. It is well known that President Juárez, upon hearing a peon decry the whipping he had received for having broken a plow blade, ordered the abolition of corporal punishments. Furthermore, Article 5 of the Constitution of 1857 tacitly prohibited debt servitude. [Several state constitutions also included laws favoring resident farm workers.]

Other agrarian problems were attacked at gunpoint. Laws, political measures and campaigns were undertaken to suppress banditry. The laws of December 6, 1856, January 5, 1857, June 3, 1861, January 25, 1862, and April 13, 1869, established methods for judging and punishing brigands. To aid in their apprehension, Ignacio Comonfort created a security guard, and Benito Juárez, five years later, a corps of *rurales.* . . . In 1861, with the name of "Defender of Commerce," the first corps went into battle, and to it were added five more corps in the following decade. *Rancheros* for the most part (and some professional killers), the *rurales* made a considerable dent in the ranks of the brigands.

The campaign against the Indian rebels was very costly indeed. . . . In 1867, President Juárez conceded Yaqui and Mayo lands to Ignacio Gómez del Campo for colonization. The Indians, who did not understand colonization, rose up. [Ignacio] Pesqueira subdued them; they rose up again in 1868 and suffered another defeat. In 1875, José María Leyva Cajeme, mayor of the Yaqui villages, organized a respectable army, carried out a massacre of *yoris* [whites], overcame the governor, and withdrew his region from the realm of the legitimate authorities, organizing an independent state with its own laws and institutions.

In Yucatán, the war against the rebellious Mayas continued sporadically. . . . At the other end of the country, the Apaches renewed their incursions, and the Comanches also began attacks. In Sonora, the generals Elías, Morales, Urrea, Carrasco, Yáñez, Flores, and Pesqueira battled day and night and without much success against the Apache tribe of Cochise. In Chihuahua, Joaquín and Luiz Terrazas won renowned victories, thanks to which they were able to turn their state into the largest livestock empire in the world. [Authorities in] Coahuila and Nuevo León, who counted on the very valuable support of the Kikapu Indians, drove out the Comanches and learned how to handle the Apaches. In 1868, the central government decided to take a hand in the matter. Congress ordered that thirty military colonies be founded in the zone threatened by the "barbarians," with the double aim of obliterating the Indians and cultivating the desert. Each was made up of a hundred well-armed and -provisioned horsemen; half would be members of the army and the others volunteers from the surrounding regions. The colonists were to receive a monthly salary, plots of land, farming tools, and construction materials; in return, they were to strictly observe military discipline, under threat of losing their lands and being made to do forced labor. . . .

War of another sort was undertaken against the ignorance and vices of the peaceful population. José María Luis Mora had said: "The most necessary element for the prosperity of a people is the good use and exercise of reason, which cannot be achieved except through the education of the masses." Ignacio Manuel Altamirano would say: "What Mexico needs . . . is to open schools of primary education everywhere, in all of the regions of the country, profusely and at once." Justo Sierra asserted that Juárez's greatest dream was of schools, above all those which would rescue "the Indian families from their moral prostration, superstition; from mental abjection, ignorance; from physiological abjection, alcoholism; to bring them to a better condition, though conditions may improve but slowly."

The Constitution of 1857 stated: "education is free." The law of April 15, 1861 ratified the freedom of education and made official education free of charge. The Martínez de Castro law, promulgated on December 2, 1867 and applicable to the Federal District and federal territories, went further in making obligatory the learning of basic literacy and giving education a positivist orientation, inspired by the ideas of Auguste Comte, brought to Mexico by Gabino Barreda. The law of March 15, 1869 rounded out that of December 2, giving special emphasis to the regularization of elementary education. The majority of the states followed the example of the Federal District in expediting laws that declared primary education free of charge, scientific, and obligatory, and they provided for sanctions for parents who were remiss. . . . [However,] such new schools, for economic reasons, were not built in the countryside. . . .

Half of the rural population, the Indians, did not achieve anything and lost what little they had. The missions had been languishing since 1821 and ceased to exist at mid-century. The Liberal regime could not establish schools for Indians. Indians could not attend the schools of the Spanish-speakers because they did not know Spanish and it was difficult to find anyone to teach them. Ignacio Ramírez vainly suggested, among other practical measures, that the Indians be taught in their own languages. Between the native and Mexican races there was a wide gulf of language. The solution was urgent, and practically impossible. The great Liberal generation, led by Benito Juárez, did not solve it and, in the end, failed to realize their dream of transporting the Indian from the remote culture in which he lived to the liberal present.

The defeat of reformist agrarianism has provided historians of both the Right and the Left the pleasure of explaining it. Some say that the agrarian plan of the Reform was not carried out in all of its parts; that it was a trick to force the poor to quench the bourgeoisie's insatiable thirst for glory, comfort, and power. Others, fanatics for discipline, claim that the democratic-Liberal governments had no creative faculty, only a capacity for destruction. Witnessed from up close, between the words and deeds of Liberal agrarianism, instead of bad faith or ineptitude, one sees the confabulation of different adverse circumstances: the opposition of the clergy, the army and the landowners, the French intervention, the division of the Liberal group into *puros* and *tímidos,* the apathy of the people, the shortage of public funds, and so forth. . . .

Note

1. The nominal head of the Ayutla revolution was General Juan Alvarez, an aging veteran of the independence wars and a large landowner and regional caudillo from Guerrero state. *Ed.*

Standard Plots and Rural Resistance

Raymond B. Craib

Some of the authors in this volume insist that the fundamental problem of Mexican agriculture was fairly simple. Enrique Florescano, for instance, holds that "in the indigenous mentality, there was no concept of individual property." Luis González concurs, claiming that Indians "lacked the spirit of individualism." This supposedly innate preference for communal forms of land ownership, most historians contend, clashed with the vision of Liberals at mid-century: witness their celebrated 1856 Lerdo Law, which ordered municipalities to divide their communal lands into individual, privately owned plots. Such land divisions, the Liberals believed, would unleash the potential of the individual Indian farmer, and help to make him a true citizen of the nation. Land reform would also put an end to murkiness of land claims by clearly delineating boundaries; and it would enable the government to collect taxes on property and property transactions. In the commonly accepted version, Indian villages resisted the drive toward individualism and private ownership but were eventually dispossessed by corrupt officials and encroaching hacendados. The anger of Mexico's rural folk would become a crucial spark igniting the violent Mexican revolution of 1910.

Given that the end result of Liberal land reform was indeed the concentration of indigenous lands in the hands of large white landowners, this version seems plausible enough. Yet until recently, little research has been done in local archives to find out how the liberal vision translated into reality on the ground. In the following essay, Raymond Craib, a young agrarian historian at Cornell University, demonstrates that the state privatization of land was far more complex and unpredictable than most historians or contemporary state makers ever imagined.

Early in the morning on July 29, 1869, Martin Holzinger arrived with instruments and plans in the village of Acultzingo, Veracruz. The Prussian engineer had been hired by the municipal authorities to survey and divide the communal lands of the *municipio* into individual plots. The plots — clearly delineated, symmetrically established and numbered — would be recorded on a master map for deposit in the municipal archive as well as in the notary's office in the district capital of Orizaba. Although Holzinger finished his calculations by sunset, his land division eventually took the better part of three years to complete. He attributed the delay to "the lethargy of the Authorities, the apathy of the Indians, and the influence of the so-called Tetíazcal [indigenous chief] who, not wanting to see the lands of this pueblo divided, devised to discredit it and put up all kinds of traps so that it would not succeed." While Holzinger's survey was, by his own estimation, one of the earliest completed land divisions in the state of Veracruz, his complaints reveal how difficult the process could be. The land division was anything but the quick and easy triumph of geometry over geography.

LEGISLATED INTO EXISTENCE by individual states, such as Veracruz in 1826, and nationally codified in the Ley Lerdo of June 25, 1856, the *repartimiento de terrenos comunales* (division of communal lands) constituted the means by which land worked in usufruct by a largely indigenous peasantry and owned collectively by municipalities would be transformed into individual, privately held plots. Yet, for much of the century, the profusion of decrees, circulars, and laws brought little real change to rural Veracruz. How can this be explained?

Surveyors, Communities and the Practice of the Survey

While federal and state officials talked much about the need for, and benefits of, a land division, they were remarkably haphazard with regard to the practical issues of implementing that division. Veracruz's 1826 land division law, for example, had little to say about who would do the surveys, pay for them, or administer the process. Moreover, both state and federal governments lacked the technical, administrative and financial ability to oversee the process. As a consequence, the surveys—including the hiring, contracting and paying of the surveyor—became the responsibility of municipal authorities. Such an approach had the dual advantage of saving the government the costs of the land division and of keeping the newly installed Liberal regime in the good graces of the rural communities, upon whom it depended for support, by allowing them a substantial measure of control over the process. On the other hand, it meant that state officials immersed the land division process in the contentious social and political world of the villages.

From the beginning questions arose: How would the survey be conducted? How would the surveyor be paid? And, more fundamental still, who would do the survey? Land divisions, in theory, were to be done only by qualified surveyors due to official concerns that speculators might otherwise take advantage of "the ignorance of the Indians," but such a provision proved problematic. In particular, as federal and regional officials repeatedly noted, there were few professionally trained land surveyors in Mexico. In addition, more lucrative work than surveying communal lands awaited with the Ministry of Development's proliferating projects. As a result, an eclectic array of individuals performed the land surveys—large landowners, military surveyors working for the federal Geographic-Exploration Commission [or CGE, by its Spanish acronym], a surprisingly high number of foreigners, as well as community officials—and while some were qualified surveyors, many were not, particularly those community officials and regional elites chosen more for political, financial or personal reasons than for their abilities.

Little wonder that municipal authorities and different factions within communities argued vehemently over who would perform the survey. A well-documented dispute that erupted in the village of Ixhuacan de los Reyes in 1886 is a case in point. When the municipal president, over the opposition of the town *síndico* (the treasurer, who theoretically oversaw the land division process), appointed a local community member as the surveyor, a number of villagers took to the streets shouting "death to the authorities, long live Señor Síndico!" Although quelled quickly, their action prompted a visit by the *jefe político* (regional political authority) who noted that the protestors were not angered by the land division per se, but rather by the imposition of a surveyor whom they deemed not to be impartial. He managed to broker an agreement in which the surveyor would remain but his work would be subject to review by the *síndico*.

Village officials were not always free to contract with whomever they wished. Regional elites and state officials had their own personal, political, and economic interests at stake, and they often were able to influence the appointment of the surveyor. The political boss of Misantla in 1902 appointed an old colleague from his days in the CGE to survey and divide the lands under his jurisdiction, and many villagers charged that he was illegally rewarded for the appointment with several choice plots of land. Political alliances and animosities could lead to violent confrontations. A merchant in southern Veracruz wrote President Porfirio Díaz in 1887 complaining that the local political boss had forced an indigenous community to contract with an Italian surveyor at an inflated price of $20,000 pesos, a sum which, along with forced Indian labor, allowed the surveyor to live in a luxurious "feudal encampment" decorated with Italian flags. Not long after he posted his letter, the merchant and his wife, young son, six servants, and a business partner were murdered. The surveyor, Victor Assennato, and his associates were the prime suspects.

The contentious process which inevitably surrounded the selection of the surveyor calls into question conceptions of surveyors as impartial technicians who mechanically implemented state plans. Surveyors were subject to influences, threats and overtures from those around them, whether it be the blandishments of the powerful or anonymous threats, such as the one posted on a surveyor's door in Misantla: "Surveyor, my friend, go back to where you come from because if you stay, we'll meet you in the woods one day." Nor were surveyors simple lackeys of the state and large landowners. They came to the field with their own politics, persuasions and interests. In some instances, the federal government imprisoned surveyors as enemies of the state for purportedly inciting villagers to violence and rebellion. On other occasions, surveyors raised the ire of *hacendados*. When Victor Assennato surveyed the district of Acayucán, he in effect "translated" the old and imprecise land measurements in the villagers' colonial titles into contemporary dimensions so that they might set the boundaries of their community and recuperate lost land. In doing so, he sparked the ire of a powerful neighboring landowner who claimed that his modern translation was based upon payoffs rather than mathematics.

Once the surveyor was chosen, municipal officials signed a contract to have the survey performed. This meant not only measuring the land into plots according to the number of registered recipients but also creating a final map of the survey to be deposited in both the municipal and cantonal archives. The final map was critical to communities. If the surveyor departed without leaving a completed and certified map, communities were condemned to resurveying their lands at their own expense. A notorious case of this sort of abuse was that of Victoriano Huerta. Huerta, a military officer who would eventually go on to overthrow President Francisco Madero in the early stages of the Mexican revolution, contracted his surveying services while in the employ of the CGE to a number of villages in central and northern Veracruz in the 1880s. He apparently left these villages upon receipt of payment without completing the survey or producing a final map of the division. Ironically, Huerta had been sent to one of the municipalities in part because another surveyor had himself been accused of not completing his duties and of trying to charge land recipients for the maps of their parcels. Such instances increased the communities' suspicions about the entire land division process, particularly when their repeated complaints to state officials garnered only perfunctory and unsatisfactory responses. To protect themselves, municipal officials began drawing up contracts in which the surveyor was paid his fee at three different stages of the survey, and the last third only upon submission of the final map.

To pay the surveyor, municipal officials had a number of options: levy a fee on all members of the community who would be receiving plots; sell portions of the village's land; or give the surveyor portions of the land in place of

"Mapa del Pueblo de San Juan Bautista Acultzingo." Hand-drawn copy of a 1559 título primordial map submitted to the Comisión Geográfico-Exploradora, May 1895. (Archivo de la Comisión Geográfico-Exploradora, exp. 7, f. 243. Photograph by Carmen H. Piña. Reprinted by permission of Mapoteca Manual Orozco y Berra.)

money. Sometimes a combination of two options would be used. Regardless, forcing communities to cover the costs often ensured that the surveys would proceed only haphazardly. The costs could be an enormous burden, particularly for smaller villages. In addition, village officials were often tempted to use available funds to construct municipal buildings or purchase portions of land rather than to pay a surveyor.

Issues of payment could dramatically impact the survey in a multitude of ways. For example, it offered opportunities for powerful factions and interests to influence the parameters of the surveyor's tasks. In Acultzingo, the municipal authorities proved delinquent in paying Holzinger's expenses and he postponed his survey for some thirteen months. He returned to work when a group of merchants offered him a weekly fee of $25 [pesos], providing he also divided portions of land of interest to them not included in the original division — *monte* [forest] land on the outskirts of the village. Holzinger agreed, claiming it was "the only means of completing the division, because if I waited for the Authorities . . . it might never have been completed." In another instance, the issue of payment sparked a whole series of questions within and between communities about exactly what land could be divided and under whose jurisdiction. Such disputes further delayed the implementation of the land divisions.

Agrarian History and Practice

Once the surveys were completed, the process of plot distribution began. At the beginning of the survey, municipal authorities posted notices of the impending division, requesting that anyone in the community with rights to land and desiring to participate, sign up in order to receive a plot. The final list of recipients would then be used as the basis for determining how many lots would be created by the surveyor as well as their relative size. Once surveyed into existence, lots were usually assigned through a *rifa* — literally, a raffle. Although designed to minimize the potential for corruption in the land distribution, favoritism could still pervade the process. Villagers from Misantla reported to the state governor that people of money or influence inevitably received the best lands in their municipality. In addition, the *rifa* faced stiff opposition once villagers became aware of its ramifications. The land division (and the *rifa*) only ensured villagers a plot of land somewhere within the village bounds. Thus, the lot they received would not necessarily encompass the land they had worked or the area in which they lived and grew their crops. In 1886, a number of villagers wrote the state governor complaining that they were to "receive our respective lots in places very distant from the *congregación*, and where for reasons of distance we cannot cultivate without sacrificing our local interests . . . abandoning our home and our families." Signatories to another letter found it "unjust" that "after having opened up virgin lands at the cost of much sweat and labor" they should now lose them. Villagers stood to lose more than the lands they had cleared. Crops such as vanilla or fruit trees required significant inputs of labor before they began to yield with regularity. They also constituted the patrimony which villagers wished to pass down to their children. In sum, the *rifa* could not account for the villagers' particular means of working the land, or for what the land meant to them.

Villagers occasionally managed to alter the land distribution in such a way as to maintain the lands they had traditionally worked. An 1889 report to the state governor on a land survey in Santiago Tuxtla observed that "some villagers received more or less land in the division" than others. The author continued that, while such a difference might at first appear unjust, it was the result of the wishes of a number of recipients "who, having possessed certain parcels from a long-ago time, preferred to conserve these, although they would have less land surface than those lots indiscriminately adjudicated." In Minatitlán the *jefe político* determined that villagers could keep the houses they had built even if they had been granted a different lot in the land distribution as long as they did not assert any permanent rights to those lots. These kinds of locally improvised solutions reveal just how complicated the land division could become once implemented on the ground, and the imaginative ways in which some people tried to modify the system to their relative advantage (or minimum disadvantage).

More problematic for cultivators, however, was that the very logic that organized land as a patchwork of permanent parcels was not necessarily logical from the perspective of agrarian practice, tenure and history. Permanent parceling could hardly account for something as complex and local as the *rueda* (wheel), a form of tenure common in one mountainous region of Veracruz. The *rueda* was not, as one contemporary noted, "a determined agrarian measure, but an extension of land considered sufficient to provide a regular harvest in order that they do not go without maize during the year." That is, the size of the *rueda* changed yearly, even seasonally, to account for the vagaries of long-term weather patterns, soil quality, changes in the size of a family, the kind of crop being grown and so forth. A very local measure, it responded to villagers' need to minimize risks of hunger or starvation rather than maximize profits. Other questions arose: How could one survey and map the "properties" of cultivators who grew plants in several different areas but did not own the land upon which it grew? How could the crops of cultivators be respected if they sowed different crops in different places? They could not, as a reply by the *jefe político* of Misantla to the protestations of a large group of vanilla cultivators in 1887 clearly reveals: starting from the premise that it would be impossible to subdivide lands "dedicated to sugar cane or vanilla which are in general very small, almost insignificant, and *irregularly established*," he suggested they instead try to rent the land upon which their crops grew from the owners of the newly created lots.

Villagers and village authorities often struggled to modify the land division in such a way as to dampen the most egregious effects of permanent parceling. One common form was *condueñazgo,* a modification of the land division process in which land would be divided into large lots, each one held communally by a determined number of community members as shareholders. Each shareholder owned a share of the lot but did not have exclusive rights to any specific plot within its bounds. *Condueñazgo*, at least in theory, permitted traditional forms of agriculture to persist by maintaining a semi-communal form of tenure. The state government grudgingly legalized *condueñazgos* in 1874 due to concerns over potential resistance to the land divisions. Modifications occurred in other ways. In Acultzingo, the majority of villagers who registered to receive land in the division expressed discontent with the parameters of the original survey contract and effectively forced surveyor Holzinger to divide the communal lands with distinct surveys: one of *riego* (land directly abutting a water channel) and one of *temporal* (land suitable for cultivation only during the rainy season). Each recipient would receive a plot of both *riego* and *temporal*. This modification made sense: the natural springs which coursed through the municipality were the lifeblood of agriculture, ensuring the success of crops such as corn, beans, chickpeas, chile and barley.

As much as they mitigated the effects of the division, modifications such as these were not lasting solutions. *Condueñazgo* persisted only until an increased financial and military capacity permitted the state to break these up into individual lots or until local power holders saw the potential benefits of the permanent titling and codification of parcels. More to the point, villagers found themselves unable to alter the process of dividing property into permanent parcels. In contrast to, say, the *rueda*, permanent parceling could hardly account for change over time. The example of Acultzingo is instructive: in an era of steadily decreasing rainfall, many plots divided as *riego* land in 1870 were little better than plots of *temporal* by 1900, particularly those at the eastern edges of the village and furthest downstream from the water sources.

The *rueda*, rights to crops rather than territory, the personal and familial histories of use: these all defied easy summation. The land division, with its emphasis upon permanent parceling, simply could not account for the flexibility of customary tenure practices or for the modifications to such practices brought about by the demands of a constantly changing environment. The issue was not necessarily that of the imposition of private property over communal property. The "communal system" often easily accommodated forms of private ownership. The ultimate aim of land division, however, was to conceive of land as a series of *fixed* parcels which could not be altered by local realities. Such fixity promised stability for buyers and sellers of land and for state bureaucrats, but it could make life very unstable for farmers accustomed to using land in accordance with their local needs and customs.

Rethinking "Indian Resistance"

By the end of the century, 70 years after the first promulgation of a land division law in the state and nearly a half-century after the passage of the federal laws of the Reform, officials in Veracruz lamented that communal lands throughout the state had still not been divided. Governor Teodoro Dehesa, in 1897, succinctly summarized the common explanation for this persistence: "the indigenous class has always tenaciously opposed the division of communal lands." Dehesa's invocation reflected two prevalent assumptions among the establishment in Liberal and Porfirian Mexico: first, that surveys did not proceed apace because of a unified resistance on the part of an "Indian class"; and second, that Indians were by their very nature opposed to the land division because of some innate anti-liberal, communitarian ethic. Dehesa effectively conflated ethnic identity (Indian-ness) with ideology (anti-liberalism). Yet a closer look at the actual process of land division has suggested that such accusations hardly account for the lethargic pace at which land divisions progressed in nineteenth-century Veracruz.

In the first place, not all Indians opposed the land division. An emphasis upon "Indian resistance" reduced Indian communities to unified and homogeneous entities. They were not. There could be, and was, unity within diversity but the fact remains that villages were also riven by different kinds of conflict: class, generational, gender, and ethnic. Within communities some supported the land division while others did not. The municipal authorities who contracted surveyors often were, after all, Indians. In Acultzingo, Domingo Guzmán, the only living descendant of the original founder of the community in 1554, served on the municipal council the very year it hired Holzinger to divide the lands. During the land division, he received a special set of lands not subject to the same prescriptions as the standard lots given to others. And while Holzinger never named the merchants who paid him to do the land division and expand its parameters, we should not automatically presume that they were non-Indians or non-members of the community. By 1908, a small number of villagers, not just outsiders, had consolidated significant amounts of land.

Moreover, the constant delays in surveys were sometimes due to local disputes and negotiations over the process of implementation rather than simple opposition. As noted, disputes often erupted over *who* should divide the land or *how* it should be done and not necessarily over the fact of land division itself. The state's dependence upon local structures of power to implement the land division meant that it inherited all of the local conflicts, rivalries and histories which inevitably foiled the creation of a simple uniform grid. Although nicely articulated in speeches and decrees, on the ground the land division appears less as some kind of carefully articulated state strategy than a widely variable and contested process, shaped by a wide range of agents: municipal, regional, and federal authorities; landowners and local elites; and, not least, villagers and surveyors.

Dehesa, of course, did not entirely imagine "resistance" when he penned his speech in 1897. But we should be careful not to assume that such resistance had always been there or that it was uniform and unchanging. Such a conception merely serves to strengthen notions of a romantic but static tradition and, even worse, locates villagers outside history. Outright opposition to the land divisions was not, as Dehesa seemed to suggest, a visceral response conditioned by some primordial anti-liberal chromosome buried deep in the Indian's genetic code. The process of implementing the land division left much to be desired in the eyes of many and resistance to surveys most likely sprung from more historical (and admittedly mundane) roots: namely, an historical memory of error-ridden or incomplete surveys, dubious surveyors, and unsympathetic authorities. Land surveys were riddled with mistakes and problems or simply not carried out in the way they were supposed to be; surveyors did not fulfill their obligations; surveyors could be imposed upon villagers by interested federal, regional or municipal officials at exorbitant costs; and they were often neither trained nor impartial.

Resistance also increased as communities learned how little control they had over the final form of land distribution and the ways in which parceling would effect their agrarian practices, livelihoods and existing properties. Holzinger's journal, for example, reveals that opposition by both villagers and village authorities developed at specific points in time *over the course of his survey,* such as when he plotted out the *fundo legal* [urban township]. When Holzinger arrived in Acultzingo, he confronted a town "without a well-demarcated *fundo legal* and only two streets that scarcely deserve the name." He thus determined to create one himself, mapping into existence seven rectilinear streets and some 64 blocks of urban plots, "each with the symmetry which Modern Towns require and conforming to the Topography of the land." His actions generated vociferous opposition among villagers and the authorities who saw the urban plots and homes they had created being reordered to conform to Holzinger's aesthetic sensibilities. Even the town priest voiced his opposition, angered as he was by Holzinger's attempts to put a road through his farm which abutted the church.

Holzinger eventually completed his survey on May 15, 1872, a day, he wrote, which "will be one of joy among the unfortunate *indígenas* in that pueblo who before did not even have a home." For too long they had been "owners of everything . . . but possessed nothing." By 1911, however, most villagers in Acultzingo owned nothing. Within thirty years of Holzinger's survey, a small minority of indigenous villagers and mestizo elites had come to own the majority of Acultzingo's land. Land did indeed become concentrated in fewer and fewer hands, and Acultzingo did in fact become a hotbed of agrarian radicalism. Yet while many cultivators in the late nineteenth century might have predicted the consequences of the land division (which they accordingly sought to modify) and the obsession with standard plots, few could have foretold a revolution. We might accordingly modify the standard plot which constitutes the conventional agrarian history of nineteenth-century Mexico, one which, in a single leap of faith, fills the temporal gap between the issuance of a legislative decree and the loss of pueblo land with ready-made actors and romanticized notions of resistance.

Offer of the Crown to Maximilian

Junta of Conservative Notables

In addition to taking lands away from those who, in the Liberals' view, would use them inefficiently—namely the Indian communities and the Church—the Reform Laws also attacked the special privileges of army officers and Catholic clergy and sought to undercut the Church's ideological influence. These measures infuriated the Conservatives, who were supported by the Catholic and military hierarchy, and in 1857 they provoked a Conservative rebellion that came to be known as the War of the Reform. The Liberals emerged victorious in this bloody three-year civil war, but owing to its terrible destruction, President Benito Juárez presided over a destitute country in 1860. Conservatives continued to decry the liberal course of the Republic, while foreigners clamored for repayment of Mexico's debts, old and newly acquired. Juárez found himself obliged to suspend all payments on the foreign debt in July 1861, whereupon England, France, and Spain opted for military intervention. They landed troops at Veracruz in October 1861. While the aggressors had formally foresworn any intention of armed conquest, it soon became clear that Napoleon III, emperor of France, intended precisely that. With the United States in the throes of its own civil war, the French emperor thought it a good time to defy the Monroe Doctrine and to stake a French claim to New World territory. It took his armies nearly two years to seize the Mexican capital from Juárez's dogged republican regime.

Napoleon III found some eager allies in Mexico's Conservatives, who had long been persuaded that republicanism was at the root of Mexico's woes and that monarchy was the only form of government suited to their country. After reviewing the available European princes, they settled on Maximilian, the Hapsburg Archduke of Austria. In the following selection, a Junta of Conservative Notables formally offers Maximilian the crown on July 10, 1863.

1. The republican system, whether it takes the form of a federation or a centralized government, has, during the many years of its existence, been a fertile source of all the many evils that afflict our country, and neither good sense nor political reason permit us to hope that it can be remedied except by destroying the sole cause of our misfortunes at its root.

2. The institution of monarchy is the only one suitable to Mexico, especially in our current circumstances, because it combines order with liberty, and strength with the strictest justification. Thus, it is nearly always capable of imposing order over anarchy and demagogy, which are essentially immoral and disruptive.

3. To found the throne, it is not possible to choose a sovereign among the natives of the country (although there is no shortage of men of eminent merit), because the principal qualities that distinguish a king are those that cannot be improvised, and it is not feasible that a simple private individual should possess such qualities, much less that they can be established, without other antecedents, by a mere public vote.

4. And finally: a prince who stands out for his clearly exalted lineage, no less for his personal virtues, is the Archduke Ferdinand Maximilian of Austria. It is he who must receive the vote of the nation so that he may rule its destiny, because he is among the descendants of the royal house most distinguished for its virtues, extensive knowledge, elevated intelligence, and special gift for governance.

The Commission, accordingly, submits for the definitive resolution of the respectable Assembly, the following propositions:

1. The Mexican nation adopts for its form of government a MODERATED MONARCHY, hereditary, with a Catholic prince.

2. The Sovereign shall take the title of Emperor of Mexico.

3. The imperial crown of Mexico is offered to His Royal Highness, Prince Ferdinand Maximilian, Archduke of Austria, for himself and his descendants.

4. In case unforeseeable circumstances prevent the Archduke Ferdinand Maximilian from taking possession of the throne that is offered him, the Mexican nation shall appeal to His Majesty Napoleon III, Emperor of the French, to indicate another Catholic prince.

A Letter from Mexico

Empress Carlotta

Maximilian and his wife Carlotta arrived in Mexico in June 1864 to begin what turned out to be a dramatic and disastrous three-year attempt at ruling a Mexican Empire. They were opposed from the start by the Liberals, led by Benito Juárez, who kept up a steady armed opposition. These Liberals were joined by nationalistic Conservatives who resented foreign domination. Maximilian made the roster of his foes complete by making it clear that he was, in fact, a liberal at heart. His draft constitution upheld the reform laws attacking the nation's Catholic Church, endorsed religious freedom, decreed the equality of all Mexican citizens under the law, forbade debt peonage and corporal punishment, and protected the rights of workers. These declarations were likely intended to win the hearts and minds of the Mexican poor, but as the following selection makes clear, their more crucial impact was to cost the emperor the support of the hardline, religious Conservatives who had previously been his greatest champions. While Maximilian and Carlotta made great show of adopting the customs of the country, it was obvious that they had a limited appreciation of Mexico's cultures; the empress's letter suggests that she held the country's inhabitants in low regard, particularly Mexican liberals, who are dismissed as so many bands of brigands. Increasingly, the monarchs found themselves almost entirely dependent on the support of the French army. As the civil war in the United States wound down, Napoleon III determined that his imperial adventure was doomed and began withdrawing his troops. Maximilian, in the words of his private secretary, was stubbornly naïve: "It was the Emperor's great illusion that if he could talk to Juárez he could attract him to his cause, make him his ranking minister, and aided by him, and freed of the intervention of the French, he could govern the Empire wisely and inaugurate for Mexico, in its entirety, an era of peace, progress, and well-being."[1]

In the following letter to the French empress Eugenie, Empress Carlotta implores the French monarchs to reconsider withdrawing their troops and outlines her vision of Mexico's future. Carlotta would leave Mexico in July 1866 to personally plead for greater French military support. In Europe, the unmistakable signs of serious mental illness became manifest, though she lived until 1926. Maximilian and two of his top generals were captured by the triumphant Liberals, court-martialled, and executed by firing squad on June 19, 1867.

Chapultepec, February 3, 1865

Madam and beloved sister,

I hope that the Emperor will effect no more reductions before he has heard General Douay. I think that if we are to do well this year, we shall require an effective force of forty thousand men, including all nationalities. This means that if a few thousand more could come to us from France, by continuing re-cruiting elsewhere, with the aid of money (though I do not know where we shall get it), we might perhaps reach this figure. It seems to me that M. Jules Favre² could not but approve of our being assisted in combating the clergy, for it is only the latter which, combined with disorder and the Juarista bands, calls for an increase of the troops. This would be far from decreasing the con-fidence felt in the future of Mexico even in Europe, for it is in fulfilling its duty that our Government is meeting with resistance from the elements which it is bound to destroy so as to clear the way to order, progress, and the true and brilliant future of this country — *European immigration.*

It will not be long before France reaps a rich harvest from what she has sown. The traffic between Le Havre and Vera Cruz was considerable last year, and who knows how many French will come and settle here?

As to what the good marshal said — that there are more organized bands from Vera Cruz to San Blas and from Durango to Monterey [*sic*] — Your Maj-esty would think I give you false reports if this were true, but nothing could be less accurate at the present moment, and General L'Hérillier is obliged to dispatch expeditions from Mexico in every direction with the greatest energy, there are so many bands.

It is also announced that a certain number of *pronunciamientos* are about to take place in favour of *"religión y fueros"* [religion and clerical privileges], at Guadalajara among other places.

It seems to me that it would be easy to send us some reinforcements from Algeria now that everything seems to be over there. Frankly, supposing that we were not supported, we should have to set aside all our projects of reform and govern as M. Gutierrez³ desired, surrounding ourselves as with a great wall of China. I quite see that this system was perfectly rational; it was also eminently Mexican and that was what was wrong with it; whereas it is our mission gently, affectionately, but none the less surely, to attract to Mexico a stream of population which shall absorb the old one, for there is nothing to be done with the existing elements. I should say it quite openly if I were not afraid that it would be repeated here. I rely upon immigration, which will perhaps begin this year, and if I were not convinced that it would be considerable, I should be bound to admit to Your Majesty that all we are doing would be to no purpose. The affair of the clergy has been the touchstone which has confirmed me in all the ideas which I formed as soon as we arrived, and I see that I was not mistaken. However that may be, it is rather fortunate that we have found out in time that Europe alone can fitly people this Empire, and if Your Majesty's gentle influence can provide us with a few more troops, the situation will be *afianzada* (secured). I do not doubt for a moment that Your Majesties will regret the reductions when you know what is going on. I therefore rely with the utmost confidence upon the hand which pressed ours on March 12 and on April 10 traced those lines which are the expression of a great power as well as of a sovereign friendship: "Always rely upon my friendship and support."

I put my trust in that hand, in Your Majesty's heart, and in him who said: "God helps those who help themselves."

It seems to me that by all these means together, we cannot fail to triumph.

The poor Holy Father is doing us a pretty service in Europe with the encyclical.[4] If I might allow myself a slight irreverence, I should say that if it comes from any spirit at all, I do not think it is the Holy Spirit. Our Lord gave peace to His Apostles and did not address them in any other terms; nowadays it is trouble that they are trying to disseminate.

Ah! if Bossuet[5] were still living, it would be he and the clergy of France, who are so able and so Catholic, to whom we should owe the salvation of Europe from a schism. If it were not for the Gallican church, confusion would fall upon men's consciences in the attempt to reconcile the irreconcilable. God did not make faith and reason to contradict each other, but to confirm each other. I find this very consoling. . . .

As for our costumes, we dress in Mexican fashion, I go out riding in a sombrero, our meals are in the Mexican style, we have a carriage drawn by mules with quantities of bells, we never use any wraps but sarapes, I go to mass in a mantilla; in short, if we have any secret thoughts of emigration, it does not look like it. It is not reforms that shock men, it is the way in which they are carried out; and so in all that is external and puerile we conform to all that is most Mexican, to such an extent as to amaze the very Mexicans themselves. My parties end after one o'clock. Next Monday will be the sixth. I dance a few quadrilles, one of which is regularly with General L'Hérillier. I am gradually inviting all the French officers, even the paymasters, who had a great longing to dance. . . .

Life here is almost like the Middle Ages; we are gay, contented, and calm,

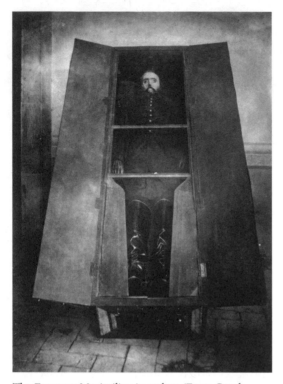

The Emperor Maximilian in casket. (From Carole
Naggar and Fred Ritchin, eds., *Mexico Through Foreign
Eyes, 1850–1990* [New York: W. W. Norton, 1993], 163).

and yet there is nothing to prevent a band of guerrillas from falling upon us
at any minute. Up here we have cannon and a system of signals for communicating with the city. But that does not prevent us from being always on the
look-out. The night before last I got up on hearing cannon-fire; it was a tumultuous celebration in honour of the Virgin of Tacubaya, as if the Presentation
had taken place at four in the morning; I suppose it was to allow for the difference of time between here and Jerusalem. All religious festivities take place
here at night, amid an explosion of fire-crackers, as if the earth were being
rent asunder. In the daytime festivals go off more quietly. There is no denying
that this country has a character all its own; Gutiérrez was quite right about
that too, except that he liked it, whereas we see nothing to respect in it and
shall act in such a way as to change it. The masses are excessively stupid and
illiberal, and it is not the *licenciados* (intelligentsia) who will stir them up; that
explains the strangle-hold which the clergy have managed to obtain on them;

it does not educate the people, and so they remain as they are, and because they are as they are, the clergy has a free hand.

Your Majesty has doubtless read Marie Antoinette's charming letters published by M. d'Hunolstein? This suggests the reflection that everything comes to light one day, whether one is celebrated or not; one does not know what may happen, and when one expresses judgments that are not very charitable, it is not at all to be desired. Your Majesty will see what I am driving at. In order to be quite sure that the Mexicans do not know what I am saying about them until a new nation is in being which will say the same, I should be glad if Your Majesty would destroy all my letters. They are intended only as conversations; once the idea is expressed, my object is attained. It would be a service on your part which I should appreciate extremely.

Meanwhile, in concluding this long letter I beg Your Majesty to be assured of the unchanging attachment with which I am

Your Majesty's good sister and friend,

Carlotta

Notes

1. José Luis Blasio, *Maximilian, Emperor of Mexico: Memoirs of his Private Secretary*, translated and edited by Robert Hammond Murray (New Haven: Yale University Press, 1934), 62. *Ed.*
2. Jules Favre (1809–1880), leader of the republican opposition to the empire of Napoleon III. *Ed.*
3. Apparently a reference to José María Gutiérrez de Estrada, a diehard Mexican monarchist who had worked since the 1840s to bring a European prince to a Mexican throne. *Ed.*
4. In 1864, Pope Pius IX (1792–1878; pope 1846–1878) angered progressive Catholics with his encyclical *Quanta cura*, which was accompanied by a so-called "Syllabus of Errors," which harshly denounced liberalism, republicanism, democracy, rationalism, and many other features of the modern world. *Ed.*
5. Jacques Bénigne Boussuet (1627–1704), French priest, regarded as one of the greatest orators in French history. *Ed.*

The Triumph of the Republic, 1867

Benito Juárez

The Liberal victory over Maximilian in 1867 was a source of patriotic pride for many Mexicans, but it was also widely interpreted as the definitive victory of republicanism in Mexico. In the following selection a triumphant Juárez issues a stirring proclamation to the Mexican people on July 15, 1867. The brief and eloquent proclamation is redolent with meanings. First, it celebrates the nation's will to survive the darkest night in its young history. During Mexico's longest foreign occupation since Bourbon times, Juárez himself became a national icon, an indomitable, peripatetic figure who kept the idea of a sovereign republic alive, sometimes only a few leagues ahead of the Empire's pursuing forces in his simple black coach. Second, the proclamation signals Juárez's determination to transcend the bitter, internecine conflict between Liberals and Conservatives that had undermined the republic's entire existence. The challenge, he points out, is to reconcile justice with national reconciliation. An example was made of Maximilian and two of his top generals, who were executed under the law, but there would be no further rounds of vengeance against fellow Mexicans. Finally, the reader will detect a certain irony in this declaration. Juárez pledges himself to uphold Mexico's free republican institutions, emphasizing that henceforth the Mexican people will be the arbiters of their fate. How ironic that Juárez's subsequent Restored Republic (1867–1872), which would usher in an era of sustained growth and stability, would also witness the creation of a formidable Juarista Liberal political machine. In laying the groundwork for both a modernizing economy and an authoritarian central state, Benito Juárez was the precursor of Mexico's quintessential order and progress caudillo, Porfirio Díaz.

Mexicans: The national Government today returns to establish its residence in the City of Mexico, from which it fled four years ago. At that time it made a resolution never to abandon its duties, which were all the more sacred when the nation's conflict was the greatest. It did this with the clear confidence that the Mexican people would fight unceasingly against the iniquitous foreign invasion, in defense of their rights and their freedom. The Government fled so that it could sustain the banner of the fatherland for as long as necessary,

Despite his stirring rhetoric about republicanism, Benito Juárez became increasingly auto-cratic in the later years of his government, and the system grew increasingly corrupt. In this cartoon, drawn by Santiago Hernández, pesos from the national treasury drop bal-lots into an electoral urn held by Juárez and his finance minister. The caption beneath the cartoon contains one of President Juárez's more unfortunate turns of phrase: "Go tell the people that they have voted and that thus speaks the Supreme Government." (Originally published in *La Orquesta,* June 30, 1869)

until it obtained the triumph of the holy cause of independence and of the institutions of the Republic.

The good sons of Mexico have achieved this triumph, fighting alone, with-out anyone's help, without resources, without the elements necessary for war. They have shed their blood with sublime patriotism, making every sacrifice, for they would never consent to the loss of the Republic and of their freedom.

In the name of the grateful fatherland, I pay tribute to the good Mexicans who have defended it, and to their worthy leaders. The triumph of the father-land, which has been the object of their noble aspirations, shall always be their greatest claim to glory and the best reward for their heroic efforts.

With full confidence in the people, the Government complied with its duties, without ever once thinking it licit to reduce any of the rights of the nation. The Government has fulfilled the first of its duties by not contract-ing any compromise overseas or in the interior of the country which could prejudice in any way the independence and sovereignty of the Republic, the integrity of its territory, or the respect due to the Constitution and laws. Its enemies tried to establish another government and other laws, but they were unable to realize their criminal intentions. After four years, the Government returns to the City of Mexico, with the banner of the Constitution and with the same laws, without having ceased to exist for a single instant within the national territory.

The Government does not wish, has never wished—especially now, in the hour of the complete triumph of the Republic—to allow itself to be inspired by any sentiment of passion against the enemies that it has fought. Its duty has been, and is, to weigh the demands of justice with all of the considerations of mercy. The restrained nature of its conduct in all of the places where it has resided has demonstrated its desire to moderate as far as possible the rigor of justice, conciliating indulgence with its strict duty to apply the laws as far as is necessary to secure the peace and future of the nation.

Mexicans: We direct all our strength to obtain and consolidate the benefits of peace. Under the Government's auspices, the protection of the laws and the authorities shall effectively ensure the rights of all of the inhabitants of the Republic.

The people and government must respect the rights of everyone. Among individuals as among nations, peace means respect for the rights of others.

We have confidence that all Mexicans, taught by the prolonged and dolorous experience of the calamities of war, will henceforth cooperate for the well-being and prosperity of the nation, which can only be achieved with inviolable respect for the laws and with the obedience of the authorities elected by the people.

In our free institutions, the Mexican people are the arbiters of their fate. With the sole aim of sustaining the cause of the people during the war, while they were unable to elect their leaders, I have had to, in accordance with the spirit of the Constitution, retain the power that was conferred upon me. Now that the struggle is ended, my duty is to convoke the people at once so that, with no pressure or illegitimate influence upon them, they may choose with absolute freedom the person to whom they wish to entrust their fate.

Mexicans: We have achieved the greatest good that we can desire, having consummated for the second time the independence of our fatherland. We shall all cooperate so that we will be able to bequeath prosperity to our children, loving and sustaining always our independence and our freedom.

Porfirio Díaz Visits Yucatán

Channing Arnold and Frederick J. Tabor Frost

In 1876 General Porfirio Díaz, a hero in the war against the French, overthrew the government of Juárez's successor, Sebastián Lerdo de Tejada (who had come to office when Juárez died suddenly at the beginning of his fourth term, in 1872). Díaz's rallying cry was "Effective suffrage, no reelection"; yet, with the exception of a four-year interregnum, he would be Mexico's dictator until 1911, presiding over an increasingly harsh and corrupt system. The pace of the global economy greatly accelerated during these years, and countries like Mexico, which depended heavily on the export of raw materials to the industrialized nations, experienced a frenzied pace of change which proved, in general, to be bad news for the laborers of the country. As the demand for Mexico's exports grew, so too did the demands on labor. Working conditions in many areas — such as the tobacco plantations of the Valle Nacional in Oaxaca, the lumber camps of Chiapas, and the henequen fields of Yucatán — gained great notoriety as regions where the most barbaric forms of "slavery" were practiced. While many travelers to Mexico may certainly be accused of using the term slavery imprecisely, the conditions they described — debt servitude, extreme exploitation, corporal and even capital punishment — were harsh by any standard.

In their grim portrayal of conditions of life on Yucatecan haciendas, British travel writers Arnold and Frost were hardly scientific in their observations and were rather sweeping in their judgments. In their haste to indict the planters of Yucatán, they occasionally fall into factual errors. Moreover, they seem intent upon proving the notion that tourists tend to view other societies with an "imperial gaze": thus, they often compare the Yucatecan elite unfavorably with their more noble British counterparts; they allow that slavery may sometimes be a justifiable means of domesticating an inferior race; they favor corrective action by the United States; and they make much of the supposed docility of the Maya — a charge that was often made, but invariably mistaken. However, in their account of Porfirio Díaz's visit to Yucatán, Arnold and Frost hit upon a key feature of the regime: its tendency to treat Mexico's most grievous problems with that simplest of strategies, denial.

Porfirio Díaz poses in front of the Aztec sunstone.
(Reprinted by permission of Fototeca de INAH, Mexico.)

There would be no hardship [for the Maya of Yucatán] if—and it is a large, large IF—the patient toiler were a free man. The Yucatecans have a cruel proverb, *"Los Indios no oigan sino por las nalgas"* ("The Indians can hear only with their backs.").[1] The Spanish half-breeds have taken a race once noble enough and broken them on the wheel of a tyranny so brutal that the heart of them is dead. The relations between the two peoples is ostensibly that of master and servant; but Yucatan is rotten with a foul slavery—the fouler and blacker because of its hypocrisy and pretence. . . .

The Yucatecan millionaires are very sensitive on the question of slavery, and well they may be: for their record is as black as [Simon] Legree's in *Uncle Tom's Cabin.* You have but to mention the word "slavery," and they begin a lot of cringing apologetics as to the comforts of the Indians' lives, the care taken of them, and the fatherly relations existing between the haciendado [*sic*] and his slaves. . . . They take just so much care of the Indians as reasonably prudent men always take of their live stock; so much and no more. . . .

A recent visit [was] paid to the country by President Díaz. It was the first time during the whole of his long reign that the great man had troubled himself about the limestone peninsula which forms the furthermost eastern part of his dominions, and the trembling Yucatecans looked to the bolts of the cupboard in which the family skeleton was hidden, and they were not oversatisfied with those bolts. They had new locks made and new and thicker doors fixed so that august presidential ears should not be offended by the rattling of those most unfortunate bones. With their teeth chattering, they hastened to put their house in order and sweep and garnish it, for they knew quite well that the eyes into which they had to throw dust were eyes which could see further than most eyes. It was all the fault of a snobbish governor. Many a henequen lord must have cursed the self-importance of their parvenu chief which had induced in him such discontent with the Spartan-like simplicity of his rule at Merida that he must needs wish to entertain presidential guests and bask in the sunshine of the mighty Díaz's approval. Díaz, they knew very well, cared little or nothing for Indians *qua* Indians. But Díaz cares immensely about the fair name of Mexico, which they knew they had done for years all they could to besmirch. Would he see the skeleton through the fatal door? If money and bribery were of any avail, those slave-owners would see to it that their terrible ruler should be fooled. But they had to calculate on more than his natural perspicacity. There was much reason to believe that ugly rumours had reached Mexico City of the slavery rife in Yucatan, and that the President's visit was not unconnected with these. That skeleton must be cemented into its cupboard with the cement of millions of dollars if necessary.

Well, the President came. Never were there such junketings: night was turned into day; roadways were garlanded; gargantuan feasts were served. Lucullus never entertained Caesar with more gorgeous banquets than the henequen lords of Merida spread before Díaz. Small fortunes were spent on single meals. One luncheon party cost 50,000 dollars: a dinner cost 60,000, and so on. The official report of the reception reads like a piece out of the *Arabian Nights*. In their eagerness to keep that skeleton in its cupboard some of the haciendados actually mortgaged their estates. One of the most notable of the entertainments provided was that of a luncheon at a hacienda ninety miles south-east of the city of Merida. At the station where the President alighted for the drive to the farm, the roadway was strewn with flowers. Triumphal arches of flowers and laurels, of henequen, and one built of oranges surmounted by the national flag, spanned the route. The farm-workers lined the avenue of nearly two miles to the house, waving flags and strewing the road with flowers, while a *feu-de-joie* of signal rockets was fired on his alighting from his carriage. He then made a tour of the farm. Having inspected the henequen machinery he (we quote from the official report) "visited the hospital of the finca, and the large chapel where the Catholic labourers worshipped; the gardens and the beautiful orchard of fruit trees; and during this tour of inspection he honoured several labourers by visiting their huts thatched with palm-leaf and standing in their own grounds well cultivated by the occupants. More than two hundred such houses constitute the beautiful village of this hacienda, which breathes an atmosphere of general happiness. Without doubt a beautiful spectacle is offered to the visitor to this lovely finca with its straight roads, its pretty village clustering round the central building surrounded by gardens of flower and fruit trees."

At the luncheon the President in the course of his speech said: — "Only can a visitor here realise the energy and perseverance which, continued through so many years, has resulted in all I have seen. Some writers who do not know this country, who have not seen, as I have, the labourers, have declared Yucatan to be disgraced with slavery. Their statements are the grossest calumny, as is proved by the very faces of the labourers, by their tranquil happiness. He who is a slave necessarily looks very different from those labourers I have seen in Yucatan." The prolonged cheers and measureless enthusiasm evoked by these words (one can understand how the conspirators chuckled at the success of their efforts at deception) were agreeably interrupted by the appearance of an old Indian, who made a speech of welcome in his own language, presenting a bouquet of wild flowers and a photographic album filled with views of the hacienda. It is not necessary to quote the fulsome stuff which had been placed in the mouth of the poor old man by his master. It is simply a string of meaningless compliments which ends with these words: "We kiss your hands; we hope that you may live many years for the good of Mexico and her States, among which is proud to reckon itself the ancient and indomitable [surely a pathetic adjective under the circumstances] land of the Mayans." Well may the official report say that "it is only justice to declare that the preparations of the feast and the decorations of the finca showed that the proprietor had been anxious to prepare everything with the most extraordinary magnificence."

This feast was a gigantic fraud, a colossally impertinent fake from start to finish. Preparations indeed! That is the exact word to describe the lavish entertainments of Mexico's ruler here and elsewhere in Yucatan. Tens of thousands of dollars were lavished to guard the haciendados' secrets. In this particular case the huts of the Indian labourers which the President visited were "fake" huts. They had been, every one of them, if not actually built for the occasion, cleaned, whitewashed, and metamorphosed beyond recognition. They had been furnished with American bentwood furniture. Every Indian matron had been given a sewing-machine; every Indian lass had been trimmed out with finery and in some cases, it is said, actually provided with European hats. The model village round which the President was escorted was the fraud of a day; no sooner was his back turned than to the shops of Merida were returned sewing-machines, furniture, hats and everything, and the Indians relapsed again into that simplicity of furnitureless life which they probably cordially preferred. We are not quoting the "faking" of this village as an example of hardship dealt out to the Indians, but as a proof of the ludicrous efforts made by those whose fortunes have been and are being built on slave labour to hide the truth from General Díaz. As for the poor old Mayan who addressed him, and as for the deputations of whip-drilled Indians who were paraded before him to express their untold happiness and loyalty, they very well knew that they had got to do exactly what they were told to do. We are not exaggerating when we state that it would have cost any Indian his life to have even attempted to make General Díaz aware of the truth. No Indian throughout civilised Yucatan could have been found to make the attempt. For nothing is sadder than the lack of all manliness and spirit which characterises the average Indian workman. . . .

If the hardship of the Indians' lot was merely slavery, it might be argued that there were slender grounds for our indictment. Slavery may under certain circumstances be far from an evil, where the backward condition of a race is such as to justify its temporary existence, and where the slave-owner can be trusted. But the slave-owner can very seldom be trusted, and he certainly cannot be in Yucatan. It is no exaggeration to say that the enslavement of the Indians of Yucatan never has had, never can have, justification. Conceived in an unholy alliance between the Church and brute force, it has grown with the centuries into a race-degradation which has as its only objects the increasing of the millions of the slave-owners and the gratification of their foul lusts. The social condition of Yucatan to-day represents as infamous a conspiracy to exploit and prostitute a whole race as the history of the world affords. Yucatan is governed by a group of millionaire monopolists whose interests are identical, banded together to deny all justice to the Indians, who, if need be, are treated in a way an Englishman would blush to treat his dog. . . .

And so, after centuries of oppression, the race is dead, a chattel, body and soul, of a corrupt and degraded people. When the task of revivifying these poor Mayans with the elixir of freedom is undertaken, if it ever is (and pray God it be), by the United States of America, it will be as difficult as nursing back to convalescence a patient sick unto death. No beings will at first understand freedom so ill. They are like prisoners who have been for weary years in the darkness of unlighted dungeons. The glare of the sunlight of freedom will be too dazzling for their poor atrophied eyes. They will shade them and cringe back into the gloom. . . .

Note

1. The term *nalgas* is a bit cruder than Arnold and Frost would have it. A better translation might be "backsides" or "rumps." *Ed.*

Scenes from a Lumber Camp

B. Traven

The mahogany camps of the southeastern state of Chiapas were among the most notoriously abusive industries in Porfirian Mexico. The abuse of Indian workers, often shanghaied from their villages, reached deadly extremes. The enigmatic German socialist writer B. Traven traveled in the region of the lumber camps as part of an anthropological expedition during the 1920s, a time when, despite the revolution, conditions in the camps had changed but little. His informants were the lumber workers themselves, and he always claimed that he represented them with unsentimental accuracy. In the following excerpt, taken from one of Traven's series of "jungle" novels, Indians newly arrived at a lumber camp are initiated into some harsh realities.

The new gang reached the south camp in the middle of the night. The men were dead on their feet with fatigue from the march through the underbrush and a two-hour struggle to get out of the heavy, sticky mud of the swamps. They let themselves fall to the ground with whatever they were carrying, and it was not until almost half an hour later that they began to have the strength to ask for something to eat. The cook told them he had nothing to give them and that unless they had brought their own provisions they would have to wait until morning. . . .

"Any of you ever been in a camp before?" [someone] asked.

"Not me," replied one of the men in a voice exhausted by fatigue. "And I don't believe that any of us know the camps."

Santiago, one of the ox-drivers, broke in, saying: "Well, you'll get to know them. You'll get to know hell and all its devils."

Nobody took up his words. The old hands smoked; the new ones waited for their beans and coffee to get warm. The fire crackled, throwing out sparks, and at last decided to burn brightly.

THE INDIANS LYING around the fire suddenly raised their heads as if they had heard the roar of a jaguar in the underbrush.

Lumber workers in Chiapas, 1940s. (Alex Harris and Margaret Sartor, eds., *Gertrude Blom: Bearing Witness.* [Photographer Gertrude Duby Blom. Reprinted by permission of Na Bolom Museum, Mexico])

"What's that noise coming from the jungle?" asked Antonio, an Indian from Sactun, listening intently.

"Do you mean those groans and moans in the underbrush?" asked Santiago, raising his eyebrows.

"Yes, that's what I mean. You'd think that somebody was tormenting gagged animals."

"By God, comrade," said Santiago ironically, "I assure you that you're sharp of hearing. You must be able to hear a flea dancing on a silk handkerchief. With hearing like that, you'll get somewhere! Besides, you're not mistaken."

"No, you're not mistaken, you've heard perfectly," interposed Matías. "They're tormenting animals, and they're holding their mouths to stifle cries that might disturb Don Acacio while he's slipping between the heavy thighs of his Cristina, the girl with the twisted nose. By the devil, she's ugly! But her ass must have some enchantment, for he takes her everywhere with him and buys her boxes of scented soap whenever the Turk comes."

"And why are they tormenting those poor beasts?" asked Antonio.

The ox-drivers laughed uproariously.

"Those poor beasts!" replied Santiago. "Yes, the poor beasts are being cruelly mistreated because in spite of the gags they can hear their screams."

And there was another outburst of laughter.

"But they're not little lambs with white fleece," explained Pedro.

"Beasts, poor beasts! No, those are not animals that are being tormented, you pack of asses! It's twenty cutters, twenty ax-men who are howling. They've hung them up for three or four hours because they haven't produced, either today or yesterday or the day before, the tons of mahogany they'd been told to. You are innocent and ignorant, but within three days you'll know what four tons are. Two tons are the normal production of an experienced cutter who's as strong as an ox. And now that son of a bitch Don Acacio wants us to cut four tons a day. Whoever can't cut that amount is hung from a tree by his four members, and even by five, for half the night. . . . Then the mosquitoes come humming around, because the thing happens at the edge of the swamps; not to mention the red ants, which arrive in battalions. But I don't have to give you any more details. In less than a week you'll know as much as I do—and by personal experience. After that you'll have been initiated into all the mysteries of a camp belonging to the Montellano brothers. You'll be soldiers of the regiment of the hanged."

Somebody said: "I thought that all they did was flog you the way they do in the prison camps and coffee fincas."

It was Martín Trinidad who seemed to be so well informed. Martín Trinidad was one of the three ragged men who had joined the column on the road and whom Don Gabriel had engaged without a stamped contract. During the three long weeks of the trek through the jungle those three vagabonds had hardly exchanged a word with the Indians. They had always remained together in a group, talking among themselves and not appearing to bother about the others. This was the first time that Martín Trinidad had spoken to them.

Santiago looked at him with half-closed eyes and an air of suspicion, with the caution a real proletarian employs in the presence of an informer.

"Where do you come from?"

"I'm from Yucatán."

"That's a long way! How did you get here? Are you running away?"

"Let's say that's right, brother."

"Right, let's say that. . . . When they've hanged you at least three times, I'll begin to believe you. Because, look, if anyone here isn't flogged or hanged we get suspicious—he may be a squealing son of a———. And even to receive some lashes doesn't prove anything, but to be strung up, to be well and duly hanged as El Rasgón, La Mecha, and El Faldón know how to do it—that's altogether another matter. After that there's no comedy. I hope you understand what I'm going to tell you. Celso and Andrés will have a little chat with your two pals in order to know more about who you are. Here nobody's afraid of anything, and nobody can match our skill in sweetly slicing the next fellow's neck for almost no reason at all. It can happen within twenty paces of the hut without the interested party's feeling it at all. Nor is any attention paid to how the loathsome soul of an informer goes down to hell. As you'll see, we don't give a thought to anything, not even their bullets—you don't shoot a man you expect four tons a day from. A dead man can't fell trees—isn't that so? The worst they can do is hang us, and we're so used to that now that it doesn't help them any more. They used to beat us savagely when we couldn't cut more than two tons. But we got hardened to beating, and it no longer served any purpose. On the contrary, the more they beat us, the less we produced. At that point the Montellanos thought up the scheme of hanging us. It's horrible, it's terrifying, but only while you're strung up. Next day you can work again, and then you cut your four tons! This new invention has really worked for them, because the recollection, the mere recollection of the suffering, the terror of being strung up again, drives you to try to cut four tons, even though after one ton your hands are skinless. Only now we've almost got to the stage where even their new invention will become useless. There's nothing they can do about Celso there, for instance. When they've hanged him for four hours and El Guapo arrives to take him down, Celso shouts: 'Hi! you son of a bitch, here you come just when I feel fine. I'm sleeping peacefully, and this is the moment you choose, you pig, to come and disturb my dreams!' Celso was the first. Now there are about six of us. This is the secret: human beings can become like oxen or donkeys and remain impassive when they're beaten or goaded, but only if they've succeeded in suppressing all their natural instinct to rebel."

Martín Trinidad did not reply. . . .

FIDEL AND TWO of his comrades went to the large hut that served as their dormitory, picked up two lanterns, and made toward the underbrush. Eight men, eight shapeless masses, were twitching on the ground. They were incredibly doubled up, as if they had been cooped up in narrow boxes for six months. Each wore only a torn pair of white breeches. They groaned quietly, like sleepers half awakened. They squirmed on the ground and slowly stirred their limbs one after another to ease the stiffness, for their arms and legs were stiff and swollen.

The ropes that had held them to the trees had been simply untied by the foremen, letting the men fall brutally to the ground. The foremen never worried about their victims, because they knew that the men would come to help them. Besides, the foremen were not required to watch over the health of hanged men. They could burst or not during the torture. The Montellanos and their bodyguards were not concerned with the possible death of the hanged men beyond the fact that a death meant the loss of a man's labor. If a cutter was lazy or weak and could not produce three tons of mahogany daily, the loss was not great, the man could die quietly. For the worker, work is a duty. If he is lazy, he has no right to live. After all, if he dies, there is one less nuisance.

The eyes of the hanged men were bloodshot and inflamed. Their bodies were covered with the bites of red ants and mosquitoes. Hundreds of ticks of all sizes had penetrated so deeply beneath their skins that infinite patience was necessary to extract them without leaving the heads behind, for if these were left under the skin the bites produced by the insects' stings would become dangerous. Wherever a tick had worked its way in, there remained, even after its removal, a terrible itching that lasted as much as a week and compelled the victim to scratch himself incessantly. The bodies of the tortured men were still covered with ants, which now began to make their escape replete with their booty of blood or flesh. On and between their toes chiggers had left their eggs deposited deep in the flesh. Spiders had invaded their hair, and some of them had begun to weave webs to catch the flies attracted by the blood and sweat of the hanged men. On their legs could be seen the sticky tracks left by snails.

The old hands picked their comrades up in their arms and carried them, still stupefied by pain, to the bank of the arroyo. They immersed them in the running water to alleviate the burning stings of mosquitoes and to rid them of ants and spiders. After this ducking they laid them out on the bank and began to stretch their limbs, massaging them at the same time.

"This isn't so bad," explained Santiago to Antonio, who was helping him revive one of the cutters, Lorenzo. "It's not so serious when they hang one near the huts. What is dangerous is when they do the hanging far from the camp as a special punishment. Because then the wild boars and wild dogs eat them, and they aren't able to defend themselves in any way."

"There's still another marvelous punishment, an invention of Don Severo," said Matías, rubbing another of the hanged men. "Toward eleven o'clock in the morning they grab a man and take him to a place where there isn't a tree or any shade of any kind. They take off his clothes, tie his hands and feet, and bury him in the hot sand to just below his mouth, leaving only his nose, his eyes, and the top of his head above ground, and all this under the caress of the sun. To you, you innocent lambs who don't yet know anything about these things, I can say that when a man has been buried once in this way, just once, he shakes like a goat's beard when he hears Don Félix say these pretty words: 'Now you'll cut your three tons, or I'll have them bury you for three hours.' Those three hours seem longer than a lifetime." . . .

When the hanged men were at last revived, thanks to the ministrations of their comrades, they could sip a little coffee and eat a few warmed-over frijoles. They got up and, staggering like drunken men, moved toward their huts, where they collapsed at full length. It was nearly eleven o'clock at night.

AT FOUR O'CLOCK the next morning la Mecha went into the huts to kick the sleeping men awake. They were still so full of pain and fright from the hanging of the preceding evening that, without washing their hands, they threw themselves on the pot of tepid beans, which they scooped up with their hands and ate ravenously. Then each of them drank a few gulps of coffee and, ax on shoulder, went off into the forest resolved to cut his four tons that day.

Throughout the entire day they had only one idea in their heads, an idea that never left them in three weeks: "By all the saints in heaven, little God, make me able to cut my four tons so they won't hang me!"

But God, who came to earth two thousand years ago to save men, undoubtedly forgot these Indians. It is certain that at that time their country was still unknown. And when at last it was discovered, the first thing the conquistadores did was to plant a cross on the beach and say a Mass. In spite of that ceremony the Indians still suffer.

"Certainly," said Martín Trinidad unexpectedly some nights later, "the Lord came to the world two thousand years ago to save men. Next time we'll save ourselves."

"Maybe so," replied Pedro, one of the ox-drivers who had some ideas about religion and priests, "maybe so. But we'll still have to wait another two thousand years for our turn to come."

Celso intervened dryly: "Why wait for the Saviour? Save yourself, brother, and then your savior will have arrived."

President Díaz, Hero of the Americas

James Creelman

While Porfirio Díaz certainly had his detractors, there were nevertheless many who greatly admired the considerable achievements of his extended regime. Between 1876 and 1910, peace and order prevailed, some 19,000 miles of railways were built, and 45,000 miles of telegraph wires were installed. Of course, each of these achievements had its downside: peace and order were established only at the cost of harsh violence and violations of human rights; most of the railways and many other key sectors of the economy were foreign-owned; and the bulk of the population remained illiterate and impoverished. Intellectual apologists for the regime styled themselves "científicos," or "scientific men," because they justified the persistence of the regime — and their own wealth and power — on the basis of "positivist" philosophy glorifying hard science, which they maintained was applicable to all aspects of life.

It is hardly surprising that among the dictator's staunchest admirers were wealthy Mexicans and foreigners. One of the most effusive apologies appeared in the now-famous 1908 article by journalist James Creelman, published in Pearson's Magazine. *Creelman's portrait of the venerable dictator is embarrassingly hagiographical, while his depiction of the Mexican masses is offensively patronizing. Despite the journalist's simplistic analysis and gushing prose, the article proved to be of considerable historical import. Creelman quotes Díaz as saying that the Mexican people, having been nurtured by his stern dictatorship, were finally ready for democracy, and that he planned to step down at the end of his term in 1910. Some pretenders to power, including Francisco I. Madero, took these words seriously and launched energetic political campaigns. Díaz's later change of heart would set the stage for the opening act of the bloody Mexican revolution.*

From the heights of Chapultepec Castle President Díaz looked down upon the venerable capital of his country, spread out on a vast plain, with a ring of mountains flung up grandly about it, and I, who had come nearly four thousand miles from New York to see the master and hero of modern Mexico — the inscrutable leader in whose veins is blended the blood of the primitive Mixtecs with that of the invading Spaniards — watched the slender, erect form,

Revolutionary muralist David Alfaro Siqueiros, in this 1957–1967 mural, depicts Porfirio Díaz surrounded by sycophants, his foot crushing the Constitution as he is entertained by dancing girls. (Museo Nacional de Historia, Chapultepec Castle, Mexico City)

the strong, soldierly head and commanding, but sensitive, countenance with an interest beyond words to express.

A high, wide forehead that slopes up to crisp white hair and overhangs deep-set, dark brown eyes that search your soul, soften into inexpressible kindliness and then dart quick side looks—terrible eyes, threatening eyes, loving, confiding, humorous eyes—a straight, powerful, broad and somewhat fleshy nose, whose curved nostrils lift and dilate with every emotion; huge, virile jaws that sweep from large, flat, fine ears, set close to the head, to the tremendous, square, fighting chin; a wide, firm mouth shaded by a white mustache; a full, short, muscular neck, wide shoulders, deep chest; a curiously tense and rigid carriage that gives great distinction to a personality suggestive of singular power and dignity—that is Porfirio Díaz in his seventy-eighth year, as I saw him a few weeks ago. . . .

It is the intense, magnetic something in the wide-open, fearless, dark eyes and the sense of nervous challenge in the sensitive, spread nostrils, that seem to connect the man with the immensity of the landscape, as some elemental force.

There is not a more romantic or heroic figure in all the world, nor one more intensely watched by both friends and foes of democracy, than the soldier-statesman, whose adventurous youth pales the pages of Dumas, and whose iron rule has converted the warring, ignorant, superstitious and impoverished masses of Mexico, oppressed by centuries of Spanish cruelty and greed, into a strong, steady, peaceful, debt-paying and progressive nation.

For twenty-seven years he has governed the Mexican Republic with such power that national elections have become mere formalities. He might easily have set a crown upon his head.

Yet to-day, in the supremacy of his career, this astonishing man—foremost figure of the American hemisphere and unreadable mystery to students of human government—announces that he will insist on retiring from the Presidency at the end of his present term, so that he may see his successor peacefully established and that, with his assistance, the people of the Mexican Republic may show the world that they have entered serenely and preparedly upon the last complete phase of their liberties, that the nation is emerging from ignorance and revolutionary passion, and that it can choose and change presidents without weakness or war. . . .

The President surveyed the majestic, sun-lit scene below the ancient castle and turned away with a smile, brushing a curtain of scarlet trumpet-flowers and vine-like pink geraniums as he moved along the terrace toward the inner garden, where a fountain set among palms and flowers sparkled with water from the spring at which Montezuma used to drink, under the mighty cypresses that still rear their branches about the rock on which we stood.

"It is a mistake to suppose that the future of democracy in Mexico has been endangered by the long continuance in office of one President," he said quietly. "I can say sincerely that office has not corrupted my political ideals and that I believe democracy to be the one true, just principle of government, although in practice it is possible only to highly developed peoples."

For a moment the straight figure paused and the brown eyes looked over the great valley to where snow-covered Popocatapetl lifted its volcanic peak nearly eighteen thousand feet among the clouds beside the snowy craters of Ixtaccihuatl—a land of dead volcanoes, human and otherwise.

"I can lay down the Presidency of Mexico without a single pang of regret, but I cannot cease to serve this country while I live," he added.

The sun shone full in the President's face, but his eyes did not shrink from the ordeal. The green landscape, the smoking city, the blue tumult of mountains, the thin, exhilarating, scented air, seemed to stir him, and the color came to his cheeks as he clasped his hands behind him and threw his head backward. His nostrils opened wide.

"You know that in the United States we are troubled about the question of electing a President for three terms?"

He smiled and then looked grave, nodding his head gently and pursing his lips. It is hard to describe the look of concentrated interest that suddenly came into his strong, intelligent countenance.

"Yes, yes, I know," he replied. "It is a natural sentiment of democratic peoples that their officials should be often changed. I agree with that sentiment."

It seemed hard to realize that I was listening to a soldier who had ruled a republic continuously for more than a quarter of a century with a personal authority unknown to most kings. Yet he spoke with a simple and convincing manner, as one whose place was great and secure beyond the need of hypocrisy.

"It is quite true that when a man has occupied a powerful office for a very long time he is likely to begin to look upon it as his personal property, and it is well that a free people should guard themselves against the tendencies of individual ambition.

"Yet the abstract theories of democracy and the practical, effective application of them are often necessarily different—that is when you are seeking for the substance rather than the mere form.

"I can see no good reason why President Roosevelt should not be elected again if a majority of the American people desire to have him continue in office. I believe that he has thought more of his country than of himself. He has done and is doing a great work for the United States, a work that will cause him, whether he serves again or not, to be remembered in history as one of the great Presidents. . . .

"Here in Mexico we have had different conditions. I received this Government from the hands of a victorious army at a time when the people were divided and unprepared for the exercise of the extreme principles of democratic government. To have thrown upon the masses the whole responsibility of government at once would have produced conditions that might have discredited the cause of free government.

"Yet, although I got power at first from the army, an election was held as soon as possible and then my authority came from the people. I have tried to leave the Presidency several times, but it has been pressed upon me and I remained in office for the sake of the nation which trusted me. The fact that the price of Mexican securities dropped eleven points when I was ill at Cuernavaca indicates the kind of evidence that persuaded me to overcome my personal inclination to retire to private life.

"We preserved the republican and democratic form of government. We defended the theory and kept it intact. Yet we adopted a patriarchal policy in the actual administration of the nation's affairs, guiding and restraining popular tendencies, with full faith that an enforced peace would allow education, industry and commerce to develop elements of stability and unity in a naturally intelligent, gentle and affectionate people.

"I have waited patiently for the day when the people of the Mexican Republic would be prepared to choose and change their government at every election without danger of armed revolutions and without injury to the national credit or interference with national progress. I believe that day has come." . . .

"General Díaz," I interrupted, "you have had an unprecedented experience in the history of republics. For thirty years the destinies of this nation have been in your hands, to mold them as you will; but men die, while nations must continue to live. Do you believe that Mexico can continue to exist in peace as a republic? Are you satisfied that its future is assured under free institutions?"

It was worthwhile to have come from New York to Chapultepec Castle to see the hero's face at that moment. Strength, patriotism, warriorship, prophethood seemed suddenly to shine in his brown eyes.

"The future of Mexico is assured," he said in a clear voice. "The principles of democracy have not been planted very deep in our people, I fear. But the nation has grown and it loves liberty. Our difficulty has been that the people do not concern themselves enough about public matters for a democracy. The individual Mexican as a rule thinks much about his own rights and is always ready to assert them. But he does not think so much about the rights of others. He thinks of his privileges, but not of his duties. Capacity for self-restraint is the basis of democratic government, and self-restraint is possible only to those who recognize the rights of their neighbors.

"The Indians, who are more than half of our population, care little for politics. They are accustomed to look to those in authority for leadership instead of thinking for themselves. That is a tendency they inherited from the Spaniards, who taught them to refrain from meddling in public affairs and rely on the Government for guidance.

"Yet I firmly believe that the principles of democracy have grown and will grow in Mexico."

"But you have no opposition party in the Republic, Mr. President. How can free institutions flourish when there is no opposition to keep the majority, or governing party, in check?"

"It is true there is no opposition party. I have so many friends in the Republic that my enemies seem unwilling to identify themselves with so small a minority. I appreciate the kindness of my friends and the confidence of my country; but such absolute confidence imposes responsibilities and duties that tire me more and more.

"No matter what my friends and supporters say, I retire when my present term of office ends, and I shall not serve again. I shall be eighty years old then.

"My country has relied on me and it has been kind to me. My friends have praised my merits and overlooked my faults. But they may not be willing to deal so generously with my successor and he may need my advice and support; therefore I desire to be alive when he assumes office so that I may help him."

He folded his arms over his deep chest and spoke with great emphasis.

"I welcome an opposition party in the Mexican Republic," he said. "If it appears, I will regard it as a blessing, not as an evil. And if it can develop power, not to exploit but to govern, I will stand by it, support it, advise it and forget myself in the successful inauguration of complete democratic government in the country.

"It is enough for me that I have seen Mexico rise among the peaceful and useful nations. I have no desire to continue in the Presidency. This nation is ready for her ultimate life of freedom. At the age of seventy-seven years I am satisfied with robust health. That is one thing which neither law nor force can create. I would not exchange it for all the millions of your American oil kings." . . .

"And which do you regard as the greatest force for peace, the army or the schoolhouse?" I asked.

The soldier's face flushed slightly and the splendid white head was held a little higher.

"You speak of the present time?"

"Yes."

"The schoolhouse. There can be no doubt of that. I want to see education throughout the Republic carried on by the national Government. I hope to see it before I die. It is important that all citizens of a republic should receive the same training, so that their ideals and methods may be harmonized and the national unity intensified. When men read alike and think alike they are more likely to act alike."

"And you believe that the vast Indian population of Mexico is capable of high development?"

"I do. The Indians are gentle and they are grateful, all except for the Yacquis [*sic*] and some of the Mayas. They have the traditions of an ancient civilization of their own. They are to be found among the lawyers, engineers, physicians, army officers and other professional men."

Over the city drifted the smoke of many factories.

"It is better than cannon smoke," I said.

"Yes," he replied, "and yet there are times when cannon smoke is not such a bad thing. The toiling poor of my country have risen up to support me, but I cannot forget what my comrades in arms and their children have been to me in my severest ordeals."

There were actually tears in the veteran's eyes. . . .

SUCH IS PORFIRIO DÍAZ, the foremost man of the American hemisphere. What he has done, almost alone and in such a few years, for a people disorganized and degraded by war, lawlessness and comic-opera politics, is the great inspiration of Pan-Americanism, the hope of the Latin-American republics.

Whether you see him at Chapultepec Castle, or in his office in the National Palace, or in the exquisite drawing-room of his modest home in the city, with his young, beautiful wife and his children and grand-children by his first wife about him, or surrounded by troops, his breast covered with decorations conferred by great nations, he is always the same — simple, direct and full of the dignity of conscious power.

In spite of the iron government he has given to Mexico, in spite of a continuance in office that has caused men to say that he has converted a republic into an autocracy, it is impossible to look into his face when he speaks of the principle of popular sovereignty without believing that even now he would take up arms and shed his blood in defense of it.

Only a few weeks ago Secretary of State [Elihu] Root summed up President Díaz when he said:

"It has seemed to me that of all the men now living, General Porfirio Díaz, of Mexico, was best worth seeing. Whether one considers the adventurous, daring, chivalric incidents of his early career; whether one considers the vast work of government which his wisdom and courage and commanding character accomplished; whether one considers his singularly attractive personality, no one lives to-day that I would rather see than President Díaz. If I were a poet I would write poetic eulogies. If I were a musician I would compose triumphal marches. If I were a Mexican I should feel that the steadfast loyalty of a lifetime could not be too much in return for the blessings that he had brought to my country. As I am neither poet, musician nor Mexican, but only an American who loves justice and liberty and hopes to see their reign among mankind progress and strengthen and become perpetual, I look to Porfirio Díaz, the President of Mexico, as one of the great men to be held up for the hero-worship of mankind."

Gift of the Skeletons

Anonymous

While many of the realities of the Porfiriato were grim, the regime was not able to suppress a vibrant popular culture. Anonymously written poetry often ridiculed the pretensions of the rich, lampooned the great dictator, or commented wryly on the injustices of early-twentieth-century Mexico. The calavera—*the dancing skeleton or grinning skull—was a staple in the popular etchings of José Guadalupe Posada, which often illustrated popular political verse of the day. These skeletal figures served to remind Mexicans that death (perhaps catalyzed by popular revolt) would level even the most extreme social hierarchy.*

The Englishman's a skeleton,
So's the Italiano.
The Frenchman is a skeleton, too,
Even Maximiliano.
The cardinals and dukes and counts,
The Pope himself in Rome;
The Presidents of Nations
And kings upon their thrones—
In the grave, they all are equal:
Just a heap of bones.

The general is a skeleton,
And all the general's men.
The colonels and comandants,
And the crazy *capitán*.
The sergeants are all lined up
In military style;
Next will come the corporals
And the other rank-and-file—
Soldiers by the hundreds
Are just skeletons in a pile.

Artist José Guadalupe Posada achieved tremendous popularity in late nineteenth- and early twentieth-century Mexico with his famous *calavera* etchings. (From Roberto Berdecio and Stanley Appelbaum, eds., *Posada's Popular Mexican Prints* [New York: Dover Publications, 1972], 3)

The drunken little martyrs
Are souls free of sin,
Because they've paid their debts
In this world that we are in.
The innocent children suffer,
In the cold, hard earth so deep,
While the sick or those in prison
Find no comfort as they weep.
They should be angels up in heaven,
Not just skeletons in a heap.

SPECIAL SECTION

Mexican History: A Photo Essay

John Mraz

*John Mraz is Research Professor at the Instituto de Ciencias Sociales y Humanidades,
Universidad Autónoma de Puebla. He considers himself as a "historiador gráfico,"
and he has been a pioneer in the use of photography, cinema, and video in recounting
the histories of Mexico and Cuba. In addition to writing numerous books and articles,
Mraz has directed an award-winning documentary video on the history of Mexican
railroad workers and is currently working on a film on agrarian struggle in Puebla
during the Mexican revolution.*

What can photographs tell us about Mexico's past? As "traces" of yesterday's
surfaces, they appear to offer a window onto history. It is not that simple:
photographs are constructed messages, composed through decisions made
during the photographic act—including the selection of subject, framing, focus, light, and lens—as well as later alterations of the original negative in the
darkroom. However, notwithstanding the dense system of mediations that
enter into making a photograph, it is still different from other visual media because of its unique capacity to embalm the appearance of things in the world.
An image is made with great ease; hundreds of photographs can be taken
in the space of minutes without much forethought because something can
always be salvaged in negative selection and darkroom cropping. A product of
mechanical reproduction, photography's singular capability to include details
which the photographer may have had no intention of documenting leaves
historians with the possibility of discovering things which were invisible to
the image maker.

This capacity for "unintentional content" is a significant factor in contem-
plating photography's value to the historical enterprise. Consider, for example, the picture by the Hermanos Mayo of preparations for a feminist march in
Mexico City during 1980 (Photo 1). As a working photojournalist (and part of a
collective whose individual members maintained control of their negatives in
order to later sell prints to other buyers), Mayo's job was to cover the march in
its entirety. Photos of preliminary activities, such as the painting of posters and

the preparation of banners, provide important background material for reporting on this event (as well as contributing to the collective's archive). In the
middle of this image, we see a young man wearing a Boston College T-shirt.
The use of such clothing—T-shirts, sweat suits, jackets, caps, sweaters, etc.—
decorated with the logos of U.S. colleges and professional sports teams is so
common in Mexico that people don't notice it. However, despite their ubiq-
uity (or better, because of it), these emblems are largely invisible to Mexicans.
On many occasions, I have shown the Mayo photograph to Mexican audiences and posed this question: "You are historians one hundred years from
now. What can you find in this photo which is an important artifact about
Mexico in the twentieth century?" They often don't see the Boston College
T-shirt, and Mayo probably didn't either. Its very invisibility is ominous, for
it is an eloquent symptom of the "Americanization" of Mexico.

As dense "technical" images, photographs would seem to offer unlimited
possibilities in developing visual histories, for pictures can be gleaned from
a wealth of sources. The richest fount is photojournalism, and the archives
of the collectives formed by the Casasola dynasty, the Hermanos Mayo, and
Díaz, Delgado y García contain among them some seven or eight million
negatives.[1] The usefulness of photojournalist collections varies in relation to
the information that accompanies the archival negatives. Thus, it is unfortunate that even in the best-catalogued archive, that of the Hermanos Mayo,
the data are limited to minimal notes that appear on the negative envelopes.
Although locating the photographs in the publications where they originally
appeared would be an arduous task, it would open up a gold mine of information. One place where photographs are found together with extensive textual
descriptions is in the Departamento del Trabajo of the Archivo General de la
Nación; here, inspectors' reports of labor conditions sometimes accompany
interesting images. Another source is family photo albums; these can often
offer invaluable insights into the past if interviews were carried out in relation
to the pictures. Photographs taken for political purposes can also be useful, as
is the case of the photos of Guillermo Treviño, the Puebla railroad union militant, who documented labor struggles from the 1920s until the 1970s. Finally,
photos taken by foreigners can offer alternative insights, as in the pictures of
C. B. Waite, William Henry Jackson, François Aubert, or Abel Briquet.

Photographs can be important historical "leads," but their worth depends
upon having trustworthy identifications. Consider the image of women protesting in the street (Photo 2) with banners declaring "TODAS PEDIMOS TRA-
BAJO" ("We all want to work"). We don't know exactly when this picture was
taken, although it is identified in the famous Casasola series, *Seis siglos de historia gráfica en México,* as dating from 1913. The image is probably from a later

date, however, perhaps around 1917. I suspect that women were incorporated into factory work when men went off to fight the revolution, but that as the veterans returned from the armed struggle the women were forced back to their domestic labors. I imagine that these women liked working outside the home and the salaries they were able to earn; when that was taken from them, they complained. The fact that we cannot trust the identifications of the photos in the Casasola series — or those of almost any of the collections of *Historia gráfica* which have been produced in Mexico — makes them problematic for historians, because we would have to locate the original publications in which the pictures appeared in order to be able to employ them with any rigor.²

Without identifications that "anchor" photographs to their reality, their esthetic force can sometimes generate myths. The famous image of "Adelita" offers one example, for this woman, hanging out of a train, has become the paradigmatic image of the *soldadera* in the Mexican revolution. As can be seen in Photo 3, the "Adelita" image was cropped out of a negative the right half of which was removed. Although that half of the original glass plate is broken, we can still see that it contained a group of women standing on the platforms of the train cars. When we ask who Adelita was, her location in the train may provide an important clue. *Soldaderas* usually traveled on top of, or underneath, the cars. The women who traveled in the cars were often the prostitutes of the federal officers. The image, as a whole, could contribute to our historical knowledge about the revolution, for it provides a "lead" about the living conditions of some women. The cropped version of "Adelita," however, only serves to further another revolutionary myth, because the vitality evinced by this woman has made her a repository for, and a symbol of, all the attributes of the legendary *soldaderas*.

The basic elements of a photograph that can be used to develop social histories may be defined without unnecessary complications.³ The first is the presence of people who are often excluded from written texts. Women and children, for example, usually buried under the proclamations of male governing bodies, are present in photographs to be rescued for history. As mentioned above, women participated actively in the Mexican revolution, though little has been written about them. They appear constantly in photographs from the revolutionary period, however, among other places, on the tops of trains (see Photo 4). Children are also a pervasive presence in photographs of Mexico's adult world, most often appearing as workers, despite the fact that Article 123 of the 1917 Constitution forbade child labor; in Photo 5, we see a little girl in a Mexico City match factory in 1919.

Social relations are also documented in photographs, which can speak volumes about the existence and the transformation of class, race, and gender

distinctions. Consider, for example, how class relations during the Porfiriato
are illustrated in Photo 6, which shows how the poor carried the better-off
across flooded streets in Mexico City. Demands relating to labor relations are
evident in the banners of a protest march from around 1911 (see Photo 7), in
which workers are reclaiming the right to have Sundays off. Another instance
of class struggle (and the democratic appropriation of the new photographic
technology) can be seen in Photo 8, taken by workers in 1924. It documents
how management employees (dressed in their suits and ties), replaced strikers
to load barrels of oil, in violation of labor agreements. The transformation
of class structure is portrayed in Photo 9, an image of campesinos carrying
rails. They are participating in the early industrialization of Mexico, which will
soon make them permanently into a proletariat.

Photography embalms gender relations as well. Hugo Brehme captured
these two children (Photo 10) as they played out the roles assigned them: the
girl washing clothes, the boy pretending to be a boatman. Women's rebellion
against their subordination can be seen in a 1930s protest (Photo 11), in which
they hold a banner which states, "We are on strike because, when we ask for
a raise in salary, they insult us, telling us to become prostitutes."

The power of photographs to capture the relations of class, race, and gender so central to history is also demonstrated in the image by Enrique Díaz of
a shoe factory during the 1930s (Photo 12). Here, dark-skinned women labor
under the gaze of well-dressed, white bosses and their visitors.

Photographs can also document particular expressions of mentalities. For
instance, in Photo 13 we see a couple posing for a family photograph in the
railroad yard of Oriental, Puebla, in the 1940s. A tiny town in the middle of nowhere, the village of Oriental offered no other way of making a living than the
railroad, and diversions were similarly limited. The centrality of the railroad
in this couple's life is demonstrated in their choice of "studio backdrop."

It is crucial to insist that we are not here arguing for a psychological reading of photographs. The term *mentalities* is used here to denote long-term,
deeply ingrained sociocultural patterns; the term *psychology*, on the other
hand, at least for its use here, describes an immediate emotional state: sadness,
joy, disappointment, chagrin. Making psychological judgments from "apparent" expressions of sentiment—for example, deducing depression from a non-
smiling face—is a great temptation.[4] However, the problem with such judgments becomes obvious if we consider exposure times. When films and lenses
were slow, people did not look happy because they could not hold a smile
for the length of time required; it became a blur. Thus, they necessarily had
to maintain a straight face (which may also have had something to do with
the ordeal of posing). Today, exposure times are usually in the range of from

1/250th to 1/60th of a second, so subjects can "smile for the camera" with no difficulty. Because of the slow exposure times of earlier eras, it would be imprudent to make any psychological analysis of subjects from that time. This can be appreciated by comparing two photographs of Zapatistas in Sanborn's restaurant during their 1914 occupation of Mexico City (see Photos 14 and 15). In the first image, the two men are almost incarnations of the image which many Mexico City residents had of them: scarred, violent men who appear ready to cut your throat for the pleasure of it. In the second image, they look like harmless campesinos, a bit disoriented by finding themselves in an unfamiliar situation. Obviously, neither of these readings offers us the "truth" about the Zapatistas.

Another important area in which photographs contribute to our understanding of social history is in the representation of material culture and daily life. Photographic images of the most mundane aspects of human existence, such as eating, drinking, housing, transportation, disasters, and expressions of popular culture, can be fundamental in allowing us to reconstruct the everyday lives of people in the past. Photographs preserve these aspects of daily life as perhaps no other medium can. However, in order truly to understand what these images convey, we must also develop a knowledge of the contexts in which they were originally taken.

Eating and drinking are fundamental activities of life that are often overlooked in written histories. Film can be an important media to show how Mexican women ground corn on metates to make *nixtamal,* or how they shaped the corn dough into tortillas, for example. Photo 16 demonstrates another way that one poor woman acquired food: by sweeping up the rice thrown at a wedding! Water vendors were a favorite subject of nineteenth-century *costumbrista* paintings and tourist postcards; an image by the Hermanos Mayo (Photo 17) that shows women waiting for the truck to dispense the precious liquid in one of the slums on the outskirts of Mexico City provides a concise representation of one facet of a poor woman's day around 1950.

Housing is yet another of the mundane yet vital elements of material culture which are embalmed in photographs. In Photo 18 we see the houses provided for miners in Mapimí, Durango, in 1920. The photograph was taken by one of the miners and sent to the secretary of labor along with a description of their living conditions. Although the image itself is eloquent, the accompanying letter, conserved in the Ramo de Trabajo, provides us with insight into the marginal existence of these people:

> The company provides houses of three square meters. They consist of one poorly built room without kitchen, bathroom, light or water. They are fit

for one person, but the company forces us to accept others in them without any concern for the inhabitants, so there are usually about four or five people from different families living together. The bathrooms—one for men and another for women—are placed next to the steepest part of the cliffs, and a slight carelessness on the part of anyone sitting there could result in their falling down the cliffs to their death.

Another image of housing from the archives of the Ramo de Trabajo shows us a woman with a child crawling under a fence in Tampico in 1923 (see Photo 19). Again, workers took the photo (almost certainly posing what was evidently a quotidian scene) and sent it to the secretary of labor with a letter detailing their complaints. It appears that the Mexican government had ordered the Pierce Oil Company to put more distance between its tanks and the workers' houses, to avoid disasters. In order not to have to relocate their tanks, Pierce constructed a fence so that the workers would move, thereby leaving the families no other alternative than to crawl under it in order to reach their homes.

Photographs are also an excellent medium for representing labor conditions. In Photo 20, we see women in the Buen Tono cigarette company, seated neatly in rows at their workspaces. While we might find this situation claustrophobic, the Buen Tono may have been a model factory of the Porfiriato, demonstrating the country's orderly development to attract investment. The next image (Photo 21) shows us the other side of the coin: Filgenio Vargas and Jorge Miranda took this photo of fellow oil workers, dead and injured by a burst line in Tepexintla, Veracruz, on January 4, 1922. They sent it to the secretary of labor, with a note: "Because the company provided no medical assistance to the victims, we felt the necessity to write down their names and take some photos to try to get them attention." Not only were the workers denied medical assistance, but Vargas and Miranda were fired for having complained. Hazardous working situations abound in Mexico, as can be seen in Photo 22, a 1951 image taken during the construction of Mexico City's Latin American Tower, where the absence of safety gear is conspicuous. Women may not normally face such dramatically dangerous circumstances, but Photo 23, which depicts a woman washing clothes next to a railroad car, shows us the sort of daily labor to which they are condemned. This picture was taken in Puebla by Guillermo Treviño to document the living conditions of railroad workers and their families during a strike in 1958–1959. Getting to and from work can be an ordeal in itself, as in the photo of a crowded Mexico City bus in the 1940s, equipped with straps for people to hang from (see Photo 24).

Popular culture and leisure activities are also preserved in photographs.

One interesting example is offered by the image of Zapatistas asking for food during their occupation of Mexico City in 1914 (Photo 25); note the cards of the Virgin of Guadalupe stuck in their sombreros, evidence of her importance for that movement and of her constant presence in Mexican history. Television has become as big a part of life in Mexico as in the rest of the world; in Photo 26 we see a television set in a poor Mexican house in 1956, where multiple beds also occupy the "TV room." Easter Week is a time to escape Mexico City's crowds, if you have the money to do so. If not, you may find yourself among the multitudes at a packed public pool, as in "Belly Flop" (Photo 27), taken by Francisco Mata Rosas.

Earthquakes occur so often in Mexico that they sometimes seem as much a part of daily life as eating or working. In Photo 28, Marco Antonio Cruz captured Tlatelolco Plaza ten minutes after the devastating 1985 earthquake struck Mexico City. If any doubts remain about what photographs can tell us about history, ask yourself how many words you would need to describe this scene.

Notes

1. The Casasola Archive is now the property of the Fototeca del Instituto Nacional de Antropología e Historia; the collections of the Hermanos Mayo and Díaz, Delgado y García are found in the Archivo General de la Nación, Mexico City.

2. See my critique in "Una historiografía crítica de la historia gráfica," *Cuicuilco* 5, no. 13 (1998): 77–92.

3. I have dealt with this question more extensively in the following articles: "Más allá de la decoración: Hacía una historia gráfica de las mujeres en México," *Política y cultura* 1 (1992): 155–89; and "De la fotografia histórica: Particularidad y nostalgia," *Nexos*, no. 91 (1985): 9–12.

4. The classic example is Michael Lesy, *Wisconsin Death Trip* (New York: Pantheon, 1973).

Photo 1: Feminist rally, Mexico City, May 10, 1980. (From Archivo General de la Nación, Fondo Hermanos Mayo, Concentrated Section, "Manifestación de mujeres.")

Photo 2: Women demanding work, Mexico City, c. 1917. (From Conaculta-INAH-SINAFO-Fototeca Nacional, Fondo Casasola, 5336.)

Photo 3: "Adelita" and other women, Mexico City, c. 1913. (From Conaculta-INAH-SINAFO-Fototeca Nacional, Fondo Casasola, 5670)

Photo 4: Soldaderas on top of train, Mexico City, c. 1913. (From Conaculta-INAH-SINAFO-Fototeca Nacional, Fondo Casasola, 543243.)

Photo 5: Girl working in match factory, Mexico City, 1919. (From Archivo General de la Nación, Departamento del Trabajo.)

Photo 6: Man being carried across flooded street, Mexico City, c. 1905. (From Conaculta-INAH-SINAFO-Fototeca Nacional, Fondo Casasola.)

Photo 7: Protest in demand of "Sunday Off," Mexico City, c. 1911. (From Conaculta-INAH-SINAFO-Fototeca Nacional, Fondo Casasola, 36373.)

Photo 8: Office employees working in place of striking oil workers, Pueblo Viejo, Veracruz, 1924. (From Archivo General de la Nación, Departamento del Trabajo.)

Photo 9: Campesinos working on the construction of the railroad, Mexico, c. 1900. (From Conaculta-INAH-SINAFO-Fototeca Nacional, Fondo Casasola, 32041.)

Photo 10: Indian children, Canal de Ixtacalco, Mexico City, c. 1920. (Photo by Hugo Brehme. From Conaculta-INAH-SINAFO-Fototeca Nacional, Fondo Brehme, 372055.)

Photo 11: Women protesting mistreatment, Mexico City, c. 1935. (From Conaculta-INAH-SINAFO-Fototeca Nacional, Fondo Casasola, 6350.)

Photo 12: Executives, visitors, and women workers in a shoe factory, Mexico City, c. 1930. (From Archivo General de la Nación, Fondo Díaz, Delgado y García, caja 27/4.)

Photo 13: Couple in train patio, Oriental, Puebla, c. 1945. (From the archive of John Mraz.)

Photo 14: Zapatistas in Sanborns Restaurant, Mexico City, 1914. (From Conaculta-INAH-SINAFO-Fototeca Nacional, Fondo Casasola, 33532/6219.)

Photo 15: Zapatistas in Sanborns Restaurant, Mexico City, 1914. (From Conaculta-INAH-SINAFO-Fototeca Nacional, Fondo Casasola, 33532/6219.)

Photo 16: Woman sweeping up rice after a wedding, Mexico City, c. 1950. (Photo by Hermanos Mayo, Archivo General de la Nación, Fondo Mayo, Concentrated Section, "Arroz en las bodas.")

Photo 17: Women waiting for water, Mexico City, c. 1950. (Photo by Hermanos Mayo, From Archivo General de la Nación, Fondo Mayo, Concentrated Section, "Agua potable.")

Photo 18: Miners' housing, Mapimí, Durango, 1920. (From Archivo General de la Nación, Departamento del Trabajo.)

Photo 19: Woman and child going out to the street, Tampico, 1923. (From Archivo General de la Nación, Departamento del Trabajo.)

Photo 20: Women working in Buen Tono cigarette factory, Mexico City, c. 1910. (From Frederick Starr, *The Story of Mexico* [Underwood and Underwood, 1914].)

Photo 21: Dead and injured oil workers, Tepexintla, January 4, 1922.
(Photo by Filgenio Vargas and Jorge Miranda. From Archivo General
de la Nación, Departamento del Trabajo.)

Photo 22: Construction worker, Latin American Tower, Mexico City, 1951. (Photo by Faustino Mayo. From Archivo General de la Nación, Fondo Mayo, Concentrated Section, "Torre latino-americana.")

Photo 23: Woman washing clothes, Puebla, 1958. (Photo by Guillermo Treviño. From the archive of John Mraz.)

Photo 24: Crowded bus with straps for "hangers-on," Mexico City, 1940s. (Photo by Hermanos Mayo, Archivo General de la Nación, Fondo Mayo, Concentrated Section, "Camiones urbanos.")

Photo 25: "Zapatistas asking for food, Mexico City, 1914. (From Conaculta-INAH-SINAFO-Fototeca Nacional, Fondo Casasola, 6267.)

Photo 26: Television and hi-fi set in a poor home, Mexico City, January 1957. (Photo by Hermanos Mayo. From Archivo General de la Nación, Fondo Mayo, Chronological Section, 10837.)

Photo 27: "Bellyflop," public pool during Easter week, Mexico City, 1986. (Photo by Francisco Mata Rosas and from his archives.)

Photo 28: Tlatelolco Plaza, ten minutes after the earthquake struck, Mexico City, September 19, 1985. (Photo by Marco Antonio Cruz and from his personal archives.)

V

Revolution

The Mexican revolution was the defining event in modern Mexican history. The long, bloody, chaotic war began when Porfirio Díaz, ruler of Mexico since 1876, declared in 1908 that Mexico was ready for democracy and, accordingly, he would not seek another presidential term. But when Francisco I. Madero, the scion of a wealthy Coahuila family, launched an energetic political campaign that threatened to land him in the presidency, Don Porfirio had him arrested and prepared for a standard round of election-fixing. This time, however, the aging dictator (who pundits had taken to calling *Don Perpétuo*) badly miscalculated. Radical activists like Ricardo Flores Magón had for years been stirring up opposition to the regime. By mid-1910, economic downturns and the dictator's increasing harshness prepared Mexicans to support that opposition. Ultimately, when the more moderate Madero called for an armed rebellion to ignite in November 1910, that call was seconded by a broad cross-section of Mexican society. A decade of violence ensued, as a bewildering array of interests clashed.

What did it all mean? Luis Cabrera, perhaps the greatest ideologue of the revolution, declared that "La revolución es revolución"—arguing that the "fundamental purpose" of revolutions is "transcendental," for they "seek to change the laws, customs, and the existing social structure in order to establish a more just arrangement." The Mexican revolution brought change, certainly, but the question of whether the postrevolutionary arrangement was more "just" remains hotly debated. Indeed, even the appropriate case of the initial letter in *revolution* is a matter of some dispute. We have chosen the lower case, to distinguish what began as a multifaceted, distinctly local process from the postrevolutionary regime's subsequent appropriation and simplification of that process—after which the revolution was always rendered in the upper case by the Party of the Institutional Revolution.

The readings that follow present the views of politicians, peasants and poets, radicals and reactionaries, the well-heeled and the dispossessed. We hope they will give readers a sense of why the interests involved in the 1910 revolution were so difficult to reconcile, why violence came to beget violence, and why the passions unleashed proved so hard to pacify. We also provide assessments of the regimes of reconstruction (roughly 1920–1934) and radicalization (1934–1940), to enable readers to better understand the complex forces that contested and represented the revolution's consolidation and, in the process, shaped modern Mexico.

Land and Liberty

Ricardo Flores Magón

Like any great social movement, the Mexican revolution had many precursors. None was quite so radical or influential as Ricardo Flores Magón. Born in 1874 in a small village in the impoverished southern state of Oaxaca, Flores Magón studied law before settling into a career in journalism. In 1900, together with his brother Enrique, he founded the journal Regeneración, *which frontally criticized the Díaz dictatorship. Within the year, Flores Magón was in prison, and by the end of 1903 he was forced into exile in the United States. In 1905 Flores Magón helped to found the Mexican Liberal Party in St. Louis, Missouri. He spent most of the remainder of his life in exile, agitating constantly against the Porfirian regime through the pages of several journals, including* Regeneración, El Hijo del Ahuizote, *and* Revolución. *In the United States, he was repeatedly incarcerated on charges of violating the neutrality and espionage laws. In 1918 he was sent to Leavenworth prison in Kansas, where he died in November 1922.*

Despite the name of his party, Flores Magón's politics were the antithesis of turn-of-the-century liberalism. He was, in fact, a staunch partisan of the international anarchist movement, which declared private property to be theft, denounced governments of all stripes, and advocated "direct action" in place of political participation. His writings envision self-governing, self-reliant, socialistic communities. It is not surprising, therefore, that Flores Magón's relations were poor with most of the revolutionary factions, which tended, to a greater or lesser degree, to cleave to nineteenth-century liberal traditions (note his disdain for Madero expressed in his dismissal of the anti-reelectionists). Ultimately, his work found its greatest resonance in the agrarian movement of Emiliano Zapata, which adopted the slogan "Land and Liberty" as its own. The essay reproduced below appeared in Regeneración *on November 19, 1910, one day before the Mexican revolution officially broke out.*

The fruit, well-ripened by ardent revolt, is about to fall—fruit bitter to all who have become flushed with pride, thanks to a situation which brings honour, wealth and distinction to those who make the sorrows and slavery of humanity the foundation of their pleasures; but fruit sweet and pleasant to all who have regarded as beneath their dignity the filthinesses of the beasts who, through a night that has lasted thirty-four years, have robbed, violated, slain, cheated and played the traitor, while hiding their crimes beneath the mantle of the law and using official position to shield them from punishment.

Who are they that fear the Revolution? They who have provoked it; they who, by oppression and exploitation of the masses, have sought to bring the victims of their infamies despairingly into their power; they who, by injustice and rapine, have awakened sleeping consciences and made honourable men throughout the world turn pale with indignation.

The Revolution is now about to break out at any moment. We, who during so many years have followed attentively the social and political life of Mexico, cannot deceive ourselves. The symptoms of a formidable cataclysm leave no room for doubt that we are on the eve of an uplift and a crash, a rising and a fall. At last, after four and thirty years of shame, the Mexican people is about to raise its head, and at last, after this long night the black edifice, which has been strangling us beneath its weight, is about to crumble into dust.

It is timely that we should here repeat what already we have said so often; that this movement, springing from despair, must not be a blind effort to free ourselves from an enormous burden, but a movement in which instinct must be dominated almost completely by reason. We [Liberals] must try to bring it about that this movement shall be guided by the light of Science. If we fail to do this, the Revolution now on the point of coming to the surface will serve merely to substitute one President for another, one master for another. We must bear in mind that the necessary thing is that the people shall have bread, shelter, land to cultivate; we must bear in mind that no government, however honourable, can decree the abolition of misery. The people themselves—the hungry and disinherited—are they who must abolish misery, by taking into their possession, as the very first step, the land which by natural right should not be monopolized by a few but must be the property of every human being.

No one can foretell the lengths to which the impending Revolution's task of recovery will go; but, if we fighters undertake in good faith [to help] it as far as possible along the road; if, when we pick up the Winchester, we go forth decided not to elevate to power another master but redeem the proletariat's rights; if we take the field pledged to conquer that economic liberty which is the foundation on which all liberties rest, and the condition without which no liberties can exist; if we make this our purpose, we shall start it on a road worthy of this epoch. But if we are carried away by the desire for easy triumph; if, seeking to make the struggle shorter, we desert our own radicalism and aims, so incompatible with those of the purely bourgeois and conservative parties   then we shall have done only the work of bandits and assassins; for the blood spilled will serve merely to increase the power of the bourgeoisie and the caste that today possesses wealth, and, after the triumph, that caste will fasten anew on the proletariat the chain forged with the proletariat's own blood, its own sacrifices, its own martyrdom, which will have conquered power for the bourgeoisie.

It is necessary, therefore, proletarians; it is necessary therefore, disinherited, that your thought be not confused. The conservative and bourgeois parties speak to you of liberty, of justice, of law, of honourable government; and they tell you that when you replace with others those who are now in power, you will have that liberty, justice, law and honourable government. Be not deceived! What you need is to secure the well-being of your families — their daily bread — and this no government can give you. You yourselves must conquer these good things, and you must do it by taking immediate possession of the land, which is the original source of all wealth. Understand this well; no government will be able to give you that, for the law defends the "right" of those who are withholding wealth. You yourselves must take it, despite the law, despite the government, despite the pretended right of property. You yourselves must take it in the name of natural justice; in the name of the right of every human being to life and the development of his physical and intellectual powers.

When you are in possession of the land you will have liberty and justice, for liberty and justice are not decreed but are the result of economic independence. They spring from the fact that the individual is able to live without depending on a master, and to enjoy, for himself and his family, the product of his toil.

Take, then, the land! The law tells you that you must not take it, since it is private property; but the law which so instructs you was a law written by those who are holding you in slavery and a law that needs to be supported by force is a law that does not respond to general needs. If the law were the result of general agreement it would not need upholding by the policeman, the jailer, the judge, the hangman, the soldier and the official. The law has been imposed on you, and these arbitrary impositions we, as men of dignity, must answer with rebellion.

Therefore, to the struggle! Imperious, unrestrainable, the Revolution will not tarry. If you would be really free, group yourselves beneath the [Liberal] Party's banner of freedom; but, if you merely want the strange pleasure of shedding blood, and shedding your own by "playing at soldiers," group yourselves under other banners — that of the Anti-reelectionists, for example, which, after you have done "playing at soldiers," will put you anew under the yoke of the employer and government. In that case you will enjoy the great pleasure of changing the old President, with whom already you were becoming disgusted, for a spick and span new one, fresh from the mint.

Comrades, the question is a grave one. I understand that you are ready for the fight; but fight so that it shall be of benefit to the poor. Hitherto all your revolutions have profited the classes in power, because you have no clear conception of your rights and interests, which, as you now know, are completely opposed to the rights and interests of the intellectual and wealthy classes. It is to the interest of the rich that the poor shall be poor eternally, for the poverty of the masses guarantees their wealth. If there were not men who found themselves compelled to work for other men, the rich would be under the necessity of doing something useful, of producing something of general utility, that they might be able to exist. No longer would there be slaves they could exploit.

I repeat, it is not possible to foretell the lengths in which the approaching Revolution's task of recovery will go; what we must do is to endeavour to get all we can. It would be a great step in advance if the land were to become the property of all; and if among the revolutionists there should . . . be the strength, the conscious strength, sufficient to gain more than that, the basis would be laid for further recoveries which the proletariat by force of circumstances would conquer.

Forward, comrades! Soon you will hear the first shots; soon the shout of rebellion will thunder from the throats of the oppressed. Let not a single one of you fail to second this movement, launching, with all the power of conviction, that supremest of cries, Land and Liberty!

Plan of Ayala

Emiliano Zapata and Others

The revolution headed by Francisco I. Madero relied heavily on the support of diverse groups and interests. Prominent among these were peasants who demanded an end to government repression and immediate agrarian reform, and who were encouraged by vague proposals contained in Madero's Plan of San Luis Potosí. Upon attaining power, however, Madero's message to those peasants was that they must disarm and demobilize before reforms could be contemplated. Meanwhile, he collaborated with the federal army and many other elements of the old regime. Not surprisingly, he quickly lost the support of agrarian elements, the most prominent of which were the southern forces of Emiliano Zapata. In 1911 Zapata and his followers issued their Magna Carta, the Plan of Ayala, from a small town in southern Puebla. For as long as the Zapatista movement survived, it regarded the Plan of Ayala as practically a sacred text. Interestingly, the plan was rather conservative, as revolutionary documents go. It included a rather unfashionable reference to God, while in agrarian matters it did not go as far, for instance, as the law issued in early 1915 by the rival faction of Venustiano Carranza, which provided for lands to be granted to any village that could prove it had insufficient land for its needs. The Plan of Ayala did not seek to eliminate the hacienda, but rather to have it coexist with the peasant villages.

Liberating Plan of the sons of the State of Morelos, affiliated with the Insurgent Army which defends the fulfillment of the Plan of San Luis, with the reforms that it believes necessary to increase the welfare of the Mexican Fatherland.

The undersigned, constituted into a Revolutionary Junta to sustain and carry out the promises made to the country by the Revolution of 20 November 1910, solemnly declare before the civilized world which sits in judgment on us, and before the Nation to which we belong and which we love, the propositions we have formulated to do away with the tyranny that oppresses us and to redeem the Fatherland from the dictatorships that are imposed upon us, which are outlined in the following plan:

1. Taking into consideration that the Mexican people, led by don Francisco I. Madero, went out to shed their blood to reconquer liberties and vindicate their rights which had been trampled upon, and not so that one man could seize power, violating the sacred principles that he swore to defend with the slogan "Effective Suffrage and No Reelection," thereby insulting the faith, cause and liberties of the people; taking into consideration that the man to whom we refer is don Francisco I. Madero, the same who initiated the aforementioned revolution, who imposed his will and influence as a governmental norm upon the Provisional Government of the ex-president of the Republic, licenciado Francisco León de la Barra, causing with this deed much bloodshed and many misfortunes to the fatherland in a cunning and ridiculous fashion, having no goals to satisfy apart from his own personal ambitions, his boundless instincts for tyranny, and his profound disrespect for the fulfillment of the preexisting laws emanating from the immortal Constitution of 1857, written with the revolutionary blood of Ayutla.

Taking into account that the so-called chief of the Liberating Revolution of Mexico, don Francisco I. Madero, due to his great weakness and lack of integrity, did not bring to a happy conclusion the Revolution that he began with the help of God and of the people, since he left intact the majority of the governing powers and corrupt elements of oppression from the dictatorial Government of Porfirio Díaz, which are not and can never in any way be the representation of the National sovereignty, and that, being terrible enemies of ourselves and of the principles that we defend, are causing the ills of the country and opening new wounds in the breast of the Fatherland, making it drink its own blood; taking also into account that the aforementioned don Francisco I. Madero, current president of the Republic, tried to avoid fulfilling the promises he made to the Nation in the Plan of San Luis Potosí, . . . nullifying, persecuting, imprisoning, or killing the revolutionary elements who helped him to occupy the high post of president of the Republic, by means of false promises and numerous intrigues against the Nation.

Taking into consideration that the oft-mentioned Francisco I. Madero has tried to silence with the brute force of bayonets and to drown in blood the people who ask, solicit, or demand the fulfillment of the promises of the Revolution, calling them bandits and rebels, condemning them to a war of extermination, without conceding or granting any of the guarantees that reason, justice, and the law prescribe; taking equally into account that the president of the Republic, Francisco I. Madero, has made of Effective Suffrage a bloody mockery by imposing, against the will of the people, the licenciado José María Pino Suárez as Vice-President of the Republic, imposing also the governors of the States, designating such men as the so-called general Ambrosio Figueroa, cruel tyrant of the people of Morelos; and entering into collaboration with the científico party, feudal hacendados and oppressive caciques, enemies of the Revolution he proclaimed, with the aim of forging new chains and continuing the mould of a new dictatorship more opprobrious and more terrible than that of Porfirio Díaz; so it has become patently clear that he has undermined the sovereignty of the States, mocking the laws with no respect for life or interests, as has happened in the State of Morelos and other states, bringing us to the most horrific anarchy registered in contemporary history. Due to these considerations, we declare Francisco I. Madero incapable of realizing the promises of the revolution of which he was instigator, because he has betrayed all of his principles, mocking the will of the people in his rise to power; he is incapable of governing and because he has no respect for the law and for the justice of the people, and is a traitor to the Fatherland, humiliating the Mexicans by blood and fire because they wish for freedom and an end to the pandering to científicos, hacendados and caciques who enslave us; today we continue the Revolution begun by [Madero], and will carry on until we defeat the dictatorial powers that exist.

2. Francisco I. Madero is disavowed as Chief of the Revolution and as President of the Republic for the reasons expressed above. We shall bring about the overthrow of this functionary.

3. We recognize as Chief of the Liberating Revolution General Pascual Orozco, second of the caudillo don Francisco I. Madero, and in case he does not accept this delicate post, we shall recognize as chief of the Revolution General Emiliano Zapata.

4. The Revolutionary Junta of the State of Morelos manifests to the Nation, under formal protest, that it adopts the Plan of San Luis Potosí as its own, with the additions that shall be expressed below, for the benefit of the oppressed peoples, and it will make itself the defender of the principles that they defend until victory or death.

5. The Revolutionary Junta of the State of Morelos will not admit transactions or agreements until it has brought about the defeat of the dictatorial elements of Porfirio Díaz and of Francisco I. Madero, for the Nation is tired of false men and traitors who make promises like liberators, and upon attaining power forget those promises and become tyrants.

6. As an additional part of our plan, we make it known: that the lands, forests and waters that have been usurped by the hacendados, científicos or caciques in the shadow of venal justice, will henceforth enter into the

possession of the villages or of citizens who have titles corresponding to those properties, and who have been despoiled through the bad faith of our oppressors, and they shall maintain that possession with weapon in hand, and the usurpers who believe they have rights to those lands will be heard by the special tribunals that will be established upon the triumph of the Revolution.

7. In view of the fact that the immense majority of Mexican villages and citizens own no more land than that which they tread upon, and are unable in any way to better their social condition or dedicate themselves to industry or agriculture, because the lands, forests, and waters are monopolized in only a few hands; for this reason, we expropriate without previous indemnization one third of those monopolies from the powerful proprietors, to the end that the villages and citizens of Mexico should obtain ejidos, colonias, and fundos legales for the villages, or fields for sowing or laboring, and this shall correct the lack of prosperity and increase the well-being of the Mexicans.

8. The hacendados, científicos or caciques who directly or indirectly oppose the present Plan, shall have their properties nationalized and two thirds of those properties shall be given as indemnizations of war, pensions to widows and orphans of the victims who are killed in the struggles surrounding the present Plan.

9. In order to execute the procedures respecting the aforementioned properties, the laws of disamortization and nationalization shall be applied, as convenient; for our norm and example shall be the laws put into effect by the immortal Juárez against ecclesiastical properties, which chastised the despots and conservatives who have always wanted to impose upon us the ignominious yoke of oppression and backwardness.

10. The insurgent military chiefs of the Republic who rose up in arms to the voice of don Francisco I. Madero in order to defend the Plan of San Luis Potosí, and who now forcefully oppose the present Plan, will be judged traitors to the cause that they defended and to the Fatherland, for presently many of them, in order to placate the tyrants, or for a fistful of coins, or owing to schemes or bribes, are shedding the blood of their brothers who demand the fulfillment of the promises that were made to the Nation by don Francisco I. Madero.

11. The expenses of war will be appropriated according to article XI of the Plan of San Luis Potosí, and all of the procedures employed in the Revolution that we undertake will be in accordance with the same instructions that are set out in the mentioned Plan.

12. Once the Revolution that we are making has triumphed, a junta of

the principal revolutionary chiefs of the different States will name or designate an interim President of the Republic, who will convoke elections for the organization of federal powers.

13. The principal revolutionary chiefs of each State, in council, shall designate the governor of the State, and this high functionary will convoke the elections for the proper organization of public powers, with the aim of avoiding forced appointments that bring misfortune to the people, like the well-known appointment of Ambrosio Figueroa in the State of Morelos and others, who condemn us to the precipice of bloody conflicts sustained by the dictator Madero and the circle of científicos and hacendados who have suggested this to him.

14. If President Madero and the rest of the dictatorial elements of the current and old regime want to avoid the immense misfortunes that afflict the fatherland, and if they possess true sentiments of love for it, they must immediately renounce the posts they occupy, and by so doing they shall in some way stanch the grievous wounds that have opened in the breast of the Fatherland, and if they do not do so, upon their heads shall fall the blood and anathema of our brothers.

15. Mexicans: consider the deviousness and bad faith of a man who is shedding blood in a scandalous manner, because he is incapable of governing; consider that his system of Government is tying up the fatherland and trampling upon our institutions with the brute force of bayonets; so that the very weapons we took up to bring him to Power, we now turn against him for failing to keep his promises to the Mexican people and for having betrayed the Revolution he began; we are not personalists, we are partisans of principles and not of men!

Mexican people, support this Plan with weapons in your hands, and bring prosperity and welfare to the Fatherland.

Liberty, Justice, and Law. Ayala, State of Morelos, November 25, 1911

General in chief, Emiliano Zapata; signatures.

The Restoration of the *Ejido*

Luis Cabrera

Emiliano Zapata was not alone in his criticism of Madero's handling of the agrarian issue. Some criticism came from within the ranks of the government itself. Luis Cabrera (1876–1954) was arguably the most important ideologue of the Mexican revolution. He had a distinguished career as a lawyer, schoolteacher, professor, and journalist in the years prior to the outbreak of the revolution. He backed the candidacy of Francisco I. Madero in 1910 and was elected a federal deputy in 1912. In the Chamber of Deputies, he headed the Bloque Renovador, a group of progressive legislators who pressured Madero to approach social reform more decisively. His most famous pronouncement on the issue came in the speech excerpted below, delivered to congress in 1912. Cabrera would go on to become a prominent figure in the government of Venustiano Carranza, during a period when violent factionalism was rampant. As Carranza's treasury secretary, he authored the Law of January 6, 1915, the regime's key initiative on agrarian reform, which would largely be incorporated into the Constitution of 1917. When Carranza was overthrown and assassinated in 1920, Cabrera's influence waned drastically and he grew increasingly conservative. Nevertheless, his advocacy of distributing ejidos (common lands) to the villages as a means of satisfying their needs while attacking the inefficient latifundista system would be of enduring significance: the government of Lázaro Cárdenas, which during the 1930s carried out one of the most ambitious agrarian reforms in Latin American history, did not view the distribution of ejidos as an urgent expedient of war but as an end in itself. Thus, the ejido—which was ultimately an ambiguous concept of property involving state ownership of the land and communal usufruct by the villages—became a cornerstone of Mexican agriculture until the neoliberal "reform" of the agrarian reform in 1992.

While considering the presentation of this Project to the House of Deputies, I made sure to ascertain [President Madero's] opinion, in the hope of finding a disposition favorable to these reforms. I must state frankly that I did not find such a disposition on the President's part. He believes, rightly or wrongly, that the work of reestablishing peace must take precedence over economic reforms that, in his view, will cause further disruptions. I disagree. In my own view, the restoration of peace should be brought about by preventive and repressive measures, but also by economic reforms that will bring conflicting social groups into a relative state of equilibrium. One of these economic measures that may help to restore peace is the restoration of the *ejidos*. . . .

DON FRANCISCO I. MADERO, in the San Luis Plan, noted that the demand for land was the cause of political unrest and promised to remedy this problem. . . . The need for land was a kind of a phantasm, a vague idea floating in a nebulous state through all minds and spirits. Everyone believed that the solution to the agrarian problem consisted in distributing land; yet no one knew where, or to whom, or what type of land. . . .

Meanwhile, the real agrarian problem, [the need to distribute] lands to the hundreds of thousands of pariahs who had none, was gradually becoming more urgent. We needed to give lands not to selected individuals, but to social groups. The fact that the people owned land in previous times made the solution simple and clear: restoration of that land to the people. All dispossessed populations naturally thought that restorations were the solution. [Many] communities . . . recalled that they had but recently lost their lands, and it was undeniable that their lands were taken by illegal means. Is it not natural for people to think that the restoration of their usurped lands will follow the triumph of a revolution that has promised them justice? [And is it not natural to suppose also] that a capitalist, however ambitious, will not willingly give up the lands that he had usurped? And that there will be some means of justice by which the unfortunate people who hunger for the land they once occupied will be satisfied and will return to living the way they lived for more than four hundred years, because their rights were established in the epoch of the Aztecs?

The logical but ingenuous system of land restorations was accepted, of course, by the Secretary of the Interior. All the populations seeking the return of their *ejidos* were invited to come forward and identify themselves and the size of their lands in order to see if restoration would be possible. But what actually happened was inevitable: it was not possible to restore the *ejidos*, because the greatest injustices in a people's history cannot be simply undone by a corresponding act of justice — they must be remedied in some other form. . . .

Let me now sketch out the problem as I understand it. At the risk of tiring the reader, I ask for your indulgence with regard to one point. I believe that politics is the most concrete of the sciences, as well as the most concrete of the arts, and extreme caution is needed to avoid rationalizations that rely on analogies with other countries and other periods. Our political system requires a personal and local knowledge of our country and our country's needs, not general principles gathered from the study of other peoples. The antecedents that I draw upon to develop the resolution to this dilemma are not found in the histories of Rome, the English or French Revolutions, Australia, New Zealand, or even Argentina. There is only one country [and history] that can teach us the solutions: New Spain. . . . Two factors must be taken into consideration: the land and the people; the land, whose possession we will discuss, and the people, to whom lands should be given.

The Spanish occupants of New Spain at the time of the conquest respected the conditions that they found and, under the wise rule of Philip II, the indigenous peoples were not interfered with; later, villages were created through "reductions"[1] and the founding of colonies. In the Spaniards' view, such villages could not survive without their *casco,* their *ejidos,* and their *propios.* The *casco* [or *fundo legal*] was the land upon which the town itself was constructed; the *ejidos* were the communal lands of the village; and the *propios* were the village's public lands.

We need not concern ourselves with the *casco* at present. The *ejidos* and *propios,* however, have been very important economic entities in our country. Anyone who studies a land title from the colonial period can read on every page the transcendental struggle between villages and haciendas. In the conflicts between the villages and haciendas, the former triumphed thanks to their privileges, their organization, and effective means of cooperation among the villagers, developed over centuries. . . . But above all, they triumphed thanks to the enormous power that the villages retained through the possession of public lands [*propios*], which brought wealth and power, and of *ejidos,* which helped to preserve their communities.

The *ejidos* assured the people of their subsistence and the *propios* guaranteed the power of the village governments; the *ejidos* ensured tranquillity of the families gathered around the village church, and the *propios* brought economic power to the village authorities. The villagers were, in effect, communal landowners rather than individual owners of large landed estates. This was the secret behind the preservation of the villages in the face of the hacienda, in spite of the great political privileges held by Spanish landowners during the colonial period.

Later, the true nature of landownership became clear. Laws were passed mandating the breakup of lands held in "dead hands,"[2] and public lands were invariably considered a very dangerous form of landownership which needed to be ended, just as the lands of lay groups and religious institutions had to be dismantled.

The communities' situation with respect to the haciendas was a notoriously privileged one prior to the 1856 law of disamortization. This law was perfectly justified economically, but I do not need to remind you gentlemen that, although the breakup of the public lands may have been necessary, the application of the law to the *ejidos* was a very serious mistake. The laws were applied to the *ejidos* in accordance with the circulars of October and December of 1856 which, rather than awarding the lands to individual tenants, stipulated that they be divided up and distributed among the villagers. This led to the disappearance of the *ejidos* and to the absolute impoverishment of the people. I would not say that all of the land was usurped, although much of it was; I will not say that all of the land was stolen with the connivance of the authorities, although there are thousands of such cases. But the distribution of the *ejidos* was naturally intended, for economic reasons, to transfer the land to those who could put it to better use. The lands eventually went from the villages into the hands of *hacendados*. You know the results of this process: in certain parts of the Republic, and principally in the area of the Central Mesa, all of the *ejidos* became part of the surrounding estates; communities like Jonacatepec, Jojutla . . . ; but, why do I need to mention Morelos? I will simply mention the Federal District: towns like San Juan Ixtayopan, Mixquic, Tlahuac, and Chalco were reduced to their own town boundaries, and in conditions so poor that even the most foolish of the Spanish monarchs or viceroys would not imagine that a people could live this way. . . . This is the situation of ninety percent of the population in the Central Mesa, which [Andrés] Molina Enríquez has called the cereal zone, where life makes no sense without the *ejidos*.

Some have fought against the disintegration of the *ejidos*, [and some villages] have even managed to preserve them. Not just one, but many villages have learned to resist the disintegration of their *ejidos*, using methods easily available to all. After distributing their lands among the villagers, they instinctively deposited their deeds with that person in town who merited the greatest confidence, until this chief . . . had collected all of these titles with the implicit charge of preserving and defending the people's land through a communal administration. In the state of Mexico, this system was used frequently, and it was perfected to the point where villages became practically cooperatives or corporations which existed with the aim of returning the village to a communal system, but using procedures more in line with modern social organization, according to the rather limited intelligence of the town clerks.

This was the means found to defend against the disappearance of communal property; but this strategy was entirely ineffective in the face of the avarice of the surrounding estates toward the distributed land. And so it went, whether through mismanagement by the small landholders or abuses by the authorities; what is certain is that the *ejidos* have passed almost entirely from the villages to the *hacendados*. As a consequence, a large number of populations currently are unable to satisfy their most basic needs. In the towns of the state of Morelos, in the southern part of Puebla, and in the state of Mexico, the villagers do not have enough land to feed a goat, or to collect what is ironically called firewood — although it is really only garbage — for the pariah's home; they do not have the means to satisfy the most basic needs of rural life, because there is not even a square meter left of the *ejidos* to provide for the population. Neither economic arguments nor scientific proof are needed to understand that people cannot live when they have no way to perform the agricultural tasks that used to ensure their survival.

The simplest means of remedying this situation is restoration of lands to the people. If the people of, say, Ixtlahuaca or Jilotepec can remember that they once had *ejidos,* what could be simpler or more natural, now that the revolution that once promised justice and lands — and it did promise these things, no matter what anyone says — has triumphed, than for the people to request their *ejidos* once again? Restorations have been attempted, but in the most unjust ways imaginable. The most recent spoliations of the villages have been ineffective; they receive no support from any party, neither from the justice ministry, nor from this Chamber. On the other hand, the distribution of lands seized from small landholders and from villagers who managed to retain some part of their *ejidos* have received some support of the most unjust sort, for it comes primarily from local authorities who believe that by encouraging the pillaging of those who still have portions of their former *ejidos,* the situation will be saved. No one seems to see that the true restorations, those we should be attempting, are the ones that aim to recover the lands that have passed into the hands of large landowners, some of whom are completely protected by their influential families. Of course, some of the large landowners are foreigners, and their interests must be respected in order to protect Mexico's domestic and foreign credit. . . .

I hesitate to mention specific individuals, for I do not wish to shame anyone; but I will, with your permission, mention some. I will mention how, under the feudal domination of Iñigo Noriega, the villages of Xochimilco, Chalco and many other villages have been unable to take back lands that were usurped through the most unjust and violent means; the authorities continue to protect Iñigo Noriega and his enormous estates, which were established by pillaging the people. By contrast, there is the case of [the relatively small landowner] Aureliano Urrutia of Xochimilco, who must deal with the agitation of some individuals and some ridiculous local authorities who provoke the people with claims that his "enormous estate" of 300 hectares is a threat to the sacred promises proclaimed by the 1910 Revolution.

Thousands of cases like Urrutia's have occurred throughout the Republic, and they have caused discontent to a great number of people. The example suggests a paradox, for it is the small landholders who are the principal victims of the restoration of lands, and they are cast as the enemies of any and all change in the economic condition of the people. Why such absurdity? Because the agrarian issue is the Achilles' heel of the Revolution. . . .

If the rural population had—as only a few communities [presently] do—lakes to fish in and lands to hunt on; or land to plant and harvest, even if under the vigilance of authorities; if there were woodlands from which people could gather material to make tiles, furniture, and firewood; [thereby solving] their food problems on a basis of freedom; if the rural working population had land where they could plant freely, even a small plot, workers could augment their salaries without relying on the hacienda; they could work on the hacienda during peak seasons for a more equitable wage, and during the rest of the year devote their energies to working for themselves. The *ejido* would give them these opportunities.

Until it is possible to create a system of small-scale agriculture to replace the current system of large estates, the agrarian problem can be resolved through the granting of *ejidos* as a means to complement the workers' salaries.

The complement to the workers' wages must come from communal possession of land for subsistence. There are some rural classes which must always serve as day laborers; but we cannot continue to use the political strength of the Government to force these classes to work all year on the haciendas for extremely low wages.

The large rural proprietors must resolve to test new agricultural systems which use workers only during the months when agriculture demands it, for the large farms do not absolutely require a permanent workforce. If the haciendas can get by with a maximum of six months and a minimum of four months of labor, and if the working population refuses to be enslaved by the haciendas and their Government allies, the workers either will take up their rifles and join the Zapatista ranks or they will find legal ways to employ their energies, exploiting the fields, plains and hills of the *ejidos*.

When a sick man lies prostrate in his bed or on the table awaiting the surgical knife, he closes his eyes, clenches his jaw and tells the doctor, "Cut," because his pain resigns him to the greatest heroics; when a man's whole head is swollen by a fearsome toothache and he goes to the dentist, he is resolved to have all his teeth extracted; but when the pain subsides, he is no longer disposed to make such sacrifices. It is the same in society: when a time of revolution arises, we must apply pressure to resolve problems; we must cut, we must demand sacrifices, because these are times when people are willing to make those sacrifices and changes can be made easily. When the storm clouds pass, however, the old system returns, responses are slower and more tempered, and we are no longer disposed to resolve the transcendental issues that brought about the revolution in the first place.

This is why we have not resolved our agrarian problem, the principal dilemma of our country and one which deserves more of our attention. If the solution does not come from here, the Chamber of Deputies, the wound will be reopened.

Notes

1. During the Conquest era, as disease decimated the indigenous population, survivors would be relocated into newly founded villages called "reductions." See the selection in Part III by Zorita. *Ed.*

2. In the liberal lexicon of the nineteenth century, non-entrepreneurial institutions such as the indigenous villages or the church were referred to as "dead hands." See the selection by Luis González in the previous section. *Ed.*

Zapatistas in the Palace

Martín Luis Guzmán

The government of Francisco I. Madero was overthrown in February 1913, and soon thereafter both Madero and his vice-president, José María Pino Suárez, were killed. The regime which took over, headed by federalist General Victoriano Huerta, was authoritarian and reactionary, and had very little popular support.

Factions arose in various parts of the country to oppose the Huerta dictatorship; the most important was led by the governor of Coahuila, Venustiano Carranza, who was tenuously recognized by the insurgent armies as "First Chief." The revolution quickly entered a tremendously violent phase, one which did not end with Huerta's ouster in July 1914.

In October 1914 the several revolutionary factions met in the city of Aguascalientes to participate in the Sovereign Revolutionary Convention, whose goal was to establish a new government for all of Mexico. Sharp disagreements and clashes among leaders quickly led to a violent rupture between Conventionists (the populist forces of Zapata and Pancho Villa) on one side, and Constitutionalists (led by the patrician Carranza) on the other. The president of the Conventionist faction was Eulalio Gutiérrez, though the real power was held by Pancho Villa in the North and Emiliano Zapata in the South. The two movements were remarkably different in character, and their prospects for a successful alliance were remote. Still, they were able to occupy Mexico City briefly from late November 1914 until late January 1915. The following excerpt presents a scene from that occupation.

Martín Luis Guzmán (1887–1976) was the son of a federal army colonel from the northern state of Chihuahua. Eschewing his father's profession, he became one of Mexico's greatest literary figures. When the revolution broke out in 1910, the young Guzmán had just begun a career as a journalist. During the fight against Huerta he served as emissary from Venustiano Carranza to Pancho Villa, an experience that provided the material for his most famous books, The Eagle and the Serpent (1928) and Memoirs of Pancho Villa (1951), both works of fiction based on Guzmán's first-hand observations. In the vignette that follows, he provides a vivid portrait of the Zapatista leadership and their ambivalence toward political power. At the same time,

Provisional President Eulalio Gutiérrez *(left)* and General Eufemio Zapata *(right)* after taking possession of the National Palace, December 4, 1914. (Reprinted by permission of Fototeca del INAH, Mexico.)

he graphically evokes the yawning cultural chasm that separated Mexico's humble peasant revolutionaries from urbane, middle-class intellectuals like himself.

Eulalio Gutiérrez wanted to visit the National Palace before he installed his government there. So that same afternoon he, José Isabel Robles [a Villista general appointed minister of war by Gutiérrez], and I presented ourselves there. Eufemio Zapata [the elder brother of rebel leader Emiliano Zapata], who was in charge of the building, came out to the main entrance to receive us and began to do the honors of the house. To judge by his air, he was taking his momentary role of receiving the new President in his government abode and showing him the splendors of his future drawing rooms and offices very seriously. As we got out of the automobile, he shook hands with each of us and spoke like a rough but affable host.

While the greetings were being exchanged, I looked around me. The car had stopped just past one of the arcades of the large patio. In the background the two lines formed by the white masonry of the arches and the shadow of the openings met at an angle. A short way off, a group of the Zapata soldiery stood observing us from the sentry chamber; others peered from between the columns of the massive white arches. What was the attitude of these men? Meek or suspicious? At the time, they aroused in me curiosity more than anything else, because of the setting of which they formed a part. That place, which I had seen so many times and which always seemed the same, gave me on that occasion, practically empty as it was, and in the hands of a band of half-naked rebels, the effect of something new and strange.

We did not go up the main stairway, but used the staircase of honor. Eufemio walked ahead of us, like a janitor showing a house for rent. He was wearing the tight trousers with a broad fold down the two outside seams, a cotton blouse tied at the belly, and a huge broad-brimmed hat; as he mounted step after step, he seemed to symbolize the historic days in which we were living, in the contrast of his person, not meek, but uncouth and clumsy, with the cultivation and refinement presaged by the staircase. A flunky, a coachman, an official, an ambassador would have been in place there; each would have had the dignity, small or great, that went with his position, and that had its place in the hierarchy of dignities. Eufemio looked like a stableboy who was trying to act like a president. When his shoe touched the carpet, there was a clash between carpet and shoe. When his hand rested on the banister, there was an immediate incompatibility between the two. Every time he moved his foot, his foot seemed surprised at not getting tangled up in brush and undergrowth. Every time he stretched out his hand, it seemed to feel in vain for a tree trunk or boulder. One only had to look at him to see that everything that should have formed his setting was lacking, and that everything that surrounded him was superfluous as far as he was concerned.

But at this moment a terrible doubt assailed me. What about us? What kind of impression would the three of us who followed Eufemio have made on anybody who saw us? Eulalio and Robles in their stetson hats, unshaven and with their unmistakable plebeian aspect, and I with that everlasting air of the civilian in Mexico who at the hour of violence goes into politics, a mere instrument assuming the attitude of intellectual adviser to a successful military leader, at best — at worst, of criminals passing themselves off as leaders?

After we had ascended the stairs, Eufemio took great pride in showing us one by one the different rooms of the palace. Our steps alternately were echoed on the waxed floors, so polished that we could see ourselves dimly reflected in them, broken by the different colors of the marquetry, or were hushed by the velvet of the carpets. Behind us we could hear the soft slapping of the sandals of the two soldiers who followed us at a short distance through the empty rooms. It was a meek, gentle sound. Sometimes it ceased for a long time while the two soldiers stopped to look at a picture or examine a piece of furniture. Then I would turn back to look at them through the long perspective of the rooms. They formed a double figure, strangely quiet and remote, as they stood close to each other, looking at things in silence, their heads with their lank heavy hair uncovered, and their palm-leaf hats humbly clasped in both hands. Something sincere and worthy of respect was unquestionably represented by their rapt, embarrassed, almost religious humility. But we, what did we represent? Was there anything fundamentally sincere and serious in us, who were making joking comments on everything we saw, and had not bothered to take off our hats?

Eufemio made some remark about everything we passed, and his observations were often primitive and ingenuous. They revealed a cheerful, childlike conception of the gubernatorial functions. "This is where the government meets to talk." "This is where the government eats." "This is where the government has its dances." It was evident that he supposed we had never seen a tapestry nor had the slightest idea of the uses of a sofa or an armchair or a corner table, and he went along illuminating us. He said everything in such good faith that it positively touched me. When we reached the presidential chair, his tone became triumphant, almost ecstatic. "This is the chair." And then in a burst of enviable candor he added: "Ever since I've been here, I come every day to look at it, just to get used to it. Because—can you imagine in it?—I always used to think when I heard them talk about the President's seat that they meant his saddle." Eufemio laughed heartily at his own ignorance and we laughed too.

For some time Eulalio had been aching to take a dig at General Zapata, and he saw his opportunity. Turning toward Eufemio and putting a hand on his shoulder, he fired this arrow in his gentle, modulated voice:

"Not for nothing is one a good horseman, partner. The day this seat becomes a saddle, you and your friends can all be presidents."

The smile disappeared from Eufemio's face as if by magic, and a gloomy, sinister look replaced it. Eulalio's witticism had been too cruel and perhaps too apt, and it had flicked him on the raw.

"Well," he said a few seconds later, as though there were nothing more worth seeing, "let's go downstairs now and see the stables. Then I'll take you to the rooms where my men and I are quartered."

We went over the stables from one end to the other, though with greater satisfaction on Eufemio's part than on ours. Amidst the array of collars, bridles, bits and halters—all smelling of grease and leather—he displayed an amazing store of knowledge. And the same with the horses; he knew all about breeding them, training them and showing them. His enthusiasm for these things took his mind off the incident of the chair, and then he led us to the quarters he and his men occupied in the palace. Eufemio—and in this he gave evidence of his sincerity—had found rooms to his taste in the poorest, most out-of-the-way rear court. He seemed well aware of how miserable his accommodations were, and to forestall criticism, he quickly explained why he had chosen them.

"I picked this place because I've always been poor and I didn't feel right in better rooms."

Really the place was abominable. I thought I should smother as I went in. The room was not large and had only one door and no windows. There must have been from fifty to a hundred officers from Zapata's army there, of all ranks, when we came in. The majority were standing up, side by side, or in groups with their arms around each other. Others were sitting on the table, and some were lying on the floor in the corners and along the wall. Many of them had a bottle or a glass in their hand. The air was foul and sour and a hundred odors were mingled with the heavy pall of smoke. Everybody was drunk, some more, some less. A soldier stood by the door to keep it shut against the light or against inquisitive eyes. Two small electric lights glimmered feebly through the asphyxiating fog.

At first nobody paid any attention to us. Then as Eufemio went from group to group, whispering something in a low voice, they began to look at us without suspicion and even make certain signs of welcome. But they were faint, almost imperceptible expressions. We had, beyond question, fallen into a world so different from our own that our mere presence was a source of perturbation in spite of everything they and we did to overcome this. With the exception of a few, they avoided looking straight at us and watched us instead out of the corner of their eyes. Instead of talking with us they whispered among themselves. And every now and then they would turn their backs to take a long swallow from their bottles or empty their glasses.

Eufemio and those around him invited us to have a drink.

"Here, let's have some glasses," shouted Eufemio. Timid hands reached out to set five or six dirty glasses on the edge of the table. Eufemio set them in a row and poured out fresh drinks of tequila on the dregs at the bottom of the glasses.

We drank in silence. Eufemio poured out more tequila. We drank again. Once more Eufemio filled up the glasses. . . .

As we drank, Eufemio began to warm up. At first he became happy, jovial, and then thoughtful and gloomy. At about the fifth or sixth glass he happened to remember Eulalio's joke about the presidential chair.

"This comrade," he said, addressing his men, "thinks that Emiliano and I, and others like us, will be presidents the day they saddle horses with seats like the one upstairs."

There was a profound silence, broken only by Eulalio's sarcastic laugh.

Then the rustle of voices began again, but there was a vague, new note in it, excited and menacing. Nevertheless Eufemio went on serving tequila as though nothing had happened. Once more the glasses were handed round and we drank upon each other's sticky leavings. But at this point Robles began to look at me hard and then, almost imperceptibly, make signs to me with his eyes. I understood; draining my glass, I took leave of Eufemio.

An hour later I was back at the palace, and Robles's entire guard was with me; but just as we came up to the entrance, I saw Eulalio and Robles calmly walking out the same door through which we had entered in the early afternoon.

"Thanks," said Eulalio when he saw me. "Fortunately we don't need the soldiers now. They were so busy drinking that they could not waste time fighting with us. But, anyway, the precaution was thoughtful. What amazes me is how you and Robles understood one another without saying a word."

Mexico Has Been Turned into a Hell

William O. Jenkins

*One of the first major battles of the ugly, factionalized war that broke out after the con-
vention of 1914 was fought in the city of Puebla, some sixty miles southeast of Mexico
City. The city was taken easily by the Zapatista forces in December 1914 when the
Constitutionalists abandoned it. The Constitutionalists, intent on retaking the city,
invaded in force in early January 1915. U.S. Consul William O. Jenkins here paints
a vivid picture of the ferocity which would characterize this phase of the revolution,
known to historians as the "war of the factions." His jaundiced view of Mexicans in
general, and of revolutionaries in particular, were typical of many foreign observers,
who were quick to find the remedy for Mexico's woes in foreign intervention and who
appeared to believe that Mexicans would welcome such a violation of their sovereignty.*

*William O. Jenkins (1878–1963) was a prominent and controversial figure in Mexi-
co's twentieth-century history. A native of Shelbyville, Tennessee, in 1901 he moved
to Mexico where he soon proved himself a shrewd — and reportedly ruthless — businessman. He built up a string of textile and stocking factories in various parts of
the country and was named U.S. Consul for the Puebla region. While he was clearly
unhinged by the events he describes below, Jenkins did not abandon his interests in
Mexico, but rather found ways to profit from the chaos and violence of the revolution,
largely by loaning money to desperate landowners and later foreclosing on them. By
the end of the war, he had become the dominant figure in the Mexican sugar industry.
His close ties to influential political figures — notably, the notorious General Maximino Avila Camacho, the political boss of Puebla during the 1930s — helped him to
acquire many other interests, ranging from popsicle-making to a nearly complete monopoly on Mexico's movie theaters. In 1960, Time magazine declared him to be the
richest man in Mexico. Perhaps Jenkins's greatest notoriety came in 1919, when he
was kidnapped and held for ransom by Mexican rebels. When the kidnappers released
him, he was immediately arrested by the government and charged (probably falsely)
with engineering his own kidnapping. The episode caused a brief flare-up in tensions
between Mexico and the United States. Jenkins is mostly remembered in Mexico today
for his vast fortune and for the Mary Street Jenkins Foundation, founded in the 1950s*

in honor of his late wife, which continues to fund hospitals, universities, and other philanthropic causes.

Puebla, Mexico. January the 7th. 1915.

Hon. Arnold Shanklin, American Consul General, Temporarily in Veracruz

Sir:

. . . The general attack was begun early on the 5th., and on the opposite side of town from my house. I saw many large bodies of Zapatistas evacuating the city without a fight . . . but it is said that many of the Zapatistas got surrounded in the city and had to fight their way out. At any rate, there was some severe fighting in the streets of the city, beginning as I have said on the opposite side of the city from my house, and gradually getting nearer, as the Zapatistas fought their way out on this side. In front of the Consulate, there was an extremely prolonged battle, lasting for more than an hour, for usually the fighting was done on the run, and no stand was made, but evidently some one got cornered in front of the Consulate, for the firing was constant for at least an hour. When it finally terminated here, it was practically over throughout the whole city, or at least I heard very few shots after that. The factory was working at the time, and of course was full of the female operators whom I employ in my knitting mill, about three hundred at the time. I was careful to get them all under cover, and no one was hurt. Of course the front of the building was struck many times, and the window glass broken up, but that is only natural considering the number of shots fired, and the poor marksmanship of these soldiers. . . .

After the firing ceased and allowing a sufficient time to elapse to not be in danger, I went out and there were 27 dead men in front of the house and one wounded. I immediately sent the wounded man to the hospital, and upon examination of the dead, found that many of them had been evidently shot after being hurt and unable to move, for their heads were blown open in many cases, sometimes stuck with knives, and everything showing that the wounded had been unmercifully finished up, after being helpless. Also I noticed many wounds made with the expansive bullets and picked up pieces of these bullets as well.

In the afternoon, when the patrols of the Carrancistas were going about over the city, examining the dead etc., I was shocked to be told that it was reported that the shots which had killed these men had been fired from my house. I immediately denied such a report, and paid no further attention to it, but about five o'clock in the afternoon, I was sitting in my office, and heard a scandal at the door, and went there only to find a crowd of drunken soldiers, abusing the doorkeeper, striking him, and firing at him twice, which he fortunately escaped, and they at once began with their abuse at me, saying that I had killed their comrades etc. etc., threatening to shoot me at once, and using all manner of abuses and indignities. I pretended to summon the authorities, but was immediately put under arrest, and threatened with instant death, and together with my brother-in-law, and the doorkeeper we were carried off through the street between files of these drunken dogs, to their cuartel [military headquarters]. We were there placed in an open lot with the horses and soldiers and threatened with immediate execution if we attempted to run away. I assure you that I had no thought of attempting it, and only prayed that we would be spared the shooting if we made no attempt to run away.

Before leaving the house, I explained to them that this building was the American Consulate and that I was the Consul, but was informed that it made no difference to them what I was, nor what the house was, as I had to pay for the death of the men in front of my house. I explained to them that I could prove by three hundred witnesses of their own people that no shots had been fired from my house, that I took no part in the matter, etc. etc., but it was like arguing a matter before a herd of swine, as they would listen to nothing, and amid insults and abuses we were carried to the cuartel.

After arriving there, I finally managed to get a talk with the captain, for it must be noted that the men who had arrested us were privates, and a sergeant or so, all equally abusive. I explained to the Captain who I was, and why I was arrested, and finally got him to return to the house with me, so that I could show him why their accusation was completely false. I was not released however, but carried back to the lot and confined there for about three hours, until a Coronel came, who immediately put us at liberty, and said that if our presence was necessary the next day, he would advise me. He assured me that I would not be molested any further and I returned home. . . .

Early the next morning (Yesterday, Jan. the 6th) I was awakened by a loud knocking at the door, and upon going toward the door, encountered about thirty soldiers, headed by another crazy sergeant, and was informed that I was under arrest, and to accompany them at once. I was not even allowed to dress properly, but was made to accompany them throughout all the house searching even the rooms where my wife and daughters were in bed, and upon venturing to inquire by whose orders this was being done, was significantly informed that their rifles were their orders, and not to question them. My brother-in-law was not taken at once, though his room was searched, and

I was again hurried down through the streets with six employees who were around the front door, to another place of confinement. These were different soldiers from the afternoon previous, but even more abusive than the other if possible. Upon arriving at their cuartel, which was full of the rest of their company, I was met with the vilest invective, curses known only to Mexicans, abuses and even blows, and it was with difficulty that we were conducted to the cell where we were to be confined. Upon seeing that my Brother-in-law was not with me, he was immediately sent for, but in the meanwhile it was decided that I should be immediately shot for aiding the Zapatistas the previous day. It was impossible to explain that I was innocent, and had nothing to do with the battle in any way, and I was hastened from the room where, confined to the Patio, and in spite of my protestations of innocence, and even pleading, I was made to stand against a stone pillar, and the whole crowd of insane fiends were preparing to shoot me. I asked permission to write a note of farewell to my wife, but was met by increased insults, and had given up all hope on earth of being saved when a captain, evidently belonging to another regiment, passed by, and asked the sergeant or cabo [corporal] who was in charge, what they were doing and why they were doing it, and upon being told, I went to him and told him who I was, that I was absolutely innocent of any charge, but was being murdered like a dog without even listening to hundreds of witnesses who would swear to my absolute innocence. Upon asking the sergeant why they were shooting me and on whose orders, it developed that they had no order at all, except a general order to shoot snipers from the General, but they had taken it on themselves to judge me guilty without any especial order, or trial whatever. Seeing in this captain at least a ray of hope, I besought him to procure a stay of execution, or rather murder I should call it, until the General's attention was called to it, and he in his turn explained to the Sergeant that it would be a dangerous matter to thus shoot the American Consul without a special order to do so. In spite of the protestations of all the soldiers, and their efforts to prevent it, this captain personally conducted me back to the cell, and a little later, I was conducted to another building, and confined there with other prisoners. This was very early in the morning, and until about 12:30. I was released through the efforts of the British Consul, Mr. W.S. Hardaker, who had upon hearing from my wife what had happened hastened to Gen. F[rancisco] Coss and Gen. Alvaro Obregon, who were commanding the Carrancista troops, and explained to them my situation and peril. Immediately on being informed, Gen. Obregon, who is in charge of the entire military force here, sent for me, and released all the men who were imprisoned with me, as well as my Brother-in-law who had also been imprisoned in another place, and gave me offers of all protection and guarantees, assuring me of his sincere regret of the occurrence, and offering to punish those who were guilty of such an act. He was extremely kind about it, which I appreciated very much, but I was unable to forget that but for a miracle I would have been shot down in cold blood by his irresponsable [*sic*] men, even though he himself had nothing but kind intentions to give protection to all. . . . These [Mexican soldiers] understand nothing. They are animals without hearts, conscience or intelligence. Their Generals may be honest men, I don't know, but the soldiers know no obedience, and are completely and utterly irresponsible, without having any other aim in war than robbery and destruction. Liberty, for which they claim to be fighting, is to them, License to rob and destroy. They know no ideals, and are incapable of comprehension. I have known this all along, but never have I so completely appreciated it as now, when I have passed through this terrible ordeal. It has made an old man of me in a day. I have lost all interest in everything and only think of getting away from this God-forsaken country, to where a man can sleep in peace. I cannot rest here but am looking all night into a thousand rifles pointed at me by as many howling devils, and undergoing the tortures of all doomed men. If I had committed a crime, and was being executed for it, I believe that I could face the firing squad with some degree of equanimity, knowing that I was only receiving my just due, or if I had to die for my country, I could do it in the knowledge that I was complying with my duty, but to be subject to assassination, to murder, such as this, and knowing that as long as this state of affairs lasts, we will all continually be subject to the same thing, [is] why, Mr. Shanklin, it has taken the very life out of me. Every sound startles me, because I have no assurance but that at any time a crowd of these devils will come and shoot me in my own room in spite of all the orders of the Generals in Mexico. There is no discipline among them. They know no order. Every common private is a law unto himself. Not only with the Carrancistas, but the Zapatistas are even worse.

As you know I have been in Mexico a long time, about fifteen years. I have worked hard and have built up a great business, completely covering the whole Republic in my line, and have made a fortune, but I am anxious to abandon it all, and get out where I can breathe free once more. . . . Mexico has been turned into a Hell, and gets worse every day, for little by little its resources are being destroyed, its riches being wasted in a senseless war, and the time is very near when there will be famine and thousands will die for lack of food. Many calculate that this will come in six months. Certainly in another year. Knowing these people as I do, I don't want to face the consequences that a famine is sure to bring, for then it will be like turning wild animals together, and no life will be respected for a moment longer than the opportunity comes to destroy it. The country is completely demoralized, and the soldiers have long since lost all conception of personal privilege or property rights, and accept as authority only some one whom they fear. . . .

. . . You have always been extremely discreet in your conversations with me as regards any criticism about any action or policy of our country as regards Mexico, and I may be overstepping the bounds of Consular propriety to ask you, if you can understand why our Government continues to allow munitions of war to be given into the hands of these irresponsible people to be used not only in murdering each other without cause or reason, but in destroying the lives of foreigners as well, and even in shooting the own [*sic*] representatives of our country, for it is no fault of the ammunition or the men who had it, that I was not murdered yesterday.

It is a cold blooded traffic in men's lives, and nothing more, and I can not possible [*sic*] understand how it can be countenanced by our Government. If the war was for a cause, or a reason, if there was any solution in sight, if it was for men's liberty, or a heritage for their children, we would all of us, who know Mexico so thoroughly, say that was for the best, but it has degenerated now into a war of pillage and destruction and the greatest evils which it started out to cure and the reforms it was to establish have been lost sight of in the maze of changes that have taken place, and the longer it is allowed to go on, the worse it will become.

I was for years violently opposed to any Intervention on the part of our Government in Mexican affairs, because I thought that the Mexicans should be allowed to settle their internal affairs in their own way, but the matter has now reached such a stage, that I am very much afraid there is no other solution. The element of Mexican citizenship which could be counted on to bring about the needed reforms in the proper way have [*sic*] long since been eliminated from the scene of action, and we have now the country governed by illiterate men, without the least capacity for helping the country in this dire need, but only capable of ruling a sufficient number of men to keep them in the fight. When I was in Mexico on Dec. the 23rd, I had an interview with President Eulalio Gutierrez, and found him a miner who worked for me in 1905 and 1906 in the state of Zacatecas, a man utterly incapable of even comprehending the position which he fills, much less understanding the thousand and one difficult problems that he has to face. It is useless to tell you, for you already know it, that he is a mere figurehead, and will serve no other purpose than to probably cause trouble when he is separated from his position. He is a good miner to earn two or three pesos per day, or to even manage a bunch of 20 or 50 peons, as he did when I knew him, but ridiculously incapable of his present exalted position.

I am therefore coming to the opinion that it will be a positive necessity for Mexico to have some assistance in straightening out this tangle, for otherwise it will gradually assume a state of anarchy that will ultimately become unbearable. . . .

Pancho Villa

John Reed

In the northern part of Mexico, a style of revolution arose that contrasted sharply with that of the settled, religious, generally conservative peasants of Morelos. Here, peasants, cowhands, miners, and petty merchants took up arms with abandon: in the unforgettable portrait painted by Mariano Azuela, the first important novelist of the Mexican revolution, the northern rebels fought "as if in that unrestrained running they were trying to take possession of the whole land"[1] and to redress the humiliations of their former lives. No one better exemplifies this spirit than the legendary northern leader, Francisco "Pancho" Villa, who is portrayed here by the American journalist John Reed (1887–1920).

Reed's work was tremendously popular and influential in molding world opinion regarding the Mexican revolution, and Villa in particular (after reading his work, Woodrow Wilson expressed great admiration for Villa). John Reed was a left-wing writer who made the most of his short life by chronicling the American labor movement, the Mexican revolution, and, most famously, the Bolshevik revolution in Russia. Only twenty-six years old in 1913, Reed approached his subject with a rare boldness, traveling alone and unprotected through revolutionary Mexico, living and fighting with the ordinary soldiers, and cultivating a relationship of mutual respect with Villa. His unrestrained admiration for the revolutionary seems somewhat naive in retrospect, though he clearly represented the romantic tendencies of his generation in viewing Villa as a noble savage, a primitive socialist, capable of reinventing Mexico while igniting hopes for change in other climes. While readers should be cautioned against Reed's tendency to over-romanticize his subject, it is worth noting that later writers—most notably, the historian Friedrich Katz, whose monumental biography of Villa was published in 1998—bear out many of Reed's main points.

The Rise of a Bandit

Villa was an outlaw for twenty-two years. When he was only a boy of sixteen, delivering milk in the streets of Chihuahua, he killed a government official and had to take to the mountains. The story is that the official had violated his sister, but it seems probable that Villa killed him on account of his insufferable insolence. That in itself would not have outlawed him long in Mexico, where human life is cheap; but once a refugee he committed the unpardonable crime of stealing cattle from the rich *hacendados*. And from that time to the outbreak of the Madero revolution the Mexican government had a price on his head.

Villa was the son of ignorant peons. He had never been to school. He hadn't the slightest conception of the complexity of civilization, and when he finally came back to it, a mature man of extraordinary native shrewdness, he encountered the twentieth century with the naïve simplicity of a savage.

It is almost impossible to procure accurate information about his career as a bandit. There are accounts of outrages he committed in old files of local newspapers and government reports, but those sources are prejudiced, and his name became so prominent as a bandit that every train robbery and holdup and murder in northern Mexico was attributed to Villa. But an immense body of popular legend grew up among the peons around his name. There are many traditional songs and ballads celebrating his exploits — you can hear the shepherds singing them around their fires in the mountains at night, repeating verses handed down by their fathers or composing others extemporaneously. For instance, they tell the story of how Villa, fired by the story of the misery of the peons on the Hacienda of Los Alamos, gathered a small army and descended upon the Big House, which he looted, and distributed the spoils among the poor people. He drove off thousands of cattle from the Terrazzas [*sic*] range and ran them across the border.[2] He would suddenly descend upon a prosperous mine and seize the bullion. When he needed corn he captured a granary belonging to some rich man. He recruited almost openly in the villages far removed from the well-traveled roads and railways, organizing the outlaws of the mountains. Many of the present rebel soldiers used to belong to his band and several of the Constitutionalist generals, like Urbina. . . .

His reckless and romantic bravery is the subject of countless poems. They tell, for example, how one of his band named Reza was captured by the rurales and bribed to betray Villa. Villa heard of it and sent word into the city of Chihuahua that he was coming for Reza. In broad daylight he entered the city on horseback, took ice cream on the Plaza — the ballad is very explicit on this point — and rode up and down the streets until he found Reza strolling with his sweetheart in the Sunday crowd on the Paseo Bolivar, where he shot him and escaped. In time of famine he fed whole districts, and took care of entire villages evicted by the soldiers under Porfirio Diaz's outrageous land law. Everywhere he was known as The Friend of the Poor. He was the Mexican Robin Hood.

Pancho Villa. (Reprinted by permission of Fototeca del INAH, Mexico.)

In all these years he learned to trust nobody. Often in his secret journeys across the country with one faithful companion he camped in some desolate spot and dismissed his guide; then, leaving a fire burning, he rode all night to get away from the faithful companion. That is how Villa learned the art of war, and in the field today, when the army comes into camp at night, Villa flings the bridle of his horse to an orderly, takes a serape over his shoulder, and sets out for the hills alone. He never seems to sleep. In the dead of night he will appear somewhere along the line of outposts to see if the sentries are on the job; and in the morning he returns from a totally different direction. No one, not even the most trusted officer of his staff, knows the last of his plans until he is ready for action. . . .

A Peon in Politics

Villa proclaimed himself military governor of the State of Chihuahua, and began the extraordinary experiment — extraordinary because he knew nothing about it — of creating a government for 300,000 people out of his head.

It has often been said that Villa succeeded because he had educated advisers. As a matter of fact, he was almost alone. What advisers he had spent most of their time answering his eager questions and doing what he told them. I used sometimes to go to the Governor's palace early in the morning and wait for him in the Governor's chamber. About eight o'clock Sylvestre Terrazzas, the Secretary of State, Sebastian Vargas, the State Treasurer, and Manuel Chao, then Interventor, would arrive, very bustling and busy, with huge piles of reports, suggestions and decrees which they had drawn up. Villa himself came in about eight-thirty, threw himself into a chair, and made them read out loud to him. Every minute he would interject a remark, correction or suggestion. Occasionally he waved his finger back and forward and said: *"No sirve"* ["This won't do"]. When they were all through he began rapidly and without a halt to outline the policy of the State of Chihuahua, legislative, financial, judicial, and even educational. When he came to a place that bothered him, he said: "How do they do that?" And then, after it was carefully explained to him: "Why?" Most of the acts and usages of government seemed to him extraordinarily unnecessary and snarled up. For example, his advisers proposed to finance the Revolution by issuing State bonds bearing 30 or 40 percent interest. He said, "I can understand why the State should pay something to people for the rent of their money, but how is it just to pay the whole sum back to them three or four times over?" He couldn't see why rich men should be granted huge tracts of land and poor men should not. The whole complex structure of civilization was new to him. You had to be a philosopher to explain anything to Villa; and his advisers were only practical men. . . .

No sooner had he taken over the government of Chihuahua than he put his army to work running the electric light plant, the street railways, the telephone, the water works and the Terrazzas flour mill. He delegated soldiers to administer the great haciendas which he had confiscated. He manned the slaughterhouse with soldiers, and sold Terrazzas's beef to the people for the government. A thousand of them he put in the streets of the city as civil police, prohibiting on pain of death stealing, or the sale of liquor to the army. A soldier who got drunk was shot. He even tried to run the brewery with soldiers, but failed because he couldn't find an expert maltster. "The only thing to do with soldiers in time of peace," said Villa, "is to put them to work. An idle soldier is always thinking of war."

In the matter of the political enemies of the Revolution he was just as simple, just as effective. Two hours after he entered the Governor's palace the foreign consuls came in a body to ask his protection for 200 Federal soldiers who had been left as a police force at the request of the foreigners. Before answering them, Villa said suddenly: "Which is the Spanish consul?" Scobell, the British vice-consul, said: "I represent the Spaniards." "All right!" snapped Villa. "Tell them to begin to pack. Any Spaniard caught within the boundaries of this State after five days will be escorted to the nearest wall by a firing squad."

The consuls gave a gasp of horror. Scobell began a violent protest, but Villa cut him short.

"This is not a sudden determination on my part," he said; "I have been thinking about this since 1910. The Spaniards must go."

Letcher, the American consul, said: "General, I don't question your motives, but I think you are making a grave political mistake in expelling the Spaniards. The government at Washington will hesitate a long time before becoming friendly to a party which makes use of such barbarous measures."

"Señor Consul," answered Villa, "we Mexicans have had three hundred years of the Spaniards. They have not changed in character since the Conquistadores. They disrupted the Indian empire and enslaved the people. We did not ask them to mingle their blood with ours. Twice we drove them out of Mexico and allowed them to return with the same rights as Mexicans, and they used these rights to steal away our land, to make the people slaves, and to take up arms against the cause of liberty. They supported Porfirio Diaz. They were perniciously active in politics. It was the Spaniards who framed the plot that put Huerta in the palace. When Madero was murdered the Spaniards in every State in the Republic held banquets of rejoicing. They thrust on us the greatest superstition the world has ever known—the Catholic Church. They ought to be killed for that alone. I consider we are being very generous with them."

Scobell insisted vehemently that five days was too short a time, that he couldn't possibly reach all the Spaniards in the State by that time; so Villa extended the time to ten days.

The rich Mexicans who had oppressed the people and opposed the Revolution, he expelled promptly from the State and confiscated their vast holdings. By a simple stroke of the pen the 17,000,000 acres and innumerable business enterprises of the Terrazzas family became the property of the Constitutionalist government, as well as the great lands of the Creel family and the magnificent palaces which were their town houses. Remembering, however, how the Terrazzas exiles had once financed the Orozco Revolution, he imprisoned Don Luis Terrazzas Jr. as a hostage in his own house in Chihuahua. Some particularly obnoxious political enemies were promptly executed in the penitentiary. The Revolution possesses a black book in which are set down the names, offenses, and property of those who have oppressed and robbed the people. The Germans, who had been particularly active politically, the

Englishmen and Americans, he does not yet dare to molest. Their pages in the black book will be opened when the Constitutionalist government is established in Mexico City; and there, too, he will settle the account of the Mexican people with the Catholic Church. . . .

The Human Side

Villa has two wives, one a patient, simple woman who was with him during all his years of outlawry, who lives in El Paso, and the other a cat-like, slender young girl, who is the mistress of his house in Chihuahua. He is perfectly open about it, though lately the educated, conventional Mexicans who have been gathering about him in ever-increasing numbers have tried to hush up the fact. Among the peons it is not only not unusual but customary to have more than one mate.

One hears a great many stories of Villa's violating women. I asked him if that were true. He pulled his mustache and stared at me for a minute with an inscrutable expression. "I never take the trouble to deny such stories," he said. "They say I am a bandit, too. Well, you know my history. But tell me; have you ever met a husband, father or brother of any woman that I have violated?" He paused: "Or even a witness?"

It is fascinating to watch him discover new ideas. Remember that he is absolutely ignorant of the troubles and confusions and readjustments of modern civilization. "Socialism," he said once, when I wanted to know what he thought of it: "Socialism — is it a thing? I only see it in books, and I do not read much." Once I asked him if women would vote in the new Republic. He was sprawled out on his bed, with his coat unbuttoned. "Why, I don't think so," he said, startled, suddenly sitting up. "What do you mean-vote? Do you mean elect a government and make laws?" I said I did and that women already were doing it in the United States. "Well," he said, scratching his head, "if they do it up there I don't see that they shouldn't do it down here." The idea seemed to amuse him enormously. He rolled it over and over in his mind, looking at me and away again. "It may be as you say," he said, "but I have never thought about it. Women seem to me to be things to protect, to love. They have no sternness of mind. They can't consider anything for its right or wrong. They are full of pity and softness. Why," he said, "a woman would not give an order to execute a traitor."

"I am not so sure of that, *mi General*," I said. "Women can be crueler and harder than men."

He stared at me, pulling his mustache. And then he began to grin. He looked slowly to where his wife was setting the table for lunch. "*Oiga*," he said, "come here. Listen. Last night I caught three traitors crossing the river to blow up the railroad. What shall I do with them? Shall I shoot them or not?"

Embarrassed, she seized his hand and kissed it. "Oh, I don't know anything about that," she said. "You know best."

"No," said Villa. "I leave it entirely to you. Those men were going to try to cut our communications between Juarez and Chihuahua. They were traitors—Federals. What shall I do? Shall I shoot them or not?"

"Oh, well, shoot them," said Mrs. Villa.

Villa chuckled delightedly. "There is something in what you say," he remarked, and for days afterward went around asking the cook and the chambermaids whom they would like to have for President of Mexico. . . .

It seems incredible to those who don't know him, that this remarkable figure, who has risen from obscurity to the most prominent position in Mexico in three years, should not covet the Presidency of the Republic. But that is in entire accordance with the simplicity of his character. When asked about it he answered as always with perfect directness, just in the way that you put it to him. He didn't quibble over whether he could or could not be President of Mexico. He said: "I am a fighter, not a statesman. I am not educated enough to be President. I only learned to read and write two years ago. How could I, who never went to school, hope to be able to talk with the foreign ambassadors and the cultivated gentlemen of the Congress? It would be bad for Mexico if an uneducated man were to be President. There is one thing that I will not do—and that is to take a position for which I am not fitted. . . ." On behalf of my paper I had to ask him this question five or six times. Finally he became exasperated. "I have told you many times," he said, "that there is no possibility of my becoming President of Mexico. Are the newspapers trying to make trouble between me and my Jefe? This is the last time that I will answer that question. The next correspondent that asks me I will have him spanked and sent to the border." For days afterward he went around grumbling humorously about the *chatito* (pug nose) who kept asking him whether he wanted to be President of Mexico. The idea seemed to amuse him. Whenever I went to see him after that he used to say, at the end of our talk: "Well, aren't you going to ask me today whether I want to be President?" . . .

The Dream of Pancho Villa

It might not be uninteresting to know the passionate dream—the vision which animates this ignorant fighter, "not educated enough to be President of Mexico." He told it to me once in these words: "When the new Republic is established there will never be any more army in Mexico. Armies are the greatest support of tyranny. There can be no dictator without an army.

"We will put the army to work. In all parts of the Republic we will establish military colonies composed of the veterans of the Revolution. The State will give them grants of agricultural lands and establish big industrial enterprises to give them work. Three days a week they will work and work hard, because honest work is more important than fighting, and only honest work makes good citizens. And the other three days they will receive military instruction and go out and teach all the people how to fight. Then, when the Patria is invaded, we will just have to telephone from the palace at Mexico City, and in half a day all the Mexican people will rise from their fields and factories, fully armed, equipped and organized to defend their children and their homes.

"My ambition is to live my life in one of those military colonies among my *compañeros* whom I love, who have suffered so long and so deeply with me. I think I would like the government to establish a leather factory there where we could make good saddles and bridles, because I know how to do that; and the rest of the time I would like to work on my little farm, raising cattle and corn. It would be fine, I think, to help make Mexico a happy place."[3]

Notes

1. *The Underdogs,* translated by Frederick H. Fornoff (Pittsburgh: University of Pittsburgh Press, 1992), 40. *Ed.*

2. Luis Terrazas (the misspelling is in Reed's original text) was a prominent Apache fighter in the northern state of Chihuahua, who rose to become one of Mexico's wealthiest and most powerful regional caudillos. Together with his son-in-law, Enrique Creel, Terrazas achieved near-total political and economic dominance in the state, a fact that is generally regarded as a major provocation of the revolution in Chihuahua. *Ed.*

3. In 1920 a new coalition led by Alvaro Obregón overthrew the government of Venustiano Carranza. The new government sought to ensure Villa's loyalty by providing him with a large, remote estate in Chihuahua for his retirement. He ran the estate very much like one of the idyllic military colonies he described to Reed. His retirement was short-lived, however, for he was gunned down on the streets of Parral in 1923, most certainly by supporters of his former Constitutionalist rivals, Obregón and Plutarco Elías Calles. *Ed.*

La Punitiva

Anonymous

On March 9, 1916, Francisco Villa led five hundred guerrilla troops across the U.S. border to attack the small border town of Columbus, New Mexico, killing seventeen Americans. The attack was in retaliation for U.S. diplomatic recognition of Villa's rival, Venustiano Carranza, as the legitimate government of Mexico. The attack caused considerable outrage in the United States, and since it was a presidential election year, it appeared some response was called for. On March 15, President Woodrow Wilson authorized the second major military intervention in the Mexican revolution (the first was the occupation of Veracruz in 1914): he sent a "punitive expedition" of six thousand (later increased to ten thousand) troops into Mexico with orders to capture Villa and disperse Villista bands operating near the border. The mission, led by General John J. ("Blackjack") Pershing, failed miserably and was withdrawn in February 1917. The details as given in the following corrido *were largely erroneous, but the sense of outraged and bellicose nationalism caused by "la punitiva" was clearly genuine. Indeed, Villa remains a beloved nationalist icon and secular saint in his native Chihuahua and among* mexicanos *along the border.*

In our Mexico, on the 23rd of February,
Carranza let the Americans cross over:
20,000 men, and 200 airplanes
were looking for Villa throughout the country.

Carranza tells them earnestly,
if they are men enough and know how to track him down:
"I give permission for you to find Villa
and you can also learn how it is to die."

When the Texas "blondies" arrived
exhausted from so much walking,
after seven hours on the road,
the poor souls wanted to go back home.

The American Punitive Expedition in Mexico. (Anita Brenner and George R. Leighton, *The Wind That Swept Mexico: The History of the Mexican Revolution of 1910–1942* [Austin: University of Texas Press, 1971], photo no. 12.)

The expeditionary searches began
and the airplanes started to fly,
they took several directions
looking for Villa in order to kill him.

When Francisco Villa saw the punitive forces
he immediately got ready, too,
he dressed as an American soldier,
and he also transformed his troops.

When the planes saw the flag
that Villa had painted with stars
they made a mistake and came down,
and Villa took them prisoners.

Francisco Villa no longer rides a horse
and his people need never ride again:

Francisco Villa is now the owner of airplanes
which he very easily acquires.

Because we are so few Mexicans
the "blondies" say they can finish us off,
it doesn't matter if they bring a thousand cannons
because they end up leaving them in the hills.

When they entered the State of Chihuahua
all of the people were just amazed
to see all those American soldiers
that Pancho Villa left hanging from the poles.

When the "blondies" entered the city of Parral
asking for flour, crackers, and ham,
men, women, and children would tell them,
"There's only gunpowder and cannon balls."

They say death stalks in Mexico,
and that people there kill each other every day;
as long as there is one Mexican alive
our flag will be waving in his hand.

Francisco Villa was a fighting man
and his artillery was always prepared,
they would have burned the last cartridge
in defense of our nation.

Just what were the Americans thinking,
that combat was like dancing a *carquis*?
With their faces covered with shame
they returned to their country once again.

It doesn't matter that the "blondies" have
battleships and vessels by the score,
and airplanes and armored cars
if they don't have what it really takes.

Pedro Martínez

Oscar Lewis

Between 1943 and 1963, anthropologist Oscar Lewis conducted extensive tape-recorded interviews with the members of a peasant family from the village of "Azteca" (actually, Tepoztlán, Morelos). The resulting volume, Pedro Martínez, *is quite likely the most detailed autobiography ever produced by a Mexican peasant family. In the following excerpt, the family patriarch, Pedro Martínez, provides a rambling account of his revolutionary years as an active Zapatista combatant, while his wife Esperanza contributes an interesting counterpoint on the hardships suffered by the families the soldiers left behind.*

Pedro

In 1910, the action was in the north. It was still possible to work, then. So, once again, there I go to the *haciendas* looking for work. But the foremen didn't do anything to us any more. They were afraid, now, and besides we didn't take it any more.

Well, there we were one day and it was time for lunch. We were all hunting for wood to make a fire. We had only cold *tortillas* to eat while those who belonged there, the permanent hands of the *hacienda,* had coffee and two pieces of bread. They would swallow it down as fast as they could and get back to work. When the call came to get to work, they were ready, but we were still gathering wood to make the fire to heat the *tortillas.* The foreman shouted, "Come on, up on your feet."

"But we haven't had lunch yet."

"What's that to me? Come on, on your feet. Time is up."

But nothing doing. Everybody said we wouldn't go back to work until we had eaten. There were about sixty of us in a big circle. So the foreman said, "Oh, so you won't, eh?" And he rode his horse into the circle and trampled the *tortillas* we were warming. The horse was about to step on one of the men but he grabbed it by the bridle. The foreman raised his whip to hit him. Then we stood up, all of us. We dropped the *tortillas,* napkins and everything, and each of us picked up a stone. In a single voice we said, "We are going to kill this one. What can they do to us? We are many."

"Are you going to let go?" said the foreman. But the man didn't let go. The foreman started to reach for his pistol, but he saw us all with stones. And we said, "Go ahead, go ahead. Draw your pistol. What are you waiting for?" And we said to the one who had his horse by the bridle, "Don't let go, don't let go!"

The foreman didn't touch his pistol now. Then we let him know that we were on the point of quitting, that we had not sold ourselves to anyone. "We're going now. Get out of here before we cut you to pieces." He left.

Then the whole gang said, "Let's go and leave the tools so we all have a right to our pay." They still owed us for three days. Then everybody said that all they do was take the shirt off our backs. We said, "If they try to do anything to us, we'll make mincemeat out of them all. Don't give in!"

The manager came, wearing boots up to here. He saw us all at the ticket tent. "Fellows! Why aren't you working?"

"Because the foreman did this, that, and the other to us."

"No, look, boys, go on and yoke up and I'll pay you the full day. And as far as that damned foreman is concerned, I'll take care of him." He went to leave his horse and came back. He didn't even stop to take off his spurs but went right to the tent. The foreman was there, making out the tickets, when he lit into him. He treated him like a dog and fired him. . . .

There was justice then! Not like now . . . In those days, it was the *caciques* in our own village who oppressed us most. They had money and rode fine horses and were always the officials. They took advantage of poor girls. If they liked a girl, they got her—they always enjoyed fine women just because of the power they had. One of the head *caciques* died at eighty in the arms of a fifteen-year-old girl. Another, José Galindo, had yokes of oxen and hired many peasants. He gave the men *tortillas* and sent them to the fields, then he would go to their homes, just for a little while, to be with the wives. These rich men worked hand-in-hand with the Díaz government and if someone complained he would be punished. . . .

The Revolutionaries entered Azteca for the first time exactly on March 17, 1911. There weren't many of them, only about thirty, led by Lucio Moreno. They wore their sombreros on the back of their heads and held their muskets in their hands as they rode in.

I was on the road at the time, almost at the entrance to the village. With the help of my neighbors, I was carrying my wife to the *temazcal* for a steam bath because she had given birth to our first child. You see, it is the husband's obligation to bring the water, to heat the stones in the bathhouse, and then to slowly, carefully, carry her there on his back with a tumpline. So that's where I was when we heard them coming. Naturally, they took us by surprise.

Moreno and his men had come to kill a few people and I was already resigning myself. I said, "Well, they will kill me because of my wife but I will not leave her." I took her into a yard and crouched down behind the wall. "Now, how will I get out? If I run, the more likely they will kill me. Better let them find me here with my wife."

Well, I stayed there and some of them rode in and didn't say anything to me. They went on riding fast, with their muskets high, running, running, until they reached the first corner of the main street. They shouted, "Long live the Virgin of Guadalupe! Long live Francisco I. Madero!" and rushed to the *palacio* and began to burn it. . . .

Everything continued to burn there because they threw gasoline on it. At that time I didn't even know what gasoline was. After that, Lucio Moreno's men remounted and left for Elotepec. No fight took place. Nothing!

The next day when we went to the *hacienda* to work, the foremen asked us what happened. "Have they entered Azteca? Did they enter already?" they wanted to know.

"Yes, they were there."

"And how many of them were there?"

"Hmm, well, about three thousand or so." That's what we told them!

"*Caramba!* And what did they do?"

"Nothing. That is, not to us. It's the *caciques* they are after. They all ran away, all the *caciques*."

"And are they well armed?"

"*Uuy!* well armed, nothing but shotguns and plenty of ammunition!"

"*Újule!* Then we are really in trouble. Look, if anything happens come and warn us."

"Sure, sure, don't give it another thought. I'll come." Of course, I wasn't going to come! Why should I? . . .

Things got tighter as time went by. Everybody left, even the chickens! Everything was lost. I was left to the four winds. At the end of 1912, going into 1913, they didn't let us work on the *haciendas* any more. So I went back to doing what I did before, making rope. But the thick rope didn't sell then, only lariats. With that we supported ourselves. I also began to plant in the hills, and that was all. That was my whole life now, planting the *tlacolol* [subsistence crops on the steep, rocky hillsides]. My wife did the same. "How else?" she said. "You can't work on the *haciendas* now."

It reached the point where martial law was declared. There was no way of getting out now. At the end of 1913, and into 1914, you couldn't even step out of the village because if the government came and found you walking, they killed you.

And the troops dug everywhere, looking for buried coins, because in my village there was a lot of money buried. Think of it, even the very poor were saving then. If a *peso,* one of those great big old silver ones, fell into their hands, they wouldn't change it and spend it but would go and pawn it to a rich man, if they needed a little money. Later they would get the *peso* out of hock and bury it. So the soldiers, the *carrancistas,* did a lot of digging.

That was when my second child, Manuel, was born. He died when he was eight months old. I was hiding in the hills when the troops took all the women to Cuernavaca. They came to take out my wife, though she was still in bed. She hadn't yet got back her strength when they made her walk from Azteca to Cuernavaca.

I was young then and we men were angry because they took away our families. About two hundred of us got together and we were thinking of rebelling and attacking the train because they said our families were going to be taken to Mexico City. We had all decided to rebel against the government, but no, we hadn't eaten for two days and we went to look for food in the village. *Uuy!* What destruction we found there. Corn was scattered in the streets . . . the *carrancistas* had destroyed everything.

Somehow we found food. Then we heard the cry, "Here come the women! They freed them in Cuernavaca and now they are returning." Esperanza was with my mother-in-law, carrying the baby. There I go running to meet them. They were unharmed but because she had walked to and from Cuernavaca, my wife had a relapse and became ill.

Then some soldiers entered my uncle Crescenciano's house to take away his daughter Berta. He was blind and mean but he was very brave. He grabbed a stick and hit whomever he could. While he was clubbing them and they were kicking him, my cousin Berta ran away with the neighbors. She wasn't violated but they practically killed my uncle. He went to Cuautla after that and died there. Later, Berta went off with the colonel. What else could she do, now that she had no one? . . .

The first village to be burned was Santa María, in 1913. I was at home when it happened and I went to see it three days later. It was entirely destroyed. The *carrancistas* had burned everything. The dead were hanging from the trees. It was a massacre! Cows, oxen, pigs, and dogs had been killed and the people, poor things, went about picking up rotten meat to eat. All the corn and beans were burned. It was a terrible pity.

The people of Santa María began to come to Azteca and that's when the typhus epidemic started there. Two families came to my house and soon my entire barrio was sick. In every house there was fever and it spread through the village. My house looked like a hospital; all the sick people came to stay and then, *újule,* I got it and my wife, too. As my mother was dead, we went to my wife's mother so she could take care of us. My brother-in-law was there and he got angry because we brought the sickness. But what else could I do? I left my wife with her mother and went to my sister, who was living in the hills. She would give me a *taco,* for with my wife sick what was I going to eat? There, my other brother-in-law got angry because I carried the sickness to them. But I decided to be comfortable and I said, "Someone must support me until I recover!"

Well, both brothers-in-law and my mother-in-law got sick. She even died. Between the epidemic and the *carrancistas* we were nearly wiped out! Two weeks later, the soldiers came and burned my house. They wanted to kill me but they saw how I was and asked my wife what I had and she said, "The fever." Then they were afraid and left me alone. They took us out and set fire to the house. It was made of cane and they threw on some hay and lighted it and reduced it to nothing. That day they burned the village and threw out people everywhere. Even the municipal building was burned down.

Before we left my house my wife said, "let's put out the fire." And I said, "If I am going to die, let it burn up. Let's go." We left it burning and went to the hills, along with all the neighbors whose houses were burned. While we were running away, Carranza was bringing in more soldiers and telling them they could do whatever they pleased in the State of Morelos because it was Zapata's state. They could sack and kill, and all civil guarantees were suspended. He gave the order to destroy us and they killed and hanged everyone, even dogs, pigs, and cattle. That's why it makes me angry when they celebrate a fiesta for him now. When I see Carranza's picture it nauseates me. I cannot bear to see it because of the ugly way he mistreated us then.

We lived in the hills for about three months. I built a little shelter for my wife and me and the baby. It was the rainy season and we had a little corn, so we managed until we dared go down to the village again. By then we lived wherever we could. . . .

The Madero Revolution was almost over, and I still hadn't joined in the fighting. Madero was already President when Emiliano Zapata began to be heard of. It was in 1913 when his name was talked about, but we just criticized. Then you began to hear about Emiliano Zapata everywhere. It was Zapata this and Zapata that. But we said that he was only a peasant, not an intellectual man. . . .

I liked Zapata's plan and that's why, when he came to my village, I went to him. I still hadn't joined but I went up in the hills with *tortillas* and water.

Instead of going to my *tlacolol* I went to see Zapata in his camp. He was in a little house but they wouldn't let me go in. They were suspicious. There were two guards right in front of the door. I stood at a distance, watching. He was sitting inside with his general staff. And he calls out to me, "What do you have there, friend?"

"Nothing, *señor.* Just my *tortillas.*"

"Come in."

So there I go and now the others didn't stop me. He was a tall man, thin, and with a big mustache. . . . He had a thin high voice, like a lady's. He was a *charro* and mounted bulls and lassoed them, but when he spoke his voice was very delicate.

"Let's see your *tortillas.* Take them out."

And I gave them all to him. How he liked my *tortillas*! He and his staff finished them off.

"And what do you have in your gourd? *Pulque?*"

"No, *señor,* water." And he drank it.

What I wanted was to speak with Zapata, to sit with him. I had ideas although I still couldn't read. . . .

After that I joined Zapata and was with him through 1914, 1915 and 1916. Luckily, I wasn't a *maderista,* I was a *zapatista.* I took up arms to go south with him. I said to myself, "I can't stand this any more. It's better that I go." My wife stayed behind.

Now we knew what we were fighting for — Land, Water, Forests and Justice. That was all in the plan. It was for this reason that I became a Revolutionary. It was for a cause! Many joined just to get rich, to steal whatever they could. Their sons are rich now, because the fathers robbed. When a plaza was captured, they would sack the houses and give half the loot to their officers. But others were true revolutionaries and joined to help Zapata.

In my judgment, what Zapata was fighting for was just. Porfirio's government took everything away from us. Everything went to the rich, the *hacendados,* those with the power were the masters, and we had nothing. We were their servants because we could not plant or make use of any lands that did not belong to the *hacienda.* So they had us subjugated. We were completely enslaved by the *hacendados.* That is what Zapata fought to set right.

I joined the Revolutionary ranks because of the martial law in Morelos, declared by Carranza. If they found you sitting in your house, they would shoot you. If they found you walking, they would shoot you. If they found you working, they would shoot you. That was what they called martial law. There was *no* law! Naturally, when I saw this, I said to myself, "Rather than have them kill me sitting, standing or walking, I'd better get out of here." And so I went to war along with the *zapatistas*.

Esperanza

I was not afraid when the Revolution began because I didn't know what it was like. After I saw what it was, I was very much afraid. I saw how the federal troops would catch the men and kill them. They carried off animals, mules, chickens, clothes. The women who came with the soldiers were the ones who took away everything.

The government soldiers, and the rebel soldiers too, violated the young girls and the married women. They came every night and the women would give great shrieks when they were taken away. Afterward, at daybreak, the women would be back in their houses. They wouldn't tell what happened to them and I didn't ask because then people would say, "Why do you want to know? If you want to know, let them take you out tonight!"

For greater safety, we would sleep in the *corral*. Our house was very exposed because the street is one of the main entrances to the village and the soldiers would pass that way. Pedro took us to a relative's house further into the village. There the soldiers never entered. The *zapatistas* were well liked in the village, because although it is true they sometimes carried off young girls, they left the majority of women in peace. And after all, every one knew what kind of girls they took. The ones who like that sort of thing!

Sometimes the *zapatistas* would come down to the village and send someone from house to house to ask for *tortillas*. At other times, the government troops did the same thing. We always gave them whatever they asked for. After all, what else could we do? But the government men were the ones who behaved the worst and did us the most harm.

One time the government called all the women together in the village plaza. I was in bed. My baby had been born a month before. Sick as I was, they made me get up and go. When they had us all there, they told us to go and grind corn and make *tortillas* for the soldiers and then come to sleep with them that night. We ground the corn and delivered the *tortillas* and went off into the hills. Sleep with the soldiers! Not for anything would we have stayed for that!

My mother remained in the village with my brother because he had corn and beans to guard. Sometimes Pedro would leave me with my mother and he would go back to the hills and come down at night. One day my mother died. She died at three o'clock one afternoon and we buried her at six o'clock because they were saying, "The government is coming." We didn't make a coffin for her, poor thing. We just wrapped her in a *petate,* put a board on either side of her and buried her. Pedro was angry when he came home that night and learned that I had already buried her.

I didn't feel my mother's death, probably on account of it being a time of revolution. Since we were always on the run from the government, I didn't grieve so much over her. After my *mamá* was gone, Pedro took me with him to the hills.

There was no work here any more and Pedro had nothing to do. There was no way to earn money for food. But I didn't want him to go as a *zapatista.* I would say to him, "Even if we don't eat, Pedro." He would answer, "What are we going to live on? If one works, the government grabs and kills him." That's why when someone cried, "Here comes the government!" Pedro would take his *sarape* and make for the hills.

One day Pedro appeared, carrying his rifle. He told me, "Well, I've done it. I've joined up." He had become a *zapatista* because they offered to give him food. I got very angry but he said at least he would have something to eat and furthermore they would pay him. Then he told me he would have to go to Mexico City with the rebels and he promised to send me money.

He went with the *zapatistas* and left me without a *centavo.* There I was with nothing and I had two children to support, the girl of two years and the boy of two months. Also, I had in my care Pedro's cousin who was about eight years old. I cried in anguish because I didn't know what to do. . . .

Pedro

Ever since [the Revolution], I bear testimony that God saved me from all dangers. Because I was a believer, that's why. Having always been a very pious Catholic, whenever I went into action I would commend myself to God and nothing ever happened to me, not even a scratch. Not then or since. Yes, I came out of the war with a lot of experience. I have been in some very tight spots, at that time and later, too, in politics. All my former political opponents are gone, all gone. And so I am a living testimony that the one who entrusts himself to God will be protected from everything. . . .

We still kept fighting. I would leave my wife in a nearby village and would go to join the battle. We had many combats over here near Santa María, and still more over toward Yautepec. Marino Solís, the general from my village, was in charge at that time. It was my colonel, Leobardo Galván, who joined us up with General Marino. Sometimes we were ahead and sometimes the *carrancistas* were. There were heavy losses, men and horses too. Fleeing all the time! Yes, sir, to the south. After they drove us out of Santa María, we went to Tejalpa. After a few days in Tejalpa, we went on to Jiltepec. One week in Jiltepec and then to San Vicente, where we hung around for a month.

The people were tired. They didn't want to fight any more. I remember well when Zapata came to San Vicente. He had been driven out of Cuernavaca and he said to us, "If you don't want to fight any more we'll all go to the devil! What do you mean, you don't want to fight?"

Everyone was quiet. They didn't respond. "Bah!" he said. "Then there's nothing I can do." We were exhausted, sleepy, tired, and the *carrancistas* kept chasing us, almost to Jojutla, near the border of Guerrero. Marino went to the general headquarters in El Higuerón and got together five or ten thousand men. He said, "Who wants to go with me? Let's go and break up their base! Our situation is desperate. We are at the state boundary. Where else can we go? Now let us go back!" Then he opened fire and his men cleared a path all the way back to the *municipio* of Azteca and made camp in the hills of Tlaya-capan. There his brother Teodoro, who was in hiding, joined him. Marino was very brave. During the night they met the *carrancistas* and overthrew them all. He killed so many in Yautepec they piled up like stones. Later, he finished off practically all the *carrancistas* of the north because they ate mangoes and got sick and while they were stretched out Marino went in and just had to take aim and *zas, zas,* he finished them. That's why they named him General Mango. At that time, the peasants brought their mangoes to Yautepec. There was nothing to eat so people ate mangoes. A detachment of *carrancistas* was there, and when the peasants entered the city carrying their net sacks the sol-diers took away their fruit and ate it. In a few days, *zas,* the entire army was shivering with chills, they were all dying of malaria. All of them! And what doctor was there then? What medicine? The streets were full of corpses and the women who followed their men in the army searched among the bodies to find their dead. But I didn't see any of that because by that time I wasn't in the army any more.

Meanwhile, Zapata followed the lines to Yautepec and went as far as Tiza-pán. He had cannons and machine guns but he lost them all. That was the last big battle of the war, there in Tizapán, in 1916.

That's where I finally had it. The battle was something awful! The shoot-ing was tremendous! It was a completely bloody battle, three days and three nights. But I took it for only one day and then I left. I quit the army and left for Jojutla, without a *centavo* in my pocket. I said to myself, "It's time now I got back to my wife, to my little children. I'm getting out!"

That's why I left the army, for my wife. How I loved my wife! I didn't leave because I was afraid to fight but because of my wife, who had to find food for herself and the children. I said to myself, "No, my family comes first and they are starving. Now I'm leaving!" I saw that the situation was hopeless and that I would be killed and they would perish. . . .

I worked in Guerrero for three years, as a plowman. They grew tomatoes and *chile* peppers there. I also planted corn for myself on the hillside. Then one of my babies died of a scorpion sting. It was a boy, too, twenty-two months old. We were making rope and had gone to eat when the scorpion stung him. It happened at about ten in the morning and he died at seven that night. We went to Buena Vista to bury him the next day. It was about two hours walk to Buena Vista. After that I joined up with another work gang and stayed with them a year, cultivating *chile* peppers.

Of our three children, now we had only the little girl María left, and she was sick, too. María was our first child and our favorite while she was the only one. My wife loved her as much as I did, and because we were ignorant you might say we were responsible for her death. Like fools, we didn't know how to take care of children so we gave her all she wanted to eat. We gave her bread every little while, bread and meat. I gave her all my meat . . . meat was cheap then. It was always, "Come, this is for my daughter for I love her so much." With that we practically killed her because her stomach went bad. She became sick with *ético* [a wasting disease accompanied by chronic diarrhea]. She lasted a long time, until she was seven, but she never got better. And the Revolution made things worse. After that we had no way to cure her. There were no doctors and she died. They say she died because we loved her too much.

On the same day my little daughter died a battle broke out in Buena Vista between the turncoats and the fleeing *zapatistas*. . . . The shooting went on for days so when it was time to bury my little girl we couldn't go to the cemetery in Buena Vista. We had to go to Tlaxmalaca and that's where we buried her.

And so we had no one left then. But the following year, in 1917, my daughter Conchita was born. She was like a first child and we favored her a lot. She would throw things and we couldn't do anything with her. That's the way she was, very bad-tempered. When we left Guerrero she was about two years old. We had been there three full years. In all that time I had no other women, absolutely none. I couldn't because I didn't earn enough. But I didn't suffer the hunger people in my village were suffering. . . .

Esperanza

[After my children died] I remained all alone. . . . The death of the children affected Pedro, but it is not the same as with a woman. He cried a little but the grief soon passed. I believe men don't feel, or they feel very little. I feel deeply. Three months went by after their death and I was still crying and crying. I kept remembering how they were . . . the way they walked, the clothing they had . . . I even wanted to sleep in the cemetery and stay there all the time looking at the piece of earth that covered them. And he, when he saw that I was crying, would scold me and that made me angrier and more resentful. . . .

I was like a new person after I started to have children again. I was no longer sad and lonely. . . . It made me so happy when Conchita was born. We loved her very much and it was as if she had been our first born. We spoiled her a lot as it was five years before the following child was born. We spoiled her, but we also beat her when she cried. . . .

We came back from Guerrero because Pedro did not want to stay there any longer. He said, "We have our own house in Azteca and that is where we belong."

I was sick, too. I think it was from "cold" as they did not bathe me in the *temazcal* [traditional steambath] after I had Conchita and I didn't always have "hot" food to eat. Pedro would go out to sell the tomatoes he had planted. He would leave me sick and alone. . . .

My trouble was that my abdomen hurt me very much. I was skin and bones and had fevers every day. Pedro had a lot of people look at me, but nobody cured me. He said to me, "As soon as I have the harvest in, we will go to Azteca. They will cure you there." That is the reason we went.

When we got to Azteca, he had a woman look at me. "It's because you are pregnant," she said. "That's why your belly is big." I was here for about five months and nothing changed. So then Pedro said, "The thing is that you are not pregnant at all." And he took me to another curer. This one said that I had "cold" in the belly. . . . I was sick and that was the reason I wasn't having children. . . . She gave me a medicine to take and smeared greases all over my body, oil of camomile, oil of rosemary, and others. . . . Then, when I was better, my aunt Gloria said to me, "Silly girl, now that you are cured, you are going to have another baby." . . .

I wanted to be cured as I never felt right. But I didn't want any more children. I have always had a horror of having children. The thought of being pregnant would frighten me and sometimes it would make me angry because I was the one who was going to suffer. I cried and cried every time I felt that I was pregnant. . . .

At night, when my husband took me I became angry because of the danger he put me in. But when I didn't want Pedro to come near me he scolded, saying, "You don't want me because you have some other man." So I had to let him and then I would be pregnant again.

I know that what happens is God's will, so I say, if children come, good, if not, so much the better!

I was glad to be back in Azteca. The village was the same but a lot of people were missing because they had died of hunger. . . . Almost none of my people were still living. My brother was alive but he was far away in Puebla. His wife had died and so had his children. . . . When he came back later, it was just to die . . . he was very sick by then.

The Revolution was almost over when we came back from Guerrero and Pedro began to work in the fields [and] planted the *tlacolol*. . . . Five and a half years after Conchita's birth, Rufina was born. It didn't matter to us whether the child was a boy or a girl. Pedro said that it was all the same to him. "Whatever the ladle brings." All children mean money, because when they begin to work, they earn.

Juan the Chamula

Ricardo Pozas

Few accounts of the revolution better illustrate its intensely factionalized nature and the shallowness of the allegiances of common footsoldiers than the following "ethnological re-creation" of the life of a Chamula Indian by Ricardo Pozas, one of Mexico's most distinguished anthropologists. Pozas based his account on fieldwork conducted in the 1940s and 1950s among the Chamulas of Chiapas, a group of about sixteen thousand people who spoke the Tzotzil Maya language and who lived in rural settlements in the highlands around the regional center of San Cristóbal de las Casas. Even today, many Chamulas live principally from subsistence farming, supplemented by contract labor on lowland coffee plantations. They practice a culture that still owes much to pre-Columbian traditions.

The principal character in this account, Juan Pérez Jolote, first leaves home in order to escape the wrath of his abusive father. He is clearly puzzled by the world outside of his village and has little understanding of the meaning of revolution or the aims of the various factions he fights for. In short order, however, the revolution revamps his identity and redirects his fortunes.

They were looking for people to work on a farm called La Flor. I contracted to go, and when I got to La Flor the patrón told me: "I'm going to give you your meals and you'll sleep here next to the henhouse, so you can scare away the animals that try to steal the chickens at night." I slept there, and woke up when I heard a noise. Then I shouted so that the animals would run away. I worked at La Flor for about three months, and got to know three men from Comitán who had women with them to cook their meals. One of them asked me, "Are you going to keep on working here, José?"[1] "Yes," I said. "Then don't eat over there in the kitchen. You can eat better here with my woman," he said. . . .

The men from Comitán used to get drunk every payday. When they were drunk they exchanged their women among themselves, but the next day they were jealous.

Chamula Indian, Chiapas. (Reprinted by permission of Fototeca del INAH, Mexico.)

"You, you cabrón!"² one of them said. "You're screwing my wife."

"And you're screwing mine."

Then the third one came over. "You're screwing my woman, too."

And the fight began:

"Why don't we ask José Pérez if it isn't true?"

"He doesn't drink, and anyway I saw you, cabrón . . ."

They asked me if it was true.

"I don't know. . . . I don't sleep here, so I don't see what happens at night . . ."

"You mean you don't want to tell us."

That was right. I didn't want to tell them because I knew what would happen, but I'd seen the whole thing and the woman who cooked for me told me about it in the morning.

They fought with their machetes. The women and I were frightened and we just watched them. One of them was killed, and the other two and the three women ran away.

I didn't know what to do. "If I run away," I thought, "they'll say I killed him." So I stayed there, watching the blood run out of his wounds.

As soon as they knew that a man from Comitán had been killed, they went to tell the authorities in Mapa. The police came out to the farm to find out what happened, and they saw me there near the corpse.

"Who killed him?"

"I don't know."

"What do you mean, you don't know! You were right here with the rest of them. If you don't tell us we'll have to take you in."

"I don't know," I said. And without another word they fastened my hands with a rope and tied me to a post. . . .

They took the dead man away, and they took me to Mapa as a prisoner and I slept there in the jail.

Early the next morning we went on to Tapachula and they put me in the jail there. I was a prisoner for eleven months and two weeks. I wove palm leaves and they paid me one centavo for each armful. A man from San Cristóbal named Procopio de la Rosa advised me not to sell the woven palm but to make sombreros out of it. "If you weave five armfuls, that's only five centavos. But if you'll make the brims of the sombreros I'll pay you three centavos apiece." I could finish two brims a day, and I earned six centavos. . . .

Later on, Don Procopio told me, "I'm going to give you your palm from now on, so you can work on account." He was the one who sold the palm to everybody. He delivered the finished sombreros by the dozen to be sold outside. Then he taught me how to make sombreros that sold for a peso and a half. . . . I didn't suffer in jail because I learned how to make all these things. . . .

When they first put me in jail I could understand Spanish well enough but I couldn't pronounce the words. I learned how to make things by watching because there wasn't anybody who knew how to speak my language, and little by little I began to speak Spanish.

While I was in jail we learned that the Government [Huerta's] was in danger of losing because they killed the President [Madero]. It was looking for people for the army so it could defend itself. Two of the prisoners wrote letters to the Government, and it told them that if they wanted to be soldiers they should put in a request. The rest of us didn't say anything, because we didn't know if we wanted to be soldiers or not, but the government didn't accept just the two who wrote letters, it accepted everybody in the jail. Even the invalids got out along with the others.

The soldiers came for us at four in the morning, and the man in charge said, "All prisoners get their belongings together. You're all going to be free." But they took us to the station and put us into a boxcar, the kind that's used for cattle and bananas. The soldiers guarded us on all sides, and two of them stood at the door of the car, poking us with their pistols and saying, "Come on, get in."

I brought five new sombreros along with me to sell on the way. We arrived at San Jerónimo and they took us off the train and put us in a barracks. They took my sombreros away from me to start a fire so they could make coffee. They gave a close haircut to everyone who had long hair. They took our extra clothing away if we had any, and gave us coats with long sleeves.

The next day we went on toward Mexico City. I could hear them naming the different places we passed: Orizaba, Puebla . . . We arrived at San Antonio, where there was firewood. They took us out of the cars to rest, and built a fire so we could warm ourselves. It was the season when the corn is ripe. After we ate, they put us back in the cars and we went on until we reached the Mexico City station. They took us to the army post called La Canoa, and the next day they signed us up. . . .

They took us to a different barracks and made us take off all our clothes. Then they examined us. Those who had ringworm . . . weren't any use as soldiers because the Government didn't want them. It also didn't want anyone with boils or tumors. The only ones they kept were the ones with clean skins, and since I've always had a clean skin, without any sores, they didn't let me go free.

They began to pay wages to those of us who were left: twenty-five centavos a day and our meals. After a few days they gave each of us a pair of huaraches, and then a pair of shoes. Later they gave us kepis, and Mausers with wooden bullets, and now that we were in uniform they paid us fifty centavos a day and our meals.

The training started at four in the morning. The corporals, sergeants, lieutenants, and captains made us form ranks and learn how to march. At six o'clock we all drank coffee. There were a hundred and twenty-five of us, and we were from many different villages because there's a jail in every village. They called us the 89th Battalion.

A few days later they taught us how to handle our guns and how to shoot. We formed ranks, some of us in front and the rest behind, and when they shouted the command we had to throw ourselves flat on the ground. At other times they ordered some of us to kneel and the others to remain standing. They lined up some of our own men in front of us, and said, "This is the enemy. We're going to practice what you'll have to do in battle. Ready! Aim! Fire!" We pulled the triggers, there was a loud noise, and the little pieces of soft wood popped out of the Mausers. We were just training, so the bullets weren't real. . . .

Finally they gave us real bullets, fifty to each man, and we began to earn a peso a day. After they gave us the real bullets we didn't fire any more, we just practiced the way they taught us before.

A little later we went out to fight Carranza. Before we left, a priest came to the post and they told us to form ranks. He stood up on a chair, we all knelt down, and he said, "Well, men, I'm here to tell you that we're going into battle tomorrow or the day after, because the enemy is getting close. When you're out there fighting, I don't want you to mention the devil or the demons. I just want you to repeat day and night the words I'm going to tell you: *Long live the Virgin of Guadalupe!* Because she's the patron saint of every Mexican, the Queen of Mexico, and she'll protect us against our enemies when we go into battle."

We left the next day. They loaded us into boxcars with our weapons, and told us we were going to Aguascalientes. We could hear artillery along the way, and when we looked out through the cracks we could see people running across the mountains. My comrades said, "It's going to be wonderful!" Some of them had guitars with them, and they played and sang because they were so happy.

We stopped in Aguascalientes, and then went on to Zacatecas. Then we just stayed there, because the train couldn't go any farther. They took us out of the cars and put us in a big house that was like a fort. We stayed there for several days. They got us up at four o'clock every morning and gave us a drink of aguardiente with gunpowder in it, to make us brave, and then gave us our breakfast. Those that had women with them were contented, they laughed and sang and played their guitars. "We're doing all right," they said, "and tomorrow we're going to the fiesta."

The time came to go out to fight. There was a mountain near Zacatecas with a little hill in front of it, and the artillery faced the mountain. The artillerymen dug a cave near their guns and cooked their meals in it.

At nine in the morning we crossed a wide field to climb up the mountain, and while we were crossing it we heard the General shout, "Spread out!" The bugle blew and we scattered across the field. The enemy was up there on the top of the mountain, because the bullets came down at us from above. We started to shoot too, but since we couldn't see where they were, and they could get a good aim at us, a lot of our men were killed. The artillery was firing at the mountain, and some other soldiers ran forward and climbed up the mountain from the side, and the enemy retreated a little.

That night we had to bring in the wounded, without even having drunk any water all day. One of them said to me, "Take me back to the artillery positions. I can't walk. And bring my Mauser." I got him to the artillery. My throat began to hurt, and when I tried to drink some water it wouldn't go down. I couldn't eat anything, either, and I was deaf from the noise of the cannons.

They sent me to the post at Zacatecas, and then to Aguascalientes. I was in the hospital there for two days, and on the third day I was sent to the hospital in Mexico City, where I almost died from my earaches. First blood came out, then pus. I was in the hospital for several months, because they wouldn't let me leave until I was well again.

The people who were taking care of us began to say, "Who knows what'll happen to us, because they're going to come here to eat people, and we don't know what kind of people they like to eat."

The sick and wounded began to cry because they couldn't leave the hospital and run away, and those others were going to eat them. We heard it was the Carrancistas that were eating people.

A little later Carranza entered Mexico City. We could hear his troops go by in the street, shooting off their guns and shouting: "Long live Venustiano Carranza! Down with Victoriano Huerta! Death to Francisco Villa! Death to Emiliano Zapata!" They only cheered for Carranza. And we just looked at each other, there in the hospital, without being able to leave.

The next day the Carrancistas came to the hospital to visit the sick and wounded. They arrived with their officers, and after greeting us they asked, "How are you? What happened to you? Are you getting better? We're all friends now, that's why we've come to see you."

The men that had been crying spoke first: "They told us the Carrancistas eat people."

"What? . . . No, we're not cannibals."

"Then it isn't true that you're going to eat us?"

"Of course not!"

So the sick and wounded were happy. "Here's two pesos," the Carrancistas said, "and stop being afraid." They gave two pesos to each one of us.

I stayed in the hospital until I was cured. As soon as they let me go I went to Puebla and worked as a mason's helper, carrying lime and bricks. I also worked for some butchers, bringing the goats and sheep in from the haciendas to be slaughtered. They gave me my meals and a place to sleep, but they didn't pay me anything.

After two or three weeks I left Puebla and walked to Tehuacán de las Granadas. A butcher let me live in his house there. I'd already worked for butchers in Puebla, so I knew they were good people. I worked for him for five months.

The butcher's father used to go to the butcher shop at two in the morning to cut up the meat, and he always took me with him because he was deaf. When we went past the army post he couldn't hear the guard shout, "Who goes there!" and he was afraid they'd shoot him if he didn't answer. I had to answer, "Carranza!" and they'd let us go past without stopping us. . . .

All they gave me was my clothing and my meals. I wanted to earn some money, so I went to the army post to talk with the captain. I said: "Captain, sir, I'd like to be a soldier."

"Good, good! What's your name?"

"José Pérez."

They gave me a shirt, a pair of trousers, and a kepis, and paid me a peso and half.

When the old [deaf] butcher found out I was a soldier, he came looking for me the next day. "Don't take him away from me," he begged the captain, "because I need him to help me. I've been good to him, too . . . I don't even criticize him. Ask him yourself."

"Is that true?" the captain asked me.

"Yes," I said. "I only left because I wanted to earn some money, but he's good to me and gives me food and clothing."

"Well, if he feeds and clothes you and doesn't hit you or anything, you ought to go back with him. What more do you want? Good food, good clothes . . . he's practically your father. You've got a home now. We don't know when we'll be called out to fight. Maybe we'll all be killed. I feel sorry for the old man because he was crying when he came in here. Go back with him, hombre." The captain gave me five pesos, and I went back with the deaf man.

But I only stayed in his house another week, because one day I met a woman who lived with one of my friends while we were fighting for Victoriano Huerta. She saw me in the street and said, "José, it's you! What are you doing here?"

"I'm just living here. Where's Daví?"

"He was killed in the battle. I'm going back home. I'll take you with me if you want. I've got enough money to pay your fare."

I went with her to Oaxaca. She told me she was going to stop there and not go any farther, but she told me I could get home from there without any trouble. We arrived at Oaxaca in the train and she took me to her house to spend the night.

I left the next morning, to go home. I started asking the way to San Cristóbal de las Casas, but nobody could tell me. I must have asked a hundred people at least, but they all told me they didn't know. Finally I got tired of walking around the city, so I went to the army post to sign up. They asked me my name and wrote it down, and I was a Carrancista again.

After I'd been in Oaxaca for about a week they sent all the soldiers in the post to Mexico City, and I had to go with them. First they sent us out to Córdoba, and then to a little village where the Zapatistas had come in to rob the houses. We stayed there for six months, guarding the village, and that's where I first had a woman.

They assigned me to a lieutenant, and when I was off duty I went to the plaza to drink *pulque.* It was sold by an old woman with white hair, and one day she asked me, "Do you have a woman?"

"No, señora, I don't."

"Then why don't you find one? This village is full of pretty girls."

"I know . . . but I don't know what to say to them."

"But you do want a woman?"

"Yes."

"And you've never had one?"

"No, señora, not yet."

"Let's go to my house."

"Good, let's go."

She gathered her things and took me to her house. She gave me something to eat, and after we finished eating she led me to her bed.

I went back to the barracks when we were all done. "Now that you know where my house is, you can come here whenever you want." . . .

She used to come to the post when she wanted me to go home with her. She'd ask the maid who worked in the kitchen, "Is José in?"

"I don't know. Go in and look for him."

She'd go in, and as soon as I noticed her I'd raise my hand to stop her, so she wouldn't speak to me in front of my friends. I was ashamed to have them see how old she was. I'd get up and go over to speak with her, and she'd say, "I'll be waiting for you tonight." And at night I'd go there.

At the end of six months they sent us to another village. The old woman who sold pulque stayed at home.

We went back to Córdoba and stayed there for a month, and then we went to Pachuca and stayed for two months. Next they sent us to Real del Monte, but we were only there for twenty days because the weather was too cold for us. We returned to Pachuca again and went out to another village, where the Villistas attacked us.

They entered the village at daybreak. We were all asleep, even the sentry, when the sound of gunfire woke us up. We all ran out and they started shooting at us. We had sixty-five men. Some of them were killed, some ran away, and twenty-five of us were taken prisoners by General Villa. They asked us why we'd become Carrancistas, and I said: "The Huertistas made us go with them, and when Carranza started winning we had to change sides."

"Where are you from?"

"I'm a Chamula."

The man who was questioning me, a lieutenant, turned to General Almazán and said, "These poor men were forced into service." .

An old man with a big moustache said: "Well, what do they want to do now?"

I said, "I just want to be on your side."

"What about the rest of you?" they asked.

"Just what our friend said, to be on your side."

"All right. But look, if you try any tricks we'll shoot you."

"No, señor, we're telling you the truth."

"We'll see about that. We're going to send you straight into battle, to find out if you're really men."

They signed us up and gave us weapons and five pesos each, and that made us Villistas. . . .

The officers paid us all the money they had with them so we could buy what we needed, and when it ran out they began paying us with stamped slips of paper. These slips were only good in the village itself, and nobody else would accept them because they weren't worth anything. The leaders kept saying, "The money will get here in a day or two," but finally there wasn't anything left to eat in the village, and we couldn't buy anything outside because they wouldn't take the stamped slips.

General Almazán got us all together, privates and lieutenants and captains, and told us: "The Carrancistas have captured all the villages and haciendas. I'm leaving, because there aren't any more villages we can stay in. You can leave too, or stay here. Or if you want to join up with the Carranza forces in Tehuacán, you can do that."

We decided to go to Tehuacán, and left the village at night. We traveled across the mountains all night long, and when it was daylight we got some sleep and let the animals graze. The next night we started out again. We came to an hacienda near Tehuacán, and the leaders sent a note to the Carrancistas who were in the village. The note said that we wanted to join them, that we were a hundred and fifty Villistas who wanted to go over to Carranza. General Almazán had accompanied us as far as the hacienda, but when the messenger came back from Tehuacán with the answer, the General said to us: "Go ahead and give yourselves up, but I'm not going with you. If I did, they'd probably wring my neck." He left us that night, and in the morning we went on toward the village.

The Carrancistas came out to meet us, and we ran into them about a league outside of Tehuacán. They all had their Mausers in their hands, aiming them at us, and we carried our own Mausers butt first to show we were surrendering. They marched us ahead of them to the barracks and took our rifles away from us at the gate, although they let us keep the rest of our things. Inside, they asked us where we'd been, and we told them about the different places we stayed at.

The next day they got us together and said; "Now that you've surrendered, what do you want to do? Do you want to be Carrancistas? If you don't, we'll let you go free, so you can go home and farm your lands."

I said, "I want to leave, I want to work in the fields."

"Where do you want to go?"

"To Veracruz," I said. Now that I could go free, I wanted to visit that town, and be a free man, not a soldier.

"You can go there, you can take the train. It won't cost you anything."

They gave me my ticket and twenty-five pesos, and above all they gave me my freedom. . . .

I worked [in Veracruz] for nine months. . . . When I got tired of working there I went to a different farm called San Cristóbal, where I worked for three months in the cornfields. I didn't like it there either, so I came back home. . . .

I went into the house and greeted my father, but he didn't recognize me. I'd almost forgotten how to speak *Tzotzil*, and he couldn't understand what I was saying. He asked me who I was and where I came from.

"You still don't know me? I'm Juan!"

"What? . . . You're still alive! But if you're Juan, where have you been? . . . I went to the farm twice to look for you."

"I left the farm and went to Mexico City to be a soldier." I was kneeling down as I said this.

"Did you really become a soldier?"

"Yes, papacito."

"Well, I'll be damned! But how come you didn't get killed?"

"Because God took care of me."

Then he called to my mother: "Come here and see your son Juan! The cabrón has come back to life!" . . .

And I stayed here, I lived in my own village again. The first night I woke up when my father started blowing on the embers of the cooking fire. I was afraid he'd come over and wake me up by kicking me. But he didn't, because I was a man now!

Notes

1. By this point in the story, Juan has taken to calling himself "José" in the hope of evading his father. *Ed.*
2. *Cabrón:* literally, a he-goat. A common insult in Mexico. *Ed.*

The Constitution of 1917: Articles 27 and 123

The ascendant Carranza faction, after defeating Pancho Villa in mid-1915, felt con-
fident enough in its hold on power to undertake the writing of a new constitution
for Mexico. The Constitutional Convention, which met in the city of Querétaro in
late 1916, was dominated by relatively radical representatives who were determined
to push social reform much further than their leader wished. The final document,
which remains in force today, was most notable for championing a fresh concept of
property. As in colonial times, the state was the ultimate owner of all of Mexico's
land, water, and minerals. Private property — sacred and inviolable in liberal concep-
tions — was made conditional, something that the state could concede to individuals
only so long as their activities did not violate the general well-being of Mexico's citi-
zens. The state was expressly permitted to intervene in private property in the name
of "public utility." This notion, most clearly expressed in Article 27, paved the way
for one of the most sweeping agrarian reforms in the history of Latin America (one
that remained on the books until the early 1990s), as well as for the expropriation of
foreign-owned oil properties in 1938. Article 27 also attacked the right of the Catho-
lic Church to own real property, becoming a factor in the religious civil war of the
late 1920s. Article 123, meanwhile, was one of the most progressive labor codes in the
world at the time of its promulgation. Of course, many provisions of the 1917 Consti-
tution were honored only in the breach, but the document's impact on the course of
twentieth-century Mexican history is beyond dispute.

ART. 27. Ownership of the lands and waters within the boundaries of the national territory is vested originally in the Nation, which has had, and has, the
right to transmit title thereof to private persons, thereby constituting private
property.

Private property shall not be expropriated except for reasons of public use
and subject to payment of indemnity.

The Nation shall at all times have the right to impose on private property
such limitations as the public interest may demand, as well as the right to regulate the utilization of natural resources, which are susceptible of appropria-

tion, in order to conserve them and to ensure a more equitable distribution of public wealth. With this end in view necessary measures shall be taken to divide large landed estates, to develop small landed holdings in operation, to create new agricultural centers with necessary lands and waters, to encourage agriculture in general and to prevent the destruction of natural resources, and to protect property from damage to the detriment of society. Centers of population that at present either have no lands or water or that do not possess them in sufficient quantities for the needs of their inhabitants shall be entitled to grants thereof, which shall be taken from adjacent properties, the rights of small landed holdings in operation being respected at all times.

In the Nation is vested direct ownership of all minerals or substances which in veins, layers, masses, or beds constitute deposits whose nature is different from the components of the land, such as minerals from which metals and metaloids used for industrial purposes are extracted; beds of precious stones, rock salt and salt lakes formed directly by marine waters; products derived from the decomposition of rocks, when their exploitation requires underground work; mineral or organic deposits of materials which may be used for fertilizers; solid mineral fuels; petroleum and all hydrocarbons—solid, liquid or gaseous.

In the Nation is likewise vested the ownership of the waters of territorial seas to the extent and in the terms fixed by the Law of Nations; those of lakes and inlets of bays; those of interior lakes of natural formation which are directly connected with flowing waters; those of the principal rivers or tributaries from the points at which there is a permanent current of water in their beds to their mouths, whether they flow to the sea or cross two or more States; those of intermittent streams which traverse two or more States in their main body; the waters of rivers, streams or ravines, when they bound the national territory or that of the States; waters extracted from mines; and the beds and banks of the lakes and streams hereinbefore mentioned, to the extent fixed by law. Any other stream of water not comprised within the foregoing enumeration shall be considered as an integral part of the private property through which it flows; but the development of the waters when they pass from one landed property to another shall be considered of public utility and shall be subject to the provisions prescribed by the States.

In the cases to which the two foregoing paragraphs refer, the ownership of the Nation is inalienable and may not be lost by prescription; concessions shall be granted by the Federal Government to private parties or civil or commercial corporations organized under the laws of Mexico, only on condition that the said resources be regularly developed, and on the further condition that the legal provisions be observed.

Legal capacity to acquire ownership of lands and waters of the Nation shall be governed by the following provisions:

1) Only Mexicans by birth or naturalization and Mexican companies have the right to acquire ownership of lands, waters, and their appurtenances, or to obtain concessions for the exploitation of mines or of waters. The State may grant the same right to foreigners, provided they agree before the Ministry of Foreign Relations to consider themselves as nationals in respect to such property, and bind themselves not to invoke the protection of their governments in matters relating thereto; under penalty, in case of noncompliance with this agreement, of forfeiture of the property acquired to the Nation. . . .

2) Religious institutions known as churches, regardless of creed, may in no case acquire, hold, or administer real property or hold mortgages thereon; such property held at present either directly or through an intermediary shall revert to the Nation, any person whosoever being authorized to denounce any property so held. . . . Places of worship are the property of the Nation, as represented by the Federal Government, which shall determine which of them may continue to be devoted to their present purposes. . . .

3) Public or private charitable institutions for the rendering of assistance to the needy, for scientific research, the diffusion of knowledge, mutual aid to members, or for any other lawful purpose many not acquire more real property than actually needed for their purposes and immediately and directly devoted thereto . . .

7) The centers of population that by law or in fact possess a communal status shall have legal capacity to enjoy common possession of the lands, forests, and waters belonging to them or that have been or may be restored to them. . . .

10) Centers of population that lack communal lands (*ejidos*) or that are unable to have them restored to them due to lack of titles, impossibility of identification, or because they had been legally transferred shall be granted sufficient lands and waters to constitute them, in accordance with the needs of the population; but in no case shall they fail to be granted the area needed, and for this purpose the land needed shall be expropriated, at the expense of the Federal Government, to be taken from lands adjoining the villages in question . . .

17) The Federal Congress and the State Legislature, within their respective jurisdictions, shall enact laws to fix the maximum area of rural property and to carry out the subdivision of the excess lands. . . .

18) All contracts and concessions made by former Governments since the year 1876, and that have resulted in the monopolization of lands, waters, and natural resources of the Nation by a single person or company, are declared

subject to revision, and the Executive of the Union is empowered to declare them void whenever they involve serious prejudice to the public interest.

ART. 123. The Congress of the Union, without contravening the following basic principles, shall formulate labor laws that shall apply to:

A. Workers, day laborers, domestic servants, artisans (*obreros, jornaleros, empleados domésticos, artesanos*), and in a general way to all labor contracts:

1) The maximum duration of work for one day shall be eight hours.

2) The maximum duration of night work shall be seven hours. The following are prohibited: unhealthful or dangerous work by women and by minors under sixteen years of age, industrial nightwork by either of these classes, work by women in commercial establishments after ten o'clock at night, and work (of any kind) by persons under sixteen after ten o'clock at night.

3) The use of labor of minors under fourteen years of age is prohibited. Persons above that age and less than sixteen shall have a maximum work day of six hours.

4) For every six days of work a worker must have at least one day of rest.

5) During the three months prior to childbirth, women shall not perform physical labor that requires excessive material effort. In the month following childbirth they shall necessarily enjoy the benefit of rest and shall receive their full wages and retain their employment and the rights acquired under their labor contract. During the nursing period they shall have two special rest periods each day, of a half hour each, for nursing their infants.

6) The minimum wage to be received by a worker shall be general or according to occupation. . . .

7) Equal wages shall be paid for equal work, regardless of sex or nationality.

8) The minimum wage shall be exempt from attachment, compensation, or deduction.

9) Workers shall be entitled to a participation in the profits of enterprises. . . .

11) Whenever, due to extraordinary circumstances, the regular working hours of a day must be increased, one hundred percent shall be added to the amount for normal hours of work as remuneration for the overtime. Overtime work may never exceed three hours a day or three times consecutively. Persons under sixteen years of age and women of any age may not be admitted to this kind of labor.

16) Both employers and workers shall have the right to organize for the defense of their respective interests, by forming unions, professional associations, etc. . . .

29) Enactment of a social security law shall be considered of public inter-

est and it shall include insurance against disability, on life, against involuntary work stoppage, against sickness and accidents, and other forms for similar purposes;

30) Likewise, cooperative societies established for the construction of low-cost and hygienic houses to be purchased on installments by workers shall be considered of social utility. . . .

An Agrarian Encounter

Rosalie Evans

In 1920, when President Venustiano Carranza tried to impose his successor in the presidency, he was overthrown by a military rebellion led by three strong personalities from the northern state of Sonora: Alvaro Obregón, who was president from 1920 to 1924, Plutarco Elías Calles, who held the office from 1924–1928, and Adolfo de la Huerta, who served as interim president in 1920. The "Sonoran Dynasty" is generally viewed as the end of the violent phase of the revolution, and the start of "reconstruction." The new national leaders made the first serious efforts to carry out some of the "promises of the revolution," one of the most notable of which was agrarian reform.

Early efforts in this area witnessed the rise of a uniquely compelling figure in Mexico's history, the agrarian cacique. In many parts of the republic, these local politicos pegged their fortunes to the agrarian issue, often using strong-arm methods to compel the federal government to seize and distribute hacienda lands. One such cacique — Manuel P. Montes, of the San Martín Texmelucan Valley of western Puebla state — met his match in Rosalie Evans, the owner of the two-thousand-acre hacienda San Pedro Coxtocán. The American-born widow waged a highly publicized, six-year fight against Mexico's agrarian reform before being ambushed and killed in August of 1924. In the following excerpt from a letter to her sister, Mrs. Evans recalls her first encounter with Montes. While Rosalie Evans was more obstreperous and uncompromising than most foreign property owners confronting revolutionary threats, her disdain for the "rabble" is typical enough.

San Pedro.

May 15, 1921.

About four I forced myself to dress and go in my little buggy to San Martin to see Don P——. At the moment of getting in the buggy I was stopped by the arch-devil of the valley, whom the Indians have elected as their "member of Congress," Manuel Montes being his name, so you will rejoice with me if he meets his death before I do mine.[1] He was dressed in a black frock coat, and a bull fighter hat; is short and square, with the cruelest little black eyes,

Agraristas in Puebla waiting to take possession of their land grant. (Reprinted by permission of Fototeca del INAH, Mexico.)

like a snake ready to strike. So dressed to impress, I suppose. With him an-other deputy with a stooping frame and a long beard, also to cause respect. Back of them the usual rabble, but only one man caught my eyes; he had a wooden leg.

He with the beard began a pompous address and handed me an order from Obregón and [Minister of Agriculture Antonio I. Villarreal] . . . which, to my utter astonishment, was entirely in my favor. I said, with real surprise: "This paper tells you to respect me and my property."

"Yes," replied he with the long beard, "but I bring an oral message from the Minister Villarreal to deliver over all your crop, at once, to these gentlemen (the rabble rout) and he will indemnify you afterward."

I said: "Do you think that on an oral order I would give you my crop?" — and the riot began.

Manuel Montes got leave from "Congress" to come down and speak to the people, so you can appreciate my danger and that of my men. It was he who had arranged the simultaneous killing of administrators that I told you of and who at eleven the same morning had made the people attack San Juan

Tetla—perhaps you will remember it, a place we once wanted to buy, now owned by [William O.] Jenkins and Arrismondi, brother of the administrator killed two years ago. Montes said that he would lead his people on San Pedro himself, and make the señora listen to reason. He leads all the strikes and, if you once let him speak, rouses the people to madness.

I determined that he should not speak on my place. He tried to harangue them and "all my rage arose," I am told, for really I did not realize it. I outspoke him, calling him a coward, assassin and my whole wicked vocabulary of insults. He trembled with rage, but I got my hand on my pistol and *he* ran—I standing up in the buggy, [hacienda administrator] Iago by the mule (which they tried to unharness). Montes was followed by the bearded hypocrite. They mounted their little ponies as fast as they could, calling to their people to take the crop by force. Iago had his pistol ready and whistled for the soldiers who were sleeping somewhere inside. There was much shouting and confusion, the man with the wooden leg making an awful stumping sound in front of the mule, when the boy captain of my soldiers ran into the midst of them crying out: "Insult me, not the señora. I will not fire yet, you are too *few* for *me*." (There were about twenty.) I saw we had won the day. They were not armed so I forbade firing, and "Satan fled murmuring" that he would be back in the morning.

I left the captain on guard. He really is a perfect little devil, about twenty-three, but does my bidding. He asked that I should bring him permission from San Martin to fire if necessary, so far he has only police authority. We then drove to San Martin. As usual, no support! We did not ask for more men, we had seven and with the three of us armed we were quite enough.

Note

1. Montes would meet a violent death in 1927. *Ed.*

Ode to Cuauhtémoc

Carlos Pellicer

Poet Carlos Pellicer (1899–1977) was born in the southeastern state of Tabasco, where he learned to admire the tropics and the indigenous societies that had long inhabited them. He moved to Mexico City in 1914 and published his first poems in 1921. He was clearly influenced by "modernist" writers such as the Nicaraguan poet Rubén Darío and the Cuban poet José Martí, who wrote exuberantly about the glories of "Our America" (as Martí habitually referred to Latin America). Pellicer was very much in tune with the strain of "indigenismo" that surfaced during the Mexican revolution — that is, he celebrated Mexico's native cultures as the true soul of the nation and its greatest glory. His work includes unabashedly romantic elegies to his heroes, principally Simón Bolívar, the leader of South America's independence movement and a staunch Latin America nationalist, and Cuauhtémoc, the young Aztec emperor who tenaciously resisted European conquest and was eventually tortured and killed by his Spanish captors. The following poem, published in 1923, was the first of several poems Pellicer wrote in honor of Cuauhtémoc. It is a good example, not only of the exuberant indigenismo *that progressive intellectuals sought to promote in alliance with the postrevolutionary state, but also of the tendency among the revolutionary generation to portray the United States as a soulless, acquisitive, and aggressive power.*

I.
Sir, your will was so beautiful
that during the tragic months of your empire
the rhythm of the great stars quickened.
The time of your most terrible sorrow
remains within me:
when you searched for allies
among the men of your race,
and your cry was lost in the jungles.
That moment of your solitary bitterness
remains within me,
and before your desolate grandeur

Carlos Pellicer was not the only member of the revolutionary generation to celebrate the heroic resistance of Cuauhtémoc. In this 1944 mural by David Alfaro Siqueiros, "Cuauhtémoc Against the Myth," the last Aztec emperor, standing atop a pyramid, hurls a flaming spear at the heart of a ferocious centaur representing the Spanish invader. In the background, Montezuma appeals to the gods, apparently immobilized by the myth of Spanish invincibility. (Tecpan de Tlatelolco, Mexico City)

I sing melodies of love and illusion,
I thunder a tragic symphony.
Before your august solitude
I unfurl my own, the solitude of a falling leaf.
Your religious upbringing
and your heroic, magnificent youth
make me a leaf that falls upon

the mountains and jungles,
proclaiming with great shouts
your grandeur, kicking awake all those who have forgotten
the prodigious course of your star.
The black arc stretched itself before the dawn
and the arrow sailed upward to pierce the last star.

II

We dedicate a mountain or a part of the sky
to the first of the Mexicans.
We delight at the magnificence of your actions.
You were handsome as the night and mysterious as heaven.
But your sorrow cannot be measured
by the orbit of the great planets,
or by the course of the sumptuous stars that shine upon our fears.
Your sorrow,
in the dark mirror of my eyes
begins to reveal to me
eternal anguish and eternal sorrow.
Cuauhtémoc was nineteen years old
when the Empire fell into his hands
like a wounded eagle.
Tenoxtitlán was the loveliest of all
the cities of the New World.
The divine Quetzalcóatl,
who was called Ku-Kul-Kan in the land of
the dear and pheasant,[1]
had announced,
many moons before,
that other men would come through the South.
Thus, he dreamed.

III

And so it is that today,
with the sun broken in my hands
I hear rolling in my destiny
as in a cactus thicket,
the curse of the gods piercing my mouth
and the holy ax of tragedy lashed to my hands.
Can no one free me from
this pain, great as a basalt wave?

Can no one give me back
the sweet hours of love and the joy
of singing in the fields?
Because my eyes now glow only with hatred
and my free hands
think only of vengeance,
hatred and vengeance.
Who can go back to watching the stars serenely
when it seems that fate must trample us
with its stone feet?
The civilized monarchies of my America fell.
Tenoxtitlán and Cuzco
were its sculpted heads.
The fine races fell
before the brutal blows of the conquerors
who overcame the archers with their
loud cavalry and wide-mouthed cannon.
The divine prophet Quetzalcóatl,
did he foretell the arrival of these intrepid destroyers?
Since then, a mournful star
flees over the plains and sinks behind the hills.
For four hundred years we have been servants and slaves!
Who can look sweetly to the heavens
when the people of my America
were forced to flee before the curses of the Europeans,
weak, ignorant and sick?
They branded men like beasts,
and throughout the countryside, and in the entrails of the mines,
they lived the cruelty, the misery, and the tedium
I see, feel, and mourn still today.
Who can gaze sweetly upon the
sweet mysteries of heaven
when ignominy and infamy would bury us again beneath their steely din?
The men of the North loot the continent and the islands at their whim,
and they help themselves to pieces of heaven.
Oh, destiny of inexorable and gigantic tragedy!
You cover the wall of my anguish
and divert the course of the arrow that aimed at some star.
I see your figure sketched in the shadow of fire.
Shall we succumb to your laws of gold and silver?

In the Antilles and Nicaragua
the sun wallows in mud and fear.
Our vain and absurd America
is rotting.
Oh! destiny of inexorable and gigantic tragedy!
Can no one stop you?
Will you return to put our feet to the flame?[2]
Will you return with brutal hands
from the land of the yankees, mediocre, orderly and fat?
Will you return amid explosions and machines
to steal, kill, buy up caciques with your inexhaustible loot?
Oh Sir! Oh great King! Tlacatecutli!
Oh solemn and tragic leader of men!
Oh sweet, ferocious Cuauhtémoc!
Your life is an arrow
that has pierced the eyes of the Sun and
still goes on flying through the sky!
But in the crater of my heart
burns the faith that will save your people.

Notes

1. That is, among the Maya of the Southeast. *Ed.*
2. Cuauhtémoc was tortured by the Spaniards, eager to learn the whereabouts of Aztec gold, by having his feet doused in oil and then set aflame. *Ed.*

The Socialist ABC's

Anonymous

During the 1920s, following the revolution's bloody military phase, several Mexican states carried out homegrown radical experiments, vying with one another for the title "Laboratory of the Revolution." The southern state of Tabasco, during the regime of governor Tomás Garrido Canabal (1922–1935), was a leading contender for that title. Much in the manner of Ché Guevara and the Cuban revolutionaries decades later, Garrido aimed to create a "new type of man," an abstemious and atheistic "man of the future." To accomplish this, he persecuted the Catholic clergy, prohibited alcoholic beverages, structured production and consumption in the state along cooperative lines, organized all citizens into "resistance leagues," formed a red-shirted paramilitary force, and adopted "rationalist" education in the state's schools. What follows are excerpts from a school primer published by the state's "Redemption Press" in 1929.

Man is a sociable being.

Anyone who isolates himself is an *egoist*.

Those who want to have everything for themselves, and who try to monopolize land and money in a few hands, impoverish the country and bring general discontent and misery to the majority.

The monopolizers of wealth exploit the workers and are humanity's worst enemies.

The worker needs to alternate between tools and books, between the workshop or field and the school, so that, cultivating his intelligence and forming his sensibilities, he will become a conscious being who thinks, feels and loves.

The worker who has cultivated his intelligence improves and dignifies both himself and his family.

The worker's ignorance is very dangerous, for it allows him to be victimized by the exploiters, priests, and alcohol.

Little Proletarian

I call you this because I know that your father is a proletarian, and you will be one also.

You lack much, and you and your family work hard for your food.

Although you are still young, you have already begun watering the soil with the sweat of your brow, and your hands are growing coarse from using heavy tools.

It is good that this is so: although small you are already manly, because as a child you still enjoy the feeling of being useful. To be useful is to be good for something, to do something, to give something, and it is the noblest aspiration one can have in life.

To be useful is to be happy.

There are very many proletarian families throughout the world who, despite their hard work, do not have what they need.

If you learn that the man who works is the man who produces, and that he has the right to enjoy the product of his labor, you will understand that there is no reason for proletarian families to suffer misery. Think about this: look around you, and you will see the cause of this injustice. Your labor and that of your family produce more than you can use; a small group lives at your expense and steals from you through deceit, and exploits you without your knowing it. It has been this way for a long time! Your ancestors endured it patiently, as did your parents; they have become indifferent and have kept their sorrow to themselves. But you were born in a century of freedom and compensation, you must win for the proletarian family the right to enjoy all that it produces.

The Society of Yesterday

Human beings need to associate in order to live.

The first union of human beings led to the formation of the family.

The grouping of families which lived in the same place, had the same customs and language, and were linked by ties of affection, resulted in the formation of society.

In our society, before the Revolution of 1910, an odious division of classes came into being. There was one class that enjoyed every consideration and which had the support of the government.

This was the privileged class.

The victims of the privileged class were the workers of the cities and of the countryside; the latter were called *"mozos"* ["servants" or "boys"] and they lived in the saddest conditions you can imagine.

They were exploited without pity, and the greatest fortunes of Tabasco were built upon their excessive labor.

The greedy capitalists packed many tears and sorrows away in their strong treasure chests.

Their wild festivals and brilliant parties prevented them from feeling like human beings, and from understanding the battle that was raging within their suffering souls. Believing that things must be as they were, they grew more and more demanding; they were helped by the clergy in their unhealthy passion to exploit; they shared their riches with the clergy in exchange for absolution, and they were blind and deaf to the sorrow of the oppressed; and, assured that their sins would be forgiven, they grew more and more tyrannical.

It was within this society, organized so unjustly and completely lacking in the principles of love and justice that must exist among men, that the Revolution broke out; the struggle was joined against the regime which protected this state of affairs, and after several years and much blood, tears, and suffering, the Revolution triumphed.

With its triumph, the workers' freedom was secured, and they abandoned the farms where they had worked as servants for many long years.

The privileged class, being opposed to the change that had come about, abandoned their haciendas. They left the state, and they pooled their money with their fellow exploiters in other states, and they tried to form a counterweight to the Revolution.

They have not yet succeeded in their efforts. The Mexican people now understand that they must occupy the place of men and citizens in their country; they compare their lives today with their sufferings of yesterday, and they stand by their conquests and do not listen to those who try to disturb the peace that they enjoy today and that they will enjoy for many years. They are men who feel true fraternity and justice and are opposed to all tyrants and exploiters.

The New Society

The current society tries to organize itself without iniquitous exploitation and without shameful servility.

The goal is the dignification of the Mexican family, and we do all we can to achieve that goal.

The principles of solidarity, a spirit of cooperation, and feelings of equality, are inculcated in the school and propagated at civic and cultural meetings.

The leaders of this social transformation seek to organize men into a more just and humane society.

The ideal of the new societies is to derive individual rights from those of the collectivity.

The supreme aspiration is to create governments that respond to man.

Socialism is the system of organization that is best adapted to reaching these goals, ideals and aspirations.

The Good Citizen

Worker of the field and city:

If you want to feel the true happiness to which we all aspire, bear in mind your duties. Once these are carried out, you will understand your rights and how to retain them when someone opposes you.

The first duty that nature has imposed upon you, whether you are a son, a husband or a father, is to provide comfort to those who depend upon you; in order to be sure that your work is justly remunerated, that work must be of high quality, since no one pays for work that is poorly done or done only out of necessity. If you do shoddy work, you will be obliged to take whatever the boss sees fit to pay you, which will never be enough to account for your needs. If your work is done well, you have the right to set the price in accordance with your needs, and you will have enough to live with decency and ease.

When you have received the product of your work, take care not to spend it unwisely; adjust your expenses to your income, reserving a part of it for savings. Although that portion may be small, it is not insignificant, since the centavos form pesos, and with pesos one can attend to unexpected changes of fortune, such as unemployment, strikes, illness, or death, in which event savings will ensure the future of the family.

Do not ask for a loan, and do not stop eating in order to save money, since savings through debt or at the cost of hunger are not savings.

Be good, work, and economize, and happiness will come to you.

The Plagues of Humanity

Campesino:

Never linger in the doorway of a tavern, and never enter that den of perversion, because there you will only find degradation and misery for yourself and your children.

Think of your home before you cross its threshold; think of what you will

be leaving in the hands of the man who exploits your laziness and weakness —
the bread of your selfless wife and your beloved children.

Think of how alcohol destroys your system, making you incapable of all
human activities which are indispensable for you and your family to live; be
aware that if you ruin your body, you enervate and pollute your spirit to the
point of allowing it to degenerate into abjection and wretchedness.

Think of the shameful spectacle of the disheveled drunkard who falls down
in the street and becomes the object of scorn or pity for passers by.

Reflect on the brutal scene one sees in the home of the drunkard when,
disorderly and demented, he mistreats his tender and long-suffering wife and
his innocent children with words and deeds.

Think of the sorrowful mornings your children will have when they ask
for breakfast, only to find the cruel anguish of hunger because the tavern-
keeper, whenever you go to the saloon, takes your wages so as to fatten his
own children, while your children grow rickety and weak.

Know that the damage you do with liquor is not limited to yourself alone,
but you pass it on to your children and they pass it on to your grandchildren,
and thus you are forging a chain of misfortune for which you, and you alone,
will be to blame.

Campesino, think, reflect, arm yourself with valor and energy, flee from
the tavern and from vice, because this depresses and dishonors you and takes
away the fruit of your labor.

Hate those who poison and despoil you!

The False Religions

Campesino:

If you need to have faith in something, have faith in yourself and in your
labor. Nothing contributes to the success of an undertaking like perseverance
and effort.

No mythical god, no supernatural cause, is capable of granting you the
recompense for a job you have not done.

Do not think or hope for aid from gods who live in heaven. The only thing
that can make you prosperous is the effort that you make to better your own
position.

The only way to achieve welfare is through work. Work that is conscious,
guided, and always striving toward perfection is what makes us prosper economically and lets us enjoy the satisfaction of having finished a job.

Do not have faith in false religions that teach you humility and force you to
renounce your rights as a conscious citizen. Do not enter into religions that

Anti-religious demonstration in Villahermosa, Tabasco, late 1920s. Demonstrators appear to have placed priestly headwear on a cow, while a man holds a sign saying "Down with the Priests." (Reprinted by permission of Fototeca del INAH, Mexico.)

counsel you to be meek when other men belonging to superior classes exploit your labor and turn you from a man into a beast of production.

Reject the religions that offer you glory in heaven in exchange for your slavery here on the earth. Live on your feet, like a man among men! There are no superior castes!

Repudiate the religions that preach and maintain the division of human beings into castes. Man must not live to be exploited by other men. Socialism, the modern doctrine of social confraternity, advocates cooperation, not the exploitation of man by man.

Recall with horror those who admonished you to be meek when you worked fourteen hours a day and lived like a beast, often worse than some of the animals which belonged to the privileged people. The ones who counseled you thus were the infamous representatives of a false god, who would permit such foul injustices and cruelties.

Think that your only god is labor, because it redeems you; but work that demands just recompense, work that is coordinated and organized by socialism, because it unites and strengthens the workers to demand their rights.

Work is an individual duty; it is also a social duty and a high moral duty, because the morality which prevails in modern society teaches that only the person who works should live, whether he works materially or intellectually, with brawn or brain; so long as, in the end, he works.

Have faith in work as a duty, and this belief will be your best religion.

The Ballad of Valentín of the Sierra

Anonymous

As the previous selection suggests, anticlericalism was a major theme in the Mexican revolution. Modernizing elites blamed the Roman Catholic Church for inculcating superstition and ignorance among the masses, and of meddling repeatedly in politics on behalf of reactionary elements. In 1926 President Plutarco Elías Calles began making serious efforts to enforce the anticlerical legislation contained in the 1917 Constitution. The most objectionable provision of that legislation, for Mexico's Catholic clergy, was one that required all clergymen to register with the government. In response to this initiative, the Church hierarchy called upon the clergy to shut down their operations and begin what was, in effect, a religious strike. In the west-central states of Michoacán, Zacatecas, and Jalisco, peasants took up arms against the government with the battle cry, "¡Viva Cristo Rey!" ("Long Live Christ the King!"). This bloody civil war, known as the Cristero Rebellion, raged for nearly three years. What follows is a corrido, a popular folk ballad that appears in scores of local versions, all of which reflect the sentiments of the Cristeros, particularly their loyalty to their village priests and comrades-in-arms. Without question the best known of the substantial repertoire of ballads devoted to the Cristero Rebellion, this corrido narrates the circumstances surrounding the 1928 death of one Valentín Avila in the sierra that joins the states of Jalisco and Zacatecas. Little is known of Avila's life or military career, though the manner in which he met his death has won this humble cristero virtual immortality.

I'm going to sing some verses
About a friend from my *tierra* [locality],
About the brave Valentín,
Who was shot and hung in the sierra.

I hate to remember
That cold winter's afternoon
When it was his bad luck
To fall into the Government's hands.

Cristeros. (From Enrique Krauze, *Plutarco E. Calles: Reformar desde el origen* [Mexico: Fondo de Cultura Económica, 1987]).

On the Fresno riverbank
Valentín met up with
The enemy *agraristas* of the valley
Who questioned him and took him prisoner. . . .

The federal general asked Valentín:
"How many men do you command?"
Valentín replied:
"The fifteen soldiers camped at the Rancho Holanda."

The general then asked him:
"How many men were in your company?"
"The eight hundred men
That Mariano Mejía brought through the sierra."

The general said to him:
"Valentín, tell me the truth.

If you tell me what I want to know
I'll give you two thousand pesos and your freedom."

Then the general said:
"I am prepared to grant you a pardon
If you will tell me
Where I might find the local priest."

Valentín promptly answered him:
"That I cannot say;
I'd rather you kill me
Than give up a friend." . . .

Before they shot him,
Before he went up the hill,
Valentín cried:
"O Mother of Guadalupe!
For your religion they will kill me." . . .

Fly, fly away, my little dove
Far from your mountain fastness.
Tell of these last rites
Paid to that brave man, Valentín.

Mexico Must Become a Nation
of Institutions and Laws

Plutarco Elías Calles

*President Alvaro Obregón fell victim to a Catholic zealot's bullet in 1928, after being
elected to his second presidential term. His death raised the specter of a major political crisis, as ambitious politicians and military men primed themselves to fill the
sudden power vacuum. Plutarco Elías Calles, the incumbent president, fully recognized the dangers of the moment, yet he remained remarkably calm. On September 1,
1928, he delivered before Congress the speech excerpted below, urging his fellow revolutionaries to seize the unwonted opportunity to effect a major transformation in the
political life of Mexico. While Calles's apparent faith in the loyalty of the military
was largely wishful thinking, and his repeated assertions of respect for the democratic
process were hypocritical—he would himself dominate Mexican politics as behind-
the-scenes strongman until 1934—the speech did indeed mark a crucial moment in
the history of Mexican politics. It was a first step toward the creation of the National
Revolutionary Party, which was supposed to be a broad and inclusive political vehicle, containing and channeling disputes toward constructive ends. The PNR would
morph into the Mexican Revolutionary Party (PRM) during the late 1930s, and finally
become the Institutional Revolutionary Party (PRI) in 1946. The PRI would control
the presidency and most important political offices for the remainder of the twentieth
century.*

The death of the president-elect is an irreparable loss which has left the country in an extremely difficult situation. There is no shortage of capable men:
indeed, we are fortunate to have many capable individuals. But there is no
person of indisputable prestige, who has a base of public support and such
personal and political strength that his name alone merits general confidence.

The general's death brings a most grave and vital problem to public attention, for the issue is not merely political, but one of our very survival.

We must recognize that General Obregón's death exacerbates existing political and administrative problems. These problems arise in large measure

Calles's stirring rhetoric was not enough to prevent a military insurrection from breaking out in 1929. In this photo, Calles (seated) is seen on a train platform in the state of Sonora personally leading the campaign to crush the rebellion. On the left, with dark jacket and hat, is General Lázaro Cárdenas, who would become president in the mid-1930s. Between Calles and Cárdenas, (leaning on doorframe) is General Saturnino Cedillo, political boss of San Luis Potosí, who would lead a rebellion against Cárdenas's government in 1938. (Reprinted by permission of Fototeca del Fideicomiso Archivos Plutarco Elías Calles y Fernando Torreblanca.)

from our political and social struggle: that is, they arise from the definitive triumph of the guiding principles of the Revolution, social principles like those expressed in articles 27 and 123 [of the Constitution], which must never be taken away from the people. At the start of the previous administration, we embarked on what may be called the political or governmental phase of the Mexican Revolution, searching with ever increasing urgency for ways to satisfy political and social concerns and to find means of governing appropriate to this new phase.

All of these considerations define the magnitude of the problem. Yet the very circumstance that Mexico now confronts—namely, that for perhaps the first time in our history there are no "caudillos"—gives us the opportunity to direct the country's politics toward a true institutional life. We shall move, once and for all, from being a "country ruled by one man" to a "nation of institutions and laws."

The unique solemnity of this moment deserves the most disinterested and patriotic reflection. It obliges me to delve not only into the circumstances of this moment, but also to review the characteristics of our political life up until now. It is our duty to fully understand and appreciate the facts which can ensure the country's immediate and future peace, promote its prestige and development, and safeguard the revolutionary conquests that hundreds of thousands of Mexicans have sealed with their blood.

I consider it absolutely essential that I digress from my brief analysis to make a firm and irrevocable declaration, which I pledge upon my honor before the National Congress, before the country, and before all civilized peoples. But first, I must say that perhaps never before have circumstances placed a chief executive in a more propitious situation for returning the country to one-man rule. I have received many suggestions, offers, and even some pressures—all of them cloaked in considerations of patriotism and the national welfare—trying to get me to remain in office. For reasons of morality and personal political creed, and because it is absolutely essential that we change from a "government of caudillos" to a "regime of institutions," I have decided to declare solemnly and with such clarity that my words cannot lend themselves to suspicions or interpretations, that not only will I not seek the prolongation of my mandate by accepting an extension or designation as provisional president, but I will never again on any occasion aspire to the presidency of my country. At the risk of making this declaration needlessly emphatic, I will add that this is not merely an aspiration or desire on my own part, but a positive and immutable fact: never again will an incumbent president of the Mexican Republic return to occupy the presidency. Of course, I have absolutely no intention of abandoning my duties as a citizen, nor do I intend to retire from the life of struggle and responsibility that is the lot of every soldier and of all men born of the Revolution. . . .

Historical judgment, like all a posteriori judgments, is often and necessarily harsh and unjust, for it overlooks the pressing circumstances that determine attitudes and deeds. I do not intend to review the history of Mexico merely to cast all blame on the men who became caudillos owing to the frustrations of our national life. Those frustrations—the inert condition of the rural masses, who have now been awakened by the Revolution; the sad, nearly atavistic passivity of citizens of the middle and lower classes, who fortunately have also been awakened—inspired those caudillos to identify themselves . . . with the fatherland itself. They styled themselves "necessary and singular" men.

I need remind no one of how the caudillos obstructed—perhaps not always deliberately, but always in a logical and natural way—the formation of strong alternative means by which the country might have confronted its internal and external crises. Nor need I remind you how the caudillos obstructed or delayed the peaceful evolution of Mexico into an institutional country, one in which men are what they should be: mere accidents, of no real importance beside the perpetual and august serenity of institutions and laws. . . .

I would never suggest such a path if I feared, even remotely, that it could cause us to take a single step backward from the conquests and fundamental principles of the Revolution. . . . [I suggest this path] out of the conviction that effective freedom of suffrage must be extended even to groups representing the reaction, including the clerical reaction. This should not alarm true revolutionaries, for we have faith that the new ideas have affected the conscience of nearly all Mexicans, and that the interests created by the Revolution are now much stronger than those represented by the reaction, even if it were to be victorious. The districts where the political or clerical reaction wins the vote will, for many years at least, be outnumbered by those where the progressive social revolutionaries triumph.

Not only will the presence of conservative groups not endanger the new ideas or the legitimate revolutionary institutions; their presence will also prevent revolutionary groups from weakening and destroying themselves through internal squabbling, which is what happens when one finds oneself without an ideological enemy. . . .

We revolutionaries are now sufficiently strong—having achieved a solid basis in law, in the public consciousness, and in the interests of the vast majority of people—that we need not fear the reaction. We invite that reaction to take up the struggle in the field of ideas, for in the field of armed combat—which is the easier of the two forms of struggle—we have triumphed completely, as those groups representing liberal ideas of social progress have always done. . . .

I would not be behaving honorably if I did not point out the many dangers that could result from dissension within the revolutionary family. If such dissension should occur, it would be nothing new in the history of Mexico, which has at times abounded in shady, backroom political dealings that brought to power ambitious, unprincipled men who weakened and delayed the final triumph of progress and liberalism in Mexico, surrendering themselves, whether consciously or not, to our eternal enemies.

I have spoken of our political adversaries with special tolerance and respect, even going so far as to declare the urgency of accepting the representatives of every shade of the reaction into the Chambers of Congress if they win in perfectly honorable democratic struggles. Having said this, I should be permitted to insist that, if one day ambition, intrigue, or arrogance should fracture the revolutionary group that for so many years was united in the struggle for a noble cause—that of the betterment of the great majorities of the country—then the conservatives will once again seize the opportunity to insinuate themselves. If this happens, it is almost certain that the reaction will not need to secure a direct military or political triumph. History and human nature permit us to foresee that there will be no shortage of disaffected revolutionaries who, upon failing to find sufficient support from the disunited revolutionary factions, would call insistently at the doors of our old enemies. This would not only endanger the conquests of the Revolution, but it would surely provoke a new armed social conflict that would be more terrible even than those the country has already suffered; and when the revolutionary movement triumphed, as it must triumph, after years of cruel struggle, Mexico would be bled dry and would lack the strength to resume the march forward from the point where it was interrupted by our ambitions and dishonor.

Finally, in my triple capacity as revolutionary, division general, and chief of the armed forces, I will address myself to the army. . . . We have an opportunity that is perhaps unique in our history. In the period that follows the interim presidency, all men who aspire to the presidency of the country, be they military men or civilians, will contend on the fields of honorable democracy. As I have so frankly pointed out, there will be many dangers for Mexico—dangers that imperil the revolution and the fatherland itself. Anyone who, during those anxious moments, abandons the line of duty and tries to seize power by any means other than those outlined in the Constitution, will be guilty of the most unforgivable criminal and unpatriotic conduct.

All members of the national army must be conscious of their decisive role in those moments. They must embrace the true and noble calling of their military career: to give honor and fidelity to the legitimate institutions. Thus inspired by the duties imposed upon them by their mission, they must reject and condemn all whispers and perverse insinuations from ambitious politicians who would seek to sway them. They must choose between doing their duty, and thereby winning the gratitude of the Republic and the respect of the outside world, and betraying the Revolution and the fatherland at one of the most solemn moments in its history. The latter course of conduct could never be condoned by society or history.

The Formation of the Single-Party State

Carlos Fuentes

An alternative, and decidedly more cynical, view of the political transformation wrought by President Calles and his fellow revolutionary leaders is found in Carlos Fuentes's novel, The Death of Artemio Cruz, *first published in Spanish in 1962. The novel is told largely in hallucinatory flashbacks, as Artemio Cruz—an idealistic revolutionary turned corrupt industrial magnate—lies on his deathbed. Cruz becomes a symbol of the generation of leaders who abandoned idealism in favor of wealth and power, leading Mexico toward moral bankruptcy. In this selection, the dying Artemio flashes back to a smoke-filled meeting of top leaders of the Sonoran dynasty, where the Machiavellian credo of the new official party is set forth. Fuentes (b. 1928) is undoubtedly Mexico's best-known living writer and intellectual.*

[1924: June 3]

. . . and that night you will talk with Major Gavilán in a whorehouse, with all your old comrades, and you will not remember what was said, or whether they said it or you said it, speaking with a cold voice that will not be the voice of men but of power and self interest: we desire the greatest possible good for our country, so long as it accords with our own good: let us be intelligent and we can go far: let us accomplish the necessary, not attempt the impossible: let us decide here tonight what acts of cruelty and force are needed now to make it possible for us to avoid cruelty and force later: let us parcel out well-being, that the people may have their smell of it; the Revolution can satisfy them now, but tomorrow they may ask for more and more, and what would we have left to offer if we should give everything already? except, perhaps, our lives, our lives: and why die if we thereby do not live to see the beneficent fruits of our heroic deaths? we are men, not martyrs: if we hold on to power, nothing will not be permitted: lose power and they'll fuck us: have a sense of destiny, we are young and we glitter with successful armed revolution: why have we fought, to die of hunger? when force is necessary, it is justified: power may not be divided: and tomorrow? tomorrow we will be in our graves, Deputy Cruz, leaving those who follow to arrange the world as best they can . . .

The Rough and Tumble Career
of Pedro Crespo

Gilbert M. Joseph and Allen Wells

Despite the hopeful rhetoric of Calles, much of Mexico's political life has long been dominated less by institutions and laws than by regional caciques of the sort described in the following reading (and in the earlier selection by Rosalie Evans) — men whose power seems to be based upon a complex and mysterious blend of charisma, patronage, violence, and manipulation. Two veteran historians of modern Yucatán, Gil Joseph and Allen Wells of Bowdoin College, analyze the ways in which these individuals gained and used power in their close-up portrait of Pedro Crespo, the political boss of a strategic portion of the state in the decades following 1910.

Temax is at the end of the road. A few blocks north of the weather-beaten plaza, the paved road from Izamal runs out; further on, *camino blanco* winds for about twenty kilometers through scrub, then mangrove swamp to the Gulf of Mexico. Eighty kilometers west of the town is the state capital, Mérida: en route one travels through the heart of the henequen (sisal) zone, glimpsing remnants of a more affluent past. Poorly tended henequen fields line both sides of the highway, which is crisscrossed here and there by the rusting and twisted rails of imported Decauville narrow-gauge tram tracks. Blackened chimneys and the ruins of once elegant haciendas similarly bear witness to the grandeur of a monoculture now in irreversible decline. To the east of Temax, henequen's bluish gray spines soon give way to denser scrub and clearings of grazing cattle; beyond the neighboring village of Buctzotz there is little to see for another seventy kilometers, until Tizimin, cattle country's new boom-town. Hot, dusty, and unprepossessing to the casual eye, Temax appears to be just another desperately poor and sleepy municipal seat that time has long since passed by.

Current appearances, however, mask a turbulent and intriguing recent past. Indeed, Temax has figured prominently in Yucatecan history since the apocalyptic Caste War of the mid–nineteenth century. Poised as it is between the dynamic henequen zone and the marginal sparsely populated hinterland, between the settled plantation society and the zone of refuge for the rebellious Maya *campesinos* who resisted plantation encroachment on their traditional way of life, Temax has been a strategic periphery or frontier. Consequently, its control has posed a significant problem for Yucatán's modern rulers. And, for much of the first half of the twentieth century, Temax's political fortunes were closely linked to the career of an extraordinary rural insurgent and political boss, Pedro Crespo. State authorities came to realize that the price of peace in Temax was a certain degree of autonomy for Don Pedro. . . . Crespo knew how to survive. [His] political career came to embody the achievements and contradictions of the larger revolutionary process.

We know relatively little about Crespo's prerevolutionary career before he burst upon the local political scene in March of 1911. . . . [He was] born about 1870, of humble village origins, like many campesinos on the fringes of the expanding henequen zone. . . . [He] grew up determined to preserve the family's status as small but free cultivators. Quite likely, he chose to enlist in the state national guard, to avoid the mechanism of debt that tied an ever-increasing number of villagers as peons to the large and powerful henequen estates.

In short order, Crespo demonstrated his prowess as a soldier and was made an officer in the local guard. How did Crespo regard his duties, which included hunting down and returning runaway people to their masters, quelling worker protests against brutal, slavelike labor conditions, and implementing the hated *leva* (conscription), which dragooned villagers and drifters into the guard? We'll never know. No doubt Crespo came to know the social world of north-central Yucatán beyond the boundaries of the rural countryside. Temaxeños remember him as a man with a foot in both worlds: "un mestizo de buen hablar"—a Maya who spoke Spanish well and could handle himself in town.[1] Through his work, young Crespo was introduced to the milieu of urban polities, to the ever-shifting layered networks of patronage and clientele, which tied the local *dzules*—powerful [white] rulers of land and men in their own right—to even more powerful patrons in the state capital.

As an officer in the guard, Crespo was compelled to play this exacting, dangerous game of late Porfirian politics. Although he initially flirted with the intrigues of a disenfranchised faction of the planter elite in 1909, by the eve of the 1910 gubernatorial election, Crespo had allied himself with Enrique Muñoz Arístegui, the "official" candidate of the "Divine Caste," an entrenched oligarchy led by the state's most powerful planter, merchant, and politician, Don Olegario Molina.

Don Olegario was a formidable patron. He was a favorite of President Porfirio Díaz, and, following a term as governor of Yucatán, he served as minister of development in Díaz's cabinet (1907–11). Molina's relations filled the upper echelons of the state's bureaucratic machine. Indeed, the power of the "Divine Caste" radiated outward from the Molina *parentesco* (extended family), which, apart from its national connections, was greatly fortified by its partnership with the principal buyer of raw henequen fiber, the International Harvester Company. Under the terms of a secret arrangement between Molina's import-export house and the North American corporation, large sums of foreign capital were periodically placed at the oligarch's disposal, enabling Molina y Compañía to affect price trends, acquire mortgages, and consolidate its hold on fiber production, communications, the infrastructure, and banking in the region. Despite the fabulous wealth generated by the *fin de siècle* henequen boom, the first decade of the new century was a veritable summer of discontent for the vast majority of Yucatecan producers, merchants, workers, and campesinos, who found themselves personally indebted or subordinated, in one form or another, to the Molina *parentesco*.

Francisco Madero's national political campaign against the Díaz regime emboldened two disgruntled *camarillas* (political factions) of the Yucatecan planter class and their middle-class allies to organize parties for the purpose of challenging Molinista hegemony in the 1910 elections. Formed in 1909, these rather loose political coalitions, the Centro Electoral Independiente and the Partido Antireeleccionista, were known popularly as "Morenistas" and "Pinistas," after their respective standard-bearers, Delio Moreno Cantón and José María Pino Suárez, who were journalists. But they were financed by their planter supporters, and each faction hastily attempted to construct alliances reaching into the urban intelligentsia and small working class, and, perhaps even more tactically, into the large and potentially explosive Maya *campesinado*.

As a rising military leader able to bridge the cultural distance between dzules and campesinos, Crespo was a valuable asset in strategic Temax and was wooed by incumbents and dissidents alike. After testing the waters of Morenismo, however, he chose to stay with the Molinista . . . puppet, Muñoz Arístegui. . . .

What, then, turned this cautious policeman into a revolutionary? Quite likely he was unable to ignore ties of blood and a claim for vengeance. Like Pancho Villa, whose sister was raped, and countless others who joined Madero's national movement in 1910, a sense of deep personal outrage set Crespo at odds with the Porfirian authorities. . . . Crespo had been left by Temax's corrupt *jefe político* [district prefect], Colonel Antonio Herrera, who also was Crespo's superior officer in the local guard detachment, to languish for thirty days in the notoriously unfriendly confines of Mérida's Juárez Penitentiary.

Crespo would later speak vaguely of differences he had had with the Temax authorities, and his lieutenants would cite the tyrannical abuses of Herrera's local rule. Some old-timers recall that Crespo had been openly critical of the jefe político's high-handed tactics in meetings with Temaxeño campesinos. But for Crespo, much more than *mal gobierno* or perhaps even personal rivalry was at issue here: Herrera had killed Crespo's father, Don Cosme Damían, under shadowy circumstances. Apparently, while Pedro was in jail, Don Cosme had balked at Herrera's arbitrary order that he do *fagina* (unpaid, forced road work), whereupon the jefe político ordered his goons to gun the old man down in broad daylight.

Soon after his release from prison, Crespo sought revenge. He mustered up a small band of his kin and clients — most of them peasant villagers — and exploded into revolt. Operating in the chaotic climate that was Maderismo in Yucatán, Crespo elected to burn his bridges behind him, joining his local vendetta to the larger regional movement against Díaz and the Molinistas. On March 4, 1911, he led his column in a lightning predawn raid on the county seat of Temax. The rebels easily overwhelmed the nine-man guard detachment of Temax's central plaza. (Later, the town police commander would charge that the guardia had been sleeping on the job.) Crespo immediately rousted Colonel Herrera and the treasury agent Aguilar Brito from their beds and hauled them, clad only in their skivvies *(paños menores)* to the plaza. All the while, as members of his band shouted "Viva Madero!" and "Down with bad government!," Crespo vented his rage on the stunned Herrera: "You bastard, you killed my father! Before you were on top and screwed me, but now it's my turn."

The tables were indeed turned. Handpicked as district prefect by the great Molinista planters, Colonel Herrera was the dominant figure in Temax's political life, and his physical presence made him even more menacing to local campesinos. Hulking in stature, with his shaved head and long gray beard, Herrera often took on the dimensions of a mad monk or an avenging prophet. Only days before, during the Carnival revels of Shrove Tuesday, although too cowed to make a statement about their jefe político, Temaxeños had mocked his subordinate, Aguilar Brito, as "Juan Carnaval," shooting an effigy of the treasury agent in front of the Municipal Palace. Now, in the same central plaza in the wee hours of the morning, Pedro Crespo was cutting the despised prefect down to size. In a final act of humiliation, Crespo strapped Herrera and Aguilar to chairs and riddled them with bullets in the same spot in front of the town hall where Aguilar had been "executed" during Carnival. The bodies were piled into a meat wagon and then dumped at the gates of the town cemetery. (It was ghastly ironic that the treasury agent would later be interred in the same coffin that "Juan Carnaval" had occupied the preceding Shrove Tuesday.)

Before he left town the next morning, Crespo emptied the municipal jail, freeing some campesinos who had been imprisoned for refusing to do *fagina* ordered by the deceased jefe político. Crespo armed his new recruits and then . . . requested food, drink, and "contributions" from local merchants, and took the 300 pesos (one peso equaled fifty U.S. cents) in the municipal treasury. Yet Crespo . . . made sure that Temax's prominent families were not physically harmed, and he strictly limited his men's intake of *aguardiente*. . . . Crespo saddled up his force—now swollen to about eighty—and divided the men into two mobile bands, one to head west toward Cansahcab, the other east, under his direction, toward Buctzotz. All wore red bands on their hats.

In the weeks and months that followed, Pedro Crespo became Yucatán's most successful insurgent. His hit-and-run tactics, based on an intimate knowledge of the local terrain, were celebrated in the pueblos and hacienda communities of north-central Yucatán, and his ranks continued to multiply. One week after his raid on Temax, his troops mushroomed to 200; by mid-April some estimates placed his strength at 400, in May, close to 1,000. Many free villagers and some hacienda peons joined his campaign willingly, eager to strike a blow against the dzules, particularly the despised jefes políticos and hacienda overseers who symbolized the encroachments and abuses of the oligarchy. In Buctzotz, a group of villagers rose up upon Crespo's arrival, took the National Guard barracks, and cut out the tongue of the municipal president before executing him. In Dzilám González, dozens of campesinos, including the town's band, defected en masse to the rebellion. The musicians brought their instruments and enlivened the guerrilla campaign in the weeks ahead with a series of impromptu Saturday night *jaranas* (folk dances) in remote backcountry hamlets.

Although many hacienda peons were recruited at gunpoint by the rebels, Crespo sought to erode planter paternalism and social control with clientelist measures of his own. At the Cauacá, Chacmay, and San Francisco Manzanilla haciendas—the estates of the largest henequen planters—he decreed "liberation," canceling all of the peons' debts. Moreover, Crespo provided amply for his recruits, derailing trains, raiding *cuarteles* (barracks) for munitions, and levying forced loans on local planters and merchants. At Cauacá, 150 peons joined Crespo, and suddenly Maya surnames were greatly outnumbering Spanish ones in his ranks. . . .

Crespo's guerrilla campaign forced the Molinista regime to expend great amounts of time, money, and manpower in a futile effort to pin down the rebels. Soon other risings against government installations and officials—like

Crespo's, nominally Maderista — spread through the countryside. During the spring of 1911 the Mérida government found itself unable to do more than hold the county seats, leaving the hinterland to the insurgents. Moreover, village-based campesinos increasingly resisted government attempts to recruit them to fight against the rebels, or mutinied following recruitment. Finally, Muñoz Arístegui was compelled to resign, and the new military governor issued an amnesty for all disaffected rebels designed to coax rebel leaders like Crespo to lay down their arms, a desperation move that did little to quell rural unrest throughout the state. . . .

By late May 1911, Díaz had fallen, and Pedro Crespo had disbanded his forces. But, far from being finished, his career was just beginning. For the next thirty years, Crespo arbitrated the political fortunes of Temax, brokering power between elites, villagers, and peons during the most volatile juncture of the revolutionary period.

In the political vacuum that resulted in Yucatan from Díaz's defeat, More-nistas and Pinistas vied for leadership, and rural violence reached dangerous new levels. But, under Crespo's sway, Temax remained relatively calm. The cacique had only contempt for noncombatant civilian politicians like Pino Suárez — soon to become Yucatán's Maderista governor and then vice president of Mexico — who during the insurrection had called upon Yucatecos to join Madero but to avoid acts of vengeance such as those committed at Temax. Unfortunately, once in power, Madero and Pino seemed intent upon employing the same nefarious "bola negra" tactics of political imposition that they had deplored during the Porfiriato. Crespo's sympathies lay with the more popular Morenistas, who now intrigued throughout the state with their former Molinista foes against the ruling Pinistas. At no point, however, during the short-lived Madero regime (1911–13) did the Pinistas feel strong enough to move against Crespo in Temax. Following Díaz's ouster, Crespo had sent his lieutenants to Mérida to serve Pino notice that, although they had been disbanded, his followers remained armed and could be activated at his command on short notice.

Like the Maderista liberals, the neo-Porfirian Huertista military leader who would supplant them (1913–14) saw the wisdom of accommodating the Crespo *cacicazgo*. Nor did the pattern change significantly when the Mexican revolution in Yucatán moved dramatically left under the socially active administrations of Constitutionalist General Salvador Alvarado (1915–18) and the Marxist Felipe Carrillo Puerto (1921–24). These progressive caudillos also found it wiser to court rather than wrangle with the powerful Crespo as they sought to mobilize campesinos behind their agrarian, labor, and educational reforms between 1915 and 1924. For his part, Crespo was a political pragmatist; he could live with—even actively support—regimes of widely varying ideological coloration, provided they favored, or at least did not intrude upon, his *cacicazgo*.

Particularly interesting is the nature of Crespo's collaboration during the twenties and thirties with the Socialist Party of the Southeast (PSS), led by Carrillo Puerto (1915–24) and his successors. Whereas General Alvarado had brought the Constitutionalist revolution to Yucatán in March 1915 with eight thousand troops, the civilian governor, Carrillo Puerto, was not always able to count on the support of a loyal, progressive military and, consequently, had to rely more heavily on the muscle of local power brokers like Crespo. Moreover, in case of hacendado-backed insurrection against the socialist revolution (a very real possibility), the geopolitics of Crespo's *cacicazgo* were critical: Temax was located on the rich eastern fringes of the henequen zone, astride the Mérida–Valladolid Railroad. Its proximity to the [Mayan populated] hinterland made it essential that Temax be secure since, if it fell into hostile hands, Valladolid and the southeastern part of the state—the base of rebel operations during the nineteenth-century Caste War—might once again be cut off from the state capital in Mérida.

To ensure Crespo's loyalty, Carrillo Puerto awarded him the plums of civil government and agrarian office, either to hold himself or to dispose of as he saw fit. Like other powerful caciques, Crespo combined the municipal presidency with leadership of the local resistance league *(liga de resistencia),* the PSS's constituent unit in Temax. Upon Crespo's recommendation, his ally, Juan Campos, was chosen as the district's federal deputy. Several years later, Crespo succeeded Campos in the Chamber of Deputies. . . .

To the day he died, Pedro Crespo lived in much the same manner as his campesino followers: He spoke Maya among friends, wore the collarless white *filipina,* and lived in the *kaxna,* the traditional wattle-and-daub cottage with thatched roof. What interested him most was political power, not wealth. The revolution had offered him a chance and he had seized it. No doubt he viewed himself and came to be regarded in Temax as a *líder nato*—a born local leader, a chief. As such, he did what was necessary to preserve, even extend, his *poderío,* or his local power base. This entailed constant political vigilance and negotiation; deals might be made with powerful planters and bargains struck with the emerging revolutionary state, but it never called upon Crespo to sell out his clientele, to accumulate great wealth and leave Temax for Mérida. Indeed, precisely because he was a *líder nato,* he was incapable of transcending his locality and breaking with the political culture that had produced him.

In return for Carrillo Puerto's preferment and patronage, Crespo performed a variety of services for the pss. Not only did he selectively bring violence to bear against local opponents of the party to ensure it a political monopoly within the state, but Crespo also doubled as an informal ward boss, guaranteeing, through a variety of incentives, the enrollment of local campesinos in Temax's liga de resistencia. Like other loyal party officials, Crespo scheduled weekly cultural events and frequent recreational activities.

Although few in the region appreciate it today, under Carrillo Puerto baseball became a strategic component of the pss's campaign to mobilize its rural-based revolutionary regime. The sport already was rooted in the regional environment. In addition to its incredible popularity among all classes in Mérida and Progreso, the principal port, campesinos in the larger rural towns had demonstrated a particular fascination with it. Now the party's goal was to mount a statewide campaign to organize baseball teams *"hasta los pueblitos"* — in even the most remote interior Maya communities. Such a program would enhance the popularity and morale of the pss, which might then be parlayed into other programs for social change. It would strike at traditional rural isolation which impeded the socialist transition, and would immediately contribute to the party's goal of social integration, even in advance of longer term efforts to improve regional communication and transportation. Carrillo Puerto had no way of knowing it at the time, but his campaign also would have the effect of institutionalizing *béisbol* as the regional pastime, an anomaly in a nation where elsewhere *fútbol* became the people's game.

Pedro Crespo and Juan Campos became energetic promoters of the game in north-central Yucatán. In 1922 these *beisbolistas* petitioned the Liga Central de Resistencia in Mérida for money for gloves, bats, balls, and uniforms, and personally organized ball clubs in Temax, Dzilám González, and surrounding pueblos and hacienda communities. Once this rudimentary infrastructure was in place, Crespo and Campos worked with the presidents of other interior ligas de resistencia to schedule country tournaments and leagues and, later, to arrange for tours by the more experienced Mérida and Progreso clubs. To this end, they frequently petitioned Governor Carrillo Puerto for free passes for ballplayers on the state-controlled railroads.

It is not surprising, then, that local nines still bear their names, or that Temax has become synonymous with high-quality baseball, periodically producing bona fide stars for the Mexican League. The backcountry ball games that these caciques promoted in the twenties and thirties likely echoed with the same patois of Maya and Spanglish that one hears on hacienda and pueblo diamonds today: "Conex, conex jugar béisbol. . . . Ten pitcher, tech quecher, tech centerfil!" ("Come on, let's play ball. . . . I'll pitch, you catch, and you play centerfield!").

Carrillo Puerto's socialist experiment ended suddenly and tragically in January 1924, when Yucatán's federal garrison pronounced in favor of the national de la Huerta rebellion and toppled the PSS government, which had remained loyal to President Alvaro Obregón. Carrillo Puerto and many of his closest supporters in Mérida were hunted down and executed by the insurgent *federales,* who had the financial backing and encouragement of Yucatán's large planters, whom Carrillo Puerto had threatened with expropriation. When push came to shove during the de la Huerta revolt, the majority of the irregular bands led by Carrillo Puerto's cacique allies proved unreliable; in fact remarkably few of them mounted even token resistance against the federales. The truth is that few of these local bosses were ideologically motivated or were organizationally prepared to become dedicated socialist revolutionaries committed to a defense of the PSS regime.

Pedro Crespo was one cacique who did not desert his *patrón.* In Carrillo Puerto's vain attempt to elude the Delahuertistas in December 1923 and, ultimately, to gain asylum in Cuba, he stopped in Temax where he was received by Don Pedro and his intimates. . . . Crespo could not persuade his patron [to wait out the siege in Temax. Carrillo Puerto] continued his flight eastward across the peninsula, a journey that soon ended in his capture and execution.

By April 1924 the de la Huerta revolt had been quelled and the PSS returned to power in Mérida, but now with a social program more in tune with the moderate politics of national leaders Alvaro Obregón and Plutarco Calles in Mexico City. The next decade (1924–34) witnessed a decline in the membership and organization of the resistance leagues, a reconsolidation of the power of the peninsular bourgeoisie, the infiltration of the PSS by that group, and a sharp falloff in agrarian reform, especially in the henequen zone. As the Yucatecan revolution reached its Thermidor, Crespo, now in the autumn of his years, adjusted with the times. In 1930 he was still president of the local resistance league, but now, more than ever, "Yucatecan socialism" was a matter of form, not substance. Led by their patriarch, Temaxeño socialists wore red shirts, spouted revolutionary slogans, and invoked their martyred Don Felipe Carrillo on appropriate public occasions. Yet few serious agrarian or labor demands emanated from Temax's liga de resistencia.

Apart from the revolution's ideological drift to the right, the economics of the period left Don Pedro and the socialists little room to maneuver. The henequen boom had crashed on the rocks of world depression and foreign competition. Temaxeños, like other Yucatecan campesinos, were experiencing severe privation and were glad for even the reduced workload that the hene-quen estates provided. Like most of the PSS's rural chiefs, Crespo was forced to seek an accommodation with the most powerful planters during the Great Depression in order to keep fields in production and minimize layoffs. Indeed, it was his ability to balance and play off the hopes and fears of both dzules and campesinos amid the roller-coaster-like political economy of the twenties and thirties that preserved his cacicazgo until his death in November 1944.

Even the renewed populist groundswell of Cardenismo, which unleashed a fury of riots and political assassinations throughout the state during the late thirties, could not topple Crespo. Newly formed radical mass organiza-tions like the "Juventudes Socialistas" denounced Crespo and the larger evil of "revolutionary caciquismo," but Don Pedro's alliances within the party and provincial society allowed him to hang on. In fact, it was Melchor Zozaya Raz, perhaps the most vocal of the young firebrands in the Juventudes So-cialistas during the late 1930s, who would become Don Pedro's protégé in the early 1940s and ultimately inherit the Temax cacicazgo upon Crespo's death.

Now properly reverential of Pedro Crespo's "revolutionary legacy," Don Melchor Zozaya ruled the district into the 1970s, until diabetes and blind-ness weakened his political grip. Although no powerful individual boss has emerged since, caciquismo as an informal institution of power and patron-age has endured in Temax. Municipal government, *ejidal* office, and access to work on private sector estates are in large part controlled by a camarilla, which corporately functions as a cacique. A favored few are endlessly recycled through the same offices, thereby assuring the Party of the Institutionalized Revolution (PRI) a large majority at all levels of government. And, while the PRI periodically excoriates bossism in the abstract, the national regime seems reluctant to tamper with the political culture of the institutionalized revolu-tion in Temax or anywhere else. This is because the Mexican state rests upon a multitiered system of patronage and clientele that always finds new aggres-sive, upwardly mobile elements to sustain it.[2]

In the Temax of the 1980s, Pedro Crespo also has been institutionalized; Yucatán's branch of the PRI has duly incorporated him into the revolutionary pantheon alongside more famous regional icons like Salvador Alvarado and Felipe Carrillo Puerto. Temaxeño popular tradition, however, has reached a more ambiguous verdict regarding Crespo's *actuación revolucionaria*. "Era ca-cique . . . gran cacique," old-timers pronounce, often with raised eyebrows or a wry smile. ("He was a boss . . . a very great boss.") This rather terse depiction reflects admiration for Crespo's courage, resoluteness, and shrewdness, but also registers a sardonic appreciation of his surmounting ambition to control and dispense power.

Notes

1. In Yucatán the term *mestizo* differs from the standard usage. It indicates a person or attribute—that is, style of dress—which is at root Maya but has been influenced over time by Hispanic culture.
2. These observations were made in the late 1980s and obviously will have to be reassessed following the PAN's victories at the national and regional level beginning in 2000. *Ed.*

A Convention in Zacapu

Salvador Lemus Fernández

During the years immediately following the Mexican revolution, the state of Michoacán became exemplary of some important trends. It was among the several states in the west-central area to be rocked by the Cristero War (1926–1929). *It was also the home state of General Lázaro Cárdenas, who served as its governor from 1928 to 1932. As governor, Cárdenas reinvigorated various revolutionary initiatives, including land reform, anticlericalism, and resolutely secular public education. He also formed the "Revolutionary Labor Confederation of Michoacán," an officially supported labor/campesino union and political organization. Cárdenas would later carry his experiments with such mass-based organizations to the national level during his presidency (1934–1940), experiments which are often viewed as watershed events in modern Mexican political history.*

The narrative below is an excerpt from the unpublished autobiography of agrarian activist Salvador Lemus Fernández, based upon his personal archive and his own memories. Lemus was born in Taretan, a small town in Michoacán, on July 23, 1908, the son of a carpenter-musician. He took an active interest in local agrarian politics from a very young age. While attending an agricultural college between 1927 and 1929, he began to support the social policies of Governor Cárdenas. In 1931 he left his home region to travel north to a revolutionary convention at Zacapu, which lies on a high plain in central-western Michoacán, an area populated principally by mestizos and Purépecha Indians. The region was dominated by large haciendas, and in the 1920s and 1930s it became the scene of bitter and bloody struggles between landowners and land-hungry peasants, who hoped to benefit from the government's land-reform program. It was also a region where the religious struggle was most intense, as Lemus's story graphically demonstrates.

The Secretary General of the State Committee of the Confederation invited me to attend a convention to be held in the town of Zacapu on the eleventh and twelfth of December, 1931. . . . A couple of my friends found a truck that would take us, even though there was no road that led there. I set off with compañero Ventura Mier, who would later be my compadre [co-parent], as well as with a compañero named Piñón and the truck driver. About half way to Zacapu, the truck broke down at a village called El Tigre. We needed to repair it with a new part before we could continue on to Zacapu. It was around 4:00 in the afternoon when we sent compañero Piñón to fetch the part from Morelia. Mier, the driver, and I intended to spend the night by the truck and wait for him to return.

Let me tell a little story here that shows the sorts of difficulties we could run into in those days. We were on the outskirts of the village of El Tigre with nothing to eat when it occurred to us to go and see if any of the people who lived there would sell us some beans or tortillas or whatever. We went to the first little house, and the woman there said that she couldn't offer us anything because she had nothing at all in her home.

Then compañero Mier brazenly said, "Hey, ma'am. Don't you have anything for the father here?" (The "father" was me, since I was dressed up as a dandy with a suit and all, making me look like a clergyman. Everyone else was wearing campesinos' clothing.)

The woman opened her eyes wide and said, "Really? This gentleman is a priest?"

"Absolutely," said Ventura. "Just don't tell anybody. Keep quiet. Surely you know that priests are persecuted, and who knows what might happen if you sold us a bit of food for him?"

"You're right! But I must have something in here. Maybe just a few eggs."

Then the woman went into the kitchen, where her husband called for her. Then he came over to us to say hello, and in a short while we were eating a pair of scrambled eggs with beans and mouth-watering tortillas. But that wasn't the end of it: The restless woman began to ask us questions. First she wanted to know why I was armed, as we all carried pistols tucked into our belts.

Compañero Mier explained, "You see, the government harasses priests, and sometimes you have to be armed to defend yourself. So he carries a gun, and we are also here to protect him. But no one can know anything. God will know it if the government ever finds out about him."

"Well all right," the woman said. "You wait here."

Night was falling when church bells from the village chapel began to peal. We heard the singing of hymns in the distance, drawing ever nearer. Then the lady said, "Listen, father. Since the fiesta of the Virgin of Guadalupe (December 12) is coming up, why don't we celebrate it today and Christmas tomorrow? Maybe you could go to the church and say a Rosary for us."

"Can't you see the situation we're in?" I asked. "Who knows how many would come?"

Drawing for a poster by Diego Rivera. The poster featured the words: "The Distribution of Land to the Poor is not contrary to the Teachings of Our Lord Jesus Christ and the Holy Mother Church. The Mexican people fought and suffered ten years desiring to find the word of our Lord Jesus Christ." The poster aimed to counter clerical hostility to the agrarian reform. (From Ernest Gruening, *Mexico and its Heritage* [New York: The Century Co., 1928], facing p. 265.)

"Couldn't you give us something? Maybe just a short sermon?"

"No I can't. I can't run the risk of letting the government find out about us and then taking us off to prison." That is how I avoided saying Mass.

In the meantime, the religious procession had arrived at the church and waited there expectantly. We left the house and headed toward the truck. On the way, we began to talk about compañero Mier's recklessness. We figured that the townsfolk might attack us if they learned what had happened, since the Cristero War was still in full force. Time passed, the evening got darker, Piñón didn't arrive, and we were afraid to approach any household to ask for shelter for the night.

Some heaps of cornstalks, which the people of the region call "bulls," were stacked up nearby. The villagers pile up their harvest—the corncobs and stalks and everything—to let it dry. So we hollowed out a little cavern in the "bulls" to make a place to spend the night. Naturally, we didn't have any blankets or anything with us. We didn't want to stay in the truck because we thought we might get ambushed. The next day, compañero Piñón arrived with the part, and we continued on our journey to Zacapu.

When we got there, we found the house in which the Governor, General Lázaro Cárdenas, was having lunch along with many of the leaders and campesinos who belonged to the Confederación. We came in and greeted him, and he invited us to eat. After we had finished lunch, compañero Mier told Cárdenas and his guests about what we had done in El Tigre. The General burst out in laughter, and, of course, all the other compañeros laughed along with him. Even we chuckled, because compañero Mier's gambit really had been quite audacious, and we had had no choice but to play along.

After a while, we returned to the work of the convention. It had opened the previous day, that is, the eleventh of December. It was now the twelfth, the day that the Catholics pay homage to the Virgin of Guadalupe, as the Spaniards had taught them. The convention took place in the yard of the town's most important church. A table of honor had been set up covered with bunting and presided over by the Governor, General Lázaro Cárdenas, and all the regional delegates were there. My friends and I also took part in the proceedings and sometimes spoke, but we preferred to let the delegates do the talking.

At one point, compañero [Antonio] Mayés Navarro called me aside. He had been standing at the dais along with the General. He got down and told me, "The General wants us to go see what is going on in the church, because there are some strange sounds coming from inside."

"Fine. Let's go," I said.

We climbed an exterior stairway that led to the loft and looked in through a window. We saw an incredible mess: broken statuary was scattered on the floor; the woven reeds that the statues were made out of had been torn up; and the depositories where the faithful placed their "offerings" had been thrown onto the ground. We went back to tell the General what we had seen. The governor grew very upset and asked us who we thought could be responsible for the disaster. Someone told him that it was probably a compañera known as Catalina, or "La Pelona" ["The Short-haired Woman"], who was traveling with us. In fact, a rumor began to circulate implying that she had done it. We asked her whether it was true. She acknowledged that she had, saying that she and a group of delegates wanted to "finish with all this once and for all." The General told us that these events did not bode well for us because the townsfolk would find out and no one could tell what might happen then. He said that we had better leave at once and that we could finish the convention elsewhere.

At that moment, the townsfolk began to realize what had happened. They rang the church bells to call together all the Catholics that had been gathering in the churchyard and in a large plaza nearby. As this went on, we carried out the closing ceremonies. The General told us to leave for Tiríndaro, but first we dismantled the equipment we had used during the convention. By this time the church bells had attracted about 500 people to the plaza, and they clearly knew what had happened inside the church. Men, women, and children began to shout insults at us all, but mainly at the Governor. We started to withdraw from town following behind the General, who led La Pelona by the arm.

We had to cross the plaza to get to our hotel, but we noticed that the number of zealots was growing. They were armed with stones, sticks, machetes, and doubtless with pistols. They seemed aggressive. We all came to a standstill in front of the antagonists. Mayés and I were walking just behind the General, and we had to stop short. It seemed like the prelude to a vicious battle. Once the crowd had forced the General to a halt, the people began to jeer at him. They yelled that he was not a governor but a murderer and an enemy of religion. The mob lurched forward threateningly, yet the General stood his ground and asked, "What do you want?"

He was answered by shouts: "We want La Pelona!"

Then La Pelona shook off the General's grip, took a step forward as if to give herself up, and cried, "Here I am!" The General took hold of the back of her dress and jerked her backward between Mayés and me. People in the crowd began to draw pistols and knives. At that point, the armed compañeros from the village home guards tried to halt the multitude's advance by raising their rifles to protect the General and the rest of the group. The guardsmen's attitude annoyed the General, who reproachfully ordered them to keep away, not to get involved, and to be calm. Then Mayés and I marched off with Catalina. We moved quickly between the two groups toward the hotel. As soon as the crowd noticed that we were taking Catalina away the people quit bothering the General and began to follow us instead. We started out at a trot and soon broke into a run, but the throng did the same thing. It was practically on our heels when we made it to the end of the street. About 100 guardsmen were there, though they did not intend to get involved since the General had ordered them not to. But the mob threatened to work itself into a frenzy if it caught us, so we ordered the compañeros to stop its advance. The guardsmen sprung into action and took up positions blocking the street. They cocked their rifles as they took combat positions, some on one knee and others standing. The compañeros' decisive action caught the crowd off guard, and we took advantage of the moment to get to the Hotel García, disguise La Pelona as a man, and rush out of Zacapu towards Tiríndaro.

But who was "La Pelona"? She was Catalina Duarte, a native of Taretan, the daughter of Jesús Duarte and Josefa Zaragoza (the latter of whom was the half-sister of Mrs. María Béjar de Ruiz, who was later my mother-in-law; she was also the cousin of my compañero Emigdio Ruiz Béjar and of my wife, María Concepción Ruiz Béjar). The family owned a butchershop. Catalina disappeared from town one day for some reason, and I later discovered that she was an active member of the Confederation. She attended nearly all the conventions. She was so brassy that she would ride yearling bulls in village rodeos (*jaripeos*) to the wild applause of the spectators. She completely gave herself over to the Confederation. Her anticlerical attitudes were entirely contrary to those of the rest of her family. Her relatives were not only practicing Catholics, they vigorously opposed the government. For example, everyone knew that one of her brothers killed a compañero named Onésimo Reyes, who was a member of the agrarian community of the Ex-Hacienda of Taretan. She once received a gunshot wound when she got involved in a problem involving a priest. That was Catalina Duarte, a.k.a., La Pelona.

At any rate, we all arrived in Tiríndaro as the General had ordered. We arrived in the village and everyone was preparing to receive the General, or rather had already prepared to do so. The brass bands began to play and the compañeras cooked *corundas, tamales,* and *atoles* for dinner. In other words, as soon as the General arrived there began a huge fiesta — complete with dancing, music, and everything else — that didn't end until the early morning hours.

The Agrarian Reform in La Laguna

Fernando Benítez

The agrarian reform carried out by President Lázaro Cárdenas during the late 1930s was the most sweeping ever undertaken in Latin America, and it certainly marked a watershed in the long history of the Mexican revolution. Unlike similar efforts during the 1920s, this reform affected even lucrative export crops such as cotton and henequen. Indeed, the two showcases of the reform were the cotton-growing region of La Laguna, which is located at the conjunction of the states of Durango and Coahuila, and the henequen zone of Yucatán. These land distributions were carried out with dizzying speed, and have often been criticized as haphazard, politically motivated acts which did little to improve the conditions of the campesinos. In the following excerpt, Mexican writer Fernando Benítez, who has written several books on the dilemmas of the postrevolutionary countryside, provides some sense of the complexity of the issue, for we find that the Cardenista reform's supposed beneficiaries, as well as its alleged victims, are ambivalent about the results.

Paradoxically, La Laguna has no lake to justify its name. This region is really a kind of American Egypt, a desert region crossed by the Nazas and Aguanaval Rivers. In between these is a gigantic crescent of alluvial soils whose richness contrasts sharply with the aridity of the surrounding landscape.

The vast fields of golden wheat and the symmetrical cotton plantations—the work of men—seem out of place next to the immobile and disorderly agaves, the spiny mesquites, . . . and the fleshy plants of the dry Mexican North. . . .

In 1930 the powerful Agricultural Commission of the Laguna Region, of which all of the large landowners were members, tried to exempt the region from any sort of agrarian reform, citing their efficiency and their economic contribution to the nation: with only 1.3 percent of the national population, they claimed, the region produced more than half of the nation's cotton and 7 percent of its wheat.

But the fabled efficiency of the hacendados was contradicted by reality.

An agricultural center of such importance attracted many people who made every effort to remain there. The landowners, in the face of that avalanche of people, gave out lands—not their good lands, of course, but marginal ones—where people settled, living very precariously. This aggravated the [agrarian and social] problem. Later [the *hacendados*] tried unsuccessfully to expel 15,000 farmworker families, leaving only 20,000 resident peons who were paid starvation wages.

Thirty-five thousand pariahs, who supported themselves by working three or four months of the year or by working odd jobs, lived amid the opulent great estates. This led to a period of conflict and organizing beginning in 1935, when the day laborers organized unions, demanded a minimum wage of one and half pesos, eight-hour workdays, and a collective contract that would cover the entire agricultural workforce of La Laguna.

. . . [I]n the first months of 1935 the struggle centered on labor issues rather than on the demand for land, and the *hacendados* fought back by organizing their peons into "white" (or company) unions; they [also] called in 10,000 campesinos from other areas, offering them good wages. In September, a strike on the Hacienda Manila unleashed many more strikes, and launched a period of intense conflict between white and red unions, complete with mass firings. These events instilled in the workers some class-consciousness. While the *hacendados* bribed the local authorities for protection, the workers received the support of the most active members of the Communist Party, the rural teachers, and the union leaders from Torreón and Gómez Palacio.

On November 6, 1936, Cárdenas arrived with a group of engineers and began to distribute lands. The landowners' arrogance disappeared as if by a magic spell. The President made them see that if they used any violence, the government would arm the campesinos, and the landowners, fearful of losing everything, folded their cards and resigned themselves to the inevitable. . . .

Cárdenas distributed the lands of La Laguna in one month, and all of the important and revolutionary measures there were taken during his administration. For the first time, the campesinos were awarded fertile lands instead of the bad, rain-fed lands they had been given earlier; and it was demonstrated beyond any doubt that a well-organized collective [*ejido*] could be as efficient as an hacienda, with the advantage that it favored hundreds of campesinos instead of a single landowning family. The destiny of La Laguna was now, essentially, that of all the *ejidos* created during the time of General Cárdenas, and if problems arose later which have persisted to this day, that was due to the inept bureaucracies and corruption that prevailed during the three decades following the reform.

Lázaro Cárdenas presiding over a land-expropriation ceremony
in Michoacán. The man at the microphone is Michoacán
governor Gildardo Magaña, who was an important figure in the
movement headed by Emiliano Zapata. (From Betty Kirk,
Covering the Mexican Front: The Battle of Europe versus America
[Norman: University of Oklahoma Press, 1942], 109. Reprinted
by permission of the University of Oklahoma Press.)

EIGHT YEARS AFTER the land distribution, a car carrying Egon Erwin Kisch
motored along the new highway between the green fields sprinkled with yellow and purple flowers. The famous Czech journalist, who had just escaped
from the Nazis, recalled the European headlines of 1936: "Theft of Land Ordered by the Government!," "Has Bolshevism Triumphed in Mexico?" And
naturally, he also recalled what the economists, politicians and bureaucrats
of Mexico City had said before he began his journey: "The distribution, as
you will see with your own eyes, has failed dismally. The old farmworkers
have only managed to lose their steady wages and benefits, becoming financial slaves of the banks and sinking into misery. The new owners of the land
are down on their knees begging their old masters to once again take over

the estates and hire them back as peons; but the landowners resist doing so, in the hope that the government will return their land en masse."

When Kisch spoke with the *ejidatarios,* they seemed to confirm the alarmist predictions, indeed even to exceed them.

"So, how is life around here?" asked Kisch.

"How do you think? It's plenty bad."

"Bad? Why? The fields are beautiful and the cotton is selling at a good price on the market."

"Sure, but we don't get the benefits; we just get a peso and a half per day."

"But I thought that was just an advance. Don't they distribute the profits when they sell the harvest?"

"Maybe so, but in practice there's never anything to distribute."

"Why is that?"

"Because we still have to settle all of the debts we've had pending since the first year, when we barely harvested anything. And we also have to pay the Ejidal Bank so it can pay the big landowners."

Kisch was reluctant to believe that the agrarian reform had turned the campesinos into slaves of the banks, since they looked rather like European industrial workers and had nothing in common with the Indians he had seen in other parts of Mexico, with their sunken cheeks and rags for clothing. He insisted:

"Yesterday I visited the hospital that you have in Torreón."

"Yes," interrupted one boy, "the hospital is very nice. But even when somebody is sick, it's not so easy to get in there."

"What? They don't admit all of the sick people from the *ejidos?"*

"And if we all went to the hospital, who would do the work?"

"And the schools? The new schools?"

"They would be fine if the children did not have to help out in the fields, especially during harvest time. They can't work and go to school at the same time. Also, there are not enough teachers."

Kisch's last optimistic sentiment withered. He had lost the battle, and he exclaimed:

"So you were all better off before?"

There was a deep silence, like a shout of protest. A woman said:

"For the love of God, sir! How can you think such a thing? That's not what we meant to say; don't misinterpret our words."

"Before," someone clarified, "we lived like beasts. Now at least we are men, and as the harvest grows we earn more."

"What? Didn't you just tell me you earn a peso and a half, no matter how things turn out?"

"Yes, but that's nothing but an advance, sir; we told you that when they figure up the accounts they give us what we've earned."

"But didn't you say that, in practice, they never give you anything?"

"Sure, naturally, because we have to meet our debts. But these debts we're repaying are from the first year when we hardly harvested anything; we told you that, sir."

"Our hospital alone," said a woman with a cranky tone and gestures, "makes us feel like people. Before, we could never call the doctor for want of money to pay him. My mother gave birth to me in an open field, out among the plants, and my husband died in the fields vomiting blood. Now, when we are sick we have our hospital."

"Then," Kisch insisted, "do I understand that you live better than before?"

Kisch later remarked that, "Anyone who believes that our interlocutors were pressured to answer cheerfully and in the affirmative does not know campesinos." Shrugging their shoulders, the campesinos again said that they lived badly, and Kisch, fearing that the long conversation would return to its point of departure, bade them farewell.

In Mexico City he spoke of the big hospital, of the new machines, of the new homes and schools; the educated people and bureaucrats, smiling sarcastically, told him:

"How naive you are! You don't understand Mexico. They never show visitors anything more than what will impress outsiders."

"But we spoke to more than a hundred *ejidatarios* and they all assured us that they live incomparably better than they did before," answered Kisch.

"Sure," they responded, "they're well coached. They don't tell anyone anything except what suits the unions. Pity the man who tells the truth! And you, sir, were you so naive that you believed them?"

KISCH CONCLUDED HIS report on La Laguna by asking: "Where have we heard this before?" And we, thirty years later, must ask ourselves, where do we continue to hear it? Because the campesinos are the same as the ones that Egon Erwin Kisch met. Zapata told Villa that the campesinos of Morelos, long after they had received lands, did not believe those lands really belonged to them. And the campesinos of La Laguna, who were only slightly better off than the boll weevil, "not unlike the Sudanese Berber, the Egyptian felah, the Hindu of Haiderabad, or the black man from Arkansas with his North American citizenship" — that is, all of the cotton cultivators of the world — "they complained bitterly of their fate, even while they refused to live in caves and in the old shacks, to toil in the fields like animals, or to support themselves for a year on two month's wages."

No, Mexico's problem is not the campesinos. They deeply felt themselves to be men and not beasts of burden driven by the whims of Mr. Purcell or the Tlahualilo Company.[1] The problem, the great and tragic problem of the country, is that it was and still is set up by the educated people, the engineers, the bureaucrats, the rectors of national life, with their colonialist education, who hate the people and can only conceive of them as peons or servants.

Pegren-Dutton, an Englishman who monopolized the cotton fiber in Torreón for twenty-five years, told Kisch:

"In reality, Torreón began to grow in 1936 when Cárdenas distributed the land among the cotton pickers. In these eight years the population of Torreón has grown by thirty per cent, and several thousand houses have been built here."

Kisch asked him if this really had anything to do with the distribution of land.

"The big landowners," answered the Englishman, "were foreigners, Spaniards for the most part, who lived in Mexico City or even Madrid, which is where they would invest their profits. Before, a *hacendado* would own up to 75,000 hectares; today, the maximum set by law is 150 hectares. Obviously, if a landowner took the precaution of putting part of his property in the name of his wife or children, he can own, together with his family, 150 hectares multiplied three or four times. But to recover the profits of the old days, farmers nowadays have begun intensive cultivation and above all they have renounced absenteeism; they no longer live in the city, far from their land, so they can personally supervise the exploitation of their lands. And although the old *hacendados* complain bitterly about the agrarian reform, as is natural, in private they recognize that they feel no great nostalgia for the old days, with their complaining peons with their many demands, since that was quite often disagreeable. Do you understand?"

"Do you authorize me, Mr. Pegren, to publish this as your opinion?"

"I've no objection, but do mention at the outset that I am not in agreement with the agrarian policy of Cárdenas."

Kisch finally summarized the problem of La Laguna and the entire nation, saying: "All this land belonged first to one person, then to a few, now to many. Only when everything belongs to everyone will we see an end to the bitter complaints that we always hear, and the eternal arguments about the advantages and disadvantages of the agrarian reform."

Note

1. William Purcell, an Englishman, owned some twenty haciendas in the Laguna region prior to the agrarian reform. The Tlahualilo Company, an Anglo-American cotton concern dating from 1883, owned vast amounts of land and had long been accused of laying claim to a disproportionate share of the waters of the Nazas River. *Ed.*

The Oil Expropriation

Josephus Daniels

In 1937 a labor dispute erupted between Mexican oil workers and the foreign-owned oil companies, most of which were based in the United States. When the oil companies resisted settling the strike in the workers' favor, flaunting the dictates of the Mexican Council of Conciliation and Arbitration, Cárdenas made the stunning announcement on March 18, 1938 that his government was nationalizing the companies' properties. The oil companies responded with a furious anti-Mexican propaganda campaign, but the crisis wound down thanks largely to the government's pledge to pay indemnities (though far below those demanded by the companies), the worsening situation in Europe which demanded U.S. attention, and the judicious conduct of the U.S. Ambassador to Mexico (1933–1942), Josephus Daniels.

In the following excerpt, Daniels describes the tremendous enthusiasm generated in Mexico by Cárdenas's decree.

With the expropriation of foreign oil properties, a wave of delirious enthusiasm swept over Mexico, heightened by bitter denunciations from other countries as people felt that a day of deliverance had come. On March 22, upon the call of the Confederation of Mexican Workers, some two hundred thousand people passed in compact files before the National Palace acclaiming President Cárdenas and carrying banners such as: "They shall not scoff at Mexican Laws." Old inhabitants said there had never been such manifestations of the unity of the Mexican people in the history of Mexico as followed the appeals to the people to uphold the Constitution and the sovereignty of Mexico. It was shared by people who lost sight of oil in their belief that Mexicans must present a united and solid front.

Closing his address to the multitude, Cárdenas told labor men they deserved the support of their government, and counseled them to discipline their ranks, increase production, and avoid insolent attacks—"to prove there is a real, individual liberty justly demanded by the Mexican people."

Many thousands of students in the Mexican University organized an enthu-

Women donate various items to help pay the indemnity for expropriated oil lands. (Reprinted by permission of Fototeca del INAH, Mexico.)

siastic parade. Its Rector, speaking to President Cárdenas, said: "The University offers you its solid support in this moment when the fatherland requires the unity of its sons. It comes to offer the youth of Mexico to be with you as you are with the honor of Mexico."

Catholics Raise Funds

Noticeable was the enthusiasm of Catholics, many of whom had been critical of the Cárdenas government, in raising funds to support his expropriation move. On Sunday, April 30, the Archbishop of Guadalajara advised from the pulpit that it was a "patriotic duty to contribute to this national fund." It was announced (April 3) that Archbishop Martínez had promised a "letter on the oil controversy during Holy Week." On May 3, a circular, approved by archbishops and bishops, was published, exhorting Catholics to send contributions. All over the country in churches collections were taken to help pay for the seized oil properties.

Women Make Expropriation a "National Religion"

Women in Mexico have generally followed an old slogan: "The place of woman is in the home." That was the attitude of women in the early part of April, 1938. Then, as by a miracle, suddenly they became vocal in their patriotism. Cárdenas had made approval of the expropriation of oil a sort of national religion. The people believed—and had grounds for their opinion—that their patrimony had been given for a song to foreigners who refused to pay living wages to the men who worked in the oil fields. When the men gathered by the hundred thousands to show allegiance to Cárdenas after the oil expropriation, the women poured out of their homes by the thousands to voice their ardent support of the leaders who had somehow made the people feel that the oil exploiters were the enemies of their country. What could they do? President Cárdenas had given his word to me on the day after the expropriation that payment would be made. The people were zealous to see that his pledge was kept. What could the women do? Pitifully little toward the millions needed, but all Mexico in a day was full of the spirit of the widow who gave her mite and was commended, having given her all as giving "more than all the rest."

Something the like of which has rarely been seen in any country occurred on the twelfth day of April. By the thousands, women crowded the Zócalo and other parks and in companies marched to the Palace of Fine Arts to give of their all to the call of their country's honor. It was a scene never to be forgotten. Led by Señora Amalia Solórzano de Cárdenas, the President's young and handsome wife, old and young, well-to-do and poor—mainly the latter—as at a religious festival gathered to make, what was to many, an unheard-of sacrifice. They took off wedding rings, bracelets, earrings, and put them, as it seemed to them, on a national altar. All day long, until the receptacles were full and running over, these Mexican women gave and gave. When night came crowds still waited to deposit their offerings, which comprised everything from gold and silver to animals and corn.

What was the value in money of the outpouring of possessions to meet the goal of millions of pesos? Pitiably small—not more than 100,000 pesos—little to pay millions—but the outpouring of the women, stripping themselves of what was dear to them, was the result of a great fervor of patriotism the like of which I had never seen or dreamed. It was of little value for the goal. It was inestimable in cementing the spirit of Mexico, where there was feeling that the Cárdenas move was the symbol of national unity. . . .

Celebration of Anniversary of Expropriation

On the anniversary of the expropriation (March 18, 1939) two thousand people attended a banquet in the bull ring in celebration, and on Sunday seventy-five thousand people gathered in the Zócalo with banners, and heard speeches by President Cárdenas, syndicate workers, and others to celebrate "the historic decree." The ringing of the Hidalgo bell was said to be the signal for throwing off the foreign yoke. The syndicate workers and Señor [Abelardo] Rodríguez, President of the Mexican Revolutionary Party, created great enthusiasm by their attacks of imperialistic policies. President Cárdenas' speech was mild in comparison, but he upheld the course he had pursued, said that no backward step would be made, and indicated that the negotiations going on between him and Mr. Donald Richberg, attorney for the oil companies, would be successful, leaving operation in the hands of the government.

His speech was enthusiastically received, particularly when he denounced the oil companies for launching a fiery campaign through the foreign press in an endeavor "to crack the domestic economy." He defended "the reincorporation of the oil subsoil rights to the hands of the nation." He declared that the oil companies had "made it a practice to obstruct the enforcement of the most fundamental laws by way of diplomatic coercion or mercenary revolt." He declared, "The potential wealth of Mexico, purely hard Indian labor, exemption from taxes, economic privileges and tolerances on the part of government constitute the essential figures of the great prosperity of the petroleum industry in Mexico."

At the same time flags were flown on the towers of the Cathedral which faces one side of the Zócalo. On one of the towers was a large Mexican flag with the eagle and snake. On the other tower was a great flag of the Mexican Revolutionary Party, and high above all was a banner reading: "The PRM extends greetings to President Lázaro Cárdenas, Redeemer of Economic Independence." I do not recall ever before seeing a political banner on the Cathedral.

Cárdenas and the Masses

Arturo Anguiano

*Lázaro Cárdenas has entered Mexican folklore as the greatest friend and benefac-
tor of the poor and marginalized. Not surprisingly, he has also been vilified by large
landowners, foreign oil companies, and conservatives of all stripes. But there is also
a significant body of literature which critiques Cárdenas from the left. Some Marxist writers, with the benefit of hindsight, have identified in his rule the origins of
many of Mexico's persistent problems: government domination of labor unions, the
continuing poverty of the peasantry, a fixation on industrialization at the expense of
human needs, and the clear triumph of state capitalism. A fairly typical example of
this perspective is excerpted below.*

The new governing forces headed by Lázaro Cárdenas knew that the class
struggle was bound to worsen. They therefore considered it necessary to guide
the mass movement of workers and peasants by winning their support and ori-
enting their struggles so as to strengthen the State, giving it power that it could
use to foment the country's industrial development. The destruction of the
large landed estates and the transformation of the old rural structures brought
Mexico into the era of mechanization and capitalist relations. Meanwhile, the
renovation and encouragement of industry, which obliged the bourgeoisie to
break with their anachronistic practice of exploiting the working class to the
point of exhaustion, were objectives that the State not only was able to carry
out, but carried out without provoking serious social conflicts that might well
have caused the incipient social and political regime to waver and break apart.
The State lacked its own social base, since the capitalist class did not yet fully
identify its interests with those of the government; only the assistance of the
masses would allow it to impose its will and realize its objectives.

In order to achieve this, Cárdenas, as the new representative of the State,
adopted a policy which, in addition to conciliating classes and conceding social reforms to the workers and peasants, took on a new character that differentiated it from all preceding governments. We shall call this policy "mass
politics," since it appealed to the masses and provoked their mobilization. . . .

Although mass politics would surely have developed independently of the person who occupied the presidency, it is certain that Cárdenas's unique personal characteristic and particular style were decisive in reestablishing relations between the State and the working masses. His austere character, firm and full of patience; his strength and dedication to labor; the simplicity of his lifestyle and his egalitarianism—all were keys that allowed him to approach the masses, beginning a new relationship of apparent equality with them. That personality manifested itself in his first acts of government, which were designed to win the sympathy of the masses. Thus, he eliminated the wearing of dress-coats at official ceremonies; he turned Chapultepec Castle, which had till then been the presidential residence, into a museum, while he continued to live with his wife in their private home and later in "Los Pinos" [the current presidential residence]; he cut in half the salaries of government officials, using the rest for "projects for the collective betterment"; he condemned gambling, closing the Foreign Club of Cuernavaca, which included some politicians and military men among its members; and he carried out other measures of this kind. Especially important was his order that the telegraph offices dedicate one hour a day, free of charge, to transmitting the complaints and opinions of peasants and other workers. Such measures had tremendous repercussions, since General Cárdenas's no-nonsense image spread to every corner of the country and won much sympathy among the most diverse social sectors. Cárdenas's image was accepted and admired by the worker and peasant masses, which easily distinguished it from that of traditional politicians.

What best allowed Cárdenas to ally himself with the masses were his constant travels, which brought him to even the most remote and unknown parts of the country. Cárdenas went in search of the masses, and he linked himself closely with them. His electoral campaign, and the trips he took during his administration, were supposed to be a means of learning the conditions of life and the needs of the people at first hand, of studying the problems of each region and the means to resolve them. During his trips, just as in Mexico City, he listened patiently for hours to the workers, peasants, and small farmers who brought him their problems and their complaints. "They have so many needs," said Cárdenas, "they lack so many things, that I can at least listen to them with patience." Cárdenas gave them advice or promised to fulfill their demands. The trips also aimed to "educate the people" in order to secure their cooperation. They taught the masses "the precise conception of their rights and obligations," even though some believe that Cárdenas hoped personally to oversee compliance with his decisions and even to control local leaders.

The trips to every corner of the country constituted one of the special elements of the mass politics that Cárdenas originated. His direct relationship with the peasants and workers, his socializing with them, allowed him to win the confidence of people who, lacking consciousness and direction of their own, saw in the president someone they could confide in, who listened to them and helped them to resolve their problems. He was not the usual "strong man," hostile, someone to be feared; nor was he the phantasmagorical president whom people heard speak from time to time and who lived in some place they knew nothing about and could not even begin to imagine. No, this president was a man of flesh and blood, a man they could talk to, who would not scold them, who encouraged them to fight for their own vindication. This political style allowed Cárdenas to obtain considerable support and enabled him to control the masses of workers and peasants. . . . Cárdenas was sprouting his "own roots," cementing his authority and power, gaining strength sufficient to achieve the key objective that the State had assigned itself, namely, the industrialization of the country, with all that that implied. . . .

Cárdenas made direct, physical contact with the workers and peasants fundamental to the practice of government. Official functionaries now had to become mass leaders of sorts. In order to ally themselves with workers and peasants they would have to seek them out in the workplaces, in the regions where they lived, with the aim of learning their problems and needs directly. By linking themselves closely with the masses, by beginning a permanent relationship with them, these functionaries would be able to guide them along institutional channels, to control them and regulate their struggle, snuffing out any rebellious tendencies and winning a broad base of support. The Cárdenas style invaded the country, and the governors, along with gubernatorial or congressional candidates, found themselves obliged to adopt the new political strategies.

Cárdenas launched before the entire country an immense propaganda campaign designed to encourage organization, unification, and discipline among the workers and peasants. In every workplace he visited, in every meeting where he spoke to workers, he insisted again and again, to the point of exhaustion, on the need for workers to organize. This would be the president's transcendental preoccupation, his obsession, and it would lead Cárdenas to become the most important propagandist and the leading promoter of the mobilization of the working masses. . . .

But Cárdenas did not just initiate and promote the organization of the workers and peasants into unions or agrarian leagues; his objective was the complete unification of workers and peasants. He criticized inter-union squabbles that arose among workers, denouncing them as "sterile and criminal," and pointing out that the bosses could take advantage of these conflicts. Organization had to result in unification, in the integration of a united front of all workers. . . . This must include those workers who were as yet unorganized, who were now encouraged to join unions.

In effect, Cárdenas prepared the way for the actions of the State, which was the promoter of worker and peasant organization. Peasants were organized directly by the State, which, through the PNR, took the task into its own hands; workers were aided and encouraged to commit themselves to the State. The president did this because he knew the advantages of worker organization. In his struggle to modernize the country, doing away with large landholdings and fomenting industrialization, Cárdenas, as representative of the State, appealed to the masses and solicited their collaboration in order to begin in earnest to transform the country's economic conditions, obliging the bosses to submit to the laws and the hacendados to accept the government's resolutions in agrarian matters. Without the collaboration of the masses of workers and peasants, "organized, disciplined and unified," Cárdenas reckoned it would be difficult to impose the State upon all social sectors, especially the privileged classes, and to create the bases necessary for the country's economic progress. . . .

The organization and unification of the workers not only served as a base of support for the State that Cárdenas headed, but also put an end to the interunion squabbles that disrupted the economy. With the workers dispersed among many organizations, each fighting for dominance, struggles were guided from within, that is, by the wage workers themselves; strikes would break out, factories would stop production, the workers would cease to collect their wages, and the factory owners' losses would force them to raise the cost of their products. This retarded industrial development, which is why Cárdenas thought it necessary to unify the workers and reestablish good relations among them. . . .

The policy of promoting the organization and unity of the workers did not run the risk of being counterproductive for the State or for the nation's capitalists. Cárdenas took care to guide the workers' struggle toward purely economic rewards, and when they were integrated into the political process, they remained subordinate to, and controlled by, the State, through the official party. The limited consciousness of the workers, which was formed by the unions and their leaders, was another guarantee that the unification of the workers would not endanger the stability of the regime. On the contrary, the workers were organized precisely in order to maintain and consolidate that stability. Moreover, the organization and unification of the proletariat gave the workers uniform objectives and strengthened them, putting them in a position to demand from their bosses better economic benefits which would redound to the benefit of the national market, since with less miserable wages the workers would increase their purchasing power and consume manufactured and agricultural products. This stimulated production and increased the profits of the capitalists. . . .

VI

The Perils of Modernity

By the 1930s Mexico's leaders had come to question the conventional wisdom of classical economics, which held that unfettered trade would benefit all peoples in equal measure and within roughly the same time frame. The international capitalist system, they claimed, favored industrialized countries disproportionately, and adverse terms of trade would keep the exporters of raw materials forever mired in poverty. Accordingly, Mexico adopted the new economic strategy of Import Substitution Industrialization (ISI), a state-led effort to replace imports with locally manufactured products. To shield fledgling factories from foreign competition, the government established protective tariffs, import quotas, and import licensing. It also gave subsidies and tax breaks to encourage private investment in industry.

By some measures, this strategy succeeded spectacularly. The Mexican economy grew at an impressive average annual rate of 6.5 percent between 1940 and 1970, and Mexico was transformed from a predominantly agricultural country to one where industry accounted for more than a third of total production. Such numbers prompted some to speak giddily of a "Mexican Miracle."

It was no miracle. While the economy enjoyed robust growth, Mexico had one of the world's most unequal patterns of income distribution. And while the government fomented industrial development, it neglected agriculture, especially the production of basic foodstuffs. The *ejidal* sector—at one time heralded as the revolution's crowning achievement—remained primitive and impoverished. Potential rural unrest was partly contained by the incorporation of the *ejidos* into the ruling party's massive bureaucracy—a bureaucracy that was plagued by extraordinarily high levels of corruption, factionalism, favoritism, and clientelism. Many peasants who found only misery in the countryside headed for the U.S. border; many more made their way to the cities, especially to Mexico City, which grew at a vertiginous pace. There, they often found themselves packed into improvised and dehumanizing slums.

Meanwhile, the overprotected industries spawned by ISI proved inefficient and uncompetitive. Most were capital-intensive—a curious thing in a country whose single greatest resource was its large and rapidly growing labor force. Problems of unemployment and underemployment have been chronic. Meanwhile, government expenditures on education, health care, housing, and social security have been notoriously inadequate.

All of the problems we have mentioned thus far were severe even during the golden age of the "Mexican Miracle." From roughly 1970 till the present, it has seemed as though fate intended to mock Mexico's modernizing pretensions with a series of cruel jokes. President Luis Echeverría (1970–1976) presided over an unprecedented expansion of the public sector without any meaningful increase in government revenues. The foreign debt ballooned. Echeverría's successor, José López Portillo (1976–1982), continued to borrow and spend wildly, albeit with greater confidence, for by the mid-1970s it had become known that Mexico was sitting atop vast untapped petroleum wealth. It made perfect sense, López Portillo reasoned, to borrow money to modernize infrastructure and pave the way for an oil-rich future. Foreign banks agreed, and they fairly inundated Mexico with loans. Unfortunately for Mexico, the early 1980s brought a global glut of oil, and Mexico's dreams of leapfrogging painlessly into the First World faded. At the end of his term, López Portillo reluctantly devalued the peso, which had been maintained at artificially high levels. The peso went from 26 to the dollar in 1982 to 2,300 to the dollar by 1987. The shock of the devaluation and the hyperinflation that followed was severe. It was made worse by revelations of grotesque corruption in the López Portillo administration, including the tawdry tale of the president's friend, "El Negro" Durazo, a portion of which is recounted in this section.

In view of its hyperindebtedness, Mexico had little bargaining power with international financial institutions like the International Monetary Fund (IMF) and the World Bank. Those institutions insisted that the solution to Mexico's crisis lay in jettisoning the old protectionist paradigm and embracing privatization and free trade. State-owned industries were sold off; price controls and subsidies were lifted; tariffs were reduced or removed. In the bargain, businesses failed and people were thrown out of work. President Carlos Salinas de Gortari (1988–1994), a Harvard-trained economist, took the next logical step in Mexico's transformation: rather than watch idly as his country was dragged kicking and screaming into the Brave New World of neoliberalism, Salinas was one of neoliberalism's most zealous pitchmen. He staked the credibility of his regime on the North American Free Trade Agreement (NAFTA), a plan to eliminate remaining tariff barriers, sell off remaining state enterprises, and enter into a relationship of unprecedented coziness with the

Colossus of the North. The methods were different, but the subtext was the same: this, at last, was to be Mexico's ticket to modernity.

No such luck. The very day the new treaty entered into effect, a serious peasant uprising erupted in the impoverished southern state of Chiapas. In December 1994, immediately after Salinas's successor, Ernesto Zedillo, took office, the overvalued peso was once again devalued, and another severe crisis was on. Equally traumatic was a series of high-level political assassinations and revelations of horrific corruption in the Salinas government. The most damning revelations involved the president's brother, Raúl Salinas de Gortari, who was charged with involvement in influence peddling, murder, embezzlement, and drug trafficking.

While most Mexicans and foreign observers alike applauded the remarkable transparency of the 2000 presidential elections—elections which brought a definitive end to the official party's monopoly on power—it seems less clear that the new president, conservative ex-businessman Vicente Fox, can finally offer Mexico a winning program. Neoliberalism in general, and NAFTA in particular, have so far brought few tangible benefits to most Mexicans. In the words of novelist Carlos Fuentes, Mexico's experience of neoliberalism "holds out the promise of Adam Smith's optimistic eighteenth-century definition of economics—the science of human happiness—and ends up confirming Thomas Carlyle's pessimistic definition in the nineteenth: the dismal science."[1]

In any case, the readings that follow seek quite deliberately to illustrate the darker side of Mexico's frustrated attempts at modernization: the impoverishment of the countryside, the unchecked growth of the megalopolis, the burgeoning slums, the blatant corruption, the ravaging of the environment—all of those trends which have routinely been shrugged off as the inevitable costs of modernization. Meanwhile, age-old problems such as racial discrimination festered, seemingly untouched by new, progressive attitudes. Many of the readings in this section are graphic and disturbing. We do not, however, intend to suggest that the Mexican people have been docile or passive in the face of these horrors, as subsequent sections will make clear.

Note

1. Carlos Fuentes, *A New Time for Mexico* (Berkeley and Los Angeles: University of California Press, 1996), 128.

They Gave Us the Land

Juan Rulfo

Juan Rulfo (1918–1986) is considered one of Latin America's literary giants despite his meager productivity, which consists of only fifteen short stories and one slender novel. He was born in the tiny village of Apulco, Jalisco, in the waning days of the Mexican revolution. During the 1920s and 1930s, his home region became the scene of considerable violence related to agrarian and religious issues. His father and several uncles were murdered in 1925, and his mother died two years later, leaving him to be raised in an orphanage run by French Josephine nuns. While he is best known for his novel Pedro Páramo, which has entered the canon of Latin American literature as one of the first works of "magical realism," his short stories provide powerful glimpses of the harsh realities of postrevolutionary Mexico. "They Gave Us the Land," which was first published in 1948, presents an almost surreal critique of the postrevolutionary agrarian reform, where government officials congratulate themselves on fulfilling the promises of the revolution by giving the worst farmland to the poorest people. These characters' unending and apparently pointless trek across a strange, desolate desert serves as a metaphor for the plight of Mexico's poor in the twentieth century.

After walking so many hours without coming across even the shadow of a tree, or a seedling of a tree, or any kind of root, we hear dogs barking.

At times, along this road with no edges, it seemed like there'd be nothing afterward, that nothing could be found on the other side, at the end of this plain split with cracks and dry arroyos. But there is something. There's a town. You can hear the dogs barking and smell the smoke in the air and you relish that smell of people as if it was a hope.

But the town is still far off. It's the wind that brings it close.

We've been walking since dawn. Now it's something like four in the afternoon. Somebody looks up at the sky, strains his eyes to where the sun hangs, and says, "it's about four o'clock."

That was Melitón. Faustino, Esteban, and I are with him. There are four of us. I count them: two in front, and two behind. I look further back and don't see anybody. Then I say to myself, "There are four of us." Not long ago, at about eleven, there were over twenty, but little by little they've been scattering away until just this knot of us is left.

Faustino says, "It may rain."

We all lift our faces and look at a heavy black cloud passing over our heads. And we think, "Maybe so."

We don't say what we're thinking. For some time now we haven't felt like talking. Because of the heat. Somewhere else we'd talk with pleasure, but here it's difficult. You talk here and the words get hot in your mouth with the heat from outside, and they dry up on your tongue until they take your breath away. That's the way things are here. That's why nobody feels like talking.

A big fat drop of water falls, making a hole in the earth and leaving a mark like spit. It's the only one that falls. We wait for others to fall and we roll our eyes looking for them. But there are no others. It isn't raining. Now if you look at the sky, you'll see the rain cloud moving off real fast in the distance. The wind that comes from the town pushes the cloud against the blue shadows of the hills. And the drop of water which fell here by mistake is gobbled up by the thirsty earth.

Who the devil made this plain so big? What's it good for, anyway?

We started walking again; we'd stopped to watch it rain. It didn't rain. Now we start walking again. It occurs to me that we've walked more than the ground we've covered. That occurs to me. If it had rained, perhaps other things would've occurred to me. Anyway, I know that ever since I was a boy I've never seen it rain out on the plain—what you would really call rain.

No, the plain is no good for anything. There're no rabbits or birds. There's nothing. Except a few scrawny huizache trees and a patch or two of grass with the blades curled up; if it weren't for them, there wouldn't be anything.

And here we are. The four of us on foot. Before, we used to ride on horseback and carry a rifle slung over our shoulder. Now we don't even carry the rifle.

I've always thought that taking away our rifles was a good thing. Around these parts it's dangerous to go around armed. You can get killed without warning if you're seen with your thirty-thirty strapped on. But horses are another matter. If we'd come on horses we would already be tasting the green river water, and walking our full stomachs around the streets of the town to settle our dinner. We'd already have done that if we still had all those horses. But they took away our horses with the rifles.

I turn in every direction and look at the plain. So much land all for nothing. Your eyes slide when they don't find anything to light on. Just a few lizards stick their heads out of their holes, and as soon as they feel the roasting sun quickly hide themselves again in the small shade of a rock. But when we have

Ejidatario, c. 1950, ploughing fields in the traditional way. (Photo by Fritz Heyle. Reprinted by permission of Henle Archive Trust.)

to work here, what can we do to keep cool from the sun?—because they gave us this crust of rocky ground for planting.

They told us, "From the town up to here belongs to you."

We asked, "The Plain?"

"Yes, the plain. All the Big Plain."

We opened our mouths to say that we didn't want the plain, that we wanted what was by the river. From the river up to where, through the meadows, the trees called casuarinas are, and the pastures and the good land. Not this tough cow's hide they call the Plain.

But they didn't let us say these things. The official hadn't come to converse with us. He put the papers in our hands and told us, "Don't be afraid to have so much land just for yourselves."

"But the Plain, sir—"

"There are thousands and thousands of plots of land."

"But there's no water. There's not even a mouthful of water."

"How about the rainy season? Nobody told you you'd get irrigated land. As soon as it rains out there, the corn will spring up as if you were pulling it."

"But, sir, the earth is all washed away and hard. We don't think the plow will cut into the earth of the Plain that's like a rock quarry. You'd have to make holes with the pick-axe to plant the seed, and even then you can't be sure that anything will come up; no corn or anything else will come up."

"You can state that in writing. And now you can go. You should be attacking the large-estate owners and not the government that is giving you the land."

"Wait, sir. We haven't said anything against the Center. It's all against the Plain — You can't do anything when there's nothing to work with — That's what we're saying — Wait and let us explain. Look, we'll start back where we were — "

But he refused to listen to us.

So they've given us this land. And in this sizzling frying pan they want us to plant some kind of seeds to see if something will take root and come up. But nothing will come up here. Not even buzzards. You see them out here once in a while, very high, flying fast, trying to get away as soon as possible from this hard white earth, where nothing moves and where you walk as if losing ground.

Melitón says, "This is the land they've given us."

Faustino says, "What?"

I don't say anything. I think, Melitón doesn't have his head screwed on right. It must be the heat that makes him talk like that — the heat that's cut through his hat and made his head hot. And if not, why does he say what he's saying? What land have they given us, Melitón? There isn't even enough here for the wind to blow up a dust cloud.

Melitón says again, "It must be good for something — for something, even just for running mares."

"What mares?" Esteban asks him.

I hadn't noticed Esteban very closely. Now that he's speaking I notice him. He's wearing a coat that reaches down to his navel, and under his coat something that looks like a hen's head is peering out.

Yes, it's a red hen that Esteban is carrying under his coat. You can see her sleepy eyes and open beak as if she was yawning. I ask him, "Hey, Teban, where'd you pick up that hen?"

"She's mine!" he says.

"You didn't have her before. Where'd you buy her, huh?"

"I didn't buy her, she's from my chickenyard."

"Then you brought her for food, didn't you?"

"No, I brought her along to take care of her. Nobody was left at my house to feed her; that's why I brought her. Whenever I go anyplace very far I take her along."

"Hidden there she's going to smother. Better bring her out in the air."

He places her under his arm and blows the hot air from his mouth on her. Then he says, "We're reaching the cliff."

I don't hear what Esteban is saying any more. We've got in line to go down the barranca and he's at the very front. He has a hold of the hen by her legs and he swings her to and fro so he won't hit her head against the rocks.

As we descend, the land becomes good. A cloud of dust rises from us as if we were a mule train descending, but we like getting all dusty. We like it. After tromping for eleven hours on the hard plain, we're pleased to be wrapped in that thing that jumps over us and tastes like earth.

Above the river, over the green tops of the casuarina trees, fly flocks of green chachalacas. That's something else we like.

Now we can hear the dogs barking, near us, because the wind coming from the town re-echoes in the barranca and fills it with all its noises.

Esteban clutches his hen to him again when we approach the first houses. He unties her legs so she can shake off the numbness, and then he and his hen disappear behind some tepemezquite trees.

"Here's where I stop off," Esteban tells us.

We move on further into the town.

The land they've given us is back up yonder.

Mexico's Crisis

Daniel Cosío Villegas

The essay excerpted below was first published in 1947 in Cuadernos Americanos, *one of Mexico's most prestigious and widely circulated journals. It appeared at the start of the administration of Miguel Alemán, a time when official Mexico was busy congratulating itself on its new maturity and embracing a vision of rapid industrial progress (it was in 1946 that the Party of the Mexican Revolution was renamed, tellingly, the Institutional Revolutionary Party, or PRI). "Mexico's Crisis" was the work of one of the greatest intellectuals of twentieth-century Mexico. Daniel Cosío Villegas (1898–1976) first rose to prominence with the so-called Generation of 1915, a group of university students who sought to realize revolutionary ideals in cultural and intellectual life. He studied at some of the finest schools in Mexico, the United States, England, and France, helped create the school of economics at the National University of Mexico, and was among the founders of Mexico's premier institution of advanced learning, El Colegio de México. Cosío Villegas founded three of Mexico's most important scholarly journals—El Trimestre Económico, Historia Mexicana, and Foro Internacional—and was the director of the monumental La Historia Moderna de México, a nine-volume, multiauthored work that examined the multiple dimensions of late-nineteenth- and early-twentieth-century Mexico. His insider's familiarity with the Mexican revolution made his judgment of its institutional ossification all the more stinging—so stinging, in fact, that President Alemán's private secretary warned him never to publish anything of the sort again. Despite the bitter disapproval with which official Mexico received his essay, his words were extremely prescient, and they stand as one of the earliest, and boldest, exposés of the moribund revolution.*

For several years now, Mexico has been in a crisis which worsens day by day; but, as in those cases in which the patient is mortally ill, the members of the family will not talk about it, or they do so with an optimism that is tragically unreal. The crisis stems from the fact that the goals of the Revolution have been exhausted, to such a degree that the term *revolution* itself has lost its meaning. As is their custom, the official political groups continue to guide their acts according to their most immediate ends, while no one seems to care about the distant future of the country.

To understand the crisis, to gauge and resolve it, these primary questions should be considered: what were the goals of the Revolution, when were they exhausted, and why? . . .

One of the main goals was that the indefinite tenure of power by one man or one group of men should be condemned; another, that the lot of the many should prevail over that of the few, and that in order to improve the fortunes of the many the government should become an active element of change; finally, that the country has interests and tastes of its own, which must be safe-guarded, and that in cases of conflict they should prevail over foreign interests and tastes. The reaction against the Porfirio Díaz regime and its ultimate overthrow was the application of the first goal; agrarian reform and the labor movement of the second; while to the third belongs the nationalist tone of the Revolution, exalting what was Mexican, distrusting, or openly fighting, what was foreign. . . .

When and why the program of the Mexican Revolution was exhausted is a very painful chapter in our history, for not only has the country lost its motive force, which until now it has failed to replace, but the failure is one of the most definite tests to which the undoubtedly creative genius of the Mexican has been subjected—and the conclusions, unfortunately, could not be more discouraging.

Let us begin, then, with the following statement: without exception all the men of the Revolution were inferior to its demands; and if, as may be argued, these demands were quite modest, one must rightly conclude that the country, in a whole generation and in the depths of one of its three major crises, could not produce one leader of great stature, of the kind who deserve to be remembered in history. The extraordinary thing about the men of the Revolution, in magnificent contrast to those of the Díaz regime, was that, bursting forth as they did from the soil itself, they seemed capable of giving the country something as solid, as well founded, and as genuine as are all things which sink their roots deep into the earth to nourish themselves directly from it, profoundly, perennially. If the Mexican Revolution was after all a democratic, popular, and nationalist movement, it seemed that no one but the men who had made it could lead it to success, because they were of the people and had been so for generations. They had felt the whiplash of injustice on their own flesh, and on that of their sons and fathers—the political boss, the priest, and the lawyer—they had known loneliness, misery, ignorance, the dense and heavy mists of uncertainty, if not complete subjection. How could one fail to hope, for example, that with Emiliano Zapata agrarian reform would be achieved—he, a poor peasant belonging to a people who had lost their lands centuries before and who had for generations demanded in vain their return? The very fact that the men of the Revolution were ignorant—the very fact that they governed by instinct rather than reason—this seemed a promise, perhaps the best, for while reason makes distinctions, instinct hits straight to the mark.

But what has been said is the truth: all the revolutionaries were inferior to the task which the Revolution had to accomplish. Madero destroyed the Díaz regime but he did not create democracy in Mexico; Calles and Cárdenas ended the great landed estates, but they failed to create a new Mexican agriculture. May it be that instinct can destroy but that it cannot create? Enough time has passed for us to judge the men of the Revolution with certainty: they were magnificent destroyers, but nothing that they created to replace what they destroyed has turned out to be indisputably better. That is not to say that the Revolution created *nothing,* absolutely nothing. During its time new institutions were born, as well as an important web of highways, impressive irrigation works, thousands of schools, a good number of public services, industries, and agricultural areas hitherto unknown. But none of these things, in spite of their undoubted importance, has succeeded tangibly in changing the country, in making it happier. Thus the achievements of the Revolution have always remained in a most vulnerable posture: exposed to the fury of their enemies, they have not engendered in their supporters the burning conviction that comes with the knowledge that the task has been well done. For the justification of the Mexican Revolution, as of all revolutions, of all movements which subvert established orders, cannot be other than the conviction of its necessity, of the fact that without it the country would be in a worse condition.

TO CREATE IN MEXICO a democracy with some aspects of authenticity is of course a task that would discourage any sensitive man. It is so complex, so arduous, and so slow that it should be conceived as the consequence or end of many other changes and not as a task in itself, to be met head on, let us say. A country whose population is scattered into an infinity of tiny settlements in which civic life is at present impossible, settlements which live isolated from each other, out of the reach of knowledge and of wealth—such a country cannot suddenly create a favorable environment for conscientious and responsible civic life. It would be necessary beforehand to increase the population, for which end our soil would have to be made more productive; to complete our physical communications, increasing our railway system five-fold, our highways tenfold, our airways one hundredfold; to create, as nearly as possible, a system for the communication of ideas as well, with complete postal and telegraphic services and all the means of expression, making these both honest and accessible (books, newspapers, radio); to inaugurate gigantic projects in hygiene, educational propaganda, and economic production aimed at saving from death so many children who today die in their first years. In short, what would be necessary is educative action — slow, consistent, and extremely costly — to give all Mexicans a common consciousness of their past, of their interests, and of their problems. . . .

Of course the Mexican Revolution did not intend to take on this Cyclopean task, much less in a systematic way. Its first act was to attack a regime which not only clung to political power long beyond its time but which with inhuman obstinacy rejected the opportunity of renewing itself by admitting fresh vitality, new blood. The Revolution, consequently, set out only to ventilate, to change the political atmosphere of the country, and, on the positive side, to create public opinion, and to make easier its expression; to provoke opposite views as well and at all events to respect them; to assure periodic and peaceful renewal of the men in power, giving admittance to new talents. The idea itself that the principal task of the Revolution was to alleviate the economic, social, political, and cultural condition of the great masses led to the hope that in these masses there would eventually awaken a genuine interest in government, and a necessity to participate in it in order to defend their new rights and interests. . . .

It was no mean feat to replace the principal government leaders at short intervals, and many times in spite of their wishes and their efforts. Thus was dictatorship avoided, and even the dominant and prolonged influence of any one man. But one cannot forget that this renewal in office has sometimes been brought about at the price of violence and even of crime; nor that the process has had a flavor of dynastic rule and palace intrigue rather than of popular choice, so narrow and so uniform has been the group from which the "elect" have come! Nor can one forget that the process has been truly fissiparous, reproducing itself after the manner of inferior biological organisms.

More significant yet is the fact that these changes in office have not undergone to date the only test that could give them a genuinely democratic character — victory at the polls of a party or group which is alien or, better, yet, opposed to the government. This last perhaps was not a matter of distressing urgency while the Revolution had sufficient prestige and moral authority to suppose that the people were with it, and that consequently it did not matter very much who was its physical embodiment. But now that the Revolution has lost this prestige and moral authority, when even its aims are confounded, now it should be necessary to submit to the people the actual naming of its leaders, for the question is no longer a matter of persons but of what is known esoterically as "the system." Then one might see whether Mexico's civic progress has been if not complete at least genuine. Moreover, let us not be deceived if this test should occur when it is too late: in six years, for example, the differences between the Mexican Revolution and the conservative parties may be so insubstantial that the latter may slip into the government, no longer as opponents but as near relations. Very much the same thing would happen if the revolutionary government made slight electoral concessions to the opposition parties, concessions which, while sufficient for the government to sprinkle itself with the rosewater of democracy, would prevent the opposition from participating in any effective way in the government, but which nevertheless would give full satisfaction to the interests of those parties, especially their economic interests, by means of a "constructive" government program. In such a case, not only would there be no democratic advance but the Revolution would reach the extremes of sterility, for all of its efforts would be expended in retaining power, with no other motive but political and economic greed.

The blackest of omens is the role played by the Congress in the revolutionary era. . . . In any democratic country the congress continues to discharge . . . important functions, acting as censor to the executive, as an organ expressing public opinion, and as final judge in acts of such great national importance as the declaration of war. If we judge our own according to this model . . . our judgment cannot be other than the most vehement and absolute condemnation. In the revolutionary legislature there never has occurred a single debate that deserves to be remembered, as do those of the legislatures of 1856 to 1876. . . . The revolutionary congresses have been as servile as those of the Díaz regime, with the difference that the latter was by definition a tyranny, and that the Revolution is, also by definition, rebellion, independence. In the eyes of the nation, without consideration of classes or groups, there is nothing so despicable as a congressman or a senator. They have become the yardstick of all human misery. That is why the civic progress that Mexico has achieved in these last years seems so vulnerable, because to expect the restoration of the Congress in its full prestige as a governmental organ essential to a democracy is hopeless. . . .

The case of Mexico's modern press is pathetic because in any European or Yankee capital, and in several of South America, there is always some newspaper which is honest and effective, to which one may turn in search of an informed and just opinion, a newspaper which not only records the facts truthfully but which comments and evaluates. That is why the press of this country must carry upon its shoulders an immense responsibility: it has exchanged the superior and lasting satisfaction of enlightening the public for the fugitive and worldly pleasure of enriching itself; it has denied to the people of Mexico, in sum, all guidance and all light.

Extreme class distinctions are a very old phenomenon in Mexico; it could be said in fact that all our history has been one long and distressing effort to diminish them. There were social inequalities among the Indian communities before the Conquest; they existed during the colonial period and during the era of the war for Independence. The Porfirio Díaz regime, therefore, cannot be saddled with responsibility for all of them; and yet, its long duration, its very stability, made these differences more apparent and more rigid, incarnate in actual persons, with that irritating ostentation which resides in the palpable.

The Mexican Revolution was in fact a revolt of the impoverished many against the wealthy few. And since the wealth of the country was agricultural, revolution was directed perforce against the great landowners. For that reason, too, agrarian reform took in large measure the oversimplified character of a mere distribution of the great riches of the few to alleviate the poverty of the many. Once it had triumphed, the Revolution made some efforts — few, weak, and almost always foolish — to justify agrarian reform on other grounds: those of jurisprudence, economics, and even agricultural technology. But the reason which made reform irresistible came from the purest Christian source: a feeling of obvious social injustice.

Unfortunately, in order to endure, even a measure justified by the best moral and social reasons needs some success to sustain it; in the case of economic activity success can be measured only in terms of profits made. These in turn depend — as economists proclaim to no avail — on the good use of factors of production. Now then, agriculture during the Díaz regime was weak in leadership and initiative since it became in large measure an extractive industry owned by absentees; it also was weak in respect to the soil because of natural limitations and lack of technology. On the other hand it was strong in regard to capital because whether much or little it all belonged to the landowner, and because the labor involved, moderate and somewhat mechanical, received an extremely low wage.

From this point of view — and it is of course the most important one — it could be said at first that agrarian reform was socially justified because it gave the peasant the satisfaction of being a landowner. But as time went on it could maintain itself only if the peasant-owner received more from his work than he had as a peasant-hired man. For such an improvement it was necessary that the new agriculture be more profitable than the old, and this required in turn that the elements of production be employed in a better fashion. It was necessary that the leadership be wiser, that a new capital advantageously replace that of the landowner, and that capital and technology be used to overcome some of our more serious natural limitations, which since times long past had been strangling Mexican agriculture.

This was a problem that required vision and initiative, technology, consistency, and honesty; and in every way the Revolution was quite inadequate to these needs. It lacked the vision necessary to grasp the panorama of our agriculture and to draw from it what might justly be called the strategy of agrarian reform. Reform should have begun in the zones where industrial crops were cultivated (sugar, coffee, cotton), the most prosperous and advanced, and not—as really took place—in the cereal zones, on the plateau, where the natural conditions of soil and climate are decidedly unfavorable. Initiative was lacking also, for the Revolution awakened too late to the idea that agrarian reform involved more than partitioning the great estates and giving the pieces to the peasants. This fact is evident: the first credit institution for the new agriculture and the initial attempt to reform teaching of agricultural methods date from 1925, that is, ten years after the first agrarian law, the famous one of January 6, 1915.

Technology was lacking; from the beginning it was not understood that merely shifting the title to the land could not produce the miracle of greater profits from labor which operated under exactly the same physical, economic, and technological conditions. No serious effort was made to discover what changes in methods and in crops could best overcome the unfavorable conditions in which our agriculture has always existed. . . .

There was also a lack of consistency, of arduous and sustained effort, the only kind which could lead to tangible and enduring results. It is sufficient to examine the consistency . . . of the ordinary . . . procedure by which the *ejidos* have been parceled out. It will be seen then that there was no consistency and that furthermore the grants of land have not always been dictated by prudence or necessity, but rather by the desire of each particular person in power to appear as the bravest dispenser of lands. Consistency in the form or logic and thoroughness also was lacking; the lands were given to the peasants but not the means to process the products which they derived from the land. The flour, rice, and sugar mills, the equipment for drying and roasting coffee beans, the cotton gins, and the oil presses remained the property of the former owners of the land, that is to say, of the enemies of the new owners under the agrarian law. Furthermore, many of the great projects of the Revolution should have been inspired by the firm belief that agrarian reform must be successful at all costs. A great part of the educational and sanitation work should have been developed in relation to the agrarian colonies; highways should never have been built merely to attract tourists until the *ejidos* had the roads necessary for their social and economic ends. The same is true of irrigation projects, public health, and social improvement.

As for honesty—is it necessary to give details?

This is not to say, nevertheless, that agrarian reform did not produce some favorable results; only that its success has not been great enough to command a favorable public opinion. The truth is that the program is in the worst condition possible. Its destructive work was harsh enough to bring down upon it all the hate and resentment of those who suffered thereby, and of those whose interests are opposed to the principles which inspired it; but in its constructive aspects its success has not been sufficiently clear to maintain the unshakable faith of those who expected of it terrestrial bliss for ten or twelve million Mexicans.

IN ITS BEGINNINGS the Mexican Revolution was more a revolution of farmers than of industrial workers, but since it always had a popular character it soon made of labor one of its most useful supports. In its turn the Revolution gave the worker such personality and strength that already in 1917, in Article 123 of the Revolutionary Constitution, the labor question was given equal importance with that received, in Article 27, by the problems of agrarian reform, of mining policy, especially the petroleum question, and in general by the problems of all the "modifications of private property" that occasioned such great alarm among the Mexican and foreign *bourgeoisie*. Labor legislation in time has become more prolix than even the legislation on agrarian reform; the activities and size of the tribunals charged with its application are in no way inferior to those of the administrative organs required by the agrarian laws. The labor movement soon became stronger and more solidly based than the agrarian. Some Mexican government leaders made "socialist" experiments in the labor field which have no parallel in that of agriculture. . . . In sum, the Mexican Revolution became, if you will, more urban than rural. At the same time, the Revolution has encountered few sources of embarrassment and disrepute like those which the labor movement has given it. Why? Because labor at its best has been confused; at its worst it has been irresponsible, dishonest, lacking in superior vision, and even in great initiative or simple political drive. But this, in turn, has its explanation. . . .

The Mexican Revolution did not have sufficient genius to devise a juridical system which, without impeding the spontaneous birth and development of labor disputes, would permit their efficacious solution in the superior interest of the community. . . . It has been so constantly and unnecessarily partial that it has "ganged up" on labor's opponents. All the risk and dignity of a contest between two honest rivals has disappeared. All labor legislation was conceived to favor the worker. It could not and should not be otherwise, since by definition the worker is the weaker party, facing the almost invincible power of wealth. But in administering the legislation, the revolutionary governments, without even condescending to play the friendly conciliator or impartial judge, have ruled almost always in favor of the worker, no matter how notoriously unjust or grotesquely puerile may have been the specific cause defended at the moment by the worker.

Not only have the courts in the majority of cases decided in favor of the worker, but they have always made the employer pay him back wages. In this manner the worker has lost the sense of danger, of risk or adventure inherent in all struggles, which he needs to strengthen him so that he may stand alone and win his own victories. The employer has lost his faith in justice; and once over his first reaction of vengeful resentment, he has set himself to corrupting the labor leaders as the only means of preventing his conflicts with the workers from reaching the courts.

The harm done to the cause of labor—which being the best of causes has a permanent value—has been illimitable and to a certain extent irreparable. In the first place an opposition has been created, so bitter that nowadays labor hardly has a defender who is sincere and disinterested: to capitalists and reactionaries all ills come from the irresponsible and excessive power of the workers; as for honest liberals, they do not want to defend labor's cause without first trying to cleanse it of all the excrescences produced by a blind governmental policy. In the second place, the government has wasted all of its many opportunities to gradually develop in the organization of labor not only a conscience and a sense of responsibility, but also a feeling of independence from official favor and of dependence on its own resources, the latter being as important as the former. The Mexican labor movement has come to depend so completely on protection and support from official sources that it has been transformed into a mere appendage to the government, whose every step it follows: good, doubtful, or frankly censurable. In fact, it is nothing but a governmental instrument and has no other role but to serve the government as a claque. This marriage has been harmful to both spouses. It has prevented the government from resolving problems of great importance to the general economy, such as those of the railroads and the oil fields, problems whose solution would have given it the prestige and authority which it so badly needs. Labor has been degraded and dishonored, and, even worse, it has been condemned to disappear or be pulverized the instant it ceases to hold official favor, leaving no trace except a memory of the sad figure it cut in life, that of the bully.

Nonetheless, the achievements of the Mexican Revolution in pursuing its three major objectives: political liberty, agrarian reform, and labor organization, have been neither slight nor meager. They would have been enough to maintain for a long time the moral authority of revolutionary governments, if in the eyes of the nation the efforts made to achieve these goals had possessed an immaculate probity. What was humanly impossible was to have faith in mediocre and dishonest officials. Thus a general administrative corruption—ostentatious and offensive, always cloaked under a mantle of impunity to which only the most refined virtue should aspire—has spoiled the whole program of the Revolution, with its attempts and its successes, to the point that the country no longer cares to know what the original program was, what efforts were made to achieve it, and whether there were any results. Mexico's sole aspiration is sweeping renewal, true purification, which can be satisfied only by a fire that will raze even the soil itself in which so much evil flourished.

It must be remembered that the Revolution was a most violent movement, whose destructive visage is gradually being forgotten. It exterminated an entire generation of men, many groups, and whole institutions: it wiped out the army and the bureaucracy of Porfirio Díaz' time; it put an end to the most powerful and richest class, that of the great and middle-sized landowners, causing most of the higher and a good part of the petty middle class to disappear; it caused many of the best sources of national wealth—transportation, the sugar industry, all raising of livestock—to languish to the point of extinction. Even some great professional groups—university teachers, for example—saw their ranks so reduced that even their cadres properly ceased to exist. The Mexican Revolution, in sum, created an enormous vacuum of wealth and unmade the social and economic hierarchy that had been fashioned in the course of almost half a century.

This nearly complete devastation of the national wealth was received by some with jubilation, by others as a happy omen that in the future Mexico's resources, though limited, would be equally distributed. At some time in our revolutionary history, the inspiring statement that in Mexico there was not a single millionaire and that large social groups were bettering their economic conditions could have been true. But sad realities soon asserted themselves in the necessity of recreating the wealth which had been destroyed. No greater burden fell on the shoulders of the men of the Revolution; it was the most severe proof of their rectitude, fortitude, and creative capacity. The failure

of the Revolution in this great moral test was the most flagrant of its short-
comings. Instead of being distributed equally among the most numerous
groups and among those in greatest need of moving up the social scale, the
new wealth was allowed to fall into the hands of a few, who of course had no
special merit of any kind. Wherefore the bloody paradox in which the government, while waving the revindicatory flag of an impoverished people, by
prevarication and by theft and embezzlement, created a new high and low
middle class which in the end dragged the Revolution and the country itself
once more to the brink of social and economic inequality.

With the Revolution the previous hierarchy disappeared, and that fact also
contributed to the general dishonesty: the whirlwind carried the rubbish sky-
wards; men suddenly found themselves making salaries of a thousand pesos,
which they tried to preserve forever by stealing a million while the whirlwind
lasted. Not among the least causes for dishonesty in government is the constant insecurity of man and woman in this land, because to the state's omnipo-
tence we must add an arbitrariness which has all the marks of a Biblical curse.
Victim of it the Mexican falls and rises, again and again, during the whole span
of his life until death permanently ends his struggle. And the man who lives
insecurely tries to protect himself, not caring whether in doing so he violates
a law or sets aside a moral precept.

Administrative dishonesty in Mexico has its causes, which we have barely
outlined. They do not mitigate its social monstrosity by a single jot or lessen
in any way its deadly political effects, for the dishonesty of the revolutionary
leaders more than any other factor has split the very heart of the Mexican
Revolution. . . .

If we judge the present situation of Mexico with any degree of severity, it
is difficult to avoid the conclusion that the country is passing through a most
serious crisis. The magnitude of this crisis leads us to think that if it is under-
estimated or ignored, if the best efforts are not immediately employed to lead
the country out of it, Mexico will drift aimlessly, without a definite course,
losing time that cannot be lost by a land so far behind in its progress; and it
will end by entrusting its major problems to inspiration, or to imitation of
and submission to the United States, not only because the United States is a
rich and powerful neighbor but because it has been successful in a way that
we have not been able to imitate. We would call on that country for money,
for technical training, for patterns in culture and art, for political advice; and
we would end by adopting unchanged its whole scale of values, so alien to
our history, our interest, and our taste. To the North American influence, of
itself overpowering, would be added the dissembled conviction of some, the
frank interests of others, the indifference or the pessimism of the majority,

making possible the sacrifice of our nationality and, more important still, of the security, authority, and happiness we may gain by forging our own destinies. Many of Mexico's problems would then be resolved; the country might even enjoy an unaccustomed prosperity. But are we sure that our people, ourselves even, would in truth be happier? Our Indian, for example. Would he gain by passing into the unredeemed status now occupied by the Negro in the United States? . . .

What remedy . . . is there for Mexico's crisis? We have said that it is grave. On the one hand, the cause of the Revolution has ceased to inspire that faith which all navigation charts must inspire if the pilot is to remain at his post; to that must be added the fact that the men of the Revolution have exhausted their moral and political leadership. On the other hand, there is no clear basis on which to found the hope that redemption may come from the Right, because of the interest which it represents, because of its antipopular spirit, and because of its lack of preparation.

The only ray of hope — quite pale and distant to be sure — is that from the Revolution itself there may come a reaffirmation of principles and a purification of men. It may not be worth the trouble to speculate on miracles; but at least I would like to be clearly understood: to reaffirm means to affirm anew, and to purify would mean to use only those men who are unsullied and honest. If principles are not reaffirmed but merely juggled about, if men are not purified but merely dressed up in their Sunday best and decorated with titles (of lawyers!), then there will be no autoregeneration in Mexico; and consequently regeneration will come from the outside. The country will lose much of its national identity, and in no long period of time.

Struggles of a Campesino Leader

Rubén Jaramillo

With the presidential election of Manuel Avila Camacho in 1940, the era of land reform and support for social change ended suddenly and the revolution veered sharply rightward. The politics of class struggle quickly gave way to a state-directed campaign to achieve the goals, and inculcate the values, of modern capitalist development within a postwar world of united, anticommunist nations. The change in the tenor of the regime is dramatically illustrated in the following selection by peasant leader Rubén Jaramillo (an autobiographical account, despite the author's peculiar use of the third person). Jaramillo was born in Tlaquiltenango, Morelos, in 1900. He joined Zapata's army at the age of 15, and became a lifelong adherent of the Zapatista causes of land and liberty for the rural poor. By the end of the 1920s he had emerged as a prominent agrarian leader. He strongly supported the Cárdenas presidency, and Cárdenas returned the favor by supporting Jaramillo's project, the cooperatively run sugar complex of Zacatepec, which was inaugurated in 1938. Jaramillo was elected to the mill's first Council of Administration and Vigilance. He immediately entered into conflict with the mill's federally appointed administrators when he uncompromisingly advocated many reforms in favor of the mill's workers. These conflicts turned more violent with the advent of the Avila Camacho era, as we see in the excerpt below.

Jaramillo would spend much of his life trying to elude death threats from corrupt local powers supported by the federal government. While underground, he remained active in organizing peasants and workers; occasionally, he managed to emerge from hiding long enough to found legal, above-ground organizations. In 1958 President Adolfo López Mateos named him special delegate of the National Peasant Confederation. Frustration with the funereal pace of the government's land reform led Jaramillo to support land invasions and the formation of a socialist collective in 1960, inviting fresh reprisals from his enemies. On May 23, 1962, judicial police and soldiers captured Jaramillo and assassinated him along with his pregnant wife and three sons. No one was ever brought to trial for the crime, which proved to be one of several high-profile episodes that darkened the reputation of the PRI in the postwar era.

Rubén Jaramillo, 1960s. (Reprinted by permission of
Fototeca del INAH, Mexico.)

General Cárdenas invited Jaramillo to dinner at the Tehuiztla spa. State governor Elpidio Perdomo also attended the dinner. This was in December of 1938, ten months after Jaramillo had been named to the [Council of Administration and Vigilance of the Zacatepec Sugar Mill]. It was at this dinner that General Cárdenas told him that General Manuel Avila Camacho was to be the next president of Mexico. Jaramillo said to Cárdenas: "Won't he betray us? You know what Don Maximino[1] is like." Cárdenas responded: "Don Manuel is a good man. Not all the fingers on a hand are the same. I want all of your campesinos to support General Avila Camacho." Jaramillo told him: "I don't like the Avila Camachos. Their history in the state of Puebla is doubtful with respect to our revolutionary ideology, which is what we hope will bring our nation out of its backward state. If this gentleman wishes to take us back to the old days, we will not be in accord." Cárdenas responded: "I'll vouch for General Avila Camacho." Jaramillo then said: "I still have my doubts about the gentleman. But we have confidence in your word, so we will help Don Manuel. But be aware, Mister President, that the lessons you've taught the people can't be taken away. The workers and peasants are revolutionaries, and if Don Manuel deviates from that, we won't stay with him." When the General heard these words, he embraced Jaramillo and offered him the gift of a horse, which he received in February of 1939. . . .

In January of 1940, the members of the Council [of the sugar-mill coopera-tive] were removed. Ambitions had been awakened and some people spoke against Jaramillo, claiming he had an easy job. No sooner was the new council in place than a movement got under way to make the director the sole power at the mill. Such propaganda spread till finally the Council gave all power to the director, at that time a so-called engineer named Severino Carrera Peña, a crafty, thieving politician from way back. From that moment on, all of the councilors of the cooperative were mere tools of the directors, who subju-gated the members of the cooperative by getting the army, the judicial police and paid gunmen to watch the directors' backs and to assassinate any mem-bers who spoke out against their injustices.

Because the Second World War was going on, peasants and workers of many cooperatives thought to ask for higher wages or a better price for their cane. The *ejido* members met and named a commission to seek these improve-ments. Jaramillo and others were named to the commission, which called itself the "Union of Cane Producers of the Mexican Republic." Jaramillo him-self was the representative of this organization in the first National Commit-tee, provisionally established in the offices of the National Sugar Syndicate. . . .

The issue of increasing the price of the cane was discussed in the offices of the Syndicate. The director of the Zacatepec mill, Carrera Peña, opposed this move and sought ways to frustrate Jaramillo's struggle. One day the Union held an assembly to inform the peasants of the results of its efforts with the government. Carrera Peña was invited to the forum, and he demonstrated his extreme hypocrisy by seeming to agree with the Union's efforts. He agreed to support the contents of Circular 16, which had been a triumph for Jaramillo because it announced measures that would bring great gains to the campe-sinos. The director offered to abide by this Circular, promising to respond to the demands it made on behalf of the mill's campesinos and workers.

When Jaramillo heard the director's words, he said: "I'm sure that the di-rector will stand by his word and that we, the peasants and workers, should stand by ours in terms of unifying to meet our true goals in this magnificent sugar industry, which undoubtedly is a prelude to the economic happiness that will come to the workers through this great Revolution. If we follow the path of simple justice, we will surely build the basis of true happiness and progress for a large part of the state of Morelos. But if we lose sight of our responsibilities as workers and campesinos and give way to selfishness, fool-ish passions, calumnies, intrigues, personal ambitions and divisions, then this mill — which today is the pride of the Revolution — will become a center of misery, vice, discord, crime and slavery. If that happens, this mill will be like a dead horse devoured by vultures. United we will be strong and respected; divided and disorganized, we will be easily defeatable victims. Thus, no campesino should separate from his compatriots, and should die before becoming a traitor. For my part, I swear to God that I speak with all the sincerity and purity of my heart, when I say that I prefer death to the smallest act of betrayal against you, men of my class, to whom I give my heart and will give my life if necessary. Regardless of the person or people, I will struggle against those who willfully become our oppressors and exploiters. Be assured that what I tell you is true, and I affirm it repeatedly because I know that we are watched over by thugs who serve their masters like dogs drooling for breadcrumbs."

Director Carrera Peña invited Jaramillo to his home. Jaramillo went, along with two old friends. When they arrived, the director offered them drinks. Jaramillo declined, his friends accepted. The director said: "Look, Jaramillo, I've called you here because I hope that from now on we can be good friends." Jaramillo interrupted him: "Sure, we can be friends, director, just as long as no harm comes to us or our interests." The director replied: "From your tone I can't tell if you mean what you say or are just showing off in front of these campesino representatives." "Look, director," replied Jaramillo, "when a hen lays an egg, we take it in our hands and we know there's a life inside, and that life will emerge after an incubation period; we know it will be a chicken, but we can't know what color it will be until it leaves the shell. That's how it is with the matter before us now, director: I only know that you and others have planned something. That's the egg. But I also know it won't be long before your evil chicken is born."

The director replied: "Make no mistake, Jaramillo; we recognize you as a worthy campesino, but we still hope that you'll come around. Don't forget that if you accept our propositions, you will rise up to our status. I'm here by order of the federal government, and I'm prepared to offer you whatever I can. I'm sure the government supports me in my dealings with you. The government and I are interested in solving the problems with Zacatepec's workers." Jaramillo answered: "Director, the campesinos and workers have you outnumbered, and they're just as resolved to win out as you are. You've made it clear that you wish to defend the interests of those who sent you here. Don't forget that you and I are from different classes and that I, like you, am ready to defend the men of my class. So we're both justified in our positions, no?" The director responded: "In any case, the terms of Circular 16 will take effect during the *next* harvest, not the one currently under way. As far as the increase in the workers' wages is concerned, for the time being there will be no change." Jaramillo said: "Why didn't you say this to the assembly? Were you hoping to bribe me? Neither you nor anyone else will be able to do that. The terms of the Circular must be put into effect *now*, not during the next harvest."

This occurred on the first Sunday of February, 1939, at around four o'clock in the afternoon. The director told Jaramillo: "Think well about what I've told you; you'll come to agree with me." "Fine, director. Wait for my reply." With this said, Jaramillo left with his compatriots. On the road, Jaramillo said to his friends: "I don't know where these friends of ours will take us. Their hearts are poisoned toward us and, well . . . Look, Chinto, I want you to go to the campesinos and tell them that on the last Sunday of this month we'll have a meeting in the union hall at ten o'clock in the morning, and we'll discuss what you just heard the director say." Chinto, a dynamic man of 65 years, did as instructed and on the last Sunday of February the hall was filled with workers and campesinos. . . . Many workers rose to express their opinions, and some suggested that a work stoppage be called in the fields and factories. Both the labor and campesino sectors agreed, and we decided to bring our demands back to the director. If he refused to comply, the strike would begin.

The petition was brought to the director, who repeated what he had told Jaramillo previously, that no modification would take place until the following harvest and that wages and sugar cane prices would remain the same. This was stated before a commission of laborers and campesinos. When the commission received this response, the members grew angry at the director's hypocrisy. They immediately notified the director of the time set by the Federal Labor Law for the initiation of a strike. Still, the director did nothing to remedy the situation.

This occurred in the month of March, 1942.[2] If we remember correctly, on April 9 of that year, at about eleven o'clock in the morning, at the sound of the whistle, everyone left the factory and the campesinos stopped cutting cane. But before this happened, Director Carrera Peña, instead of working out a fair and reasonable agreement with the workers, had gone to Governor Perdomo and given him $50,000, suggesting that Rubén Jaramillo be assassinated. Perdomo personally went to Zacatepec with General Pablo Díaz Dávila, chief of the 24th Military Zone, and two police officers, to detain Jaramillo, who at that moment was signing some documents of the Sugar Cane Workers' Union.

A man nicknamed "El Chícharo" ("The Pea"), one of Perdomo's assistants, arrived to invite Jaramillo to the director's house where Perdomo was waiting to discuss the price of cane and the workers' wages. Jaramillo was a fighter, but he was not malicious or mistrustful. When he finished signing the documents, he went with "El Chícharo" to the director's house, where Perdomo sat with a drawn face. The governor, with no explanation, ordered his men to put Jaramillo in the car, said goodbye to the director, and set out on the road to Cuernavaca. . . .

They went to the Cortés Palace, where Governor Perdomo had his office. Upon entering, Perdomo ordered José Urbán and Professor Alfonso Casales to look for some papers, undoubtedly the director's denunciation of Rubén M. Jaramillo.

The two could not find those papers. Then Perdomo, with two of the most bloodthirsty gunmen of his staff flanking the door, their hands on the triggers of their pistols, said to Jaramillo: "Sit down." The two men sat face to face.

Perdomo, in a haughty voice that betrayed his arrogance at being governor, said to Jaramillo: "I'm fed up with your nonsense." "Nonsense?" replied Jaramillo. "Shut up, you son of a . . ." said Perdomo, "I'm talking, damn it! You go around telling the campesinos that they're victims of injustice, living in misery because the government exploits them. You must know that the happiest, luckiest men in the world are those who've received a parcel of land from the Revolution. And how can you, who know them, defend these malcontents? Why do you defend these lazy communists? Today you threaten the director—a wonderful person—with a strike, just to pacify these lazy campesinos and workers. If you carry out this strike, I will have you shot. Don't forget that Cárdenas ruled in the past, but that now it's Avila Camacho who leads the country."

To this Jaramillo responded: "I think you're my judge and I'm your prisoner, and you have to let me talk. If you don't, you're as guilty as I am." Then Perdomo said: "Talk, then, let's see what you have to say."

Jaramillo began: "You say that I know absolutely nothing about cane, but I can assure you that now I am more informed of the cultivation and processing of sugar than ever before. When I promise better benefits for the campesinos, it's because I know what I'm doing with my petition, which is legal and does not endanger the state or federal treasuries. My petition is based on justice and not on the whims of the workers. We must not forget or abandon the millhands and campesinos, because they are all workers. They are not lazy, as you say. The Fatherland owes all of its strength and grandeur to them. As for your suggestion that the workers are communists, I don't understand that doctrine."

Then Perdomo interrupted: "Do you mean . . ." Jaramillo said: "I have the right to speak, no? This business about how yesterday we had Cárdenas and today we have Avila Camacho, I've nothing to say about that. I'm not a follower of men. I am a follower of justice and of the people, the rest does not concern me. You say I claim that the campesinos suffer greatly while you maintain that they are the luckiest, happiest men in the world with the parcels that the Revolution gave them. I ask you: why did you leave your own plot abandoned, all covered with weeds and gone to waste, forgetting the happiness that the *ejido* gave you? Well, what do you have to say? I say you abandoned that plot because with it, it would be impossible for you to build houses here and there, have a new car each month, have lots of women and money in the bank—all those things that exploitative politics makes possible. You've even forgotten your own family because you're all puffed up with the vanity of power."

At this Perdomo grew furious, and growling like a caged lion he said to Jaramillo: "No son of a . . . has ever talked like that to me." Then he lunged at Jaramillo with his fists flying, and Jaramillo, defending himself, said: "Look, this is not the proper place for what you want to do." Perdomo responded: "Wherever, you son of a . . ." Jaramillo said: "We just came through the countryside where we could have knocked each other silly, you miserable miser." During this attack, no one—not Professor Urbán, Professor Alfonso Casales or the gunmen—was able to contain the ire of that jackal, who defamed that temple of justice while they looked on.

Finally, hot and tired, Perdomo said to Jaramillo: "Now get out of here and go to [hell]." To which Jaramillo responded: "Only you know the way there." The gunmen retreated from the door to the interior of the office. Perdomo said: "If you go through with the strike, I'll have you shot." And Jaramillo replied: "Pilate, I've written what I've written."[3] Jaramillo left. . . . This was seven days before the strike.

The workers and campesinos, upon hearing of these events, went looking for Jaramillo, and they found him in Temixco, Morelos, together with Isaac Hain. They returned with Jaramillo to Zacatepec and immediately, in spite of everything, agreed to proceed with their plans for the strike.

At about two o'clock on the afternoon of the inauguration of the strike, the director visited the factory and found it empty except for Adolfo Arenal, the chief mechanic. Everything was in disorder because the factory was still running. It was a scandal. The cane juices flooded the factory, so that the director said to Arenal: "What do we do? The factory may explode. How many soldiers will it take to get this factory back in order?" Arenal told him: "No, director, the soldiers can only handle rifles, machine guns, cannon and planes, when they are trained to do so; this industry needs skilled workers, not soldiers. There is nothing to do but to shut down the factory." "Well, do it at once," said the director. And so it was.

At about three in the afternoon, the director ordered an ex-Zapatista by the name of Teodomiro Ortiz, "El Polilla" ("The Moth"), a hired thug, to take a car and five of his soldiers to the *ejidos* to invite campesinos to take the places of the workers. At about eleven o'clock that night, several trucks arrived carrying campesinos who were immediately put to work in the factory in place of the millhands. Although it was far from perfect, they got the factory running, creating the impression for the government that there was no strike. Thus, with great losses, director Carrera Peña went on with his plan.

Within a day or so, "El Polilla" received an order to take 25 soldiers with him to force the peasants to cut and haul the cane, and to pursue the most conspicuous figures in the working-class movement. As a result, Filiberto Vigueras, Lucas Alonso and Félix Serdán Nájera were arrested and sent to the penitentiary in Cuernavaca.

The campesinos, unaccustomed to working-class movements and facing the threats of "El Polilla," were intimidated and, lacking respect for their own ideals, agreed to work. The workers held out for a month and a half, although many—frightened, hungry and urged on by people outside of the union— turned themselves over to the director, asking forgiveness and soliciting work. Others stood firm, resolved to achieve a just and honorable outcome. Those workers and campesinos, conscious of their civil rights, held out for a little over two months; but ultimately, because they posed an imminent threat to the administration, they were dismissed from their jobs.

During all this time, Jaramillo and others made great efforts to keep up the fight, a difficult task because it involved a government enterprise. As a result of the events described above, Jaramillo was removed as a member of the cooperative, though he continued to cultivate sugar cane.

Finally, in October of 1940, Carrera Peña, plagued by his conscience, had the good grace to visit Rubén M. Jaramillo on his plot of land, offering him every form of assistance if he would abandon the campesino movement. The director said that those campesinos would never improve their lot because they didn't know the difference between those who treated them well and those who treated them poorly; "they are always the same, always disloyal."

To this, Jaramillo said: "Look, director, I'm a campesino and I don't think I'm disloyal or ungrateful. I've always been firm, loyal, sincere and dedicated to my duties and ideals. I don't know what you and others mean by these accusations against the poor farmers. If the campesinos are as you describe, it's your own fault, because you've neglected the responsibility of educating them, and whatever education you *have* given them is false, hypocritical and lacking in all truth and sincerity. So the campesinos are what they are. But there will come a day when these people that you, their exploiters, so despise, will rouse themselves and unite, and then we'll see what's in store . . ."

Jaramillo remained uneasy. He was constantly glancing over his shoulder due to the threat from the government, the director's gunmen, and the campesinos corrupted by the politicians, both large and small.

Eventually, Elpidio Perdomo left the government. His secretary, Jesús Castillo López, took his position and followed the same policies. Don Severino Carrera Peña also left his position as director, leaving the office to his son, who followed the same route as his father.

Rubén M. Jaramillo suffered all manner of intrigues, insults and threats, and no authority would hear his continued protests. Finally, at seven o'clock on February 12, 1943, "El Polilla," the director's henchman, and 15 other men, came to lay siege to Jaramillo's house and assassinate him, but fortunately he had been warned. He and his family had gone to another house, leaving the doors locked. The assassins beat down the doors. When they didn't find him, they left, but that was not the end of it. Three days later, on February 15, five agents of the judicial police, the most criminal of government agents, went to Jaramillo's plot where, despite all his vicissitudes, he was busy working on his cane. By the time they arrived, he was already in the hills to the south. The agents questioned the man in charge of the fieldwork, who told them that Jaramillo was in Zacatepec. The agents left, thinking that they would find him there.

Jaramillo now thought that the situation could not be resolved by means of the laws and the authorities, which were all in league against him. None of the authorities was willing to hear his arguments. This state of affairs continued until Wednesday, February 17.

On that day, Mario Olea was on the bridge at La Cantora with six well-armed agents, awaiting Jaramillo's return home. At about four o'clock in the afternoon of the 17th, Felipe Olmedo came to Fidel Brito's land, where Jaramillo had some sugar cane, and told him: "I just passed the bridge at La Cantora, and Mario Olea is there with six men. They have their pistols and two machine guns. I think they're waiting for you there. You might want to take other measures." Olmedo had barely given this warning and left, when Jaramillo's wife came to say that four agents from the judicial police had come to their home demanding that she give him up. By now, Jaramillo understood that the danger was very serious and he left immediately on the horse that General Cárdenas had given him. That horse was named "El Agrarista." . . .

It was around six o'clock in the afternoon. Jaramillo had gone to the colony of Manzanares, where he sent a friend to inspect the road. The friend returned and told him that the path was clear. Jaramillo went home and told his wife: "You know, I think I must abandon everything now and give all my attention to protecting myself. If I don't they'll kill me like a miserable dog, and I can't let that happen. I'm convinced that doing the right thing—speaking on behalf of the campesinos — is a crime in the eyes of this government, and I believe that's what's happening to me. God knows, I can't be accused of any other crime. They're doing this to me because I haven't let them bribe me to betray those campesinos they call ignorant, stupid and disloyal. That makes me mad because I'm a campesino myself, a member of the suffering, backward class, and I'll never abandon them. To the contrary, I'll work as long as God lets me, to see that one day these men, who now are mocked and abused, can get the justice they deserve. I know that they are what they are because of ignorance."

Jaramillo added: "You are everything to me, and it hurts me to tell you that bitter days await us, that this little bit of happiness that God has given us will end and we will pass through waters of bitterness, through fires of sorrow, and through fields of trouble, but at the end, God willing, we'll have peace." Saying this, he took all of his papers, set aside the most important ones, and burned the rest. . . .

Finally, after taking care of everything he thought necessary, at about three in the afternoon of Friday, February 19, . . . Jaramillo saddled his horse, "El Agrarista," put his poncho over the horse's haunch, changed his clothes, embraced and kissed his young wife, . . . mounted his horse and left.

Notes

1. Maximino Avilo Camacho, brother of president-to-be Manuel, became governor in 1937. His corruption and propensity for ruthless violence — often at the expense of the state's peasantry — were legendary. *Ed.*

2. This date is as it appears in the original text, though it seems likely that Jaramillo intended to say 1940. *Ed.*

3. In 1939 Governor Perdomo had a crisis in the State Chamber of Deputies and he asked Jaramillo for help. Jaramillo managed to win him popular support and served as his intermediary before the President of the Republic. From that time, Perdomo considered Jaramillo his protector. This is why Jaramillo allowed himself to speak this way during the interview recounted above.

Art and Corruption

David Alfaro Siqueiros

During the 1920s, under the auspices of Education Minister José Vasconcelos, the Mexican government began sponsoring artists to adorn public buildings with ambitious murals celebrating the forging of the Mexican nation in a series of popular struggles that began with the Conquest and culminated in the epic Revolution of 1910. The most celebrated of these muralists were Diego Rivera, José Clemente Orozco, and the present author, David Alfaro Siqueiros (1896–1974). In 1922 their Union of Technical Workers, Painters, and Sculptors issued a manifesto that denounced bourgeois art in favor of a monumental public art that would be uniquely Mexican. Siqueiros was the most technically innovative of the great muralists, and also the most outspoken and resolutely Marxist; indeed, for decades he played an active role in the Mexican Communist Party. He would pay for his convictions with several stints in prison and in exile—including the entire six-year term of President Adolfo López Mateos (1958–1964)—most often for the crime of "social dissolution." In the following excerpt, written in the late 1960s, Siqueiros looks back rather bitterly on the postrevolutionary state's faded idealism in the aesthetic sphere.

[When the Mexican mural movement first began in the early 1920s,] the new political fervor that would later shape our painting had not yet become manifest; the new social generator, the source of the highest voltage, had barely begun to appear. But what *did* appear was the enemy. Already some people had begun to insist that painting had no place as a proselytizing force, as a stimulant for polemics, as an ideological tool. They claimed that photography and cinematography were better suited to such purposes. "Abandon propaganda painting," they told us. The reactionary university professors had paid no attention when we painted symbols of eternity—the natural elements, Boticellian Madonnas—into our murals in the National Preparatory School. Those same professors, who would smile amiably when they viewed our works-in-progress, began to incite the reactionary students and to provoke the entire country against us, once we began painting other themes. They said our paintings were obscene; that we were destroying architecture with paintings that did not complement the marvelous colonial style of the buildings; that the State should immediately call a halt to our grotesqueries, because our aims were subversive. The professors complained that the mural painters were trying to push the Government into taking more radical attitudes in agrarian reform, in defense of the workers, in social security, in the struggle against imperialism. They even grumbled about how, in early 1924 in the pages of our [Communist] newspaper, *El Machete,* we had made the absurd demand that petroleum be nationalized.

The inevitable happened: groups of armed students attacked and partially destroyed our murals. To defend the murals, we had to engage in gunfights with the students—even though we, in terms of age and the inception of our movement, were students ourselves. But that counter-revolutionary offensive—which was also an offensive against the Mexican Revolution, of which our work was a manifestation in the field of art—led to the mobilization of the people, which allowed us to talk loudly and with far greater resonance about the importance of our movement. The workers' unions and the agrarian organizations gathered around us in great numbers. In one magnificent instance, a battalion of Yaqui Indians who were staying in the building occupied by the National School of Jurisprudence came to the National Preparatory School to say they were putting themselves at our service in the defense of paintings which were conceived with the political aim of bringing about the social transformation of our country.

The theorists who had denounced our paintings as politically useless now took a different tack. They began to accuse our murals of being academic and backward, arguing that they were far removed from the "civilized" painting that was being done in Europe. In other words, they wanted to return Mexico to the Porfirian period, when our painters could only imitate European currents and fashions, using absolutely none of their own creative talent or national idiosyncrasy. But these criticisms did not accomplish much, because the government at that time was still ascending along a revolutionary path. Before long, of course, it would begin to change its political line. To a certain point, then, the government was still interested in mural painting—it served to adorn its demagogy, giving it a popular tone. Our murals allowed the government to present itself to the people as a government which favored an advanced revolutionary program.

When the political activity of the painters increased, and when our means of ideological communication grew wider and more efficacious, the now-capitulating government called us to account: "If you continue publishing your newspaper *El Machete* in opposition to the policies of the Government, using its pages to defend the points of view of the radical sectors of the working class, you will have to abandon mural painting, because we will withdraw your contracts."

The painters who were members of the union met and discussed the problem, and unfortunately we split. Corruption had appeared. There were some who said: "Even if we have to sell our soul to the devil, we will keep on painting murals." Others thought: "If politics impedes us from continuing to paint murals, we will leave Mexico and go to the United States." But there were some who obstinately insisted: "If we don't have the stationary walls of public buildings, we will have the mobile walls of our newspaper's pages."

What was "public art"? "Public" meant public for everyone, for the citizenry, not just for one sector of it, not just for the elite. . . . Public art had disappeared several centuries before, and its techniques were forgotten. Mural painting, as a collective movement, had been extinct since the end of the Renaissance. The bourgeoisie, with its concepts of individualism and private property, took art out of the crowded places, away from the places where the masses congregated. They simply stuffed it in a bag and carried it off to their homes. The bourgeoisie had no interest in getting close to the masses. Thus they created private art as we know it today, which is prevalent throughout the world. There was an increase in landscape painting, portraiture, pictures of dead nature; unilateral currents arose, leading to abstractionism and then to tachism,[1] pop-art and op-art, to the many and very frivolous and pointless variations on these styles. The bourgeoisie, the rich — who were the only ones buying artwork, the only ones who had the right to be interested in works of art — no longer wanted dolorous religious scenes in their homes: No more descents from the cross, no more Magdalenas bathed in sorrow. They did not need that; they wanted happiness, tranquility, something that showed their euphoria as a class in power. They did not want always to be shown the misery they themselves had created, or to be reminded of how they had betrayed their own people. They wanted to enjoy their fortunes quietly.

In our Mexican movement, we felt we had no reason to produce what they tried to make us produce. We sought out places where we could create our public art; but we were still bohemians, and aesthete attitudes were not totally annihilated in us (that virus does not die as easily as is supposed), so we chose buildings for their architectonic beauty, not taking into account the sorts of people who passed through them. Our confusion was a natural byproduct of the world we lived in. It was necessary that the working class should appear and tell us: "You don't want to help us, you want to help the Mexican Revolution. But down here things are very bad. You must adopt a thematic, you must begin with political content, with subjects that correspond to the primordial proposition you have proclaimed." . . .

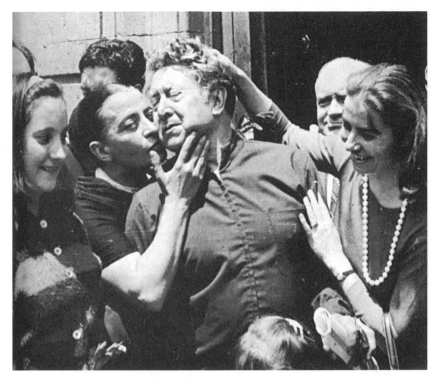

David Alfaro Siqueiros being greeted by his wife and daughters upon leaving the penitentiary, July 14, 1964. Siqueiros had served four years for the crime of "social dissolution." (Reprinted by permission of Fototeca del INAH, Mexico.)

Art cannot break down the barriers which society erects, except in a relative way, as is the case of the monumental painting of Mexico. We carried out our work under singularly difficult conditions. At the beginning, our art was based upon the best aspects of the Mexican Revolution, which was still alive then. Afterward, the government's intention of dominating our ideology became apparent, and our struggles began. The struggles of many of my colleagues were positively heroic: I believe them to be the most heroic liberation struggles carried on by any artists in any part of the modern world. I believe there is a huge difference between the Mexican pictorial movement and the contemporary movements of other capitalist countries. Our movement had—and has—a different sense. We have fallen and we have picked ourselves up; we have been in and out of jails; but always we have made every effort to create an art that could reach the multitudes. We might do this well, very well, fairly well, or very badly; but our position is just and our attitude is just. We have linked ourselves to the popular struggles and we have tried to heed the mandate of the people. We were not heartbroken when the people, upon viewing our earliest works, told us: "We don't understand what you're trying to say." We joined with the people and worked together to acquire a political education. The artist who joins with the people and their revolution in a purely emotional sense will never be able to bring the force of the revolution into his own work. The artist who does not delve into ideology always thinks that art is one thing, and society another.

When, in 1964, the People's Electoral Front postulated me as a candidate for senator of the Republic, I declared: "One of the fundamental points of my activity in trying to win this position in the national congress will be to struggle for the freedom of artistic creation in all orders, and, accordingly, for the defense of our mural movement, the fruit of the Revolution in Mexico." At that moment I recalled the attitude of President Alvaro Obregón, who favored the development of radical muralism, and granted us much bureaucratic protection — particularly to our *compañero* of the Union of Painters and Sculptors, Diego Rivera — at the same time that he ordered the confiscation of entire editions of our newspaper *El Machete,* the official organ of the aforementioned union, and had its editors jailed. There were also many "friendly" calls for us to understand that the government was not an enemy of the revolutionary political content of our paintings, as was demonstrated by its attitude toward muralism: the government, they claimed, opposed only those portions of our movement that condemned concrete attitudes that the government had adopted out of necessity or due to international pressure. The reason General Obregón's government confiscated an edition of *El Machete* and jailed its editors was because we published a drawing by José Clemente Orozco condemning, with strong sarcasm, the first serious toleration of the illegal political activities of the clergy. This was the logical reaction of an oligarchy that was beginning to develop. The presidents Plutarco Elías Calles, Emilio Portes Gil, Pascual Ortiz Rubio and Abelardo L. Rodríguez continued, expanded, and deepened that repressive line, which was manifested on occasion by a reduction in the numbers of commissions for mural painting. During the administrations of Manuel Avila Camacho, Miguel Alemán, and Adolfo Ruiz Cortines, the persecution and censures of the Mexican pictorial movement — fruit of the Mexican Revolution in the field of culture — were extended from graphic to monumental art. A work by Rivera was removed from the Palace of Fine Arts because it eloquently criticized the bellicose international policies of the United States, France, and England. The National Institute of Fine Arts began, in rather dissembling fashion, to restrict the freedom of philosophical-political expression. Thus, the most important official artistic institution adopted the inquisitorial line sponsored by the United States. . . .

Every revolution in social life brings with it an equivalent transformation in artistic forms, and consequent modifications in esthetics. The French Revolution did away with feudalistic forms in economics and culture, replacing them with the new forms of capitalism. In painting, new styles were produced that were most appropriate for widescale individual acquisition, since painting had become a physical and spiritual complement to the bourgeois home. The religious and aristocratic art of the Middle Ages and the Renaissance disappeared. The easel painting is the pictorial form most suitable to capitalism, it is the materialization of its market. . . .

In general, easel painting is limited by the environment, and mural painting is constrained by reduction of physical space. But artists believe themselves to be free only because they are not contracted to do works on themes that are determined beforehand. Currently, the standard practice is for the buyers to go see works that are already completed, instead of commissioning works with a certain content and of certain dimensions, as they did before. But the commission is implicit: the environment dictates the themes which used to be set by the buyers. Speaking of artistic freedom, Picasso told me one day that the bourgeoisie never imposed any theme upon him; but Picasso knows as well as I that modern buyers always prefer something light and amiable. Although the artist creates for man, it is *class* that determines art. The true artist creates for everyone, but the rich man hides art away wherever he pleases. This fact determines many aspects of art. I myself have, on many occasions, had to make art for the private homes of the rich. There are those who confuse the cause with the consequence, and very dramatically denounce the "commercial capitulation of artists," but they do this with a totally anti-didactic method worthy of puritan mystics and pharisaic moralists. When in 1953 I did a portrait of the architect Carlos Lazo, I declared: "I will sell you the portrait, but not my ideology. The fact that I am painting a portrait of the architect Carlos Lazo does not in any way mean that I am retracting my ideas about neo-Porfirianism in architecture. I will sell you the portrait, but not my ideology, just as I suppose you do not surrender your ideology in exchange for the portrait." I have done portraits of beautiful ladies and of ugly bureaucrats. Naturally, the ugliest have been those who have capitulated in the social struggle, or who have been the frank enemies of the progress of the people; I have included these people in my murals.

The tourist market of the United States also contributed powerfully to the distortion of pictorial production in the generations following my own, in a most lamentable way. First, it took young artists away from muralism and brought them around to easel painting; next, it led them from dramatic themes to "Mexican curios" which became increasingly innocuous; and fi-

nally, it led them to adopt formal styles that changed with the speed of speculations on the Stock Exchange. What is really worrisome is that the youngest
generation, as a consequence of this, has no contact with the living realities
of the country, and this is worrisome because that generation has lived its
life in the climate of capitulation to the government oligarchy. An immense
political cowardice has filtered down to the bone-marrow of the majority of
artists, thanks to several decades of ideological lackeydom. Archaeologism—
the superficial imitation of remote antiquity—is characteristic of plastic, pictorial, and sculptural production at the present time. In dealing with tradition,
the artists of today eat the husk and throw away the fruit. That is what the
radicals of the artistic vanguard do. They extract styles—or rather the culmination of phenomena—totally forgetting the causes that determined those
styles. For them neither the tools, nor the materials, nor the historic concept
of reality, nor socio-political function have had anything to do with the creation of artwork. They are stylish stylists, and in this anti-realistic attitude, in
its essence, we must find the catastrophe of formalistic manipulation.

Many critics have tried to separate the work of Picasso, for example, from
the socio-historical oxygen that determined it. They have tried to see in the
work of Picasso a kind of celestial exception in the midst of generalized decadence, when in fact they are dealing with the most ingenious and active expression of that decadence. . . .

I have always maintained, and I still maintain, that democratic governmental organization leads to democratic expressions in art, to commodities that
are within public reach and which contain, in the most profound sense possible, the fundamental transformations of a people. I do not forget that the
basic problem is one of class, and that the class that governs is the one that
gives its orientation to culture. But in Mexico we must always bear in mind
that our Revolution, the one that began in 1906,[2] has made it so that we artists
have a closer relationship with the masses. Mexico is possibly the only country in the capitalist world where the multitudes continue to sympathize with
the Mexican pictorial movement. The people follow us, they surround us, because our movement gets close to the people and lives from them, from them
it extracts it juices and its essences. We understand that a democratic State
must liberate, or aid in the liberation of, artists: it must patronize them. . . .

I am one of the pioneers of the Mexican muralist movement, and, without
being fatuous, I believe that it is up to me to see that that movement not be
destroyed or detained. The great threat comes from the policy of imperialist
penetration in the realm of culture, and of submission to this policy. If the government does not advance along the road toward perfect democracy, if it does
not apply the principles of the Mexican Revolution that are still lacking . . .

then it will be moving backward, at least as far as public art is concerned. The Mexican State still accepts the production of murals, but each day political discrimination grows more visible. They maneuver to replace socially conscious muralism with murals that are exclusively ornamental.

Only the state can promote transcendent art, as we have seen in the best periods of our past. But we must not forget that only revolutionary states have promoted art, states which established and developed an ideology of profound social progress. The struggle for a positively progressive State is, therefore, the duty of all Mexican artists, regardless of differences we may have in the realm of esthetics.

Notes

1. A method of painting where paint is splashed or dribbled on the canvas, apparently at random. *Ed.*
2. The Mexican revolution is commonly considered to have begun in 1910. No doubt Siqueiros has in mind the precursor movements among workers and activists, organized primarily by the radical Magonistas. *Ed.*

The Two Faces of Acapulco
during the Golden Age

Andrew Sackett

After World War II, as the official party promoted Mexico at home and abroad as a politically stable, economically dynamic, and socially progressive nation, tourism became a particularly strategic arena. No other state in the western hemisphere invested as much in the creation and promotion of a national culture than the Mexican central government. This investment began in the 1920s and 1930s in public education, archaeology, and the plastic arts; it was epitomized, perhaps, by the great works of the muralists, which stirred the imaginations of Mexicans and foreigners alike. By the 1940s, the PRI had dramatically expanded its efforts in radio, film, comic books — and tourism. In the 1950s it would invest heavily in the new medium of television. It is not surprising, therefore, that Mexicans have come to identify the postwar decades (c. 1940s–1970), which witnessed an economic boom tied to domestic manufacturing and consumption, as a "golden age" of consumer culture, particularly in the areas of journalism, the electronic media, and tourism.

This golden age was also marked by a heightened sense of patriotism and mexicanidad. Through such common terms of reference as movie stars Pedro Infante and Cantinflas, telenovelas, and Sabritas (a popular brand of Mexican junk food), Mexicans came to share in a consumer language forged through state-sponsored cultural nationalism, import-substitution industrialization policies, and, ironically, closer ties with the United States, invariably the "silent partner" in the most dynamic sectors of Mexico's postwar economy. In the process, certain icons and symbols of national identity (such as ranchera *singer Infante and the Ballet Folklórico) were successfully exported by this powerful alliance of state and private sector; internationally, they projected a colorful but increasingly cosmopolitan (and safe) image of Mexico.*

Acapulco was very much a part of this new image; indeed, during the 1950s and 1960s, it became Mexico's most alluring showcase for foreigners while still serving as a magnet for the nation's nouveau riche. The personal project of golden-age president par excellence Miguel Alemán, Acapulco became an object and center of modern desire and fantasy. Alemán's genius as tourist entrepreneur was his ability to promote re-

gional sites as diverse as Acapulco and Chichén Itzá; to juxtapose modern beaches and quaint folkloric displays like the jarabe tapatío (more vulgarly known in this country as the "Mexican hat dance"); and to persuade countrymen and foreigners alike that both represented lo mexicano. In the following selection, Andrew Sackett, a young Canadian historian who is writing a book on the social, cultural, and environmental consequences of tourist development in Acapulco, attempts to look behind the veneer of Acapulco's tourist promotion. Based on extensive oral histories and underutilized archival collections, his essay reveals a face of modernization that the state-promoted industry strenuously sought to hide. As an added bonus, we include the lyrics to a song from Elvis Presley's period film, "Fun in Acapulco," which provides a barometer of the attractions of the "Mexican Riviera" in the North American imagination.*

Travel brochures promoting Acapulco in the 1950s and 1960s said it was a land of magic landscapes sparkling like jewels around the blue crescent of its bay. It was. They said the golden beaches glistened in the sun, while rocky cliffs dropped precipitously into the ocean. They did. They would describe the luxurious hotels, sultry sea air, swinging singles scene, and generally languorous lifestyle that readers could purchase by the day, week, or even a lifetime.

But they wouldn't mention that this wasn't life for the majority of Acapulqueños. They omitted descriptions of the segments of the shoreline and the streets that sparkled with effluent from the city's rudimentary sewer systems. While the hotel pools remained full and the nightclubs shimmied until almost dawn, most people experienced frequent water and electricity outages, assuming that their neighborhoods were even connected to the city's infrastructure. Crime against tourists or the more frequent violence among the city's growing population, didn't rate even a mention, and prostitution (if it made an appearance) was merely one of the possible diversions for a playful male visitor.

This disjuncture between image and reality was not accidental. The Mexican state constructed both the physical infrastructure necessary for tourism in Acapulco and the image of Acapulco as a glittering locus of recreation and relaxation. The idealized Acapulco found in tourist publications was thus not merely fluff for ignorant readers. It was a reflection of what the state was attempting to create, both through advertising and the forced relocation of people who belied the image—peasant farmers on valuable coastal land or indigent ambulatory vendors wandering among tourists on the beaches. The image, though, was often challenged by the popular classes of Acapulco, who appropriated land owned by developers and the state and used it for housing instead of hotels.

By the end of its golden age (c. 1970), Acapulco had become, for Ameri-

Two tourists enjoy the afternoon sun overlooking the
Pacific from La Quebrada, in Acapulco. (Photo by Fritz
Henle. Reprinted by permission of Henle Archive Trust.)

cans, Europeans, and wealthy Mexicans, the international center of recreation,
relaxation, even hedonism, described in the brochures. Tropical, exotic, easy-
going, sexualized, and debauched—this was Mexico for the middle-class and
wealthier vacationers who could easily afford a week on the beach. They went
looking for the "Fun in Acapulco" that Elvis Presley sang about in his 1963
movie of the same name, where he observed, "No one's in a hurry, No one
seems to worry / Why they're all so happy is very clear / Every day siesta, every
night fiesta / I think I'm gonna like it here."

Although for tourists in this golden age Acapulco may have seemed like
a tropical paradise, tens of thousands of local residents faced a much more
prosaic reality. For them, life in Acapulco was a daily struggle. There was a
lack of housing; municipal services such as paved streets, water, and sewerage
were intermittent or completely absent; and the cost of living was very high.
Meanwhile, migrants from the rest of the state of Guerrero (then, and now,

one of Mexico's poorest) surged into Acapulco, putting further pressure on housing and services.

Acapulco is located on the Pacific Coast of Mexico, about 450 kilometers south of Mexico City. It's isolated from the interior by mountains, which rise steeply from the shore to a height of 690 meters, and surround a crescent-shaped bay which measures 2,413 meters from east to west, ringed by long, sandy beaches and palm trees curving into the sky. The physical setting— even today, surrounded by a large Third World city—is stunningly beautiful, and it distinguished Acapulco from the hundreds of other possible beach resorts on the Mexican Pacific. The experience of arriving in Acapulco was breathtaking: the contoured shores, indented peninsula, crescent-shaped bay, and backdrop of high mountains. Although there were dozens of places along Mexico's Pacific Coast that offered the cooling breezes, broad white-sand beaches, sea of turquoise blue, and swaying palm trees, none offered the phenomenal scenery combined with the stable climate of Acapulco.

Tourism to Acapulco began in the 1930s, after the first major road was completed in 1927. Before that, the only ways to reach the city were by boat or mule train. The railroad from Mexico City never made it farther than halfway. Acapulco had been an important port during the colonial era, but had since declined in importance. By the time of the Mexican revolution, it was a small, crowded town with narrow streets, considered "unhealthy" by commercial observers. Trade was dwindling, and much of the town had been damaged by a hurricane in 1912.

The 1920s was a time of rapid change in Acapulco, as in much of Mexico. With the completion of the Mexico City–Acapulco highway in 1927, travel between the two cities was cut to less than a day—and with continued improvements the trip was reduced to only eight hours by the 1940s and six by the 1950s. The first airport was also built in the late 1920s, opening the possibility of speedy flights from Mexico City. With very little promotion, Acapulco quickly became a destination for people from the capital during important national holidays, such as Semana Santa [Holy Week]. In 1933, for example, ten thousand people went there for the week, sleeping on the beaches and in their cars. What appealed to these visitors? Acapulco's splendid natural setting, certainly not its limited hotels and restaurants.

In these early days, state and national politicians, familiar with both the appeal of Acapulco and the growing tourist industry in Mexico, began to acquire land in and around the town. Their actions, although corrupt and often unjust, were relatively minor compared to the wheeling and dealing that took place in the city after Miguel Alemán Valdés became the president of Mexico in 1946. During his tenure, the small port of Acapulco was completely transformed;

in short order the groundwork was laid for its development into a glamorous international playground in the 1950s, and for the partition of Acapulco into tourist resort and Mexican city.

In his political speeches to the people of Acapulco before the election, Alemán claimed that it was not enough that hotels and suburbs of villas were being built. He promised hospitals, parks, schools, and potable water. If all that he promised had been delivered, Acapulco would have become a modern city with the infrastructure required for its citizens to lead healthier and more productive lives. Instead, the public funds that poured into Acapulco promoted displacement and heightened inequality, as the two faces of Acapulco began to harden. The federal organization charged with developing Acapulco, the Junta Federal de Mejoras Materiales de Acapulco [Acapulco Federal Committee on Material Improvements], in spite of its purported mission to develop the city's water, drainage, road, and educational networks, instead directed almost all its resources to expropriating land from *ejidos* (communal farms), building scenic highways, improving beaches, planting ornamental shrubs, and paving parking lots for tourists. Only a minute percentage of government resources went to schools, hospitals, or street and sewer construction in the rapidly growing residential neighborhoods where ordinary people lived.

By contrast, the 1950s and 1960s were certainly a golden age for Acapulco's tourist industry. In spite of the occasional downturn in the number of visitors, it was a growing industry, with large investments in hotels and real estate development. In 1952, there were 123 hotels with 2,423 rooms. By 1962, this had more than doubled, to 5,474 rooms. This trend continued well into the 1970s. In the early 1950s the change from a small fishing village and port to a resort had begun to draw the attention of international travel writers. Sydney Clark, author of more than ten guides to European and South American destinations, commented on the infrastructural improvements of the Junta within the areas frequented by tourists—the downtown, coastal roads, and airport: "The reeking dust of the town's Zócalo and radiating streets is no more. Every street has been paved . . . and the bumpy little pasture that formerly served as airfield is replaced by the fine modern airport." In the *Standard Guide to Mexico and the Caribbean,* the authors were explicit about the comparison, lamenting the passing of quiet beauty but ignoring the misery that accompanied development. "Boulevards curve where thatched huts once stood among the coco-palms. Residential suburbs spread deeper and farther into what was jungle. The juke box sings where late the crocodile basked."

At this time, the best hotels, like the Reforma-Casablanca, Los Flamingos, and El Mirador, were all on the Peninsula de las Playas, to the east of the downtown, not on the larger bay. The industry was actually divided among these hotels, with the comforts American tourists expected—fans and air conditioning, tennis courts, swimming pools, and bars—and those closer to the beach, generally owned by Mexican families, and far less self-contained. By 1958 this geographic distinction had been eclipsed, as newer hotels sprang up along the beaches and elsewhere, and there were too many hotels for any guidebook to attempt a complete list. Instead, guides to Acapulco suggested the "very best" in various categories: large deluxe, first-class, and inexpensive hotels that, although aimed at the Mexican market, happily accepted American tourists as well. Thus, an updated version of Frances Toor's *New Guide to Mexico* in 1957 went from listing three hotels as the best-known and popular in 1944—El Mirador, Los Flamingos, and Papagayo, along with two less expensive options—to six "De Luxe" and twelve "first-class operations."

There were no direct flights to Acapulco from the United States until 1964, meaning that American tourists generally went through Mexico City. Arriving in the nation's capital, they continued to Acapulco by air or land. The former was, of course, considerably faster, taking around an hour and costing around $25 round-trip. There were numerous flights: during the peak of Semana Santa, 150 planes made the trip each day. Going by land was recommended as a better way to experience an "authentic Mexico." Travelers could stop in the mountain cities of Cuernavaca and Taxco, encountering the "colonial" Mexico before experiencing the modernity of Acapulco.

Once in Acapulco, a tourist had hundreds of choices of accommodation. A quick review of English-language guidebooks published between 1954 and 1962 finds about a hundred suggested establishments, and there were at least another hundred aimed exclusively at the Mexican market. When a tourist arrived at one of these hotels, what did he or she find? Generally, an experience as far removed from the life of the average Acapulqueño as Manhattan is from rural Guerrero. Two of the most exclusive and fashionable hotels were the Pierre Marqués and El Presidente. The former was located on a 167-acre site off by itself about eleven miles southeast of the bay. Built by oil magnate J. Paul Getty in 1958 (and subsidized by the Mexican government), it was managed by the Hotel Pierre of New York. It was there that U.S. President Dwight Eisenhower stayed when he met with Mexico's President Adolfo López Mateos in 1959. All 101 rooms, suites, and bungalows were air-conditioned, and each had a private terrace overlooking the beach. Set in magnificently landscaped grounds, it had tennis courts, a golf driving range, two pools, a bar, cocktail lounge, terraces, and a dining room with excellent food. For these deluxe amenities tourists paid up to $46, fifteen to twenty-five times what Mexican hotel workers earned in a day. So that guests weren't subjected to the negative aspects of living in the countryside of a poor tropical country, the hotel had its own electricity and water purification plants. *Playboy Magazine,* in its 1960 cosmopolitan's guide to Acapulco, noted that it was a "favorite of New York's top callgirls, with their patrons in tow." The Presidente was a modern high-rise hotel, the kind now associated with Mexican beach resorts. It also opened in 1958. Eleven stories high, it began with 140 rooms and within a few years had expanded to 200. Located on Los Hornos beach on the bay, it had circulating purified ice water, radios, and "hi-fi" music in the rooms. It had an excellent restaurant, one of the swankiest nightclubs — the Jacaranda — and poolside luncheon service. Guests lounged under the thatched roof of the Palapa Bar, sipping the hotel's designer cocktail — the "Presidente," a tropical mix of pineapple, orange, and grapefruit juices fortified with gin and apricot brandy.

During the day, tourists who tired of the swim-up bars at their hotel pools could hit Acapulco's twenty-one beaches, starting with Caleta, the "morning" beach. The more active could water-ski, sail, or go deep-sea fishing. Most of the hotels were on the "American Plan," meaning tourists usually ate where they stayed. When they ventured out, the Focolore, attached to El Presidente but separate from the hotel dining room, was the most elegant restaurant in Acapulco, with "Langostines à la Bordelaise" and sensational Mexican specialties.

There were two shows tourists wouldn't miss: the "Holiday on Skis" at the Club de Esquies, and the high divers of La Quebrada. The former consisted of sitting on a waterfront patio eating Oysters Rockefeller while 28,000 watts of spotlights illuminated forty-two skiers in a dazzling, rather gaudy show. The latter has become one of the most enduring symbolic images of Acapulco, as the "Clavadistas de Acapulco" dove 136 feet off a rocky cliff into the crashing surf in a narrow inlet by torchlight. The image was reproduced in media as diverse as postcards and souvenir plates to Elvis's escapades in the 1963 film *Fun in Acapulco* (although Elvis actually filmed all his scenes in California!).

At night, at least during the December–April high season, Acapulco was a party town for gringos and wealthy Mexicans. "Young men in search of companionship" would move from nightclub to nightclub, including the Turquoise Room at the Club de Pesca, or the always jammed Dali bar (including custom artwork by the artist) at the El Presidente. They would then go dancing, or take in an "authentic Mexican folk dance."

For some, there was the added allure of a well-known and easy to find red-light district, whose workers were accustomed to dealing with English-speaking tourists. The clubs, like Rio Rita's, were (again, according to *Playboy*'s tacky but complete "cosmopolitan guide") filled with "dozens of girls of all colors and ages, waiting for someone to buy them a drink or ask them to dance or to retire into the cubicles behind the club where the major business of the establishment is consummated for anything from forty cents up."

During the winter months, Acapulco often accommodated sixty thousand tourists at a time. Scattered among them were expatriate Americans, who lamented the good old days. "Why, there were only a half dozen hotels. And the beaches! Nobody on them. And prices—you could live on $5 a day." By 1960, tourists could no longer live on $5 a day in Acapulco, but numerous Mexican families survived on less; indeed, waiters often supported families of four or more on $3 or less a day. With this, they paid some of the highest rents in the country (as demand far exceeded supply), living in tenements unfit for human habitation, tiny rooms where ten, twelve people lived, sharing sanitary facilities with their many neighbors. The city was also faced with a growing pollution problem, for many of the houses were not connected to the rudimentary sewer networks; thus, human waste mixed with household garbage and dead animals in the streets and open drainage canals that ran down through the city to the bay.

Meanwhile, up the hills from the swanky surroundings of the El Presidente, and just two months before it opened, on January 6, 1958, the largest and most successful land invasion in Acapulco's history took place. The neighborhood known as "La Laja" ("The Flagstone") was founded under the direction of Alfredo López Cisneros. Known as "Rey Lopitos" ("Little King López"), he ruled La Laja with an iron hand until his death nine years later. The popular barrio quickly grew from an agglomeration of cardboard shacks perched amid scrub-brush and boulders into one of the largest neighborhoods in Acapulco, and became a political force indispensable to local politicians. The development of La Laja demonstrates how poor Acapulqueños sometimes successfully challenged the state's focus on Acapulco as a place for tourists. The face of Acapulco usually hidden to tourists was pushed into view as thousands of indigent migrants from the countryside joined the urban poor and successfully invaded and held a large parcel of vacant city land in the face of political pressure and violence.

The process of organizing three thousand people to take a large piece of land was, obviously, not carried out overnight. During a series of meetings to challenge merchants who were charging more than the government's authorized prices for the most basic foods, corn and beans, someone yelled out that that wasn't the only problem. "There needs to be a Unión Inquilinaria de Acapulco (Acapulco Tenants' Association) because the landlords charge high rents, don't provide electricity or potable water, and because the tenements are true pigsties and we have to get out of them." It was these people facing ever bleaker living conditions that Rey Lopitos led into founding La Laja. Although it was not the first or the last successful land invasion in Acapulco, La Laja was certainly the biggest.

After various unsuccessful attempts to invade vacant lands around the city, the disgruntled tenants were told by the general who had earlier dislodged them from land destined for military housing that there were some lands being disputed in court by various owners—the area known as La Laja. The first group to settle there was relatively small, but once the neighborhood was established, word spread incredibly fast. At the end of two months, there were five thousand residents, and Lopitos began to charge two pesos per person per month to cover the costs of organization and vigilance. Soon, the neighborhood had grown to over twenty thousand residents, who came from the tenements of the older barrios in the center of Acapulco and from the desperately poor countryside of Guerrero.

The landscape the settlers faced was a difficult one. It was rocky and uncultivated, of variable elevation, and covered with vegetation. To make things worse, it was not near any established mass transit routes, making travel to markets and work difficult. Still, in spite of extremely rough conditions, the settlers persevered. As one of Lopitos's sons explained in an interview:

> It was better than being in the hands of the landlords, who were constantly raising the rents. . . . The houses were inadequate, because the growth of Acapulco had been anarchic from the traditional neighborhoods to the recent ones. It was better for many to live in these conditions . . . with the hope that any moment those lands would be their own. They sacrificed much with the intention of obtaining their own property.

The settlers immediately began to delineate lots. Although the police attempted to dislodge them several times, without success, López Cisneros quickly came to an accommodation with the President of the Republic, Adolfo López Mateos. The rapidity of the understanding they reached can be dated to a public event in which López Cisneros deployed roughly five thousand Lajeños fourteen months after the invasion. He turned them out at the airport, to welcome López Mateos and U.S. President Dwight Eisenhower, who, as we have seen, held a high-profile summit in Acapulco.

By 1966, López Cisneros had parlayed his status as the "king" of La Laja into a position of official political power. A year and a half later, on his way home from an evening with two teenage girlfriends in some of Acapulco's trendiest nightclubs, Lopitos and one of his bodyguards were murdered in a hail of gunfire. Eventually, six people were arrested for the crime, most prominent among them Acapulco's chief of police, Simón Valdeolivar Abarca (a.k.a. "El Tuba"). During sentencing, El Tuba accused the ex-governor, Raymundo Abarca Alarcón, of hiring professional gunmen to commit the crime and then framing him and his associates. The six were sentenced to twenty years in prison, where El Tuba quickly became president of the prisoners' association. Shortly after the trial, however, the ex-governor died of a mysterious heart attack and a federal injunction set the convicts free for lack of evidence. No one else has ever been convicted, but the predominant theory holds that the governor ordered the killing because his chosen candidate for mayor had been defeated, and both he and the national PRI were concerned about their inability to coopt the Lajeños, a local political force spiraling out of control behind Acapulco's glitzy façade.

The settlement and growth of La Laja altered the pattern of development in the city. Parts of Acapulco have grown in a pattern fairly typical for Latin America, with the poorest residents located in shantytowns on the least stable areas, high on the hills. The exception to this pattern is the area called Las Brisas, where the most expensive homes in the city are located. The owner of what became La Laja would have continued the pattern of Las Brisas, building villas and other hotels in the mountainous terrain, with the fabulous views and refreshing sea breezes that went along with a hilltop location. Instead, Lopitos and the Lajeños hijacked the land and turned it into an area for the common people of Acapulco, relieving the pressure on housing and creating the possibility of owner-occupied housing for some of Acapulco's poorest residents.

How could tourists come to Acapulco and only see its pleasant side? The architecture of new hotels, like the Presidente, improved people's experiences by having *all* the terraces and balconies face the bay — which allowed the aesthetic pleasure of an ocean view but also obscured the teeming, unstable, polluted city that was growing only a few hundred meters away from the shore. The axis of development in Acapulco was the Costera Miguel Alemán (Miguel Alemán Coastal Highway), a grand boulevard that curves around the bay. Nearly all the restaurants, nightclubs, hotels, and beaches were along this boulevard, meaning that there was rarely any need for tourists to enter the city where Acapulqueños actually lived.

This dual nature of Acapulco would eventually produce a conflict that could not be resolved. The pollution of the streets and a few small beach areas spread to the entire bay, while the city eventually grew too large to hide. The combination of these two factors killed Acapulco as a first-tier resort. The problems that arose from having the city of workers adjacent to the tourist district led to a new philosophy of Mexican tourist planning in the 1970s, 1980s, and 1990s. With the development of resorts like Cancún, Ixtapa, and Huatulco, planners more consciously separated the tourist and resident areas, in an effort to better mask the two distinct faces of tourist-led development that endure up to the present.

Mexico

Words and music by Sid Tepper and Roy C. Bennett

Mexico, Mexico
They've got muchas, mucha-chas, amigos
Latin features, never saw such adorable creatures
Love to dig, ooh the nights here

We live it up and love it up amigo
Life begins when you're in Mexico

You never order water
When you order south of the border
In to kiss a lovely señorita
Ooh . . . the samba, la bamba
I'll go where you go
Life begins when you're in Mexico

Mexico, Mexico
They've got muchas mucha-chas, amigos
Never saw such adorable creatures

We'll live it up and love it up amigo
Life begins . . . when you're in . . . Mexico . . .

The Dark Deeds of "El Negro" Durazo

José González G.

One of the perennial plagues of twentieth-century Mexico has been official corruption, which reached something of a high-water mark during the administration of José López Portillo (1976–1982). While the López Portillo administration was marred by several high-profile scandals, most paled beside the case of Arturo "El Negro" Durazo, whose infamous career spawned a best-selling book by his aide, José González (a notorious gunman in his own right). Durazo was a childhood friend of López Portillo, even though the two hailed from very different social backgrounds. While López Portillo followed a career path typical of aspiring politicos — law school at the National University, a series of bureaucratic appointments — Durazo worked as a bodyguard, postal worker, bank employee, and finally traffic cop. The salaries of Mexican police are scandalously low, a fact which inspires many to enhance their wages illegally. Clearly, Durazo was never renowned for honesty: in 1976, when López Portillo named him police chief of Mexico City, he was under grand jury indictment in the United States for drug trafficking. Of course, Durazo did not introduce corruption into the Mexico City police force; but he was able to escalate it to unprecedented levels, turning the force into a virtual criminal syndicate involved in drug trafficking, torture, extortion, and bank robbery. He also lived regally on his meager salary of 65 dollars per week. As López Portillo's term neared its end, Durazo begged the president to secure him immunity from prosecution by fixing him up with a seat in the national senate. When that strategy failed, he managed to escape into exile, but in 1984 he was arrested in Costa Rica and extradited to Mexico two years later, where he faced charges of illegal possession of firearms, tax evasion, extortion, and multiple homicide. Durazo was given a sixteen-year sentence, but served only six years before retiring in great comfort. Meanwhile, the administration of President Miguel de la Madrid, as part of a much-touted "moralization" campaign, seized Durazo's properties, including his Ajusco "chalet," which was turned into a "museum of corruption." Durazo died in August 2000, whereupon his sons launched a legal offensive (still unresolved at this writing) to regain the confiscated properties.

El Negro Durazo and his wife, who had lost all conception of reality due to their power and the large sums of money that Durazo was taking illegally, stumbled upon a chance to buy some communal lands in the highest part of the Ajusco heights. Their proposal was to build a chalet like those found in the Swiss Alps, a perfect complement to their "little home" at kilometer 23.5 of the federal highway to Cuernavaca.

Durazo paid the residents more than what their lands were worth; so as to avoid later problems and to protect his hide, he involved them in his dirty dealings. He told them, "Look, Mr. So-and-so, I've paid you very well for your little piece of land; now, do you have a son or daughter? Yes? Good, good, I'll give him an important position in the police force, just have him stop by."

Naturally, they all accepted his offer. But three or four months later, Durazo called together the residents and told them, with his usual arrogance:

"Look, folks, don't go and raise a stink with your little pieces of land. Your sons and daughters are committing a crime by collecting a salary from the government without working, and I can send them to prison any time I please. I tell you this in case you decide you no longer want to be my pal."

These poor people, caught unawares and lacking any assistance or recourse, had to accept the situation without complaint. As soon as the lands were acquired, I rode out on horseback with El Negro Durazo, his wife Silvia, and the chief of the Office of Urban Security and his advisors, to the plot where the aforementioned chalet was to be built. The Señora, with her architectural visions already well-established by the construction of the "little house" at kilometer 23.5 (a project costing billions of pesos that included a casino, race track, discotheque, artificial lakes, a farm and more) began to direct the building of the chalet.

Durazo asked the architect Vázquez, "Let's see, now, how many people do you need?"

"Well, sir, in order to finish by the time requested by the Señora [about eight months], I would need at least 150 workers."

"Tomorrow, you will have 650 police officers here."

"Perfect, my general," said the architect. Then he added, "Where would you like to put the road, so that we can break ground and bring the material here?"

I should clarify that the nearest road to the plot where the Chalet was to be built is almost a kilometer away. Señora Durazo intervened: "No, no, architect! I don't want any road here, because wherever roads are built, humans always follow!"

The architect replied, "Señora, do you have any idea how much material we need to bring here in order to complete the construction? If there's no road, the men will have to carry it all on their backs!"

"That doesn't matter one bit to me—that's why you will have 650 men. It's their problem!"

To my mind, the construction recalled the building of the Egyptian pyramids: the lines of police officers carrying the many heavy materials needed for the construction were the longest I could imagine. There were interminable lines of policemen, all paid by the Mexican government—with our tax money—ignoring their duty to the citizens' peace and security. They reminded one of the slaves of ancient times who worked till they dropped for their Egyptian masters. Only now the police officers had to carry their own food, and the only help they got was that they were carried to and fro in official police vehicles. That created another large problem, because the police department needed vehicles for its official participation in demonstrations, parades, civic acts, and so forth. For this purpose, they asked for buses from the city's bus-lines, to the detriment of ordinary citizens. Of course, El Negro Durazo didn't pay a penny from his own pockets. It all came out of departmental funds.

These police officers–masons–laborers, who felt degraded, frustrated and belittled by their situation, could not seek recompense because anyone who complained was punished by the omnipotent El Negro. Some malcontents were packed off to be rural guards in the remote hills or plains; others were accused of crimes and thrown in prison. Durazo relied on the servile collaboration of Pancho Sahagún Baca [director of the Division of Research for the Prevention of Delinquency and one of Durazo's top aides] to carry out such orders.

Another frustration for the laborers was that Señora Durazo chose to observe the Masons' Day (May 3), but did not honor Policemen's Day (December 22). Regarding this insult, many of the police officers commented to me: "Boss, we are not masons. We are policemen."

But they did each get a bit of barbecue, a piece of meat and a beer. Of course, the celebration was paid for by some area police chief. Durazo did not pay one penny from his own pocket.

When the Chalet was nearly finished and such a large number of workers was no longer required, approximately 150 officers were sent to [the Pacific resort town of] Zihuatanejo to help build the famous Parthenon [another of Durazo's opulent residences]. The rest continued with the inane project of building the house at kilometer 23.5, which as I have stated above was [also] about one kilometer from the federal highway. The entrance to the mansion was very noticeable because the long driveway was twice as wide as the federal highway. Durazo also had a huge sign that read "Kilometer 23 and a half" erected so that his guests could find their way.

The construction of the chalet lasted a bit longer than eight months. In order to decorate it, interior decorators of authentic Swiss Alpine chalets were "imported." I conservatively estimate the cost of this enterprise to have been at least 100 million pesos, at the value of the peso prior to the two devaluations of López Portillo.

Once the Chalet was finished, and before any "humans" would dare set their vulgar feet in the place, the first guest to visit was [President] López Portillo. Obviously, because of the lack of any road to the Chalet, the guest had to be brought in by helicopter. When the President saw the construction, he was perplexed and said to Durazo:

"Durazo, you jerk! You've outdone yourself! Make me one just like it, don't be a stingy son-of-a-bitch."

Almost immediately, El Negro Durazo began building the infamous "Black Dog Hill," which, once completed, far outshone the Parthenon of Zihuatanejo. . . .

The President always spurred him on, and Durazo complied! In his usual fashion, he acquired a larger plot of land by tricking the *ejidatarios,* and there, away from the house, he built a club complete with a casino, game hall, indoor pool, and discotheque. Because his son Yoyo had admired the famous "Studio 54" on a recent trip to New York, El Negro Durazo ordered his staff to buy exact replicas of all the discotheque's electronic devices and lights so they could be installed in his club. As I recall, the cost was somewhere around 58 million pesos.

Apart from the club, the house at kilometer 23.5 also included stables, a farm, a sports arena, a track for horse and dog races, and other luxuries. . . .

The parties at the Chalet were normally held on weekends, lasting through Sunday night. Guests were transported from the house at kilometer 23.5 by two police helicopters since, as I have mentioned, there was no road up to the Chalet. The number of guests would range from 200 to 300.

The Chalet had no kitchen, because the Señora believed that in kitchens everything smelled of grease. So enormous grills, spits and picnic tables would be erected outside to accommodate all the necessary preparations. The food and drink (all imported) were acquired and paid for by some local boss with fees he would extort from his subordinates.

The necessary staff—chefs, waiters, bouncers, and so on—was formed entirely of police officers. . . . Some of those officers commented to me: "Boss, if there is a party at the Chalet, I'd rather slit my wrists than go there."

These officers were not fortunate enough to be able to bring all of those plates, pans, linens, silverware, and so forth up to the Chalet by helicopter; they had to carry this stuff from the highway, a kilometer away. When the parties ended around three or four in the morning, only intimates of the Durazos would remain in the Chalet. Then Durazo would call me: "Listen, Slim, take the staff and we'll see you tomorrow at seven. See to the house's security."

This task consisted of stationing officers from the Mounted Police, armed with machine guns, on the surrounding hillsides.

The staff would leave in the dark of the night. Many fell and hurt themselves, which is not surprising, for there was no electricity in the area around the Chalet. As for the Chalet itself, there was a power-line with more than 100 poles, all paid for by the police department, of course.

The following day, Durazo would contact me by radio to have the heroic peregrination begin again, this time with the men hauling sweetbread, chilaquiles, and everything needed to cure a hangover up the hill to the Chalet. At noon, the meals would begin again, with cooked meat, barbecue, carnitas and tamales (Señora Durazo's favorite dish), followed by special pastries from "El Globo" bakery. Every weekend, 40 trays of pastries would arrive at the Chalet, including five or six of a special sort which fascinated the Señora. . . .

Everything to be consumed in the Durazo house was ordered in industrial quantities: legs of serrano ham from Spain, all kinds of cheeses from Holland, caviar, preserves, marzipan, foreign produce—all in such enormous quantities that much of it spoiled before it could be eaten. Neither Durazo nor his wife allowed anything to be thrown out until it was in a perfect state of decomposition. It seems not have occurred to them that, with all that food on the verge of rotting, they might be able to help the poor, hungry people living nearby.

Four giant refrigerators were needed to hold all of the food that was accumulated. When the Christmas turkeys arrived, we would find the refrigerators still full of last years' turkeys. Durazo and the Señora did not decide to throw away any food until it was infested with worms. Never did they consider sending the food to any of the nearby hospices, institutions, or shelters that could have made good use of it.

The Durazos were so stingy that the employees were forbidden even to ask for a cup of coffee, and we all had to bring our own food to the house. Pity the waiter who dared to bring food to the security staff! He would be severely reprimanded and locked up for a long time. The parties happened every weekend, and they were attended by [many people with lofty government positions].

As I said earlier, the decoration of the Chalet was suited to the Señora's wishes, and by way of the architect Carreño, her personal director, all the materials were brought from Switzerland by plane. The cost of this endeavor was more than 100 million pesos; it was important to Durazo and the Señora that the Chalet and its surroundings have all the ambience of the genuine Swiss Chalets which so fascinated them. And remember that the Chalet was situated at the highest point of the Ajusco.

YOU MAY BE wondering about the spoiled heir of the Durazo family. At the time that I met him, this troglodyte was seventeen years old. He was named Francisco Durazo Garza, but he had been given the endearing nickname "Yoyo" by his parents. I'll tell about a few of his "stunts."

Yoyo's eyes are always glassy and dilated due to his use of stimulants. He is the sort of person who hates the entire world, and who glories in his own importance. His *mamita*, Silvia Garza de Durazo, loved to encourage in her son an attitude of absolute superiority over all other human beings—over us, that is, or anyone not named Durazo Garza.

Thanks to this style of "education," Yoyo loved to amuse himself at others' expense, and in this he was insatiable. He would be accompanied by at least two patrolmen and eight "select" agents, the most belligerent and ignorant of the corps. His car had to be reinforced on all sides so that no one could block his way: anyone who dared get in his path would be assailed by this "war tank" masquerading as an automobile. The boy also felt well protected by eight gunmen bearing German machine guns, and by patrol cars manned by thugs who at any given moment would deliver the "coup de grace" to anyone who dared to protest the outrages of their young boss. How would you like to meet up with this fiendish boy on the beltway around Tecamachalco, the route he took each day to the private school he attended, the Colegio Irlandés?

Speaking of the Colegio Irlandés, which is particularly renowned among our celebrated politicians, I remember an anecdote about Yoyo that reveals his barbarity as well as the sheepishness and opportunism of those who, for whatever reason, interacted with El Negro Durazo.

One day in June or July of 1978, Yoyo came to speak with me in Durazo's office: "Listen, you little shit of a lieutenant colonel, I just worked over one of my teacher's cars because the bastard failed one of my friends, so if they come to complain to my dad, don't let 'em in."

What had sweet little Yoyo actually done to the teacher's car? Well, when the teacher got into his car to leave the school, Yoyo and his buddies caught up to him and, with their automatic pistols, they shot up the car's windows, trunk, chassis and tires, and all this while the poor teacher remained inside, imprisoned by fear, the doors securely locked. Having had his little joke, Yoyo left with his assistants and friends, boasting of his prowess.

The next day, the director of the Colegio Irlandés, an Irish priest, together with the assaulted professor and three other priests (also Irish), appeared in Durazo's office to present their complaint. I told Durazo the purpose of their visit, and he said to me: "Look, Slim, call Sahagún and bring 500,000 pesos from the green box in my closet. Then show those idiots in."

I expected a real protest due to the seriousness of Yoyo's deeds, but the Irish School's director had something else in mind: "My general, I apologize for coming to bother you with these little details, but we must concern ourselves with the education of your son 'Paquito,' who is clearly quite brilliant."

"Father, there is nothing in life that has no remedy," responded Durazo. "I have just told Colonel Sahagún here to buy a new car of whatever make and color the professor chooses; and for you, I have here a small gift of 500,000 pesos for your school so that you can continue to bestow upon our children such a fine education. You know that our Mexican schools are very inadequate and there's no sign that they will improve any time soon."

The Irish priest, the teacher, and the others left the office completely satisfied, especially because Sahagún Baca, interpreting the sentiment of his patron, had told them that color television sets with remote control and stereo speakers awaited each one of them in the basement of the house, as tokens of the family's esteem and affection.

Another of Yoyo's little pranks took place at his house at kilometer 23.5 from Cuernavaca, where he was hanging out with his buddies. Bored and with nothing to do, he ordered his "assistants" to detain the waiters and cooks so that he could inject Coca-Cola into their gluteal regions. He and his friends waited to see how these poor people would react. A waiter called "El Grande," who is now the chief of dining services for General Ramón Mota Sánchez, the current director of the Mexico City police, could tell you more about this incident.

Another favorite diversion of Yoyo and his friends was to send someone to buy a bunch of eggs, and then they would paint a sign that said: "Throw these at the police." After using marijuana, cocaine and psychotropic drugs washed down with Amaretto, they would throw the eggs at the uniformed officers on duty at the house. Obviously, the policemen had to bear this humiliation. If they ceased to humor her "baby," as Yoyo's mother called him, they would have to face her sanctions.

In 1979, the fearless Yoyo killed a cyclist who dared to cross his path. He also attacked and killed an old woman in an open-air market, despite the presence of many people, and he overturned his sports car at more than 250 kilometers per hour on the beltway, causing the death of a schoolmate. Of course, these bloody events were of little consequence thanks to papa Durazo's interventions.

When he would come home from school, accompanied as usual by friends from the same mold, he would amuse himself with another of his stunts. This one involved ordering his aides to block the traffic of the beltway near the Channel Eight television station. His only intention was to have the beltway to himself so that he could do acrobatics on his motorcycle in order to impress a model who worked at the station. Obviously, Yoyo was unconcerned by the frustration and powerlessness of the people who were stuck in the rush-hour traffic until he ended his spectacle. And no one dared to complain in the presence of eight gorillas armed to the teeth.

One time, when Yoyo left for Acapulco with his friends, he managed to get a Mexicana Airlines flight delayed with all of its passengers on board. This was because, with his usual arrogance, he grievously offended a lady who was about to board the plane, and the woman turned out to be the wife of the pilot. When the pilot found out about Yoyo's behavior, he tried to call attention to the transgressor without knowing who he was dealing with. He only succeeded in getting a savage beating by Yoyo's thugs which sent him to the hospital.

Thereupon, agents of the Federal Judicial Police stationed at the International Airport detained Yoyo and his friends. Of course, they had to be released when El Negro Durazo found out about the events. Señora Durazo's only reaction, when her "baby" came home after this scandal, was to call me in and say: "Look Pepe, I can't allow those barbaric gunmen you send to guard my son to traumatize him or interfere with his trip. Order that damn Sahagún Baca to send for Yoyo and rent an executive jet to take him to Acapulco with his little friends."

Of course, her orders were carried out. Durazo, for his part, invited the directors of the pilots' syndicate of Mexicana Airlines to a breakfast in the dining room of his office and presented them with police credentials and other gifts. Thus the "little incident" was resolved.

The Sinking City

Joel Simon

Arguably the most egregious cost of Mexico's desperate attempts to modernize is a major environmental catastrophe. Although Mexico's environmental problems are diverse and multifaceted and have affected virtually every corner of the country, they have come to be symbolized by Mexico City's world-famous air pollution. Horror stories about Mexico City's air abound: it has been linked to chronic respiratory and gastrointestinal ailments, headaches, sore throats, exhaustion, irritability, skin disease, heart attacks, and mental retardation. Simply breathing in Mexico's capital has been likened to smoking two packs of cigarettes a day; it is, in the words of New York Times *correspondent Julia Preston, "one of the most dangerous places on the planet to take a breath."*[1]

Given horrors of such magnitude, Mexicans can scarcely take comfort in journalist Joel Simon's assertion that air pollution is not the worst of the city's environmental woes. Simon's remarkable book, Endangered Mexico, *details the clash between a mentality that emphasizes "progress"—conceived in terms of epic infrastructural projects, massive consumption of resources, and monumental growth—and a delicate ecosystem ill-suited to such ambitions. Mexico City's growth in the past decades has been phenomenal. In 1950, its population was a modest three million; today, according to some estimates, it tops twenty million. In 1940, it covered 43.3 square miles; today it accounts for about 571 square miles. Mexican authorities apparently have not found such growth as alarming as one might expect. To the contrary, it has been a source of great pride, a clear indication that Mexico was in step with the modern, industrial world. Indeed, perhaps the most troubling aspect of Simon's work is his account of the attitudes he encounters among both high officials and ordinary folks, who seem to regard their country's environmental debacle as either an unfortunate inevitability—one exaggerated in the media—or as a reasonable price to pay for the blessings of modernity. Among the many costs of Mexico's development strategy is the severe exacerbation of a problem dating back at least to the start of the Spanish colony: Mexico City's troubled relationship with its water supply.*

Anyone who has lived through Mexico City's rainy season, when the sky blackens each afternoon and lets loose a thunderous deluge, would never suspect that the city is running out of water. . . . But that is only because they cannot see what is happening under their feet. The underground aquifer that provides 70 percent of the city's water is being rapidly emptied—its useful life can be measured in decades.

Air pollution receives so much attention because it is so obvious. It is everywhere and its effects are immediate. The water threat is long term—and it takes a trained eye to see the damage. The only visible evidence that the city is running out of water is the fact that it is sinking. So much water has been pumped out of the underground aquifer that the clay soil underlying the city has contracted like a sponge left to dry in the sun. The sinking is not uniform; it varies from street to street, from building to building. After a century of slow subsidence, downtown Mexico City resembles a fun house at an amusement park. Streets are buckled; buildings are pitched forward or balanced at impossible angles. . . .

The problem would be bad enough if only the buildings were affected. But of course, pipes, cables, subway tunnels and the whole underground infrastructure are sinking along with the rest of the city. So many water pipes have burst that 30 percent of the water flowing through the system is lost to leaks. The sinking undermines foundations, making buildings vulnerable to collapse in the earthquakes that periodically strike the city. Sometimes the ground simply collapses and a sinkhole swallows a piece of the city. On July 6, 1996, Pati Ortiz was selling quesadillas on the street corner of a poor neighborhood called Iztapalapa when she heard a loud crack. She grabbed frantically at the skirt of her friend Hortencia Gener, but the ground had fallen away and she was sucked screaming into a twenty-foot sinkhole. The falling earth ruptured an abandoned septic tank, filling the sinkhole with poisonous methane gas. Ortiz and three bystanders who jumped into the sinkhole to save her were all killed.

Because nearly twice as much water is being pumped out of the aquifer as naturally flows in, the water has higher and higher concentrations of salts and other minerals. And because the water level is subsiding at a rate of about three feet a year, it is more and more costly to pump it up from the depths.

Thirty percent of the city's water is piped from distant reservoirs at enormous cost. In fact, 10 percent of Mexico's total energy output is used to meet Mexico City's water needs—pumping drinking water into the city and pumping waste water out.

The situation is clearly untenable. "We've looked at all of the alternatives—every one," said Alfonso Martínez Baca, the head of Mexico City's Water Commission, when I met him in his wood-paneled office. "Not one of them is viable." Martínez Baca has the unenviable task of managing the city's water system. "There is no nearby source that can give us the water we need," he said. "Some people have pointed out to me that we have an inexhaustible source of water, which is the Gulf of Mexico. But you'd have to transport it four hundred kilometers and raise it two and a half kilometers. It's impossible. It would be cheaper to move Mexico City to Veracruz."

Martínez Baca leaned across the conference table and spoke in a conspiratorial whisper. "Water is the most serious threat facing the city," he said. "Tomorrow everyone could ride on bicycles and the air pollution would clear up. But where on earth are we going to get our water from?" . . .

[Editor's summary: The Spaniards, according to Simon's account, destroyed the sophisticated hydraulic works of the Aztec city of Tenochtitlán, which led to problems of chronic flooding. In the early 1600s, the Spaniards began the greatest engineering project of the colonial era: the famous *desagüe*, or drainage canal, which siphoned off the waters of Lake Texcoco. (See the selection by Zorita in Part III.) The project brought flooding under control, but created a host of new problems, including depletion of the water content of the soil, which caused the city to sink, and perennial shortages of potable water. In the late nineteenth century, the modernizing dictator Porfirio Díaz attacked these problems with new engineering feats, which included digging new wells to tap the water of the aquifer and constructing a "Gran Canal," a thirty-six-mile drainage ditch which finally dried up what was left of the lakes that had once covered 736 square miles of the Valley of Mexico.]

AFTER THREE CENTURIES of abuse, the valley's hydrology had been permanently and irreparably damaged. Buildings were cracking, water pipes were snapping, and no one could figure out exactly why. It was not until 1946 that the problem was finally solved. Engineers announced that so much water was being pumped out of the underground aquifer that the ground supporting the city was collapsing.

The Mexican government was not ready to hear the bad news. The economy was poised for takeoff and Mexico City was a big part of the plans. Commercial agriculture had been largely dismantled by President Cárdenas, who had put through the largest land reform in Mexican history. The new landowners were told not to grow crops for the gringos, but for the new factory workers in Mexico City. World War II had spawned the country's great industrialization. Nothing could stand in the way of Mexico's bright future, not even nature itself.

Despite the report on the sinking, the Mexican government went right on pumping water from the aquifer. Between 1948 and 1951 the city sank 4.4 feet; the next decade it sank another 4.75 feet. In one single year—1950—it sank a remarkable 18 inches.

By the mid-1950s, Mexico City was no longer merely the capital of the country. It had become, like Tenochtitlán, an imperial city that demanded tribute from the hinterlands. The tribute was brought in various forms—campesinos provided cheap corn, the rural migrants provided their labor, raw materials from throughout the country were channeled to Mexico City. Like Tenochtitlán, the ever-larger Mexico City embarked on an era of expansion in which it subdued its neighbors and took their water. While the Aztecs could only capture water from within the valley, new technology allowed Mexico City to look farther afield. In the late 1930s, the city's gaze fell on Almoloya del Río, a backwater town of four thousand fishermen on the other side of the 12,620-foot Ajusco volcano.

Eladio Casteñeda was a thirty-one-year-old schoolteacher when President Cárdenas motored into town with a group of engineers. They all took a quiet walk along the lakeshore, staring intermittently down at the water and up at the 14,600-foot Nevado de Toluca, a snow-covered volcano rising above the valley like a jagged crown.

The villagers were honored by the visit but did not think too much about it—not until 1942, anyway, when the engineers returned in droves with slide rules and note pads. They set up camp along the lakeshore in a field where water percolated up through the ground "like it was overflowing from a boiling pot," according to Casteñeda. The water trickled down into Lake Chiconahuapan ("nine waters" in Nahuatl) and then formed a series of other, smaller lakes before settling down to become the Lerma River. The Lerma flows through the states of Querétaro and Guanajuato before emptying into Lake Chapala, near Guadalajara.

"This was the source of the Lerma River," Casteñeda said with a certain pride as he waved a hand over the landscape visible outside his second-story home. "The whole plain was covered with water—and it was clean, Señor. You could see the fish." Casteñeda had spent his childhood fishing and scavenging in the lake. The Mazahua- and Otomi-speaking Indians who had first settled the valley eight hundred years ago had lived much the same way.

The plan to bring the water to Mexico City got off to a poor start. The engineers dynamited the spring in an attempt to increase the flow of water, but instead the water stopped flowing altogether. Undaunted, the engineers sank pumps into the ground. They sucked up 1,600 gallons of water per second and sent it along a large pipe parallel to the old river channel. In the town of Atrasquillo, the pipe turned east at a ninety-degree angle and climbed the Sierra de las Cruces. Then the water flowed through a three-mile tunnel into the Valley of Mexico. The hundreds of springs in Almoloya quickly ran dry.

The inauguration in September 1951 drew a long line of dignitaries from Mexico City. Once again, the public was assured that the new system would end Mexico City's water problems forever, and that the sinking city would be quickly stabilized.

Meanwhile, Eladio Casteñeda watched as the lake that had sustained him, his village, and his ancestors slowly dried up. "It was like a dream," he said. "One day we woke up and it was gone." More than thirty years later, Caste-ñeda took me for a walk along what used to be the lakeshore. With the springs gone, what remains of the lake is now filled by sewage and runoff. A small flock of pelicans rested on the water. Casteñeda laughed when I asked if it reminded him of his childhood. "Oh, it was much bigger," he said. "The lakes were not deep, but you could go in a canoe from here all the way to Lerma."

When I asked Casteñeda whether he missed the village life of his child-hood, he was less definitive. The engineers who took the water later brought roads, schools, sewage systems, potable water, and a wave of industrial growth. The town's economy shifted from fishing to shoe making and the standard of living rose accordingly. Among Casteñeda's nine children one is a doctor, another a lawyer, and a third an engineer. During a later visit to Almo-loya, I asked seventy-eight-year-old Taurino Ariscorreta whether he missed the lakes. He sat back in his chair and thought for a few moments. "It was a beautiful life," he said finally. "But we were very, very poor.

Meanwhile, the diversion of the water from Almoloya to Mexico City meant that the Lerma River now began downstream. Unfortunately, it was exactly the same spot where the government of Mexico State had decided to build an enormous industrial park. Today, the Lerma begins its journey carry-ing 1,000 gallons per second of partially treated sewage and industrial waste. Along its route, it is fed with chemicals from tanning factories, tar from a Pemex plant, and pesticides and fertilizers from the fields that line its banks. It disgorges the muck into Lake Chapala.

The sacrifice of the Lerma River bought Mexico City only partial relief from its water woes, and for only about fifteen years. In 1965, with demand for water continuing to increase and with downtown Mexico City continuing to sink, authorities decided to expand the pumping around the headwaters of the Lerma from 1,500 gallons per second to 4,000 gallons per second. Five hundred new wells were drilled throughout the Ixtlahuaca valley north of the town of Lerma. But the engineers had vastly overestimated the size of the aquifer. By 1970 the land was sinking so rapidly that cracks began to open up in the ground. Still they kept pumping until the aquifer was completely depleted. Today only 1,400 gallons a second can be pumped from the Lerma Valley—a mere drop in the bucket of Mexico City's water needs.

The government had known from the beginning that the Lerma system would buy the city only a few more years. A report released at the time that the Lerma system was inaugurated acknowledged that the next water crisis was only a few years away. . . .

[IN 1952], MEXICO CITY was hit with a terrible flood. As in colonial times, people moved through downtown streets in canoes. The city flooded because, after decades of pumping water from the aquifer, the city had sunk below the level of the drainage canal and the flood water could not be evacuated. When the Gran Canal del Desagüe was built in 1900, it was graded to carry the sewage downhill and out of the valley. After the 1952 flood, pumping stations were installed to take the water uphill. Authorities recognized that this was only a temporary solution. As the city grew, more and more water needed to be drained. The pumps consumed large amounts of electricity, and the city remained vulnerable because they could always break down.

Attacking the underlying problem by reducing water consumption and thereby stabilizing the sinking would have been politically unpopular and would have brought the country no glory. Authorities argued that the development process required the consumption of large amounts of resources, and they were convinced that technology and growth would create a solution. Enormous public works were always favored over conservation because they strengthened the power of the central government and became a source of national pride. Mexico would solve the flooding problem with an infrastructure project on the scale of [the colonial] *desagüe*.

Studies for a deep drainage tunnel began in 1959, but ground was not broken until May 1967. The plan was to build a fifty-mile tunnel at a depth of 650 feet, making the system impervious to the sinking. Thirty thousand workers labored on the project, raising 4.57 million cubic yards of dirt from the depths. Workers hoisted from the bowels of the earth had to be put in decompression chambers to avoid getting the bends. The official cost of the project was $43.2 million (540 million pesos), a figure many believe to be far less than the actual investment.

Completing the tunnel took nearly a decade. President José López Portillo personally opened the floodgates in 1975. Supporters were bused in and given T-shirts and banners and instructed to cheer the president and thank him for liberating them from the floods. Officials made a host of self-congratulatory political speeches. . . .

It was another decade before the deep drainage canal was operating at full capacity, but the Gran Canal continues to handle the bulk of the city's sewage. The pumping stations, viewed as a stopgap measure, still move the water along its uphill journey out of the valley.

There was one last detail to be worked out. What do you do with the 23,200 gallons of raw sewage and industrial waste that Mexico City produces every second? In order to find out, I decided to follow the Gran Canal. It was easy to find—I could smell it from blocks away. The canal begins appropriately enough just behind the Mexican Congress. I followed it a few blocks north and stopped at the first bridge to take a look. The "water" was a thick black sludge, the consistency of syrup. It did not seem to flow so much as percolate. I drove through working-class neighborhoods and stopped again at the border of Mexico State, where the canal intersects with the Rio de los Remedios; the sludge carried by the river backed up with the canal, forming an enormous swamp of sewage that spread out over acres. I had to hold my breath as I ran across a hanging bridge to a dusty soccer field. Jesús Fuerte García, a sixty-year-old truck driver, covered his mouth with a handkerchief as he crossed behind me and then spat on the ground. "It's a source of infection, of course," said García as we watched the soccer game together. "It hurts your throat. The kids who play soccer here are always getting sick. And when it rains, it overflows the banks."

When I crossed back over the bridge to return to my car I noticed a large object floating under the bridge. It was the carcass of a dog. I recognized it only because of the outline of a jaw poking through the muck.

Despite the stench, houses line the banks of the Gran Canal as it passes through the shantytowns north of the city. Then it flows through open fields until it reaches the town of Zumpango. There, it ducks into a tunnel and then reappears outside the valley in the state of Hidalgo. . . .

I caught up with the black waters in Hermanejildo Estrada's cornfield. Detergents agitated by the passage through the tunnel floated along the irrigation ditch. Foam was everywhere, blowing through the landscape like sagebrush across the prairies. The water is used to grow vegetables. The Mexican government has repeatedly claimed that there are no health risks, but in 1992 a United Nations study found extremely high levels of arsenic, chromium, and selenium and moderately high levels of cadmium, nickel, and zinc in the soil. What effects, if any, these high levels could have on human health is much debated, and from a scientific standpoint the answer is by no means clear. But logic would suggest that there are health risks associated with eating anything grown in raw sewage. Certainly, there are serious risks to the farmers and to the land itself.

When I visited the Mezquital Valley in 1991, cholera was raging through the region. Doctors at local hospitals told me there had been hundreds of cases but added that the government was not releasing the official figures. Farmers, however, defended the waters, saying the organic waste fertilized their fields. Estrada, for example, was undaunted by the recent outbreak. "I've worked with the black waters for twenty years and I've never gotten sick," he told me as we stood beside the toxic canal. "If cholera gets me, so be it."

Cornelio Rosas, meanwhile, was back in his fields only a day after suffering a cholera attack. The doctors told him to wash his hands better. "The black waters don't do anything bad," insisted Gerardo López as he loaded squash into the back of his pickup truck. "We will never let the authorities take them away from us."

As the black waters retreat, they leave the fields coated with a thick crust of salt. The Tula and Salado Rivers, which receive the effluence from the Valley of Mexico, empty into the Moctezuma River. The Moctezuma, like every river in the whole watershed, is dead. In most of the world, large cities are in valleys, along river banks, or on the coast, so that if you hike up into the mountains you can find a less-disturbed landscape. But Mexico City's sewage feeds the headwaters of several major rivers. Even if you hike into a remote canyon downstream, you will have to wade through a river full of foam and chemicals.

The black waters have a second destination as well, as I discovered during my travels along the city's sewage canals. On the highway from Mexico City to the city of Texcoco, signs announced a government-funded "ecological rescue" project to restore Lake Texcoco. I pulled off the highway on a dirt road and drove half a mile to a locked gate. A policeman, dressed in black and carrying a machine gun, emerged from a small cubicle. "Entry is prohibited," he told me. "Those are my orders."

The effort to revive the lake began in 1971 as a means of controlling the dust storms caused when dried sediment is whipped up by strong winds. Engineers who began work on the project discovered a major obstacle: the city had sunk so far that Lake Texcoco, once the lowest point in the valley, was now six feet higher than the city center. Allowing the lake to fill with water would have created a serious flood risk. So the engineers did what they knew best—they begun pumping water from the soil around Lake Texcoco until the whole area started to sink. Today Lake Texcoco, which is filled by partially treated sewage water, is two feet below the city. It seems absurd that in an area once covered with water, lake beds have to be created artificially. It is equally absurd that up to 23,200 gallons—both sewage and rainwater—are artificially channeled out of the basin, while approximately 5,300 gallons are pumped in from neighboring valleys. The city is running out of water, and yet it is perennially flooded.

Something in the policeman's tone suggested to me that he thought his orders to keep me out were as stupid as I did. Since he was unmoved by my press pass, I started chatting about the ancient lake. I told him that five centuries ago we would have been under water—or if we were lucky, in a canoe. We could have paddled from where we stood to the town of Texcoco, where the poet-king-engineer Nezahualcóyotl once ruled. We could have paddled or poled across the shallow waters to Tenochtitlán; we would have seen the pyramids rise into the sky as we drew close. If we had some business there, we could have paddled through the streets of the city, directly into Moctezuma's palace. We could have paddled to Lake Chalco, or among the *chinampas* (floating gardens) of Lake Xochimilco. The lakes would have been full of ducks and pelicans; we would have been able to see the fish swim below us.

I do not know if I bored or amused him, but he finally realized that the easiest way to get rid of me would be to let me see the lake. He opened the gate. "Park your car in the bushes," he said. "I could get in trouble."

I walked a few hundred yards over a rise and looked down across a dark lake. Yes, the lake had returned, but the water had not been sent by Tlaloc, the water god. Lake Texcoco was filled with the sewage from Mexico City. The freshwater springs that once filled the lake had been replaced by millions of flushing toilets and the industrial waste from thousands of factories. The tragic cycle had been completed. The pelicans did not seem to notice. They gathered along the lakeshore and flapped lazily into the darkening sky.

As I walked back to my car for the drive back into the smoggy city, I thanked the policeman for breaking the rules. He seemed strangely disappointed that I was leaving. The poor guard was going out of his mind with boredom. "This is my job," he said, as I climbed into my car. "But I hate it. There's nothing here. This spot is so lonely you can't imagine." . . .

IN 1972, AROUND the time that air pollution finally became a public concern, the government was working quietly to find a new source of water. The millions of newcomers were a problem, not only because they needed water but also because they often settled on the aquifer's wooded "recharge" areas. As trees were cut down and roads were paved, less rainwater was absorbed into the aquifer.

The 1965 strategy to increase pumping in the Lerma Valley was clearly a failure—the friatic level (the depth at which water is found) was dropping rapidly, and water could be guaranteed for only a few more years. The Mexico

City aquifer was being exploited at full capacity, and the sinking, though slowed, continued to be a serious problem.

The solution to the water crisis had to be another massive infrastructure project. Los Angeles, it was pointed out, had brought water from the Colorado River two hundred and fifty miles away, and Mexico City could do the same. In fact, it would have to do more. Los Angeles is at sea level, and the water from the Colorado is carried in an aqueduct that flows downhill. At an elevation of 7,347 feet and surrounded by mountains, Mexico City is on one of the highest plateaus in Mexico. Water from surrounding river valleys would have to be pumped at tremendous cost.

On a map, the engineers drew concentric circles around Mexico City. They evaluated various factors—the distance the water would have to be transported, the height of the intervening mountains, the existing infrastructure. The engineers noticed a major dam built in the 1940s at Valle de Bravo in the pine-forested mountains of Mexico State. There was a second dammed reservoir forty miles away at Villa Victoria. The engineers calculated that they could tie the two dams together and then send the water to Mexico City through the tunnel that had originally been built to bring the water from the Toluca Valley. There was only one problem: Valle de Bravo is at 5,700 feet and Mexico City is nearly 1,700 feet higher. Not only that—there is an even higher pass (8,300 feet) between the two. Getting the water to Mexico City would require building dozens of miles of aqueduct, a ten-mile tunnel, a five-mile canal, six power plants to raise the water up the mountains, and an enormous water treatment plant, plus the installation of pipes and tunnels to distribute the water once it reached the city. The system would be a project to rival Hoover Dam. It would fundamentally transform the entire landscape and put it at the service of Mexico City.

When ground was broken on the Cutzamala ("watershed") project in 1974, Mexico was flush with oil money, and future growth seemed ensured. The government did not flinch at the prospect of subsidizing the water delivery system, since its actual cost would be well beyond the means of most Mexicans. But by 1982, when the first part of the system was brought on line, oil prices had collapsed, and Mexico had begun a decade of deprivation and economic stagnation. Still, the work continued apace. In 1985, 1,600 gallons of water per second were being pumped from the Valle de Bravo dam. Over the next few years several other small dams were added to the system, and in 1995 the third phase was completed, bringing the total output of the system to 4,200 gallons per second—about one quarter of the 16,400 gallons per second consumed by the city. It takes 1,650 million kilowatt-hours per year to pump the water to Mexico City—approximately 6 percent of the city's total energy consumption.

The use of surface instead of subterranean water has made the Cutzamala system the most reliable of all of the city's water sources. But it is some of the most expensive water in the world.

One day I tried to follow the aqueduct from the Valle de Bravo back to Mexico City. Valle de Bravo is a quaint cobblestoned village where the Mexican elite have their weekend houses. To get there, I drove through the treeless plains around Toluca and then followed a snaking road that descended from the plateau into a pine-covered valley.

What is ironic about the Cutzamala system is that a city that first trashed its own hydraulic system and then that of its neighbor is now dependent on the conservation and careful management of a third one. All dams have a limited life; over decades they fill with sediment washed down in tributaries, and their capacity diminishes. When the Valle de Bravo dam was built in 1944, the capacity of the reservoir was 108 million gallons; today sedimentation has reduced it to 89 million gallons. Preventing deforestation and erosion in the Valle de Bravo is the responsibility of Santiago Zepeda González, the local delegate from Probosque, the federal forestry agency. With a tiny office and an annual budget of $10,000, Zepeda tries to stop illegal logging, prevent forest fires, and encourage reforestation. In an area in which the Mexican federal government has invested billions of dollars in infrastructure, it has been miserly in funding programs to protect that investment. "Illegal logging is the biggest problem," said Zepeda. "You can get 200–300 pesos for a tree. That's a lot of money for a poor campesino."

The next morning I followed the road to Los Berros, the enormous water treatment plant that purifies the water sent to Mexico City. Five pumping stations raise the water 2,300 feet from Valle de Bravo. What surprised me was that what had appeared as a solid mass of trees was actually forest interspersed with cornfields. Some of the cleared areas were plowed and planted with corn in anticipation of the summer rains: others were eroded and abandoned. At a clearing full of shacks made from freshly cut timber, I talked to Genaro Mari Carranza, who along with about a dozen other men was returning from an afternoon fighting a small forest fire. "It's volunteer work," said Carranza. "We want to save something for our children."

Rangers patrol the woods to ensure that only dead trees are logged, but cutting down a live pine is an incredible temptation for families without enough to eat. Carranza and the 155 Mazahua Indian families who settled in the clearing in 1993 subsist on the corn they produce. But the land they cultivate has been depleted of nutrients; every year they have to add more fertilizers. Carranza leaned against the hoe he was carrying when I asked if logging should be allowed. "For the people who live here, yes, but the government says it's illegal." It must seem nonsensical to be told essentially that a tree is more important than the lives of their hungry children.

Just a few miles up the road was a sad example of why the government is taking a hard line. The forest revealed itself as a veneer, a tree theme park. The trees simply vanished as I drove through them and emerged onto an open plain full of small towns and scraggly cornfields. A few miles farther on I reached the Los Berros water treatment plant, the center of operations for the whole Cutzamala system. In Mexico City I had been told that all visits to the plant had been suspended for "reasons of security," but after a little cajoling Absalón Domínguez, the engineer who runs the facility, consented to give me a tour. We stood in the control room amidst blinking yellow and red lights, as Domínguez used a wall-sized map of the Cutzamala system to make his points. "The Villa Victoria dam was built only fifty years ago and is already full of sediment," he said. "It's only got another fifteen to twenty years of useful life. Valle de Bravo is in much better shape — I give it thirty years, assuming that there is no more deforestation." He pointed to light green spots on the map where the forest had been removed. "This is what worries me," he said. "At some point we'll need to find more water."

The enclosed pipe that carries the water to Mexico City ran across a field and disappeared over an 8,300-foot ridge. From there it is all downhill. The water flows through lonely valleys, across the Toluca plains and through a tunnel in the Sierra de las Cruces before arriving in Mexico City. By the time it comes out of the tap, the cost of a gallon of water is nearly four-tenths of a cent (a liter costs one-tenth of a cent). What you pay, if you pay at all, is less than half that amount. That means that every time you open the tap and take a drink of water in Mexico City (assuming you are brave enough to do so), you strain Mexico's national treasury. The government picks up 60 percent of the tab every time you flush the toilet, take a shower, wash your car, or water your lawn. The total deficit according to Mexico City officials is $125 million a year. An independent study of the water system came up with even more alarming numbers: although the real cost of a cubic meter (1,000 liters) of water is one dollar, the government recovers only ten cents. The annual deficit for water services is $1 billion. Subsidizing the water not only strains the budget; it encourages the illusion that water is plentiful and that there is no reason to conserve it.

The lesson to be drawn from the Cutzamala system is that it is not economically feasible for the government to transport water from other basins. Not only is the infrastructure investment prohibitive, but the government must also make an indefinite commitment to covering the annual budget shortfall. The only way to restore some sort of environmental equilibrium is to treat the valley as much as possible as a closed system. Nearly thirty inches of rain fall in the Valley of Mexico each year, enough to provide a good deal of the city's water needs if it were properly managed. The problem is that the rains in Mexico City are torrential, and the terrain in the surrounding mountains is extremely steep. Left to its own devices, the rainwater would refill the dried lake beds. Unfortunately, they are now occupied by millions of people. The handful of reservoirs within the metropolitan area are used not to store potable water but rather raw sewage, which cannot be accommodated by the city's overloaded drainage system. Because of the danger of flooding, the city must pump rainwater runoff out of the valley as quickly as possible. There are simply no places left in the valley to store large quantities of water for human consumption.

But there is another option: the aquifer itself. The city needs to do a careful study of the exact composition of the aquifer and then inject rainwater collected in smaller reservoirs equal to the amount that is being extracted. One of the greatest untapped sources of water in the city is the water system itself; the sinking has ruptured so many pipes that 30 percent of the water is lost. Alfonso Martínez Baca told me that if he could cut that figure in half, he would suddenly have another 18,000 liters (4,760 gallons) per second of water available for distribution. The city also has a billion-dollar plan to improve drainage and build water treatment plants. If the authorities can find a way to better police industry so that the sewage is less contaminated by chemicals and heavy metals, the water could be treated sufficiently so that it could be reused by industry or perhaps reinjected into the aquifer. There is simply no other solution: Mexico City must find a way to live within its means.

NEARLY FIFTY YEARS after the first scientific report confirmed that extracting water from the aquifer was causing the city to sink, 70 percent of Mexico City's water continues to come from wells in the valley. Once you develop a trained eye you can spot the pumps throughout the southern part of the city—in highway medians, parks, and abandoned fields, and on street corners. There are 4,820 of them, and they pump 11,000 gallons a second out of the aquifer—double the amount that flows in naturally. Because of the "overexploitation" of the aquifer, the friatic level drops more than three feet a year. The danger is not so much that one day the wells will run completely dry, but rather that the quality of the water will continue to deteriorate. More and more of the water pumped up is "fossilized," meaning it has been in the aquifer for an eon. It is so full of minerals and salts that it is not potable. The sinking threatens not only the buildings and the streets but the aquifer itself. In many areas, the direction of the natural drainage has changed; waste water that used to accumulate on the less permeable clay soils of the former lake now flows toward the recharge areas where it filters down into the aquifer. The sinking has opened deep fissures in the surface of the valley. During the 1985 earthquake an enormous crack opened up in Lake Xochimilco, and millions of gallons of untreated sewage poured into the aquifer. Contaminants from the open-air garbage dumps also eventually migrate down to water level. As the friatic level drops, the concentration of both natural and artificial contaminants increases. Since the water has to be pumped from about three feet deeper each year, it is also becoming more expensive.

Beginning in the 1950s, the city began using wells to the south of the valley rather than downtown. This change has reduced the sinking in the city center from a high of eighteen inches a year in 1951 to only four inches a year today— still a very dangerous amount. Meanwhile, the sinking has intensified in the south. Chalco, for example, a squatter settlement built partially on the extinct lake bed, sank about a foot a year between 1985 and 1990. As the south has become increasingly urbanized, it has begun to confront the same problems the city center has; foundations are cracking, roads dip for no apparent reason, overpasses pull away from the main road, and floods are growing worse. A depression formed by the sinking around Chalco becomes a fetid lake during the rainy season. In heavy rains it overflows and floods the town. Xochimilco— once a lake, now a suburb—has had similar problems. On October 4, 1990, fourteen-year-old Sol Aguilar Gallardo stepped off a city bus and was swept away in the raging river that had replaced the street.

Despite the fact that the city depends on the aquifer for its survival no one I talked to would give me a straight answer when I asked how much longer it would be able to provide water. "I wouldn't dare to guess," said water commissioner Alfonso Martínez Baca.

"But since the city would disappear if the aquifer ran dry," I asked, "why haven't you done a detailed study to find out how much water it contains?"

"There are a lot things that haven't been done," he said.

Even in the unlikely event that the aquifer is able to meet the city's water needs for the next few decades, the cost of the centuries-long battle against the water has already been paid in thousands of lives. At 7:19 in the morning on September 19, 1985, off the coast of Michoacán, the land ruptured along an area 240 miles long and 50 miles wide. The quake, which measured 8.1 on the Richter scale, killed tens of thousands in Mexico City and reduced whole neighborhoods to rubble. Certainly the earthquake was a "natural disaster." The impetus was a cataclysmic event that could not have been controlled or predicted. But a great deal of the tragedy was also manmade, a result of centuries of environmental abuse in the Valley of Mexico.

While the earthquake leveled the small town of Lázaro Cárdenas near the epicenter, forty miles away the damage was relatively minor. That was because much of the energy liberated by the seismic motion was absorbed by the surrounding bedrock. But when the seismic waves passed under the mountains and entered the Valley of Mexico two hundred and fifty miles from the epicenter they were suddenly revitalized. The dried lake bed on which the city is built is made up of volcanic ash and sediments washed down from mountains over millions of years. The soil is highly saturated—in effect, Mexico City is built on mud. The seismic waves were trapped in the spongy soils under the ancient lakes; they bounced around wildly, hurling themselves against the denser basaltic rock that once marked the lakeshores, and then vibrating back through the soft soil until they hit something solid. It was as if four people, each holding onto a different corner, tried to shake out an enormous blanket. Buildings were pulled in two directions at once. In the marshy soil underlying the city center, the destructive force of the earthquake matched that at the epicenter. Meanwhile, in tony neighborhoods like Coyoacán and Lomas de Chapultepec, which were built on firm rock, the intensity was fifty times less.

Above the remains of Lake Texcoco, dust rose into the air. Nowhere was the damage more severe than around the Alameda [Park, near the center of the city]. Pumping from the aquifer had caused the park to sink more than twenty-five feet since the turn of the century, weakening the foundations of many of the hotels and government office buildings surrounding it. The Hotel Regis, the Hotel del Prado—both spilled their guts into the street, a tangled mass of twisted girders, concrete slabs, electrical cables, splintered furniture. Under tons of rubble were hundreds of bodies. Some were extracted and buried in common graves; others, never found, disappeared into the landfill along with the broken concrete. A block from the Hotel Regis, Lucas Gutiérrez stood outside his restaurant, the Super Leche, "and watched as a hole opened up in the ground into which disappeared his restaurant along with an apartment building in which 300 people had lived." Wrote Mexican journalist Elena Poniatowska: "It was as if a giant vacuum cleaner had sucked it up."

The earthquake represented a terrible payback for the centuries-long battle against the valley's natural environment. Despite clear evidence of its potentially disastrous consequences, city authorities continue to pump water from the aquifer.

The Aztecs believed that the fifth sun, the sun of motion, would be destroyed by earthquakes. Whether or not that prophecy is fulfilled, Mexico City must live under the weight of its history and with the consequences of poor decisions made long ago. The Spanish city has a shallow hold on the land. Despite nearly four and a half centuries of progress, despite an enormous investment in monumental infrastructure projects, the city cannot escape the destiny ascribed to it by the Aztecs. Mexico City is condemned forever to be a city on the brink.

Note

1. "A Fatal Case of Fatalism," *New York Times*, February 14, 1999.

Ciudad Nezahualcóyotl: Souls on the Run

Roberto Vallarino

A portion of the area that, centuries ago, was under Lake Texcoco has become, thanks to the ambitious drainage projects described in the previous selection, a dry salt flat. Now located some ten miles east of downtown Mexico City, this unhealthy region became home to many thousands of migrants fleeing deteriorating conditions in the countryside. The squatter settlement grew willy-nilly: the migrants built makeshift huts of cardboard and other discarded materials. Eventually, it emerged as one of the world's largest and most infamous slums, Ciudad Nezahualcóyotl. Named after the illustrious poet-king (1402–1472) of the city-state of Texcoco, Ciudad Nezahualcóyotl grew from a shantytown of about ten thousand souls in the late 1950s to over three million by the late 1980s, making it Mexico's fourth-largest city.

The following essay was published by Roberto Vallarino (b. 1955) in the daily newspaper Unomásuno *in October 1982. Vallarino has served as cultural attaché of the Mexican embassy in Yugoslavia. He has published several volumes of essays, poetry, and short stories. His powerful exposé is clearly intended to provide the reader with an apocalyptic vision of the hell of urban poverty. It is worth noting, however, that largely as a result of community organization and popular struggle, "Neza" has witnessed tangible improvements in the past decade. Such developments run counter to Vallarino's suggestion that the residents of hell are powerless to affect their own destinies. Although Neza remains far from paradise, the impression of utter helplessness, despair, and anomie conjured up here can be rightly characterized as overdrawn.*

First Movement

Federal District: two words that the middle class keeps within strict parameters, a place they identify with their own everyday social customs. Federal District: the monster of concrete that has grown uncontrollably, creating around itself strips of misery that spring up at a dizzying pace. Matrix of power, but also the matrix of misery, loathing, and the complete lack of identity found in places like Ciudad Nezahualcóyotl. . . .

We enter by the Calzada Ignacio Zaragoza. Traffic is heavy. Clouds of diesel smoke and smog spiral up from the buses and cars. Before us is the highway to Puebla. To one side, Seventh Avenue. We turn in. As the car enters, the urban environment changes: little by little, the stores disappear, the buildings give way to a horizontal series of squat gray houses. The south of Neza: the civilized part of the villa of misery that everyone, every resident of Mexico City, has helped to create. The car advances slowly over tortuous, irregular pavement, arriving at the intersection with Pantitlán Avenue, and we begin to understand where we are. A sign, pocked and rusted, its surface scarred, confirms our suspicions:

"Welcome to Nezahualcóyotl.

The city of change."

The acrid smell of diesel and gasoline fumes is behind us. An odor enters our nostrils, sweet at first, then earthy, finally rotten. First image: the wide and desolate avenue without trees. In a corner, stretched out in the dirt, two dead dogs, their eyes open and infected, their skin sickly, with greenish, frothy drool hanging from their crushed snouts: the first sign of death, abandonment, decomposition, violence.

The senses immediately recoil: our noses refuse to accept the effluvia of fecal matter and urine, of nitrates and mire. . . . Our eyes react to contact with the dust and trash that float in the air. Our stomachs churn. In that instant we are no longer residents of a *colonia* in southern Mexico City.

Everything seems like a dream scene in a black and white movie through which we pass in color; then, as the car advances, we change color, we become part of this desolate, uniform landscape. This is a vision from the Apocalypse, I think. An idea occurs to me: end of the century. Correction: end of the millennium, beginning of the end of civilization, of human identity, rupture of development, putrefied head of the entire Hydra of our system. End of the century. End of the millennium.

The heart of Seventh Avenue is like a dry river. The horizon lacks any dimension. Soon, up on a ridge we see something bright red and yellow: the tent of a traveling circus, with its deformed conical structure. Next to it, the always exciting presence of the animal kingdom in captivity: three elephants, small, dark-eyed, with dirty skin and languid faces, no tusks, shackled with chains, walking in a tiny space. There are two camels standing with their backs to us. A male and a female. The female opens her legs and urinates for a long while. Clouds of flies circle over their heads. Farther on, a pair of Peruvian llamas with bent necks, eating ochre-colored grass.

Outside the tent is a group of faceless men. There is no aggression or menace, no sweetness or sadness in their eyes: there is absence. Their faces are blank. As if some omnipresent hand had erased their features. We begin to

Lomas de Tecamachalco, a typical Mexico City slum, 1960s. (Reprinted by permission of Fototeca del INAH, Mexico.)

feel that here the humans are nothing but extensions of the animal kingdom. Mutants, horrible mutants with the forms of men. And soon, for the first time, we see those beings whose dolorous presence will be repeated incessantly in our journey: vague ghosts of children who play with pieces of plastic garbage, seated on the hinges of soggy wooden doors or on pieces of metal rusted red and ochre. There is a chorus of teenagers making dirty jokes about the elephants' trunks. The drowned, bitter laughter echoes in our ears and our minds, laughter of child-adults, elderly children, ancient children, children who are themselves parents, who often steal to eat, children who are dead in life: premonition of grown-up ghosts.

We advance by the open roadway like an alligator's snout. The cadavers of dogs and cats multiply as we move further into this shadowy realm. We see the carcass of an automobile splayed out in the middle of a road. Surely, I think, it is the home of some vagrant, of some prostitute, of some orphan. We pass in front of several signs with civic slogans. All are destroyed, leaning, their supports broken. We advance. To our left rise asbestos pipes that should carry sewage underground. There is political graffiti on the sides of the pipes, washed out by the rain. . . .

Somewhat further on we hear the babble of a group of washerwomen. . . . The women and the girls wash their clothes and the clothes of others in water that flows from a broken pipe. We come closer. They all smile, with fresh, unforgettable smiles. When they see Marta Zarak's camera they don't get angry, nor are they disconcerted. They ask what newspaper we are from. They smile again: the sound of their laughter echoes in my mind. A man who had been watching us draws near and says, after introducing himself and offering his hand: "That water has been spilling out of there for seven years. They take lots and lots of pictures, but it never gets fixed."

Before returning to the car, we see on a placard a graffiti that defines this environment: "Souls on the run." A couple, embracing, stops in front of the slogan. Souls on the run: consciences that touch each other primitively and flee, finding refuge in coitus because here there is no other way to feel alive. Men and women who copulate, not out of love, not in order to procreate, but to feel alive. The men, in the psychotic selfishness that this marginal life has driven them to, hope to feel ejaculation (not orgasm) and know that they exist; the women, to know that something, that being they carry inside them, is theirs, that they own something . . . not someone. Souls on the run.

Second Movement

I am Nezahualcóyotl
I am the poet
Tzontecochitzin ("Big headed parrot")

Ciudad Nezahualcóyotl is the empire of souls on the run. The buses pass, vomiting their diesel smoke, pouring out murderous gases from their mufflers. Seventh Avenue ends and we arrive at the Vía Tapo, on the banks of what remains of Lake Texcoco.

Reflected in the gray surface of the lake are the pillars that mark the existence of the Ancient Avenue of los Remedios, now known as Xochiaca. This is the place that must be haunted by the ghost of the Indian poet, the spirits of old hunters and beautiful women with olive skin who once bathed naked in its waters. Buses and tractor-trailers pass over Xochiaca. We see them enveloped in a dense cloud, then they're lost from sight. For an instant one gets the impression that those vehicles are running over the waters. But then we remember that only Christ has accomplished such a feat. And here Christ does not exist. He fled with the souls of the nezahualcoyotitlos.

In the distance we see the gates at the back of the airport. A plane takes off almost over our heads. Its inverted image is reflected in the mud. We move toward the point where the Vía Tapo and Xochiaca merge, a point known also as Devil's Curve since countless cars have left the highway and plunged to the bottom of the lake. The children tell of one car in which an entire family was traveling: when the remains of the car were brought up, the twisted corpses of the family were found covered with a thick coating of nitrate, mud and brine. Yes, brine. That is the greenish, dense liquid that fills what is left of Lake Texcoco.

We return by the Vía Tapo and the "tapahoyos" appear. They are children who dig holes in this part of the avenue and wait for cars to pass by. When the cars slow down, the children ask for handouts. Then they go up to the windshield, their faces wearing sad expressions, form their right hands into a conch shell, raise their mouth and in a mournful, rapid voice they say: "for a soda, for a soda, for a soda . . ." If the driver gives them some coins, the ritual continues. If he doesn't, the same hand that served as a megaphone moves as if impelled by hidden springs and forms an obscene gesture behind the driver's head. For the last time I see what remains of Texcoco. Again I think of the Indian poet:

> Where are we going, oh, where are we going?
> Are we dead or do we yet live?
> Where did time stop? Is there perhaps still time?
> A few here on earth become real. . . .

We arrive at the Colonia of the Sun. Colonia of eternal eclipse, I think. This sun does not brighten, nor provide warmth: it makes one sick, it petrifies the children, softens the daily promiscuity. We leave the car at a corner and go on foot along the streets made of mud and puddles and trash and urine. The odor of a corpse grows intense. We walk along the railroad tracks: this is the border. To one side are the marshy remains of Lake Texcoco. To the other side, below, the empire of misery: rude shacks made of cardboard and plastic, created with the refuse of the city.

We walk and we see, outside of the houses, puddles of urine and fecal matter. Clouds of flies buzz around us. Three boys, seated on the train tracks, watch us approach. We say hello. They smile, but do not speak. In one, mental retardation is evident. He smiles with an odd mouth, his right eye missing. We continue along the railroad track. There is not so much as a shrub here. I feel more and more heartsick, angry and alienated. A bit like a dead man, like a zombie. At that moment a woman with subtle features, hardened by shame, leaves her shack with a full chamberpot. She stops at the train track and hurls the waste into the boggy pools on the other side. Perhaps she is unaware that the rain will carry that waste back to her own house. She returns and tosses the chamberpot in a corner where there stands a heap of mutilated tricycles, twisted steel and plastic: the children's toys. Farther on, many children play with a whiffle ball and a piece of wood that serves as a bat, practicing baseball. A little baby girl who can barely stand upright leaves her hut, toddles intrepidly to where her brothers are playing. One of them, the one with the bat, strikes her down carelessly. Her pained cries mix with the voice of [popular singer] Javier Solís, which echoes through this musty afternoon:

Shadows, nothing more,
between your life and mine.
Shadows, nothing more,
between your love and mine.

At that moment, David Zamorano, who is our guide because he has been doing research and social work in Neza and environs for seven years, greets a middle-aged man who comes up to us. This is Rubén, the artist of the slum. Rubén paints. He paints for hire and for pleasure. After greeting us, he brings a painting from his house: it is a copy of a work by Blanchard, painted in 1867, which depicts the Moulin Rouge and certain streets of nineteenth-century Paris. The windmill has no blades yet. Rubén has made Toulouse Lautrec the central figure in his painting. Dogs dart out from everywhere. They come near us. They smell us. They grunt. Rubén shoos them away. Finally, he tells us that last week the train decapitated his own dog, one he loved very much. He says it with apparent coldness. But in his opaque eyes we see courage and sorrow as he tells us this. We say goodbye to this man, who waves his hand and grows smaller as we retreat. We again walk along the railroad track. Now there are more children seated on the rails. One of them has a spinning top in his hand. I tell him to throw it. He looks at me as though I were a rare bug. A hard smile fights to emerge from the depths of his soul. Then, with a rapid movement, he throws the top, which lands in the center of his world — a piece of land saturated with feces and flies — and, for one instant, in that boy's mind, the order of the universe is restored.

Third Movement

The image of these elderly children stays in our minds. We go once again to the car and a pack of hungry, mangy dogs, one of them missing an eye, wanders by us. We hold our breath and pretend to throw a stone, which is enough to drive them away. I feel the adrenaline run through my shoulders. We leave the Colonia of the Sun. We don't speak among ourselves. We have become huge eyeballs that have witnessed the rupture between man and society, the return to the prehistoric: the neo-prehistoric. Once again the car runs along the Vía Tapo. . . .

We travel across a space that two years ago functioned as a garbage dump, and where now a sports field is being constructed. The blue color of the recently painted fence contrasts with the grayness of the foundation. We recall that all along this avenue the government of Mexico State planted thirty thousand trees. The ones that survive are so scarce that we cannot avoid thinking again of the sterile, briny land.

We arrive at the Colonia of San Lorenzo, one of the areas most affected by the rainy season. The images are swamp-like. This place smells, literally, like shit, human shit, not animal. This is Chimalhuacán. Again my memory weaves its unexpected web: here, between 1974 and 1975, mayor Ruperto Flores took over these lands, and when the residents of Nezahualcóyotl began to invade them he saw that they were fractioned out among the supporters of the PRI. It was then that the famous feud broke out between the people of Chimalhuacán and Neza. Then the armed forces occupied the zone and brought more death to this cemetery. . . .

The hills that mark the entrance to the Puebla highway are growing closer. We cross a bridge under which the foul "black waters" run: but the water is not black, it is greenish, yellowish at the banks, clammy waters in which flies with outsized bodies and blue wings nest.

On foot, we enter the Colonia San Lorenzo. Around a corner comes one of the thirty-three youth gangs who sow terror in this desolate parcel. One of them takes out his penis and shouts provocatively. When they recognize David, though they continue shouting insults at us, they walk away, disappearing down an alleyway. We can only see the interminable perspective of the miserable huts crowded together, one after another: the sensation of infinity.

Soon, upon arriving at the corner, we see here and there infected puddles. The rain has caused them to rise to within a yard of the walls of the houses. Many of these puddles are tinged with colors. Stagnant water, some painted red, some yellow. In this neighborhood, many families make a living by painting soccer balls, and they throw out the leftover ink which now brightens the puddles, giving color to those sepia images.

We approach one of the largest puddles. We see on its edges a dark stain: they are flies, filthy flies of three, four centimeters, which fertilize their eggs in these stagnant waters. We must walk slowly so as not to disturb the bees that buzz ever louder. Some kids play at the other edge of the water, in which is reflected the cubic brick structure that forms the School With No Name. The flies buzz in concentric circles above us. A rat the size of a cat runs from one corner and does a spectacular jump over the puddle. The kids play, eat pieces of decomposed chicken, stop there, observing our alien presences.

We return, preceded by a flying, buzzing retinue. We get into the car and head toward our final stop: the main trash dump of Nezahualcóyotl. Fences enclose this immense space, which shows off its hills of refuse. A creamy white color predominates. Behind it is the last stagnant pool we can see. We cannot avoid the reflection: what is beneath that infected water, which reveals only the semicircular forms of tires and the fantasmal figures of plastic bags? David reads my thoughts and clarifies them with a terrible confession: this is where they have found the corpses that the federal police discard in order to hide their criminal actions. I imagine the bottom of the pool covered with decomposing bodies mired in the mud, with mutilated human limbs resting in the ooze.

The car stops, and with it my hallucination about the pool. There is another apocalyptic image: a bulldog, or a cross between a bulldog and boxer, covered . . . with a blue sheet, one eye open, a bullet hole in one side, his fangs showing. The flies circle the corpse, which is splayed out atop a trash pile.

We enter the junkyard. There is the desolation of the ephemeral: mattress springs, pieces of grimy cloth, beer cans, sardine cans, rusted metal, bottles, used tissues, mud-covered shoes, skeletons of chairs, furniture, toys, flasks, cardboard boxes, crutches, dead rats, and children and men and women who wait for the trucks to dump off tons and tons of garbage.

One of those trucks arrives. It advances ponderously. It stops there, at the base of the trash pile. A group of dark children appears and they are immediately submerged in the mountain of trash, looking for useful things, be they objects or food. They are twisted kids: they sniff glue and poverty, and they hasten toward the end of this thing which is not life, but a heavy walk over shit and misery. The trashpickers walk here and there: some pick up cardboard, which they tie up and stack in the center of the trashyard; others pick up flasks and fill sacks with them; still others specialize in plastic, glass, metallic objects. A girl carries a sack full of bottles. Her sweaty face expresses bitterness, impotence, weariness.

Soon it is impossible to move forward because the trash obstructs the central roadway. We back up. We see a pair of old people (we had not yet seen any old people on our trip) made of grime. Their skin covered with black scabs. Their eyes sunk into prominent cheekbones. Their hands like animal claws. Before entering again into the Vía Tapo we see several orange bulldozers near the fence around the junkyard. We ask a boy what they are used for.

"Look here," he says, "they flatten the trash and make holes to bury stuff. Although . . . to tell the truth, one time I came here very late at night and they were making holes and tossing dead people in them."

We leave. We are mute. We stop before arriving at Zaragoza Avenue and buy six cans of beer. We drink but the bitter, earthy taste remains on the palate and on the tongue. We leave this dead land that is stretching rapidly out toward Puebla. Again the odors change. The diesel and the gasoline fumes scatter through the atmosphere. But now it is different. The odor of Ciudad Nezahualcóyotl and environs doesn't leave our nostrils. And although we recognize that in that moment the only thing we want is to get home to our petite bourgeois homes and take a bath and wash away the presence of Neza, we know that we will never forget its existence.

Neza lives. There it is: around the corner, close to our daily lives. Soap and water will not get rid of it. It remains in our eyes, in our conscience, like a burning, maddening, spasmodic and terrible stain.

Modesta Gómez

Rosario Castellanos

Few Mexican writers have written as gracefully or as poignantly about the inequali-
ties of class and the intersecting dynamics of race and gender as Rosario Castellanos
(1925–1974)—themes that are brilliantly invoked in "Modesta Gómez." Castellanos
was raised on her affluent family's ranch in southern Chiapas, near the Guatema-
lan border, where she witnessed firsthand the cruelties and ambiguities inherent in
Indian–white relations. She later studied in Mexico City, earning a master's degree in
philosophy from the National University in 1955, where she later taught comparative
literature and also served as press and information director. Castellanos published
two highly regarded novels, some theatrical works, and several volumes of poetry,
essays, and short stories, including City of Kings, *about San Cristóbal de las Casas,*
in which the following selection appears. In 1971 she was named Mexico's ambassador
to Israel, where she was electrocuted in a tragic accident in 1974, at the age of 49.

How cold the mornings are in Ciudad Real! A mist covers every thing. From
invisible places you hear the chimes of the first mass, the creak of massive
doors opening, the wheeze of mills beginning to turn.

Huddled in the folds of her black shawl, Modesta Gómez was shivering as
she walked back and forth. Her friend, Doña Agueda, the butcher, noticed:

"Some people don't have any stomach for this sort of work, they pretend
they're too delicate, but what I think is that they're just plain lazy. The bad
thing about being an ambusher is that you've got to get up so early."

I've always gotten up early, thought Modesta. That's how my mother raised
me.

(No matter how she tried, Modesta couldn't remember her mother's scold-
ing words, that face bending over her in early childhood. Too many years had
gone by.)

They sent me away when I was just a little girl. One less mouth at home
was a great relief for everyone.

Modesta could still remember the clean change of clothes they had dressed
her in for the occasion. Then, suddenly, she found herself standing before an

enormous door with a bronze knocker: a finely sculpted hand, with a ring entwined on one of its fingers. It was the house of the Ochoas: Don Humberto, owner of the "La Esperanza" store; Doña Romelia, his wife; Berta, Dolores and Clara, his daughters; and the youngest, his son Jorgito.

The house was full of marvelous surprises. What a feeling of wonder when Modesta discovered the drawing room! Cane furniture, wicker holders with fans of multicolored postcards spread out against the wall, the floor made of wood. Wood! A pleasant sensation of warmth rose from Modesta's bare feet all the way up to her heart. Yes, she was happy to stay with the Ochoas, to know that from now on this magnificent house would also be her home.

Doña Romelia led her to the kitchen. The servants gave the waddling little girl a hostile reception, and when they discovered that her hair was swarming with lice they unceremoniously dunked her into a vat filled with ice-cold water. They scrubbed her with soap-root, over and over again, until her braids were squeaky clean.

"All right, then. Now you look good enough to be presented to the *señores*. They're finicky enough already. But they really take a lot of pains with little Jorgito. Since he's the only boy . . ."

Modesta and Jorgito were almost the same age. And yet, she was the baby-carrier, the one who had to take care of him and keep him entertained.

"They say that my legs got twisted from carrying him around so much, because they weren't strong enough yet. Who knows?"

But the little boy was really spoiled rotten. If he couldn't have his own way, he went "completely nuts," as he himself used to say. They could hear him screaming all the way out to the store. Doña Romelia would hurry over.

"What did they do to you, lambkins, my little darling?"

Without breaking his wails even for a second, Jorgito would point to Modesta.

"The carrier?" the mother nodded. "We'll fix her so that she doesn't lay a finger on you again. Look, a smack here, right in the noodle, a yank on the ear and a whack on the behind. Is that better, my little dumpling, little apple of my eye? All right, you're going to have to let me go now; I have things to do."

In spite of these incidents, the children were inseparable. Together they suffered through all the childhood illnesses; together they discovered secrets; together they got into mischief.

Although this sort of intimacy relieved Doña Romelia from the extreme attention that her son demanded, it still struck her as uncalled-for. How could she ward off the risks? The only idea that occurred to Doña Romelia was to put Jorgito into primary school, and to forbid Modesta from using the familiar *vos* when she addressed him.

"He's your master, your *patrón,*" she explained condescendingly, "and you can't be so chummy with the *patrones.*"

While the boy was learning to read and count, Modesta was busy in the kitchen; feeding the fireplace, hauling in water, and gathering up slop for the hogs.

They waited until she was a little bigger, until she'd had her first period, to give Modesta a more important position. They put away the old mat she had slept on since first arriving, and replaced it with a cot that was going unused since a cook had died. Under the pillow Modesta placed her wooden comb and her mirror with its celluloid frame. By this time she was a robust little pole, and she liked to put on airs. When she went out to the street to run an errand, she washed her feet very carefully, scrubbing them with a stone. The starch in her skirts crackled as she walked past.

The street was the stage for her triumphs: young men, barefoot like her but with decent jobs and ready to marry, courted her with rough compliments; the "swells," Jorgito's friends, propositioned her; and wealthy old men offered her presents and money.

At night Modesta dreamed of being the lawfully married wife of an artisan. She could imagine the humble little house on the outskirts of Ciudad Real, having to scrape to make a living, the life of sacrifices that awaited her. No, better not. There would always be time enough for a legal marriage. Better to sow her oats first, to have a good time like bad women do. An old bawd would sell her, the kind that offers girls to gentlemen. Modesta could see herself in a corner of the brothel, wrapped in a shawl with her eyes lowered, while drunken, scandalous men made bids to see who would be the first to possess her. And then, if everything went well, the man who made her his mistress would set her up in a little business so she could support herself. Modesta would not hold her head up high, she wouldn't be a model of purity as though she had left the charge of her *patrones* heading for the church, all dressed in white. But maybe she would have a child with good blood, and a little savings. She would learn some trade. With time her reputation would grow, and they would call on her to grind chocolate or to cure evil spells in the homes of well-off people.

But instead, she had ended up being an ambusher. What a topsy-turvy world this is!

One night Modesta's dreams were interrupted. The door to the servants' room opened quietly, and in the darkness someone moved toward the girl's cot. Modesta felt heavy breathing close to her, and a rapidly beating pulse. She crossed herself, thinking it a ghost. But a hand fell brutally upon her body. She tried to scream, and her scream was smothered by another mouth covering her own. She and her adversary struggled while the other women slept soundly. From a scar on his shoulder, Modesta recognized Jorgito. She didn't try to defend herself any longer. She closed her eyes, and submitted to him.

Doña Romelia had suspicions about her son's hanky-panky, and the servants' gossip removed all doubt. But she decided to pretend that she knew nothing. After all, Jorgito was a man, not a saint; and he was at that age when the blood starts to boil. Besides, it was preferable for him to find release in his own home, instead of going around with tramps who teach boys bad habits and bring them to ruin.

Thanks to his rape of Modesta, Jorge could brag about being a "real" man. For several months he had been smoking in secret, and he had gone off and gotten drunk two or three times. But in spite of the taunts of his friends, he still hadn't dared to go with women. He was afraid of them: all painted up, so vulgar in their gestures and the way they talked. But with Modesta he felt comfortable. The only thing that worried him was that his family might find out what was going on between them. To mislead them, in front of everybody he treated Modesta coldly, and even with exaggerated harshness. But at night he again sought out that body he knew through long familiarity, in which the smells of home and childhood memories mingled together.

But as the saying goes, "What night hides is revealed by day." Modesta's complexion began to take on a mottled look; there were dark circles under her eyes and her movements were listless. The other servants made comments, accompanied by obscene winks and malicious laughter.

One morning Modesta had to stop her work grinding corn because a sudden attack of nausea swept over her. A tattletale went to notify the *patrona* that Modesta was pregnant.

Doña Romelia showed up in the kitchen like a fury.

"You ungrateful little slut. You would have to go off the deep end. And what did you think would happen? That I was going to cover up your carrying-on? Not on your life. I have a husband that I have to answer to, daughters that I need to have good examples for. So I want you out of here right now."

Before she left the Ochoas' house, Modesta was subjected to a humiliating search. The lady and her daughters went through the girl's clothing and possessions to make certain that she hadn't stolen anything. After that they formed a sort of barricade in the entryway, and Modesta had to go through it in order to leave.

Fleetingly, she glanced at those faces. Don Humberto's, ruddy from fat, with its watery little eyes; Doña Romelia's, twitching with indignation; the girls', Clara, Dolores, and Berta's, curious and slightly pale with envy. Modesta looked for Jorgito's face, but he wasn't there.

Modesta had reached the town limits of Moxviquil. She stopped. Other women, barefoot and badly dressed just like her, were already there. They looked at her with distrust.

One of them spoke up for her: "Leave her alone. She's a Christian like anybody else, and she's got three kids to support."

"And what about us? Are we some kind of rich women?"

"Did we come here to sweep up money with a broom?"

"What this one takes isn't going to get us out of the poor-house. You've got to have a little pity. She was just left a widow."

"Who was her husband?"

"Alberto Gómez. The one who just died."

"The bricklayer?"

"The one who drank himself to death?"

(Although it was spoken in a low voice, Modesta could hear the remark. A violent flush spread across her cheeks. Alberto Gómez, the one who drank himself to death! Filthy lies! Her husband didn't die like that. All right, it was true that he did his share of drinking, even more than his share lately. But the poor man had good reason to. He was tired of wearing the pavement out looking for work. Nobody builds a house, nobody has repairs done when it's the rainy season. Alberto got tired of waiting on porticos or in doorways for the rains to stop. That's what got him going into bars in the first place. Bad company did the rest. Alberto neglected his obligations, he mistreated his family. You had to forgive him. When a man isn't in his right mind, he does one awful thing after another. The next day, when the haze wore off, it scared him to see Modesta all full of bruises, and the children in a corner, trembling with fear. He cried with shame and remorse. But he didn't change. Vice is stronger than reason.

While she waited up for her husband at all hours of the night, Modesta tortured herself thinking about the million things that could happen to him on the streets. A fight, a stray bullet, being run over. Modesta imagined him carried in on a stretcher, covered with blood, and she wrung her hands wondering where she was going to find money for the burial.

But things happened differently. She had to go get Alberto because he had fallen asleep on the sidewalk, and there the night found him and the evening dew fell on him. Alberto had no visible cuts or bruises. He complained a little about a pain in his side. They made him an ointment out of animal fat just in case he had taken a chill; they put cupping-glasses on him; he drank embered water. But the pain only got stronger. The death rattle was brief, and the neighbor women took up a collection to pay for the coffin.

"The cure turned out to be worse for you than the disease," Modesta's friend Agueda told her. "You married Alberto so you'd be under a man's hand, and so the son of the famous Jorge would grow up with some respect. And now you end up a widow, not a penny to your name, with three mouths to feed and nobody to look out for you."

It was true. And true also that the years Modesta was married to Alberto were years of pain and hard work. True that when he was drunk, the brick-layer beat her, throwing in her face how Jorgito had abused her, and true that his death was the biggest humiliation of all for her family. But Alberto had come through for Modesta at just the right time: when everyone had turned their backs on her so as not to see her dishonor. Alberto had given her his name and his legitimate children; he had made a lady out of her. How many of these beggars in widows' weeds talking behind her back wouldn't have sold their souls to the devil to be able to say the same thing!)

The early morning mist began to lift. Modesta had sat down on a rock. One of the ambushers approached her.

"*Yday?* Weren't you one of the clerks in Doña Agueda's butcher-shop?"

"I still am. But I don't make enough money there. With me and my three little ones I needed something extra. My friend Agueda told me about this."

"We only do it because when you're poor, you lead a dog's life. But being an ambusher wears you down. It's hardly worth it."

(Modesta searched the face of the woman talking to her, suspicious. What was the point of saying awful things like that? Probably to scare her off so she wouldn't be any competition. That was a big mistake. Modesta was no pansy: in other places she had gone through her own hard times. Because the business of being behind a butcher counter was no paradise either. Nothing but work all morning long: keeping the place clean — and with the flies there was never any end to it; taking care of the merchandise; bargaining with the clients. Those maids from rich houses who were always demanding the fat-test pieces of meat, the best cuts, and the cheapest price! She had to give in to their wishes, but Modesta took out her revenge on the others. The ones who looked poor and badly dressed, the women who had stands in the mar-ket place and their employees, she held strictly to account; and if they ever tried to get their meat at another stand because it was a better deal, she would scream at them and never wait on them again.)

"Yes, handling meat is a dirty job. But it's even worse to be an ambusher. Here you have to fight with Indians."

(And where don't you have to? thought Modesta. Her friend Agueda had instructed her right from the start: for Indians you saved the spoiled or grainy meat, the big lead weight that tilted the scales, and your howls of indignation if he made even the slightest protest. The women who ran the other stands

Chamula Women. (Photographer Gertrude Blom. Reprinted by permission of Na Bolom Museum, Mexico.)

would come running over when they heard the outburst. A fight would break out, with gendarmes and people who were just curious joining in, egging on the participants with sharp words, insulting gestures and shoves. The outcome of the scuffle, invariably, was the Indian's hat or bag that the victor held up in the air like a trophy, and the vanquished's frightened run to escape the threats and mockery of the crowd.)

"Here they come now!"

The ambushers stopped talking in order to look toward the hills. Now they could make out some figures moving around in the mist. They were Indians, loaded down with the merchandise they were going to sell in Ciudad Real. The ambushers moved forward a few steps in their direction. Modesta imitated them.

The two groups were face to face. A few brief seconds of anticipation went by. Finally the Indians began walking again, their heads lowered, their eyes fixed obstinately on the ground, as if the magical recourse of not looking at the women could make them non-existent.

The ambushers threw themselves upon the Indians tumultuously. Stifling screams, they struggled with them for possession of objects they didn't want to damage. Finally, when the wool blanket or the net of vegetables or the clay utensil were in the ambusher's hands, she would take a few coins from her blouse, and without counting them, let them drop to the ground, where the fallen Indian would pick them up.

Taking advantage of the fight's confusion, a young Indian girl tried to escape, running away with her burden intact.

"That's one of yours," one of the ambushers shouted jeeringly to Modesta.

Automatically, just like an animal trained for a long time in the hunt, Modesta threw herself after the fugitive. When she caught up to her she grabbed her skirt, and the two of them tumbled to the ground. Modesta fought until she was on top of her. She pulled her braids, slapped her cheeks, dug her fingernails into her ears. Harder! Harder!

"You damn Indian! Now you're going to pay me for everything!"

The Indian girl writhed in pain. Ten thin lines of blood ran from her earlobes down to her neck.

"No more, Ma'am, no more . . ."

Inflamed, panting, Modesta held on to her victim. She didn't want to let go of her, not even when the Indian handed over the wool blanket she had been hiding. Another ambusher had to intervene.

"That's enough," she said forcefully to Modesta, pulling her to her feet.

Modesta staggered like a drunk while she used her shawl to wipe her face, dripping with sweat.

"And you," continued the ambusher, turning to the Indian, "quit sniveling: that's no way to act. Nothing's happened to you. Take this money and God help you. Be thankful we're not taking you to the Courthouse for causing a disturbance."

The Indian girl hastily picked up the coins, and quickly ran away. Modesta watched, uncomprehending.

"Let this be a lesson to you," the ambusher told her. "I'm keeping the blanket since I paid for it. Maybe tomorrow you'll have better luck."

Modesta nodded. Tomorrow. Yes, she would come back tomorrow, and the day after tomorrow, and forever. It was true what they said: an ambusher's job is hard, and there's not much profit in it. She looked at her bloody fingernails. She didn't know why. But she was satisfied.

VII

From the Ruins

The shocks attending Mexico's postwar modernization came in the form of growing rural and urban poverty, environmental destruction, political corruption, official manipulation of workers and peasants, and selective, locally administered violence of the sort that took the lives of Rubén Jaramillo and his family. However, by far the most spectacular instance of state violence in postrevolutionary Mexico occurred on October 2, 1968, when troops and police opened fire indiscriminately into a crowd of student protesters and bystanders at the Plaza of Three Cultures in Tlatelolco, killing several hundred. In view of the growing popularity of the underdog student movement and its generally nonviolent nature and modest demands, the massacre at Tlatelolco struck many as a hideous overreaction. Indeed, it seemed further evidence of the growing paranoia of an unpopular and unrepresentative regime that would stop at nothing to project an image of stability and modernity on the occasion of the nation's hosting of the summer Olympic Games.

Dissident movements have never been lacking in Mexico, but according to some observers—most notably Carlos Monsiváis and Elena Poniatowska, who are both included in this section—it took such debacles as Tlatelolco and the government's inept handling of the disastrous earthquakes that struck Mexico City in 1985 to bring such movements above ground and make them more inclusive of Mexican society at large. A series of dramatic social, political, and natural events—the student movement; the earthquakes and their aftermath; the fraud-riddled presidential campaign of 1988; the signing of NAFTA and the immediate outbreak of the Zapatista rebellion in Chiapas; the subsequent revelations of corruption in the regime of President Carlos Salinas de Gortari; and several high-level political assassinations—have registered substantial impacts on civil society, and a number of encouraging developments have emerged from the ruins of Mexico's frustrating attempts to modernize. Perhaps most significant, in July 2000, after seventy years of rule by the PRI, the official party was defeated by the candidate of the center-right National

Action Party (PAN), Vicente Fox. This epochal succession of events indicates that there are limits to what the Mexican people are prepared to endure, and that change can, for the most part, be brought about peacefully.

The Student Movement of 1968

Elena Poniatowska

Many students of modern Mexico see October 1968 as an important watershed in the country's history. Certainly, the mass mobilization of students and the government's brutal response had far-reaching effects. Although some Mexicans applauded their government's decisive action, many more were impressed by the appearance of such a unique, massive, and essentially peaceful protest movement, and appalled by the violence that extinguished it. In the aftermath of Tlatelolco, the state was forced to struggle mightily to regain some semblance of credibility, while social activists found the experience both traumatizing and empowering. If the optimism of social critic Carlos Monsiváis is well founded, then the student movement must be seen as the seedbed of Mexico's burgeoning "civil society."

Perhaps the writer who has contributed most to a judicious evaluation of the events of 1968 is Elena Poniatowska, one of Mexico's most celebrated living authors. Born in Paris in 1932 and descended from Polish royalty, she was raised amid great privilege. With the outbreak of World War II, her family moved permanently to her mother's homeland, Mexico. In the 1950s, Poniatowska launched a career in journalism and eventually founded La Jornada, one of Mexico's most respected dailies. She is best known for her unique blending of journalism and literature, which includes several "testimonial" novels and artfully arranged collections of interviews. Her book La Noche de Tlatelolco (1971) was a best-seller which spliced together eyewitness accounts of the violence with memories of former participants in the movement. The following essay, published in 1980, presents a more personal response to the same events. Poniatowska has increasingly come to identify herself with the popular classes and their efforts to bring about meaningful change.

In the years that followed the revolution of 1910 with its million dead, poor Mexico knew only authoritarianism. The peasants were given back part of the land, but without water or credit or the tools to cultivate it; the workers never got anything except bosses, both foreign and domestic, who exploited them. . . .

In 1968, a kind of silence pervaded the country. Then suddenly a movement broke out that was dynamic, autonomous, and—why not say it?—infuriatingly unexpected, a movement of pure and incorruptible men . . . , and of thousands of young people united by an indissoluble bond: courage. The people marching in the streets were not peasants or workers. This was a rebellion made by readers and writers. Against what? The apparent pretexts could have been anything, but fundamentally they protested against misery, imposition, and corruption.

These young people had been destined to join the very government they were rising up against. The so-called "cadres" were the government's future leaders. They came from the UNAM [the National Autonomous University], from the Polytechnic School, from the Agricultural School at Chapingo, from the preparatory schools. Nevertheless, in Mexico, universities are the places where the country's problems are discussed. In the absence of strong political parties, the universities have become redoubts in which professors and students freely express their ideas. This influences the young, it drives them to action; one need only tour University City and read the signs to realize that the students there support the strike of doctors from the General Hospital, the mothers of the "disappeared" and of political prisoners, the Amnesty Law, the Subway Sanitation Workers who have yet to unionize; they use very good slogans to denounce *charrismo* and *tapadismo*[1] and the politicians who divvy up the country every six years.

In Mexico there is an age to be idealistic, another to be a *guadalupano* [a devotee of the Virgin of Guadalupe], another to be anti-imperialist, another to be anti-government, and another to become a *priísta*. One becomes a *priísta* upon attaining maturity. All of the other stages are youthful follies. How many men who were once leftists now recall their youthful years with a pat on the back and a mischievous little smile? In 1968 Mexico was young, and it made everyone young. The student movement did this. It was the most intense period in many years and, once things calmed down, many came to appreciate that it was the most intense moment of their lives. Something was irremediably lost in 1968 (death is always irremediable), but something was won. . . .

This chronicle tries to follow the trajectory of the student movement of 1968, not to redeem its errors, but . . . because no homage to that great moment in our history is excessive.

IT IS DIFFICULT to describe Mexico in the fifties and sixties in anything other than a social chronicle, because that was the prevailing style, or at least it was the style we lived. What did the student movement of 1968 do? In the first place, it destroyed the official image of Mexico. That image was lustrous, full of blue skies and promises. Above all, it suggested that we were different from the rest of Latin America; we were proudly Mexican. (What does that mean? Who knows, but it is a cliché from which we have not yet freed ourselves.) All of the countries to the south — or rather, down below — were backward (even Brazil, with its drums and gorillas), and they looked up to us; we should be the leader, the spokesman for the continent. The Mexican revolution was the precursor, the interrupted elder sister of other revolutions. In 1939, the great revolutionary family began its take-off; the eagle, seated on the nopal cactus, would take flight, and would dominate the skies of the entire continent.

THE SECOND WORLD WAR gave a great boost to the Mexican economy. The closure of foreign markets restricted imports, and Mexico was able to accumulate an enormous quantity of foreign reserves that it later invested in machinery, so as to begin its industrialization. Already during the war we exported henequen, *ixtle,* minerals, silver, cotton clothing and large quantities of chickpeas to Spain . . . ; by the end of the conflict we had developed industries in construction, cement, corrugated metal, electricity, glass, paints and, collaterally, in shoes and apparel. Mexico financed this development with foreign loans. During the term of [Manuel] Avila Camacho [1940–1946] the loans barely reached seven million dollars, but during [Miguel] Alemán's term [1946–1952] they rose to 43 million, then nearly tripled under [Adolfo] Ruiz Cortines [1952–1958] to 125 million, and they exceeded 397 million dollars with [Adolfo] López Mateos [1958–1964]. Since then we have continued to go into debt, happy to have a country worthy of credit, while our own money is devalued vertiginously.

Of course, the great Revolutionary Family not only established the foundations but also set the rules of the game. It was renovated every six years, although its members were always the same: they were *avilacamachistas, alemanistas, ruizcortinistas, lopezmateístas, diazordacistas.* Never did an opposition party (officially) win an important election, never more than a mayoralty. . . . The *"istas"* had a common denominator: they had breakfast together; some had been members of others' cabinets; they owed one another favors; they were all quite familiar with the gears, the intricate machinery of our Institutionalized Revolution. They used terms and expressions like "democracy," "effective suffrage / no reelection," "economic growth"; slogans like "Only one road: Mexico," "God helps those who are early to rise," "Twenty million Mexicans cannot be wrong," "There is no place like Mexico," "Fair distribution of wealth," and all the other "postulates and principles emanating from the Revolution." According to statistics — and plain sight — the Revolution had produced thousands and thousands of prominent millionaires.

THIS PLEASANT AND prosperous image lasted nearly forty years. There was no organized political criticism, and very few truly dissident intellectual positions. There was no Flores Magón. . . .

Mexican politicians, cunning as they were effective, were and still are consummate masters of the techniques of personal enrichment and aggrandizement. Whatever for whomever: they rarely forget their friends, their banking buddies: *"My friend, for you, anything; don't even mention it."* They entered into shady schemes; they had many ways of fixing things; and politics were always carried out in secret . . . if word ever got out, forget about Watergate! They drank in the 123 Club of Luisito Muñoz, who was as enigmatic and crafty as a mountain lion; or in Fatso Bloomy Blumenthal's Cyro's. Carlos Denegri, a boisterous journalist, set the tone of daily events, both in his sometimes excellent reporting, as well as in his personal conduct. If a woman he was chasing took refuge on a ranch up north, he would go after her, angry and hungover, and with the governor's help he would order the highways blocked off. They were pure machos. *Guard your hens well, my rooster is on the loose! No old lady runs away from me! Hey, bring me another drink; these ones are on me!*

While the macho environment of the cantina invaded Mexican politics, the social pages tried to dignify the *official* lives of those same politicians. Alongside the carousing there were debutante balls; alongside the drinking sprees, there were sweethearts covered in their tulle veils, solemn funeral honors, rosaries in La Profesa; and Archbishop Luis María Martínez, in his strapless cassock, would render even the nightclubs decent with his benedictions. . . .

THE FEDERAL DISTRICT (Mexico City) grew. It spread out to cover an area of 1,499 square kilometers; it stretched upward (the Hotel de México is 218 meters from the ground to the top of its antenna); it swelled . . . ; and it prospered (on University Avenue alone there were four Burger Boys). The single-story houses disappeared overnight, and multifamily houses and condominiums sprang up like mushrooms; viaducts and beltways, with many uneven stretches, were enlarged; self-service stores and residential communities sprouted. . . . It was delirious. For years, Mexico was nothing more than a city of pickaxes and potholes, detours and bottlenecks: *"Work in progress, pardon the inconvenience,"* and so on. Everything was construction, progress, well-being. *"Buy now, pay later."* There were systems of generalized credit, magic little cards that included even the waiter's tip, the chance to own one's own car, one's own home, . . . *"There is a Ford in Your Future," "Malena and her Volkswagen,"* furniture on installments, bank loans, the ISSSTE, Social Security, theaters, grand movie houses, good and cheap, public parks, sports fields in the suburban neighborhoods, Chapultepec Park for the poor, this Happy World.

Never had the hotel chains—the Hiltons, the Sheratons, the Ramada Inns—enjoyed such a meteoric rise as in our country: docile little Mexico, Chiquita Banana, *"very good flavor,"* a stage for Frank Sinatra and the jet-set. . . . *"Please come in, and pardon this, your poor home,"* the mayor would say, offering up the tropical paradise of Acapulco.

Ninety-five percent of the tourists who came to Mexico were from the United States. In every part of the world, even the deserts, the United States had established its hotels and imposed the American Way of Life, the cocktail lounge, the lobby, the bathroom with its seat covers and toilet paper (smooth as a rose petal), so that the North Americans, who embarked on a veritable fever of traveling, would feel at home everywhere; even in Chalchicomula they would find the ambience to which they were accustomed and which always brought them a feeling of security. Mexico was North Americanized. Tourism was our industry without smokestacks. If we were unable to process our own products, we would at least sell them our folklore: the anthropologists of the world would lean toward our swarthy faces to fathom the Mexican soul and remove its two masks: the indigenous and the Spanish.

Among the great condominium projects that sprang up was one that surrounded the little colonial church of Santo Santiago: Tlatelolco, with one hundred and two buildings and a population of around 70,000. Many of them daily crossed a plaza: the Plaza of the Three Cultures.

OF COURSE, THERE had been some chinks in our country's official image, but they were scarcely perceptible. Do you remember, for example, when the miners of Nueva Rosita, Coahuila, marched more than a thousand kilometers on foot to Mexico City in 1952 to present their demands? Do you know about professor Othón Salazar, who, together with the Ninth Section of the National Union of Education Workers, occupied the patio of the Secretariat of Public Education for several days in 1958, asking for a salary increase for the primary school teachers whose wages condemned them to inevitable martyrdom?

In 1958 and 1959, the union-government-church-bosses-press chorus had no fissures in the face of the railroad workers' movement headed by Demetrio Vallejo. All of the chambers of commerce and industrialists condemned their petitions for a pay raise as wild pretensions. Demetrio Vallejo, the top leader, and Valentín Campa spent eleven and a half years deprived of their freedom. There was a generalized persecution throughout the country; the activist railroad workers, followers of Vallejo, were jailed, kept under surveillance, beaten, denounced as communists, bad Mexicans, unpatriotic sell-outs to a foreign power. . . . The railroad workers who were fired in 1958 have not yet been rehired, although twenty years have passed. Also imprisoned in the first years of the period of López Mateos were David Alfaro Siqueiros and Filomeno Mata. Their crime: directly criticizing the President of the Republic, the Untouchable One.

On May 23, 1962, the peasant leader Rubén Jaramillo died, riddled with bullets. The photograph of his embrace with President López Mateos appeared on the cover of the magazine *Política*. Rubén Jaramillo was assassinated in Xochicalco, state of Morelos, along with his wife Epifania García Zúñiga, who was eight months pregnant, and his sons Ricardo, Enrique and Filemón. Jaramillo had been a Zapatista soldier. He fought the landlords and obtained for the peasants rights to the lands of Michapa and Los Guarines, in Morelos. His daughter Raquel told how soldiers with Thompson machine guns came to her father's house in armored vehicles and military jeeps. They were the ones who committed the multiple murder. None of the guilty parties ever came to trial.

In the first months of the [Gustavo] Díaz Ordaz government—in 1964—the doctors' movement was also repressed. Only the magazines *Sucesos* and *Política* defended them, but in general the press, the misinformed public, and the media applauded the government measures. How was it possible for the doctors to go out on strike without abandoning the sick, risking their patients' deaths, just so they could get an increase in salaries that were already 650 pesos a month . . . ? Was this not a criminal attitude? It was blackmail to go on strike and put the lives of the sick in danger; the striking doctors were murderers. . . . Result: Díaz Ordaz fired them all. After that, we lapsed into the approving drowsiness that seems to characterize us, and the doctors who led the movement were left destitute.

EXCEPT FOR THESE events, which were promptly stashed away in the archives, our national life continued to present a postcard image: the Mexican sky, intensely blue; the Mexican rose, exported along with our popular handicrafts; Mexican white, the very white Sunday clothes that our Indians wore, the embroidered *huipiles* [shifts] of Yucatán; Mexican yellow, the straw sombrero beneath which the muleskinner dozes peacefully in an eternal siesta, for, as he would say, everything can be put off till tomorrow. . . . Mexico was marvelous; the tourists were fascinated by the cheapness of our silversmith shops, our awe-inspiring landscapes, our unpronounceable volcanoes, and the meekness of "those sweet little Mexican Indians" in Taxco who would pester them in English. It was fitting that Mexico City should be the site of the Olympiad; no other country in the world was more appropriate than ours; it shone like a gold coin in the midst of the jungles and undiscovered regions of Latin America, a horn of plenty . . . ; that song of mariachis, with their strumming guitars: *"I am like a green chili pepper, sad lady, hot but tasty!";* this paradise that runs from the Atlantic to the Pacific. . . . Mexico, site of the Olympiad! A prized trophy, cost what it may! (the important thing is not to win but to play the game); the Olympic games in Mexico would be the gold medal, the culmination of the efforts of Mexico's politicians and of an ascendant economic development, ruled by the PRI, which devours all.

The XIX Olympiad was to begin in Mexico on October 18, 1968. Before that, on June 23, the Spiders and the Ciudadelans, two gangs of vagrants—not students—sporting the insignias of the Vocational School #2 and the Isaac Ochoterena preparatory school, got into a fight that would have amounted to nothing more than a simple skirmish if the riot police—the *granaderos*—had not intervened. The key to the official anti-student movement lies in the suspicious intervention in this affair of three hundred *granaderos,* armed to the teeth, who, after pacifying the boys on Lucerna Street, went on to flush out the students and teachers of Vocational School #5, who were totally uninvolved in the altercation. Thus, an apparently insignificant conflict (there were a few broken windows) unleashed the student movement of 1968, which ended in the massacre of October 2, ten days before the inauguration of the Olympic festival.

IN THAT ATMOSPHERE—prosperity, peace, evident economic growth, the absence of social conflicts, the permanence of the PRI which ensured the political stability of the country—the student movement of 1968 was the political awakening of the young. Their unity belied the traditional rivalry between the Polytechnic students and those of the university, who struggled together to carry out an organized action. The students held daily meetings in their respective schools, be it at the UNAM or the Poli, and there they had an ideal center from which to promulgate their ideas, to communicate among themselves . . . , to organize, to call the students to assemblies and meetings, and to plan a united action, creating a feverish climate of enthusiasm and courage. . . . The UNAM, thanks to its tradition of autonomy—despite the fact that it was wholly supported by the Federal Government—remained free of uniformed police and armed interventions. It could carry out political and social work: there were mimeograph machines, buses, sound equipment, stencils, paper, and printing presses, all at the disposition of university people. No one came around to impede them . . . [The novelist] Luis González de Alba remembered how the halls of the Faculty of Philosophy and Letters were crammed full; how buses were used as improvised pulpits; the return of the brigades after the protest marches, when boys and girls would set themselves to folding banners like sheets, storing placards . . . then climbing aboard their already crowded school buses to return to guard duty on the rooftops; the sandwich at three or four in the morning, the tacos at a *taquería* on Insurgentes Avenue, the hot coffee, the laughter, the happiness that brings triumph. . . . On the other hand, so many endless and aimless sessions always made it difficult for the students to respond to stimuli; [frequently] they were left behind by events; while they were making a decision, events would have already overtaken them. Salvador Martínez della Roca, "el Pino," put it very well . . . "They would talk of class struggle, about the means of production being in the hands of the bourgeoisie, of the class in power, and that sort of thing, instead of going out to distribute handbills and finding a common language with the people."

When the repression picked up — there had already been several disappearances — the students began to sleep at the UNAM, which functioned as a true alma mater, a loving mother that shelters with her protecting wings. Luis González de Alba slept on the eighth floor of the Rectory tower, sometimes in an armchair, sometimes stretched out flat on the carpet. All night he would hear the noise of the mimeograph machine. He felt good. By contrast, the Poli, with its poorer, more marginal population, was always at the mercy of the *granaderos*, who could attack with impunity. . . .

SINCE 1958, NO ONE had dared to protest; the young people, thanks to their privileged situation, did dare. Why them? In the first place, because they had nothing to lose (except their freedom and, as we saw on October 2, their lives); and, in the second place, because they were young and believed that ideas could make a difference, and they wanted to put those ideas immediately into practice. They were also encouraged because they never imagined the extremes of perversity to which a paranoiac system — personified at that time by "the Mandril" [President Díaz Ordaz] and his band of assassins — would go. The young are the ones who question society; they are the ones who get indignant about the injustices they encounter, they are the ones who get a hard jolt from reality and rebel. Everything must be resolved completely and at once. So the students rush in. Between July and October of 1968, all of Mexico was young, and it lived intensely. Each day brought news of clashes between *granaderos* and students in different parts of the city; or of lightning meetings in the doorways of factories, of street gatherings, of manifestos published in *El Día.* . . . In those days, everyone opened newspapers with real eagerness; the student movement managed to infect even the most indifferent. . . .

In those months the government spent a good deal on whitewash to cover up the murals that appeared on nearly every wall in the city. The sanitation workers of the Federal District walked around the streets with their brushes and pails, wiping out slogans like "Justice and Liberty"; "Free the Political

Gustavo Díaz Ordáz meets ex-President Lázaro Cárdenas while campaigning for president in 1964. (Reprinted by permission of Fototeca del INAH, Mexico.)

Prisoners"; "Dictatorship, No, Democracy, Yes"; "Victory"; "We Shall Overcome." Meanwhile, other cruder slogans appeared alongside the Olympic rings and the conventional words that tourists from all parts of the world were supposed to see: "Welcome," "Bienvenus," "Bienvenidos a México." . . .

ON SEPTEMBER 18, 1968, when the army entered University City — an act which still inspires outrage — the government nevertheless authorized the payment of university employees and professors . . . demonstrating that the government was willing to sustain the university even despite the military occupation. As for the famous "autonomy" of the university, everyone interpreted it as they pleased. The students saw the university as extra-territorial, free territory of America; the government, on the other hand . . . said that the university's autonomy had been violated by the irrational groups that had taken over the buildings, and it justified the army's intervention as a matter of returning the buildings to the appropriate authorities and, in consequence, as a preservation of the university's autonomy. . . . Nevertheless, the university's rector, Barros Sierra, allied himself with the students and declared that autonomy meant that the university had the right to administer itself.

IN 1968, THE GOVERNMENT's terror continued to rise till it reached a boiling point. The eyes of the world, it was said, were upon us. What kind of spectacle were we creating? Three billion pesos had been invested in the Olympics; the problems in the countryside, the frightening public debt, the labor problem, the housing problem, all had been put to one side so that Mexico could be transformed into a showcase. In the hotels, telephones rang and telegrams arrived, bringing cancellation after cancellation. "In view of the student disturbances, we do not wish to expose ourselves. . . ."; foreign correspondents—especially photographers—were more interested in interviewing students than in touring the stadium where the Olympic games were to be inaugurated. . . . There were many rumors: a bomb would explode in Azteca Stadium during the opening ceremonies, and everyone would be blown up, athletes, guests, and especially the Big Mouth [Díaz Ordaz] with his thousand teeth. We must act quickly, once and for all! While the students were young and impetuous, the government never abandoned the paternalistic posture that characterizes our presidential regime. The president is the father, our little papa, and in 1968 he reached out to us, . . . an angry father who smashed a chair over our head and killed his disobedient child. Everyone knows the consequences of governmental anger and fear; a still-not-established number of students, men, women and children (325 according to the English newspaper, *The Guardian*) fell murdered in the Plaza of the Three Cultures on October 2, 1968. From that moment on, the lives of many Mexicans were divided in two: before and after Tlatelolco.

OF THE REPORTERS' accounts of the Tlatelolco massacre, that of Félix Fuentes of *La Prensa* gives an almost cinematographic image of the actions of the Olympia Battalion and the police with their white gloves. *La Prensa* is a tabloid-style newspaper that can be read on the bus, so its opinion is less partial than that of the newspapers which defend business or state interests. That's why its version of the facts is important:

> Fear spread among the students, reporters and police. The latter, every so often, called out: "Olympia Battalion!" And the firing continued. The present writer was swept up by the crowd near the Ministry of Foreign Relations building. Not far away a woman fell to the ground; it was not known if she was wounded by some projectile or if she fainted. Some young people tried to help her, but the soldiers stopped them. For twenty minutes the shooting was intense and the bursts of machine gun fire caused panic. The soldiers shot at the buildings, too; who knows why. Soon it was impossible to know the number wounded or dead; the military operation surrounded and confined the crowd, and many soldiers must have injured other soldiers, for as they closed the circle the bullets flew in all direc-

tions. The hum of the bullets caused as much terror as the shooting itself; there were desperate women who hugged their children as they fled the zone, not realizing that this exposed them to greater dangers. Hundreds of women, students and adults found refuge in the thousands of apartments of Tlatelolco, but many people sought refuge . . . in the stairwells. People who had nothing to do with the student movement, but who were nevertheless enraged by the military's actions, took out their pistols and shot through their windows at the soldiers. The shouts, the weeping, and the desperation were mixed together in that episode, which lasted only thirty minutes but which seemed to last thirty centuries. In the midst of the chaos, there were young people who confronted the army, but they were met with blows from the butts of rifles. A colleague, who writes for a daily paper, shouted out that he was a reporter, and a soldier answered, "Pleased to meet you!" Then the soldier threw him against a wall, with his arms raised. A photographer was forced to release his camera at bayonet point. Our photographer, Raúl Hernández, was thrown to the ground by soldiers who showered him with the worst insults while spent cartridges shot out of the automatic weapons all around him, and he heard the hum of bullets fired by other soldiers. A man who was shot next to Raúl Hernández never stopped praying. We supposed that police agents . . . were awaiting the arrival of the army to set it against the student leaders. During the thirty minutes that the shooting lasted, the ambulances of the Green and Red Crosses were not allowed to enter the Plaza of the Three Cultures. A Green Cross ambulance driver told *La Prensa* that he was told he could not approach while the shooting lasted. By 6:30 P.M., one could still hear firing, but the shots were sporadic now. Some foreign cameramen filmed the scenes, and a soldier helped them to escape from that inferno. A Japanese journalist ran around with his hands to his neck; no one could understand him, but it was supposed that he was asking for help. Around seven at night the ambulances were allowed to enter the area, and an unbearable howling of sirens was unleashed, which rattled the nerves of all those who had been in the midst of the shootout.

The army's aggression came just as the meeting was nearly over, and when a student leader had asked the crowd "if they would rather suspend the rally that was planned for the Casco de Santo Tomás."

AFTER THE MASSACRE, the same October 2, taxis, cyclists, and pedestrians passed by the Plaza of the Three Cultures as if nothing had happened. Life returned to an insulting normality. There were few public protests. Either the government silenced them, or the people were terrified. . . . What in another

Protesting students rally in the Zócalo (main plaza) of Mexico City, August 1968. (Reprinted by permission of Fototeca del INAH, Mexico.)

country would have unleashed a civil war disturbed only a few Mexicans. This lack of reaction on the part of other social sectors is due to several causes: de-politicization, union repression, disinformation, and so forth. The students never really managed to communicate with the workers, they did not share a common language, because for the majority of them, even today, the problem of the working class is a problem they have only read about in books; they can feel it, but they do not know it. To many workers, the students' casual misbehavior was their undoing; they felt real and profound anger toward the young people who acted up in the buses, their disorderliness, their shouting, their long hair, their vanity. "They have an opportunity that we never had, and they spend their time playing golf. The fact is those losers have no mother" [a common insult in Mexico]. The father of Andrés Montaño Sánchez, a worker on the railroad cars in Ciudad Sahagún, prohibited his son from joining the movement: "I've had to work much too hard for you to go to Mexico City and get yourself involved in scraps." So the student problem did not concern the working class very closely, and it was confined to the closed circle in the halls of higher learning. . . . The lack of politicization, the disinformation published in our blessed press—whose principal task is to deliver blows of amnesia from one day to the next—did not favor the movement of '68. The reports on television were always condemnatory. Our country returned to its silence. . . .

IN 1968, IN THE STREETS, in the Paseo de la Reforma, in the Zócalo, the voice that had been hushed for so many years—to the point where one spoke about Mexican muteness, Mexican lassitude, Mexican indifference—suddenly exploded. In 1968, thousands of Mexicans left their homes to shout their courage, their non-compliance. Suddenly, not only did they demonstrate their repudiation of the government, but they proved that they were willing to demand that their petitions be acted upon, shouting it beneath the presidential balcony. The student movement acted as a detonator. The rancor of years, which was handed down from fathers to sons, now broke through the surface. The sons had begun to suffocate in that atmosphere where they heard whispers of *"better not,"* of *"in the end, there's nothing we can do,"* of *"talk won't change things,"* and so forth. Now they could shout loudly and form that critical mass—determined and mobile—which so frightened and irritated the government that it carried out that tragic and criminal insanity which shredded our public life.

The repudiation of the government was made still more patent in the presidential elections of [1970]. Despite continuous speeches and massive propaganda, abstentionism was at 36 percent. This was more than a third of all registered voters. Mario Moya Palencia called it "the abstentionist party," and he spoke of the profound deception within the democratic system. The number of ballots annulled was a whopping 26 percent. If we consider that the number of registered voters was 21,700,000 in 1970, this was dispiriting and hardly flattering for the PRI's candidate [Luis Echeverría], whose hyper-tense campaign was stronger, more dynamic, and more active than anyone could possible have anticipated. Thirty-six percent of voters refusing to vote is a bitter pill for a future president to swallow.

TWO YEARS LATER the consequences of the student movement and of the night at Tlatelolco would flourish in the attitude of the government of Echeverría (1970–1976). If the student slogan was "to win the streets," Echeverría's slogan seemed to be "to win the students," because he dedicated much of his energy to that objective. In *The Ideology of the Student Movement in Mexico*, Abelardo Villegas writes: "The gravest thing, the greatest enemy of the student movement, is not violent repression, but governmental assimilation." President Echeverría spent much of his valuable time conquering intellectuals who had had access to power from a relatively early age. . . .

Echeverría's government carried the stigma of Tlatelolco,[2] which it tried to remove at all cost. . . . If the government had lost credibility with the public, it tried to reclaim it by uniting with the young. [The poet] Gabriel Zaid once told me of a Guatemalan president who, whenever he saw a protest rally against him, would go down from the presidential balcony and lead the opposition to his own government. With Echeverría, roughly the same thing happened: the president set out to conquer the students with a vehemence that would have been unthinkable without Tlatelolco. . . . In Baja California, some students asked him for two buses. Echeverría gave them six. . . .

A large part of Echeverría's attention was centered on young people: young people in his cabinet, young people in the governorships of states, young people in political and administrative posts; so the voice of the young was heard, even though it became official, captured by the governmental machinery. The government of Echeverría recognized that the student movement, with all its faults and virtues, was a very important force, a vital force in the country. Would it be possible to govern without it? . . . Public discussion, the appearance of critical attitudes, the demonstration that in Mexico "it is possible to mobilize large sectors of the population at the margin of the official controls," the interest in the universities, both national and provincial, seemed in the [Echeverría] *sexenio* [six-year term] to constitute another student victory. . . .

Ten years have passed since Tlatelolco. Many of the young people of '68 are now activists in political parties, their revolutionary enthusiasm still intact. . . . None take themselves too seriously. I have seen them sitting on flower planters, laughing and looking out at the Paseo de la Reforma which once was theirs. What is our image now? It continues to be rather murky. The Sanborns, the Denny's, the Lyni's, the Burger Boys, the Tom Boys, the Holiday Inns, the Sheratons, the Ramada Inns, the supermarkets, continue to spring up. The flowers, now devalued, constantly change in the sidewalk planters and in the city parks; glass replaces *tezontle* [stone]; Mexico still has one of the world's highest birth rates, 3.2 percent; the PRI is doing very well, thank you; Fidel Velázquez [for five decades the boss of the official labor confederation] is very robust; the rich are very powerful despite — or perhaps because of — the devaluation. Apparently everything has stayed the same. And yet, at times the wind brings a rumor of protests, of rejoicing in the streets, of that momentum that dazzles everyone, and one feels that the boldness of '68 is still alive in the youth. Only now there is greater reflection, a more profound sense of things — a sense that we might wish to divine the sure and determined route to our historical salvation.

Notes

1. *Charrismo:* government-controlled labor unionism; *tapadismo:* the Mexican practice whereby the president chooses his successor. *Ed.*
2. Luis Echeverría, president from 1970 to 1976, served as Secretary of the Interior (*Gobernación*) in the Díaz Ordaz government and is widely believed to have been instrumental in the decision to open fire on the student gathering at Tlatelolco. *Ed.*

El Santo's Strange Career

Anne Rubenstein

It seems safe to say that most readers of this book will have at least a nodding acquaintance with the Mexican "macho," that volatile, violent, unpredictable character who sneers and smirks his way through so many Hollywood westerns, who is immortalized in ballads of smugglers and bandidos, and who was transformed into a veritable archetype by such intellectuals as Octavio Paz and Samuel Ramos. It may surprise some readers, then, to learn that one of the most popular Mexican media icons of the 1950s, 1960s, and 1970s was in fact a sober, decent, pious, and fatherly fellow in white tights and a silver lamé mask who called himself "El Santo" (the Saint). From the wrestling ring to the silver screen, El Santo battled evil in gentlemanly fashion, gaining a fanatically devoted following in the process. For the thousands of poor migrants who poured into Mexico City and other urban centers from the countryside in search of work and the attractions of modern life after World War II, pastimes such as lucha libre (wrestling) and the movies not only represented life's simple pleasures, but also taught new behaviors and ways of negotiating the tricky urban environment. As Anne Rubenstein of York University argues in the following essay, El Santo was a uniquely Mexican phenomenon, one who must be taken seriously for what he represented as well as for the legacy he left behind. Rubenstein's writings have significantly advanced our understanding of Mexican popular culture since 1940, particularly the influence that forms of mass culture (for example, the movies, comic books, and lucha libre) have had in shaping the identities of working-class men and women.

The first thing about El Santo — to his fans, anyhow — was that he was beautiful. To look at him now, captured on film in his heyday as the champion wrestler and most important professional athlete of the twentieth century in Mexico, you might think he was just a slightly flabby man in tight white pants and a silver lamé mask. But watch the geometric precision with which he rolls out from under his opponent, the contained force with which he bounces from the ropes toward his partner: this is a gorgeous display of masculine grace and dignity. El Santo in the ring was not so much a sports star as he was a brilliant dancer, working in close collaboration with the referees and the lesser stars who fought him. The esthetic beauty of his movement suggested the moral worth of his actions.

As in the rest of the world, professional wrestling in Mexico (where it is called lucha libre) is more an entertainment than an athletic contest—that is, most of the bouts have fixed endings. But this form of entertainment has political and moral implications. The world of lucha libre is divided between *los rudos,* who fight dirty and usually win, and *los técnicos,* who play by the rules and often lose. Mirroring postrevolutionary political reality, the referees often refuse to enforce the rules evenhandedly, ignoring the misdeeds of the rudos; often, the técnicos can win only by breaking the rules themselves. But técnicos and rudos both have their fans, and both present themselves as co-workers or relatives. El Santo told Elena Poniatowska in 1977, "in the ring we are all enemies, but when the fight is over everyone is a friend . . . the sport makes us all a big family." As in workplace and in family relations, struggles for dominance can take symbolic forms. In lucha libre, a final victory is marked by the unmasking of the loser, which has enormous symbolic importance as a loss of face, of masculine status. In Mexican wrestling, the mask can be a mark of a real man. And El Santo, in more than five thousand bouts, never lost his mask.

El Santo started his career as a teenage rudo, fighting under his own name, Rodolfo Guzmán. But a referee, spotting his star potential, convinced Guzmán to name himself after the referee's favorite comic-strip character, the Saint. Guzmán put on the silver-lamé mask that became his trademark, and a matching silver cape. Gracious in victory, conspicuously religious, he developed the dignified bearing that seemed to suit his title. Some years later he became a técnico, but by then he was already a beloved star. His real name remained a secret, but his audience soon learned the outline of his life story from radio announcers, newspaper sports sections, and fan magazines. El Santo's life started out resembling many of his fans' biographies: born into rural poverty, in his youth he migrated with his family to Mexico City, where they lived in urban poverty instead. As a teenager—as if he were starring in one of the *radionovelas* and comic-book melodramas that were Mexico's most popular form of mass media at the time—Guzmán's athletic prowess lifted his family into the new middle class. Fans also learned of the prayers El Santo recited before each match, his close relationship with his older brother, his marriage, and his ten children. El Santo became a working-class hero at the precise moment when Mexico's urban industrial working class reached the peak of its power and prosperity.

El Santo greets fans in Chapultepec Park, mid-1950s. (Collecíon Enrique Díaz, Fototeca del Archivo General de la Nación, Mexico City. Reprinted by permission.)

Surrealist Cartoons

And at that moment, too, he began to reach a far broader audience: he became a comic-book character. The agent of this transformation, the cartoonist and publisher José G. Cruz, was himself extraordinarily important to Mexican popular culture, a popular and prolific creator of the melodramatic adventure serials that most suited readers' tastes at the time. His innovation was the *fotonovela,* a serial narrative conveyed through posed photographs rather than drawings; in the 1940s he produced them nearly single-handed, sometimes putting out episodes of three daily serials at a time. Cruz used whatever came to hand—photographs, drawings, old prints, whatever he could find—to meet the seemingly insatiable public demand for these comic books. In the early 1950s, Cruz set up his own publishing house. Among his new projects was a fotonovela called *El Santo, el Enmascarado de Plata.* Cruz hired El Santo to "act" in weekly installments beginning in 1953. This fotonovela was an immediate hit; within a year, Cruz was producing three installments a week. By 1977, he was printing 900,000 copies of every issue. It helped make Cruz— though not El Santo—rich. Rodolfo Guzmán was to discover in 1977, when he sued Cruz for royalties, that the publisher had long since taken out a copyright on the name and image of El Santo.

The fotonovela gave El Santo a whole new set of opponents. Instead of fellow wrestlers with whom he was complicit, El Santo now fought werewolves, witches, vampires, and sometimes even the devil himself. The fotonovelas' plots usually featured an innocent young working-class boy, but sometimes a pretty young middle-class woman, who discover that they are in terrible trouble, often supernatural. Nobody believes them until a wise friend or neighbor or relative (inevitably an older male) advises them to seek out El Santo. The victimized person finds El Santo in his Mexico City office. The wrestler listens gravely and vows to help. Then he goes to the arena for a wrestling match. That interruption over with, he tracks down the villains and brings them to justice if they are human, or to church if they are not. In especially difficult moments, Santo implores the aid of the Virgin of Guadalupe. She always answers, often appearing in the pages of the fotonovela in the form of a picture cut from a mass card.

The Santo of the fotonovela was not the Santo of the wrestling arena. The version of El Santo pictured in the fotonovela lacked visual consistency; it still was cobbled together from old photographs recycled with new word balloons, new photographs with other actors in El Santo's costume, and posters and stills from El Santo's movies, wrestling matches, and other public appearances.

This new El Santo had changed social class. In the arena, El Santo was clearly a worker: his fans could see him engaged in sweaty, physical labor in close collaboration with his fellow laborers on the "shop floor" of the arena. In the fotonovela, however, El Santo wore a suit (even though he kept his mask on) and usually appeared at the beginning of a new story working alone, behind a desk, in an office. He used new "scientific" gadgets to help him, a conspicuous display of higher education. And, like a businessman or bureaucrat, he aided clients who came to his office for help. El Santo, in sum, joined the new Mexican middle class when he entered the world of the comic book.

The Movie Star and Los Churros

By the middle of the 1950s, El Santo was ubiquitous in Mexico. The fotonovelas were selling well. He wrestled frequently, all over the country, sometimes losing a match but always remaining champion. His audience in these arenas was largely working-class people—a ticket for a cheap seat at the luchas cost slightly less than a cheap seat at the movies. Between 1955 and 1957 the most important wrestling matches were televised, helping this new form of media become an important part of the decor in most Mexican barbershops, bus stations and taco stands. Watching El Santo wrestle on television was for most people as communal an experience as going to the luchas in person. From television and fotonovelas, it was a natural step to cinema. El Santo did not star in a film until 1959, seven years after the first lucha libre movie was released. But his first picture—*El Santo versus the Evil Brain*—became the biggest hit that the Mexican film industry had produced in years. El Santo went on to make more than fifty more movies over the next two decades, while maintaining a full-time wrestling schedule through 1977.

None of these movies were particularly good. El Santo cheerfully admitted to being a bad actor, claiming that his fans went to see his films only out of pity for him. Carl J. Mora, an eminent scholar of Mexican cinema, calls the era in which their production began as "the darkest days" of the nation's film industry. Other recent histories of Mexican cinema simply ignore El Santo's movies altogether, thus avoiding the awkward business of denouncing the most profitable Mexican movies made from the 1950s until the release of *Like Water for Chocolate* in 1993. Such movies are commonly called *churros,* a reference to ubiquitous, machine-made crullers: not nutritious, but quick and cheap, delicious, and somehow profoundly Mexican.

The plots of El Santo's churros followed much the same pattern as his fotonovelas, as does the form, which was conditioned by low budgets, tight schedules, episodic format, and Rodolfo Guzmán's other obligations and minimal acting abilities. Most of these movies were designed to be shown on television, so they are black-and-white (until about 1968) and written to fall into three or four more or less self-contained segments. They also made extensive use of stock footage—for instance, one shot of somebody in a Santo suit, who may or may not have been Guzmán, climbing a wall, appears six times in *El Santo Fights the Witches*. Every movie filled time with film of El Santo's real-life wrestling matches. And because he was a bad actor and because his time was so valuable, Guzmán did not speak his own lines; other actors looped in his dialogue, sometimes to comic effect.

There was one way in which the Santo movies differed radically from the fotonovelas. Both the fotonovelas and the films portrayed El Santo as an educated bureaucrat, a member of the upper middle classes with a fancy car, suits, an office, and the latest gadgets. But in the fotonovelas his clientele (who of course stood in for the audience) were poorer than he was, often boys not much different than the boy whom the audience knew El Santo once had been. In the films El Santo most often saves light-skinned, well-dressed women who also drive fancy cars. His clientele, in other words, had joined El Santo in the Mexican elite, leaving the vast majority of his audience behind.

El Santo's Posthumous Career

El Santo retired from professional wrestling in 1977, after thirty-five years in the arena. Toward the end, it required elaborate strategies to enable El Santo to participate without making it too obvious that the rudos were letting him win. After retirement, he unsuccessfully sued José G. Cruz for royalties, and Cruz shut down the fotonovela. Rodolfo Guzmán died two years after his last movie appeared, in 1984, and was mourned vigorously; not since the death of the great singer and movie star Pedro Infante had a celebrity's funeral attracted such crowds.

But El Santo's career did not end with Rodolfo Guzmán's funeral. Artists and film-makers adapted the masked wrestler's image to their own purposes, often returning El Santo to his origins as a manual laborer (and not always a victorious one). In a variety of art films and comic strips produced in the 1990s, El Santo is cast either as a benevolent but detached apparition or as an ordinary man, one who takes the metro, farts, and has trouble with women. An interesting twist on the theme of the masked wrestler who defends the poor, the weak and the innocent came with the advent of the political activist Superbarrio (who may or may not also be a "real" wrestler). Unlike the avant-garde cartoonists and independent filmmakers who had previously created El Santo's posthumous career, Superbarrio could draw a crowd. Playing on the familiar themes of lucha libre, this housing-rights crusader realized that the Mexican state could not co-opt or corrupt an anonymous person. So he borrowed the persona of a masked *luchador* to confront landlords, organize demonstrations and attend government meetings, speaking on behalf of the organized groups of homeless and poor people in Mexico City. In the aftermath of the devastating 1985 earthquake and the equally devastating 1994 economic crisis, he was a sign of hope for city-dwellers. (He has taken to commenting on world issues, too, as when he offered his services as a poll watcher to the United States after the November 2000 election debacle.) Other masked wrestlers have taken up other issues in defense of children, gay men, and lesbians, and the environment. The most notable of these other "social wrestlers" is Ecologista Universal, whose activism brought the struggle against the Laguna Verde nuclear power plant into public view. Even the ski masks used by the Zapatistas in Chiapas might refer to the powerful place of the benevolent masked wrestler in Mexicans' imaginations.

El Santo vs. The Macho

A single thread connects all of El Santo's positions within Mexican popular culture both before and after Guzmán's death. No matter what his social position is or what activities he engages in, the figure of El Santo always personifies a particular image of the good Mexican man: the virtuous man, in stereotype, as the opposite and twin of the stereotypical Mexican macho. Mexican mass media deploys two contrasting stereotypes in presenting an image of the good man.

Mexican descriptions of machismo often seem both affectionate and mocking. Alma Guillermoprieto reported on the self-conscious use of macho behavior (drinking and weeping at parties, in this case) as an enjoyable catharsis for middle-class men who clearly understand that they are playing a slightly ridiculous role. And in one of the earliest portraits of machismo, the 1946 movie hit *Los tres García,* writer/director Ismael Rodríguez made all three of the film's macho men—the slick womanizer, the dreamy poet, and the drunken lout played by Pedro Infante—look foolish, though charming, as their ferocious grandmother bosses them around. (And the least macho of the three, the gentle poet, gets the girl.) Indeed, outside of Octavio Paz, it seems that relatively few Mexicans in the twentieth century have seen machismo as a unitary, definable, and entirely serious condition.

Using El Santo's career as evidence, we can see at least two forms of ideal masculinity, which can be defined by contrasts. Call one the macho and the other, the counter-macho. This counter-macho is self-controlled while the macho is impulsive; he is orderly while the macho is unruly; he is celibate or monogamous while the macho has many women (though perhaps only one true love); he nurtures a family while the macho keeps his distance from his children; he is sober while the macho is drunk, and modest where the macho is boastful. But the two stereotypes share important characteristics. Neither is a loner: the counter-macho looks out for his own children and perhaps for other people who may be more or less clients of his, and the macho shares powerful bonds of loyalty to his male peers and has strong feelings for his mother. Both are powerful: the counter-macho rules through quiet commands and self-discipline, and the macho through persuasive displays of violence. Both are highly sexual: stories about counter-macho characters frequently include scenes in which they reluctantly turn down the advances of the women who are overwhelmingly attracted to them (as El Santo does in nearly all his films), while stories about machos frequently take as their theme the macho's destruction at the hands of an unsuitable lover. Both display patriotism, though the counter-macho may be thinking of the good of the nation while the macho more often speaks of and represents his local region, as characters played by Pedro Infante and Jorge Negrete so often did in their *charro* (cowboy) movies of the 1940s and 1950s. These stereotypes define two possible positions for male stars to take, both of which can be—usually are—seen positively. At the wrestling arena, Mexicans root for both rudos and técnicos. Television in Mexico, and in the Mexican diaspora in the United States, endlessly recycles the old movies that star machos like Jorge Negrete as well as counter-machos like El Santo; both have remained heroic figures.

El Santo should be seen as an exemplary counter-macho. His style as a wrestler emphasized suave control of his opponent rather than brute force. In his films and fotonovelas, he was forever turning away the advances of gorgeous women—both the innocent victims of the female vampires, and the attractive monsters themselves—because audiences knew that the "real" El Santo had a happy home life, a long-standing marriage, and many children. Neither El Santo nor the "real" Rodolfo Guzmán drank or smoked in public, as constantly reiterated by movie dialogue praising his purity. In the wrestling ring he was often called in to "rescue" other técnicos from the violent wiles of their cheating rudo adversaries, while in the movies and fotonovelas he made a career of rescuing people from the forces of evil. His rare public pronouncements conveyed his piety and modesty.

The figure of El Santo, through its many transformations over half a century, reminds us that this stereotypical image of the good man can be found in representations of all classes, but perhaps not all ages. Recall that Rodolfo Guzmán began wrestling as a rudo, waiting years before taking on the identity of a técnico, and that the older he got, the more audiences loved him. The counter-macho must rely on—and display—a certain authority which would sit oddly on the shoulders of a teenager. And this authority is both the essence and the political function of the stereotype.

Consider, for instance, the split between the public images of the Avila Camacho brothers, just at the moment that El Santo's career got underway in the 1940s. Manuel Avila Camacho, who was president from 1940 to 1946, was an exemplary counter-macho, with a deliberately constructed persona as a homebody, a church-goer, a prude, and a calm compromiser. His brother—army general and Puebla governor Maximino Avila Camacho—had well-publicized designs on the presidency, exotic mistresses, many out-of-wedlock offspring, a powerful physique, and a violent and infamous political career. Maximino embodied the macho stereotype, at least in the national imagination. It is very unlikely that these men deliberately designed their public behavior for media purposes. But their story both fell into and helped to reinforce the categories of macho and counter-macho. This, in turn, supported two related, central political aims of Manuel Avila Camacho's presidency. He hoped to convince Mexicans that the revolution was over; and he had to show that his government was the legitimate heir to the revolution. The figure of his charismatic brother helped remind the citizenry that such macho revolutionaries can also be unpredictable, violent, and dangerous. Perhaps such admirable men would be best left slightly to the side of contemporary politics. The President's social and political conservatism, by contrast, looked modern (and safe). Yet the familial relationship and political partnership between the two men also reminded Mexicans of the connection between the two styles of politician, suggesting that this form of the post-revolutionary did draw from a revolutionary heritage.

The macho, in other words, is always receding into the past. (The ultimate macho wears ranchero costume, after all, referring to a past that is no less real for being mythological). The counter-macho, conversely, lives in the future—perhaps an Institutional Revolutionary future of perfect justice, perhaps a modernized future of technological progress and material abundance. El Santo represented the future and often battled with dangerous figures of a storybook past: ageless witches or aristocratic vampires or werewolves from "the old country." Both stereotypes are means of legitimizing present-day structures of authority, which the macho does through the invocation of "tradition" and the counter-macho does by offering the hope of transcendence.

A Conclusion

Look again at El Santo's apparitions after the death of Rodolfo Guzmán, and you can see that the figure of the counter-macho (like the figure of the macho) is now open to question. In the movies and the funnies, this exemplary counter-macho has also become a part of the past, under threat by an onrushing future in which he no longer has a secure place. Maybe the stereotype is disappearing, or maybe both stereotypes have been reduced to mere kitsch. But as we consider the political activist Superbarrio, other possible futures for the anti-macho style of Mexican masculinity emerge: a new style of authority, a new set of temptations that the good man must refuse, perhaps even a new class position from which it may be possible to hope.

After the Earthquake

Victims' Coordinating Council

On September 19, 1985, a powerful earthquake, followed by a second devastating tremor, struck the heart of Mexico City, killing at least eight thousand people, leaving many more injured or homeless, and damaging about $4 billion worth of property. The government's often slow and self-serving response to the emergency angered many people, and out of the rubble grew several important organizations. Probably the most important was the CUD (Coordinadora Unica de Damnificados, or Victims' Co-ordinating Council), which was itself composed of some twenty neighborhood groups formed to demand greater government responsiveness to the disaster. As detailed in the recollections of CUD activists reprinted in this section, the immediate response to the Coordinating Council's efforts was practically magical. With few resources or means of communication, the CUD was able to mobilize impressive demonstrations and get tangible results. In the late 1980s, however, without an emergency to respond to, the Council was shaken by lack of direction and political infighting. Nevertheless, some observers claim that the earthquake spawned a new spirit of urban social activism that had a powerful influence on both the 1988 presidential election, which many claim was won by opposition candidate Cuauhtémoc Cárdenas and stolen by the PRI, and the historic election of July 1997, which resulted in Cárdenas's becoming the first non-priísta mayor of Mexico City.

Paco Saucedo:
Reconstruction was made possible by the popular organizations that already existed and by those that were created, and also by a great, well-channeled solidarity. I believe that this was the first defeat the PRI suffered. I first realized this one day . . . when Cosío Vidaurri, Secretary General of the Government of Federal District, arrived with his famous water barrels, the ones that were brought by an international society to provide us with drinking water. We got the word that those barrels had been held up for four or five days because they had to put the PRI's logo on them; so when Cosío arrived the people were very angry and they showed him their displeasure at how the aid was being manipulated. . . .

Leslie Serna:

At Isabel la Católica #91 and 93 there lived some people who worked with my mother. They knew her because she had been the union director at the Secretariat of the Agrarian Reform, so they came to ask her for help because their neighborhoods had been affected [by the earthquake]. So we went with them to have a look and we convoked a meeting that, supposedly, would be only of those two neighborhoods, but word got around and many more showed up. By September 29 there were sixty neighborhoods and with them we formed the Tenants' and Victims' Union of the Center (Unión de Inquilinos y Damnificados del Centro).

The Historic Center of the city was cordoned off by the army. During the first days it was impossible to enter if you couldn't prove that you lived there. Little by little we broke down the cordons and established the first street encampments. The organization spread rapidly. We didn't have much of an idea of what to do, and we didn't have any great plan; we did one thing at a time, and things had their own dynamic. Suddenly we were an organization and we had named commissions and a board of directors.

The zone where we operated was a bastion of the PRI, so we had to fight to the death against Deputy Jarmila Olmedo who, unfortunately for us, was the only PRI deputy who decided to fight in earnest; so we had to confront her constantly in the neighborhoods.

The *priístas* were shameless in the way they tried to use the tragedy to gain clients. In December a little baby died from the cold in one of our encampments, and we were very indignant and made a public denunciation. We had a wake for the baby in the house where we held the Union meetings. Victoria Reyes showed up there—she was a deputy in the next legislature—to offer condolences and support. She was wearing an apron with an enormous PRI logo on it.

That same December we solicited the Cuauhtémoc Delegation to donate chickens so we could prepare a New Year's dinner for the homeless. They gave us the chickens, but they sent them along with the deputy and the photographers. We sent them away, chickens and all. They were very vulgar. The *priístas* tried to make political use of the aid, as if it were an election campaign. . . .

Ernesto Jiménez:

We grew by 500 percent. The Union was founded by ten families. Before the earthquakes they were there, but the growth began with the earthquakes because we were the only group organizing in the *colonia*. The PRI disappeared. The people of the PRI were not from here, they were people who came to exercise control from the outside. There were some bases of the PARM[1] and the Union. We grew a lot, and I recall that from December of '85 to February of '86 there was a tough fight with the PRI, which recovered and tried to compete.

Jesús Salazar Toledano took over as president of the PRI in the Federal District. To this day, every time I see him it sends me into a rage. One time he called out to those of us who were in what is today the Amanecer del Barrio, the Central Morelos Union, and those of us from Valle Gómez. He didn't have a clue about our politics, he figured we were natural leaders like other people from around here. He called us into the PRI building, and he openly offered us everything: money, grants, whatever, so that we would join the PRI. We never told him that we were all from the Socialist Movement.

It was a tough fight, from neighborhood to neighborhood; whenever we would leave, the PRI would enter. They had everything they might need; they would arrive in brand new pickup trucks with maybe fifteen people, go into the neighborhoods and distribute stuff. Their goal was to get people to leave the Union.

Paco Saucedo:
La Peña Morelos was a cultural group, and the Tenants' Union was a very small group prior to the earthquakes. Afterwards, there were amazing assemblies, there were thousands of people, sometimes in packed streets. When I think about those meetings, I tell myself that I will never experience anything like them again. People came to la Peña from all sides. I think it was a beautiful experience, I was delighted, it was very plural. I, as a militant, thought that if we didn't get together in this, when would we ever get together? You saw the need to unite, you saw it humanly and socially. . . .

Gloria Amador:
I lived in the "Arteaga" building of Tlatelolco. I grew up in Tlatelolco, and in '85 I was very young, 17 years old, and I was very, very frightened by the earthquake because in my house tiles and vases began to fall. There was a feeling that we might lose our lives at any moment, and then it grew calm. The calm was a disaster because you knew you had to leave your house, walk from one family's house to another's. . . .

One day, when I went from my grandmother's house—she lived in a less-damaged building of Tlatelolco—to my house, I found myself at a meeting and they were inviting people who might want to participate to gather around. I didn't start to get involved so much on account of my own house, but because they were saying that the government wanted to leave the victims homeless, that they wanted to demolish all the buildings and leave everyone in the street. I joined because it seemed very unjust to me that they could do such a thing. I would go with Peter, who was a *compañero* of the PRT. And from that time on I began a daily routine of distributing fliers, going to meetings, and that happened all at once, like the disaster itself; as if suddenly I had no prior life, as if my life began right then.

Peter was a close neighbor and he invited me to discussion meetings at his house. He was obsessed with teaching people, so he organized little courses in Marxist thought. One time he even managed to get Ernest Mandel to come and give us a talk. I remember that once he invited Mr. Raymundo, who was a very old man, and Peter put us all to reading Marxist economics. And Mr. Raymundo said: "I'm reading this, I'm reading this, and I'm reading this," pointing out the pages, "and I don't understand a thing." But I really liked the fact that there was political training in the movement, so I stayed on.

Dolores Padierna:
A friend of mine named Marilú, an earthquake victim from the Colonia Doctores, invited me to participate with her. We began a new history that would change my life radically. I joined the Union of Residents of the Colonia Doctores and from that time I tried to promote, first, refugee shelters, and then housing. There were a few days when we were invited to participate in the organization of the victims of the Historic Center. The residents of the Historic Center were seriously harmed by having to live in old neighborhoods. We began to work in the northern part of the Center, which was a zone without experience in self-motivated and independent organization.

We founded, then, the Union of Residents of the Central Colonia on October 20, 1985. The panorama was very desolate: one month after the tragedy practically nothing had been done; there were abuses by landlords, evictions from places that were still inhabited, reclaiming of possessions, burial of the dead, every day. Women, men, and children who sought refuge, food, protection, found themselves totally abandoned. We offered them organization and they accepted. I remember how we built huge squatter encampments in the streets, how we impeded the eviction of the refugees in the church located on Torres Quintero Street, how we converted parks into homes, how we negotiated for water and services in the subdelegation. The women organized us to get food for everyone and we solicited donations of clothing, furniture, blankets, cots. We set up . . . nurseries to protect the babies and young children. Soon more help arrived, more experience, more organization, and also more needy people. The homeless numbered in the thousands, and the problem grew every day. . . .

Alejandro Varas:

It was said that in order to confront the disaster, Plan DN-III would be implemented, but days and weeks passed and no one knew what that plan was. From what I could see, in cases of disasters in other places, Plan DN-III meant giving control to the army. So it didn't work for the City of Mexico in September in 1985, since there was a great civil reaction that awakened an anti-authoritarian sentiment that would not tolerate military manipulation of the situation. In fact, the citizens demanded that the army's cordons be withdrawn.

There was much indignation at so much bureaucracy. You should not be told that they can't act on a given request because all of your papers were lost. The first attention the government gave the situation was to offer housing to the homeless. They put modules from SEDUE [Ministry of Urban and Ecological Development] in various places. The solution they had in mind was for the people to move to the outskirts of the city, or even to the provinces. Certainly the few victims who went to those places were not well received.

Cuauhtémoc Abarca:

The official policy was always to minimize the problem, to create an image that nothing was going on here, to use the communications media to tell the people: "stay home, don't go out," something that, happily, the people ignored.

On the afternoon of the 20th [of September] we had a meeting with the director of FONHAPO,[2] the architect Enrique Ortiz Flores, and his team. . . . This meeting was brusquely interrupted by the earthquake of September 20. We then pressured the director to attend a meeting in the Cinco de Mayo Theater, and now his response was that he had no response, that the proposals we had made were now excessive and that the government was incapable of responding. So we asked him: "Who are your superior authorities, to whom must we appeal for an answer?" He said the SEDUE was in charge of the sector, along with the city government, and, in the particular case of Tlatelolco, Banobras[3] was financially responsible.

The Department of the Federal District washed its hands of us, saying that they were as much victims as we were, that they didn't order the earthquake, it wasn't their fault. They were really stupid responses, but at least they were responses. The director of Banobras went into hiding, he would not make appointments; when he heard we were coming, he would go running for his private elevator.

The SEDUE began to receive us, they planned to scold us, to treat us as if we were little kids who were misbehaving. . . . One time, for instance, we went to a meeting and they couldn't find the key to the auditorium, and it was necessary to knock down the door. Well, that had to be done by the private secretary of the Subsecretary himself. . . .

Alejandro Varas:
In the case of the Juárez multifamily dwelling, half of building "A" fell in, and the same happened with the buildings on "D" block. All of the buildings that fell did so because they were not reinforced. Many people died in "A" and in "c-4"; that is probably the most serious case in the "Nuevo León" neighborhood. The people who lived there were workers in the service of the state, and the state had a lot of control. In any case, they created an organization there that belonged to the cud.

What the government did was to demolish the buildings, and thus take away the rights of the workers who rented those apartments at minimum cost. Those multifamily dwellings were an achievement for the workers, but it was cheaper for the government to demolish them and make gardens than to maintain the buildings. About the Multifamily Juárez, I recall the image of the survivors gathering up what was left of the possessions from the rubble. It was very sad.

I remember that when our building fell, my mother was looking among the remains when a man came by; I don't know where he came from. He commented that we looked like garbage pickers. My mother said: "Look, mister, we've lost so much that anything we can get back is of enormous value to us."

Oscar Cabrera:
On September 25 we proposed that we march to Los Pinos [the presidential residence] on the 27th. We convoked a press conference and a bunch of journalists arrived that we didn't know. There were reporters from *Proceso;* Monsiváis was here in the *colonia,* Cristina Pacheco, Raúl Monge, Oscar Hinojosa; several reporters arrived and we had coverage that was much grander than we had anticipated.

We began to assemble the people, and on the 27th at 9 in the morning the whole of Labradores Street, from Congreso de la Unión to Ferrocarril de Cintura, was already full and people kept coming. We had to delay the march from 10 to 12:30 because people kept on coming.

We planned to march with our mouths shut and carrying empty pots as a symbol, and the march was silent. The argument was: "We are protesting in silence because we are in mourning and because it is a way of showing the government our anger, but it is also a way of showing the government our dignity." It was very nice. . . .

The march was impressive. The people from the Guerrero neighborhood decided to participate also, and we joined up with the contingent from that community. . . . It was very interesting because we didn't have so much as a car or truck with a loudspeaker, but word got around and a whole bunch of people arrived. . . .

We stopped in Chivatito and we were told that [Emilio] Gamboa Patrón [private secretary to President Miguel de la Madrid] would receive a commission [of earthquake victims]. There we crouched down and drew up a petition in which we proposed the expropriation of real estate, cheap credit for rebuilding, reinstallation of water and electric services, and establishment of Red Cross encampments.

A large commission was formed, not just of the usual leaders but also people from the neighborhoods, homeless people. Gamboa Patrón received us, but not the President, and that angered the people very much. From there we went to the SEDUE to see Carrillo Arena, but we could only get meetings with his assistants. . . .

Paco Saucedo:

On the morning October 2nd, a guy came to the Peña-Morelos who was the representative of the President of the Republic, one Raúl Zorrilla, and I was there with several friends and this guy comes up and says: "I've come for you, we want to fix things with the President, to see if we can have an interview and open the lines of communication; the leaders who were there on September 27 are going to come." We went to an office on Constituyentes and met up with other *compañeros*. . . . There, Zorrilla told us: "I've brought you here because we want to have an interview with the President of the Republic." We were deeply moved because, even though that had been our demand, in those days *nobody* got to see the President. . . . They never gave you an interview, they always channeled you through Secretaries who never resolved anything, so when they told us this we were very serious.

It was around 12 noon and the interview would be at 4:30. Zorrilla told us: "I brought you here right now so that you could reach some agreement; in a minute I'll be back to see if you want to eat something, but first, talk among yourselves, reach an agreement; the interview with the President will last five minutes." He closed the door and left, and we were all looking at each other, and we said: "Fine, we will decide our purpose, what to ask for," and very soon we were in agreement. We would ask for expropriation of the lands, neighborhoods, and buildings affected by the earthquake; the second point was the restoration of public services in some of the affected zones; and finally, we would outline a popular program of reconstruction. . . .

Zorrilla asked: "Who is going to coordinate the session with the President?" We started talking, and they suggested me. I was very nervous. We got to Los Pinos, to the Salón Venustiano Carranza. When De la Madrid entered, so did the reporters and they began to photograph everyone. The flash bulbs put out a lot of heat, and I was very nervous and I even started to sweat. . . . The five-minute interview became fifty minutes. On the expropriation, De la Madrid said that was a very difficult juridical matter that could take a long time, that we'd better think of something else.

Cuauhtémoc Abarca:

We planned a march from the Angel to Los Pinos on October 12. This march was very important with regard to the participation of the residents of Tlatelolco, thousands responded to the call; there were contingents by building, by section; it was a very beautiful thing, there was a very strong combative spirit among the people. There was a mixture of emotions: sadness, rage, joy at being alive, at being together, joy to be fighting for the same cause. We agreed that the march would be headed by a contingent of children carrying little placards that said things like: "Mr. President, fix our houses, we want a solution"; "we want to live in security"; the children themselves had made those signs in their own writing. After them came the contingents from Tlatelolco headed by the survivors of the "Nuevo León."

The march went off without much difficulty, more or less till we got to the Anthropology Museum, where we were stopped for the first time. They asked us not to continue, they said we should form a commission there of two or three to go and talk to the President's front man. I remember the very combative attitude of many of the women, especially when we were speaking with the men from the President's Guard—they protested and demanded in no uncertain terms that we be allowed to pass. We arrived at Molino del Rey Avenue and when we were close to the building that housed the Presidential Guards, to the side of Los Pinos, we stopped again; and again we waited and relaxed, and while we argued with the police the children kept walking and they got to the front door of Los Pinos. There were maybe two or three hundred kids who passed right through the ranks of soldiers and police. Next thing you knew, the mothers started yelling for their kids and neither the police nor the soldiers could detain them. They made such a fuss that the soldiers stepped aside, since they saw that the crowd was already upon them; it was this infiltration of children that allowed the march to carry on.

They asked us to form a commission of twenty people. We named representatives from Tlatelolco and of a group of homeless people from the Center who also participated in the march. Gamboa Patrón insisted that we agree to be received by Gabino Fraga, because the President wasn't home. We kept on insisting, and I remember something that I've never mentioned publicly: in one of so many displays of solidarity that we had, one of the soldiers from the Presidential Guard who was there came up to me very discreetly and said in my ear: "Insist, Doctor, the President *is* here." Then he went off stone-faced, as if nothing had happened. Then I said, we're not moving. And then, magically, the President appeared.

Oscar Cabrera:
On October 11 the first expropriation decree was issued. . . .

Evangelina Corona:
We women who worked as seamstresses had horrible working conditions. What the earthquake did was to reveal this reality. In the factories there was a lot of diversity, different forms of exploitation. The factory officers, the chief of personnel, of accounting or engineering—they were all determined to dominate the entire workspace, so that the workers would not be able to even raise their heads because those bosses had their eyes on them all the time. It was a kind of psychological pressure applied from a distance. Another of the conditions of work was that the tasks were too complicated for us to be able to make minimum wage. In many factories we found that the seamstresses were made to work extra hours without any pay at all. Workers told stories of being punished. In some cases, the boss arrived, opened the door for the workers, they entered, the door was closed and they couldn't leave; that was another of the reasons why many seamstresses remained under the rubble after the earthquake, because they couldn't open the doors. That is a very severe form of repression, you're there but you're not free even to leave. They didn't have any freedom at all, not even to make urgent telephone calls; there were no permits. If you got to work late they would charge you, you had to pay for the time, but not the three or ten minutes you were late, but half an hour, an hour, or more. There were inhuman forms of repression—punishments and torture—if workers revealed these conditions. They would then be put to work at things that were deliberately intended to damage their health. . . .

Another thing that came to the public's attention was sexual harassment: many of the workers were told they'd be given a job if they agreed to have relations with the boss, with the accountant, with the engineer. Unfortunately, in the factories the bosses are all men, they've reserved this privilege for themselves.

After the earthquake, the *compañeras* who were in the same factory talked with the boss, we made a demand in the Attorney General's office, and there the boss told us he didn't have any money. They offered us twenty percent of what the law mandates in case of accidents. We definitely didn't accept. We'd been initiated into the organization, not of the union itself but of that first movement that was formed by the seamstresses in their struggle.

We began to hang around with the advisors who came to help us out. They started to tell us what our rights were, why we needed to fight, that we mustn't accept what they were offering, that we could surely get more. They gave us confidence; we believed in those people who brought us together and organized us after a fashion. There were teachers, students, men and women; there was the lesbian group, the feminist group; there were party militants, an endless stream of people who wanted to help us. They taught us to make fliers, everything. We appreciated all that very much, that they had helped us, that they taught us things that we'd never known. One of the most important things was they taught us our rights. After that, we came to appreciate more what exploitation is all about, what sexual harassment was, what the results of our labor were worth, and what was the exact value of the wage we received.

We had sent the President our petition and on Friday, October 18, we went to find out the reply in the big march. It was an enormous march, beautiful, one I believe that no one will ever forget. Finally we had it down, word for word, telling the President our demands. De la Madrid picked up the phone and talked to the Secretary of Labor. He didn't want to assume the responsibility that corresponded to the bosses, but he turned us over to the secretary because in the petition we had asked for a union of garment workers, headed by seamstresses. We got buses to take us to the secretary in Ajusco. There we were received by [the secretary], who asked us for the requisites to form a union.

October 19, our advisors were gathering information to take the census and form the union, including the factories that we had united. Others were copying the statutes, the principles. It was a very hard job for them, because I want to point out that the seamstresses never thought about a union because supposedly we were already unionized, so we didn't want just another union, we'd already learned that unions are worthless and worse—sometimes the workers were repressed by their own leaders.

On Sunday, October 20, the meeting was in the encampment at San Antonio Abad. When we got there we found that some of the *compañeras* were on the list to form the Executive Committee. I don't know how the advisors made their evaluation, but there was a list of 30 people. I became general secretary. . . .

After the organizational meeting we went to the secretary with all the documentation. We got there more or less at 11 in the morning and we left at about 10 at night with the union charter. From that time we began to fight for the re-opening of the factories, the reinstallation of the workers or indemnification for those who could no longer work. It was a movement that grew tremendously. We were proud to say that from the ruins [of the earthquakes] was born the seamstresses' union. . . .

Marco Rascón:
In the middle of '87, our Assembly of Neighborhoods was holding talks with [top left leaders] Cuauhtémoc Cárdenas and Porfirio Muñoz Ledo, but we were afraid this would cause problems because the Assembly had never had any political affiliation. We realized that we had not moved in this direction so we could conserve the good feelings of the struggle for housing without getting involved in political struggles. We had a very heated discussion with Paco Saucedo because they were supporting Rosario Ibarra,[4] and Javier Hidalgo and I were backing Cuauhtémoc Cárdenas. So as not to get involved in a fight, we decided that Superbarrio would be our candidate, but then Superbarrio's candidacy turned out to be for real.

By September 19, 1988 everything was "Cárdenized" to death. The speech that we'd begun to invent said that '85 was the start of the social participation of the citizens, the break with all of the old mechanisms of control in the city; but its political expression was in '88. 1988 could not be explained without 1985: Cuauhtémoc may have been the new rallying point, but the people had known about a mechanism of autonomous participation at the margins of the PRI; they were not afraid of losing their corporative privileges because they'd already gained much outside of the PRI's auspices.

We said that there had been a natural earthquake, now there would be a political one in which there was a continuity of actors. I believe that this is what justified and sustained the discourse of the break with the PRI by Cuauhtémoc and the "Democratic Current"; . . . it was because '85 had happened and, in a certain sense, we annulled the [PRI's] representation and . . . brought it to the *cardenista* movement. . . .

Cuauhtémoc Abarca:
I think I played a central role in the CUD because I didn't have any commitment to either party x or z, or to any political current, and I could function as a point of communication, a point of connection and equilibrium among

many people and tendencies. This functioned during the heady times, the difficult stage, when we secured the agreements for reconstruction. When the movement entered a more relaxed stage, when it began to make plans for the future, to try to transcend the matter of the city's homeless, when the emergency was over, along came the questions of political parties, of political currents, and all that got really noisy. In this stage I became an obstacle, like the referee at a boxing match when everybody is hitting everybody else, till finally I was pushed to the side.

The disappearance of the CUD depends on what lens you use to look at it. You can see it as a weakening of the urban struggle, but on the other hand you can see that it was the enormous vitality of the CUD that generated and nourished a very broad spectrum of organizations which have tackled different aspects of the democratic urban struggle in our country.

Paco Alvarado:
We're accustomed to thinking more of our successes than of our errors. I think the conditions of the country incline us to think of the unity of the movement, of the necessity of thinking more about the collective interest than of the interests of each organization. Together we can put a stop to the voracity and intolerance of this government.

Notes

1. Authentic Party of the Mexican Revolution, one of several minority opposition parties. *Ed.*
2. FONHAPO: Fund for Popular Housing, which provides loans for low-income housing. *Ed.*
3. Banobras: A federal government development bank charged with funding infrastructural development, housing and public services. *Ed.*
4. Rosario Ibarra: Since the 1970s, when her son disappeared while in police custody, Rosario Ibarra has been one of Mexico's most zealous crusaders for human rights. In 1982 she became the first woman to run for the Mexican presidency. She ran again in 1988, representing a small Trotskyite party. *Ed.*

Letters to Cuauhtémoc Cárdenas

Anonymous

The 1988 presidential election was marked by an unusually strong and popular opposition campaign. Cuauhtémoc Cárdenas, son of 1930s leftist president Lázaro Cárdenas, was a former priísta who bolted the party and ran with the support of a coalition of several small leftist parties. His campaign won widespread grassroots support, and it is commonly held that he actually won the majority of votes. The PRI, however, claimed the election for its candidate, Carlos Salinas de Gortari, who would later order that all records from the election be destroyed. A year after the disputed election, some of Cárdenas's supporters from the intellectual community published a compendium of letters the candidate had received from ordinary Mexicans. The letters, which evoke the memorials of the downtrodden to viceroys, kings, and presidents in centuries past, provide a fascinating glimpse into the needs, fears, hopes, and complaints of the poor and marginalized. A few are translated below. Our translations have sought, as much as possible, to reflect the grammar, capitalization, and punctuation (though not, of course, the spelling) of the original letters.

Sir: You are the Hope of all The Poor You must sit in the presidential chair so as to put a stop to all these diabolical functionaries who only think about how to raise the price of everything with you as president in 6 years you will be able to put everything in order you will visit all of the poor neighborhoods and get to know the poor people you will hear all of the commentaries of the people who have been dragged along by the PRI in its cycle the people are very wrought up they no longer believe in it. You are the hope you must give all you have to the poor people you being president we are going to invite the people to sell all they can and give you all the money we collect so as to pay the debt sir. forgive the poor writing and lack of penmanship but go with all the heart of a Mexican citizen who desires with all his family and friends your triumph for the well being of the Mexican people thank you.

Tampico, no date

We hope to see you in triumph, because we don't want to even listen to salinas much less have him for president, what will happen to our fatherland, if we let those sell-outs take it, if now we allow them to steal votes, then what next, we will struggle for your triumph, the mothers of veracruz would like to collect twenty or thirty thousand, to carry the struggle onward and rise to triumph, because the PRI, we know and know very well where it wants to take Mexico, that even though the mexicans have nothing to eat, in the end we are not part of their family, if i could take every woman who suffers to maintain her family to help throw out that crusty, corrupt PRI we would do it.

Another of the greatest necessities we have in the state of Veracruz, that [Laguna Verde] nuclear plant, we are worried because we know that that plant is twenty years old now, that iron in salt water, how are they going to respond, only to finish us off, no more, that plant, the first reactor had to function for 6 years and the second twelve, and they're twenty-one years old and the two reactors can't function, neither, that is to say, they only serve to do away with us; on the 21st day of this month, Mr. Mario de la Garza said that the reactors are ready to overload; i only tell them; that someone should take responsibility for the genetic damage and the human lives, and for this reason we ask you mr. CARDENAS that you help us say NO TO THE LAGUNA VERDE.

MR. CARDENAS it's not right to go to tesonapa there is much caciquismo.

Veracruz, 24 September 1988

In view of the support you offer to the poor people I saw the necessity of writing you this letter I hope you read it and I can count on your help.

i am a woman sick from embolism and poor i cannot work i had my family but now there's just my husband who is old and our sustenance was our son who was 19 years old in him we had put as they say our faith but unfortunately some dope fiends [*mariguanos*] killed him very cruelly and sadistically they used him in a way that you cannot imagine and it hurts what they did and my son never did anything to deserve that they martyred him taking off pieces of his skin.

i have 2 children who are very small and who i can't send to study because we cannot work i would like it if you would give us some help give us some protection from the assassins because we are not free to leave because they have already tried to kill my other son who is younger because he is growing up and they say that they want to finish off the whole family in the past those people laughed at us, the father of the dope fiend who came to take my son from the house because he's rich he laughs at us and the president when we went to take care of those problems laughed and said in front of the fine-collector that those poor people could be treated as if they were dogs. So around here everyone goes around very freely because the law has no effect because we are poor we can't fix nothing. that's why i ask for your help and protection for my other 2 small children that i have, i can't send them to school for 2 reasons 1. economic, 2. because of the threats of the assassins. Due to the misfortune we suffer i am without any land i sold my parcels to pay all of the expenses of the burial. Now i can't afford even to fix the house. When it rains all of us get wet because my house is no good for anything I won't say more because now there isn't time i hope you understand me and forgive this humble mother. god bless you. and i await your reply or help.

1 July 1988

The person who is writing this letter is a citizen of this Mexican Fatherland, today so embittered, sad, malnourished, and dying of hunger; we are the majority, and you will know how many we are if you know the wage-workers like myself. and even more, the peasants without land who are the inhabitants of the *Ejidal* villages without hope or secure work now that the parcels are in the hands of *Ejidal* caciques [who are] putting them in the names of their families notwithstanding that another resident of the Ejido purchased them; they go to the cacique. I am speaking of an *Ejido* in the State of Veracruz. This Congregation is composed mainly of native "Totonac" people. Five or six people who are not indigenous have managed to dominate everything, they distribute the *ejidal* offices only among themselves, no one else may occupy those posts, and what's more the elections are among themselves alone. When they call an assembly it is only so the cacique can say:

["]Gentlemen, my little friend, Mr. So and So, is the new 'Municipal Agent' and the compadre of my compadres is the new Ejidal Delegate and the *'topiles'* (police) who are replacing the old ones I will name right now and don't you argue; because it's an obligation and anyone who says otherwise will be jailed.["]
I believe that this is what life is like in all the *ejidal* villages. The caciques buy the lands (twelve hectares) for livestock, not for crops, and they still make those who work their parcels with a machete, hoe or mattock because they have no other means of doing it, telling them, ["]Sell me your parcel! I need it for my livestock. Corn and beans are only cultivated by jerks! Or rent it to me.["] If an investigation is made in this village it will find that the *ejido* is now in the hands of two or three caciques. . . . The loans that the "Banjidal" gave out were for only six *ejidatarios*. There are a hundred and twelve

owners of parcels, but to whom did they give the loan? To the six who lead the congregation, and they're not farmers they're ranchers. And they're so clever that they keep track of and collect the harvests of those who *do* farm, and in order to make sure they don't have to repay the loan to the functionaries of the Bank, they always claim bad harvests. How is the countryside supposed to progress if there are no honorable Government functionaries? If there are caciques who always say, ["]We gotta screw these dumb Indians out of their wages and their labor.["] They get economic benefit out of all of them. . . . 24 Hectares of School Land has the cacique's livestock on it. The Municipal President is the son of the cacique. His eldest daughter is the Municipal Agent. The son-in-law of another daughter is President of the Family Association. And there are many things I haven't noted down.

Today, 19 June (Father's Day), come to Salina Cruz. I don't have time for more, Mister Cuauhtémoc Cárdenas S. I'm sure you'll win the elections, but only in votes, they won't let you take power. It doesn't suit the dictatorship that an investigation be made of the fortunes of the all the Ex-Presidents which they've got from the United States Government, which gives or lends them bribes of millions and millions of dollars, and they incur thousands of obligations daily; and if there is some politician who doesn't let himself be bribed he's accused of being a Communist or a Drug Trafficker and they organize coups to overthrow him like they did to Salvador Allende of Chile, Getulio Vargas of Brazil, Jacobo Arbenz of Guatemala. They claim those are countries that menace the security of the United States. . . .

It would take a long time to tell how I got to this place, just that it's my destiny in my already long life of 68 years.

Very cordially, your admirer and supporter.

Oaxaca, June 18, 1988

So as to be brief, I will tell you that a group of approximately two hundred persons were contracted to pick asparagus that a North American company grew on a ranch near this village, and at first they told us that they were going to pay us a fair wage, and when we showed up they revealed that the gentlemen of the gringo company had in fact intended to pay us well, but there was one of those bad Mexicans who had got into the good graces of the gringos without caring about our poverty, and he told them that around these parts they usually don't pay but so much for workers and they were going to spoil us, and that's why the gringos named a group that you might call overseers who don't leave us alone and don't even let us take a short rest during the workday; and they also pay wages according to scales, first, second, and third, and it's understood that the first are those persons who are their favorites and who, according to them, work harder, and the second and third, you should see how they're treated, and many of my friends tell me that this is what's happening, it seems as if we've returned to slavery, or as if we're in some foreign country, because they don't even give us Social Security cards or any other benefits, because according to them we are just seasonal workers.

Mr. Candidate: It is urgent that you put a stop to this and other situations that occur in this place, and I urge you to hurry and authorize us to open some offices of our Party here and soon we'll have a group of thirty people who can begin to work to organize so we won't be easy victims of the ambitious exploiting people, and at the same time we can help other *compañeros* who are in the same conditions as us and who cannot do anything, WE HAVE ALREADY ENDURED A LOT!, and as I said before, I ask that you authorize us to open and organize a group of the Cardenista Campesino Central, and our aim is to end the oppression and to have a truly free Mexico.

Baja California Sur, July 31, 1988

i am that humble woman who with tears in my eyes asks you for help for all of the fishermen who for three years have been fighting for the liberation of this cooperative, but the man . . . because he has money to buy the corresponding authorities for that reason we cannot do anything because here he is king we are in the bank *banpesca* of this port filling out a statement of protest because this man took away the boats from members of the cooperative so he could work them and all the people are without work and it's been three seasons that all the members of this cooperative have not gone out to work because this man spreads the word that they can't work anywhere and look here i have five kids who are all fishermen and since my son and husband are the ones who fight for the cooperative for that reason they've sent people to kill us look here my oldest son was kidnapped and I was beaten by this man's thugs through some miracle of God they didn't kill me how do you think i live here with such fear and so much repression thinking that whenever my kids go out in the street to ask for help just so as to get a tortilla in their mouths they go out with their children and i stay here thinking that only God knows if they will return alive and if i'll ever see them again because this man is the power here he orders killings and kidnappings and jailings and how do you think we are living right now that this man is the president elect we want to get out of here but we don't have anything to eat because God knows that no one in the world has less than we have to help us move someplace else . . .

August 5, 1988

Mr. Cardenas . . . I would like for you to help me, because when I was 18 years old I had an accident and it left me lame in one foot and i can hardly work in the fields since there is only work maybe two times a week and they pay three thousand pesos a day and with three thousand pesos i make do i have two kids. I would like it if you would help me, i like music very much i even compose songs. and i would like for you to help me if it's not too much to ask, with a guitar, or an organ or whatever so then i could join a musical group. That is my dream. It's just that i'm very poor physically and i live in crisis. Well that's all i have to tell you. I just ask you for help even though i can't pay you but god can.

Thank you.

No name or date given

i put my situation in your hands we the women are very mistreated by our husbands they persecute us and want to kill the children and much more persecuting them and wanting to kill them i ask for a solution to this problem and also in our *colonia* there is no drainage or pavement or public service. I ask for a solution.

Thank you for listening to me Mr. Cardenas.

June 1988

This is a complaint from *ejidatarios* from the provinces massacred by the PRI after obtaining triumph, all the zone of Oaxaca has suffered despoilments killings men women and children complain to the authorities and are not listened to the *priista ejidal* agents negotiate parcels and home lots they despoil the old men without compassion, throughout the country it is known how the mexican families were despoiled and thrown out of their houses and their parcels sold and not having any work or a place to live they emigrated to the capital to become swindlers just to subsist with the families and what they gain is to save their lives from the bullets of the *priistas* for this reason we are not willing to support the PRI any more and for that reason we are voting for Cardenas and we will demand the vote till out efforts are exhausted because we want justice and truth . . . no more deceit no more lies no more intrigues death to Imperialism death to oppression death to demagogy long live CARDENAS who will support the poor and will support the humble who protects the humble mexican who will stand up for justice and truth because he is mexican like us Death to foreign toadies we will transform Mexico and defend it. Long live Mexico!

Oaxacan woman, no date

Corazón del Rocanrol

Rubén Martínez

When most people think of Mexican music, they think of mariachi bands or romantic balladeers; some, perhaps, conjure images of jarocho singers with their white suits and harps, or corridistas with their cowboy hats and accordions. Such native musical forms are among the richest features of Mexico's cultural heritage. Rock and roll, on the other hand, is a bit more problematic. Much Mexican commercial pop music differs little from the generic product familiar in other parts of the world, which would lead many to assume that Mexican rocanrol is merely derivative. In fact, as the following article by Los Angeles–based writer Rubén Martínez and the accompanying lyrics to a hit song by the group Maldita Vecindad make clear, some Mexican rock bands — not unlike some wrestlers! — have emerged as significant spokespersons for a vital counterculture.

Mexico City, December 1990

Under a zinc-colored sky, a block away from the railroad tracks and next to a buzzing electrical substation, a young man with hair immaculately slicked back, wearing an oversize gray jacket, a starched white shirt, a fat 1940s tie and black baggies with fob swinging low, takes giant strides as he leads me down the asphalt corridor toward the crowd ahead. "Now, you're going to see the true history of Mexican *rocanrol!*" he calls back over his shoulder, flapping along through the warm, smoggy breeze.

I scramble after him as we dive into the marketplace. Throngs of Mexico City youth in all manner of *rockero* regalia surround us: *chavas* in leather miniskirts or torn jeans, *chavos* wearing Metallica T-shirts, James Dean leather jackets or Guatemalan-style *indígena* threads. We walk past stall after rickety stall, scraps of splintered wood and twine holding up faded blue tarpaulins, where the vendors — young *punkeros* or *trasheros* (thrash fans), leathered heavy *metaleros,* Peace and Love *jipitecas* and the working-class followers of Mexican raunch-rock heroes El Tri known as *chavos banda* — sell cassettes, CDs, LPs and singles, bootlegs and imports, as well as posters, steel-toed boots, skull

Punk-rocker leaping. (Photo by Pablo Ortiz Monasterio, from his book *The Last City* [Santa Fe, N.M.: Twin Palms Publishers, 1995.] Reprinted by permission of Pablo Ortiz Monasterio.)

earrings, fan mags, spiked bracelets and collars, incense and feathered roach clips. Ghettoblasters blast Holland's Pestilence, Mexico's El Tri, Argentina's Charly García, Ireland's U2.

"*¡Tenemos punk, tenemos heavy metal, tenemos en español y en inglés, tenemos al Jim Morrison y El Tri!*" yells a young vendor, exactly as any one of Mexico's army of street vendors hawks rosaries or Chiclets. His is but one voice among hundreds at El Chopo, as the sprawling swap meet is known.

It's a Saturday afternoon, some ten years after this institution was born, and the vendors tell me that the crowd of about three thousand is on the light side. "What's *chingón* is that there's no divisions here between the different *rockeros*," proclaims Ricardo, a high-school kid in a T-shirt emblazoned with the logo of the punk band Lard, a Vision Streetwear beret and hip-hop hi-tops. "It doesn't matter whether you're hardcore or *trashero*."

Mexican authorities haven't distinguished between styles either: all are equally suspect. El Chopo is often raided by police eager to club skinheads and longhairs alike, Ricardo and his young punk friends say, as a *jipiteca* strolls by with a gleaming white Fender Precision bass, telling everyone that he'll let it go for one million pesos.

It isn't long before my zoot-suited guide is recognized. "Don't you play with la Maldita?" kids inquire, before asking for autographs. Roco, the lead singer of Maldita Vecindad y los Hijos del Quinto Patio (roughly, the Dammed Neighborhood and the Sons of the Tenement) greets all comers effusively. "And don't forget to make the gig tonight! At LUCC, about midnight! *'¡Ahórale hijo!'* "

"We've received influences from all over," he adds, the words spilling out rapid and vowel-twisted, in classic Mexico City, or *chilango,* slang. "From the North, from the South, from Europe. It might be true that rock began in the North, but now it's all ours."

"ROCK EN *español,*" reads the publicity slogan, "Music for a New Generation." Since the mid-1980s, in Mexico, Argentina, and Spain, *rocanrol* has been billed as the perpetual Next Big Thing. Record labels, mostly the Spanish and Latin American subsidiaries of majors like BMG, Sony, or WEA, signed dozens of bands. Stadium gigs drew huge crowds at most of the big capitals in Latin America.

Key groups lived up to the advance publicity: Mexico's Caifanes, a dark-pop band reminiscent of The Cure, sold a respectable 100,000 copies of their first album; a subsequent *cumbia* single, "La negra Tomasa," moved half a million. Other acts, such as Radio Futura and La Unión from Spain, Los Prisioneros from Chile, and Miguel Mateos and Soda Stereo from Argentina, sold well and garnered airplay throughout Latin America.

Impresarios also looked toward the United States and its relatively untapped Latino youth market: there have been impressive Latin-rock gigs in Los Angeles and other major American cities since 1988. "L.A. is a meeting ground for rock from Latin America and Spain," says Enrique Blanc, a dee-jay at Rancho Cucamunga's KNSE, one of the few Spanish-rock supporters in the States. "And there are plenty of people with money who are interested." Marusa Reyes, a transplanted *chilanga* producer living in Los Angeles who handles both Caifanes and Maldita Vecindad, succeeded in convincing Jane's Addiction to book a few shows with a special added attraction: none other than Maldita Vecindad y los Hijos del Quinto Patio.

Roco and the Chopo crowd want to shake Mexican culture down to its very roots. But these heavier *rockeros* are still on the margins—and not because they necessarily like it there. It's the pop rockers like Menudo that have become megastars. As one veteran of the Mexico City rock wars put it, "The joke here has always been that *this* is the year real *rocanrol* is going to make it—and we've been saying it for thirty years."

In the summer of 1985, a group of *chavos* from different Mexico City *barrios* began holding jam sessions: a piano player, a vocalist and six percussionists (water bottles, pots and pans), but nothing experimental about it. "Either we waited to save up and buy equipment, or we played with what we had," recalls Roco, his leg bounding nervously up and down on the bar stool.

The city around them was on its knees, again, enduring the worst economic crisis since the revolution of 1910. A profound malaise contaminated all areas of life. Then, on the morning of September 19, 1985, Mexico City lurched over its liquid foundation, the ancient volcanic lake it was built upon.

"It was total devastation, *cabrón*," Roco says, leaning into me and yelling over UB40's "Red Red Wine." "Whole *barrios* darkened, without electricity, water running everywhere, people carrying coffins, looking for their loved ones. The people of the *barrios* had to organize themselves to survive. All of a sudden, people I'd seen my entire life but didn't know, I knew."

Citizens' committees organized relief efforts much better than the government, which had spurned international aid for the first two days after the quake, claiming it had "everything under control," until a second devastating *terremoto* made it clear that nobody controlled anything.

The city was transformed by the experience. Out of the rubble there arose all manner of new populist political personalities, including Superbarrio, a masked wrestler, whom the earthquake turned into an activist / performance artist who to this day shows up in his yellow cape and red suit wherever slumlords do their foul deeds. Cuauhtémoc Cárdenas nearly tossed the ruling PRI (Partido Revolucionario Institucional) dynasty out of office. . . . In the midst of this upheaval, Maldita Vecindad y los Hijos del Quinto Patio were born.

The other members of La Maldita join Roco and me at our table, weaving through a crowd whose attire would fit in well in New York's East Village or on L.A.'s Melrose Avenue. These *niños bien* have paid 50,000 pesos (about $17) for Maldita's *tocada*, their gig. We're in the Zona Rosa, the Pink Zone, at Rockstock, a club whose logo bears a suspicious resemblance to the Hard Rock Café's.

In comes Pato, curly locks peeking out from under his trademark gray fedora, a veteran of several vanguard Mexican bands. Sax, at twenty-two the youngest of the group, is leaning toward a U2 look with long, straight hair and loose, gauzy white shirt. He's Maldita's purest musical talent, and moonlights with mariachi bands in the famous Garibaldi Plaza. Lobo, a dark, leathery *rockero*, is the quiet one who batters the congas. Elfin-smiling and clean-cut Aldo, born in Argentina but now a full-fledged Mexico City boy, is on bass. And Pacho, the oldest at twenty-nine, with head shaven close on one side and exploding curly on the other, is the drummer, an intellectual who studied anthropology at Mexico's finest university, UNAM. (Roco, too: he's finishing his degree in journalism.)

La Maldita huddle close together sipping Coronas and smoking Marlboros in Rockstock's cagelike no-smoking section. Their look—resonances of James Dean, Tin Tan (a Mexican comedic great of the 1940s and 1950s, who popularized a Chicano/Pachuco swing style), U2, and the Mexico City barrio kids of Buñuel's *Los Olvidados*—clashes wildly with that of the surrounding scenesters. Roco's wearing a pair of mammoth black work boots. He notices me eyeing them.

"They're just like my father's, *cabrón*," he says, lifting his foot up and inviting me to tap the steel toe. "They cost sixty thousand pesos, *cabrón*—not like those European ones that all the *niños bien* wear, that sell for three hundred thousand here in the Zona Rosa."

Maldita and other young bands, like Café Tacuba, Santa Sabina, and Tex Tex, lash out at the Americanization of the Mexican middle class, a tendency led by media giant Televisa. This corporation prides itself on nationalism, a tune that's made it millions and that the PRI government has also used to help keep itself in power for the last seventy years. It's a bastion of national pride, but Televisa is also accused of promoting "*malinchismo*," a term that goes back five hundred years to la Malinche, Hernán Cortés's Aztec translator, the most famous traitor of Mexico's history.

Televisa's is a no-lose strategy; by backing both national and gringo, mainstream and underground, it's cornered all markets. But somehow, the Americanized acts always seem to fill the screen. Pato tells the story of the time Maldita did *not* meet Madonna at L.A.'s trendy Club Vertigo. Seems that somebody told somebody that Madonna was in the club the night of the band's first L.A. appearance. Though the band members swear that they never met her, tabloid headlines hit home instantly—the blonde goddess had given the sons of Mexico her blessing. Upon returning to Mexico City, the band was deluged with press queries about their all-night party with Madonna.

"They wanted to know about her, nothing about us," recalls Aldo. Horrified, the band called a press conference to set the record straight. "But it made no difference," Aldo says, finishing his beer before he heads backstage. "They still ask us about her all the time."

When Maldita bounds on stage, they start without so much as a hello. They play with a precise fury, styles merged, overturned and burned. Ska gives way to funk, funk to rap, rap to *son veracruzano*, to *danzón*, to *cumbia* and mambo on one of their anthemic numbers, "Bailando":

> No tengo ni puta idea porque quiero hoy salir
> Lo último de mis ahorros me lo gastaré en ti
> En la fábrica dijeron, "Ya no nos sirves, Joaquín"
> Para no perder dinero nos corrieron a dos mil

Hoy es viernes por la noche todos salen a bailar
Yo me apunto en el desmoche tengo ganas de gritar:
¡Ya no aguanto más, quiero bailar![1]

A few kids sing along, some skitter perfunctorily about the dance floor. It seems the *niños bien* don't want to risk tearing a thread. But Roco doesn't care: he's bouncing up and down, splaying his legs like Elvis being chased by *la migra,* diving down and nearly kissing the floor with the mike stand. His face flashes a grin, a sneer; now he jerks his head back repeatedly, as though he's being slapped by interrogators, while rapping his way through "Apañón," a song about police abuse of *barrio* youth:

En un sucio callejón, despiertas sin recordar
Nada de lo que pasó, te duelen hasta los pies
No traes dinero no traes zapatos y a no traes pelo
Sales de ese callejón ¡ODIANDO![2]

Jesus, I'm thinking, Maldita have blasted on the wind of free-jazz sax past decades of balding folk trios, put the lie to the World Beaters by merging mambo, *danzón,* R&B, ska and rap—within each song—exploding it all on one stage with the rage and rapture of boys possessed by the most sacred of rock demons, and these kids (black-stockinged *chicas,* Mel Gibson *chavos*) aren't seriously dancing?

When Maldita's roadies begin to break down the equipment, UB40's "Red Red Wine" again blares through the speakers. Suddenly, five hundred Zona Rosa kids are singing along in English, dancing so cool.

While the *niños bien* pride themselves on their Americanized hipness at Rockstock, elsewhere in the city a bunch of long-haired, wannabe *gringo* kids from Tampa, Florida, are playing before another crowd, having been billed as death-metal heroes from the North. On Televisa, surely, there is a fake blonde reading the news off a prompter. And all across the city on billboards and posters hung in liquor stores, buxom blondes are tonguing beer bottles, sucking cigarettes. Looks like la Malinche is alive and well and as sexy as she was five hundred years ago.

Yo lo único que quiero hacer
es bailar rocanrol . . .[3]
—Los Locos del Ritmo, circa 1960

The battle for the cultural soul of Mexican youth may well be as old as la Malinche. And Mexico City intellectuals are only half joking when they say that postmodernism actually originated here five hundred years ago, with the Conquest and its clash of radically different sensibilities. The tango, swing and mambo have each arrived from distant lands and transformed the city's style. Even so, most of what was promoted on radio, vinyl and the silver screen through the first half of the century was the sacred *cultura nacional*—mariachis and romantic balladeers like Agustín Lara or Pedro Infante.

When the first leather jackets and Elvis pompadours appeared on the streets of the *barrios,* the over-forty guardians of culture, nervous that Mexico City youth would arm themselves with switchblades and roar Harleys through elegant Zona Rosa establishments a la Marlon Brando in *The Wild One,* mounted on an all-out assault. Films like *The Blackboard Jungle* were pulled from movie theaters and newspapers apprised the populace of the dangers of *rocanroleando:* gang violence, lax morality, and, especially, the destruction of *la cultura nacional.* Maybe the single thing the government, the Catholic Church and the Marxist Left could all agree on was that Mexican youth was imperiled by the Protestant, decadent and individualistic North. But *bandas* like Los Locos del Ritmo, Los Apson Boys, Los Hooligans, Los Crazy Boys, and Enrique Guzmán y los Teen Tops all had avid followers.

Most songs from the early years were covers sung either in English or awkwardly translated into Spanish ("Hotel Descorazonado," "Rock de la carcel," "Pedro Pistolas," "Un gran pedazo de amor"). Gradually, however, the translated covers of American hits became more than literal adaptations; Mexican *rockeros* began rewriting the lyrics. "Under the Boardwalk," for example, became "En un café." While these tunes were often fluff, the feel of the songs was subtly shifting toward a Mexicanness that, many years later, would come to exemplify the best of the country's rock.

Lest the Old World version of *cultural nacional* be forever buried, the *oficialistas* made one final attempt to crush the *rockeros.* Elvis Presley, undisputed king in 1957, was their weapon. In what was probably an unsubstantiated story, Elvis was quoted in a border newspaper as saying, "I'd prefer to kiss three Negro women than one Mexican."

Headlines across the country: "¡INDIGNACION POR INSULTO A LAS MEXICANAS!" "¡INICIA FUERTE BOICOT CONTRA EL INSOLENTE ARTISTA!" Radio stations sponsored massive public record-shatterings. "Love Me Tender" was yanked from playlists. But, as Federico Arana, Mexico's premier rock historian, points out in his *Guaraches de ante azul (Blue Suede Guaraches),* the conspiracy was bound to fail. "The best that you can do for a person or group to reaffirm their ideals is to persecute them and surround their lives with prohibitions," writes Arana. "The story of the three kisses actually helped Mexican *rocanrol.*"

Ayer tuve un sueño, fue sensacional
Los pueblos vivían en paz . . .[4]
—Los Pasos (Spain), circa 1970

In the late sixties and early seventies, rock reached into every corner of Mexico, Central and South America as more bands bypassed covers and explored the peace and love idealism of the time, with original songs in Spanish. In Mexico, rock had become a solid underground christened la onda, or "the wave" (a term that survives today in all manner of colloquial speech: "*¿Qué onda?,*" "*¡Qué buena onda!*").

In 1971 at Avándaro, on the outskirts of Mexico City, anywhere between one hundred thousand (government figure) and half a million (*rockero* version) *chavos de la onda* attended a two-day festival featuring bands like Three Souls in My Mind, Love Army and El Ritual. The spectacle was a mirror image of Woodstock, right down to one of the organizers stepping up to the mike and warning the kids about a bad batch of LSD. The authorities braced for a predicted riot, but the *rockeros* camped out peacefully under the rain with little food or warm clothes and, yes, plenty of pot and acid.

"The fact that so many kids got together in one place really scared the government," recalls Sergio Arau, who later formed Botellita de Jerez, one of the most important bands of the eighties. The government had every reason to be nervous. It was the first large gathering of youth since 1968, the year the army massacred several hundred protesting students in the Tlatelolco district of Mexico City. Since Avándaro, the Mexican government has rarely granted permits for large outdoor rock concerts.

For Carlos Monsiváis, one of the Mexican Left's best-known essayists, *la onda* still seemed more of an imitation of the North's hippie culture than an authentic national discovery, except in one important regard. "*La onda* was the first movement in modern Mexico that, from an apolitical position, rebelled against institutionalized concepts [of culture]," he writes in *Amor perdido,* a collection of essays on the sixties in Mexico. "And it eloquently revealed the extinction of cultural hegemony."

THROUGHOUT THE EARLY seventies, *jipitecas* wearing *guaraches,* loose sandals with auto-tire soles, hitchhiked across Mexico on hallucinogenic pilgrimages, a tattered copy of *Las enseñanzas de don Juan* stuffed into their rucksacks. Even Joaquín Villalobos, today the top comandante of El Salvador's FMLN guerrilla army, admitted that there is room for *rocanrol* in *la revolución*—probably half the cadres of any given guerrilla army listened to groups like Los Pasos in the mid-1970s, not to mention Pink Floyd and Led Zeppelin. Salvadoran Marxist friends have boasted to me of sneaking a few tokes of pot and listening to rock on battered tape recorders, breaking away from clandestine military training on El Salvador's remote beaches.

By the early eighties, however, Mexican rock was on the verge of extinction. Only a handful of Mexican bands survived the doldrums of the late seventies—punk hadn't arrived to save *rocanrol* here as it had in the North—and El Tri, formerly Three Souls in My Mind, was the only solid draw. The battle between English and Spanish, North and South, had been virtually conceded to the *gringos*. The city had a bad case of Saturday Night Fever.

After generations of *rockeros* had done their best to overthrow the *cultura nacional* by singing in English and bleaching their hair, it took a few radicals to discover the obvious—that they didn't need to go north to take back rock-'n'-roll. Botellita de Jerez announced the birth of a new sound: *"Guacarock"* (*guaca* as much a reference to *guacomole,* the sacred national snack, as to *guacatelas,* an onomatopoeic term for vomiting). Botellita reclaimed popular traditions like the *norteña* and *cumbia,* as they ridiculed American rock megaheroes and *el PRI.* Mexico City youth were joining their cultural roots with the heart of rock-'n'-roll.

Considering how well these worlds merged, one begins to wonder whether rock is really foreign to Mexico City at all. Ask Roco, and he'll say that the blues could have begun only here, what with the city's deep ties to Afro-Caribbean culture, its long-standing love affair with death. And rock itself? Where else could it have exploded into being other than in the biggest city in the world, where soot and sex and social unrest are legendary? Even rap: Roco claims the music actually originated in Mexico with Tin Tan and fellow golden-era comedian El Piporro. "Just listen to the raps on the streets of the city," he says. "The vendors are the best rappers in the world!"

After Botellita, frenetic movements ensued: hardcore punk (Atóxxxico, Masacre '68), industrial disco rap (Santa Sabina), roots rock (the perennial El Tri and younger bands like Tex Tex), dark pop (Caifanes), straight pop (Neón, Fobia, Los Amantes de Lola), and bands like Maldita and Café Tacuba, with their crazy blends of styles from North and South—all churning out Spanish-only product.

"There was an explosion," says Luis Gerardo Salas, executive director of Núcleo Radio Mil, a network of seven radio stations in Mexico City, one of which is dedicated full-time to rock. "Everyone in Mexico seemed to want to be a *rocanrolero.* People discovered that there was rock in Spanish with the same quality as in English."

The *hoyos fonquis,* underground clubs that spontaneously appeared in poor neighborhoods, were the heart of the new scene. Bands would set up in the middle of the street, running electricity straight from somebody's living room. "All of a sudden, you'd see smoke rising around the stage," says Lalo Tex, lead singer of Tex Tex. "But it wasn't from a smoke machine. It was the dust being kicked up by the kids dancing on the asphalt."

A childlike awe overwhelms me as we pull up to the block-long monolith that houses the biggest media conglomerate in Latin America. We walk past the security checkpoint and wait in an antiseptic hallway. I glance at a pair of memoranda on the wall: one says you'll be fired if you're fifteen minutes late, the other urges employees to attend a seminar entitled "How to Enhance Your Image." Tonight Maldita enters Televisa's domain, for a live appearance on Galavisión, a cable infotainment network.

To be inside the monster, finally! After nearly three decades of watching it in my Mexican grandmother's bedroom in Los Angeles: all those macho heroes and child stars, Jacobo Zabludowsky, the dour-faced anchor with the Mickey Mouse earphones, and Raúl Velasco, variety show host with the sweet "This is our glorious national culture" voice. Zabludowsky and Velasco are among the most powerful men in Mexico, friends to presidents and corporate executives the world over.

Though it is often considered synonymous with *el Pri,* Televisa may be more powerful than the party. It is one tentacle of the country's most powerful business cartel, the Monterrey Group, which owns over 90 percent of television outlets, numerous radio stations, an important record label, and to boot, the country's biggest brewery. If you want to reach the masses, Televisa is the only way.

Maldita lounge about smoking cigs, antsy to get the performance over with. "Our real audience is in the *barrios,* at the universities," Pacho says, a little defensively. So entering into the realm of Televisa is a contradiction, right? "We aren't just going to do Televisa's bidding—we aren't about that," he scoffs.

The Marxist youth of the sixties and seventies would never have walked through Televisa's glass doors—except with machine guns. Even today, some look upon *rockeros* like Maldita and Caifanes (who have been on several Televisa shows) as *vendidos,* sellouts. Maldita insist that reaching a mass audience is crucial. But what will happen on the day that they decide to sing a song, say, about political prisoners on a Televisa program? Or burn the Mexican flag? Or use profanity on a single?

While the anchors read the news off prompters a few feet away, the band takes its place on the pristinely waxed stage, before elegant bronze urns gushing water. The newscast breaks for a commercial and, a few seconds later, on a talk-show set at the other end of the studio, entertainment hosts Rocío Villa

García and Mauricio Chávez (she an aging, tall fake blonde in a red dress, he a light-complected innocent in preppy sweater and black tie) shuffle papers and listen to the countdown. "And now, with us tonight is a group of fine young men . . ." The studio fills with a loud recording of the only song that's gotten airplay, "Mojado," the tale of a father who makes the perilous journey to the USA but dies along the border "like a pig, suffocated in a truck." These tragic lyrics are set, somewhat bizarrely, to a blend of highly danceable tropical and flamenco rhythms.

Televisa staffers crowd the plate-glass windows that seal off the newsroom, watching the band make an only half-serious effort to lip synch to the recording. Restrained at first, Roco begins jumping tentatively, but it's not until the second song, the Veracruz-style "Morenaza," that the band really loosens up. Sax spreads his arms and snaps his fingers, twirls about. Pato sneers, scratching ska-ishly at his guitar. Pacho and Lobo are bashing away on percussion — which, apparently, you're not supposed to do when lip-synching — you can hear the skins being pummeled even above the deafening monitors. Aldo plucks his bass with a vengeance. And Roco is now all over the waxed floor, collapsing his legs, flailing them outward in a leap, skidding and sliding. This image is being seen live all over Latin America and Europe, I'm thinking, but twenty minutes from now, it'll be back to the soap operas and wheezing professors discussing the Aztec legacy. And then I notice it: from the moment he hit the stage, Roco's black work boots (just like his father's) have been scuffing the Televisa floor like jet tires on a runway. Rocío Villa García is drop-jawed in horror. Technicians are making exaggerated hand signals, trying to settle Roco down. But no! Roco is blind to the world, on the verge of knocking himself out dancing as the song slowly fades.

Out bounds Villa García, all smiles for the interview. "Roco," she bubbles, "just how is it that you can dance around with those heavy boots?" Roco looks down at them and for the first time notices the dozens of black streaks radiating out from his mike. Before he can answer, Villa García is already into her next question.

"Now just what is this about Madonna showing up at your concert in Los Angeles?"

IN THE LATE 1980s, encouraged by the success of such Argentine *rockeros* as Soda Stereo and Charly García, as well as by the birth of *guacarock* in Mexico, the labels began signing again. BMG's Ariola led the way, producing Mexican acts Los Caifanes, Maldita Vecindad, Fobia, Neón, and Los Amantes de Lola. A suspiciously supportive Mexican government also helped by allowing a few rock acts from Argentina to stage large outdoor gigs. At the Plaza de Toros in 1987, twenty-five thousand rockeros attended the biggest *rock en español* gig since Avándaro.

In 1988, the hit that promoters, label execs, radio program directors and *rockeros* had all been waiting for arrived: "La negra Tomasa" by Caifanes. The song was a slightly electrified, *cumbia*-style cover of an old Cuban standard, and it sold over half a million copies—more than any other Mexican single in the thirty-year history of *rocanrol*. It seemed as if rock's Latin hour had finally come.

Not quite. No other band came close to matching the sales of "La negra Tomasa": most acts topped out at well under 50,000 units. Maldita barely managed 25,000. "There was a crash," says Jorge Mondragón, a Mexico City rock promoter. "People were saying that *rock en español* had only been a fad."

The reasons cited for the crash were familiar: bad label promotion, unscrupulous concert promoters, conservative radio, government censorship.

"Let's face it," says Giselle Trainor, an Ariola label manager. "It's not as easy to sell this concept as it is to sell Lucerito." The teen star's voice is nonexistent, but her long legs and fair hair have made her a Televisa darling. "And if other labels don't start supporting rock, it's going to collapse."

Soon after the initial boom, pop rockers like "Mexican Madonna" Alejandra Guzmán (daughter of Enrique Guzmán of Los Teen Tops, the *rockero* heroes of the sixties) achieved stardom, propelled by Televisa's massive promotional machine.

"Rock was taken over by people who aren't *rockeros*," says Núcleo Radio Mil's Gerardo Salas. "Sometimes I think that the whole *rock en español* movement was planned and promoted in such a way that pop rockers like Timbiriche and Menudo would end up winning."

Pop rock, one Televisa promoter told me, is most successful with the middle class, Mexico's strongest consumer force, and the bulwark of the PRI. Working-class *chavos de banda,* who are more likely to listen to the underground, are not part of the equation. "They're dirty, violent," I was told by the promoter, who complained about violence at *hoyos fonquis* and at some of the few larger-scale concerts (a violence, *rockeros* say, that is usually provoked by the authorities). "The underground may just as well roll over and die. We don't want to have anything to do with that crowd, and we never will."

BOUNCING AROUND EL LUCC, a dingy concrete vault light-years away from Rockstock in the south of the city, Roco has his arm around Saúl Hernández, lead singer of Los Caifanes, slurring: "Come on, *cabrón,* admit it. You guys sound like The Cure. *Ya no mames, güey."* And Saúl comes back, rocking back and forth on his heels: "Not everything has to be so obvious like in your songs. There's an interior landscape, too, *cabrón."*

By the time Maldita stumbles onto the stage, the walls of the club are sweating. Everyone's hair is pasted onto their foreheads in the dripping-wet air. I inch my way through the crowd, slipping on stray bottles on the unseen floor below. The balconies seem on the verge of collapse, dozens of kids hanging over the railing.

The sound coming from the stage convulses, lurches: Roco, Sax, Pato, Aldo and Lobo are floating away on tequila-inspired riffs (they've been partying since early afternoon), steam rolling crazily toward a great abyss, drunk boys daring each other as they look down into the darkness and laugh. The anarchy doesn't perturb the crowd in the least. On the dance floor a thousand bodies match Maldita's wild energy leap for leap.

Roco loses his breath during the melodramatic held note on "Morenaza." Sax stumbles through solos, barely keeping up with the rushed rhythms, flapping across the stage in his loose shirt, waving his arms, giggling. Lobito is oblivious of everything but his own private torpor, slamming away at bloodied congas (he ripped his hand open during the second song).

Punkish youths leap on stage and tumble back into the crowd. Now Roco himself takes a diving leap of faith into the mass of steaming bodies. Now Sax. Now Roco is pushing Pato, guitar and all, into the pit.

The band launches into "Querida," a hardcore cover of pop megastar Juan Gabriel's hit. Roco leaps skyward so high that he bangs his head on the red spotlight overhead. Saúl Hernández suddenly climbs onto the stage in all his tall, dark elegance, plays with a microphone-become-penis between his legs, hugs Roco like a long-lost brother, throws his head back, closes his eyes, and then without warning he too dives out onto the dance floor, where the slamming youths edge ever closer to absolute madness.

As the crowd files out afterward—punks, ex-hippies, ex-Marxists, kids from the *barrios*—Lobo is nursing his hand, bleary-eyed in the arms of his girlfriend. Aldo is downing more beer at the bar. Pacho, the only one who played the gig straight, is talking with a small group of fans. Roco is nowhere to be found. Sax is back behind the percussion section, weeping into a friend's arms—in a few minutes he'll make a bizarre attempt at taking off his pants and pass out.

Tonight, Maldita have fallen apart. Tomorrow they'll wake up, hungover as hell, in the city where *rocanrol* never quite dies.

Notes

1. I don't have a fucking idea why I want to go out tonight / But I'll spend the last of my savings on you / At the factory they said, "We don't need you anymore, Joaquín" / They fired two thousand so as not lose any more money / It's Friday tonight, everyone's going out to dance / Sign me up in the madness, I really want to scream: / I can't stand it anymore, I want to dance!
2. In a dirty alley, you wake without remembering / Anything about what happened, even your feet hurt / You don't have a jacket, you don't have money, you don't have shoes and you don't even have hair / You leave that alley, HATING!
3. The only thing I want to do / is to dance rock & roll.
4. Yesterday I had a dream, it was great / all the nations lived in peace. . . .

I Don't Believe Them at All

Maldita Vecindad y los Hijos del Quinto Patio

Today I saw on TV that the country is not so bad off:

"With Jorge Campos we'll win the World Cup."
I don't know who they think they're fooling,
the street is not on the TV screen.

They lie a lot, I don't believe them at all.
They lie a lot, I don't believe them at all.

Today I saw on the TV that the peso will not be devalued,
the radio said: "Unemployment will come to an end."
And in the city, wherever you look you see
people trying to earn their bread.

They lie a lot, I don't believe them at all . . .

What do they say?
The newspapers say
that there haven't been any massacres,
just people who've shot themselves in the back.
There is no rebellion,
it's an Internet war.

They lie a lot, I don't believe them at all . . .

Today I saw on the TV that the shooting will be stepped up
and that the army has a new arsenal.
Many troops and reserves,
they want peace, the peace of the grave.

They lie a lot, I don't believe them at all . . .

Identity Hour, or, What Photos
Would You Take of the Endless City?
(from *A Guide to Mexico City*)

Carlos Monsiváis

The almost unremittingly bleak portrait of Mexico's sprawling capital city presented in some earlier readings is rendered somewhat perplexing by the fact that millions of people live in Mexico City, and more arrive each day. A surprising number of these people profess that they have no desire to live elsewhere — indeed, cannot imagine living anywhere else. What, one must ask, accounts for this attitude? What is the attraction?

Carlos Monsiváis (b. 1938) attempts to answer this question in the following selection. Mexico's leading social and cultural critic, he contributes regularly on politics, literature, cinema, and pop culture. He has been one of the leading advocates for Mexico's "civil society," that slippery phenomenon that is neither quite the public nor the private sphere, but which constitutes the space for broad-based mobilization to secure a wide variety of improvements in people's lives and greater responsiveness from their government. In the essay that follows, Monsiváis pays an affectionate and humorous tribute to his hometown — especially its characteristic brand of postmodern (or, as he prefers, "post-apocalyptic") civil society. While he certainly does not minimize Mexico City's many problems, he ultimately paints a picture of a uniquely attractive place populated by uniquely resourceful people, a special environment where "radical optimists" celebrate the "incredulous."

Visually, Mexico City signifies above all else the superabundance of people. You could, of course, turn away from this most palpable of facts toward abstraction, and photograph desolate dawns, or foreground the aesthetic dimension of walls and squares, even rediscover the perfection of solitude. But in the capital, the multitude that accosts the multitude imposes itself like a permanent obsession. It is the unavoidable theme present in the tactics that everyone, whether they admit it or not, adopts to find and ensconce themselves in even the smallest places the city allows. Intimacy is by permission only, the "poetic license" that allows you momentarily to forget those around you — never more than an inch away — who make of urban vitality a relentless grind.

Turmoil is the repose of the city-dwellers, a whirlwind set in motion by secret harmonies and lack of public resources. How can one describe Mexico City today? Mass overcrowding and the shame at feeling no shame; the un-measurable space, where almost everything is possible, because everything works thanks only to what we call a "miracle" — which is no more than the meeting-place of work, technology and chance. These are the most frequent images of the capital city:

- multitudes on the Underground (where almost six million travellers a day are crammed, making space for the very idea of space);
- multitudes taking their entrance exam in the University Football Stadium;
- the "Marías" (Mazahua peasant women) selling whatever they can in the streets, resisting police harassment while training their countless kids;
- the underground economy that overflows on to the pavements, making popular marketplaces of the streets. At traffic lights young men and women overwhelm drivers attempting to sell Kleenex, kitchenware, toys, tricks. The vulnerability is so extreme that it becomes artistic, and a young boy makes fire — swallowing it and throwing it up — the axis of his gastronomy;
- mansions built like safes, with guard dogs and private police;
- masked wrestlers, the tutelary gods of the new Teotihuacán of the ring;
- the *Templo Mayor:* Indian grandeur;
- *"piñatas"* containing all the most important traditional figures: the Devil, the Nahual, Ninja Turtles, Batman, Penguin . . . ;
- the Basilica of Guadalupe;
- the swarm of cars. Suddenly it feels as if all the cars on earth were held up right here, the traffic jam having now become second nature to the species hoping to arrive late at the Last Judgment. Between four and six o'clock in the morning there is some respite, the species seems drowsy . . . but suddenly everything moves on again, the advance cannot be stopped. And in the traffic jam, the automobile becomes a prison on wheels, the cubicle where you can study Radio in the University of Tranquillity;
- the flat rooftops, which are the continuation of agrarian life by other means, the natural extension of the farm, the redoubt of Agrarian Reform. Evocations and needs are concentrated on the rooftops. There are goats and hens, and people shout at the helicopters because they frighten the cows and the farmers milking them. Clothes hang there like harvested

maize. There are rooms containing families who reproduce and never quite seem to fit. Sons and grandsons come and go, while godparents stay for months, and the room grows, so to speak, eventually to contain the whole village from which its first migrant came;

- the contrasts between rich and poor, the constant antagonism between the shadow of opulence and the formalities of misery;
- the street gangs, less violent than elsewhere, seduced by their own appearance, but somewhat uncomfortable because no one really notices them in the crowd. The street gangs use an international alphabet picked up in the streets of Los Angeles, fence off their territories with graffiti, and show off the aerial prowess of punk hairstyles secure in the knowledge that they are also ancestral, because they really copied them off Emperor Cuauhtémoc. They listen to heavy metal, use drugs, thinner and cement, destroy themselves, let themselves be photographed in poses they wish were menacing, accept parts as extras in apocalyptic films, feel regret for their street-gang life, and spend the rest of their lives evoking it with secret and public pleasure.

The images are few. One could add the Museum of Anthropology, the Zócalo at any time (day or night), the Cathedral and, perhaps (risking the photographer), a scene of violence in which police beat up street vendors, or arrest youngsters, pick them up by the hair, or swear that they have not beaten anyone. The typical repertoire is now complete, and if I do not include the *mariachis* of the Plaza Garibaldi, it is because this text does not come with musical accompaniment. Mexico: another great Latin American city, with its seemingly uncontrollable growth, its irresponsible love of modernity made visible in skyscrapers, malls, fashion shows, spectacles, exclusive restaurants, motorways, cellular phones. Chaos displays its aesthetic offerings, and next to the pyramids of Teotihuacán, the baroque altars, and the more wealthy and elegant districts, the popular city offers its rituals.

On the Causes for Pride that (Should) Make One Shiver

It was written I should be loyal to the nightmare of my choice.
—Joseph Conrad, *Heart of Darkness*

Where has the chauvinism of old gone for which, as the saying goes, "There is nowhere like Mexico?" Not far, of course: it has returned as a chauvinism expressed in the language of catastrophe and demography. I will now enumerate the points of pride (psychological compensation):

- Mexico City is the most populated city in the world (the Super-Calcutta!);
- Mexico City is the most polluted city on the planet, whose population, however, does not seem to want to move (the laboratory of the extinction of the species);
- Mexico City is the place where it would be impossible for anything to fail due to a lack of audience. There is public aplenty. In the capital, to counter-balance the lack of clear skies, there are more than enough inhabitants, spectators, car-owners, pedestrians;
- Mexico City is the place where the unlivable has its rewards, the first of which has been to endow survival with a new status.

What makes for an apocalyptic turn of mind? As far as I can see, the opposite of what may be found in Mexico City. Few people actually leave this place whose vital statistics (which tend, for the most part, to be short of the mark) everyone invents at their pleasure. This is because, since it is a secular city after all, very few take seriously the predicted end of the world—at least, of *this* world. So what are the retentive powers of a megalopolis which, without a doubt, has reached its historic limit? And how do we reconcile this sense of having reached a limit with the medium- and long-term plans of every city-dweller? Is it only centralist anxiety that determines the intensity of the city's hold? For many, Mexico City's major charm is precisely its (true and false) "apocalyptic" condition. Here is the first megalopolis to fall victim to its own excess. And how fascinating are all the biblical prophecies, the dismal statistics and the personal experiences chosen for catastrophic effect? The main topic of conversation at gatherings is whether we are actually living the disaster to come or among its ruins; and when collective humor describes cityscapes, it does so with all the enthusiasm of a witness sitting in the front row at the Last Judgment: "How awful, three hours in the car just to go two kilometers!" "Did you hear about those people who collapsed in the street because of the pollution?" "In some places there is no more water left." "Three million homes must be built, just for a start. . . ."

The same grandiose explanation is always offered: despite the disasters, twenty million people *cannot leave Mexico City or the Valley of Mexico, because there is nowhere else they want to go; there is nowhere else, really, that they can go.* Such resignation engenders the "aesthetic of multitudes." Centralism lies at the origins of this phenomenon, as does the supreme concentration of powers—which, nevertheless, has certain advantages, the first of which is the identification of liberty and tolerance: "I don't feel like making moral judgments because then I'd have to deal with my neighbors." Tradition is destroyed by the squeeze, the replacement of the extended family by the nuclear family, the wish for extreme individualization that accompanies anomie, the degree of cultural development, the lack of democratic values that would oblige people to—at least minimally—democratize their lives. "What should be abolished" gradually becomes "what I don't like."

To stay in Mexico City is to confront the risks of pollution, ozone, thermic inversion, lead poisoning, violence, the rat race, and the lack of individual meaning. To leave it is to lose the formative and informative advantages of extreme concentration, the experiences of modernity (or postmodernity) that growth and the ungovernability of certain zones due to massification bring. The majority of people, although they may deny it with their complaints and promises to flee, are happy to stay, and stand by the only reasons offered them by hope: "It will get better somehow." "The worst never comes." "We'll have time to leave before the disaster strikes." Indeed, the excuses eventually become one: outside the city it's all the same, or worse. Can there now really be any escape from urban violence, overpopulation, industrial waste, the greenhouse effect?

Writers are among the most skeptical. There are no anti-utopias; the city does not represent a great oppressive weight (this is still located in the provinces) but, rather, possible liberty, and in practice, nothing could be further from the spirit of the capital city than the prophecies contained in Carlos Fuentes's novel *Christopher Unborn* and his short story "Andrés Aparicio" in *Burnt Water.* According to Fuentes, the city has reached its limits. One of his characters reflects:

> He was ashamed that a nation of churches and pyramids built for all eternity ended up becoming one with the cardboard, shitty city. They boxed him in, suffocated him, took his sun and air away, his senses of vision and smell.

Even the world of *Christopher Unborn* (one of ecological, political, social and linguistic desolation) is invaded by fun ("relajo"). In the end, although the catastrophe may be very real, catastrophism is the celebration of the incredulous in which irresponsibility mixes with resignation and hope, and where— not such a secret doctrine in Mexico City—the sensations associated with the end of the world spread: the overcrowding is hell, and the apotheosis is crowds that consume all the air and water, and are so numerous that they seem to float on the earth. Confidence becomes one with resignation, cynicism and patience: the apocalyptic city is populated with radical optimists.

In practice, optimism wins out. In the last instance, the advantages seem greater than the horrors. And the result is: *Mexico, the post-apocalyptic city.* The worst has already happened (and the worst is the monstrous population whose growth nothing can stop); nevertheless, the city functions in a way the majority cannot explain, while everyone takes from the resulting chaos the visual and vital rewards they need and which, in a way, compensate for whatever makes life unlivable. Love and hate come together in the vitality of a city that produces spectacles as it goes along: the commerce that invades the pavements, the infinity of architectonic styles, the "street theater" of the ten million people a day who move about the city, through the Underground system, on buses, motorbikes, bicycles, in lorries and cars. However, the all-star performance is given by the loss of fear at being ridiculed in a society which, not too long ago, was so subjugated by what "others might think." Never-ending mixture also has its aesthetic dimension, and next to the pyramids of Teotihuacán, the baroque altars and the more wealthy and elegant districts, the popular city projects the most favored—and the most brutally massified—version of the century that is to come.

The COCEI of Juchitán, Oaxaca: Two Documents

Leopoldo de Gyves de la Cruz and COCEI

The cold war years in Latin America witnessed the birth of several revolutionary movements that combined radical politics with pride in Indian-ness. Although less well known than its counterparts in Central America, Peru, and Bolivia, a social movement rooted in the Zapotec communities of Mexico's southern state of Oaxaca emerged in 1973 and has been a powerful political force ever since. The formation of the Worker–Peasant–Student Coalition of the Isthmus of Tehuantepec (COCEI) marked a new style of political mobilization in Mexico. Relying heavily on the community's strong ethnic identity, the alliance used direct action—land invasions, political mobilization and educational activities, strikes, protests, and occasional violence—to secure better living and working conditions for the region's poor. Surviving repeated attacks by opponents, COCEI was strong enough by 1980 to ally with the Communist Party and run one of its leaders for mayor of Oaxaca's second largest city, Juchitán. The victory of that candidate, Leopoldo de Gyves, began the brief tenure of a left-wing opposition "people's government" in Juchitán, a decided anomaly in a country where all important cities were still controlled by the PRI. Opposition groups, some of them quite violent, stepped up attacks on the organization, giving the state's PRI government a pretext to oust the COCEI from Juchitán in 1983, ushering in a period of military occupation and severe repression. Despite the regime's campaign, COCEI prevailed, winning municipal elections again in 1989.

The COCEI is an acknowledged source of inspiration for the more widely celebrated Zapatista Army of National Liberation (EZLN), which made a special point of stopping in Juchitán on its September 1997 and April 2001 marches to Mexico City to demand recognition of indigenous rights and culture. COCEI provides an example both of the enduring resilience of indigenous groups in Mexico, and of the artful political balancing act that long characterized the PRI, a strategy that alternated repression with acceptance, encouragement, and cooptation.

Here, we reprint two key documents of the COCEI struggle: Mayor Gyves's inaugural speech of 1981, and COCEI's political manifesto of 1982. We conclude with an evocative photo essay on the women of Juchitán by Jeffrey Rubin, historian at Brown University who has written an award-winning study of the movement, Decentering the Regime: Ethnicity, Radicalism, and Democracy in Juchitán *(Duke University Press, 1997). Juchitecas have played a distinctive cultural and political role in the community's life for centuries, and Rubin's camera captures their determination and independent spirit in the courtyards and markets of the city during the late 1990s.*

INAUGURAL SPEECH AS MAYOR OF JUCHITÁN
by Leopoldo de Gyves de la Cruz

March 10, 1981

My fellow Juchitecos, all of my *compañeros:*

At this moment, no one can deny a great truth: Today the Juchiteco people govern themselves. The road to this great victory has been long. It began in 1911 with Che Gómez in the lead and continued in 1931 with Valentín Carrasco and Roque Robles. There were seventy years of constant struggle to gain respect for the popular will. The long road traveled by the Juchitecos has been fertilized with the blood of Juchitán's most worthy sons; with the blood of José F. Gómez, Roque Robles, Valentín Carrasco, Lorenza Santiago Esteva in 1974, José Yola on January 1, 1978; with the imprisonment of Polo de Gyves Pineda in 1978; and with the recent jailing of six *compañeros* in Mexico City for the seizure of the Guatemalan and Indian embassies.

Fertilized with the sacrifices of many Juchitecos, that road today bears fruit with our conquest of municipal power. We have now written the most brilliant pages of our history. With the occupation of City Hall on November 20, 1980, and the takeover of the embassies on February 18, 1981, we taught the Mexican people that, in order to win, registration and voting are not enough. It is also necessary to maintain ironclad unity, to struggle combatively, and to have the full support of the people. We have set a great example. We have demonstrated that our enemies, the exploiters, are not invincible. We have shown that with unity, struggle, and national support it is possible to take away their power. Today, my countrymen, Juchitán governs itself.

Beginning today, we will plan great projects, and we will confront new problems. If we strengthen the unity of Juchitecos, remain permanently mobilized, and can continue to count on the support of the Mexican people, we will overcome all obstacles. We have struggled for a new type of government, and for the elimination of the puppet regimes composed of *priístas* and run by the state government. Now we want to establish a relationship of mutual respect and equality between the people's government and the state government. From this forum, we appeal to the people of Juchitán to remain united and vigilant and to make sure the state government fulfills its promise to grant to Juchitán a three-year budget exceeding 300 million pesos, which will serve as the basis for furthering the great projects we have proposed and for carrying out the popular measures Juchitán needs in order to escape once and for all from backwardness and neglect.

Today, more than ever, it is clear that our electoral victory would not have been possible without the Juchitecos' trust and great faith. This victory is the greatest homage to the martyrs of the people of Juchitán.

Our enemies, the caciques, exploiters, and land barons, have initiated a campaign to prevent this town from having a new government. In their first offensive, our enemies were defeated. Juchitán now has its new government, but new attacks will come. Smear campaigns have already begun against the Coalition: "Subversives take over City Hall, armed men and delinquents from terrorist organizations occupy City Hall." Newspapers like *Noticias* and the magazine *Tesis* are trying to ruin the reputation of this new government, but no slander campaign can be effective in our town. All campaigns of lies will shatter in the face of the Juchitecos' confidence in their organization, the Worker–Peasant–Student Coalition of the Isthmus of Tehuantepec (COCEI).

ALTERNATIVES FOR STRUGGLE: THE CONTEXT OF THE COCEI ALTERNATIVE *by COCEI*

The inhabitants of the Oaxacan Isthmus of Tehuantepec conserve their autochthonous culture and, as part of this, their language, Zapotec. From birth, children are educated according to the traditions and customs of the region. For that reason, the vast majority are monolingual, that is, they speak only Zapotec.

The children of peasants, fishermen, artisans, [and] musicians . . . enter the first phase of education lacking any knowledge of Spanish. Primary education is given in Spanish, which is difficult for them. On the other hand, there is another kind of child, who comes from the families of the dominant classes. These children have the advantages of preschool education and knowledge of Spanish, and because of this are granted many privileges and facilities. Consequently, children of the popular classes are treated as if they were handicapped. Education, then, benefits the children of the dominant classes.

This educational contrast is due to the fact that the workers' children do not have access to preschool, where the other children learn Spanish and how to work with class materials. We should also point out the lack of bilingual teachers. These deficiencies carry on into future studies.

Another factor that intervenes in the educational environment is the economic conditions of the parents. On one hand, the children of the rich have the means to obtain books, private tutors, or assistance from their parents, who have enough education to be able to help them. These children have enough time to dedicate to their studies and are well nourished and healthy. On the other hand, the children of the poor, in the majority of cases, have to work from a young age as shoeshine boys, paper boys, or gum sellers to sustain their families. They therefore neglect their studies. Their parents are illiterate and cannot help them. They are victims of malnutrition and diseases resulting from unhealthy conditions. All of this contributes to, and is directly reflected in, the deficiencies in their education. When these children go on to secondary school they take with them the same economic and social problems. Now they must confront teachers who, because of family ties or economic interests, or because they identify fully with the sons of the exploiters, represent the caciques. Scholarships, the highest grades, and other facilities are destined for the privileged ones. The humble students are attacked, humiliated, and mistreated in the classrooms.

High school and post–high school education have one goal: to create technicians to serve the privileged classes. Hence the students study to become industrial, agricultural, and fishing technicians. Because of the low level of industrialization in the Isthmus, peasants' children have a difficult time finding work. The few available jobs are set aside for the caciques' children. As a result, there are many unemployed technicians who, because of the lack of funding to continue their education, are forced to work as peons and unskilled laborers, thus wasting their studies.

Because of poverty or because the colleges reject them as a result of their academic deficiencies, there are fewer poor students at the university level. Of those who do make it to college, the majority have to work to support themselves. Economic problems, together with a lack of study time, lead to a high dropout rate.

The situation outlined herein is not an isolated case; it forms part of the social reality of the country. Throughout the country, misery, injustice, and oppression permeate both the countryside and the city. The peasants are marginalized with minimal incomes and no education or medical care. They live with the illusion that one day the State will give them a piece of land. They have been soliciting land for ten or twenty years, and the documentation for land redistribution cases has turned yellow from sitting in the files so long. The life of workers in the city is much the same.

When the rural and urban workers organize to demand their rights they are brutally repressed. Protest is countered by jailing or even assassination.

The State also employs its organs of social control to implant modern models of Mexican dependent capitalism. A clear example of this is the Echeverría regime [1970–1976]. Without pretending to make a profound analysis of what the Echeverría regime represented, we will point out some central elements of his government. This will be the second reference point for locating the COCEI alternative.

The Mexican political system has dressed up the national model of capitalist development in new clothes. Echeverría used populist politics to gain a social base. From this foundation he proposed the modernization of capitalism and fortification of the State so that it could efficiently carry out its role as the guardian of capital. Modernization involved increasing production. In both the countryside and the city it entailed modernization of the instruments of production. To achieve this, it was necessary for Echeverría to look abroad in search of capital and technology.

To advance his project he needed to strengthen the State, which was then in crisis because of the brutal repression of the previous regime. Echeverría mounted a campaign, demagogically proclaiming that, at that moment, there was a greater margin for democracy. His famous "democratic opening" signified a supposed dialogue with different sectors of society and an announced, but not respected, freedom of the press.

This project had a strong impact on the countryside. The sold-out organizations denounced the existence of *latifundios,* raised demands for collective *ejidos,* and so forth. This can be explained. Collectivization implemented by the State is the basis for modernization of capitalism in agriculture. The new Federal Agrarian Reform Law gives legal recognition to *ejidos* so that they can obtain credit. This permits modernization of the means of production, initiation of capital accumulation in the countryside, and the creation of an *ejido* elite. It promotes the renting and monopolization of land.

Peasants have been struggling for many years to reclaim the country's *latifundios.* Echeverría used *agrarista* jargon and promised to turn over the solicited lands. Nevertheless, only a minimal portion of the *latifundios* were affected, many of which have not been turned over to the peasants because they are protected by restraining orders.

The modernization project came into conflict with the most reactionary elements of the national and international bourgeoisie, who could not comprehend that Echeverría was neither an *agrarista,* nor a unionist, nor (even less) a communist, as some called him. Instead, he was the faithful guardian of the long-term interests of the bourgeoisie.

With the advent of López Portillo, the situation changed for the reasons mentioned, particularly in the countryside. López Portillo declared that there was no land left to distribute and proclaimed the alliance for production. He attempted to reconcile his government with that fraction of the bourgeoisie that had clashed with Echeverría. This defines López Portillo's agrarian politics and permits us to predict repression against organizations independent from the State that struggle to improve workers' living conditions.

This brand of politics has begun in the Isthmus of Tehuantepec. We are aware that the State, given its class character and the interests it represents and defends, is incapable of solving the economic, social, and political problems of the region or the country. These problems can be resolved to the benefit of the popular classes when those classes are exclusively responsible for resolving them. In the meantime, the people of the Isthmus and COCEI prepare to assume their responsibilities in this historic moment. . . .

Women of Juchitán

Jeffrey W. Rubin

What enables poor people to rise up in rebellious movements and compete in elections? What provides the spark for political innovation?

On one of my trips to Juchitán, a Zapotec town in southeastern Mexico, I brought a gift for Petra, a young woman who had befriended my wife and me and sold us vegetables from her stall in the market. The stall had changed hands, however, and no one seemed able or willing to tell me where Petra had gone. My search led me from market to family courtyards and back again, until one of Petra's brothers, who lives in a radical squatter settlement, confided the truth: Petra had moved in with another woman, and her family had disowned her.

Such a prohibition came as a surprise to me, because what seems unusual elsewhere is often the norm in Juchitán. Zapotec painters and poets have long been known in Mexico City's cultural world for their subversion of Mexican and European conventions, often through eroticized imagery of iguanas and other animals. Men known in Zapotec as *muxe* (pronounced moo-sháy) sport women's clothes, adopt women's hairdos and body features, and dance with one another at fiestas. Well-heeled professionals wear traditional dress and encourage their children to speak Zapotec. And a radical leftist political movement, the Coalition of Workers, Peasants, and Students of the Isthmus, or COCEI (ko-sáy), has challenged the Mexican government and army, with unprecedented results.

In the 1970s COCEI supporters were gunned down in the streets by paramilitary squads, and leaders of the movement were thrown in jail. In 1983, when the Mexican army entered Juchitán and Zapotec Indians refused to leave the town hall, Daniel López Nelio, a COCEI leader, explained a central aspect of the town's political battle: "What is our concern? For our children to know how to speak Zapotec and play in Zapotec. For the continuity of our history, so that in one hundred years or in three centuries we can continue eating iguana."

COCEI's placing of Zapotec culture at the heart of politics eventually paid off. The movement has governed Juchitán since 1989, winning elections and initiating programs that garner widespread support, from public works carried out honestly and efficiently to oral history and social welfare projects. It is unusual for an Indian movement in Latin America to survive and rarer still for it to gain political power, reorient regional politics, and stimulate new forms of art and identity in an already vibrant Indian culture.

Women have been a major force behind this reorientation. Joaquina Peral, known as "the mother of us all," was eighty-one years old when I met her, and she still walked the length and breadth of the town to deliver babies. At first glance, she fit the image of the traditional Zapotec midwife, practicing techniques that had been handed down for generations from mother to daughter. COCEI used this cultural image to galvanize political support. But Joaquina's story, like Petra's, contained surprises.

It turned out, as my wife and I learned over Jell-O in her quiet kitchen, that Joaquina was born to Spanish parents in another part of the state. When her parents disapproved of the man she wanted to marry, they banished her to Juchitán. Once there, Joaquina explained, she asked her Japanese brother-in-law, a doctor, to teach her to deliver babies, to spite her mother.

Joaquina's story changed my notion of what Zapotec culture is and how political activism happens. Culture in Juchitán means daily activities that take on the outside and make it Juchiteco, but that also modify what is Zapotec in the process. In the words of Víctor Mesa, a local writer, "We learn about modernity from our grandparents." Zapotec midwives maintain their prestige and secure economic position not by refusing Western medicine, but by attending government-sponsored classes and referring women to doctors when that seems the best option. As a result, 70 percent of the babies in Juchitán are delivered by midwives, an astounding figure in a city filled with doctors. The descendants of immigrants to Juchitán, from places as near as Chiapas and as far as Lebanon, wear traditional dress and speak Zapotec. The grandson in one Lebanese-Juchiteco family, who attended an agricultural university near Mexico City, brought friends home during a school vacation. When they saw the young man's mother leave the house to go to the market for groceries, the friends asked him, "Why does she dress like an Indian?"

Juchitecas have been romanticized and mythicized by foreign visitors and local writers alike. Charles Brasseur, a nineteenth-century French traveler, wrote of his fascination with a Zapotec woman "so beautiful that she enchanted the hearts of the whites . . . I also remember that the first time I saw her, I was struck by her proud and arrogant demeanor." Magdalena María, a Zapotec woman arrested after a seventeenth-century Indian rebellion against the Spanish, was convicted of having sat on the dead Spanish mayor, pounding

him with a stone. The scornful invective with which she accompanied this violence is central to the legend today. In the words of Elena Poniatowska, one of
Mexico's foremost writers, "You should see them arrive like walking towers,
their windows open, their heart like a window, their nocturnal girth visited by
the moon." Zapotec women, Poniatowska continues, "wear their sensuality
on their shirtsleeves. Sex is a little clay toy; they take it in their hands, mold
it as they please, shake it, knead it together with the corn of their *totopos.*"

In Juchitán, things go together that are kept apart in other places. Men who
dress like women have prominent public roles in fiestas and commerce, market women accumulate money for cattle and university tuitions, and Zapotec
political leaders negotiate with the Mexican government with extraordinary
deftness. As a foreigner, I am simultaneously rebuffed by this culture and invited in. I am pressed to change my name—to Julio, because people can't
pronounce Jeff—and then laughingly informed that Jeffrey is fine because
it rhymes with "refri," the slang for refrigerator. I am asked slyly about the
whereabouts of my wife as I walk through the market and gleefully called
guëro, or "whitey" by the sharp-tongued fish-sellers, then praised by the flower
vendors for my burgeoning Zapotec skills. I am mocked in a skit at the Cultural Center, but when I comment on this later to the wife of the Center's
director, she responds with a pleasant shrug, as if such a thing were scarcely
imaginable.

DURING THE YEAR I spent researching my book, COCEI leaders refused to talk
to me. I was forced to learn about politics and culture by indirect means. A
key moment in my understanding occurred in the sprawling central market,
where I usually stood in front of one or another stall, discussing prices, gos-
siping, and catching up on the events of the day. One morning a woman I
knew invited me to sit down behind the table on which her produce was displayed. This space was where vendors stood or sat as they sold their wares,
talked with each other or with family members, and ate their meals. "They
came by and told us you were a spy," the woman informed me. "Are you a
spy?" She went on to tell me, in characteristically robust fashion, about the
years when her husband had had to migrate for work, about her children's
search for educations and jobs, and about her family's long involvement in a
tempestuous struggle for social change. Out of this conversation and many
others emerged these portraits of Zapotec women in a town famous for its
strong will.

Wedding celebration. (Photo by Jeffrey W. Rubin)

Laughing Vendors. (Photo by Jeffrey W. Rubin)

Family Courtyard, I. (Photo by Jeffrey W. Rubin)

Family Courtyard, II. (Photo by Jeffrey W. Rubin)

Fiesta. (Photo by Jeffrey W. Rubin)

Bar Owner. (Photo by Jeffrey W. Rubin)

Shrimp. (Photo by Jeffrey W. Rubin)

Midwife. (Photo by Jeffrey W. Rubin)

Inauguration of COCEI Health Center. (Photo by Jeffrey W. Rubin)

Altar. (Photo by Jeffrey W. Rubin)

EZLN Demands at the Dialogue Table

Zapatista Army of National Liberation

On January 1, 1994, the very date when the North American Free Trade Agreement (NAFTA) was supposed to enter into effect, Mexico was shocked by an uprising in Chiapas led by a group calling itself the Zapatista Army of National Liberation. This largely indigenous peasant uprising was surprising for a number of reasons. First, such insurrections were widely supposed to have become obsolete with the end of the Cold War. Most Latin American leftist guerrilla armies had laid down their weapons, and those that remained in the field—such as the Revolutionary Armed Forces of Colombia (FARC)—were generally regarded to have lost their ideological direction. Second, the uprising seemed to have a different character. Its leading spokesman, who called himself Subcomandante Marcos, smoked a pipe through his ski mask as he bombarded the national and international press with opaque letters full of parables and poetry. Indeed, it quickly became apparent that the movement was more concerned with the tactics of guerrilla theater than guerrilla warfare, its main objective being to win the hearts and minds of Mexicans. To prevail in this ideological war of position in a transnational environment, the EZLN made full use of the new internet technology: it sought to build international solidarity in opposition to the market-driven doctrines of neoliberalism, which, it argued, favored large corporations seeking cheap and docile labor, readily exploitable resources, and lax environmental regulation in places like Chiapas.

Although the uprising began with violence and has since seen occasional violent episodes, the history of the movement since its inception has been mostly characterized by a tense standoff between the Zapatistas and the Mexican government forces and sporadic bouts of unproductive negotiation. As of this writing, the conflict remains unresolved. The roots of the rebellion, which can be gleaned from the following list of demands made by the EZLN as it first entered into dialogue with the government, lie in the drastically unequal and exploitative socioeconomic structure of Southern Mexico. Some of the ills of that structure can be seen in readings elsewhere in this volume, notably in those by B. Traven and Rosario Castellanos.

COMMUNIQUÉ FROM THE CLANDESTINE
REVOLUTIONARY INDIAN COMMITTEE–GENERAL
COMMAND [CCRI–CG] OF THE EZLN, MEXICO

March 1, 1994

To the people of Mexico
To the peoples and governments of the World
To the national and international press

Brothers and sisters,

The CCRI–CG of the EZLN addresses you with respect and honor in order
to inform you of the list of demands presented at the bargaining table in the
Meetings for Peace and Reconciliation in Chiapas.

"We are not begging for change or gifts; we ask for the right to live with
the dignity of human beings, with equality and justice like our parents and
grandparents of old."

To the People of Mexico:

The indigenous peoples of the state of Chiapas, having risen up in arms in
the EZLN against misery and bad government, hereby present the reasons for
their struggle and their principal demands:

The reason and causes of our armed movement are the following problems, to which the government has never offered any real solution:

(1) The hunger, misery, and marginalization that we have always suffered.

(2) The total lack of land on which to work in order to survive.

(3) The repression, eviction, imprisonment, torture, and murder with
which the government responds to our fair demands.

(4) The unbearable injustices and violations of our human rights as indigenous people and impoverished campesinos.

(5) The brutal exploitation we suffer in the sale of our products, in the work
day, and in the purchase of basic necessities.

(6) The lack of all basic services for the great majority of the indigenous
population.

(7) More than sixty years of lies, deceptions, promises, and imposed governments. The lack of freedom and democracy in deciding our destinies.

(8) The constitutional laws have not been obeyed by those who govern the
country; on the other hand, we the indigenous people and campesinos are
made to pay for the smallest error. They heap upon us the weight of laws we
did not make, and those who did make them are the first to violate them.

The EZLN came to dialogue with honest words. The EZLN came to say its word about the conditions that were the origin of its righteous war and to ask all the people of Mexico to help find a solution to these political, economic, and social conditions that forced us to take up arms to defend our existence and our rights.

Therefore we demand. . . .

First. We demand truly free and democratic elections, with equal rights and obligations for all the political organizations struggling for power, with real freedom to choose between one proposal and another and with respect for the will of the majority. Democracy is the fundamental right of all peoples, indigenous and non-indigenous. Without democracy there cannot be liberty or justice or dignity. And without dignity there is nothing.

Second. In order for there to be truly free and democratic elections, the incumbent federal executive and the incumbent state executives, which came to power via electoral fraud, must resign. Their legitimacy does not come from respect for the will of the majority but rather from usurping it. Consequently, a transitional government must be formed to ensure equality and respect for all political forces. The federal and state legislative powers, elected freely and democratically, must assume their true functions of making just laws for everyone and ensuring that the laws are followed.

Another way to guarantee free and democratic elections is to recognize in national, state, and local law the legitimacy of citizens and groups of citizens who, without party affiliation, would watch over the elections, sanction the legality of its results, and have maximum authority to guarantee the legitimacy of the whole electoral process.

Third. Recognition of the EZLN as a belligerent force, and of its troops as authentic combatants, and application of all international treaties that regulate military conflict.

Fourth. A new pact among the elements of the federation, which puts an end to centralism and permits regions, indigenous communities, and municipalities to govern themselves with political, economic, and cultural autonomy.

Fifth. General elections for the whole state of Chiapas and legal recognition of all the political forces in the state.

Sixth. As a producer of electricity and oil, the state of Chiapas pays tribute to the federation without receiving anything in exchange. Our communities do not have electric power; the export and domestic sale of our oil doesn't produce any benefit whatsoever for the Chiapanecan people. In view of this, it is vital that all Chiapanecan communities receive the benefit of electric power and that a percentage of the income from the commercialization of Chiapanecan oil be applied to the agricultural, commercial, and social-industrial infrastructure, for the benefit of all Chiapanecans.

Seventh. Revision of the North American Free Trade Agreement signed with Canada and the United States, given that in its current state it does not take into consideration the indigenous populations and sentences them to death for the crime of having no job qualifications whatsoever.

Eighth. Article 27 of the Magna Carta [Constitution of 1917] must respect the original spirit of Emiliano Zapata: the land is for the indigenous peoples and campesinos who work it—not for the latifundistas. We want, as is established in our revolutionary agricultural law, the great quantity of land that is currently in the hands of big ranchers and national and foreign landowners to pass into the hands of our peoples, who suffer from a total lack of land. The land grants shall include farm machinery, fertilizers, pesticides, credits, technical advice, improved seeds, livestock, and fair prices for products like coffee, corn, and beans. The land that is distributed must be of good quality and include roads, transportation, and irrigation systems.

The campesinos who already have land also have the right to all the above-mentioned supports in order to facilitate their work in the fields and improve production. New *ejidos* and communities must be formed. The Salinas revision of Article 27 must be annulled and the right to land must be recognized as per the terms of our Magna Carta.

Ninth. We want hospitals to be built in the municipal seats, with specialized doctors and enough medicine to be able to attend to the patients; we want rural clinics in the *ejidos,* communities, and surrounding areas, as well as training and a fair salary for health workers. Where there are already hospitals, they must be renovated as soon as possible and include complete surgical services. In the largest communities, clinics must be built and they too must have doctors and medicine in order to treat people more quickly.

Tenth. The right to true information about what happens at the local, regional, state, national, and international levels must be guaranteed to indigenous peoples by way of an indigenous radio station independent of the government, directed by indigenous people and run by indigenous people.

Eleventh. We want housing to be built in all the rural communities of Mexico, including such basic services as electricity, potable water, roads, sewer systems, telephone, transportation, and so forth. And these houses should also have the advantages of the city, such as television, stove, refrigerator, and washing machine. The communities shall be equipped with recreation centers for the healthy entertainment of their populations: sports and culture that dignify the human condition of the indigenous people.

Twelfth. We want the illiteracy of the indigenous peoples to come to an end. For this to happen we need better elementary and secondary schools in our communities, including free teaching materials, and teachers with a university education who are at the service of the people and not just in defense of the interests of the rich. In the municipal seats there must be free elementary, junior high, and high schools; the government must give the students uniforms, shoes, food, and all study materials free of charge. The larger, central communities that are very far from the municipal seats must provide boarding schools at the secondary level. Education must be totally free, from preschool to university, and must be granted to all Mexicans regardless of race, creed, age, sex, or political affiliation.

Thirteenth. The languages of all ethnicities must be official and their instruction shall be mandatory in elementary, junior high, and high school, and at the university level.

Fourteenth. Our rights and dignity as indigenous peoples shall be respected, taking into account our cultures and traditions.

Fifteenth. We indigenous people no longer want to be the object of discrimination and contempt.

Sixteenth. We indigenous people must be permitted to organize and govern ourselves autonomously; we no longer want to submit to the will of the powerful, either national or foreign.

Seventeenth. Justice shall be administered by the same indigenous peoples, according to their customs and traditions, without intervention by illegitimate and corrupt governments.

Eighteenth. We want to have decent jobs with fair salaries for all rural and urban workers throughout the Mexican republic, so that our brothers and sisters don't have to work at bad things, like drug trafficking, delinquency, and prostitution, to be able to survive. The federal Labor Law shall be applied to rural and urban workers, complete with bonuses, benefits, vacations, and the real right to strike.

Nineteenth. We want a fair price for our products from the countryside. Thus we need the liberty to find a market where we can buy and sell and not be subject to exploiting *coyotes* [middlemen].

Twentieth. The plunder of the riches of our Mexico and above all of Chiapas, one of the richest states of the republic but where hunger and misery most abound, must come to an end.

Twenty-first. We want all debts from credits, loans, and taxes with high interest rates to be annulled; these cannot be paid due to the great poverty of the Mexican people.

Twenty-second. We want hunger and malnutrition to end; it alone has caused the death of thousands of our brothers and sisters in the country and the city. Every rural community must have cooperative stores supported economically by the federal, state, or municipal governments, and the prices must be fair. Moreover, there must be vehicles, property of the co-ops, for the transportation of merchandise. The government must send free food for all children under fourteen.

Twenty-third. We ask for the immediate and unconditional liberty of all political prisoners and of all the poor people unfairly imprisoned in all the jails of Chiapas and Mexico.

Twenty-fourth. We ask that the Federal Army and the public security and judicial police no longer come into rural zones because they only come to intimidate, evict, rob, repress, and bomb campesinos who are organizing to defend their rights. Our peoples are tired of the abusive and repressive presence of the soldiers and public security and judicial police. The federal government must return to the Swiss government the Pilatus planes used to bomb our people, and the money resulting from the return of that merchandise shall be applied toward programs to improve the lives of the workers of the country and the city. We also ask that the government of the United States of North America recall its helicopters, as they are used to repress the people of Mexico.

Twenty-fifth. When the indigenous campesino people rose up in arms, they had nothing but poor huts, but now that the Federal Army is bombing the civilian population it is destroying even these humble homes and our few belongings. Therefore we ask and demand of the federal government that it compensate the families that have sustained material losses caused by the bombings and the actions of the federal troops. We also ask for compensation for those widowed and orphaned by the war, for civilians as well as Zapatistas.

Twenty-sixth. We as indigenous campesinos want to live in peace and quiet, and to be permitted to live according to our rights to liberty and a decent life.

Twenty-seventh. The Penal Code of the state of Chiapas must be revoked; it doesn't permit us to organize in any way other than with arms, since any legal and peaceful struggle is punished and repressed.

Twenty-eighth. We ask for and demand an immediate halt to the displacement of indigenous peoples from their communities by the state-backed *caciques*. We demand the guaranteed free and voluntary return of all displaced peoples to their lands of origin, and compensation for their losses.

Twenty-ninth. Indigenous women's petition:

We the indigenous campesina women ask for the immediate solution to our urgent needs, which the government has never met:

(1) Child-birth clinics with gynecologists so that campesina women can receive necessary medical attention.

(2) Day-care centers must be built in the communities.

(3) We ask the government to send enough food for the children in all the communities — necessities such as milk, corn starch, rice, corn, soy, oil, beans, cheese, eggs, sugar, soup, oatmeal, and so forth.

(4) Kitchens and dining halls, with all the necessary equipment, must be built for the children in the communities.

(5) Corn mills and tortilla-makers must be placed in the communities according to the number of families in each area.

(6) We should be given the materials necessary to raise chickens, rabbits, sheep, and pigs, including technical advice and veterinary services.

(7) We ask for the ovens and materials necessary to build bakeries.

(8) We want craft workshops to be built, including machinery and materials.

(9) There must be a market where crafts can be sold at a fair price.

(10) Schools must be built where women can receive technical training.

(11) There must be preschool and day-care centers in the rural communities where the children can have fun and grow up strong, morally and physically.

(12) As women we must have sufficient transportation to move from one place to another and to transport the products of the various projects we have.

Thirtieth. We demand political justice for Patrocinio González Garrido, Absalón Castellanos Domínguez, and Elmar Setzer M.[1]

Thirty-first. We demand respect for the lives of all members of the EZLN and a guarantee that there will be no penal process or repressive action taken against any of the members of the EZLN, combatants, sympathizers, or collaborators.

Thirty-second. All groups and commissions defending human rights must be independent, that is, non-governmental, because those that are governmental only hide the arbitrary actions of the government.

Thirty-third. A National Commission of Peace with Justice and Dignity should be formed, the majority of constituents being people with no government or party affiliation. This National Commission of Peace with Justice and Dignity should be the agency that ensures the implementation of the agreements reached between the EZLN and the federal government.

Thirty-fourth. The humanitarian aid for the victims of the conflict should be channeled through authentic representatives of the indigenous communities.

As long as there is no answer to these fair demands of our peoples, we are willing and determined to continue our struggle until we reach our objective.

For us, the least of these lands, those without face and without history, those armed with truth and fire, those who came from the night and the mountain, the true men and women, the dead of yesterday, today, and forever . . . for ourselves nothing. For everyone, everything.

Freedom! Justice! Democracy!

Respectfully,

From the Mexican Southeast

CCRI–CG of the EZLN

Mexico, March 1994

Note

1. Castellanos Domínguez was governor of Chiapas from 1982 to 1988; he was succeeded by González Garrido. When González Garrido was named Interior (*Gobernación*) Secretary by President Salinas in 1993, Elmar Setzer was named interim governor. All were denounced for corruption and abuse of power by the Zapatistas. *Ed.*

The Long Journey from Despair to Hope

Subcomandante Marcos

The uniquely charismatic and mysterious Subcomandante Marcos is the best-known spokesman for the EZLN, yet he vehemently denies that he is in fact the group's "leader," for it is officially a leaderless army. About a year after the start of the uprising, the government identified Marcos as Rafael Sebastián Guillén Vicente, a native of Tampico who was then in his late-30s. Marcos has steadfastly refused to acknowledge his identity or to remove his mask publicly. In the years since the Zapatista uprising, Marcos has published voluminously. His writings show him to be a gifted literary figure and impassioned critic of globalization, exploitation, commercialization, the polarization of wealth, and other trends that have been placed under the general rubric of "neoliberalism."

September 22, 1994

THE NATION AND ITS SORROWS SPEAK

They have struck me
pained,
like a piece of land, scarred, with wounds that do not heal,
with beatings and falls. They have struck me like a never-ending curse,
like a home left to ruin and bitterness.
Oh, the weight of history!
I am filled with treachery and thefts,
every added humiliation grows,
each new misery accumulates.
The imperial eagle tears at my insides
and powerful men divide among themselves
my seas and mountains,
my rivers and deserts,
my valleys and streams.
These are my afflictions,
great and never ending:

the pain of my mangled ground,
the pain of my impoverished land,
the pain of my son betrayed,
the pain of my battle lost . . .

One can reach this country through the penthouse or through the basement. . . .

1994: Reaching the Mexican Penthouse

One arrives by plane. An airport in Mexico City, Monterrey, Guadalajara, or Acapulco is the entrance to an elevator that neither goes up nor down, but rides horizontally across the land of the twenty-four richest men in the country, the paths of modern-day Mexico: the government offices where neoliberalism is overseen, the business clubs where the national flag fades more with each passing day, the vacation resorts whose true vocation is to mirror a social class that does not want to see what is below their feet: the long spiral stairway, the labyrinth that leads all the way down to Lower Mexico, Mexico on foot, a Mexico of mud.

Above the blood and clay that live in the basement of this country, the omnipotent twenty-four are busy counting $44,100 million, a modern-day presidential gift. Penthouse Mexico simply has no time to look down; it is too busy with complicated macroeconomics calculations, exchange of promises, praises and indexes of inflation, interest rates and the level of foreign investment, import-export concessions, lists of assets and resources, scales where the country and dignity have no weight. The public debt guaranteed, long range, has gone from $3,196 million in 1970 to $76,257 million in 1989. In 1970 the private, nonguaranteed U.S. debt was $2,770 million. In 1989 it was up to $3,999 million. In 1989 the short-term public debt reached $10,295. At the beginning of the 1990s, Mexico owed $95,642 million.

Each year this country pays off more debt, yet each year it owes more. The use of International Monetary Fund credits went from $0 in 1970 to $5,091 million in 1989. The industrial and commercial economic growth takes its toll on the Mexican countryside: in agriculture, in the period of 1965 to 1980, production grew at an average national rate of 3 percent; in the period from 1980 to 1989, only by 1 percent.

Meanwhile, in foreign trade, imports speak their complicated language of numbers: grain imports in 1974 were only 2,881 thousand metric tons; in 1984 they reached 7,054 thousand. Of the total, in 1965 only 5 percent of imports were foodstuffs; in 1989 food imports reached 16 percent. On the other hand, in the same period, machinery and transportation equipment imports were reduced (50 percent in 1965, 34 percent in 1989). Exports confirm: in total, the sale of combustibles and minerals increased from 22 percent in 1965 to 41 percent in 1989. Foreign sales of machinery and transportation equipment increased from 1 percent in 1965 to 24 percent in 1989. The export of products of prime necessity were reduced from 62 percent in 1965 to 14 percent in 1989.

In Penthouse Mexico Mr. Carlos Salinas de Gortari is president—but of a board of stockholders. During these modern times, Mexican neopolitics make public functionaries into a species of retail salespeople, and the president of the republic into the sales manager of a gigantic business: Mexico, Inc. The best business in the country is to be a politician in the state party in Mexico. . . .

The Neo-elect, Ernesto Zedillo, is repeating the fallacy of the American Dream (poor children who grow up to be rich, that is to say, to be politicians), and the modernistic economic program—which is forty-eight years old!

The smokescreen about the lack of solvency, credit, and markets will again blind the heads of medium to large businesses. The "law of the jungle," free trade, will repeat its dictates: more monopolies, fewer jobs. In neoliberal politics, "growth" simply means "to sell." To practice politics, one must practice marketing technology. Sooner or later, the "citizen" of Penthouse Mexico will be named Man of the Year by some foreign institution. To achieve this he must follow:

INSTRUCTIONS TO BE NAMED MAN OF THE YEAR

1. Carefully combine a technocrat, a repentant oppositionist, a sham businessman, a union bully, a landowner, a builder, an alchemist in computational arts, a "brilliant" intellectual, a television, a radio, and an official party. Set this mixture aside in a jar and label it "Modernity."

2. Take an agricultural worker, a peasant with no land, an unemployed person, an industrial worker, a teacher without a school, a dissatisfied housewife, an applicant for housing and services, a touch of honest press, a student, a homosexual, a member of the opposition to the regime. Divide these up as much as possible. Set them aside in a jar and label them "Anti-Mexico."

3. Take an indigenous Mexican. Take away the crafts and take a picture of her. Put her crafts and the photo in a jar and set aside. Label it "Tradition."

4. Put the indigenous Mexican in another jar, set it aside, and label it "Dispensable." One must not forget to disinfect oneself after this last operation.

5. Well, now open a store and hang a huge sign that says, "Mexico 1994–2000: Huge–End-of-the-Century Sale."

6. Smile for the camera. Make sure the makeup covers the dark circles under the eyes caused by the many nightmares the process has caused.

Note: Always have on hand a policeman, a soldier, and an airplane ticket out of the country. These items may be necessary at any time.

PENTHOUSE MEXICO HAS no foreign vocation; for this it would have to have a nationality. The only country mentioned with sincerity on that increasingly narrow top floor is the country called money. And that country has no patriots, only profit and loss indexes; history happens only within the stock markets, and its modern heroes are Good Salesmen. For some reason, due to the other history (the real history) that top floor, instead of expanding, is contracting quickly. Every day, fewer and fewer are able to reside up there. Sometimes with delicacy, other times with brutality, the incapable ones are forced to go down—those stairs. The door to Mexico's penthouse elevator opens to the great international airports; it does not go up or down. To leave the penthouse, one must descend those stairs, go down farther and farther until . . .

To Get to Middle Mexico . . .

. . . One goes by car. It is urban, and its image is a carbon copy that repeats itself throughout the country, throughout Mexico City. It is an image of concrete that cannot deny the contradiction that the extremely rich and the extremely poor coexist. Middle Mexico smells bad. Something is rotting from within, while the sense of collectivity is being diluted. Middle Mexico does have a foreign vocation. Something tells it that to rise to Penthouse Mexico, the road passes through a country that is not this one. In order to "triumph" in Mexico, one must go abroad. This does not necessarily mean to leave physically, but to leave behind history, to leave behind goals. This vocation of exile as a synonym to triumph has nothing to do with the physical crossing of a border. There are those who have left and are still with us. And there are those who, although still with us, are gone. . . .

Middle Mexico survives in the worst possible way: believing that it has a life. It has all of the disadvantages of Penthouse Mexico: historical ignorance, cynicism, opportunism, and an emptiness that import products can only fill partially or not at all. It has all the disadvantages of Lower Mexico: economic instability, insecurity, bewilderment, sudden loss of hope—and what's more, on every street corner misery knocks on the windows of the car. Sooner or later, Middle Mexico must get out of the car and, if he still has some change left, get into a taxi, a collective taxi, a subway, reach a bus terminal, and start the journey down, all the way to . . .

Lower Mexico . . .

. . . which one can reach almost immediately. It coexists in permanent conflict with Middle Mexico. Half of the people in the seventeen Mexican states in the middle, low, and very low indexes of marginalization live in cramped conditions, in poverty, with two or more persons to a room. 50 percent of each unit earn less than two minimum wages daily. In Tlaxcala, three-quarters of the population lives in poverty.

In Aguascalientes, Chihuahua, Jalisco, Colima, Tamaulipas, Morelos, Quintana Roo, Sinaloa, and Tlaxcala, a third of the population over fifteen years old has not completed primary school; in Nayarit more than 40 percent have not. One-third of the population in Tlaxcala has no sewers or plumbing. Quintana Roo and Sinaloa have a fourth of their inhabitants living on dirt floors. The states of Durango, Querétaro, Guanajuato, Michoacán, Yucatán, Campeche, Tabasco, Zacatecas and San Luis Potosí have high indexes of marginalization. Nearly half the people over fifteen have not completed primary school; one-third have neither plumbing nor sewers; nearly two-thirds live in crowded conditions; and more than 60 percent earn less than two minimum wages per day.

Lower Mexico does not share; it battles for an urban or rural space, notwithstanding the existence of its own internal dividing lines, its borders. In rural areas, estates, haciendas, and large agricultural concerns impose upon *ejidos* and peasant communities. In urban *colonias* it is not necessary to state the level of income, social position, and political vocation. It is enough to say in what *colonia* of what city one lives: the name and the location, the services, the manner of speaking of their people, the way they dress, their entertainment, education — everything limits and classifies, trying to order, to accommodate, the chaos that rules Mexican cities. Within one city there are thousands of cities, fighting, surviving, struggling. In the countryside it is the mode of transportation, the way one dresses, and the attention one receives from the bank manager that indicate one's class — a person's standing can be determined by how long it takes him or her to be received in the reception areas of the financial or political world. In Lower Mexico the manor house on the Porfirian hacienda has been replaced by the inner office of the bank. This is how modern times have penetrated rural Mexico.

Lower Mexico has a fighter's vocation; it is brave, it is solidarist, it is a clan, it is the "hood," it is the gang, the race, the friend; it is the strike, the march, and the meeting; it is taking back one's land, it is blocking highways, it is the "I don't believe you!" it is the "I won't take it anymore!" it is the *"órale!"*[1] Lower Mexico is the master tradesman, the mason, the plumber, the factory worker, the driver, the employee, the subway/bus/shared-cab student, the street cleaner, the truck driver and logician, the housewife, the small businessman, the traveling salesman, the farmer, the mini and micro entrepreneur, the miner, the colonizer, the peasant, the tenant farmer—from the provinces, yet living in the capital—the peon, the longshoreman in port cities, the fisherman and sailor, the used clothes dealer, the butcher, the artisan. It is all the etceteras that one finds on any bus, on any street corner, in any given nook of any given place of any Mexico . . . of Lower Mexico.

Lower Mexico is the substance of the imprisoned, of the dispossessed, of garnishments, of liens, of layoffs, of evictions, of kidnappings, of tortures, of disappeared, of hassle, of death. Lower Mexico has absolutely nothing . . . but hasn't realized it. Lower Mexico already has overpopulation problems. Lower Mexico is a millionaire if one sums up its misery and its despair. Lower Mexico shares both urban and rural space, slips and falls, battles and downfalls. Lower Mexico is really far down, so far down that it seems that there is no way to go farther down, so far down that one can hardly see that little door that leads to . . .

Basement Mexico . . .

. . . One arrives on foot, either barefoot, or with rubber-soled huaraches. To get there one must descend through history and ascend through the indexes of marginalization. Basement Mexico came first. When Mexico was not yet Mexico, when it was all just beginning, the now–Basement Mexico existed, it lived. Basement Mexico is "indigenous" because Columbus thought, 502 years ago, that the land where he had arrived was India. "Indians" is what the natives of these lands have been called from that time on. Basement Mexico is: Mazahuan, Amuzgan, Tlapanecan, Nahuatlan, Coran, Huichol, Yaqui, Mayan, Tarahumaran, Mixtec, Zapotecan, Chontal, Seri, Triquis, Kumiain, Cucapan, Paipain, Cochimian, Kiliwan, Tequistlatecan, Pame, Chichimecan, Otomi, Mazatecan, Matlatzincan, Ocuiltecan, Popolocan, Ixcatecan, Chocho-popolocan, Cuicatec, Chatino, Chinantec, Huave, Papagan, Pima, Repehuan, Guarijian, Huastec, Chuj, Jalaltec, Mixe, Zoquean, Totonacan, Kikapuan, Purepechan, Oodham, Tzotzil, Tzeltal, Tojolabal, Chol, Mam.

Basement Mexico is indigenous . . . However, for the rest of the country, it does not count—it does not produce, sell, or buy—that is, it does not exist. Check out the text of the Free Trade Agreement, and you will find that, for this government, the indigenous do not exist. Furthermore, read Addendum 1001.a-1 to the Free Trade Agreement, dated October 7, 1992 (yes, just five days before the "festivities" of the 500th anniversary of the "Discovery of America"), and you will find that Salinas' government has "forgotten" to mention the National Indigenous Institute on the list of federal government entities. We have been in the mountains a very long time, and perhaps the National Indigenous Institute has been privatized. But it is still surprising that such well-known organizations as the Patronage for Aid to Social Regeneration, and Aid for the Commercialization of the Fishing Industry, and the Doctor Andres Bustamante Gurría Institute for Human Communication appear listed as "government entities." On the other hand, in Canada there is the Department of Indian Affairs and Northern Development.

Basement Mexico amasses traditions and misery; it possesses the highest indexes of marginalization and the lowest in nutrition. Six of the thirty-two states have a very high index of marginalization, all six of which have a large indigenous population: Puebla, Veracruz, Hidalgo, Guerrero, Oaxaca, and Chiapas. . . .

In Basement Mexico one lives and dies between the mud and blood. Hidden, but in its foundation, the contempt that this Mexico suffers will permit it to organize itself and shake up the entire system. Its burden will be the possibility of freeing itself from it. For these Mexicans, the lack of democracy, liberty, and justice will be organized. It will explode and shine on . . .

JANUARY 1994 . . .

. . . When the entire country remembered that there was a basement. Thousands of indigenous, armed with truth and fire, with shame and dignity, shook the country awake from its sweet dream of modernity. "Enough is enough!" this Mexico calls out—enough dreams, enough nightmares. Ever since steel and the gospel dominated these lands, the indigenous voice has been condemned to resisting a war of extermination that now incorporates all of the inter-galactic-technological advances. Satellites, communications equipment, and infrared rays keep watch on every move, locate rebellions, and on military maps pinpoint the places for the seeding of bombs and death. Tens of thousands of olive green masks are preparing a new and prosperous war. They want to cleanse their dignity in serving the powerful with indigenous blood. They want to be accomplices in the unjust delivery of poverty and pain.

The indigenous Zapatistas will pay for their sins with their blood. What sins? The sin of not being satisfied with handouts, the sin of insisting on their demands for democracy, liberty, and justice for all Mexico, the sin of their "Everything for everyone, nothing for us."

Those who deny the indigenous Mexican peasant the possibility of understanding the concept of Nation, who force him to look to his past—which separates him from the rest of the country—and prohibit him from looking to the future—which unites the nation and which is the only possibility for survival of the indigenous people—reiterate the division, not of social classes, but of categories of citizens. The first is the governing class, the second is the political parties of the opposition, and the third is the rest of the citizens. The indigenous would be in the very inferior category of "citizens in formation." They are Basement Mexico, the waste pile where one goes, every once in a while, to look for something that could still be used on the upper floors, or to fix some imperfection that could endanger the stability or balance in the building.

Basement Mexico is the gravest threat to the season of sales that is being organized by Penthouse Mexico. Basement Mexico has nothing to lose and everything to win. Basement Mexico does not give up, can't be bought, resists . . .

In August 1994 a voice arose from Basement Mexico, a voice that does not speak of war, that does not plan to turn back the clock of history by 502 years, that does not demand the vanguard, that does not exclude its miseries. "Everything for everyone, nothing for us," speaks the language of the millennium. The voice of those without a face, of the unnamable, became familiar in the National Democratic Convention. This voice calls to Basement Mexico, it speaks to Middle Mexico: "Don't let our blood be wasted. Don't let death be in vain," say the mountains. Through the word separate roads join. Let the rebellion also embrace . . .

THE WOMEN: DUAL DREAM, DUAL NIGHTMARE, DUAL AWAKENING

If among men the division of Mexicos is evident, to a point, with women it produces novel effects that make possible submission and rebellion.

In Penthouse Mexico, women reiterate their filigree status: being a trinket for the world's executives, the wise and "efficient" administrator of familial well-being—that is, measuring the dosage of weekly dinners at McDonald's. In Middle Mexico, women perpetuate the ancient cycle of daughter-girlfriend-wife and/or lover-mother. In the Lower and Basement Mexicos, the duplication of the nightmare where the man dominates and determines is endemic.

With the exception of respect, for the women of Lower and Basement Mexicos everything is duplicated: the percentage of illiteracy, the subhuman living conditions, low salaries, and marginalization. These add up to the nightmare that the system prefers to ignore or disguise under the makeup of general indexes, which hide the exploitation of women, and make general exploitation possible.

But something is beginning not to fit in this dual submission; the dual nightmare begins to duplicate an awakening.

Women from Lower and Basement Mexico awaken fighting against the present and the past, which threatens to be their future.

The conscience of humanity passes through female conscience; the knowledge of being human implies they know they're women and struggle. They no longer need anyone to speak for them; their word follows the double route of a self-propelled rebellion — the double motor of rebel women.

Note

1. *Órale* is a Mexican expression equivalent to "Right on!"

A Tzotzil Chronicle of the Zapatista Uprising

Marián Peres Tsu

Marián Peres Tsu worked for many years as a driver of a collective taxi, shuttling market vendors to the marketplace of San Cristóbal de Las Casas from their homes in squatter settlements to the north of the city. This work afforded him privileged access to the news and rumors that circulated in the community. He had long written poems and stories in his native language (Tzotzil). Upon the outbreak of the Zapatista uprising, he began to transcribe some of the stories he heard from fellow taxi drivers, market vendors, and other workers and local inhabitants. According to anthropologist Jan Rus, this may be "the first history of the new urban and indigenous society seen from the inside, by one of its own members." Peres Tsu's chronicle conveys something of the excitement, empowerment, confusion, and even dark humor that has attended the EZLN uprising, as long-suffering Maya Indians saw their chance to finally defy their exploiters. It also reveals some of the frustration at the conflict's lack of resolution and the tensions within the ranks of the popular movement.

Jan Rus, who translated the work from Tzotzil, is an American anthropologist who has worked in highland Chiapas continuously since the 1970s, studying the history and lore of the region's indigenous groups. Since the late 1980s, Rus has also worked for the Instituto de Asesoría Antropológica para la Región Maya (INAREMAC) in San Cristóbal de las Casas, helping native writers prepare and publish community studies, life histories, and short stories in Tzotzil and Spanish.

Early January 1994: Preparations and Visits

Before the invasion of San Cristóbal, everyone always talked about how the soldiers at the army base overlooking the southern approach to the city had spread booby traps all around their land, how they had fixed it so no one would ever dare attack them. If the poor Indians ever came to make trouble, everyone said, the soldiers would finish them off right there, before they even got out of the forest. The army officers are *maestros* of killing, they said, and all they have to do every day, their only chore, is teach the young soldiers to kill too. And as if all of that weren't enough to scare away a bunch of raggedy peasants, they said, the soldiers also have mounds of bombs stored behind their fort. Nothing but special bombs for killing Indians!

K'elevil, look here. According to what people said, the soldiers had strung a special wire around their barracks that was connected to a bomb every few steps. If the damn Indians ever did come around, they said, all the soldiers would have to do was lean out of their beds and touch the wire with a piece of metal—like, say, a beer can—and the bombs would all blow up. And if the Indians tried to cut the wire, it would also blow up. But of course, the soldiers are famous for never sleeping, so the Indians would never even get close to the bombs in the first place. No one, the soldiers figured, would ever get past them.

But after all those preparations, what happened? On January first, the soldiers were asleep when the Zapatistas arrived in San Cristóbal! But snoring! They didn't see the Zapatistas go by their check-points with the other passengers on the second-class buses! They didn't notice the Zapatistas get out of their buses at the station and walk into the center of town! They didn't see anything! And when the soldiers woke up, the Zapatistas had already seized the *Palacio de Gobierno* and set up their own guards around the city! After all, it was the Army that was left outside of town, safely holed up in its barracks! The Zapatistas won by just ignoring them! Not until two days later, when they had finished their business in town, did the Zapatistas finally go to pay a visit on the soldiers! [The Zapatistas attacked the army post at Rancho Nuevo on January 3rd, as they were retreating from San Cristóbal.]

The Zapatistas are only Indians, but what the army officers forgot is that Indians too are men. And since they are men, they also could be armed and trained, just like the army. All they needed was the idea. And as it turned out, their thinking was better than the army's! They fooled the officers, who are maestros of killing! Since that day, all of us, even those who are not enemies of the government, feel like smiling down into our shirts.

If there is a sad part to all of this, it is that even though the Zapatistas are men, they will have to live in hiding from now on. They won't be able to sleep in their own beds in their own houses, but will have to stay at all times in caves in the jungle. If they want to make babies like everyone else, they'll even have to screw in the caves. Like armadillos!

Early January: Uncertainty in Chamula

When word first came that the Zapatistas had occupied San Cristóbal, all the Chamulas said that they weren't afraid. But that was a lie: they were. Just to keep up appearances, though, everyone said that the only one who really had anything to be scared of, the single person responsible for all the bad things that have happened in Chamula, was the municipal president. In truth, of course, they all knew that they too had participated in the round-ups and expulsions of their Protestant neighbors, and they were all afraid the Zapatistas were going to come and exact justice. They had also all heard that the Zapatistas were well armed and figured they wouldn't waste a lot of time listening to excuses, that they would just kill all the Chamulas who had beaten the Protestants and burned their property. And what could the Chamulas do about it? They don't have any good weapons, just some .22 rifles, a few pistols, and one or another old shot-gun, enough to scare their unarmed neighbors, maybe, but against real soldiers they wouldn't have a chance. Instead of fighting, they all said everyone in the whole town would be better off if they just stayed in bed and screwed one last time.

As you can imagine, though, if everyone else was worried, the municipal president himself was terrified. He was so scared about what the Zapatistas and Protestant exiles would do to him if they ever caught him that he walked around for a week with a hard-on. But stiff! He better than anyone knew all of the terrible things that had been done. But he wasn't alone. To tell the truth, the whole town was afraid.

Finally, since there was no other defense, the *presidente* announced that the whole town should offer candles and incense at the sacred caves and mountain tops and ask for the protection of God and the saints. Since Chamula's *j-iloletik* (shamans) are famed for their power, this seemed like such a good idea that the officials of the *municipios* of Zinacantan, Amatenango, Mitontic, and Huistan decided to join in as well. Together, they thought, maybe their prayers would be powerful enough to keep the Zapatistas away.

On the appointed day, scores of officials and dozens of chanting shamans, all dressed in their ceremonial clothes and many carrying candles and *yavak aletik* of burning incense, assembled at the church in Zinacantan. From the church and sacred mountain of Zinacantan, they proceeded together to the sacred cave at the border of the *municipio* of San Andrés, and then to the sink-hole of Chaklajun on the sacred mountain of Chamula. They prayed for more than an hour at each site. *Kajval!* (Lord): There was so much incense it was like fragrant fog, and the whole entourage seemed to hum like bees as each man murmured somberly in his own prayers:

Have Mercy, Kajval.
Have Mercy, Jesus
Make yourself present among us, Kajval
Make yourself present in our incense, Jesus

With us, your daughters
With us, your sons
We have brought you food, Kajval
We have brought you drink, Jesus
To awaken your conscience
To awaken your heart
That you might lend us your feet
That you might lend us your hands
That you might discharge your rifle
That you might discharge your cannon

What sin have we, Kajval?
What guilt have we, Jesus?
Don't you see that we are here, sacred lightning?
Don't you see that we are here, sacred thunder?
We beg that you close the roads to your sons who are coming [the
   Zapatistas]
We beg that you close the roads to your daughters who are coming
That you bind their feet
That you bind their hands
That you silence their rifles
That you stifle their cannons
If only for an hour
If only for two hours, Kajval
Although they come at night
Although they come in the day
Although they come at sundown
Although they come at sunrise. . . .

As the days passed and the Zapatistas never came, it seemed that the prayers
had worked. . . .

Late January: Toward a Free Market

For the first two weeks or so after the seizure of San Cristóbal, not a single
kaxlan official[1] showed his face in public — not a policeman, not a parking officer, not a collector of market fees. Not one. They disappeared! They were so
terrified of the Zapatistas that they hid. But the moment they were sure the
Zapatista Army was gone and wasn't coming back, Ha!, immediately the parking officers were back unscrewing license plates, the municipal police beating
up drunks and the market collectors chasing away poor women trying to sell

tomatoes and lemons on street corners. With the Zapatistas gone, suddenly they were fearless again. But when the Zapatistas were here, they stayed in their bedrooms with the shades closed, quaking with fear. They couldn't even get it up with their wives they were so scared.

You see what that means? They were afraid of Indians because that's what the Zapatistas were, Indians. When we other Indians realized that, we felt strong as well. Strong like the Zapatistas. The *kaxlanetik* of San Cristóbal have always pushed us around just because we don't speak Spanish correctly. But now everything has begun to change.

One example of this is that in mid-January, when the *kaxlan* officials were all still hidden, the Indian charcoal sellers got together and formed the "Zapatista Organization of Charcoal Sellers." Then, without asking anybody's permission, they moved from the vacant field where they had always been forced to sell in the past to the street right next to the main market. The thing is, *ak al* is really dirty—everything around it gets covered with black dust—so the market officials had always kept it far away from the part of the market frequented by "decent people" and tourists. With no one to stop them, however, the charcoal sellers came to be near everyone else.

But there are a lot of other Indians who have always been relegated to the edges of the market, too. When these people saw that the charcoal sellers had changed their location without asking anyone's permission, they started coming around and asking if they could change as well. *¡Hijole!* [Son of a gun!] Suddenly there were a couple of hundred people sitting in orderly rows selling vegetables and fruit and charcoal in what used to be the parking lot where rich people left their cars! The first day they gathered there, the leader of the charcoal sellers gave a speech. "Brothers and sisters!" he cried, "Don't be afraid! There are too many of us selling here in this street now! Let all of those who have been forced to sell out of the backs of trucks, all of those who have been driven to the edges of the market, come sell right here in the center with us! Let them come and take a place here in these rows we have made, and then we'll see if the *kaxlan* officials dare say anything! Only one thing to all of those who join us: I don't want to hear anyone talking about being afraid! If we remain united and firm, we have nothing to fear!" All the Indian peddlers jumped to their feet. "We're with you!" they responded joyfully.

So every morning early all of these people came and formed themselves into neat rows and spread their goods out on the ground. But then the day finally came when the Market Administrator returned. Since he's the boss of the market and all the surrounding streets, he stomped up to the first charcoal seller he saw and demanded. "Who gave you permission to sell here?" "No one had to give us permission because we belong to an organization."

"What fucking organization? Pick up all this shit and get the hell out of here before I lose my temper," the Administrator screamed, "I don't want to hear another word from any of you assholes. Are you going to fucking obey or not?" Mother of God! He seemed pretty mad. "No, we're not going to move. We're poor and hungry, and we have to sell to eat," the Indian said stubbornly. Then the leader of the charcoal sellers spoke. "You sound brave now," he said evenly to the Administrator, "but when the Zapatistas were here you didn't say anything because you were hiding behind your wife's skirts. Not until now have you had the balls to talk. So who's the asshole? Maybe it would be better for you if you kept quiet, because if you run us off we're going to make sure the sub-comandante of the Zapatistas gets your name, and then we'll find out how much of a man you are. You might win today, but maybe you ought to think about what it's going to cost you in the long run."

¡Hijo! [Boy!] The Administrator had never been talked to like that by an Indian before! He started to tremble, who knows whether from fear or rage, and then he turned and fled without saying another word, taking all of his fee collectors with him.

And that's where things remain at the beginning of March. Thanks to the Zapatistas, the Indians are learning to stand up for themselves. . . .

Early February: The Governed Do Not Consent

Then there's what happened in Teopisca [the next town south of San Cristóbal, mainly ladino]. In February, some Indian squatters from outside the town seized the *kaxlan* municipal president. They said he hadn't kept his campaign promises, and just grabbed him. He tried to make excuses for himself. "I already spent my entire budget on you," he begged. "I paved your streets, I brought electricity to your houses, I brought you water faucets, I made new roads for your trucks . . . What more do you want?" But according to all of the people, none of what he said was true. The streets aren't paved, there's no electricity, no faucets, no roads; nothing. In truth, the president and his friends just stole all the money.

Well, the squatters almost lost their heads and killed the president. Some wanted to hang him and they say someone even took a shot at him. But eventually others calmed the crowd down, and in the end all they did was truss him up like a pig, throw him in a pick-up truck, and send him back to the state government in Tuxtla.

The thing is, those squatters were Indians, Chamulas! There was a handful of poor ladinos among them too, but most were Chamulas! And they managed to capture and depose the president of a *kaxlan* town! Of course it was the president's own fault; no one forced him to steal the municipality's money. But now all the politicians have to be careful. We "poor dumb Indians" aren't afraid the way we used to be. Now we've all learned from the Zapatistas how to meet our collective problems: with unity. Obviously, the squatters didn't have machine guns and grenades like the Zapatistas—just .22s and shotguns. No; it was their unity that gave them strength!

Mid-February: The Festival of Games

Since everyone in Chamula was still afraid at the beginning of February that the Zapatistas were coming, *K'in Tajimol* (the Mayan New Year, celebrated at Carnival [Mardi Gras]) didn't go well this year. Instead of coming and staying two or three days as in the past, visiting with their friends and sleeping on the ground, everyone came down from their hamlets to watch for just a few minutes before scurrying back to their houses and closing the doors. Nobody wanted to be part of a crowd in the town center.

As if that weren't enough, the army had forbidden fireworks [traditional at all festivals in Los Altos]. No one could have skyrockets . . . , firecrackers, or pinwheels. Nothing. The head religious officials were able to have just a few *cohetes* [rockets] for the celebration itself, but only by getting a special permit from the army. The municipal president had to go ask in person, and only won out after explaining that the religious officials had been saving for 20 years each to put on the fiesta, and that it—and their lives—would be ruined without rockets.

In San Cristóbal, on the other hand, fireworks are absolutely prohibited. No exceptions. But cohetes are just as much a part of their traditions as ours, so all their fiestas are very sad. Of course, there are still marimba bands, games, and always a little bit of liquor. Nevertheless, the fiestas are sad and fearful. The soldiers don't even want anyone to drink; if they catch a drunk, they beat him up. They don't want anyone to be noisy or out of order.

After all, though, neither the army nor the Zapatistas came to Chamula's *K'in Tajimol*. Not many other people came either, for that matter. The fiesta didn't go well.

Mid-February: Mayan Justice

When the negotiations with the government began in mid-February, the Zapatistas, as a sign of good faith, freed the former governor, Absalón Castellanos Domínguez, whom they had captured at his ranch at the beginning of the revolt. They say he got sick at the end, that he wouldn't eat anything.

Maybe it was because his hands were tied behind his back for six weeks, who knows . . . Personally, I think he got sick because he couldn't stand the Zapatistas' cooking! It was nothing but Indian food: corn and a little beans. No meat. There is no one in the Zapatistas' camp in the jungle but Indians, and Indians aren't used to eating meat. We can never afford to buy it, and even if an animal dies we have to sell it. Poor old don Absalón: since he's rich, he's not accustomed to going without meat every day . . .

Still, when they freed him, outside of his hands, which were a little swollen, he seems to have been okay. That's more than you can say for Indians who are arrested by the authorities, rebellion or no rebellion. When Absalón was Governor, they were always beaten, whether they were guilty or not, even before they were questioned, "so they would learn to have respect." All the Zapatistas did to Absalón, on the other hand, was take his ranch away from him and divide it among peasants who have no land. Who knows whether they will get to keep it . . .

March 1994: When the Indians Ruled

It was said that the first of March the Zapatistas killed a cow near the neighborhood of Cuxtitali, to the northeast of San Cristóbal. They had a hankering for meat, and so they stole and slaughtered the cow. But we all knew that this was not the real Zapatista Army, that the thieves just called themselves Zapatistas to avoid being arrested. In the first place, they didn't have good weapons, just old .22 rifles. And second, they stole the cow from a poor family, and the Zapatistas do not do that. The thieves knew the government was afraid of the Zapatistas—that they sat down to negotiate with them because they couldn't defeat them—and the thieves took advantage of that.

But the real Zapatistas have no reason to steal! They're already talking directly to the government, and it looks like they're going to get everything they've asked for. They say that when the talks began, the new governor, Javier López Moreno, tried to tell them that they were not going to win anything, that he had more arms and soldiers than they did. But the subcomandante [i.e., Marcos] answered that if he wanted to test his strength, by all means, do it! And although the governor got real mad, neither he nor his people could shut him up or stop him, because whenever they blinked, Marcos would turn into a plant or a fly or who knows what, and disappear. The poor governor would be talking with the sub, and suddenly he'd find himself all alone! That's why those men got so mad, because not only could they not do away with the Zapatistas, they couldn't even find them! They say that on Caracol Hill there was a cave where more than 22,000 Zapatista soldiers were hidden. The na-

San Andrés, Chiapas, July 1995. "Newsboards" mounted by the EZLN in the street outside the Peace Dialog to inform supporters of the state of negotiations. (Reprinted by permission of D. Rus.)

tional army went looking for them there. The soldiers went on foot, but they had an airplane to guide them. But the Zapatistas had an apparatus there that looked like a giant griddle [i.e., a parabolic antenna] that they used to shoot down the plane and chase the soldiers away. Those men had good reason to be frightened. . . .

January 1996: Changes in Justice

The leader of one of the marketplace unions had just gotten one of his members out of the jail in San Cristóbal. They say that the man owed 33,000 pesos to a ladino, and that he had not made payment on his loan for over a year. Then, as always happens, the ladino went to ask for help from the municipal police, and the commander and two policemen went and grabbed the debtor. They arrested him for theft, because they said that to borrow without repaying was the same as stealing. When the leader of the union heard this, he went at midnight with seventy or eighty of his people, all with rifles, pistols, clubs, machetes, pickaxes, sticks. . . . They all went to rescue their *compañero*. They grabbed the poor asshole who was guarding the jail and they gave him a whipping. I mean they whipped him good! And just when they were about to free the guy who owed the money, the *licenciado* who worked in the police station tried to argue with the leader: "How can you take this thief out of jail? What's it to you that he was arrested? He give you money or something?" "Shut up, asshole," said the union leader. "Who gave you money to arrest him? Now we are going to teach you to respect the Indians!" And they started in giving the *licenciado* a beating! *"Ti pakuj, ti pakuj!"* went the blows. "Now you see that it matters to me, moron!" shouted the leader. "This can't be," the *licenciado* whined. "You are Indians, it's not your place to give the orders here!" "Oh no?" asked the leader, and he hit him again.

And that's how the debtor got out of jail. He didn't have permission to leave; his union decided the matter.

January 1997: The Thieves Take Advantage

The corn farmers blocked the roads to the hot country, saying the government didn't pay them a fair price for their corn and beans. And although the corn was already in the government warehouses, the government still agreed to give a bit more to the farmers. Everyone says they just did it because old Marcos and the Zapatista Army were there; that really they are the ones who give the orders, and if not for them the government wouldn't have done anything.

But on the other hand, the government has not yet signed a peace accord with the subcomandante, and if it does so, if he agrees, then I say, great! First, because that would mean we're not going to die in a war. But also, ever since the Zapatistas rose up there's lots of crime everywhere. There always has been crime, but now there's more. . . . More robberies, rapes—even rapes of 11 or 12-year-old girls—killings, car theft . . . Now there are thieves who aren't afraid to rob a bank in broad daylight, or to wait for people to come out so they can rob them right there in the street. Also, at night, when we go out alone, they assault us. They also do not respect the forest and its workers: they take chainsaws to the trees without caring, and if the forest rangers come along they tie them up. Old Marcos is not to blame; he's not in charge of all those people. But since the government no longer has a presence, there are lots of bad people who take advantage.

July 1997: Electoral Fraud

Weeks after the elections of July 6, the representative of the *colonia* spoke to our meeting. *"Compañeros,"* he said, "I'm ashamed, because I told you that the PRI candidate for Federal Deputy had promised cardboard roofing planks for everyone, and later he promised sheets of galvanized metal; later, he even promised us houses. But now it seems all that was a lie. Today I went to the office to investigate, and they said that there was no longer any budget for that. I even spoke with the chief of the campaign. I reminded him that we had supported his candidate, and that he pledged his word to give twenty sheets of galvanized metal to everyone. "No, no. It can't be done," he said. So it turns out that it was all a fraud! That's why I feel bad, compañeros, and I ask your forgiveness. I don't know what you think, but I believe that from now on we shouldn't vote for the PRI."

It doesn't matter, that's just the way it is. I hoped to replace my laminated cardboard roof with one of galvanized metal, but now that won't be possible. We're very poor, and we all need new roofs. And that's just what they promised us. But now they say they'll just send the soldiers to fix the houses roofed with flattened cans [*botes*]. They didn't say if it would be with sheets of laminated cardboard or galvanized metal. . . .

I feel real bad for the poor *colonia* representative. When the campaign began and he talked at our meeting about how to vote, he told us he thought it would be good if we all committed ourselves to vote for the PRI. And he told us what the candidate had promised. Some *compañeros* said they wanted to vote for the PRD. But then someone from the water committee spoke, and he told us that he had voted for the PRD the last time and nothing had come of it. They didn't care if we died of hunger and cold; after the deputy of the PRD won the election, he had not given out so much as a single T-shirt. So for his part, the man from the water commission said, he was inclined to commit to the PRI, to see if things went any better. And so, one by one, everyone said the same. "We're going to do a test," they said, "to see if things turn out better." Then the representative said that if we were all in agreement, two or three buses would come by the school in the morning to take us off to participate in the campaign. But we would all have to go, men, women and even children; they would give us shirts and hats if we participated. And we all went that day and other days, thinking about our new roofs.

But they didn't give us anything, not then and not later. No hat, no shirt, and now no roofs. It was pure electoral fraud.

August 1997: Why the Soldiers Fled San Cayetano . . . and Why They Returned

It seems that the solders there in the jungle, in San Cayetano, were afraid of a snake. I'm talking about a gigantic snake, something like two hundred meters long. Of course, this is the *ch'ulel* of subcomandante Marcos, his animal soul. So the frightened soldiers said to their superior, "Well, it's best we return to the barracks. That damn animal is too big, and if we stay it's sure to eat us." "Return?" said the sergeant or lieutenant, or whatever he was, "No, we can't. But don't be afraid, that snake doesn't bite; it just goes out to lie in the sun and move around. At most it eats a little bit, but don't be afraid, it's definitely not the soul of subcomandante Marcos. That asshole has no strength, much less of the supernatural kind. There are lots of snakes in the jungle. . . ." But the truth is that the soldiers really didn't want to be there in the woods. They were afraid of the snake, and they wanted to go home.

I don't know how much power President Zedillo has; if he's the one who decides if the soldiers stay out there or not. Nor do I know if all that's true about the snake. It could just have been an excuse to leave the jungle. It's awfully damp and cold in the jungle, and the poor soldiers don't get to see their girlfriends. I don't know why they didn't just kill that snake and get it over with, since they have the best weapons around. But anyway, there the soldiers were, out there in the jungle and wanting to leave, when a meteorite passed over the hills. . . . Worse yet, the poor boys were traveling on foot through the woods, without being able to see more than a little piece of the sky over their heads. And they say that the meteorite, apart from being like fire, made a tremendous noise. And they were deep in the jungle, far away from everything! Well, of course they remembered that the subcomandante has more power than all of them put together!

Híjole, but the meteorite was so big you could even see it here in San Cristóbal; even in Oaxaca, they say! It passed by very late at night, very late, and
many people saw it. But the soldiers really saw it well, and they were still
frightened. And if they'd been afraid of Marcos as a big snake, now that they'd
seen him turn himself into fire and speed across the sky—now they just
wanted to flee, to not go any deeper into the jungle. *"Híjole,"* they said, "but
that son of a bitch of a subcomandante is strong! He can make himself into
a serpent and live inside a hill, and just when we get him surrounded he can
turn himself into fire and fly through the sky!" And so their officer gave the
order for them to retreat, even though he claimed not to be afraid himself.
Damn, but those soldiers were happy! Not only because they could return to
their barracks, not only because they wanted to flee, but also because in the
city there were girls walking around the streets. . . .

So, of their own accord, the soldiers broke camp and returned to the barracks. But no sooner had they left than some *priístas* from San Cayetano went
to the army headquarters to ask that the soldiers be sent back. They even went
to Tuxtla to talk to the governor. . . . "Don't be mean," they said, "help us.
There in the village there are bandits, there are people who beat up community members in broad daylight, there are rapists. . . . Don't leave us alone
with our enemies! Please, we want there to be soldiers around to protect us
from our neighbors." "Is this true what they say?" asked the governor. "How
awful!" And so it was that a few days after retreating, the soldiers went back
to San Cayetano with all their pistols, rifles, and machine guns.

January 1998: What We Understood After Acteal

On January 8, the governorship of Ruiz Ferro was cut short, supposedly because he was to blame for the *J-ajte'al* [Acteal massacre].[2] He's the one who
gave the weapons for the assassinations, they say. They were good new rifles.
According to the ladinos in the marketplace, they're worth around five or six
thousand pesos each, and he handed out over a hundred of them. And the bullets cost something like eight pesos each. It's absolutely certain that the *priístas*
of Chenalhó didn't buy them; the governor handed them out. Of course! we
thought. The government won't help us because it says it has no money. It
can't provide houses, or galvanized metal sheets, or sheets of laminated cardboard, or seeds; it won't help us get our own tortilla bakery. . . . The money
ran out because it was secretly used to buy guns! We asked for the wrong kind
of help!

February 1998: The March

On January 28 there was a march on San Cristóbal to complain to the government because it had not attended to the requests of the Zapatistas, it had only killed them. "We'll march there so they'll listen to us," the organizers said. "We won't let them forget that we're still here!"

Well, at first the government promised to give land and assistance to the Indians. But now it only offers tiny parcels of land for sale. What's more, here in the city they want to charge us for every little thing: Not only do we have to pay every month for electricity, but we even have to buy the posts and cables; and not just drinking water, but the pipes and everything. They even charge us for trash collection. And meanwhile, they help the rich for free, giving them policemen to guard their wire fences in the countryside, or to run us off when we try to sit down and sell a little something in the city center.

So, many people are starting to think again that maybe the Zapatistas were right; that the government doesn't listen to us, and that without the Zapatistas nothing is going to change. We have to pay for every little thing, but what if there's no work here? Lately there are twelve families that have left their homes in the *colonia* because they can't pay the fees and expenses. Where will they go? We can sell popsicles in the street, or maybe a few vegetables on the sidewalks, but we only earn five or seven pesos a day, barely enough to buy tortillas, much less pay for electricity. It seems the government doesn't want to recognize how much we're suffering. We want them not to charge us for everything, and it would be good if they'd lower the price of corn, beans, sugar, coffee, soft drinks, meat, everything! The organizers said that the march was to "level" everything. I don't know exactly how to do it, but many people feel that things cannot go on the way they are, and that's the reason for the march.

February 1998: Yet Another Governor

The new governor, Roberto Albores Guillén, came to the *colonia* last week with the municipal president and the chiefs of several ministries and departments. He told us that the government had already given us paved streets and sidewalks, and that we should not be afraid, that there would be still more public works, that he alone was in charge in Chiapas. It was clear that the EZLN and subcomandante Marcos were not going to help us, he said. More likely they were going to have to return to the bargaining table, because he, the governor, was going to give us everything we wanted: schools, roads, soccer fields, housing. [He told us] that we shouldn't despair, that we should all work together. But the thing was, he said, for the moment [the government] had unfortunately run out of money. . . . But surely more would come by May or June, and then [they] would once again undertake those works together.

So there you have it. The only thing is, we don't play soccer.

Notes

1. Pronounced "kashlan": a corruption of the Spanish word *castellano,* it is the Tzotzil word for non-lndians.

2. On December 22, 1997, a group of about seventy well-armed men attacked the town of Acteal in the Chiapanecan highlands, killing forty-five people, all but seven of them women and children, and wounding twenty-five more. The killings were blamed on paramilitary forces acting on orders from the local PRI. *Ed.*

Debtors' Revenge: The *Barzón* Movement's Struggle against Neoliberalism

Heather Williams

Indigenous Zapotec and Mayan peasants in the South were by no means the only Mexicans nurturing grievances with the neoliberal market reforms implemented by the Salinas and Zedillo governments. In the mid- to late 1990s, the PRI's economic policies received a severe challenge from another, unexpected quarter: middle-class Mexico. Devastated by skyrocketing interest rates on their homes and businesses—rates which were part and parcel of the austerity measures that accompanied the U.S.-brokered bailout of the Mexican economy after the peso's "meltdown" in 1995—respectable ranchers and small businessmen in north-central states such as Zacatecas and Guanajuato galvanized a formidable debtor's movement. Popularly known as El Barzón, the new social movement rapidly gained adherents throughout the country. Like the Zapatistas, the Barzonistas were adept at using the media, dark humor, and public spectacle to advance their message. Unlike the Zapatistas, the Barzonistas eschewed collective violence and moved more quickly to channel their efforts into electoral politics, with mixed results. In the selection that follows, Heather Williams, a political scientist at Pomona College, who accompanied the Barzonistas on several of their uproarious political actions and conducted scores of interviews with the movement's leaders and followers, provides an engrossing anatomy of El Barzón's rise and decline.

In pressed T-shirts and shiny leather boots, with cell phones hooked to their belts and business cards at the ready, members of the Mexican debtors' movement called *El Barzón* certainly don't look radical. Men's hair is short and their beards are trimmed; women are coifed and made up fashionably. Most of the time, they begin their meetings by singing the national anthem. It may take the newcomer by surprise, then, to hear members of this group call themselves revolutionaries.

"We are struggling to save Mexico from the clutches of a global class of speculators," explained one leader at a gathering in Mexico City. The organization's new Web site states that its members "radically oppose a politics of dispossession carried out by the most favored sector of the regime: financiers and speculators." The Barzón movement, it explains, emerged from "a moral imperative: to confront the unjust actors who have intentionally ruined millions of homes and livelihoods, who have condemned millions of children to poverty, and left young people with no future."

Class traitors? Card-carrying university socialists? Trotskyite backers of an all-out war on capitalism? Far from it. The members of this group, though sympathetic to progressive labor unions and indigenous rights struggles, are for the most part middle-class citizens who have organized to defend their rights to conduct private enterprise, to protect their property, and to maintain modestly comfortable lifestyles.

The Barzón movement, which at its peak in 1995 through 1998 claimed anywhere from one to three million members, is one of the largest social movement organizations to emerge in Mexico in recent years. A movement with members nationwide for a time, the Barzón movement captured headlines in Mexico and abroad during the troubled administration of President Ernesto Zedillo Ponce de León. Their militant but nonviolent actions targeted private banks, courts, moneylenders, securities brokers, and government officials. Using direct action, civil disobedience, lawsuits, and mutual aid, the Barzón movement framed itself as an urgent call to Mexican patriots to re-take their country from the hands of a corrupt class of elites who, they charged, had mortgaged the country's future for the sake of short-term, personal gains.

When it comes to peoples' opinion of the movement, descriptions will vary. Bankers and their colleagues in government who have been vilified by the movement spare no barbs in their declarations. "Deadbeats," "a culture of nonpayment," and "blackmailers" are favorite epithets used by treasury officials and members of the Mexican Bankers' Association to describe a movement of borrowers who have refused to accept repossession orders, restructure their debts with government-imposed terms, or pay triple-digit interest rates. "A self-defense movement of middle-class merchants and credit-card holders," explain news hounds and casual onlookers who observe intermittent gatherings and protests of housewives and thick-girthed *comerciantes* in meeting halls or on street corners. "Heroes," declared a taxi driver one morning to the author, as the cab passed a gathering of people with signs and white T-shirts outside a store. He then pulled out his own identification card with the organization's trademark green tractor logo. "I'd have lost everything without them," he asserted. "I had a loan for this taxi and then the interest payments went through the roof. But I'm not going broke for lack of hard work," he continued. "I'm in this car fourteen, sixteen hours a day, from five in the

La Jornada, one of Mexico's premier newspapers, has long featured analysis and criticism of the trend toward neoliberalism. Here are a few samples:

"Neoliberal Zapatismo" by Rocha. The capitalist is telling the peasant, "Wow, what a coincidence! I too have always wanted land and liberty." (From *La Jornada,* December 6, 1991. Reprinted by permission of Gonzalo Rocha González.)

"Twelve Years Later" by El Fisgón. The man on the left asks, "And now, how do we get out of here?" The man on the right, who is reading a book called *Neoliberalism for Beginners,* answers, "Well it says right here we should keep on digging." (From *La Jornada,* February 17, 1995. Reprinted by permission of *El Fisgón.*)

"Debts, Micro and Macro" by Rocha. The protestors in the background carry placards protesting debts and high interest rates. The caption reads, "It's about time the government sends one of its advisors to tell them what to do in case of insolvency: Ask for more loans so they can keep on paying the banks." (From *La Jornada,* June 28, 1995. Reprinted by permission of Gonzalo Rocha González.)

"The Doctors of the IMF" by El Fisgón. The doctor with the notepad is saying, "What we don't know is if he's finally stabilized from his monetary crisis or if rigor mortis has set in." (From *La Jornada,* May 23, 1995. Reprinted by permission of *El Fisgón.*)

morning until ten or eleven at night sometimes. It's the only way I can support my family." And then, he offered a lament all-too-common in neoliberal Latin America, *"Soy ingeniero, sabes?* I have a degree in engineering from the university, but I couldn't find work in my field. . . ."

Civil role models to some, scoundrels and troublemakers to others, the emergence and trajectory of the Barzón movement reflect important shifts in the structure of wealth and power in Mexico, as well as evolving public views about the roles of government and civil society in managing the economy. The movement, which expanded in the wake of a peso devaluation that sent floating interest rates on commercial, farm, and home loans to triple digits, went far beyond a mass public petition for debt relief. Instead, the movement provided a public forum where people could collectively discuss alternatives to global free trade and unfettered capital mobility. Conservative in the sense that it called for the preservation of property and a rehabilitation of national production, and progressive in the sense that it called for democratization, labor rights, and an end to financial speculation, the Barzón movement found allies in a broad array of political actors, including the Catholic Church, the Zapatista Army of National Liberation (EZLN), the (hard-left) Independent Proletarian Movement, and for a time, then-Governor Vicente Fox of Guanajuato.

Origins of the Barzón Movement

Although many associate the Barzón debtors' movement with the devaluation crisis beginning in December 1994, the Barzón movement emerged some time before that in the Mexican countryside. In the early 1990s, then-President Carlos Salinas de Gortari's bold economic development strategy was claiming its share of victims. Despite accolades from foreign and domestic investors, Salinas's aggressive project of trade liberalization (seen most prominently in the North American Free Trade Agreement), privatization of state industries, and government downsizing had drastically reduced incomes among significant portions of the population. In particular, declines in domestic manufacturing and agriculture following a flood of imports threatened millions of laborers, farmers, small businessmen, and suppliers. To make matters worse for these sectors, Salinas's team maintained an overvalued exchange rate to control inflation and provide inexpensive food for urban workers laboring under government-imposed wage caps. For farmers and certain types of domestic entrepreneurs, this was disastrous far in advance of any devaluation crisis because it made imported food, capital goods, and consumer items artificially cheap compared to Mexican goods. Maintaining an overvalued peso also meant high interest rates on commercial, farm, and home loans because such a currency peg could only be maintained through massive borrowing on foreign markets at high rates. These interest rates, plus a generous retail premium, were passed on to Mexican bank clients.

The effect of these policies on domestic production was nowhere more dire than in agriculture. Not only did farmers face dwindling prices at the market and rising credit costs. Millions more faced bankruptcy and loss of their land due to still other policies introduced under Salinas. In 1992 the government pushed through a series of changes to Article 27 of the Mexican Constitution, thereby ending the government's commitment to land reform and the administration of peasant agriculture. With lands in the *ejido* sector now privatized, debts signaled imminent loss of inherited land parcels. Finally, the government slashed its farm credit and subsidy structures in order to streamline social spending and presumably to bring Mexico's agricultural policy in line (incidentally, far in advance of its First World competitors) with the mandates the Uruguay round of the General Agreement on Tariffs and Trade. From 1991 to 1993, for example, the government-run Rural Bank (the only source of credit for *ejidatarios* and small private farmers) closed one-third of its branches and cut lending by half. Meanwhile, government silos were put up for sale, and electricity prices were allowed to float to open market levels, raising the price of irrigation by 500 percent in the arid north of the country.

Large and small farmers alike were quickly brought to the edge of ruin. By 1993, bankruptcies in the countryside had risen to twenty times their levels in 1990, according to the Mexico City daily *La Jornada*. Seeming official indifference in the face of farmers' problems prompted a wave of popular discontent. As is well known, this anger would soon fuel an armed insurgency in Chiapas in early 1994, and in Guerrero in 1995. Elsewhere, popular discontent took the form of blockades, occupations, and furious protests. In states as diverse as Nuevo León, Guanajuato, Zacatecas, Michoacán, Chihuahua, and Tabasco, farmers took over highways and bridges, spilled grain and milk in the streets, and burned effigies of government officials.

The Barzón movement began as simply one of many protests occurring in Mexico in 1993. In August of that year, a group of some 7,000 Jalisco farmers marched on the city of Guadalajara to protest their debt loads, which had risen to $344 million pesos among them (the equivalent of about U.S. $100 million). Notably, this sum was not evenly distributed. While this protest included some smaller farmers, it was in fact led by some of the wealthiest and most powerful tomato growers in western Mexico. This was unusual, because typically it was smaller, private farmers and peasants from the *ejido* sector who were forced to turn to direct action in order to be seen by public officials.

The demonstration got the attention of officials rapidly, both for who the protesters were and for their form of protest. The demonstrators took their name, "El Barzón," from a revolution-era folk song in which a hacienda peon laments that his *barzón,* or the strap attaching his plow to his ox yoke, has ripped apart. He then must borrow money from his boss to resume farming, but sinks deeper and deeper into debt as the usurious interest rates mount over time. For the sake of the *barzón,* then, the peasant ends up indentured for life. The song tells a melancholy tale but is nonetheless funny in the vein of a lot of Mexican humor, which alludes to a sort of perpetual misfortune of the common man at the hands of the gringo, the moneylender, the *patrón,* or the cacique. It is set to a tumbling, lopsided melody in which each verse begins slowly, and then whirls out of control as the story of entanglement with the landlord gets more and more involved.

This movement with the funny-sad name seemed to appeal to Guadalajarans at the end of a quiet summer. Well-heeled farmers had driven hundreds of tractors into the central plaza and cheerfully invited passersby to mingle among them. Recalling this event and others like it that would occur in the Mexican West and North in the ensuing months, a farm leader from Sinaloa recalled families strolling through the encampment, taking pictures of children atop tractors and donkeys. "There were people who brought food and blankets," one participant said, "and there was always a barbecue going. I never ate so well as during those protests."

Unquestionably, the lenience and sympathy afforded demonstrators by a conservative local media, urban onlookers, and even the governor of the state had much to do with the class and ethnic background of the protesters. These were, after all, the favored sons of the then-ruling party, the Institutional Revolutionary Party (PRI). Neither downtrodden clients nor angry peasant or indigenous dissidents whose rancor might have unnerved middle-class urban residents, these were instead the people who weren't supposed to lose their farms and homes, who didn't have to send their young sons north to work in California, whose floors were done in smart linoleum, and whose wives wore high heels to mass on Sundays.

Notably, attempts by officials to conciliate the Barzonistas (President Salinas himself met with Barzón leaders after a time) did not soften their protests. In fact, it appeared to fuel the campaign. Despite fairly hasty offers from several banks and treasury officials to restructure loans on generous terms, Barzón leaders dug in their heels, calling for an entirely new scheme of agricultural finance, including codes whereby banks and farmers would share risk for crop losses and low prices. The protest in Guadalajara meanwhile spread to three other cities in the state of Jalisco, and within two months groups of farmers in twelve other states were pledging solidarity with the Barzón and organizing similar protests. The most aggressive companion protests emerged in next-door Zacatecas, where again the initiative for the movement came from relatively better-off farmers in the most prosperous agricultural region of the state. In Zacatecas, protesters took an even more militant stance than growers in Jalisco, eventually carrying out threats to block the Pan-American Highway and burn a tractor rather than allow the banks to repossess it. "We really raised hell," commented a farmer of those actions.

What irked officials most (and terrified bankers) was the growing insistence of Barzonistas that credit and the terms of its use should be negotiable by civil society. Farm bankruptcy under conditions such as existed, protesters argued, was not due to borrowers' mismanagement, but instead to a grand scheme by which banks and speculators maneuvered their capital so as to consolidate control over Mexican resources and labor.

At least two factors seem to explain why this normally quiescent group of farmers became so militant. The first has to do with the leadership of the movement. Though the movement began in Jalisco, three of four leaders who would eventually emerge as the architects of the national organization were from Zacatecas. These individuals had participated through the years in various campaigns on the Mexican left, including the student movement in the National Autonomous University of Mexico in the 1980s, the nuclear workers' movement, and later the Party of the Democratic Revolution. All had ranching backgrounds but ran hobby farms at the time, and they viewed the Barzón movement as a means of mobilizing public energy against a PRI-led neoliberal project. The second factor had to do with the larger contradiction of the neoliberal project itself: whereas draconian market-oriented changes require that the state maintain control over those who stand to be dispossessed, such control is difficult to maintain when the state is being downsized. Thus, unlike in past instances in which aggravated debts had driven farmers to petition the government for relief, this time bankruptcy was not due to natural disaster or temporarily low prices. Instead, crisis had much to do with the wholesale exit of the state from agriculture altogether. As the central government divested itself piece by piece from the countryside, there was less and less that local interlocutors for the PRI could offer to farmers. Grain prices reflected going rates of corn and beans on the Chicago Board of Trade, and interest rates mirrored the bond yields demanded by New York brokerages. Similarly, storage and transport could only be subsidized here and there through modest discretionary funds dispensed from the federal government to farmers through state intermediaries. In this environment, there was a palpable sense among farmers that they dwelled at the edge of market oblivion. So scarce was fresh bank credit that farmers feared they would not be able to purchase seeds for the spring-summer crop cycle. Many felt they had little to lose by radical action.

Events elsewhere in the country strengthened the Barzonistas' militance. On January 1, 1994, the uprising of the EZLN pulverized President Salinas's claims to have globalized the economy with the full consent of the population. The appearance of half-starved indigenous combatants fearlessly defying the armed forces with little more than sticks belied Salinas's smug declarations abroad that his market-oriented project promoted growth and equity. Barzonistas, at that time in a rancorous occupation in the city of Zacatecas, leapt at this opening. Immediately declaring their solidarity with the combatants in Chiapas, protesters marched in support of the EZLN and declared that such a rebellion might be imminent elsewhere. "The North will boil!" warned protesters at a march organized shortly after the uprising had begun. Barzonistas publicly applauded Subcomandante Marcos and pledged to send food to the rebels to help sustain the struggle.

Thus, even prior to the cataclysmic devaluation crisis that exploded in December 1994, the Barzón movement was veering leftward and maintaining a defiant, politically autonomous position. An increasingly militant stance on government policies made it possible for the Barzón to represent debtors as a particular constituency but also declare the movement a general struggle for economic reform. The Barzón's means of framing the issue of debt made its message remarkably portable. This put the movement in the right place at the right time when financial disaster of immense proportions befell Mexico.

Out of the Campo: The Barzón's Emergence as a National Movement

The "error of December," as it was genteelly referred to by elites in the financial sector, will undoubtedly occupy space in economics textbooks for decades to come. Dubbed the first economic crisis of the twenty-first century because of the role of one-click investment banking that made it possible for the wealthy to vacate over 2 billion U.S. dollars a day from Mexican markets, the devaluation crisis of 1994–1995 shattered the image of outgoing President Salinas and his successor, Ernesto Zedillo, as saintly Ivy League–trained technocrats. With this, the fourth consecutive crisis to occur at the changing of the *sexenio,* or six-year presidential term, Mexicans at the same time realized that the system of political spoils and plunder at the top remained unchanged.

In the chaotic months after the initial crack of the peso, the currency value dropped by two-thirds. One million workers joined the unemployment rolls and tens of thousands of businesses failed within weeks. Political bosses could do little to suppress popular fury at yet another bungled presidential transition. Workers marched in defiance of pro-government union leaders, campesinos defied their patrons in the official peasant confederation. Fishermen marched alongside schoolteachers and indigenous militants denouncing electoral corruption and government malfeasance. And, in a novel vein, debtors in the form of taxi drivers, homeowners, merchants, and even manicurists took to the streets. As Jorge Castañeda wrote of the debacle in *The Mexican Shock,* "The devaluation was a surprise to the millions of Mexicans who had bought into the fond dream of entering the First World, into the countless delights of imported goods. . . . It was a surprise to those businessmen who had become indebted in dollars — the only alternative to the outrageous cost of credit in pesos — or had switched from their domestic suppliers to foreign imports."

The rapid mobilization of tens of thousands of bankrupt people in the spring and summer of 1995 can only be explained by the severity of the crisis and the fit of the Barzón's nationalist message. "Your debt," as leader Juan José Quirino Salas explained, "is unpayable." Fingering predatory bank practices, ill-liquidity (the government had contracted the money supply by one-third in order to rein in supply-side inflation), and regressive new taxes imposed hastily in order to make up for budget shortfalls, Quirino Salas declared to audiences around the country that debtors' woes were a scourge visited upon them by outside forces who would destroy Mexico.

As a collective force, these better-off citizens were an entirely new category of militant. Whereas many individuals from comfortable backgrounds had played important roles in civil society up to that point — as champions of electoral reform, government accountability, environmental issues, and women's rights, for example — the idea of a class of politicized *bank clients* had little precedent in Mexico. Unlike in the United States, where citizens have organized for some time along consumerist lines, in Mexico protest over distributive issues has tended to work along lines of production.

The novelty of the Barzón movement's constituency was matched by its protest tactics. So colorful and media-savvy were certain actions, in fact, that they came to define the organization. These included protests similar to the Barzón's earlier demonstrations over farm debt, but the presence of urban participants in the ranks of the movement somehow made it different and funnier. Now, the Barzón continued to bring farm animals to protest, but with a whimsical and patriotic twist. Urban protesters, including dainty housewives and bespectacled merchants, marched among tractors and horses in raucous displays of public defiance. References to revolution-era heroes such as Pancho Villa and his *División del Norte* were explicit, as with one protest in 1999, for example, in which two hundred horsemen rode from Chihuahua to Mexico City to occupy the federal Senate chambers. Pigs, sheep, and donkeys were taken along on many protests as well, and were often set loose in banks and law offices threatening debtors with repossession. In other protests, Barzonistas staged rowdy public satires with effigies of President Salinas in a striped suit behind bars, or with masks of public officials or bankers dressed up as mad surgeons dispensing medicine from giant syringes. This was a reference to the medical terminology that financiers and the International Monetary Fund used when discussing the need for Mexico to take the "bitter medicine" of austerity in order to "cure" its economic woes. Barzonistas frequently used coffins in protests and occupations in order to make their points, holding mock funerals in front of mortified bank personnel in order to highlight the inhumanity of creditors. Though the protests were high-energy and spiced with jokes and laughter, they carried a serious message as well. The mock funerals referred in part to banks as "killing" debtors with compound interest. With triple-digit interest rates raging through the summer of 1995, debtors often ended up owing the banks many times the amount borrowed. A simple car loan, for example, might cost the debtor his car, his furniture, and his house. The funerals also referred to the hundreds of debtors who had committed suicide under the strain of debt and harassment from banks and their lawyers.

At least two things prompted even reticent citizens who had never attended so much as a protest rally before to participate in such bald high jinks. First, the protests emphasized nonviolence and good humor. Policemen and repossession agents found themselves in impossible positions when crowds of determined matrons and middle-aged men marched onto car lots and into warehouses with wire cutters and blow torches and simply took their things back in full daylight. Neighbors and onlookers, who like as not were in dire straits themselves financially, often would stroll by and cheer on the protesters, perhaps stopping to take a pamphlet and a free soda pop and tamale offered by the Barzonistas. (No action ever went uncatered by the Barzón.) Second, the protests were functional. Actions frequently ended with lawyers and bankers agreeing to meet at a specified date to arrange partial repayment of existing capital and interest charges. In this manner, direct actions were intimidating but not always a total loss for the institutions targeted by them. Balance sheets and repossession orders aside, local bankers often knew privately that they would have a terrible time liquidating debtors' assets. Things such as used furniture and appliances, pots and pans, smallish land parcels located on bad roads, gutted commercial buildings in small towns, and well-used tractors would not yield much cash at auction, even if bankers succeeded in selling them. Recognizing this, the Barzón movement maintained its public position that interest charges on overdue loans were illegitimate, but privately offered lenders some chance to recover some of their losses. The key to this exchange was that the debtor and the lender were sharing responsibility for bankruptcy.

Yet another tactic the Barzón used to highlight its claims and resist bank repossession was legal action. Attorneys working for the movement pioneered methods of stalling banks by preparing papers for thousands of debtors and submitting them to creditors all at once. Combing through banking codes, attorneys found arcane articles stipulating minor things such as time limits on repossession proceedings. With these in hand, they charged the banks with violation of the law if they proceeded with repossessions past legal deadlines. In one case in Zacatecas, for example, the law required banks to provide upon request a full account history to any debtor facing repossession within two weeks. Barzonistas then promptly prepared ten thousand such requests and dropped them off in file boxes in the bank lobby of a local Banamex branch after marching through town in chains and striped prison pajamas.

Finally, the Barzón movement solidified its reputation as a civic-minded organization in localities throughout the country by offering its members a range of services at little or no cost. In addition to legal help, debtors could access low-cost financial or business planning or locate national suppliers and retailers for their businesses or farms. In many localities, the Barzón offered psychological counseling for distraught debtors at the edge of breakdown.

As a movement providing debtors with some means of protecting their property and converting private shame into public indignation, the Barzón was without parallel. However, the direct actions undertaken by the Barzón functioned in a stopgap manner and were difficult to maintain. As one leader in the city of Culiacán pointed out to the author during a protest, "We're constantly putting out fires here. We can't keep doing this. In the long run, we won't be able to organize a protest every time a bank issues a threat to a debtor." Indicating the people milling around in an empty lot waiting for repossession agents to come by, he explained, "These merchants have their businesses to attend to, and they lose money every time they leave." The larger problems of faltering demand, regressive taxes, and the unavailability of fresh lending capital remained critical obstacles to recovery for farmers and merchants. These issues could not be resolved through direct action and presented the Barzón movement with its most serious dilemma. Leaders bickered over whether the movement should remain decentralized and focused on local campaigns or whether it should transfer greater resources to a national struggle for broad-based reforms.

From the Streets to the Congress

Over time, the Barzón movement attempted to maintain its struggle on both local and national levels. Throughout its existence, the organization oscillated between putting up leaders for public office and distancing itself from electoral politics and declaring itself independent of all partisan affairs. Whereas putting Barzonistas up for office might offer the organization an opportunity to craft pro-borrower legislation and to conduct official investigations of fraud in government and the banks, doing so posed a very real threat to the unity of the movement. Despite some reservations, then, leaders decided to re-enter partisan politics in 1997. With changes in the electoral code offering the prospect of fairer campaign finance and more balanced media coverage, the Barzón plunged into the race and three leaders were elected to the federal Congress. It was an auspicious moment because the PRI had lost its majority in the lower house for the first time in history.

Although this turn of events provoked some discord in the ranks of the organization, with several state chapters removing their backing from the national executive committee, the Barzón's new prominence in Congress helped transform the way the Mexican legislature functioned. Until 1997, the Congress had been viewed as a rubber-stamp tool of a powerful president, but now it had quickly become a roiling cauldron of contention over key issues such as taxes, social spending, and privatization of utilities. Although a good deal of this was only smoke—the National Action Party tended in the last instance to throw its support behind the technocratic wing of the PRI on core economic tenets—it nonetheless made it very difficult for Zedillo and his cabinet to sweep embarrassing issues under the rug. One such issue was the bailout of the banking system. Barzón leader Alfonso Ramírez Cuellar's deft use of media and committee powers to reveal its staggering costs and exclusive club of beneficiaries would leave the Zedillo presidency forever tarnished.

Although a taxpayer-funded bailout of the banks was finally approved by a PRI–PAN alliance, most voters are now acutely aware of the price tag, which will run about U.S. $140 billion through 2020—a sum equivalent to more than one-third of Mexico's GDP. The Barzón's critique of the banks has prompted people to decry this arrangement and also to complain that the bailout has done little for the average citizen. Credit remained unavailable to most Mexicans in 2001, despite the recovery of growth at the national level. According to a *Business Mexico* report in May 2001, credit availability has dropped every year after 1995, falling 25 percent in 1995, 27 percent in 1996, 21 percent in 1997, 1.5 percent in 1998, 12 percent in 1999, and 4 percent in 2000.

Potential and Limits of the Barzón Movement

In the final analysis, the Barzón's greatest influence beyond its own survival may be in the field of civil politics. The movement pioneered new forms of protest and expanded the use of older types of protest. Indeed, it has created many movement "joiners" and political activists among normally noncommittal middle-class people. In establishing new networks linking private citizens to the press and to one another, the movement has trained a great many people in how to organize collective action and how to use a combination of direct action, the vote, and the courts to protect their interests against extremely powerful opponents.

The Barzón movement, like the Mexican crisis itself, may be an indicator of things to come in an era of financial globalization. Its explosive growth suggests that crises borne of volatility in global markets, combined with well-developed critiques of free-market policies, may contribute to new forms of collective action and protest. For scholars of politics and society, these new forms of protest and participation may be the most important aspect of economic crisis because they indicate much about the terms upon which citizens in Mexico will engage in public affairs in the new millennium.

Mexicans Would Not Be Bought, Coerced

Wayne A. Cornelius

In July 2000 Mexicans resoundingly elected Vicente Fox of the center-right Partido Acción Nacional (PAN), Mexico's oldest opposition party, over the candidate of the ruling PRI, Francisco Labastida. Mexico City mayor Cuauhtémoc Cárdenas, running for the third time as the standard bearer of the left-of-center Partido Revolucionario Democrática (PRD), finished a distant third. As this book went into production, it remained to be seen how momentous a political transition this election would prove to be. At a minimum, it broke the PRI's iron grip on the presidency and augured serious changes in the distribution of power and patronage. In the following selection, political scientist Wayne Cornelius, founder and director of the Center for U.S.–Mexican Studies at the University of California at San Diego, who was an observer of this historic vote, assesses the tenor of the campaign and speculates on its consequences for Mexico's democratization from the perspective of one of the PRI's traditional redoubts, the southeastern state of Yucatán.

PETO, YUCATAN. "Take the gift, but vote as you please." That was the advice dispensed to the Mexican people by opposition party candidates in the campaign just ended as well as by the head of the independent Federal Electoral Institute (IFE). But operatives of the ruling Institutional Revolutionary Party (PRI) incessantly delivered a starkly different message: "We've helped you; now you help us!"

Until 8 o'clock on election night, when exit-poll results were announced, the key unresolved question of Mexico's first national election of the twenty-first century was: Whose advice would the voters take?

With the crushing defeat that they administered to the PRI, at all levels and in most parts of the country, the Mexican people gave their answer, loud and clear.

Americans would have difficulty imagining the intensity of the psychological warfare to which Mexicans were subjected during the campaign of 1999–2000. They were alternately threatened and materially rewarded by PRI-

A rally for PAN candidate Vicente Fox, July 2000. (Photo by Tim Henderson. Reprinted by permission of Tim Henderson.)

affiliate public officials, from national party leaders on down to neighborhood-level "vote promoters."

In Peto, a town of some 22,000 — most of them Maya-speaking Indians — in the southeastern state of Yucatán, the *priísta* state governor gave thousands of families cement floors for their houses, each emblazoned with his name and the logo of a major federal government program closely identified with the PRI. Numerous residents also received portable washing machines, bicycles, sewing machines, and corn grinders from the state government in the run-up to the elections. Payment of annual cash subsidies to small farmers had been advanced from November to June. Two days before the election, the PRI municipal government distributed tons of free corn and rice. Dozens of pigs and cattle were slaughtered to provide meat for elaborate meals to which voters were invited, after they had "done their duty."

But in Peto and every other small town that I visited in Yucatán, residents had also been systematically threatened by the PRI. The party's operatives had gone door-to-door, asking people to provide the numbers of their IFE-issued voter credentials. This was a shameless intimidation tactic: Once the voter's name and credential number had been taken down, she was likely to feel committed to voting for the PRI, because "the computer will know" how one voted. In some places, PRI agents called on those who had been selected randomly by IFE as polling place officials to discourage them from showing up, warning vaguely of violence.

Rumor-mongering was rampant: If the center-right National Action Party (PAN) wins the presidential election, all social welfare programs that benefit poor families will be terminated. Scholarships for school children and milk rations for women with infants will be taken away. The era of "slavery" on large haciendas will return. The PRI and the government will know how votes were cast because secret cameras will be installed in polling places. PRI poll watchers will be armed with pocket-sized computers to record how everyone voted. Satellites flying overhead will also be watching.

Remarkably, the vast majority of Mexicans in Yucatán and elsewhere resisted the relentless psy-war. Pulling out all the stops, the PRI had cynically tried to exploit the economic vulnerability of the poorest Mexicans, but data from exit polls suggest that fewer than one out of ten voters may have succumbed to fear, intimidation, or vote-buying.

Even in Yucatán, a state governed for the past nine years by one of the PRI's most effective, authoritarian "dinosaurs," Víctor Cervera Pacheco, the machine's candidates for president and Senate seats were defeated. Many voters — especially in Mexico City — split their tickets, choosing the nominally conservative Vicente Fox for President and candidates of the center-left Party of the Democratic Revolution for mayor and legislative posts.

On election day 2000, the Mexican people passed a huge test of civic and political maturity, with flying colors. They and the IFE, whose nine "citizen councilors" courageously and tenaciously defended the reformed electoral system put into place in the 1990s, deserve full credit.

But IFE needs to have its regulatory powers expanded to enable it to police against the kinds of abuses that were still evident in the 2000 presidential campaign, especially hard-to-prove vote buying schemes. And the Office of the Special Prosecutor for Electoral Crimes, part of Mexico's Ministry of Justice, must be thoroughly overhauled to increase the probability of punishment for both individuals and political parties that commit such infractions.

Fortunately, these and other necessary political reforms are more likely to be made under a Fox presidency and a Congress in which the PRI has been reduced to a minority party in both the Senate and the Chamber of Deputies. Mexico's protracted and highly uneven transition to a fully democratic system should now advance steadily to completion.

VIII

The Border and Beyond

Readers undoubtedly will have noticed that the United States is a major presence in this anthology of writing about Mexico. Indeed, since the early days
of the republic, a diverse array of U.S. actors and agencies have powerfully
shaped Mexico's destiny and fired Mexicans' imaginations. They alternately
lament and celebrate the geographical accident that placed their country in
such close proximity to the world's wealthiest and most powerful country —
a country that has often treated Mexico with aggression, indifference, and
contempt. The two countries went to war in the 1840s, and the result was a
humiliating defeat for Mexico that cost it half of its national territory. Aggressive U.S. capitalists have long wielded inordinate power in Mexico's economy,
a predicament which helped to provoke the revolution of the early twentieth century. Powerful U.S. cultural influences have prompted Mexican intellectuals to fret about their country's loss of cultural identity for generations.
The priorities of the U.S. government in such matters as anticommunism, the
"war on drugs," and "free trade" have exerted a strong influence on the policies of Mexican leaders, not always in positive ways. Moreover, in the second
half of the twentieth century, the United States emerged as a major destination for desperate, job-seeking Mexicans. Whether these neighbors like it or
not, the destinies of their two countries are intimately intertwined. The nature
of the problematic relationship was probably characterized most famously by
the dictator Porfirio Díaz, who is alleged to have said, "Poor Mexico! So far
from Heaven, so close to the United States!"

With such disparate cultures and economies, it is not surprising that the
region where the two countries merge should be unique. In fact, the 2,000 or
so miles of border land, which stretches from San Diego–Tijuana in the west
to Brownsville–Matamoros in the east, constitutes a region like no other. It
has long been populated by a colorful cast of characters—smugglers, rustlers,
bandits, Indians, cowboys, Rangers, gun runners, drug traffickers—whose
mythification has often detracted from our understanding of the lives and folk-
ways of everyday men and women. The landscape is arid and almost surreal

in places, lending it a further air of mystery and foreboding—just witness its exaggerated depiction in bleached-out yellows and browns in the 2000 Oscar-nominated film, *Traffic*. One of the most intriguing aspects of the border is its permeability. Despite much-publicized efforts by the United States over the past decades to stem the flow of undocumented migrants and illegal drugs, knowing participants in these efforts tend to shake their heads and sigh at the sheer enormity and impossibility of the task. In addition to presenting formidable (and perhaps intractable) problems for law enforcement, the border presents unique challenges in the areas of environmental and social policy and for the study of transnational cultural forms—challenges daunting enough that Border Studies/Estudios Fronterizos has become a thriving discipline in colleges and universities in the region and beyond.

The readings that follow illustrate some of these challenges. We hope they will persuade readers unfamiliar with the region that the border is an immensely exciting and creative place, but also one plagued by serious troubles. Most of those troubles promise to be among the major public policy issues for years to come—to wit: the increasing militarization of the border that has accompanied the war on drugs; the persistence of undocumented immigration which has helped to make Latinos the largest minority in the United States but has deprived many of their dignity and fundamental rights; and the transnational industrialization of the region and the severe—potentially catastrophic—environmental costs it entails. Indeed, there is much to ponder in William Langewiesche's conclusion that the border, "to spite us all, . . . looks like the future."

Plan of San Diego

Anonymous

The historic racial, ethnic, and nationalist tensions of the border region are perhaps most dramatically illustrated by the mysterious "Plan of San Diego" (Texas), which appeared in 1915, at the very height of the Mexican revolution. The authorship of the manifesto is unknown — in fact, its authenticity has never been verified — and it does not appear to be the work of any cohesive group of revolutionaries. The plan, which called in no uncertain terms for a bloody Mexican insurrection without quarter against the United States, appeared at a time of high racial tension in the border region of the lower Rio Grande Valley, when Mexicans and Mexican Americans complained quite plausibly of abuse at the hands of Anglo police and citizens' groups. That persecution was only exacerbated by the release of the plan, which, although never taken seriously by U.S. officials, served as a pretext for reprisals against Mexicans and Mexican Americans.

We, who in turn sign our names, assembled in the revolutionary plan of San Diego, Texas, solemnly promise each other on our word of honor that we will fulfill and cause to be fulfilled and complied with, all the clauses and provisions stipulated in this document and execute the orders and the wishes emanating from the provisional directorate of this movement and recognize as military chief of the same Mr. ——, guaranteeing with our lives the faithful accomplishment of what is here agreed upon.

1. On the 20th day of February, 1915, at 2 o'clock in the morning, we will rise in arms against the Government and country of the United States and North America, one as all and all as one, proclaiming the liberty of the individuals of the black race and its independence of Yankee tyranny, which has held us in iniquitous slavery since remote times; and at the same time and in the same manner we will proclaim the independence and segregation of the States bordering on the Mexican nation, which are: Texas, New Mexico, Arizona, Colorado, and Upper California, of which States the Republic of Mexico was robbed in a most perfidious manner by North American imperialism.

2. In order to render the foregoing clause effective, the necessary army

corps will be formed under the immediate command of military leaders named by the supreme revolutionary congress of San Diego, Texas, which shall have full power to designate a supreme chief who shall be at the head of said army. The banner which shall guide us in this enterprise shall be red, with a white diagonal fringe, and bearing the following inscription: "Equality and Independence"; and none of the subordinate leaders or subalterns shall use any other flag (except only the white for signals). The aforesaid army shall be known by the name of "Liberating Army for Races and Peoples."

3. Each one of the chiefs will do his utmost by whatever means possible, to get possession of the arms and funds of the cities which he has beforehand been designated to capture in order that our cause may be provided with resources to continue the fight with better success, the said leaders each being required to render an account of everything to his superiors, in order that the latter may dispose of it in the proper manner.

4. The leader who may take a city must immediately name and appoint municipal authorities, in order that they may preserve order and assist in every way possible the revolutionary movement. In case the capital of any State which we are endeavoring to liberate be captured, there will be named in the same manner superior municipal authorities for the same purpose.

5. It is strictly forbidden to hold prisoners, either special prisoners (civilians) or soldiers; and the only time that should be spent in dealing with them is that which is absolutely necessary to demand funds (loans) of them; and whether these demands be successful or not, they shall be shot immediately, without any pretext.

6. Every stranger who shall be found armed and who cannot prove his right to carry arms, shall be summarily executed, regardless of race or nationality.

7. Every North American over 16 years of age shall be put to death, and only the aged men, the women, and children shall be respected. And on no account shall the traitors to our race be respected or spared.

8. The Apaches of Arizona, as well as the Indians (redskins) of the territory shall be given every guarantee, and their lands which have been taken from them shall be returned to them to the end that they may assist us in the cause which we defend.

9. All appointments and grades in our army which are exercised by subordinate officers (subalterns) shall be examined (recognized) by the superior officers. There shall likewise be recognized the grades of leaders of other complots which may not be connected with this, and who may wish to co-operate with us; also those who may affiliate with us later.

10. The movement having gathered force, and once having possessed ourselves of the States above alluded to, we shall proclaim them an independent

republic, later requesting, if it be thought expedient, annexation to Mexico without concerning ourselves at the time about the form of government which may control the destinies of the common mother country.

11. When we shall have obtained independence for the Negroes we shall grant them a banner which they themselves shall be permitted to select, and we shall aid them in obtaining six States of the American Union, which States border upon those already mentioned, and they may from these six States form a republic and they may therefore be independent.

12. None of the leaders shall have power to make terms with the enemy without first communicating with the superior officers of the army, bearing in mind that this is a war without quarter, nor shall any leader enroll in his ranks any stranger unless said stranger belongs to the Latin, the Negro, or the Japanese race.

13. It is understood that none of the members of this complot (or any one who may come in later) shall, upon the definite triumph of the cause which we defend, fail to recognize their superiors, nor shall they aid others who with bastard designs may endeavor to destroy what has been accomplished with such great work.

14. As soon as possible each local society (junta) shall nominate delegates, who shall meet at a time and place beforehand designated, for the purpose of nominating a permanent directorate of the revolutionary movement. At this meeting shall be determined and worked out in detail the powers and duties of the permanent directorate and this revolutionary plan may be revised or amended.

15. It is understood among those who may follow this movement that we will carry as a singing voice the independence of the Negroes, placing obligations upon both races, and that on no account shall we accept aid, either moral or pecuniary, from the government of Mexico, and it need not consider itself under any obligations in this, our movement.

EQUALITY AND INDEPENDENCE.

The Mexican Connection:

Un Pueblo, Una Lucha

Rudolfo Acuña

For too many North Americans, the border has always been associated with nefarious goings-on. Yet the stereotypical image of the region has changed over time. In the early part of the twentieth century, it was seen as a land of hostile Indians, revolutionaries, bandits, and desperados. After World War II, it came to be associated more with smugglers, illegal immigrants, impoverished and sinful border towns, and maquiladoras—factories where goods are assembled by low-paid Mexican workers for re-export to the U.S. market. The problems associated with the border region, however, must be viewed within a framework of multidimensional encounter that brings the people, ideas, commodities, and institutions of two very different and unequal nations together there. In the following selection, Chicano historian Rudolfo Acuña argues that dramatic population growth in Mexico and aggressive expansion by U.S. multinational corporations combined in the 1960s to produce a highly dependent, exploitative, and potentially explosive situation on the border—one that diminished the prospects of Mexican migrants and Chicanos alike.

Rudy Acuña is one of the most influential and controversial figures in the field of Chicano studies. He has been lauded for his passionate indictments of racism and the abuses of free-market capitalism and also harshly criticized for his lack of objectivity. In 1991 the University of California at Northridge refused to rehire him in its Chicano Studies Department, claiming that he was an "inveterate polemicist and pamphleteer." Acuña brought a successful discrimination suit against the University of California system, later publishing a book about the experience in which he excoriated U.S. academia for hewing to accepted versions of the truth (what he calls the "American paradigm") and denouncing those who sought to challenge the "official thinking." Readers will surely find his views—excerpted from his popular text, Occupied America—*provocative.*

After the mid-1960s, the migration of documented and undocumented Mexicans to the United States steadily increased. The migration itself had multiple

Mexican *braceros* en route to the United States. (Reprinted by permission of Fototeca del INAH, Mexico.)

effects on the Chicano. First, after World War II, a marked trend toward assimilation had occurred and many Mexican American parents refused to teach their children Spanish. This trend [toward what Acuña and others refer to as *pochoization*] was reversed by the growth of cultural nationalism and the presence of larger numbers of Mexican nationals. Rather than a rejection of Mexican heritage, cultural nationalism created a renaissance in Mexican consciousness. This phenomenon was the most noticeable in California, where . . . *pochoization* was the most advanced. And, second, events in Mexico increased its importance to Mexican Americans. It became clear to many Chicanos that their own status would not improve until the growing subservience of the Mexican nation to the multinational corporations ended. The image of a weak Mexican nation reinforced stereotypes of weak, dirty, lazy Mexican Americans. These caricatures were used to justify the exploitation of Mexican Americans.

Mexican migration itself was a response to industrial conditions in the United States. Increased division of labor brought about the rapid expansion of low-skilled jobs in agriculture, the service sector, and light industry—jobs that most Anglo-Americans would not accept because the pay was below the minimum wage or they were socially undesirable. This in turn created a demand for cheap labor in the United States.

The population boom during the 1960s threw millions into the labor pool.

In 1950 Mexico had a population of 25.8 million, jumping to 34.9 million ten years later, and rushing toward 50 million by the end of the 1960s. Mexico's annual population growth had dramatically increased from an average of 1.75 percent (1922–1939) to 2.25 percent (1939–1946) to 2.8 percent (1947–1953) to well over 3 percent after 1954.

Although Mexico had the fastest growing gross national product (GNP) in Latin America, it could not absorb the population boom as the first wave entered the workforce in the 1960s. Mexico, like many Third World countries, had launched a program of development and modernization after World War II, expecting to cure its economic and social ills. Modernization, however, did not solve the problem of the poor but accelerated the deterioration of their status. The mechanization of agriculture worsened the plight of the peasant and helped bring about the elimination of many subsistence farmers while increasing the division of labor—further widening the gap between rich and poor.

Industrialization made Mexico more vulnerable to the world market and encouraged U.S. penetration of the Mexican economy. Mexico's dependence on the United States was proved by the abrupt end of the *bracero* program, which had administered migration to the United States for special interests. Instead of attempting to lessen its dependence on the United States, Mexico substituted another U.S. program for the bracero, allowing greater North American control over the Mexican economy.

After World War II, multinational corporations (those doing business in more than one country) moved to dominate the marketing of Mexican agricultural products. Del Monte alone by 1967 had offices in 20 Latin American countries and ranked as the world's largest canning corporation. By 1964 Mexico shipped 334 million pounds of vegetables north; 13 years later, the flow increased to 1,108 million pounds, supplying, at certain seasons, 60 percent of U.S. fresh vegetables.

Anderson-Clayton, extensively involved in Third World nations, monopolized the sale of cotton in Mexico through credit and marketing. It loaned more credit to Mexican growers than El Banco Nacional Ejidal. Anderson-Clayton manipulated prices and kept Mexico in line by either dumping or threatening to dump cotton on the world market at depressed prices. The process of monopolization, like mechanization, accelerated the elimination of subsistence and small farmers and led to the production of crops for export rather than staples such as corn and beans.

U.S. economic penetration into Mexico during the 1960s totaled $1.1 billion; total profits of $1.8 billion in the form of payments abroad in interest, royalties, and patents were drained out of the economy annually. The United

States's monopoly of technology forced Mexico to purchase machinery, transistors, wires, generators, and similar equipment from it to the exclusion of other industrial nations. This kept Mexico constantly in debt and dependent on the World Bank and the International Monetary Fund for new loans.

Contrary to popular myth, North American and other foreign investors did not create jobs. During the decade, over 60 percent of the new foreign investment went to purchase already existing corporations. Between 1963 and 1970, the workers employed by foreign corporations increased by 180,000; however, 105,000 of these jobs already existed. In fact, foreign companies controlled 31 percent of the total value of Mexican industrial production and employed only 16 percent of the industrial workforce.

Changes in the world market since World War II also affected Mexico. Simply, after the war, the decolonization of the Third World produced a restructuring of the multinationals. Under colonialism, governments protected and regulated their national corporations doing business in countries under their flag or within their sphere of influence. With the end of colonialism, multinationals sought to maintain their control of markets and natural resources in their former colonies. They also expanded their own spheres of influence beyond former limits. As a result of decolonization and their economic growth and technological explosion following the end of World War II, many multinationals became superpowers and, by the 1960s, were assuming the character of transnational corporations. Their principal place of business was not in one country. As the transnationals grew in economic power, they became more ungovernable and often acted independently of the home country.

Immediately after World War II, the United States had no competitors on the world market. Government contracts accelerated the growth and power of U.S. multinationals. However, by the 1960s, competition from Japanese, German, and other European nations threatened North American hegemony. U.S. transnationals sought to cut their costs by relocating the production of many commodities to Asia and Latin America. . . . Labor in those regions was just as much a commodity as natural resources. Buying labor cheaply meant higher margins.

By the mid-1960s, the phenomenon of the runaway shop was well advanced in the electro-electronic and garment industries. The restructuring was made possible through special privileges extended to North American multinationals by loopholes in the U.S. Customs Simplification Act of 1956. Section 806.30 allowed the processing abroad of metal goods that returned to the United States for finishing. Section 807, passed in 1963, laid the basis for apparel, toy, and similar "light" industries to relocate overseas. Understandably, U.S. labor opposed these loopholes, but it lacked sufficient power to stop the flow of jobs out of the United States.

Meanwhile, conditions in Mexico worsened with the termination of the bracero program. Mexico had become dependent on renting out its workers. The border areas became an object of special concern for the Mexican government because of the accumulation of people who responded to the pull north as the Mexican economy deteriorated. In the early 1960s, it initiated *La Nacional Financiera* (PONAF), a program intended to (1) substitute Mexican manufacturing for U.S. goods which Mexicans commonly bought, (2) promote the sale of Mexican goods abroad, and (3) upgrade the social environment along the border. PONAF's success was mixed. As unemployment mounted, Mexico responded by accepting more overt U.S. penetration.

Mexico agreed to the Border Industrialization Program (BIP). The purpose of the BIP was to create jobs, to attract capital, to introduce modern methods of manufacturing in assembling, processing, and exporting, and to increase consumption of Mexican raw materials. The Mexican government waived duties and regulations on the import of raw materials and relaxed restrictions on foreign capital within 12.5 miles of the border (this area has continuously been expanded); 100 percent of the finished products were to be exported out of the country, with 90 percent of the labor force comprised of Mexicans. In 1966, 20 BIP plants operated along the border. This number increased to 120 in 1970 and to 476 in 1976. The majority were electro-electronic and apparel plants.

In reality, although these *maquiladoras* did create jobs (20,327 in 1970), they did not ameliorate the unemployment problem, since they hired mostly from a sector of Mexican labor that was not previously employed. The BIP workforce, over 70 percent women, was paid minimum Mexican wages. North American employers gave no job security and the maquiladoras could move at the owner's whim. The BIP failed miserably as a strategy for development. The Mexican government had hoped that the maquiladoras would purchase Mexican parts; this did not occur. The BIP left relatively little capital in Mexico. The program itself provided multinationals an alternative to Taiwan and Hong Kong, dramatically cutting down transportation costs. BIP projects grew rapidly during the decade that followed. Just like the bracero program, it increased Mexican dependence on the United States, making both Mexico and its rented slaves more vulnerable to multinational penetration.

Exploitation of Mexican labor was not confined to the BIP program nor multinational activity. Both documented and undocumented workers flowed freely into the United States in order to ensure a surplus of cheap labor for growers and other domestic interests. The commuter program served farmers, small businesses, and corporations along the border. The McCarran-Walter Act removed the alien contract provision from the immigration code and introduced "a system of selective immigration giving special preference to skilled aliens urgently needed in this country." It authorized the secretary of labor to grant a limited number of permits (green cards) for temporary residence if the workers did not compete with domestic workers. U.S. immigration and labor authorities constantly abused the commuter program, even losing count of the number of permits issued. As in the case of the El Paso Payton Packing Company strike of 1960, growers also received special treatment; they did not have to bother to pay living wages to attract U.S. workers. They just had to petition the Department of Labor for temporary workers and allege that they could not find sufficient numbers of domestic workers and that an emergency existed.

By the mid-1960s, Chicano militancy concerned growers and other employers. The purpose of immigration policy was to control not only Mexicans but Chicanos. After 1965, this policy became more restrictive, designed to regulate both the flow of workers and the wages paid. Essential to this strategy was the criminalization of Mexican labor, which devalued and degraded the work performed by Mexicans and Chicanos. Criminalization intensified the division of labor and resulted in Chicanos, to avoid discrimination, pecking down on the undocumented worker; it also justified increased use of police power against all Mexicans, whether documented or undocumented.

The first step in the criminalization process was the passage of restrictive legislation that directly affected the documented immigration of Mexicans. Liberals such as Senator Edward Kennedy sponsored legislation in 1965 designed to correct the past injustice of excluding Asians from legal entry. Nativists took the opportunity to broaden the legislation and, for the first time, placed Latin America and Canada on a quota system. The law specified that 170,000 immigrants annually could enter from the Eastern Hemisphere and 120,000 from the Western. Up to this time Mexico had been the principal source of Latin American immigration; the new law put a cap of 40,000 from any one nation. Unfortunately, few Chicanos or progressive organizations protested the law. And it was not until the 1970s that its full impact was felt; at that time it became a popular cause for progressives.

The *Maquiladoras*

William Langewiesche

Key sticking points during the NAFTA negotiations of the early 1990s involved the treatment of labor and the environment. Critics charged that NAFTA was merely a ploy by transnational corporations to increase their profits by taking advantage of unprotected low-wage workers and lax environmental standards. Their fears were certainly not unfounded: to bolster their case, these critics needed only point to the region immediately south of the United States border, where maquiladoras—plants where goods were assembled using tax-free imported materials and then returned to be marketed in the United States—had been in operation for some time. William Langewiesche, a correspondent for The Atlantic Monthly, *describes working and environmental conditions in the Lower Rio Grande Valley of Mexico on the eve of NAFTA's passage.*

After hundreds of miles of virtual wilderness, the border . . . is blighted by urban desperation. Before emptying into the Gulf of Mexico the Rio Grande snakes across a semitropical coastal plain, a green and hazy flatland known locally as the Lower Valley. The north side, where 80 percent of the residents are Mexican-American, has long been weakened by corruption and political bossism. *Colonias,* decrepit farming towns, and three decayed cities—McAllen, Harlingen, and Brownsville—attest to the lack of opportunity. Publicists there speak of a rich cultural heritage. No doubt. But as measured by income, health, and education, the Lower Valley is among the poorest regions in the United States. And to spite us all, it looks like the future.

Across the river, Mexico is poorer still. Life is dominated by the presence of American manufacturers, who have set up some of the border's largest *maquiladoras.* Reynosa, which lies on the Rio Grande, is a flat industrial city of perhaps 300,000 people, about seventy miles from the Gulf. To get there from Texas, you cross a big modern bridge, passing a mile of trucks waiting to clear Mexican customs, and an equally long line waiting to enter the United States. The trucks attest to the vigor of business and binational trade. Zenith alone employs ten thousand workers in Reynosa.

Colonia Roma is typical of the districts where they live. It sprawls across a swampy lowland beyond the Pemex refinery—a large and desolate slum, strewn with trash, where vegetation does not survive. The shacks are made of scraps discarded from the factories. Children wear rags and go barefoot. Here and there, a Coke sign hammered to a wall indicates a small grocery, a place perhaps with electric power. A paved road passes beside the neighborhood, on higher ground, and crawls with buses blowing smoke. During the shift changes at the *maquiladoras,* workers stream between the shacks and balance on planks across mud and sewage. The women dress in pressed skirts and blouses; they look like office workers from a better neighborhood in a better city. Many go into debt to achieve this effect. Inflation has outpaced wages in Mexico. The average *maquila* worker in Reynosa labors forty-five minutes for a quart of milk or a pound of chicken, two hours for a bottle of shampoo, three hours for two boxes of cornflakes or a toddler's used sweater, twenty hours for sneakers, and over a hundred hours for a double mattress.

Drainage in Colonia Roma is poor. The district flooded the week before I got there, and residents waited for the water to subside by perching with their belongings on their beds. This seems hardly noteworthy to the family I went to see. Their yard was a mess of cinder-block rubble imbedded in mud. They lived in a single-room plywood house that was almost filled by two iron beds pushed together. On subsequent visits I counted eight people who slept there, but I may have missed a few. The oldest was a toothless Indian grandmother who questioned me about my religious beliefs. I was cautious: she wanted to talk about God's grace and the afterlife. The youngest resident was a girl, perhaps five, who seemed ill. One of the sons, who in his mid-twenties had been working three years at Zenith, was small, thin, and discouraged.

I asked, "How is the job?"

He answered, "Good." But his eyes were furtive.

"Good?"

"Little good. The problem is there is no money."

"And the union?"

"It can't protect us."

"How long will you stay?" I asked.

"I don't think about it."

The shack smelled of lard and garbage. Smoke from a refuse fire drifted by the open door. Chairs hung from nails on the walls because there was no place for them on the floor. A pair of prized cowboy boots stood under the bed, by a stack of clothes. The kitchen consisted of a camp stove, a water jug, and an insulated box. There was a kerosene lantern, a transistor radio. The buzzing of flies mixed with the shouts outside.

Seen from a distance—say, in a photograph—such poverty evokes powerful feelings. Close up, however, it can seem unreal. It is bewildering that people
you can touch, who share the air with you, can be suffering in conditions so
different from your own. I have experienced this before in Africa, in the midst
of starvation. We carry our own world with us and it is numbing.

IT IS AN ENVIRONMENTAL future to be feared. When people live in cities built
on industrial waste, they suffer. In the Lower Valley, miscarriage, birth defects,
disease, and cancer rates are high. For this and the other calamities of their
lives, the workers have begun to blame the United States. In Matamoros, the
city of a half million that lies across the Rio Grande from Brownsville, Texas,
I talked to a labor organizer named María Torres. She said, "Americans say
they can save us from starvation. But all of us who have come to the north,
if we had stayed where we were, we would not be dying of hunger. Here on
the border, we are just slaves."

That word *slave* kept reappearing. Upriver I had seen graffiti scrawled defi-
antly across a bridge: NO SOMOS ESCLAVOS! We are not slaves! And in Reynosa's
Colonia Roma, I had talked to a man whose greatest wish was for his children
to work in the *maquiladoras*. He said, "In the past we were nothing but the
slaves of the rich. And if we are still slaves today, at least the *maquiladoras* pay
us more."

I quoted him to Torres. She became calmer and said, "No one is against
the plants. No one wants to close them down. We ask only for better conditions and we are willing to compromise. But we refuse absolutely to be used
as a dumping ground for industrial wastes. The president of Mexico claims
he won't allow contamination. He claims environmental enforcement will be
part of free trade. But why should we believe him? We've seen what they do:
they close down the companies that contaminate the least and they leave the
big polluters alone." She named them for me and said, "There are strong interests involved. The neighborhoods around the plants have denounced them,
but nothing is done."

In Matamoros the best-known case of this occurred around a chemical
plant called Chemica Flor, which sits by a mountain of its own waste. The
plant, partly owned by DuPont, produces hydrogen fluoride, a volatile, toxic,
and highly corrosive acid shipped to the United States for use in the manufacture of Teflon coatings. The risks of having such a facility within the bounds of
a city are considerable. When nearby residents objected, Mexican authorities
ordered the permanent evacuation of neighborhoods within two kilometers
(1.25 miles) of the stacks: ten thousand people were affected. The residents
marched in protest. Finally, the authorities "backed down" and allowed the

people to remain. Such false concessions have sustained the Mexican government for decades. But the technique has its limits.

Across town, I visited a General Motors facility that makes bumpers. The buildings were big, square, and anonymous. They had nice little lawns. I arrived during the shift change, when several thousand workers—again, mostly young women—streamed out and climbed onto the colorful buses waiting to take them back to their shacks. I went around the side of the main building, to the ditch into which the plant's outflow pipes drain. Activists from the United States have taken samples here showing massive levels of xylenes, ethyl benzene, acetone, toluene, and methylene chloride. I did not need a test tube— from a hundred yards away I could smell the solvents. They dribbled from the outflow pipes in paint-colored water and floated off through the city in the ditch.

Senior General Motors spokesmen have denied these conditions, and in all sincerity. The corporation does not intend to pollute. Workers are provided with tanks into which to purge their paint guns. But to save time, they simply purge the guns into the drains, which empty into the ditch. Mexico has adopted strict laws regulating toxic wastes, but government technicians measure the outflow water only for feces and bacteria. In addition, Mexican laboratories are notorious for falsifying results. So for a variety of reasons, the industrial chemicals do not officially exist. If they did, nothing would be done anyway. General Motors' Mexican landlords were legally obligated to build a treatment plant, if not for chemicals, at least for sewage. Instead they dug the ditch. This was not unusual. General Motors' ditch empties into a larger flow, the central canal, where it mixes with untreated municipal sewage and the poisonous outflow from an entire city of unchecked industry.

I spoke to a chemist in Brownsville, who said, "G.M.'s problem is they empty directly into a ditch. Other plants empty into other pipes, which empty into the main canal. It's practically impossible to trace their spills." Speaking of *maquiladoras* in general, he said, "The companies hide in their own corporate structures. They pass responsibility upward. If they go high enough, they can find people who don't know what's going on. They don't have to lie."

The central canal in Matamoros flows through residential neighborhoods. When residents complained, Mexican federal cleanup money was used to cap it for a mile or two and hide it from view. The covering was made in part of rock and gravel, which was later discovered to be toxic waste. A string of playgrounds was built on it. Word got out and the playgrounds lie unused. The canal does not empty into the Rio Grande. The discharge emerges from the city, flows southeast, and twenty miles below the border feeds into the Gulf of Mexico, where fish swim it north again.

The fear of poisoning is not an abstraction. Industrial accidents in Mata-moros have sent hundreds of people to the hospital and forced thousands of others to evacuate their houses. On the night of December 6, 1990, a tank in the center of town overheated, blew a valve, and leaked a cloud of toxic vapor. The vapor entered the ventilation system of another *maquiladora,* a manufac-turer of electric blankets, about three blocks away, and sent fifty women to the hospital. Slowly dissipating, it drifted over the Rio Grande into Brownsville, where the stench caused terror in the streets.

María Torres, the labor organizer, took me to a neighborhood sandwiched between two chemical plants: one brewed pesticides, the other detergents. By the standards of Matamoros, the neighborhood was middle class. The houses were made of rough, unpainted wood, but they had electricity, running water, and small yards. Most of the families had moved there in the 1930s, when cot-ton dust was the biggest nuisance.

A chemical smell wafted through the area and burned softly in my throat. The day was hot and I had a headache. A stout woman with crooked teeth, a friend of Torres's, invited us into her house. We sat on chairs covered in padded red vinyl in a room the size of a closet. Through a doorway veiled by a beaded curtain I heard a television. An open fuse box was fixed to the wall, and a Coors-shaded light hung from the ceiling. A new telephone stood on the cabinet.

The woman offered me a glass of water and I declined. I asked her if she worried about the chemicals next door. She said, yes, ever since the explosion of 1983, when a pipe had burst at the insecticide plant and sprayed poisonous foam over the houses. I asked her to describe it. She said, "It snowed foam. We were afraid and ran with the children, thinking only of saving ourselves. Where we touched the foam, we got sores on our feet. The next day it rained, and the poison spread through the neighborhood. We were kept out for eight days. Our clothes were contaminated and destroyed. We had to kill our ani-mals. Pigs, chickens, dogs, cats. We had seven ducks. They were all buried in a trench in the company compound."

I wandered across the street and talked to an old man who told me of dig-ging holes and smelling chemicals in the groundwater, which lies close to the surface. The detergent factory had built evaporation ponds next to his house. When they overflowed, his chickens picked at the water and died. Chickens in Matamoros are like canaries in a mine — but here when the canaries die the miners stay on.

Later, Torres took me for a walk along a ditch where discharges from bor-dering plants sink into the soil. The water was black and it turned milky when I tossed rocks into it. Families live there along the railroad tracks, in a district called *Chorizo* because it is long and narrow like a sausage. They drink from tainted wells and hang their clothes to dry on the fences that separate them from industry. The border is full of these fences. . . .

MARÍA TORRES, WHO wanted so for me to see her industrial nightmare, is a woman well known to the poor of Matamoros. . . . I first met her at a café in the heart of the city to talk about her efforts to organize women workers in the *maquiladoras.* At forty-eight, she has a gentle face coarsened by hardship. For most of her adult life she worked on the production lines in Matamoros for a company called Kemet, which manufactures capacitors. Now she works for an organization called *Comité Fronteriza de Obreras,* or the Border Committee of Working Women. The committee collects no dues and has no membership rolls, but is well known to thousands of *maquila* workers along the lower Rio Grande. Its approach is low-key: it does not exhort the women to march or strike, but rather encourages them to meet discreetly in small groups in the shantytowns. They teach themselves about their rights under Mexican federal labor law and about the occupational dangers in the factories. Torres helps them to learn, as she herself learned. She encourages them to ask for small improvements from the *maquila* managers and better representation from the huge Mexican union, the CTM. Faced in their offices with delegations of women who are calm and resolute, the managers and union sometimes give in to the demands. As a result, wages and working conditions in Matamoros are slightly better than elsewhere on the border. Torres has nourished herself with these small victories. She is a strong woman who has grown stronger with age.

I heard she went to Mexico City with a coalition of Mexican and American union men concerned about the effects of free trade. They met with scholars in a conference room at the Colegio de México. Someone gave a presentation. The discussion that followed was too theoretical for Torres's taste. She butted in and said in Spanish, "What I want to talk about is not free trade. What I want to talk about is, I worked eighteen years in the *maquiladoras.* I washed parts in methylene chloride with my bare hands. No one told me it was poisonous. No one gave me safety equipment." Looking annoyed at the interruption, some of the academics pushed back from the conference table. Torres persisted. She had brought along the label from a spool of lead solder, and because it was in English, she asked an American to read it: CONTAINS LEAD WHICH MAY BE HARMFUL TO YOUR HEALTH. LEAD IS KNOWN TO CAUSE BIRTH DEFECTS OR OTHER REPRODUCTIVE HARM. FEDERAL AND STATE LAW PROHIBIT THE USE OF LEAD SOLDER IN MAKING JOINTS IN ANY PRIVATE OR PUBLIC POTABLE (DRINKING) WATER SUPPLY SYSTEM. AVOID BREATHING FLUX

FUMES EMITTED DURING SOLDERING. FLUX FUMES MAY CAUSE PULMONARY
IRRITATION OR DAMAGE. AFTER HANDLING SOLDER, WASH HANDS WITH SOAP
AND WATER BEFORE EATING OR SMOKING. Torres said, "There are thousands
of women handling solder who have no idea what this warning says. They are
told nothing."

When I met her in Matamoros she continued the story. "They don't have
time before lunch to wash. They eat greasy tacos, which become black from
their hands." She spoke from experience, the source of her power.

Torres was born in 1944 in Cárdenas, a large town in the state of San Luis
Potosí, about 250 miles south of the border. Her father was a railroad laborer
who died by falling off a train when she was a baby. Her mother went to work
as a domestic for other railroad families. They could not afford to pay but
provided food and a place for the night. María . . . grew up in their shacks,
sleeping in blankets on the floor. When she was seven she caught typhoid and
nearly died. She spent a year recovering. At the age of ten, having completed
the third grade, she gave up on school and went to work with her mother.

Her mother dreamed of working in the United States. "My mother . . . had
the dream of crossing into Texas and we came here to the border, to Matamoros, when I was sixteen."

It was 1960. The bracero guestworker program was still in full swing. Mexicans could cross the bridge into Brownsville without documents; it was
thought of as part of the natural border traffic. Nonetheless, moving to the
United States was a big step. Mother and daughter hesitated for eight months
in Matamoros, working in the upper-class neighborhood.

When finally they ventured into Brownsville, they quickly found live-in
jobs. Torres became the nanny of four children, for eight dollars a week. She
stayed three years, until she was twenty, saved a little money, and went often
to the dances. Then she and her mother moved to Harlingen, the next town
north, where again they found jobs in separate households. Harlingen lasted
a year, until someone called the Border Patrol. When the agents came, Torres
ran into the field and hid in a furrow. Afterward, her employers drove her
back to Brownsville, where her mother, too, had taken refuge.

By then you needed a Border Crossing Card to take the bridge. The women
had a friend in Mexico who was sleeping with someone in American Immigration, who got them the card. They found work in Brownsville. Torres wanted
to return to Mexico; her mother did not. They argued about it.

I asked Torres why she wanted to return. She said, "I felt alone in the United
States and this loneliness was overwhelming me. . . ."

One Saturday when she was in her mid-twenties, Torres crossed the bridge
from Brownsville and rented a room in an old house on Morelos Street, in the

central district of Matamoros. Her mother did not approve of the expense. Torres bought the basics: a bed, a two-burner stove and a tank of gas, a frying pan, two cups, and two plates. Her mother stayed with her for the weekend, but returned on Monday to Brownsville. That morning, Torres went to the union office looking for a job.

It took two months to get one, at a pottery factory. After the first week she learned she would not be paid because she was "in training." She wondered how she was going to survive. There were twenty workers there, and they told her this was standard. She answered, "If they haven't paid you either, then you should ask for your money."

They told her not to make trouble.

When the owner arrived, she said to him, "I won't work here anymore, but you owe me for the work I've already done." She pointed to the pots she had made. "I did all this and I'm sure you'll sell it. I won't leave until you pay me."

The owner refused.

Torres raised her voice. Using strong language, she said, "These other women have been here for months, and have never been paid for their training either. You owe them, too."

The owner hushed her and agreed to pay. He wanted to write her a check, but she had never in her life been to a bank and she demanded cash. Leaving the factory, she waved the money at the other workers and cried, "Look! Look!" She heard later that they, too, were paid.

The next factory was a clandestine operation making knitted handbags. There were twelve workers. They had no chairs or tables, but sat on newspapers on the floor. One day a union man arrived and got into a shouting match with the owner, who was Italian. The union man took out a pistol and made the owner pay the workers then and there. Then he said, "Any who want to work in an electronics factory, come with me in my car." The car was a black Buick. Torres was the first one in. The others crowded in after her, until the union man barely had room to steer. Somehow he drove them to his office.

The electronics factory was an American *maquiladora,* set up by the Electronic Control Corporation to manufacture electrical coils. The union was supplying the workers. There were two hundred. Torres was given a three-month probationary contract with a promise of permanent employment if she performed well.

At the café in Matamoros she showed me what the job entailed: she folded a paper napkin and with deft and reflexive fingers simulated wrapping wire around a spool. The company required the women to produce two boxes of four hundred coils a day, six days a week, for about eighteen cents an hour. Despite swollen and bloody hands, Torres caught on quickly, and by her second week was producing four boxes a day. The supervisors were pleased, but after eight months the company still had not given her a permanent position. Then, just before Christmas and the mandatory two-week bonus, all two hundred workers were fired.

Torres was in trouble. Her savings were gone, and her clothes, which she had been given while working as a nanny, were wearing out. Her mother moved in with her to help with the rent, and both women took occasional day jobs in Brownsville. But Torres was determined to stay in Mexico. Every morning she walked to the union hall. Another eight months went by. She knew already about the difficult conditions at Kemet, the *maquiladora* where she was to work for eighteen years. She took the job there because she felt she had no choice. It was 1969 and she was twenty-five.

Kemet was as bad as they said. She worked in the department of injection molding, forming capacitor bodies from hardening epoxy. She washed the bodies bare-handed in methylene chloride, a volatile solvent that turned her skin papery and white. Methylene chloride is chlorinated hydrocarbon, linked to liver damage, birth defects, and cancer. It is in the same chemical family as chloroform and it can have similar soporific effects. The warning labels cautioned in English against breathing the fumes and mentioned narcosis, respiratory failure, and death. The workers did not understand the dangers. Their supervisors probably did not, either.

They were all under constant pressure to increase their production. "Once they brought in a man who stood beside us, watching the clock, and wouldn't let us go to the bathroom. Every hour he came by with a file to check the production. Many women felt it necessary to work right through the breaks. He told us not to talk. If we looked up, he ordered us to work."

I asked what his orders sounded like.

"With just a glance, he ordered us." She laughed. "He wanted us to sit there like statues. I rebelled by talking, by singing, by getting others to sing. If he accelerated the belt, I loaded it up with too many units so they would fall off. Sometimes I sabotaged the machine, and while the mechanics tried to fix it, I took a rest."

I asked, "What happened in the end?"

Her answer surprised me. "Eventually the man relaxed. He became our friend. When he had to leave he threw a party for us. That was before I knew about my rights."

I asked, "And now, would he still be your friend?"

She smiled. "Probably not."

She was never a docile employee, and over time she grew angry. "I felt they were constantly loading more work on us. I began to ask the others, 'Don't *we* have any rights?' One day my friend Ludivina told me her brother, who was a law student, had mentioned a federal labor law to her. This was the first I heard of it."

By then Torres had put in eleven years at Kemet. The idea of a comprehensive labor law, its mere existence, strengthened her resistance to the supervisors. But she did not know where to find this law or how to use it. She kept asking questions. Eventually she discovered that an American was coming from across the river and holding meetings in a Matamoros church, teaching Mexican workers about their rights. The American was Ed Krueger, then fifty, a soft-spoken man who had spent years helping the migrant farm laborers of Oklahoma and Texas. In February 1981, Torres went to her first meeting and took fifteen Kemet women with her. . . .

Dompe Days

Luis Alberto Urrea

*Luis Alberto Urrea, born in Tijuana and raised in San Diego, has a lifetime's famil-
iarity with the border. He saw the region anew, however, beginning in 1978 when
he became involved with a group of Baptist missionaries led by one Erhardt George
von Trutzscheler III, better known simply as Pastor Von. The group, known as "Spectrum Ministries," worked among the poor in the orphanages and garbage dumps of
Tijuana. Urrea's sobering realization of the depths of poverty in his hometown provided the inspiration for two remarkable collections of essays. These essays depict a
level of poverty that is intense and unremitting, albeit leavened by the humor, compassion, and resilience of the poor.*

One: The Infinite Swirl

Imagine this: a muscular storm came in during the last days, and as we drove
into the Tijuana dump, we were greeted by an apocalyptic scene. Let me try
to describe it. The dump, as you know, is cheek by jowl with a rangy home-
built cemetery. In fact, many of the graves are partially covered by trash. The
garbage used to be in a canyon about 150 feet deep; it is now a hill about 40
feet high. Above this hill is a seething crown of 10,000 gulls, crows, pigeons.
But mostly gulls. Imagine, further, mud. Running yellow mud; brown, reddish, black waste-water mixed with dust, ashes, and clay. The few graves with
cement slabs over them glisten with the rain. The mud is a gray so dark it
verges on black. The sky is raging. Knots of clouds speed east, far above the
gulls, and the gulls rise so high that they seem an optical illusion: from huge
birds to nearly invisible specks in the sky, they seem to hang on wires, a mad
museum display, held in place by the violent wind.

Now we drive in, and the muddy graves are pale blue and pale green and
pale brown as their wooden crosses fade; the cement headstones are all white
or streaked rainy gray. And from the hill of trash, hundreds, perhaps thousands, of plastic bags—tan bags, blue bags, white supermarket bags, black
trash bags, yellow bread wrappers, and video store bags—along with stream-

ers of computer paper, sheets of notebook paper, newspapers open like wings, ribbons of toilet paper, tissues like dancing moths, even half-dead balloons, are caught in a backdraft and are rising and falling in vast slow waves behind the hill, slow motion, a ballet in the air of this parti-colored landscape, looking like special effects, like some art department's million-dollar creation, Lucifer's lava lamp, silent, ghostly, stately, for half a mile, turning in the air, rolling, looping.

And up top, exposed to the elements, the garbage is flying like a snowstorm. We lean into it at angles, held up by the wind. The garbage-pickers are wrapped in bags to keep the rain off them. Huge tractors, two stories tall, churn through the mud. And the goo squishes up to our ankles. Boxes, panties, magazines, more bags, always plastic bags, flying and bouncing and shooting off the summit to snow down on the distant village. I watch paper drift down onto the roofs; advertisements for stoves and dog food form sentimental snowdrifts on the housetops.

Beneath us, the slowly revolving magic bags. Above us, the infinite swirl of gulls. And garbage hurricanes lift off all around us: the photographer thirty yards away from the young woman and me is dwarfed by a whirlwind of trash—it rises twenty, thirty feet above his head, and he stands at the apex, shooting us with our arms around each other, holding on in the wind. Her breasts are wet and running with milk. She tells me it tastes sweet and makes her want to vomit. Our eyes run tears from the wind. A pack of dogs tries to attack us, and a mad Indian woman breaks off from signaling passing Aeroméxico jets, hoping they'll land in the *dompe* and take her on a trip. Her name is Doña Chuy. "They'll kill you!" she yells. "The dogs! They'll kill you!" She wades into the pack and knocks them aside with her knees. They snap at her skirt. "Out of my way," she says. "Can't you see a plane is coming in?"

She thinks anti-union death squads are after her.

"I am a revolutionary," she says.

The young woman swirls her finger beside her temple.

"*Está loca,*" she says.

"They held a machine gun to my head," say Chuyita.

One scraggly bitch breaks away from the dog pack and runs at me. She has long dark teats that swing beneath her belly, and one eye is ripped out of its socket, and pus and blood are caked to her face, and she makes me want to vomit and run but throws herself at my legs and reveals herself to be the world's sweetest dog, and she rubs herself on me and wags and grins and begs to be petted. So I try to find a spot free of pus.

Behind us, as the rain begins again, a funeral procession wends its way down the narrow mud tracks. Men in wet cowboy hats and boots pull shovels out of a station wagon and wrestle a coffin over the hillocks to a likely spot; ladies with lace veils are buffeted by the wind; endless plastic bags blow between them like fleeing ghosts.

And later, in the warmth of her shack, the young woman I have known since she was six nurses her daughter, and we smile as the little mouth gobbles the huge black nipple, both the mother and I aware that she has chosen today to allow me to see her bare breasts, and we hold hands as the rain hammers at the tar paper.

Can you imagine such a scene?

Two: Boys' Life

Nobody knew what happened to the boys' parents. Not even the boys—Chacho, Eduardo, Jorge, and Carlos (fake names)—could explain what had happened to them. As is so often the case on the border, one day the boys woke up and their parents were gone. Papá had apparently gone across the wire, into the United States. Mamá blew away like a puff of smoke. The four brothers were alone in the Tijuana garbage dump.

For a few nights the younger boys wept as Chacho, the fierce elder brother, pulled together a small homestead amid the garbage. They went hungry for a while, not having any dump survival skills. The trash-pickers gave them what food they could spare, but that wasn't much. And missionaries came to the dump with goodies, but Chacho didn't trust gringos, so he kept the boys away. Besides, the gringos gave baths, and nobody was going to get Chacho naked.

One day an old man appeared in the dump. He wore grimy old suits and had no past and no home. His left arm had come out of the socket years before, and he had wandered, half crippled, from dump to dump, looking for people to care for him. Although there is no lack of ferocity in the *dompes*, there is also a high degree of compassion and fraternity. Still, if you have no food or room to spare, what can you do? Slip him a gringo doughnut (*una dona*) and see him off with a blessing. The evil ones, circling through the waters of the night, kicked him around for fun, stole the *dona*, and left him in the dirt.

Chacho came across him after one such beating. He made the old man a deal: if he would look out for the younger boys, Chacho and Eduardo would share their trash-pickings with him. And Chacho would beat up anyone who threatened the old man. They engineered a new family unit that day.

The old man, keeping his part of the bargain, scrounged a cast-off Maytag appliance box. He cut a door in its side and upended it, open top to the ground. Then he carpeted the dirt floor with newspaper, plastic bags, and cardboard. They used scavenged clothes and rags for a mattress and blankets. The little ones played in the dirt outside while the old man lay in the dark box crying, hallucinating and seeing visions—dead women he had loved, angels, demons, strange creatures, his mother coming to feed him, gringos with bags of beans, which turned out to be us, though I was never sure if he knew he wasn't dreaming.

He had a passion for avocados, and he collected them in rotting mounds inside the box.

For his part, Chacho built a real shack out of scrap wood, and he placed it on a low rise near the Maytag house, where he could watch over his brothers. For whatever reason, it never occurred to him to build them a house—that was the old man's job. Somehow Chacho acquired a pistol. Then he stole a pony from a neighboring ranch and built it a corral made of bedsprings and stolen wood. Chacho was a small warlord, surveying his kingdom.

His brothers watched the clean kids coming out of the gringo baths. They didn't envy the washed faces or clean clothes. They envied the doughnuts and chocolate milk and bananas. They marched into the bathing room and took off their blackened clothes.

Eduardo brought home animals—unwanted puppies, piglets swiped or bartered, a pathetic skeletal cat.

Chacho used his pony to steal cows.

NOBODY KNOWS WHAT happened to the old man. He was such a phantom that he passed through this story without a name. Perhaps he grew tired of being a dad, of living on a floor of smashed avocados and mud. Or he simply forgot them as the rising tide of mania and tequila ate his brain. Or he was taken by a car in the gloom of the highway canyons. Maybe he tried to go across the border. Any guess, any guess at all, is valid. The boys were out working the trash, and when they came home, he was gone. He had taken their ball of twine, so they knew he had tied his arm to his side. This suggested to them that he was planning a substantial journey.

Like abandoned children everywhere, they felt fear and talked themselves into feeling hope. *He'll be back. Maybe he'll bring us some food.* They huddled around the door of the box all night. When morning came, they knew they were alone again.

They marched up to Chacho's bandit's roost to seek help, to move in with him at least. But Chacho was a busy man. He was a *pistolero* and a cattle rustler, and he was suspected of being an undercover snitch for the police. He had *socios* (what we would call homeboys) running errands and fencing goods for him. He had a television. And he had his pistol.

Look, boys, he told them, the point is that life's shit. Who coddled me? Nobody. Who felt sorry for me? You see this house? These horses? This *pistola*? I did this. You've got to go out there and make your lives. Be tough or die.

This, in Chacho's eyes, was love.

Eduardo, Jorge, and Carlos failed to be moved by Chacho's warm sentiments. But they had to obey. He was, after all, their big brother. The closest thing to an elder they had. He was also macho, and they were afraid that if they whined too much, he'd pull his six-shooter and do them in. He wore it jammed in his belt, and even wore it to intimidate the missionaries. I once heard him say, near Pastor Von's van, "I'd better like these doughnuts. I'd hate to shoot anybody." This statement, as all macho bon mots, was delivered with a scowl that hid a tremendous laughter. Pancho Villa is the patron saint of machismo, and Pancho Villa is the in-dwelling spirit of every macho. Anyone who has survived in a tough area knows: machos are philosophers, and they are also weary judges of all they survey. If their variable code of ethics is betrayed, they are often called upon by their inner demons to be executioners. *A man's gotta do what a man's gotta do.* A macho can explode in unreasoning fury or act with benign munificence, at a moment's notice. Machos are sentimentalists, like all true fascists. Robin Hood or Vlad the Impaler—whichever it is, you have to have what it takes to back up the pose.

Chacho didn't like it, but he sent them away. That is not to say that Chacho lost any sleep over his brothers. Not yet.

BOYS LIVING ON the edges of the dump have a vast playground of sorts. Collecting trash is hard work, even if the trash-picking is off to the side, where the small ones can go. The brothers played and romped in the mounds, found the occasional toy, found clothes and tins of food, found waterlogged magazines with pictures of nude women, which they took to Chacho. Once they even found a load of fetuses dumped on the edge of the trash. "Dead babies," everyone was saying. "A sacrifice." People were afraid, able to envision only something desperately evil, something monumental that would kill so many babies, then toss them into the dump. The boys poked at the cold fetuses with sticks. To them, living in such squalor, something even more squalid was a revelation.

Although Eduardo loved animals, for example, the sight of a diseased dog being pounced upon and eaten by other dogs was exciting.

The boys had rats to kill, fires to set, food to steal, huts to spy on. No wall in that neighborhood was particularly solid, and they could peek in through the cracks and see just about anything. And there were always the fights to watch: drunks and gang members and warring young turks from alien barrios and young women throwing punches like the meanest macho. Small Huck Finns on a sea of trash, they floated through life, avoiding schooling and being educated by the harsh classroom all around them.

They even had their own swimming hole.

On the hill above Chacho's horse pens, the city had built a huge *pila* to hold water for the downhill communities. The part of the reservoir above ground was the size of a *maquiladora* or a warehouse, and it didn't take long for the boys to break through an upper corner of the cinderblock structure. They climbed in through the hole with their pals and sat on the walkways in the shadows within. They loved to swim in that cool green water. They loved to urinate in the water, imagining their pee going down the hill to the fine stucco homes.

The one game they loved the most was the most dangerous. Everyone, even Chacho, warned them about it. Everyone told them to stop. But they loved it to the point of madness. The boys loved to jump on the backs of moving garbage trucks.

EDUARDO THOUGHT he had a firm grip on the back of the big truck.

Retired from San Diego, the truck was rusty and dented. It was heavy with trash, and greasy fluids drained out of its sides like sweat. Its hunched back was dark with dirt, and its smokestack belched solid black clouds.

The boys had spent the morning running up behind the trucks as they entered the dump, hopping on the back ends, hanging on to any handhold they could grab. Sometimes, if they missed, they caught the sides and hung there like little spiders, swinging over the wheelwells as the trucks banged over the mounds.

Eduardo had run behind the truck, had flung himself at it and caught the upper edge of the open maw in back. He swung back and forth, doing an impromptu trapeze act, and the other boys called insults: "Faggot!" and "Coward!" He turned once to laugh at them, hanging by one hand and starting to flash them a hand sign. The truck slammed on its brakes. Eduardo flew inside, hit the steel wall, and was flung back out, hitting the ground on his back, hard enough to knock the breath out of him.

The boys were laughing wildly, and Eduardo tried to rise, pasting a game smile on his face though the blow must have hurt. He probably couldn't catch his breath. He lay back, just for an instant, to breathe.

The truck ground its gears and lurched into reverse. The boys yelled for Eduardo to get out of the way, but it must have sounded like more taunting. He raised one hand. The truck backed over him and the hand was twisted down to the ground, and the double wheels in the back made Eduardo disappear.

Carlos and Jorge stood staring, imagining somehow that Eduardo would get up after the truck had passed over him. But he was deep in the soil, in a puddle of his own mud. The truck driver shut off the engine and stepped out to unload the garbage, but he couldn't understand why the boys were screaming.

Three: Boot Hill

The dump people don't always knit together. Sheer survival makes it difficult to look out for their fellows. But death sometimes unites them, if the death is sad enough. Or the threat of death, if the threat is vivid enough.

Everyone knew Eduardo's story. They had all said at one time or another that someone should do something about those boys, but nobody had done much. They had all seen the Maytag box, the old man, the truck-surfing. Guilty and ashamed, the neighbors resolved to do something about Eduardo's death.

They collected money. Centavos came from hidden beer money, from the jar under the bed, from the schoolbook fund, from Christmas savings. The *americanos* gave funds. People worked extra hard that day to get a few more pesos.

They bought Eduardo a small suit. His first and last fancy clothes. Some of the Mixtec men collected raw particleboard and hammered together a coffin. They set it inside the room where the missionaries gave baths. This was done very quickly. No undertaker ever saw Eduardo, no papers were ever signed. No official ever knew he had existed, and none would be told he had died.

Since he wasn't embalmed, they had to hurry. The suit was bought and pulled onto his twisted corpse by nightfall. The coffin was built by eight P.M., and he was laid out under candles by nine. The women had washed his face. Eduardo was finally clean.

They would bury him in the morning.

CHACHO TOOK a bath. He stuck his pistol into his belt, got drunk, and walked over to weep over Eduardo. All the tough guys in the dump lost it over Eduardo. None of them knew how to deal with this tragedy. It was somehow worse than all the other tragedies. The men wept openly, inconsolably. Perhaps Eduardo had come to symbolize their own abandonment. Perhaps this small boy, thrown into the trash, left to die there, and facing a burial there, was too much like all of them. There was no way they were going to bury him in the trash too. In being killed, Eduardo had become everybody's son, everybody's brother. One family boasted that they had fed him often, another bragged that he wore their old shoes. Girls wrote his name on little torn bits of paper—hearts and flowers in blue Bic ink. Every boy there claimed Eduardo as his best friend. You would think somebody had actually loved him.

Chacho got one of this *socios* to drive a pickup. They hammered the lid on the box, then wrestled it up on their shoulders. The people who had not gone to work—mostly wives and daughters—stood silently. A woman or two worked her rosary beads. Some cried—nothing overwhelming, but there were tears. The boys lifted the box over the side and placed it carefully in the bed. Chacho and his remaining brothers climbed in with Eduardo.

Directly behind the pickup was a flatbed. It was filled to capacity with mourners. They passed a bottle of rum. Chacho would be drinking plenty that night and the next. People would steer clear of his robber's cabin, because Chacho would be in the mood to shoot.

Bringing up the rear of this funeral procession was one gringo van with a few missionaries. That one detail has lived on in the neighborhood, that the *americanos* came to bury Eduardo. Nobody asked them. They just appeared. Mourning. It was the most anyone had ever done for the people on the hill.

Ironically, a busload of fresh-faced American Jesus Teens from the suburban church had pulled up and unloaded thirty happy campers into the middle of the funeral. They bounded about Praising the Lord and Ministering to the Poor. They were no doubt shocked to find the poor rather surly and unappreciative of their Witness. Their youth pastor, being no slouch, took the opportunity to send them into the shed before Eduardo was sealed into his box. He wanted the kids to learn what real life was like. For his part, Eduardo gave them a devastating sermon, lying there in his already dusty suit, flat and angry-looking. A mute testimony.

All the bounce gone out of their strides, the teens mounted their bus again and motored away, easy answers scrubbed right out of their skulls.

During all this, Carlos, the youngest of the brothers, stayed outside, playing marbles. He didn't show the least interest in Eduardo's corpse. As Chacho was standing beside the coffin, crying out his pain, Carlos used him as a sort of shield, peering around him at Eduardo. He reached out and prodded Eduardo's face with his fingers, apparently to make sure his brother was really dead. He then went out and joined the marble game.

THEY COULD HAVE been going to work, hauling some junk to the dump.

The small procession headed off across the hills, winding through small valleys and into regions never visited by gringos. They left the road entirely and drove across dead fields. Up a hill. Some of the dump people had created their own graveyard there. Little crosses made of sticks dotted the hill. The dead here were squatters. One day the landowner would find out. But really, how can you fight with the dead?

One American said, "It's Boot Hill."

The men traded turns with the shovel, cracking, then scraping out the rocky soil. It took quite a while to make the hole, but between them, they managed it. Nobody complained.

They manhandled the box into the hole and stood around looking at it. Chacho almost fell in, he cried so hard. The men quietly went back to work, pushing dirt and rocks back in. Others who couldn't get close to the shoveling went from grave to grave, pulling dry weeds and picking up paper. Some of the crosses needed straightening. A couple of guys made borders of rocks around unmarked graves.

Jorge never went near Eduardo's grave.

But if you paid close attention, you could see Carlos moving in behind Chacho. He peeked out from between Chacho's legs. Then, at the last possible moment, he grabbed a little handful of dust and pitched it into the hole.

Pedro P., Coyote

Judith Adler Hellman

With Mexico's economy seeming to hover chronically on the verge of collapse since the 1980s, it is no wonder that as many as 150,000 Mexicans are driven to migrate illegally to the United States each year. Scarcely a month goes by without one of America's big-city newspapers carrying a major story on the transborder journeys of Mexican and Latin American migrants in search of a better life or merely the short-term opportunity to remit greatly enhanced wages to loved ones back home. Increasingly, many Mexicans have come to participate in migrant circuits that enable them to live truly transnational lives north and south of the Rio Grande.

Sadly, much of the media's coverage concerns the deplorable conditions and risks that migrants face in their efforts to elude U.S. immigration authorities ("la migra") along the two-thousand-mile border. Every year hundreds of migrants are killed in accidents: they drown in overflowing canals, fall beneath moving trains, and suffocate in sealed railroad cars and automobile trunks. Others fall victim to human predators, many of whom carry guns and badges. According to Mexican immigration officials, illegal migration has become very big business: international syndicates have turned the smuggling of migrants into a criminal enterprise comparable in profits and ruthlessness to those of the drug trade. The coyotes, or polleros (border-crossing middlemen), who lead undocumented migrants (known as pollos, or chickens) across the line, frequently overcharge and then abandon their clients at the first sign of a run-in with the migra. Often coyotes leave their human cargo cooped up and in deadly peril, exposed to bandits or corrupt policemen who rob migrants of their savings and possessions. Not for nothing, then, has President Vicente Fox vowed to create a special office for the investigation of immigrant smuggling.

Yet, as sociologist Judith Hellman tells us in her portrait of "Pedro P.," not all coyotes are unscrupulous opportunists. This Tijuana-based pollero is a decent independent entrepreneur, whose business depends on word of mouth and his ability— literally—to deliver. Her account takes us with Pedro on his nightly rounds and sheds light on his values and aspirations as a potential migrant himself. Based on extensive interviews, Pedro's story is one of fifteen portraits Hellman provides in Mexican

Lives, which chronicles the struggles of rich and poor alike to adapt to the changes set in motion by the nation's neoliberal reforms.

At six in the afternoon the crowd assembled on the Mexican side of the border fence begins to grow larger and turn jittery. Within an hour, darkness will fall and the most eager and restless of the migrants will make their move. Some will climb the twelve-foot corrugated metal fence. Others will pass under the barrier through one of the dozen or so holes that perforate its fourteen-mile length as it stretches from the Pacific Ocean at Playas de Tijuana, past the official border station, around the airport, up onto the Otay Mesa where the assembly plants cluster, and out onto the desert. Here the fence ends—far from the cities and connecting roads in canyons and badlands that no sensible person even thinks about crossing on foot.

At sunset the crowd swells. But almost any time of the day, immigrants can be found at "El Bordo," as this section of the fence is known. They nervously pace back and forth. They negotiate with the "coyotes," or "*polleros*," who offer to guide them across. They peek through or over the fence to study the moves of the *migra*—the agents of the U.S. Immigration and Naturalization Service (INS). They gaze up at the hill that rises steeply behind the U.S. border station where the border patrol's infrared scopes are mounted, ready to pick out migrants scattered—running and hiding—in the bushes below.

In the narrow strip between the border fence and the highway that runs along the edge of Tijuana, a half-dozen men and women march back and forth hawking tacos, tortas, candy, and soft drinks—food that sustains those migrants who sit by the fence all day, watching, waiting, and looking across into San Ysidro on the U.S. side. In the evening more vendors appear. These people sell the large plastic bags that migrants use to cover their shoes and legs as they wade, shin or knee-deep, across the Tijuana river. Only some of the clandestine routes to San Ysidro involve crossing the river, an open sewage ditch that rises in the mountains south of Tijuana, runs through the city in a concrete channel, and then makes its way northwest across U.S. territory to empty into the ocean near Imperial Beach. But the vigilance of the border patrol in the other sectors along the fence is so intense that increasing numbers of migrants and their coyotes are choosing to cross at the western end of the line, the path that involves fording the river and plodding through wetlands.

The movement of Mexican migrants has not always taken this form. During World War II, Mexicans were encouraged to come to the United States to meet the labor shortages produced by the war. In the 1950s, U.S. agribusiness successfully lobbied for the creation of a *bracero* program that brought hundreds of thousands of seasonal farm workers to harvest crops through the Southwest. But even as the *braceros* were arriving in the United States under government contract, the first large waves of illegal immigrants began to flow across the border. And when the *bracero* program was terminated in 1965 under pressure from organized labor in the United States, illegal migration from Mexico continued because the demand for cheap labor never slackened.

The illegal migrants of the 1960s and 1970s were mostly peasants who sought work in the fields of California and Texas. Generally, they did not come on their own. Rather, they were recruited by agents who traveled through the poorest rural areas of central Mexico collecting farm laborers and loading them into open trucks. The labor contractors transported the peasants to the border, packed like chickens in a poultry truck. This is how the migrants came to be called chickens, or *pollos,* and the agents, *polleros.*

Once at the border, the methods used to bring the undocumented workers across were crude because vigilance was light: they were loaded into the back of trucks, concealed with cargo, or marched across the desert backlands. Some died on the way.

Today increased surveillance at the official border crossings and the effort to interdict drugs makes it impossible to bring people across concealed in the trunks of cars or vans. The work of the *pollero* has changed drastically and become differentiated and specialized. A team of coyotes generally works together to complete the transfer from Tijuana to Los Angeles. Moreover, the *pollero* no longer recruits his clients in rural Mexico and hauls them to the border. The would-be migrants are now mostly urban people who reach the border cities under their own steam, traveling by bus, train, or even airplane. Once they arrive at the *frontera,* they cross on their own or engage the services of a coyote to get them into the United States.

While migrants cross at all the major border cities, half of all undocumented Mexicans who make their way into the United States do so at Tijuana. This westernmost border town is almost twice as far from the densely populated regions of central Mexico as Nuevo Laredo. . . . Moreover, the Tijuana crossing is more difficult and dangerous than some of the others. In Ciudad Juárez, for example, the streets run right up to the river that separates the Mexican city from El Paso, Texas. Here people just take off their shoes, wade across, put their shoes back on, and stride into a neighborhood on the other side. But the migrant who crosses in Texas is still more than a thousand miles from Chicago, not to speak of New York. In contrast, crossing at Tijuana puts the migrant within three hours of Los Angeles and the greater Los Angeles metropolitan area of fifteen million. For this reason the majority of migrants come to Tijuana and find a *pollero* to help them evade capture by the eight hundred INS agents assigned to guard the U.S. border at this point.

I am at the fence with a *pollero* named Pedro P. He has been recommended to me as a "coyote's coyote" — a man with a nearly perfect record of success at his trade. Once, in 1988, in what still stands as the crowning achievement of his career, Pedro single-handedly guided twenty-three *pollos,* including seven children, over the border and across the river, delivering them safely to the K-Mart in San Ysidro, where a truck was waiting to take them to Los Angeles.

This evening Pedro has five paying customers at the fence. He plans to move them in a group sometime after 8 P.M. It is a slow night for Pedro, who sometimes makes as many as three separate trips in an evening. When he is running at full throttle, he takes the first group of *pollos* under the fence just after sunset, escorts them as far as San Ysidro, passes them along to his contacts on the other side, returns to Tijuana to pick up the next group, and repeats this routine twice more before the sky begins to lighten at dawn.

Pedro had just such an evening the previous night, working three shifts before returning at 5 A.M. to the house in a working-class neighborhood in the center of Tijuana which he shares with his wife, Patti, and his four children. Under the circumstances, I had trouble making contact with Pedro, although, as instructed, I left messages at a café, a pinball parlor, a billiard hall, an autobody shop, and a bar, all on the street where I had been told I would find him. As it turned out, Pedro had slept in after his night's labors and did not stop by to check his messages until noon. But even though he got off to a late start, Pedro managed to line up some business for the evening: five men from Durango who hoped to reach East L.A. by the following afternoon.

Pedro is thirty-two, tall, and dressed not in the leather jacket, designer sunglasses, and gold jewelry he can afford but in a windbreaker, cotton shirt, worn jeans, and a baseball cap. There's nothing slick about Pedro; he looks like the people he guides to the other side. His appearance, he says, inspires confidence in the migrants who come to him on the recommendation of friends and family. Pedro looks like someone they can trust. He looks like someone from their hometown.

More important, Pedro explains to me, his choice of clothes is critical in the event he and his *pollos* are picked up by the *migra* as they make their run for San Ysidro. If they are apprehended, Pedro's goal is to remain undetected as a *pollero* among the *pollos.* As long as the *migra* does not take him for the coyote in the group, and assuming none of his customers "finger him," as he puts it, the consequences of his capture by the border patrol are minimal. Along with his clients he signs the form waiving his right to a hearing, he is loaded into the bus that takes them back to the border station and is deposited on the Mexican side. Depending on the hour and emotional state of the group, Pedro and his charges are likely to try again that same evening.

If, on the other hand, Pedro is identified as the *pollero,* he is in big trouble:

The *migra* is going to catch you from time to time. It's inevitable. It happens to everyone—to me, perhaps, less than to others because I've been very lucky and I don't take too many chances.

Once, however, I was caught with my pollos and the gringos decided— I don't know why—that I had to be the coyote for the whole group. I think one of the agents recognized me as someone he'd picked up before. My clients were sent back to Mexico, but I was put in the San Diego city jail.

The next day I was transferred to the Federal Penitentiary in Pecos, Texas. This is the place where they take coyotes, drug smugglers, and *contrabandistas.* But I can tell you one kind of person you don't find serving time in Pecos. That's the Americans who employ the illegals. These guys are smart and they pass along the risk to "labor contractors" who vouch for the workers, saying that their papers are all "in order." It's the contractors who end up in Pecos charged with falsification of documents and transport of illegal aliens.

ON THIS OCCASION, Pedro was charged with transport of illegal aliens and held for thirty days. He says he was not mistreated during his incarceration.

To tell you the truth, I would rather spend a month with the gringos in Pecos than one day in a Mexican jail. Other coyotes have told me some bad stories about beatings and other stuff that went on when they were in custody in the U.S. But, in my case, the only thing I suffered was worry for my wife and my kids, who didn't know what had become of me and had nothing to live on while I was gone.

PEDRO IS CONCERNED he may be caught again. The penalties for a second offense are severe. For this reason he is meticulous about briefing his five clients before they begin their attempt to cross. If they are caught, it is imperative that everyone behave in a way that suggests that they are just six guys from Durango who have decided to make it across together.

In the ten years I've worked as a *pollero,* I've brought thousands of people across—men, women, and children. And in all those years, no one has ever ratted on me. Mexicans are good people in this way. Besides, no one has any reason to finger a coyote who deals honestly with his customers.

This question of integrity is one that Pedro returns to again and again in our conversation. Pedro explains that virtually all his business is based on recommendations and repeat customers. Some clients reappear every year in January after returning to Mexico from Los Angeles to spend Christmas with their families. Almost all his clients are referred by friends and relations he has "passed" before. Pedro says,

> The stories you hear about coyotes who rob the *pollos,* who collude with *asaltapollos,* the bandits who assault the *pollos* while they're in no-man's-land—all these things really do happen. You hear about coyotes who rape the women they have promised to deliver safely to the other side, or who abandon people who have broken a leg or twisted an ankle jumping over the fence. These stories are true. But it is only a few *polleros* who do these things. This is a business like any other; you're going to find all kinds of people, good and bad, doing this work.
>
> My business is based on trust, on the recommendations of people I have passed to the other side. Folks come to me because I have a reputation for skill and reliability. I work with very competent people in San Ysidro—guys in whom the *pollos* can have confidence. People think of me as someone who is serious, who doesn't take stupid chances. I would never do anything that would put my name at risk.

PEDRO GOT HIS START as a coyote by assisting relatives and friends from his village who sought his help to get across. Sent to Tijuana as a boy to live with an aunt and uncle, by the time Pedro was a teenager, he had sneaked into the United States more times than he could count. By the age of seventeen, he had washed dishes in San Jose, picked cherries in Washington State, and scrubbed floors and washrooms in a large office building in downtown Los Angeles. Each time he crossed the border, Pedro says, he came to understand more about the movements and strategies of the *migra.* Once back in Tijuana, based on what he drew from these experiences, he was able to guide others—first his brothers and cousins, and then an ever-widening circle of acquaintances from his home region in Durango. Pedro says that when he realized he had a flair for getting people across, he turned professional.

Pedro's approach to business is shaped by the fact that he works on the basis of personal recommendations. While other coyotes make the rounds of the cheap hotels, stand around in bus and train stations, or patrol the area around the fence looking for clients, Pedro tells me he just hangs out in one of his usual spots downtown, and waits for people to come around asking for him. "This saves me a lot of sweat," he explains:

Apart from everything else, I don't have any hassles with other coyotes. Some of these guys can get real nasty if they think you're out looking for *pollos* in what they consider to be their corner of the bus station or their section of the fence.

When a potential client makes contact with him, Pedro requests the phone number of the friends or relatives who are supposed to be underwriting the trip. He then phones Los Angeles to check that these people have the cash on hand to pay his associate when he delivers the *pollo* to Los Angeles. Pedro prefers to operate, as he puts it, "c.o.d.," because this arrangement reduces the risk in several ways. The migrants have less to lose if they are set upon by bandits at any point in the journey, and Pedro himself is not carrying large amounts of cash at the vulnerable moments he is conducting his group from the fence to San Ysidro.

Once the contact is made with the sponsors in Los Angeles, Pedro briefs his client, sets a time and a place to meet, and takes the individual or group to the fence by taxi. Here he is joined by Jaime, his partner. Jaime's job is simple: when night falls and Pedro is ready to move the group, Jaime goes under or over the fence to draw the attention of the *migra,* while Pedro passes his clients under the fence at another point. Pedro always moves his people under the barrier. Although it constrains his range of choice in selecting a spot to cross, he says it is much faster and safer for the *pollos.*

Once over the fence, Jaime either runs forward or ducks back under the fence, whatever it takes to give Pedro the chance to move his *pollos* out of the range of the *migra*'s surveillance. Pedro explains,

With the *migra* it's always a game of cat and mouse. You study their moves, you figure out how many men and what kind of equipment they're using that night. And you rely on the fact that you know that they know that they can't stop everyone who decides to cross on a given day. The trick is not to be one of the people they catch that day.

When Pedro reaches San Ysidro, he escorts his clients to a prearranged spot, where he is met by the coyotes who will take them on to Los Angeles. At this point, Pedro usually takes his cut of the total fee (one hundred dollars per head), which is an advance on the three hundred dollars his associates will collect on delivering the *pollos* to Los Angeles. When Pedro "sells" the *pollos* to other coyotes, he turns around and heads back to Tijuana, either to escort another group or to go home. Generally speaking, in an increasingly differentiated profession, Pedro specializes in "leaping the fence."

When business at the fence is slow, Pedro will take his clients all the way to Los Angeles, the San Fernando Valley, or points north. On these occasions Jaime is waiting in San Ysidro with a van, and the group proceeds north on Interstate 5 until just before the INS checkpoint at San Clemente, an hour up the highway from the border. The checkpoint is a serious obstacle because, when it is in operation, all traffic is slowed to a crawl. Then, anyone who looks likely to be transporting undocumented immigrants — anyone, in short, who looks like Jaime at the wheel of his van — is pulled over for inspection.

When the checkpoint is in operation, Jaime drops Pedro and the *pollos* at a point south of San Clemente. Pedro then proceeds overland with the group through the hills above the highway. Jaime collects the group at a prearranged spot north of the checkpoint.

> The *migra* knows all the regular overland routes that we can use, and they patrol these with horses and helicopters. So we just have to invent new routes. To do this work, you have to believe that there's got to be one last way the *migra* hasn't thought of yet. The other thing to remember is that the people we guide are very needy. They're very desperate. So they'll put up with a lot to reach Los Angeles.
>
> Once past San Clemente, we can relax, especially as we get closer to East Los Angeles, where everyone speaks Spanish and looks like us. My job is to deliver the client safe and sound to an address in East L.A. Then I collect my $300 and leave. If, three minutes later, the guy I just dropped off sticks his head out the door to put out the garbage and is grabbed by the *migra*, that's not my problem. I just bring him there. Staying out of the way of the *migra* afterwards — that's his problem.

Pedro explains that the rates charged the *pollos* vary from $250 to $350. The exact price depends on age (children travel for less) and distance. Three hundred dollars is standard for Los Angeles; $350 will take you to the San Fernando Valley. For a good deal more money, some coyotes — working through contacts at southern California airports — provide connections to destinations throughout the West. Pedro claims that he can get me to Chicago in two days if that's where I need to go. But, he adds, 99 percent of his work involves the standard Tijuana–L.A. run at the standard price.

Pedro says that it was once the case that women, like children, were charged less than men:

> The *polleros* used to give a special rate to the women and the kids because they were crossing as part of a family. But now a lot more women are crossing. About a quarter or a third of the people I guide are women. And they're not traveling with their husbands or on their way to join husbands who

are waiting in Los Angeles. These women are on their own, and they're headed to L.A. to look for jobs. And they get good jobs, too, because most of them have more schooling, more preparation than the men. So now, most coyotes charge them the same rate as men. . . .

Having learned what the *pollos* pay, I ask Pedro if he doesn't make bundles of money each week. . . . Pedro replies,

It's true that I can take in thousands of dollars in a week—sometimes a thousand in a single night. But I also have my expenses. Apart from the calls to L.A., I pay a twenty-five-dollar finders fee to anyone who sends me a customer. I pay twenty bucks for the taxi to the fence. Whatever is left of the hundred per pollo I collect in San Ysidro, I split fifty-fifty with Jaime.

At the end of the day, I make a lot of money, but I have some very big hidden costs. The federal judicial police, the state judicial police, the municipal police—you name it—they come around as often as once a week to shake me down. They know more or less what I make so they want as much as a thousand dollars a pop. And, believe me, they get a lot more than that from the drug runners.

Pedro says that even members of the Grupo Beta are now "on the take." This elite corp of federal police was formed to coordinate with the INS to halt the worst abuses that occur on the border—the rapes, armed robbery, and murders. Pedro points out that the Grupo Beta has made the border zone safer for everyone. But, he says, some of the agents have been corrupted:

It's logical, isn't it? These guys are supposed to protect the *pollos* from the *polleros*. Thus, they are in a perfect position to extort bribes from the coyotes because they have all kinds of information on us: where we live, where we cross, where we recruit our customers. The Grupo Beta is supposed to be especially honest and upright. But the temptation to shake us down is too great for some of these guys. They come around to your house and either you pay up or they expose you to their buddies, the *migra*.

I ask Pedro if he is ever afraid. He says,

Of course, I'm often afraid. Everyone who does this kind of work is afraid. I'm scared of the police on this side and the *migra* on the other, and the bandits who attack you in between. The worst thing is the bandits, because they carry knives and guns, and they go after you when you're on your way back from San Ysidro and you have all the money you earned that night in your shoe.

A border patrol round-up of illegal immigrants. (Photo © Ken Light.)

Pedro says that his wife worries a lot and prays a lot. Patti attends an evangelical church and he often attends with her, although he still considers himself a Catholic and continues to go to Mass.

> As for my children, they're too young to worry. The oldest boy is ten. They don't really understand what I do for a living. But Jaime's kids are older, and his wife tells them that their father works in a saloon and that's why he comes home so late and why they can't visit daddy at work.

I mention to Pedro that I have noticed that most of the coyotes are men in their twenties or early thirties, and I ask him how long he sees himself doing this work. Pedro shakes his head and replies by describing to me the jobs he has held in Mexico and what he earned at each: ten pesos per day working *ejido* lands as a *jornalero;* fifteen per day in construction; forty pesos as a cab driver. In the United States he has worked as a dishwasher, busboy, waiter, janitor, checkout cashier, custodian, bricklayer, plasterer, and bar bouncer.

He has also picked cherries, apples, grapes, peaches, strawberries, oranges, grapefruits, tomatoes, lettuce, and squash.

He says,

I continue to work as a *pollero* because it is the only job I can get in Mexico where I can make really good money. My problem is that I don't want to live on the other side. I don't want to bring up my kids in the United States. I want them to live here, in their own country, where they can feel proud of who they are.

But I'll tell you what my dream is. My dream is to get papers: to get a real green card, not a fake. Then I could work in construction on the other side, and live here in Tijuana with my family. I'd like to operate the heavy equipment. I know how, and you make great money doing that in the U.S. I'd just go across every day to work, and then I'd come home to Tijuana at night. I could be really happy with that kind of life. Not just economically OK, but really happy, really content.

There's a Party Going On in Texas

Anonymous

Mexicans and Mexican Americans have historically tended to have ambivalent and often tense relations, despite sincere efforts to nourish pride in "La Raza." The two groups too often find themselves competing for work and divided by prejudices. They do, however, share many cultural traits and pastimes. Since culture is something that lives and is constantly reinvented, it should surprise no one that some fairly recent cultural developments have acquired transnational importance, as is illustrated by the following article on lucha libre (freestyle wrestling) by the Associated Press.

SAN ANTONIO, August 26, 2000. There is a new sports spectacle in San Antonio on Saturday nights, but you will not find the action at the Alamodome, the Freeman Coliseum or in the fancy SBC Center once the ribbon is cut for that new arena. There are no million dollar–salaried athletes or salary caps.

Luxury suites? The only season tickets belong to those with back yards in the barrio.

Facilities? The guy who started it traded an old red Pontiac for an unused wrestling ring.

Lucha libre is back. And growing crowds in San Antonio's South Side are having a big time watching small-time pro wrestlers dressed in tights and fierce masks, Mexican-style, beat the sense out of each other in a makeshift outdoor ring. It costs $5, and directions are needed to the Colt .45 Baseball Field off Highway 16, to check out the latest trend in street entertainment in a city that makes an art of the outdoor fiesta. And lucha libre is fiesta, South Side–style: part blood sport, part fantasy and definitely part pachanga, or backyard neighborhood party.

It is not fancy, but it is entertaining and definitely different. There is no air-conditioning. The fans sweat right along with the masked wrestlers in the Texas heat. Bleacher seating is limited; fans bring lawn chairs. Look for the solitary mesquite tree if you need some shade.

Every Saturday night, Lasero Martinez leaves his identity in the parking lot of a nearby baseball field. By the time he climbs into the ring to face an opponent, the 41-year-old, self-employed tile worker has become El Ilegal — the illegal one — a masked villain taunted by 100 boisterous fans.

"You have to love what you're doing because the crowd can get pretty vicious," Martinez told the *San Antonio Express-News*. "They yell a lot of junk."

Salvador Anguiano, a San Antonio cement contractor who wrestled for more than 30 years as El Salvaje (The Savage), swapped his 1979 Pontiac Firebird for the beat-up ring and revived the matches in April 1999.

"A friend of mine owned it and had it on his property; it wasn't being used or anything," said Anguiano, who still trains with other wrestlers on weekday afternoons. "The flood of '98 washed it away and split it into pieces. I traded a car for it, and the rest is history."

He has had decent crowds and they, in turn, have attracted many local wrestlers. All have full-time jobs, since their expenses are barely covered by gate receipts.

Tradition keeps the fans coming back. Spectators are treated to two hours of matchups that often are a kind of morality play, with symbolic good guys and bad guys. Another plus, many of the regulars agree, is the intimate setting. The action is only a few feet from the screaming fans.

"For us, this is a hobby," Anguiano said. "Nobody's going to get rich. The money we raise is for upkeep and we have to cover expenses for wrestlers who travel here each week."

Lucha libre matches can be found in Houston, Dallas, and other cities in the United States with large Mexican and Mexican American populations. Wrestlers from Mexico travel the circuit of the United States arenas to keep fresh faces in the rings.

The sport is an important part of the culture, said Javier Martinez, assistant to the president at the University of Texas at Brownsville, who has done extensive research on both the Mexican and United States styles of pro wrestling.

"In Mexican lucha libre you'll find that the wrestlers are more than likely locals who are heavy-set, while in the wwf [the highly visible, professional World Wrestling Federation] they're more muscular," he said. "The Mexican wrestling has also been a sounding board for political issues for poor people. El Santo fought corrupt Mexican officials in his movies and was the poor people's hero."

A wrestler from Monterrey, Mexico, named Fuego Sagrado, or Sacred Fire, lost his match the first time he wrestled in San Antonio, but he enjoyed the crowd and said the experience was similar to what is found throughout his homeland.

Wearing aqua blue tights and a yellow, orange and red mask with matching boots, Fuego Sagrado looked every bit the comic book superhero.

"I've been wrestling for five years, and everyone in Mexico grows up watching lucha libre," he said.

He declined to give his real name, saying: "It's just like showing someone my face. It's tradition and I'd have to stop wrestling if I told you my name or had my mask ripped off."

Masks are an integral part of lucha libre, Anguiano said. He wore a mask for 15 years in a career that took him to cities across Mexico and the southwestern United States. One night he suffered the humiliation of being unmasked in the ring.

"It's something no wrestler wants to experience," he said. "Outside of the ring all of the men are friends, but inside it's every man for himself. But the mask is your manhood."

On a recent sweltering Saturday night, the fans—young and old—were out in force, and the four wrestlers in the ring did not disappoint.

"Hey, what are you? A Teletubby? My sister can wrestle better than that!" shouted Simon Herrera, a fan and crowd favorite who heckles from the sidelines in Spanish.

Marisela Mello, Herrera's daughter, said she grew up watching lucha libre on Mexican television. On most Saturday nights, she can be found sitting with her father.

"It's all done in fun and it's good entertainment," said Mello, who was there to watch her husband, known as El Atrevido, or the Risk Taker, wrestle, matched with El Rayo de Texas, or the Ray of Texas, against two opponents. El Atrevido keeps his face hidden behind a purple and yellow mask. He and his teammate were hoping to demolish El Ilegal and El Bruto, or the Brute. After about 40 minutes of body slams—in and out of the ring—El Ilegal and El Bruto were declared the winners, much to the chagrin of many in the crowd, including Mello.

"It's different from w.w.f., but that's what makes it fun," Mello said. "There's a lot more tumbling and we know the wrestlers."

Injuries, Anguiano said, are rare.

"There's no closed-fist hitting, no choking or no hammer hits," he said.

The regular practices—two hours, three times a week—can be tough on the working people who suit up on weekends, but they are committed to their avocation. Martinez said he kept coming back for the entertainment and the exercise.

"This is a good thing for San Antonio," he said. "I'm really glad we're able to do it."

Two Poems about Immigrant Life

Pat Mora and Gina Valdés

Latin Americans have for many years comprised the bulk of immigrants, both legal and illegal, to the United States. While today there are relatively few parts of the country that do not have significant immigrant populations, the strength in numbers does not eliminate the many hardships faced by those seeking to adapt to a new language and culture. Below we present two poems by well-known Mexican American writers with very different takes on the clash of languages. They tell us of the difficulties of immigrant life while at the same time reminding us of the ways in which these immigrants have made U.S. culture more vibrant and diverse. Pat Mora, a native of El Paso, Texas, has taught English at all levels and has published several books of poetry, as well as memoirs and children's books. Gina Valdés was born in Los Angeles, California, and was raised on both sides of the U.S.–Mexico border. She has taught Spanish at several universities throughout the United States and has published several works of poetry and fiction.

ELENA, *by Pat Mora*

My Spanish isn't enough.
I remember how I'd smile
listening to my little ones,
understanding every word they'd say,
their jokes, their songs, their plots.
Vamos a pedirle dulces a mamá. Vamos.
But that was in Mexico.
Now my children go to American high schools.
They speak English. At night they sit around
the kitchen table, laugh with one another.
I stand by the stove and feel dumb, alone.
I bought a book to learn English.
My husband frowned, drank more beer.
My oldest said, "*Mamá*, he doesn't want you

(From Virgil Hancock, *Chihuahua: Pictures from the Edge,* photographs by Virgil Hancock, essay by Charles Bowden [Albuquerque: University of New Mexico Press, 1996]).

to be smarter than he is." I'm forty,
embarrassed at mispronouncing words,
embarrassed at the laughter of my children,
the grocer, the mailman. Sometimes I take
my English book and lock myself in the bathroom,
say the thick words softly,
for if I stop trying, I will be deaf
when my children need my help.

ENGLISH CON SALSA, *by Gina Valdés*

Welcome to ESL 100, English Surely Latinized,
inglés con chile y cilantro, English as American
as Benito Juárez. Welcome, muchachos from Xochicalco,
learn the language of dólares and dolores, of kings
and queens, of Donald Duck and Batman. Holy Toluca!
In four months you'll be speaking like George Washington,
in four weeks you can ask, More coffee? In two months

you can say, May I take your order? In one year you
can ask for a raise, cool as the Tuxpan River.

Welcome, muchachas from Teocaltiche, in this class
we speak English refrito, English con sal y limón,
English thick as mango juice, English poured from
a clay jug, English tuned like a requinto from Uruapán,
English lighted by Oaxacan dawns, English spiked
with mezcal from Juchitán, English with a red cactus
flower blooming in its heart.

Welcome, welcome, amigos del sur, bring your Zapotec
tongues, your Nahuatl tones, your patience of pyramids,
your red suns and golden moons, your guardian angels,
your duendes, your patron saints, Santa Tristeza,
Santa Alegría, Santo Todolopuede. We will sprinkle
holy water on pronouns, make the sign of the cross
on past participles, jump like fish from Lake Pátzcuaro
on gerunds, pour tequila from Jalisco on future perfects,
say shoes and shit, grab a cool verb and pollo loco
and dance on the walls like chapulines.

When a teacher from La Jolla or a cowboy from Santee
asks you, Do you speak English? You'll answer, Sí,
yes, simón, of course. I love English!
And you'll hum
a Mixtec chant that touches la tierra and the heavens.

The Deadly Harvest of the Sierra Madre

Alan Weisman

Despite occasional complaints from U.S. officials, Mexico has generally been an ally of the United States in the "war on drugs." It has, however, not always been happy with the alliance. Mexicans are quick to note that their drug problem owes its existence almost entirely to the presence of an immensely lucrative market for illegal drugs in the United States. While the often devastating consequences of drug abuse and drug-related crime will be well known to most readers, the consequences of the drug trade in Mexico will perhaps be less familiar. They include vastly increased violence, subversion of already shaky law enforcement institutions, and environmental and cultural destruction. Many Mexicans are naturally less than sympathetic toward the U.S. "war on drugs," which is weighted heavily toward eradication, interdiction, and punishment of drug offenders and which has tended in recent years to become increasingly militarized and irrational. They also tend to note the obvious fact that the war on drugs has been a monumental failure, one which has not merely failed to solve the problem, but which has made it demonstrably worse. Journalist Alan Weisman creates a harrowing portrait of the damage done by the drug trade to one of Mexico's most remote and beautiful regions, and to one of its least-known indigenous groups.

There wasn't much more the old Tarahumara Indian could do for the man taking refuge in Pino Gordo, high in Mexico's western Sierra Madre: All the medicine that grows in the Sierra couldn't reverse the damage that automatic weapons had wreaked upon 30-year-old Gumersindo Torres. Nevertheless, he entered his dream to ask his god, Onurúame, what might bring the broken young man some relief.

Presently, the One Who Is Father appeared behind his closed eyelids, looking much like Ramos himself: headband, single-thonged sandals strapped to bare legs, breechclout secured by a tasseled girdle covering his loins. Onurúame directed the old man to prepare poultices and teas of verbena and chuchufate, plants found in Pino Gordo's ancient forest, to soothe Torres' bruises and restore his tranquillity.

Tarahumara runner. (Reprinted by permission
of Fototeca del INAH, Mexico.)

Torres had come because his own ancestral village, two days away either
by foot or truck via the new logging road, was now the most dangerous place
in the Sierra. His community, Coloradas de La Virgen, lies at the edge of a
monstrous abyss in the Mexican state of Chihuahua called the Barranca Sin-
forosa, about 250 miles south of El Paso, Texas. Tarahumaras have lived and
gathered there for at least 6,000 years, but until the family of murderers who
now ruled the area could be brought to justice, no Indian in Coloradas de La
Virgen was safe.

On that chilly night in November 1992, when Torres was left for dead, two
of the killers had burst into the church where Tarahumara men and women
were swaying to the violins and drumbeats of their ritual prayer dance. First
the gunmen shot Torres' brother, the local Indian vice-governor, just as they
had slain his uncle, a commissioner, a year earlier. With Torres, who they
suspected was involved with environmental groups lately meddling in these
mountains, they took their time, blasting him in the right shoulder, then the
left, then shattering one of his hips with an AK-7.

He survived because their parting shot to his head, fired as he writhed on the floor, only creased his scalp. Afterward, unable to walk in his fields or chop firewood, Torres was taken to Pino Gordo and then given a small stipend from funds that had trickled down to the Indians through a succession of international environmental organizations. Among his objectives: to help this community resist the scourge of opium and marijuana that had poisoned his own village and whose spreading cultivation now threatened one of the continent's most crucial ecosystems and its people.

But how? The bullet holes that Torres insisted on showing me, sprinkled around his broken body by Coloradas de La Virgen's narcontraficantes, were sickening reminders of how defenseless one of Mexico's largest Indian tribes had become. For centuries, the Tarahumara, who today number 50,000, had mostly known peace and seclusion. They lived in tiny enclaves dispersed through the Sierra's labyrinthine terrain, which they bridged by becoming the world's greatest distance runners, often covering 60 miles between settlements in a single jaunt. (In their own language, the Tarahumara call themselves Rarámuri—foot runner.) Now I was hearing that many non-Indians who had invaded this precipitous country in recent years to steal the Tarahumaras' timber were also clearing their land to reap a growing harvest of pot and raw opium gum.

Indians who protested have been routinely shot, and local authorities have been either too intimidated or too implicated to protect them. Few of the mild, agrarian Tarahumara own firearms or would use them on humans if they did. Had any of their dream-healers, I asked, pressed God for a cure for the narcotic-induced death now spreading throughout the Sierra?

In fact, old Agustín Ramos told me, he had tried several times: lately, the dreaded plantíos were blossoming even around his remote Pino Gordo, among freshly charred remains of some of the oldest trees in Mexico. Each time, though, he got the same frustrating answer:

"Onurúame can't destroy plants that are also part of his creation," he said. "We will have to save ourselves from narcotráfico."

WHEN, FOR WHATEVER divine motive, Onurúame created opium poppies, enabling humans subsequently to manufacture heroin, he did so not here but in Asia. Chinese traders who settled in the town of Culiacán—today northwestern Mexico's leading cocaine distribution center—brought the first seeds during the 1930s. The vast mountain range that paralleled the Pacific coastal plains seemed a logical, virtually unpatrollable place to cultivate both the colorful flowers and another Far East import, *Cannabis sativa*—marijuana. Few human beings then realized the troubling implications, not only for Tarahumara Indians but for the Sierra itself, because no one yet understood that Mexico's Sierra Madre Occidental was the richest biosystem in North America.

Some 50 million years earlier, this region had simply exploded, spewing enormous quantities of volcanic dust into the atmosphere, which settled and metamorphosed into powdery layers of gray tuff and pink rhyolite. Then, as the shifting Pacific plate ripped Baja California away from mainland Mexico, runoff draining toward the widening trench that became the Gulf of California rapidly eroded the soft cap rock into a network of deep canyons. At the same time, huge blocks of crust were collapsing along innumerable faults as western Mexico continued to thrust upward. Eventually, all this tumult left a jumble of colossal barriers interspersed with immense chasms.

Within the myriad riches of this elaborate landscape evolved a woodland like no other. Here grow more different pines than anywhere else on earth and more than 200 oak species. Recently, biologists have realized that for sheer diversity, the western Sierra Madre surpasses even Mexico's cloud and rain forests. In pockets of human habitation, ethnobotanists have discovered an unprecedented genetic repository here: scores of heirloom strains of beans, squash, gourds, chiles, melons, herbs, medicinal plants and, especially, corn. Indian farmers instinctively had assured the success of nearly 20 distinct races of maize by cross-pollinating them with stands of teosinte, corn's prehistoric ancestor, found growing alongside their fields.

This splendid cache remained relatively isolated until 1962 when, 87 years after construction commenced, the Chihuahua al Pacífico Railroad finally succeeded in spanning the tangled Sierra Madre. The route instantly became famed for thrilling vistas of the geological complex known collectively as the Barranca del Cobre, or Copper Canyon—a system of four gorges bigger and deeper than Arizona's Grand Canyon. Bird watchers and backpackers thronged to view collared trogons and magpie jays with two-foot tails; oaks whose leaves ranged from slivers to giant, velvety lobes, and pines with drooping needles so long that Indians wove them into baskets. The fabulously picturesque Tarahumara themselves—bronzed, beautifully muscled—formed an idyllic portrait of indigenous people thriving in pristine innocence as they trotted easily up steep canyon trails, entire haystacks of corn fodder strapped to their backs.

But by 1988, when I first saw the Barranca del Cobre, the purity was becoming sullied. For two weeks, five companions and I had hiked over snow-covered rim country and descended into barrancas more than a mile deep, where green parakeets flitted through tamarind and citrus trees. When we finally reached the town of Batopilas, site of a Jesuit mission to the Tarahumara, we promptly located a restaurant. But inside we found a white-faced cook sitting with a pile of metallic blue automatic rifles heaped on his trembling knees. At one table, four men wearing reptile-skin boots and clumps of gold jewelry regarded us with silent stares, and nobody moved for the next 45 minutes while they finished eating.

The next morning, a priest whispered that the two Tarahumara families huddled in the mission chapel were hiding from these men: five Indians, he said, had just been massacred for refusing to tend illicit crops. Down river, the captain of a Mexican army patrol, his olive-drabs brightened by the addition of lizard footwear and half a pound of gold chain, reassured us that all was serene. We trudged on; a day later, four men on horseback, leading a string of well-laden mules, nodded politely but kept their weapons trained on us while we passed.

Just last Christmas, a group of Tucson naturalists I knew unwittingly strayed where they were not welcome; two of the men were pistol-whipped and one woman raped. Now I was in the Sierra Madre again, this time in the back of a four-wheel-drive Ford pickup, flanked by three Mexican federal police officers carrying Chinese-manufactured AK-47s equipped with 35-cartridge banana clips. Wedged into nylon holsters on their belts were 9-millimeter Smith & Wesson semiautomatic pistols. Our mission: to find where marijuana and opium growers were burning this precious forest to sow illegal crops, terrorizing Indians in the process.

Since Mexico's federales are famed more for collusion than combat with drug thugs, my escorts did not instill great confidence, but I had no choice. They were sent by Teresa Jardí, the new federal attorney general for the state of Chihuahua, who assured me that I was in trusted hands.

"These are fresh from the police academy. It takes a few months before the narcotraficantes contaminate them."

"And then?"

"I get rid of them and bring in another batch."

In Mexico, any attempt to accurately gauge progress in stemming the unmeasurable tonnage of drugs that flows across the border each day is effectively undermined by such systemic graft. According to recent U.S. State Department reports, drug trafficking has declined here since 1990, but locals in Chihuahua scoff at such pronouncements, pointing out that they're based on figures supplied by the Mexican government.

Just last February, Jardí, then a veteran human-rights advocate, was leading a campaign to throw the federal attorney general's office out of Chihuahua, so thoroughly polluted had it become by drug money. Then, in the wake of the drug-related slaying of the Catholic cardinal of Guadalajara, her old law school classmate and founder of Mexico's Human Rights Commission, Jorge

Carpizo, took over the country's legal system. As national attorney general, Carpizo assigned Chihuahua to Jardí: Mexico's biggest state, with 480 miles of largely unguarded border with the United States and regarded by U.S. drug-enforcement officials as a lawless void. By August, Jardí had purged more than 50 corrupt federal comandantes and district attorneys, and, she now boasted, was actually "fielding police without entire jewelry stores hanging from their necks."

A petite, graying woman in her early 50s, Jardí was especially proud that Chihuahua's jails were no longer filled with peasants and Indians coerced at gunpoint to plant contraband, then nabbed during bogus raids while the true mafiosi roamed untouched. But this past fall, the week before I arrived, her success began to wear thin. Jardí had requisitioned three helicopters from Mexico City and invited Tarahumara leaders, whose pastures lately had been filling with poppies, on a search-and-destroy mission. The pilots dutifully sprayed several small patches with defoliant. But when the Indians directed them to a field that stretched for several acres, two of the choppers fled. When Jardí ordered her pilot to continue, he landed next to the plantation's isolated headquarters and told her to discuss it with the people inside. She refused to leave the helicopter, a decision that possibly saved her life, and the poppy farm remained intact.

Back in Chihuahua City, Jardí soon discovered that she had a rat among her new police officials. She had assembled her comandantes to meet with Edwin Bustillos, director of the Consejo Asesor Sierra Madre, a nonprofit group promoting environmentally sound farming and timber practices. Bustillos, a 29-year-old mestizo agricultural engineer, grew up among the Tarahumara and credited their healers for his recovery from a near-fatal accident. Now he was trying to help them preserve their shrinking resources, but lately he found himself spending more time saving humans than trees.

It was Bustillos who took Gumersindo Torres to Pino Gordo and then collected enough testimonies from witnesses that bloody night in Coloradas de La Virgen to actually jail two gunmen, Tacho Molina and Agustín Fontes. Now, in secret meetings, he was requesting Madame Attorney General to pursue Fontes' uncle Artemio, whom he alleged to be the real strongman behind illegal logging, cattle rustling and dope growing on Indian lands around Coloradas de la Virgen, as well as the ruthless author of many murders.

The accusation surprised no one. Artemio Fontes was a well-known and well-connected cacique of the Sierra, whose powerful but reckless family had yanked themselves violently from rural poverty. During the early '80s, Artemio Fontes's brother Alejandro was named head of the Chihuahua state police, a position he enjoyed until the army shot him down in a plane stuffed with marijuana. Fontes's men often engaged in blood feuds with outsiders and frequently with each other. Each week, wealthy Fontes widows could he seen driving fine four-wheel-drive vehicles into town from the rancho to shop.

Attorney General Jardí called another meeting to examine information that Bustillos claimed linked Artemio Fontes to several Tarahumara deaths in Coloradas de la Virgen. Caciques elsewhere in the Sierra, he warned, were increasingly emboldened by Fontes's impunity. Artemio Fontes could be seen frequently in restaurants in Chihuahua City, where he now resided in an elegant neighborhood: a man with silver-flecked hair and gold-tipped boots, in the company of friends like former Chihuahua Governor Fernando Baeza. Meanwhile, three to four Tarahumara and neighboring Tepehuán Indians were being killed each week. Bustillos again had a stack of testimonies with signatures or thumbprints. Jardí was sufficiently persuaded to order a formal investigation. Someone else at this confidential gathering apparently was also impressed: a day later, gunmen shot up Bustillos's house in the Sierra.

The next day, in Chihuahua City, Bustillos met with his U.S.-based funding partner, Randall Gingrich, director of the tiny Arizona Rainforest Alliance. Gingrich, who wrote his master's thesis on deforestation in the Sierra Madre, had garnered a small chunk of USAID money administered through a coalition of World Wildlife Fund, the Nature Conservancy and the World Resources Institute, earmarked for easing biological impacts of Third World Development. But the threats to the environment listed in their proposal had not included the armed men they now could see parked outside their office.

They managed to slip away and headed for the border. Gingrich tried to convince Bustillos to lie low in Tucson awhile, but within a week he was restless and returned to Mexico. Now, seated on an ammunition box between me and the federales, he was heading off to find some flowers.

VIDAL VALENCIA HAD drunk a lot of tesgüino, the corn beer that accompanies all Tarahumara gatherings, before he finally raised his hand. The occasion was an assembly of Redondeados, his community deep in southern Chihuahua, where human-rights workers were asking whose lands had been invaded lately. Valencia wasn't sure which was more frightening: the new poppy fields he found every time one of his cows strayed, or what might happen if he reported them. But Edwin Bustillos had promised that the police now intended to help Indians, not to beat and jail them as in previous dope raids. And they knew of the risk Bustillos, a marked man, was taking to come here.

We were driving in a light rain through the wedge between the states of Durango and Sinaloa known as Chihuahua's Golden Triangle. "Pick your gold:

our richest forests or richest drug crops," Bustillos said. Severed from the rest of the state by the great canyons to the north, the region was tied closely to Culiacán, source of the weapons and South American cocaine that were luring more young local mestizos into choosing narcotráfico.

A World Bank loan recently proposed for this area, intended to make Chihuahua's timber industry more competitive, had been delayed by international protests when road building began before required environmental assessments were made. Bustillos, originally hired by the Mexican government's regional manager of a World Bank-funded forestry-development program, was one of the critics, because new roads would enter virgin Indian lands. Now, after two slapdash impact studies were successfully challenged, the World Bank was ready to resume disbursements, as soon as Mexico came up with its matching portion, $48 million. Besides the predicted habitat damage and erosion from increased logging, Bustillos feared that better roads would be a gift to narcotraficantes, currently bulldozing their way into places once never imagined.

Mexico, however, was in enough debt already and not inclined just yet to turn these primitive Sierra lumber trails into passable highways. The fractured bedrock and slick rhyolite clays we were bouncing over had already eaten one of the police vehicles, a Chevy Suburban van, that was supposed to take us up to Vidal Valencia's mountain pastures. A backup four-wheel-drive pickup had arrived from headquarters in Parral, Chihuahua, 10 hours away, without a spare tire. His budget was so thin, Comandante Serafin Cocones of the narcotics squad told us, that it wasn't just tires: he and four men had to buy their own ammunition.

Now we were following a borrowed Datsun with a cracked chassis, crammed with Tarahumaras, as well as a contingent of five municipal police armed with hunting rifles and ornate pistols, whom Cocones had mustered that morning simply for more firepower. Since most local police are assumed to augment their $200 monthly salaries with narcotráfico themselves, there was some question as to which way they might aim in the event of a shootout. "What choice is there?" Cocones lamented. "If someone really wants to defend these plants, we'll need 50 men against their weapons."

The road dissolved into a giant gully. We continued into the forest on foot, which made the Tarahumaras much happier. I half-walked, half-ran to keep up with Vidal, a thin, taciturn man in a red plaid shirt, and his 80-year-old cousin, Tirso Téllez, who leaped over outcroppings and scrambled up mountain arroyos where we stopped to drink from streams and catch our breath. These men had grown up playing rarajípari, Tarahumara kick-ball, over courses that sometimes stretched 50 miles. Their great-uncle Tibursio, Téllez told me, once ran the 110-mile round trip to Culiacán to deliver a message the day before an important match and returned in time to pace his team to victory.

Above us, thick-billed parrots frisked through the Chihuahua pines, showering us with droplets that hung from the elongated needles. We heard the triple hoot of a Mexican spotted owl but saw no mammals except for the flash of a white-tailed deer's rump. The last grizzlies were killed here some years ago, but, Téllez was telling me, jaguar, and Mexican gray wolves still stalk this pine-oak-juniper maze. Suddenly, Vidal stopped and pointed. At his feet was a steaming pile of fresh dung, surrounded by mule-shoe prints. Instantly, Comandante Cocones motioned for the police to fan out.

They spread across the hills, running silently along the ridges. The rest of us crept behind Cocones, scanning the perimeter and treetops for snipers. We inched forward and listened. Nothing. Finally we crested a small rise and looked down. Even the Indians gasped.

Below us, a swath of miraculous color burst from the dark green forest: pinks segueing to purples, pale lavenders, bright crimsons—big papery flowers that intermixed nearly the entire blue-red spectrum, fluttering on waist-high stalks. To see a field of poppies such as these is to begin to grasp the irresistible, addictive nature of opium. These plants did not belong here, and their presence signified great danger. But for a few moments everyone simply gazed at their beauty, so soft and seductive, like lotus blossoms floating atop the blood and violence.

We had found roughly an acre of blooms surrounded by three strands of new barbed wire, in a clearing of downed trees that had been burned. A ragged shirt and a pair of old jeans tied to a stick served as a scarecrow. There was a moment of confusion: The federales had forgotten wire cutters, but I had a pair on my utility knife. As the fence tumbled, the police and the Tarahumaras picked up sticks and began whacking the olive-green stems.

Whoever tended this field evidently had just departed, because the round bulbs left on plants that had already dropped their petals had been freshly scored. One of the local police, looking a little bereaved, showed me how to cut and squeeze the bulb until milky white syrup bubbled out every drop of which harvesters collected in vials made from battery casings, where it coagulates into brown gum. In Parral, he said, the goma brings 10,000 pesos per gram: slightly more than $3.

Resting that afternoon on a log in the 10th field Vidal showed us, while the police built a bonfire of 200 pounds of marijuana they'd also discovered growing there, Bustillos and I did some calculating. About 10 poppy bulbs yield a gram of opium gum, and a bulb can be milked from three to 10 times. Bustillos, who had paced the boundaries of each plantío, reckoned that we'd destroyed about 12 acres. Figuring 10 bulbs per square yard, that represented at least 150,000 grams of opium gum, worth $450,000 at its crudest stage.

About 10 grams of opium gum produce a single gram of heroin, which brings anywhere from $80 to $500 in the United States, depending on the city. In a few hours, I realized, we had removed millions of dollars' worth of untaxed goods from the market, plus at least another hundred grand for the pot now going up in flames. No matter at what point in the processing and shipping Artemio Fontes took his cut, I guessed that he would be upset, because we had just relieved him of a small fortune.

"These plants don't belong to Fontes. He's from over there," Bustillos replied, pointing northwest toward Coloradas de la Virgen.

"Whose then?"

He shrugged his thin shoulders. "Who knows? There are so many growers now."

Behind us, the Sierra Madre dropped into Arroyo Hondo, a minor canyon compared to the barrancas to the north, but sufficiently vast to convey the impression that no one could ever eradicate dope cultivation here.

"Frankly," Bustillos said, "I don't care if they do. I just want growers to stay out of the last hidden sanctuaries and stop bothering the Indians who know how to care for them."

"But they choose those places because growing dope is illegal. How can you keep them out?"

"Simple. Legalize it."

BEFORE WE LEFT, I asked Vidal Valencia, who now looked a little worried, what the Tarahumaras thought of legalization. After rephrasing the question twice, I let it drop: The concept of plants being unlawful was alien to him. All he knew was that, despite the Mexican constitution that recognizes Indians' rights to defend their land, someone was going to be mad about this. "When the police go, they could grab us," he observed.

For the next two days, we struggled up 40 miles of atrocious roads toward Pino Gordo, where Teresa Jardí and another helicopter were meeting us for more raids. At times we passed through deforested stretches where loggers had taken the best pines; without sufficient cover, the smaller trees left for seed stock had dried up. At lumber mills, we saw Tarahumaras working the worst jobs, hauling sawdust and dragging huge trunks to the blade. Supposedly, Bustillos's funding was designated to help Indians gain control of and properly manage wood resources that were legally theirs, but the fallout of drugs had become a constant distraction. In every village, we heard of shootings.

The road rose through spruce and aspen, then traversed hairpin ledges where waterfalls gushed between enormous boulders. We were nearing Pino Gordo, which has the largest stand of old-growth forest left in the Sierra Madre. Comandante Cocones grew edgy because of a rumored 5-million-peso ($1,600) bounty on policemen in the area. In the valley below was Coloradas de los Chávez: Some members of the extended Chávez family were reputed to be as charming as the Fontes. Last year, the Tarahumaras of Pino Gordo had found their first marijuana plantation. By this spring there were nine, and by autumn, 17. Armed men from Coloradas de los Chávez were appearing in Pino Gordo, offering money and corn in exchange for labor in the plantíos. They arrived over the same new road we were traveling, illegally opened by loggers, and made it plain that they were coming in with or without the Tarahumaras' cooperation.

In the past, it wasn't unknown for a Tarahumara to agree to plant a little pot in exchange for food or a few pesos, but with people dying and large chunks of their forest disappearing, the situation was now getting out of control. That afternoon, the men and women of Pino Gordo gathered at the log cabin schoolhouse. They hoped to see Bustillos and the federal attorney and police who promised to help rid them of narco-terror but by then we were long gone. Teresa Jardí and the helicopter had never appeared. Later I learned that, despite her livid denunciation of the pilots she had recently flown with, she had been sent the same crew again. Without air support, Cocones refused to destroy any plantíos here.

"There's only one road," he said. "Without air cover to get us out of here, they can roll a tree trunk or boulder across one of those ledges, then pick us off like pigeons."

To raid Pino Gordo properly, Cocones added, would require 100 men on the ground and 20 giving air support. It would take a week here, with tents and sleeping bags—things he didn't have. There was no budget. Cocones, with a plastic right shoulder joint as a memento of his last drug shoot-out, was getting no argument from his green troops. "I'll try to return with reinforcements," he told the Tarahumaras.

Yet if he did, I realized, these Indians would then be sitting ducks, and Pino Gordo would become another Coloradas de la Virgen. Cocones couldn't refute this. "Then how can you ever stop the killing?" I asked.

"Easy," he said. "Legalize drugs. They'll lose so much value that they won't be worth killing for." He snapped open the folding stock of his Galil. "It's the only way. Instead of public safety, we have shootings. We shoot one narco-traficante and another steps into his place. Instead of prevention and reha-bilitation, our budget goes into uprooting plants. And they just keep planting more."

I had heard this proposal a few years earlier; in Colombia, where so many people were dying that the government in Bogotá openly contemplated de-criminalizing drugs simply to halt carnage. The United States warned that such a move would put diplomatic relations at risk. Since then, however, Americans such as former Secretary of State George P. Shultz, columnist William F. Buckley Jr., economist Milton Friedman, several federal judges, the mayor of Baltimore and, most recently, U.S. Surgeon General Joycelyn Elders have argued that too much time, money and blood are being wasted in a futile war on drugs. Legalization advocates cite the example of Holland to show that decriminalization doesn't cause a surge in addiction, any more than ending Prohibition here increased alcoholism, and that drug-related crime actually drops. The potential tax revenues from legal drugs could help pay for a massive national drug education program, to say nothing of reallocation of the United States' current $8.3-billion drug-enforcement budget.

U.S. Drug Enforcement Administration officials counter that legalization would fill our highways and workplaces with stoned drivers and employees and needlessly jeopardize the mental and physical health of future generations of productive citizens. The DEA also denies that the war on drugs is hopeless, citing Department of Health and Human Services figures showing that usage in fact is declining. When I inquired about the source of these figures, however, I learned that they are derived from door-to-door samplings of households, a seemingly dubious measure of illegal activity. An HHS statistician defended the method, which uses an anonymous questionnaire, but admitted that the polls were probably worthless in monitoring heroin abuse, which even the DEA admits is rising.

For or against, none of these arguments mention the human sorrow and ecological loss being wreaked upon neighbors beyond our borders. I decided to ask Artemio Fontes, whose number I found in the Chihuahua City directory, what he thought. After several tries, one of his bodyguards told me that, "Señor Fontes says anything you want to know about him, ask the attorney general. She seems to have all the facts." This apparently didn't trouble Fontes: weeks later, a 64-page file Jardí submitted to a panel of judges, charging Fontes with both homicide and drug trafficking, failed to produce a warrant for his arrest.

"They tell me they are very behind," Jardí explained. How long? "Months. Maybe a year. Who knows?"

I took a taxi to Fontes's house. The watchman said he was out. Standing there, I realized that Artemio Fontes certainly wouldn't want drugs legalized if in fact their value, bloated by virtue of being forbidden, had afforded him this agglomeration of carved wooden doors and shiny white brick, surrounded by rosebushes and iron bars.

ON MY LAST DAY in the Sierra, I accompanied Edwin Bustillos to his home village, Guachochi, where he broadcasts a weekly radio show in four dialects to educate Indians about their rights and their priceless environment, encouraging them to unite against unscrupulous lumber caciques and narcotraficantes. He was pleased, he told me, because he had obtained from witnesses the license number of the truck whose occupants had fired at his house, which he was passing along to Teresa Jardí.

We walked outside. The truck with offending license plate, from the state of Sinaloa, was parked next to his car.

"We better get out of here," Bustillos sighed.

Two Songs about Drug Smuggling

Salomé Gutiérrez and Paulino Vargas

A number of factors have operated to convert smugglers into Mexican and borderlands heroes. The illegality of such enterprises has meant fabulous profits for people willing to take big risks. The lure of wealth and danger is widely celebrated in the macho culture of Mexico and the border. Add to that a measure of nationalistic resentment of the United States and its border patrols, the practice of modest philanthropy on the part of successful smugglers, and a long tradition of venerating bandits and rebels—many of whom struck a blow against the corrupt and violent Mexican police and their counterparts, "los Rinches" (the heavy-handed Anglo-Texan, New Mexican, and Arizona Rangers)—and you have the makings of a "contrabandista" culture. Smuggling even has its own "holy city," Culiacán, Sinaloa, whose souvenir shops sell items glorifying smugglers and drug lords as romantic outlaws, and its own patron saint, Jesús Malverde, a bandit who, according to lore, stole from the rich and gave to the poor, and was hanged in 1909. Ordinary folks come to pay homage at his shrine in Culiacán, while drug smugglers offer him thanks for successful shipments.

Below we translate a pair of songs that deal with the topic of drug smuggling on the border. The first, "El Gato Negro," was written by Salomé Gutiérrez and made famous by San Antonio–based Rubén Ramos and his band, the Texas Revolution. The second, "La Banda del Carro Rojo," was composed by Paulino Vargas and performed most famously by the duo Los Alegres de Terán.

EL GATO NEGRO

They call me the Black Cat,
all the lawmen are searching for me.
They say I'm dangerous,
a soul-less criminal.

Since I was very young
I've devoted myself to vices,
I know every kind of evil.

I know all the traffickers and criminals
of the region.

From the mountains of Chihuahua,
with a white cargo I would travel.
I would cross through the customs stations
right between the sheriffs' whiskers.

With whole cargoes of pot
I would go to Chicago and New York.
Several times, my luck ran out and
I landed in prison.

Over in Laredo the sheriffs set up
an ambush; I split for Alice,
shooting northward,
I didn't even fear death.

I passed through San Antonio by night
arriving at Houston, I don't know why.
The patrolmen had been advised
and I just escaped capture.

Terrible jail at Kansas City,
Famous jail of San Quentin.
From the new jail in San Antonio
I left from the fifth floor.

The Black Cat doesn't say good-bye,
he just disappears.
When you see me all in black,
with dark eyes, you'll know that's me.

THE RED CAR GANG

They say they came from the south
in a red car;
they were carrying 100 kilos of cocaine,
they were on their way to Chicago.
So said the informer
who had turned them in.

They'd already passed through customs,
the one at El Paso.
But in Las Cruces the cops
were waiting for them.
They were the Texas Rangers
who ran that county.

A siren wailed and the sergeant shouted
that they must stop the car
so it could be registered,
and not to resist
because if they did they'd be killed.

An M-16 roared
as it opened fire,
and the light from a patrol-car
circled through the air.
So began the battle
where the great massacre took place.

Lino Quintana told them:
"This had to happen.
My companions are dead,
now they won't be able to talk;
and I'm sorry, sheriffs,
I don't know how to sing."

Only the crosses remained
of the seven who died;
four were from the red car,
the other three from the government.
Don't worry about them,
they'll all go to hell with Lino.

Some say they came from Cantín,
others say they were from Altar,
a few even say they were from Parral.
The truth was never known,
for no one came to claim them.

The New World Border

Guillermo Gómez-Peña

Performance artist Guillermo Gómez-Peña adds a critical yet exuberant voice to any discussion of the border and its meanings. Born in Mexico City in 1955, he first came to the United States in 1978 and he has been crossing, challenging, and pondering physical, cultural, and linguistic borders ever since. Gómez-Peña believes his calling is to "live smack in the fissure between two worlds," and the complexities of "cultural otherness" have long been his principal preoccupation. Through his writings and performances, he invites us to think expansively about the border and the question of identity. In the "New World Border" and "The Border Is (A Manifesto)," the border is not simply a geographical place, nor is identity readily reducible to questions of racial or national traits. Rather, the border becomes a contentious, interactive, almost mystical concept, and identity an intoxicating cultural cocktail. Gómez-Peña would agree with William Langewiesche that the border "looks like the future;" but for him, it seems, the future is as exciting as it is frightening.

The New World Border

I am a migrant performance artist. I write in airplanes, trains, and cafés. I travel from city to city, coast to coast, country to country, smuggling my work and the work and ideas of my colleagues. I collaborate with artists and writers from various communities and disciplines. We connect with groups who think like us, and debate with others who disagree. And then I carry the ideas elsewhere. Home is always somewhere else. Home is both "here" and "there" or somewhere in between. Sometimes it's nowhere.

I make art about the misunderstandings that take place at the border zone. But for me, the border is no longer located at any fixed geopolitical site. I carry the border with me, and I find new borders wherever I go.

I travel across a different America. My America is a continent (not a country) that is not described by the outlines on any of the standard maps. In my America, "West" and "North" are mere nostalgic abstractions—the South and the East have slipped into their mythical space. For example, Quebec seems closer to Latin America than to its Anglophone twin. My America includes different peoples, cities, borders, and nations. For instance, the Indian nations of Canada and the United States, and also the multiracial neighborhoods in the larger cities all seem more like Third World micro-republics than like communities that are part of some "western democracy." Today, the phrase "western democracy" seems hollow and quaint.

When I am on the East Coast of the United States, I am also in Europe, Africa, and the Caribbean. There, I like to visit Nuyo Rico, Cuba York, and other micro-republics. When I return to the U.S. Southwest, I am suddenly back in Mexamerica, a vast conceptual nation that also includes the northern states of Mexico, and overlaps with various Indian nations. When I visit Los Angeles or San Francisco, I am at the same time in Latin America and Asia. Los Angeles, like Mexico City, Tijuana, Miami, Chicago, and New York, is practically a hybrid nation/city in itself. Mysterious underground railroads connect all these places — syncretic art forms, polyglot poetry and music, and transnational pop cultures function as meridians of thought and axes of communication.

Here/there, the indigenous and the immigrant share the same space but are foreigners to each other. Here/there we are all potential border-crossers and cultural exiles. We have all been uprooted to different degrees, and for different reasons, but not everyone is aware of it. Here/there, homelessness, border culture, and deterritorialization are the dominant experience, not just fancy academic theories.

The Fourth World & Other Utopian Cartographies

The work of the artist is to force open the matrix of reality to introduce unsuspected possibilities. Artists and writers are currently involved in the redefinition of our continental topography. We see through the colonial map of North, Central, and South America, to a more complex system of overlapping, interlocking, and overlaid maps. Among others, we can see Amerindia, Afroamerica, Americamestiza-y-mulata, Hybridamerica, and Transamerica — the "other America" that belongs to the homeless, and to nomads, migrants, and exiles. We try to imagine more enlightened cartographies: a map of the Americas with no borders; a map turned upside down; or one in which the countries have borders that are organically drawn by geography, culture, and immigration, and not by the capricious hands of economic domination and political bravado.

Personally, I oppose the outdated fragmentation of the standard map of America with the conceptual map of Arte-America — a continent made of people, art, and ideas, not countries. When I perform, this map becomes my conceptual stage. Though no one needs a passport to enter my performance continent, the audience is asked to swallow their fears and to question any ethnocentric assumptions they might have about otherness, Mexico, Mexicans, other languages, and alternative art forms.

I oppose the sinister cartography of the New World Order with the conceptual map of the New World Border—a great trans- and intercontinental border zone, a place in which no centers remain. It's all margins, meaning there are no "others," or better said, the only true "others" are those who resist fusion, *mestizaje,* and crosscultural dialogue. In this utopian cartography, hybridity is the dominant culture; Spanglish, Franglé, and Gringoñol are the *linguas francas;* and monoculture is a culture of resistance practiced by a stubborn or scared minority.

I also oppose the old colonial dichotomy of First World/Third World with the more pertinent notion of the Fourth World—a conceptual place where the indigenous peoples meet with the diasporic communities. In the Fourth World, there is very little place for static identities, fixed nationalities, "pure" languages, or sacred cultural traditions. The members of the Fourth World live between and across various cultures, communities, and countries. And our identities are constantly being reshaped by this kaleidoscopic experience. The artists and writers who inhabit the Fourth World have a very important role: to elaborate the new set of myths, metaphors, and symbols that will locate us within all of these fluctuating cartographies.

The Free Trade Agreement

The North American Free Trade Agreement (NAFTA), signed by Canada, the United States, and Mexico, has created the largest artificial economic community of the planet. In terms of geography and demographics, it is much larger than the European Union or the Pacific Rim. Sadly, out of all the possible trade agreements that could have been designed, the "neoliberal" version is not exactly an enlightened one. It is based on the arrogant fallacy that "the market" will solve any and all problems, and it avoids the most basic social, labor, environmental, and cultural responsibilities that are actually the core of any relationship between the three countries.

Many burning questions remain unanswered: Given the endemic lack of political and economic symmetry between the three participating countries, will Mexico become a mega-*maquiladora* [assembly plant] or, as Chicana artist Yareli Arismendi has stated, "the largest Indian reservation of the United States," or will it be treated as an equal by its bigger partners? Will the predatory Statue of Liberty devour the contemplative Virgin of Guadalupe, or will they merely dance a sweaty *quebradita*? Will Mexico become a toxic and cultural waste dump for its northern partners? Given the exponential increase of American trash- and media-culture in Mexico, what will happen to our indigenous traditions, our social and cultural rituals, our language, and national psyche? Will Mexico's future generations become hyphenated Mexican-Americans, brown-skinned gringos, or Canochis (upside-down Chicanos)? And what about our Anglo partners? Will they slowly become Chicanadians, Waspbacks, Gringotlanis, and Anglomalans?

Whatever the answers are, NAFTA will profoundly affect our lives in many ways. Whether we like it or not, a new era has begun, and a new economic and cultural topography has been designed for us. We must now find our new place and role within this bizarre Federation of U.S. Republics.

The Free Trade Art Agreement

Artists are talking about the need to create a structure parallel to NAFTA—a kind of Free Art Agreement—for the exchange of ideas and noncommercial artwork, not just consumer goods and hollow dreams. If formed, the task of this network of thinkers, artists, and arts organizations from Mexico, the United States, and Canada (and why not the Caribbean?) would be to develop models of cross-cultural dialogue and interdisciplinary artistic collaboration. Through multilingual publications, radio, film, video, and performance collaborations, more complex and mutable notions of "North America" cultures and identities could be conceived. . . .

The Hybrid

An ability to understand the hybrid nature of culture develops from an experience of dealing with a dominant culture from the outside. The artist who understands and practices hybridity in this way can be at the same time an insider and an outsider, an expert in border crossings, a temporary member of multiple communities, a citizen of two or more nations. S/he performs multiple roles in multiple contexts. At times s/he can operate as cross-cultural diplomat, as an intellectual *coyote* (smuggler of ideas) or a media pirate. At other times, s/he assumes the role of nomadic chronicler, intercultural translator, or political trickster. S/he speaks from more than one perspective, to more than one community, about more than one reality. His/her job is to trespass, bridge, interconnect, reinterpret, remap, and redefine; to find the outer limits of his/her culture and cross them.

The presence of the hybrid denounces the faults, prejudices, and fears manufactured by the self-proclaimed center, and threatens the very raison d'etre of any monoculture, official or not. It reminds us that we are not the product of just one culture; that we have multiple and transitional identities; that we contain a multiplicity of voices and selves, some of which may even be contradictory. And it tells us that there is nothing wrong with contradiction. . . .

THE BORDER IS . . . (A MANIFESTO)

Border Culture is a polysemantic term.

Stepping outside of one's culture is equivalent to walking outside of the law.

Border culture means boycott, complot, ilegalidad, clandestinidad, contrabando, transgresión, desobediencia binacional: en otras palabras, to smuggle dangerous poetry and utopian visions from one culture to another, desde allá, hasta acá.

But it also means to maintain one's dignity outside the law.

But it also means hybrid art forms for new contents-in-gestation: spray mural, techno-altar, poetry-in-tongues, audio graffiti, punkarachi, video corrido, anti-bolero, anti-todo: la migra (border patrol), art world, police, monocultura; en otras palabras y tierras, an art against the monolingües, tapados, nacionalistas. . . .

But it also means to be fluid in English, Spanish, Spanglish, and Ingleñol, 'cause Spanglish is the language of border diplomacy.

But it also means transcultural friendship and collaboration among races, sexes, and generations.

But it also means to practice creative appropriation, expropriation, and subversion of dominant cultural forms.

But it also means a new cartography; a brand-new map to host the new project; the democratization of the East; the socialization of the West; the Third-Worldization of the North and the First-Worldization of the South.

But it also means a multiplicity of voices away from the center, different geo-cultural relations among more culturally akin regions: Tepito–San Diejuana, San Pancho–Nuyorrico, Miami–Quebec, San Antonio–Berlin, your home town and mine, digamos, a new internationalism ex centris.

But is also means regresar y volver a partir: to return and depart once again, 'cause border culture is a Sisyphean experience and to arrive is just an illusion.

But it also means a new terminology for new hybrid identities and métiers constantly metamorphosing; sudacá, not sudaca; Chicarrican, not Hispanic;

mestizaje, not miscegenation; social thinker, not bohemian; accionista, not performer; intercultural, not postmodern.

But it also means to develop new models to interpret the world-in-crisis, the only world we know.

But it also means to push the borders of countries and languages or, better said, to find new languages to express the fluctuating borders.

But it also means experimenting with the fringes between art and society, legalidad and illegality, English and español, male and female, North and South, self and other; and subverting these relationships.

But it also means to speak from the crevasse, desde acá, desde el medio. The border is the juncture, not the edge, and monoculturalism has been expelled to the margins.

But it also means glasnost, not government censorship, for censorship is the opposite of border culture.

But it also means to analyze critically all that lies on the current table of debates: multiculturalism, the Latino "boom," "ethnic art," controversial art, even border culture.

But it also means to question and transgress border culture. What today is powerful and necessary, tomorrow is arcane and ridiculous; what today is border culture, tomorrow is institutional art, not vice versa.

But it also means to escape the current co-optation of border culture.

But it also means to look at the past and the future at the same time. 1492 was the beginning of a genocidal era. 1992 will mark the beginning of a new era: America post-Colombina, Arteamérica sin fronteras. Soon, a new internationalism will have to gravitate around the spinal cord of this continent — not Europe, not just the North, not just white, not only you, compañero del otro lado de la frontera, el lenguaje y el océano.

Suggestions for Further Reading

*There is a vast amount of good writing on Mexico in several languages. Our inten-
tion here is merely to suggest some important works in English that engage the major
themes of this volume. Where an English translation exists for works that were initially published in Spanish, we have listed it, though we encourage those who can to
go to the original. Several of the works below pertain to more than one heading. We
have also included a section featuring a variety of excellent Web sites where readers
may explore Mexican historical themes and current affairs.*

I. The Search for "Lo Mexicano"

Fuentes, Carlos. *The Buried Mirror: Reflections on Spain and the New World.* Boston: Hough-
ton Mifflin, 1992.

Gutmann, Matthew C. *The Meanings of Macho: Being a Man in Mexico City.* Berkeley:
University of California Press, 1996.

Lomnitz-Adler, Claudio. *Exits from the Labyrinth: Culture and Ideology in the Mexican
National Space.* Berkeley: University of California Press, 1992.

———. *Deep Mexico, Silent Mexico: An Anthropology of Nationalism.* Minneapolis: University of Minnesota Press, 2001.

Monsiváis, Carlos. *Mexican Postcards.* Edited and translated by John Kraniauskas. London:
Verso, 1997.

Paz, Octavio. *The Other Mexico: Critique of the Pyramid.* Translated by Lysander Kemp.
New York: Grove Press, 1972.

Ramos, Samuel. *Profile of Man and Culture in Mexico.* Translated by Peter G. Earle. Austin:
University of Texas Press, 1962.

Simpson, Lesley Byrd. *Many Mexicos.* 4th ed. rev. Berkeley: University of California Press,
1966.

II. Ancient Civilizations

Adams, Richard E. W. *Prehistoric Mesoamerica.* Rev. ed. Norman: University of Oklahoma
Press, 1991.

Aveni, Anthony F. *Skywatchers.* Austin: University of Texas Press, 2001.

Carrasco, David. *Religions of Mesoamerica: Cosmovision and Ceremonial Centers.* San Francisco: Harper and Row, 1990.

Clendinnen, Inga. *Aztecs: An Interpretation*. New York: Cambridge University Press, 1993.

Coe, Michael D. *The Maya*. 6th ed. New York: Thames and Hudson, 1999.

Freidel, David, Linda Schele, and Joy Parker. *Maya Cosmos: Three Thousand Years on the Shaman's Path*. Photographs by Justin Kerr and MacDuff Everton. New York: Morrow, 1993.

Hassig, Ross. *Aztec Warfare: Imperial Expansion and Political Control*. Norman: University of Oklahoma Press, 1988.

———. *War and Society in Ancient Mesoamerica*. Berkeley: University of California Press, 1992.

Schele, Linda, and David Freidel. *A Forest of Kings: The Untold Story of the Ancient Maya*. Color photographs by Justin Kerr. New York: Morrow, 1990.

Schele, Linda, Mary Ellen Miller, and Justin Kerr. *The Blood of Kings: Dynasty and Ritual in Maya Art*. Photographs by Justin Kerr. Fort Worth, Texas: Kimball Art Museum, 1986.

III. Conquest and Colony

Brading, David A. *The First America: The Spanish Monarchy, Creole Patriots, and the Liberal State, 1492–1867*. Cambridge: Cambridge University Press, 1991.

Chevalier, François. *Land and Society in Colonial Mexico: The Great Hacienda*. Edited by Lesley Byrd Simpson, translated by Alvin Eustis. Berkeley: University of California Press, 1963.

Clendinnen, Inga. *Ambivalent Conquests: Maya and Spaniard in Yucatán, 1517–1570*. Cambridge: Cambridge University Press, 1987.

Farriss, Nancy M. *Maya Society under Colonial Rule: The Collective Enterprise of Survival*. Princeton: Princeton University Press, 1984.

Florescano, Enrique. *Memory, Myth, and Time in Mexico: From the Aztecs to Independence*. Translated by Albert G. Bork with the assistance of Kathryn R. Bork. Austin: University of Texas Press, 1994.

Gibson, Charles. *The Aztecs under Spanish Rule*. Stanford, Calif.: Stanford University Press, 1964.

Gruzinski, Serge. *Man-Gods in the Mexican Highlands: Indian Power and Colonial Society, 1550–1800*. Translated by Eileen Corrigan. Stanford, Calif.: Stanford University Press, 1989.

Lockhart, James. *The Nahuas after the Conquest: A Social and Cultural History of the Indians of Central Mexico, Sixteenth through Eighteenth Centuries*. Stanford, Calif.: Stanford University Press, 1992.

Stern, Steve J. *The Secret History of Gender: Women, Men, and Power in Late Colonial Mexico*. Chapel Hill: University of North Carolina Press, 1995.

Taylor, William B. *Drinking, Homicide, and Rebellion in Colonial Mexican Villages*. Stanford, Calif.: Stanford University Press, 1979.

———. *Magistrates of the Sacred: Priests and Parishioners in Eighteenth-Century Mexico*. Stanford, Calif.: Stanford University Press, 1996.

Thomas, Hugh. *Conquest: Montezuma, Cortés, and the Fall of Old Mexico*. New York: Simon and Schuster, 1993.

IV. Trials of the Young Republic

Anna, Timothy E. *Forging Mexico: 1821–1835.* Lincoln: University of Nebraska Press, 1998.

Beezley, William H. *Judas at the Jockey Club and Other Episodes of Porfirian Mexico.* Lincoln: University of Nebraska Press, 1987.

Hale, Charles A. *Mexican Liberalism in the Age of Mora, 1821–1853.* New Haven, Conn.: Yale University Press, 1968.

————. *The Transformation of Liberalism in Late Nineteenth-Century Mexico.* Princeton, N.J.: Princeton University Press, 1989.

Mallon, Florencia E. *Peasant and Nation: The Making of Postcolonial Mexico and Peru.* Berkeley: University of California Press, 1995.

Reed, Nelson A. *The Caste War of Yucatán.* Rev. ed. Stanford, Calif.: Stanford University Press, 2001.

Sierra, Justo. *The Political Evolution of the Mexican People.* With Notes and a new introduction by Edmundo O'Gorman, prologue by Alfonso Reyes, translated by Charles Ramsdell. Austin: University of Texas Press, 1969.

Tenorio-Trillo, Mauricio. *Mexico at the World's Fairs: Crafting a Modern Nation.* Berkeley: University of California Press, 1996.

Tutino, John. *From Insurrection to Revolution in Mexico: Social Bases of Agrarian Violence, 1750–1940.* Princeton, N.J.: Princeton University Press, 1986.

Van Young, Eric. *The Other Rebellion: Popular Violence, Ideology, and the Mexican Struggle for Independence, 1810–1821.* Stanford, Calif.: Stanford University Press, 2001.

Vanderwood, Paul J. *The Power of God against the Guns of Government: Religious Upheaval in Mexico at the Turn of the Nineteenth Century.* Stanford, Calif.: Stanford University Press, 1998.

Wasserman, Mark. *Everyday Life and Politics in Nineteenth-Century Mexico: Men, Women, and War.* Albuquerque: University of New Mexico Press, 2000.

Wells, Allen, and Gilbert M. Joseph. *Summer of Discontent, Seasons of Upheaval: Elite Politics and Rural Insurgency in Yucatán, 1876–1915.* Stanford, Calif.: Stanford University Press, 1996.

V. Revolution

Benjamin, Thomas. *La Revolución: Mexico's Great Revolution as Memory, Myth, and History.* Austin: University of Texas Press, 2000.

Brading, D. A., ed. *Caudillo and Peasant in the Mexican Revolution.* New York: Cambridge University Press, 1980.

Folgarait, Leonard. *Mural Painting and Social Revolution in Mexico, 1920–1940: Art of the New Order.* Cambridge: Cambridge University Press, 1998.

Gilly, Adolfo. *The Mexican Revolution.* Translated by Patrick Camiller. Exp. and rev. ed. London: Verso Editions, 1983.

González y González, Luis. *San José de Gracia: Mexican Village in Transition.* Translated by John Upton. Austin: University of Texas Press, 1974.

Hart, John M. *Revolutionary Mexico: The Coming and Process of the Mexican Revolution.* 10th anniversary ed. Berkeley: University of California Press, 1997.

Henderson, Timothy J. *The Worm in the Wheat: Rosalie Evans and Agrarian Struggle in the Puebla-Tlaxcala Valley of Mexico, 1906–1927.* Durham, N.C.: Duke University Press, 1998.

Joseph, Gilbert M. *Revolution from Without: Yucatán, Mexico, and the United States, 1880–1924.* Rev. ed. Durham, N.C.: Duke University Press, 1988.

Joseph, Gilbert M., and Daniel Nugent, eds. *Everyday Forms of State Formation: Revolution and the Negotiation of Rule in Modern Mexico.* Durham, N.C.: Duke University Press, 1994.

Katz, Friedrich. *The Secret War in Mexico: Europe, the United States, and the Mexican Revolution.* With portions translated by Loren Goldner. Chicago: University of Chicago Press, 1981.

———. *The Life and Times of Pancho Villa.* Stanford, Calif.: Stanford University Press, 1998.

Knight, Alan. *The Mexican Revolution.* 2 vols. Cambridge: Cambridge University Press, 1986.

Meyer, Jean A. *The Cristero Rebellion: The Mexican People between Church and State.* Translated by Richard Southern. Cambridge: Cambridge University Press, 1976.

Vaughan, Mary Kay. *Cultural Politics in Revolution: Teachers, Peasants, and Schools in Mexico, 1930–1940.* Tucson: University of Arizona Press, 1997.

Womack, John Jr. *Zapata and the Mexican Revolution.* New York: Knopf, 1969.

VI. The Perils of Modernity

Centeno, Miguel Angel. *Democracy within Reason: Technocratic Revolution in Mexico.* University Park: Pennsylvania State University Press, 1994.

Davis, Diane E. *Urban Leviathan: Mexico City in the Twentieth Century.* Philadelphia: Temple University Press, 1994.

Fowler-Salamini, Heather, and Mary Kay Vaughan, eds. *Women of the Mexican Countryside, 1850–1990: Creating Spaces, Shaping Transitions.* Tucson: University of Arizona Press, 1994.

Krauze, Enrique. *Mexico, Biography of Power: A History of Mexico, 1810–1996.* Translated by Hank Heifetz. New York: HarperCollins, 1997.

Lewis, Oscar. *Five Families: Mexican Case Studies in the Culture of Poverty.* New York: Science Editions, 1962.

Middlebrook, Kevin J. *The Paradox of Revolution: Labor, the State, and Authoritarianism in Mexico.* Baltimore: Johns Hopkins University Press, 1995.

Simonian, Lane. *Defending the Land of the Jaguar: A History of Conservation in Mexico.* Austin: University of Texas Press, 1995.

Smith, Peter H. *Labyrinths of Power: Political Recruitment in Twentieth-Century Mexico.* Princeton, N.J.: Princeton University Press, 1979.

Warman, Arturo. *"We Come to Object": The Peasants of Morelos and the National State.* Translated by Stephen K. Ault. Baltimore: Johns Hopkins University Press, 1980.

VII. From the Ruins

Harvey, Neil. *The Chiapas Rebellion: The Struggle for Land and Democracy.* Durham, N.C.: Duke University Press, 1998.

Joseph, Gilbert M., Anne Rubenstein, and Eric Zolov, eds. *Fragments of a Golden Age: The Politics of Culture in Mexico since 1940.* Durham, N.C.: Duke University Press, 2001.

LeVine, Sarah, in collaboration with Clara Sunderland Correa. *Dolor y Alegría: Women and Social Change in Urban Mexico.* Madison: University of Wisconsin Press, 1993.

Pilcher, Jeffrey M. *Cantinflas and the Chaos of Mexican Modernity.* Wilmington, Del.: Scholarly Resources, 2001.

Poniatowska, Elena. *Massacre in Mexico.* Translated by Helen R. Lane. Columbia: University of Missouri Press, 1991.

———. *Nothing, Nobody: The Voices of the Mexico City Earthquake.* Translated by Aurora Camacho de Schmidt and Arthur Schmidt. Philadelphia: Temple University Press, 1995.

Ross, John. *Rebellion from the Roots: Indian Uprising in Chiapas.* Monroe, Me.: Common Courage Press, 1995.

Rubenstein, Anne. *Bad Language, Naked Ladies, and Other Threats to the Nation: A Political History of Comic Books in Mexico.* Durham, N.C.: Duke University Press, 1998.

Rubin, Jeffrey W. *Decentering the Regime: Ethnicity, Radicalism, and Democracy in Juchitán, Mexico.* Durham, N.C.: Duke University Press, 1997.

Womack, John Jr., ed. *Rebellion in Chiapas: An Historical Reader.* New York: New Press, 1999.

Zolov, Eric. *Refried Elvis: The Rise of the Mexican Counterculture.* Berkeley: University of California Press, 1999.

VIII. The Border and Beyond

Andreas, Peter. *Border Games: Policing the U.S.–Mexico Divide.* Ithaca, N.Y.: Cornell University Press, 2000.

Fernández-Kelly, María Patricia. *For We Are Sold, I and My People: Women and Industry on Mexico's Frontier.* Albany: State University of New York Press, 1983.

García Canclini, Néstor. *Hybrid Cultures: Strategies for Entering and Leaving Modernity.* Translated by Christopher L. Chiappari and Silvia L. López. Minneapolis: University of Minnesota Press, 1995.

Gutiérrez, David. *Walls and Mirrors: Mexican Americans, Mexican Immigrants, and the Politics of Ethnicity.* Berkeley: University of California Press, 1995.

———, ed. *Between Two Worlds: Mexican Immigrants in the United States.* Wilmington, Del.: Scholarly Resources, 1996.

Herzog, Lawrence A., ed. *Shared Space: Rethinking the U.S.–Mexico Border Environment.* La Jolla: Center for U.S.–Mexican Studies, University of California at San Diego, 2000.

Martínez, Oscar J. *Border People: Life and Society in the U.S.–Mexico Borderlands.* Tucson: University of Arizona Press, 1994.

Pitti, Stephen J. *The Devil in Silicon Valley: Mexicans and Mexican Americans in Northern California.* Princeton, N.J.: Princeton University Press, 2003.

Quiñones, Sam. *True Tales from Another Mexico: The Lynch Mob, the Popsicle Kings, Chalino, and the Bronx.* Albuquerque: University of New Mexico Press, 2001.

Sánchez, George S. *Becoming Mexican American: Ethnicity, Culture, and Identity in Chicano Los Angeles, 1900–1945.* New York: Oxford University Press, 1993.

IX. Mexico Web Sites

University of Texas Latin American Network Information Center gateway to resources on Mexico. http://lanic.utexas.edu/la/mexico/

El Instituto Nacional de Estadística, Geografía e Informática (INEGI) is one of the best sources for statistics about Mexico. Mostly Spanish. http://www.inegi.gob.mx/

La Jornada is the country's largest progressive national daily. http://www.jornada.unam.mx/index.html

Two of the most complete sites on the Zapatistas, including links, articles, analysis, images, and communiqués, are http://www.ezln.org/ and http://www.utexas.edu/students/nave/

A list of other Mexican newspapers online: http://www.lib.utsa.edu/Instruction/helpsheets/mexstates2.html

Acknowledgment of Copyrights

"Sentiments of the Nation, or Points Outlined by Morelos for the Constitution" by José María Morelas, from Ernesto de la Torre Villar, Moisés González Navarro, and Stanley Ross, eds., *Historia documental de México,* vol. 2 (Mexico City: Universidad Nacional Autónoma de México, 1964), 111-12. Translation by Tim Henderson.

"Plan of Iguala" by Augustín Iturbide, from Ernesto de la Torre Villar, Moisés González Navarro, and Stanley Ross, eds., *Historia documental de México,* vol. 2 (Mexico City: Universidad Nacional Autónoma de México, 1964), 145-48. Translation by Tim Henderson.

"Women and War in Mexico" from Frances Calderón de la Barca, *Life in Mexico* (Garden City, N.Y.: Dolphin Books/Doubleday, [1843]), 238-58.

"The Glorious Revolution of 1844" from Guillermo Prieto (Fidel), *Memorias de mis tiempos,* vol. 1, *1828 á 1848* (Paris and Mexico City: Librería de la Vda. de C. Bouret, 1906), 357-60; and vol. 2, *1840-1853,* 150-55, 160-67. Translation by Tim Henderson.

"*Décimas* Dedicated to Santa Anna's Leg" from Vicente T. Mendoza, *La décima en México: Glosas y valonas* (Buenos Aires: Ministerio de Justicia e Instrucción Pública de la Nación Argentina, Instituto Nacional de la Tradición, 1947), 283-84. Translation by Tim Henderson and Gabriela Gómez-Cárcamo.

"War and Finance, Mexican Style" by Juan Bautista Morales in *El Gallo Pitagórico,* from Ernesto de la Torre Villar, Moisés González Navarro, and Stanley Ross, eds., *Historia documental de México,* vol. 2 (Mexico City: Universidad Nacional Autónoma de México, 1964), 214-18. Translation by Tim Henderson.

"A Conservative Profession of Faith" by the Editors of *El Tiempo,* from Gastón García Cantú, *El pensamiento de la reacción mexicana: Historia documental, 1810-1962* (Mexico City: Empresas Editoriales, 1965), 251-57. Translation by Tim Henderson.

"Considerations Relating to the Political and Social Situation" by Mariano Otero in *The View from Chapultepec: Mexican Writers on the Mexican-American War,* edited by Cecil Robinson (Tucson: University of Arizona Press, 1989), 5-31. Copyright © 1989 The Arizona Board of Regents. Reprinted by permission of the University of Arizona Press.

"Liberals and the Land" by Luis González y González, from "El agrarismo liberal," *Historia Mexicana* 7, no. 4 (April 1958): 469-96. Translation and editing by Tim Henderson.

"Offer of the Crown to Maximilian" by Junta of Conservative Notables, from Alvaro Matute, *México en el siglo XIX: Antología de fuentes e interpretaciones históricas* (Mexico City: Universidad Nacional Autónoma de México, 1972), 298-99. Translation by Tim Henderson.

"A Letter from Mexico" by Empress Carlotta, from Egon Caesar Count Corti, *Maxi-*

"Pancho Villa" from John Reed, *Insurgent Mexico,* new ed. (New York: International Publishers, 1969), 122–45.

"La Punitiva" from Guillermo E. Hernández, ed., *The Mexican Revolution: Corridos about the Heroes and Event, 1910–1920 and Beyond,* CD collection, Arhoolie Records, Folklyric, 7041–44. The translation appears on pp. 72–74 of the accompanying booklet.

"Pedro Martínez" from Oscar Lewis, *Pedro Martínez: A Mexican Peasant and His Family* (New York: Vintage Books, 1964), 73–116. Reprinted by permission of Harold Ober Associates Incorporated. Copyright © 1964 by Oscar Lewis.

"Juan the Chamula" from Ricardo Pozas, *Juan the Chamula: An Ethnological Re-creation of the Life of a Mexican Indian,* translated by Lysander Kemp (Berkeley: University of California Press, 1962), 22–26. Permission granted by The Regents of the University of California and the University of California Press. Copyright © 1962 The Regents of the University of California.

"The Constitution of 1917: Articles 27 and 123" from Gerald E. Fitzgerald, ed., *The Constitutions of Latin America* (Chicago: Henry Regnery Co., Gateway Editions, 1968), 151–56, 185–88; and Eyler N. Simpson, *The Ejido: Mexico's Way Out* (Chapel Hill: University of North Carolina Press, 1937), app. C: 749–50.

"An Agrarian Encounter" from *The Rosalie Evans Letters from Mexico* (Indianapolis: Bobbs-Merrill, 1926), 148–51.

"Ode to Cuauhtémoc" from Carlos Pellicer, *Primera antología poética,* edited by Guillermo Fernández (Mexico City: Fondo de Cultura Económica, 1969), 233–36. Translation by Tim Henderson. Reprinted by permission of Fondo de Cultura Económica.

"The Socialist ABC's" from Carlos Martínez Assad, ed., *Los lunes rojos: La educación racionalista en México* (Mexico City: Secretaría de Educación Pública, 1986), 101–8. Translation by Tim Henderson.

"The Ballad of Valentín of the Sierra" from Recording no. 20, *Corridos de la Rebelión Cristera* (Mexico City: Instituto Nacional de Antropología e Historia, 1976). Translation by Gil Joseph.

"Mexico Must Become a Nation of Institutions and Laws" from Carlos Macías, ed., *Plutarco Elías Calles: Pensamiento político y social. Antología (1913–1936)* (Mexico City: Fondo de Cultura Económica, 1988), 163–74. Translation and editing by Tim Henderson.

"The Formation of the Single-Party State" from Carlos Fuentes, *The Death of Artemio Cruz* (New York: Farrar, Straus and Giroux, 1964), 117. Translation by Sam Hileman. Excerpt from [1924: June 3] from *The Death Of Artemio Cruz* by Carlos Fuentes.

"The Sinking City" from *Endangered Mexico,* by Joel Simon. Copyright © 1997 by Joel Simon. Reprinted by permission of Sierra Club Books.

"Ciudad Nezahualcóyotl: Souls on the Run" from Roberto Vallarino, "Las almas en fuga de Ciudad Nezahualcóyotl," in *El fin de la nostalgia: Nueva crónica de la Ciudad de México,* edited by Jaime Valverde and Juan Domingo Argüelles (Mexico City: Nueva Imagen, 1992), 157-69. Translation by Tim Henderson.

"Modesta Gómez" from Rosario Castellanos, *City of Kings,* translated by Robert S. Rudder and Gloria Chacón de Arjona (Pittsburgh: Latin American Literary Review Press, 1993), 50-57.

"The Student Movement of 1968" from Elena Poniatowska, "El movimiento estudiantil de 1968," in *Fuerte es el silencio* (Mexico City: Ediciones Era, 1980), 34-77. Translation and editing by Tim Henderson. Reprinted by the permission of the author.

"After the Earthquake" from *¡Aquí nos quedaremos . . . !: Testimonios de la Coordinadora Única de Damnificados,* edited by Leslie Serna (Mexico City: Unión de Vecinos y Damnificados 19 de Septiembre, A.C. and Universidad Iberoamericana, A.C., 1995), 47-54, 59-67, 69, 87-89, 147, 155-156. Translation by Tim Henderson.

"Letters to Cuauhtémoc Cárdenas" from Adolfo Gilly, ed., *Cartas a Cuauhtémoc Cárdenas* (Mexico City: Ediciones Era, 1989), 72, 123-24, 129, 131-33, 135, 148, 208-9. Translation by Tim Henderson.

"Corazón del Rocanrol" from Rubén Martínez, *The Other Side: Notes from the New L.A., Mexico City, and Beyond* (New York: Vintage Press, 1993), 150-65. Copyright © 1992 by Rubén Martínez. Published by Vintage Books, a division of Random House, Inc., New York. Originally published by Verso. Reprinted by permission of Susan Bergholz Literary Services, New York. All rights reserved.

"I Don't Believe Them at All" from the CD *Baile de Máscaras,* BMG Music, © 1996. Translation by Tim Henderson

"Identity Hour, or, What Photos Would You Take of the Endless City? (from *A Guide to Mexico City*)" from Carlos Monsiváis, *Mexican Postcards,* translated by John Kraniauskas (London and New York: Verso, 1997), 31-35. Reprinted by the permission of Verso.

"The COCEI of Juchitán: Two Documents" by Leopoldo de Gyves and COCEI, from Howard Campbell, Leigh Binford, Miguel Bartolomé, and Alicia Barabas, eds., *Zapotec Struggles: Histories, Politics, and Representations from Juchitán, Oaxaca* (Washington, D.C.: Smithsonian Institution Press, 1993), 183-90. Translations by Howard Campbell.

"Women of Juchitán" from Jeffrey W. Rubin, "Women of Juchitán: Creating Culture at the Heart of Politics," *Hopscotch: A Cultural Review* 4, no. 1 (1999): 56–77. Reprinted by permission of the author.

"EZLN Demands at the Dialogue Table" from *Shadows of Tender Fury: The Letters and Communiqués of Subcomandante Marcos and the Zapatista Army of National Liberation,* translated by Frank Bardacke, Leslie López, and the Watsonville, California, Human Rights Committee (New York: Monthly Review Press, 1995), 155–62.

"The Long Journey from Despair to Hope" from Juana Ponce de León, ed., *Our Word is Our Weapon: Selected Writings of Subcomandante Insurgente Marcos* (New York: Seven Stories Press, 2001), 60–69. Reprinted by permission of Seven Stories Press.

Portions of "A Tzotzil Chroncle" by Marián Peres Tsu, appeared in Kevin Gosner and Arij Ouweneel, eds., *Indigenous Revolts in Chiapas and the Andean Highlands,* Latin American Studies, no. 77 (Amsterdam: CEDLA, 1996). They were translated from Tzotzil into Spanish and English by Jan Rus. Other portions were translated from Tzotzil to Spanish by Jan Rus and from Spanish to English by Tim Henderson and Gil Joseph. Reprinted by permission of Marián Peres Tsu and Jan Rus.

A shortened version of "Mexicans Would Not Be Bought, Coerced" by Wayne A. Cornelius was published in the *Los Angeles Times,* July 4, 2000.

"Plan of San Diego" from Records of the Department of State Relating to the Internal Affairs of Mexico, 1910–1929, 812.00/1583, U.S. National Archives Microfilm Publications, microcopy no. M-274, pp. 145–48; reprinted in Oscar J. Martínez, ed., *U.S.-Mexico Borderlands: Historical and Contemporary Perspectives,* Jaguar series, no. 12 (Wilmington, Del.: Scholarly Resources, 1996), 139–41.

"The Mexican Connection: Un Pueblo, Una Lucha," excerpt pp. 320–24 from *Occupied America: A History of Chicanos,* by Rudolfo Acuña. Copyright © 1981 by Rudolfo Acuna. Reprinted by permission of Addison-Wesley Educational Publishers, Inc.

"The Maquiladoras" from William Langewiesche, *Cutting for Sign* (New York: Pantheon Books, 1993), 213–30.

"*Dompe* Days" from *By the Lake of Sleeping Children: The Secret Life of the Mexican Border* by Luis Urrea, copyright © 1996 by Luis Urrea. Used by permission of Doubleday, a division of Random House, Inc.

"Pedro P., Coyote" from Judith Adler Hellman, *Mexican Lives* (New York: New Press, 1994), 171–84. Copyright © 1994 *Mexican Lives* by Judith Adler Hellman. Reprinted by permission of The New Press. (800) 233-4830.

"There's a Party Going On in Texas" by Associated Press from *New York Times,* August 27, 2000, sec. 8, p. 5.

"Two Poems about Immigrant Life" by Pat Mora and Gina Valdés, from Lauro Flores,

Index

GILBERT M. JOSEPH is Farnam Professor of History and Director of
Latin American Studies at Yale University. He is the Series Editor, with
Emily Rosenberg, of American Encounters/Global Interactions (Duke).
He has authored (with Allen Wells) *Summer of Discontent, Seasons of
Upheaval: Elite Politics and Rural Insurgency in Yucatán, 1876–1915* (1996);
and *Revolution from Without: Yucatán, Mexico, and the United States* (1988).
His edited works include: *Reclaiming the Political in Latin American
History: Essays from the North* (Duke, 2001); (with Anne Rubenstein and
Eric Zolov) *Fragments of a Golden Age: The Politics of Culture in Mexico
since 1940* (Duke, 2001); (with Ricardo Salvatore and Carlos Aguirre)
*Crime and Punishment in Latin America: Law and Society since Late Colonial
Times* (Duke, 2001); and (with Catherine C. LeGrand and Ricardo D.
Salvatore) *Close Encounters of Empire: Writing the Cultural History of U.S.–
Latin American Relations* (Duke, 1998). TIMOTHY J. HENDERSON is
Associate Professor of History at Auburn University Montgomery. He is
the author of *The Worm in the Wheat: Rosalie Evans and the Agricultural
Struggle in the Puebla-Tlaxcala Valley of Mexico, 1906–1927* (Duke, 1998).

Library of Congress Cataloging-in-Publication Data
The Mexico reader : history, culture, politics / edited
by Gilbert M. Joseph and Timothy J. Henderson.
   p. cm. — (The Latin America readers)
Includes bibliographical references and index.
   ISBN 0-8223-3006-7 (cloth : alk. paper)
   ISBN 0-8223-3042-3 (pbk. : alk. paper)
1. Mexico—History. 2. Mexico—Social conditions.
3. Mexico—Economic conditions. I. Joseph, G. M.
(Gilbert Michael). II. Henderson, Timothy J. III. Series.
   F1226 .M53 2002   972—dc21   2002009112